Financial Accounting and Reporting

Second Edition

Financial Accounting and Reporting

John McKeith and Bill Collins

Second Edition

London   Boston   Burr Ridge, IL   Dubuque, IA   Madison, WI   New York   San Francisco   St. Louis
Bangkok   Bogotá   Caracas   Kuala Lumpur   Lisbon   Madrid   Mexico City
Milan   Montreal   New Delhi   Santiago   Seoul   Singapore   Sydney   Taipei   Toronto

Financial Accounting and Reporting, Second Edition
John McKeith and Bill Collins
ISBN-13 9780077138363
ISBN-10 0077138368

 **Education**

Published by McGraw-Hill Education (UK) Limited
Shoppenhangers Road
Maidenhead
Berkshire
SL6 2QL
Telephone: 44 (0) 1628 502 500
Fax: 44 (0) 1628 770 224
Website: www.mcgraw-hill.co.uk

British Library Cataloguing in Publication Data
A catalogue record for this book is available from the British Library

Library of Congress Cataloguing in Publication Data
The Library of Congress data for this book has been applied for from the Library of Congress

Acquisitions Editor: Leiah Norcott
Development Editor: Stephanie Frosch
Senior Production Editor: James Bishop
Marketing Manager: Alexis Thomas

Text Design by HL Studios
Cover design by Adam Renvoize
Printed and bound in Spain by Grafo Industrias Graficas

ISBN-13 9780077138363
ISBN-10 0077138368

Dedication

To Evelyn

Brief Table of Contents

The following chapter is available online at www.mcgraw-hill.co.uk/textbooks/mckeith:

Detailed Table of Contents

The following chapter is available online at www.mcgraw-hill.co.uk/textbooks/mckeith:

Preface

As business becomes more complex, accounting in its contribution to reporting financial information does also. The importance of a solid understanding of the basic underpinnings of accounting has never been more important. Complicated accounting transactions have become the norm in many organizations, with the result that a top-down approach to learning is no longer possible. For the business student of today, such transactions, and their implications, can be fully understood only when the individual has a firm theoretical and practical understanding of the accounting issues involved.

New to this edition

The pace of change in accounting and financial reporting is dynamic. The number of new standards, amendments to standards and exposure drafts issued since the first edition of this text was published confirms this. This second edition has been fully updated to reflect the content of the international accounting standards currently in force as well as explaining the effects of exposure drafts in issue should they in time become full IFRSs.

All of the features of the first edition have been retained and new examples and questions have been added to enhance the understanding of the topics and the ultimate application of the standards in the progress points, review questions, exercises and online resources. In addition, the use of real-life examples has been extended to further clarify the position in practice and the Logica extracts used to illustrate disclosure in practice have been fully updated.

Finally, in response to reviewer requests,

- New coverage of fair value accounting has been added to **Chapter 1.** The chapter has been restructured, and the section on Income, Value and Capital has been further developed in a new online chapter on *Alternatives to historical cost accounting* (**Chapter 14**).
- Revenue Recognition and Construction Contracts are now being dealt with in a new chapter, **Chapter 6**.
- Full coverage of share-based payments has been added to **Chapter 7**.
- More in-depth coverage of financial instruments and in particular the technical aspects of the phased introduction of IFRS 9 to replace the existing standards are included in **Chapter 8**.
- Improved coverage of ratios with increased explanation and improved links to the rest of text have been added to **Chapter 13**.

A full overview of the chapter contents can be found at the end of this preface.

Aim of the book

The aim of this textbook is to bridge the gap between introductory and so-called 'intermediate' textbooks. Many current intermediate texts fail in their attempts to get the main points across to students because they are too complex; examples used in such texts are usually too long and try to illustrate too many issues at one time. Often the organization of material is complex and there is no clear structure to follow. This book's intention is to build on the basic knowledge gained by students from an introductory course and take them to a full level of understanding of the issues involved. Examples are used frequently throughout each chapter to deal with issues on a point-by-point basis, rather than trying to cover all points at once. Having acquired the basic knowledge and understanding, the book then leads the student to evaluate existing practice and, hence, encourages them to challenge it. This builds confidence in dealing with accounting issues, and provides a better way to acquire essential knowledge.

The audience for the text

Although the book is aimed at second-year accounting students at universities, the emphasis placed on explaining the accounting issues involved in the introductory sections of each chapter will also make it useful to students undergoing professional training who perhaps have no prior accountancy knowledge.

The stepped approach will also make the book useful to those students undertaking professional examinations. Finally, the chapter summaries make this a useful text for accountants in practice by providing a quick reference for specific technical points, issues or problems.

Unique section-by-section approach

This text is unique in its approach to achieving its aims: each chapter is divided into three sections – **Basic Principles**, **Intermediate Issues** and **Advanced Aspects**.

Section 1: Basic Principles

The basic, or introductory, sections set out the basic concepts and introduce the accounting issues involved so that the student is aware of the accounting problems relating to that particular topic. Many of the issues will already have been introduced at Level 1, so this is useful revision and also extremely helpful in ensuring that the student is actually aware of the reasons why certain accounting treatments are being adopted. This text does not encourage the adage 'that's what you do because that's what you do'. These introductory sections explain and explore principles rather than confusing the reader by making reference to accounting standards and legislation. Many examples illustrate accounting issues; however, the authors are also very much of the opinion that practice makes perfect so each chapter has several **Progress Points** for students to test their understanding. Progress Points are a mixture of discussive and numerical questions, and are distributed throughout each chapter to give the student an opportunity to put into practice their earlier reading. Each Progress Point has a fully worked solution so the workings can be understood.

Section 2: Intermediate Issues

The intermediate sections allow students to build on the knowledge gained from the basic sections with references to accounting standards and legislation. Having acquired the 'tools' to do so in the introductory sections, the book encourages the student not simply to accept current practices but to evaluate and challenge them. Examples and Progress Points are used to consolidate learning. As is often the case in accountancy, a full understanding of a particular topic necessitates references to other concepts that, although essential to the understanding of the initial concept, have themselves not yet been explained. This book recognizes this problem and ensures that there is a logical, step-by-step flow to each chapter.

Section 3: Advanced Aspects

The advanced aspects sections consider advanced accounting applications and situations as well as covering current issues relevant to the chapter topic. Each section within each chapter is a complete, self-contained unit. It is therefore not necessary to cover the whole of a chapter before moving on to the next chapter.

Theory and practice

This is a practical book, but one that does not shun the importance of theoretical underpinnings. What it does not do is prescribe a theoretical approach. Unlike other texts, a 'what if' approach is taken with the examples so that several permutations of a problem are dealt with to ensure a deeper level of understanding so that new problems encountered in academia, or indeed professional work, can be dealt with. Each chapter contains a critical appraisal of the existing treatment of particular accounting situations. The accounting practices and procedures prescribed by the standards are critically reviewed and their abilities to provide the user of the financial statements with their required information questioned. Accounting standards do not simply remain set in stone; they evolve as new issues arise and new complexities are introduced. By adopting an unbiased approach to explaining the accounting issues involved, and by using numerical examples to illustrate the principles, this book will stimulate students to challenge the theory behind the practice.

The IASB Framework

It is generally accepted that the basic objective underlying the preparation of financial statements is to provide useful information for decision making. Frequent reference is made throughout the book to the

IASB's Framework for the Preparation and Presentation of Financial Statements. This book follows the conclusion reached by the Framework that not all of the information needs of the various user groups can be met by financial statements. In doing so, the rationale is to strive for solutions. It is essential that the standard of reporting is continually improved if examples such as Enron are to be stopped from bringing this elegant discipline into disrepute. Throughout the text, emphasis is given to the usefulness and effectiveness of the information provided by adhering to accounting principles and standards.

Learning features

At undergraduate level, the study of accounting can often feel far removed from reality. The text overcomes this problem by including within some chapters coverage of the 'Position in practice'. These sections outline the problems the practising accountant faces in relation to the treatment of certain accounting situations, and explains how they are dealt with in practice.

Most texts refer to examples from public limited companies, which often bear no relation to the topic being explained and can be confusing. They overlook the most important issue in using **real-life examples**. The whole purpose of financial reporting is the presentation of financial information within sets of financial statements. The use of extract details from real-life accounts is the final product of the computations. Real-life examples are therefore used to illustrate disclosure requirements and are explained, linked and integrated with the text.

Please see the Guided Tour on page xvii for a full summary of the learning features in the text.

Chapter content

- **Chapter 1**: the regulation of accounting is introduced where it complements the form and content of financial statements prescribed by IAS 1. The components of financial statements are outlined, and their preparation illustrated and demonstrated. Corporate governance issues arising as a result of previous accounting scandals are also dealt with. The Conceptual Framework is reviewed and a study made of some of the alternative measurement bases to historical costs which exist. In particular, fair value accounting is examined in detail. The chapter concludes with coverage of the accounting procedures which are necessitated by changes in accounting policies, accounting estimates and errors.

- **Chapters 2 and 3**: non-current assets are dealt with, and in particular the recognition and measurement issues arising as a result of following a historical cost basis of accounting as well as the alternative treatments that are available. The quality of the information being presented by following generally accepted accounting principles is questioned, particularly in relation to intangible assets and goodwill.

- **Chapter 4**: this chapter looks at leasing and off balance sheet finance, again questioning the usefulness of the information provided by following the prescribed accounting standard treatment. The proposed changes to lease accounting are examined in detail.

- **Chapter 5**: deals with inventories. Here the emphasis is on the accounting for such items but with extensive coverage of the measurement issues arising and the problems the accountant in practice can face when dealing with inventory measurement and valuation.

- **Chapter 6**: this new chapter deals with revenue recognition and construction contracts. The current standards relating to these areas are both under review and are likely to be superseded in the near future. The history behind the current standards is given together with the reasons why a new standard – Revenue from Contracts with Customers – has been proposed.

- **Chapter 7**: this chapter looks at share capital and reserves and then, in relation to capital maintenance, the increase and reduction of share capital is examined in detail. Full coverage of share-based payments and IFRS 2 is given in the Advanced Aspects section.

- **Chapter 8**: following an examination of the Conceptual Framework's definition of a liability, this chapter considers in detail the importance of the distinction between those liabilities that are third-party liabilities and those liabilities that are due to the owners, as well as the recognition and measurement problems associated with provisions. In this respect the corroborative and clarifying effects of Events after the Reporting Period are examined in detail. Finally, consideration is given to financial instruments and the measurement and presentation issues which surround this increasingly complex area of accounting.

- **Chapter 9**: the accounting for taxation and in particular the concept of deferred tax is covered in this chapter. Emphasis is on the explanation of the 'tax base' concept and the usefulness of the information given to users by adhering to the accounting standards in providing for deferred tax.

- **Chapter 10**: this chapter examines the preparation and usefulness of statements of cash flows. In particular, a step-by-step approach to the preparation of the statement is taken to explain clearly the link between the statement of comprehensive income and the statement of financial position, and to ensure a solid grounding in this area of accounting which students often find problematic.

- **Chapter 11**: accounting for group structures and the preparation of consolidated financial statements is covered. Both practical issues and theoretical underpinnings of group accounting are considered in detail as well as the requirements of the new IFRS issued to deal with group accounting.

- **Chapter 12**: this chapter looks at foreign currency issues and covers the accounting treatment of single transactions through to the accounting requirements for a foreign-based subsidiary in accordance with IAS 12. Consideration is also given to the various alternatives to the current prescribed treatments which have been proposed over the years to deal with foreign currency translation.

- **Chapter 13**: having covered the component parts making up a set of financial statements, this chapter analyses the information given within a traditional set of financial statements. It deals with the interpretation of financial statements and, while the calculation of key ratios is demonstrated, the emphasis is on the interpretation of these ratios, and how they can be used to explain what has happened and to predict what will happen.

- **Chapter 14**: this new online chapter deals with alternatives to historical cost accounting by identifying and explaining alternative concepts of income, value and capital. It also examines the strengths and weaknesses of historical cost accounting as well as the accounting treatment to be adopted in hyperinflationary economies.

Many texts fail to take account of the fact that their readers may be coming across issues for the first-time and appear to take the view that, simply by reading chapters, students will automatically gain the required understanding. This text has been written with a strong emphasis on readability and understandability from the introductory sections through to the advanced aspects. It has been written with the student in mind.

About the Authors

John McKeith is a partner in a firm of Chartered Accountants and a part-time lecturer at the University of Stirling where he teaches Financial Accounting and External Reporting at both undergraduate and postgraduate levels.

Bill Collins is a former Senior Lecturer at the University of Stirling where he previously taught External Reporting at undergraduate level. He is now a part-time lecturer at the University of Glasgow where he teaches Financial Accounting to Postgraduates and Financial Reporting to Masters students.

Acknowledgements

Author's acknowledgements

Time, when you are writing a book, is a very mixed blessing. On the one hand you need as much of it as you can get to enable you to write, while on the other the passage of time means that there is more chance of your first written material becoming out of date. A balance needs to be struck and I hope that this has been achieved with this edition of the book.

This book considers in detail the reporting requirements of the International Financial Reporting Standards (IFRS) and the International Accounting Standards (IAS). As such it refers to their content, and extracts from the standards are used frequently throughout the book to illustrate their meaning and effects. I would like to thank the International Financial Reporting Standards Foundation for permission to use these extracts from various IASB standards.

The person at the sharp end who miraculously navigates her way along the arrows, lines and hieroglyphics is my secretary Brenda Soreide to whom I am most grateful for once more typing the manuscript. My colleague Graeme Tough CA also helped at various stages of the book and I am extremely grateful to him for his assistance.

I would also like to thank all the reviewers who gave up their time to read the draft manuscript and for their comments and suggestions – many of which have been incorporated into the text.

The McGraw-Hill team has also been superbly supportive. I would like to thank Leiah Batchelor for getting the ball rolling on the second edition before going on maternity leave and to Stephanie Frosch who most expertly saw the second edition through to a conclusion.

Finally, I once more thank my wife Evelyn for her patience and understanding over the last year while this second edition was written. I think that the truce on the use of the dining room table worked for both of us.

John McKeith

Publisher's acknowledgements

Our thanks go to the following reviewers for their comments at various stages in the text's development:

Michel Charifzadeh, ESB Business School, Reutlingen University, Germany
Qiwei Chen, Brunel University
Chris Coles, University of Glasgow
Ian Dewing, University of East Anglia
Sheila Ellwood, University of Bristol
Rachel English, De Montfort University
Dimitrios Gounopoulos, University of Surrey
Omaima Hassan, Brunel University
Robert Jupe, Kent University
Dave Kolitz, University of Exeter
Suzanne O'Brien, Canterbury Christ Church University
Ciaran Ó hÓgartaigh, University College Dublin
Ivana Raonic, Cass Business School, City University, London
Clare Roberts, University of Aberdeen
John Stittle, University of Essex
Chris Soan, Newcastle University

Every effort has been made to trace and acknowledge ownership of copyright and to clear permission for material reproduced in this book. The publishers will be pleased to make suitable arrangements to clear permission with any copyright holders whom it has not been possible to contact.

Learning Outcomes

After studying this chapter you should be

☑ explain the differences between the fi
company

☑ identify and explain the features unique to

☑ explain the need for accounting regulations

☑ prepare financial statements of a company

☑ prepare a statement of comprehensive inc
in equity of a company in accordance with

Learning Outcomes

These set out the knowledge and skills you should have acquired by the end of each chapter.

Section 1: Basic Principles

1.1 Types of business structure

e are many different ways in which a business can
e divided into two categories: unincorporated an

ncorporated

nincorporated business is one without a separate
ucted through the names of the persons behind i
is a sole trader. A sole trader is a business run by
name (e.g. Robert Smith trading as RS Carpets). T
he sole trader has personal liability for the debts a
ts of the business, and is taxed personally on the p
A partnership is another common type of unincor

Sections

Each chapter is split into three sections, *Basic Principles, Intermediate Issues* and *Advanced Aspects*, to progress your learning in a step-by-step manner. Each section is a self-contained unit.

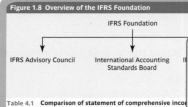

Figure 1.8 Overview of the IFRS Foundation

IFRS Foundation

IFRS Advisory Council   International Accounting
Standards Board

Figures and Tables

Figures and tables are distributed throughout chapters, as well as many financial statements to help you apply theory to practice.

Table 4.1 Comparison of statement of comprehensive inco

	Actuarial			Sum o	
Period	Depn	Finance	Total charge	Depn	Finance
	£	£	£	£	£
1	871	249	1,120	871	257
2	871	174	1,045	871	171

Example
The following trial balance is taken from the records

Ordinary share capital (£1 each)
Preference share capital (£1 each)
Share premium
Revaluation reserve
General reserve
Retained earnings at 1 January 2012
Long-term loan (debentures)
Land and buildings
Patents
Motor vehicles
Opening inventory
Accounts receivable
Accounts payable

Examples

The text is bursting with fully-worked examples to explain concepts, and real-life examples to illustrate disclosure requirements. Logica, a leading IT and business services company, is referred to throughout the chapters to demonstrate financial accounting in practice. All examples are explained, linked and integrated with the text.

Progress Point 1.1

Explain the term 'regulatory frame

Solution

The term regulatory framework re
and includes legislation, accounti
needed so that shareholders and other

Progress Points
These are a mixture of text and numerical questions which give you an opportunity to put into practice your earlier learning. Each Progress Point has a fully worked solution so the workings can be understood.

Section summary
The IASB Conceptual Framework consists o
derlie financial accounting.
Its purposes include assisting in the de
harmonization of accounting standards
ucing the number of alternative accoun

Summaries
Each section concludes with a brief summary of the main issues covered. There is also a Chapter Summary which provides a synopsis of the main provisions of the accounting standards relevant to each topic. These summaries offer you a further opportunity to consolidate and check your understanding of each topic.

pter summary

1: *Presentation of Financial State*

Financial statements should comprise a s
sive income, a statement of changes in ec

✓   Key terms for revie

Definitions can be found in the glo

Accounting policies
Audit
Conceptual framework
Dividend
Measurement
Ordinary shares
Preference shares

Key Terms for review
These are highlighted throughout the text and cross-referenced at the end of each chapter. Definitions can be found in the glossary at the end of the text.

?   Review questions

1. Define the term intangible asset and
low should an intangible asset be
ransaction?
connection with IAS 38 *Intangibl*
a) distinguish between *research* exp
b) explain the accounting treatm
xpenditure.
ive some examples of intangible a
the reason for their exclusion.
Explain the effects of using the cos

End of chapter questions
Review questions allow you to check and assimilate the knowledge acquired from the chapter. *Exercise questions* offer an opportunity to test and demonstrate your learning. Questions range from foundation level through to a level found in most professional examinations.

Online Learning Centre

Visit www.mcgraw-hill.co.uk/textbooks/mckeith today!

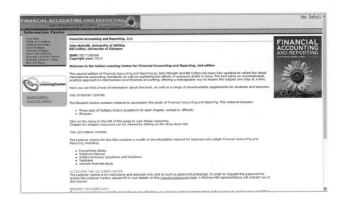

Students – Helping you to Connect, Learn and Succeed

We understand that studying for your module is not just about reading this textbook. It's also about researching online, revising key terms, preparing for assignments, and passing the exam. The website above provides you with a number of **FREE** resources to help you succeed on your module, including:

- **Self-test questions** to prepare you for tests and exams
- **Glossary** of key terms to revise core concepts

Lecturer support – Helping you to help your students

The Online Learning Centre also offers lecturers adopting this book a range of resources designed to offer:

- **Faster course preparation** – time-saving support for your module
- **High-calibre content to support your students** – resources written by your academic peers, who understand your need for rigorous and reliable content
- **Flexibility** – edit, adapt or repurpose; test in EZ Test or your department's Course Management System. The choice is yours.

The materials created specifically for lecturers adopting this textbook include:

- **Solutions manual** providing answers to the review questions and exercises in the textbook
- **Additional essay questions and solutions** to accompany each chapter
- **PowerPoint presentations** to use in lecture presentations
- **Image library** of artwork from the textbook

To request your password to access these resources, contact your McGraw-Hill representative or visit **www.mcgraw-hill.co.uk/textbooks/mckeith**.

Test Bank available in McGraw-Hill EZ Test Online

A test bank of hundreds of questions is available to lecturers adopting this book for their module through the EZ Test online website. For each chapter you will find:

- A range of multiple choice, true or false, short answer or essay questions
- Questions identified by type, level, and chapter to help you to select questions that best suit your needs

McGraw-Hill EZ Test Online is:

- **Accessible** anywhere with an internet connection – your unique login provides you access to all your tests and material in any location
- **Simple** to set up and easy to use
- **Flexible,** offering a choice from question banks associated with your adopted textbook or allowing you to create your own questions
- **Comprehensive,** with access to hundreds of banks and thousands of questions created for other McGraw-Hill titles
- **Compatible** with Blackboard and other course management systems
- **Time-saving** – students' tests can be immediately marked and results and feedback delivered directly to your students to help them to monitor their progress.

To register for this FREE resource, visit **www.eztestonline.com**.

Mc Graw Hill create

Make our content your solution

At McGraw-Hill Education our aim is to help lecturers to find the most suitable content for their needs delivered to their students in the most appropriate way. Our **custom publishing solutions** offer the ideal combination of content delivered in the way which best suits lecturer and students.

Our custom publishing programme offers lecturers the opportunity to select just the chapters or sections of material they wish to deliver to their students from a database called CREATE™ at:

www.mcgrawhillcreate.co.uk

CREATE™ contains over two million pages of content from:

- textbooks
- professional books
- case books – Harvard Articles, Insead, Ivey, Darden, Thunderbird and BusinessWeek
- Taking Sides – debate materials

Across the following imprints:

- McGraw-Hill Education
- Open University Press
- Harvard Business Publishing
- US and European material

There is also the option to include additional material authored by lecturers in the custom product – this does not necessarily have to be in English.

We will take care of everything from start to finish in the process of developing and delivering a custom product to ensure that lecturers and students receive exactly the material needed in the most suitable way.

With a **Custom Publishing Solution**, students enjoy the best selection of material deemed to be the most suitable for learning everything they need for their courses – something of real value to support their learning. Teachers are able to use exactly the material they want, in the way they want, to support their teaching on the course.

Please contact your local **McGraw-Hill representative** with any questions or alternatively contact **Warren Eels: warren_eels@mcgraw-hill.com.**

Chapter 1

The Preparation, Presentation and Regulation of Company Financial Statements

Learning Outcomes

After studying this chapter you should be able to:

- ✓ explain the differences between the financial statements of an unincorporated business and a limited company
- ✓ identify and explain the features unique to company financial statements
- ✓ explain the need for accounting regulations and the main sources of regulations
- ✓ prepare financial statements of a company for internal use
- ✓ prepare a statement of comprehensive income, a statement of financial position and a statement of changes in equity of a company in accordance with IAS 1
- ✓ outline the history and make-up of the International Accounting Standards Board and its associated bodies
- ✓ explain the purpose of international financial reporting standards and list the main steps in the standard-setting process
- ✓ identify and explain the respective roles of the directors, accountants and auditors in the preparation and publication of financial statements
- ✓ explain the term conceptual framework
- ✓ state the main purposes and explain the main sections of the IASB Framework
- ✓ explain the measurement bases that are identified in the Framework
- ✓ explain what is meant by fair value accounting and define fair value in accordance with IFRS 13
- ✓ outline the criteria to be applied in the selection and change of accounting policies
- ✓ account for changes in accounting policies, accounting estimates and errors and prepare the related disclosure in accordance with IAS 8.

Introduction

Financial accounting is concerned with the recording, classifying, summarizing and reporting of those transactions undertaken by an entity which are of a financial nature. It is also concerned with the construction of a theory of accounting, with identification of rules of measurement, and with regulation of the content of financial reports.

This first chapter outlines the main requirements in the preparation and presentation of financial statements for limited companies. It is assumed that a knowledge of the format of basic financial statements is possessed, for both sole traders and partnerships.

After an introductory section that examines the nature of limited companies and the regulatory requirements that have developed in order to safeguard financial statements users' interests, the following section examines how company financial statements are constructed. In particular, the detailed requirements of IAS 1 are explained and illustrated.

The chapter concludes with an overview of the conceptual framework within which accounting information is accumulated and reported, together with a study of fair value measurement. Finally, consideration is given to the selection of appropriate accounting policies to be adopted by an entity in preparing its financial statements and the reporting requirements necessary when changes are made to these policies.

Section 1: Basic Principles

1.1 Types of business structure

There are many different ways in which a business can be structured. In broad terms, the type of structure can be divided into two categories: unincorporated and incorporated.

Unincorporated

An unincorporated business is one without a separate legal personality. This means that the business is conducted through the names of the persons behind it. The most common type of unincorporated business is a sole trader. A sole trader is a business run by an individual either in his own name or under a trade name (e.g. Robert Smith trading as RS Carpets). The basic characteristics of a sole-trader business are that the sole trader has personal liability for the debts and obligations of the business, owns personally the assets of the business, and is taxed personally on the profits and gains of the business.

A partnership is another common type of unincorporated business. A partnership is a business run by two or more persons in common with a view to profit. The basic characteristics of a partnership are that each partner has personal joint and several liability for the debts and obligations of himself and the other partners that are incurred in the ordinary course of partnership business, has the right to share in the profits and assets of the partnership business, and the right to take part in the management of the business.

Incorporated

An incorporated business is one with its own legal personality. This means that it has a legal identity that is distinct from that of its owners or managers. This provides many benefits but is accompanied by greater regulation.

Limited liability companies

As noted above, with both sole trader and partnership businesses, a very real risk is that of losing personal possessions if the business fails. Moreover, as businesses tend to grow in size, the extent of that risk is increased as are these businesses' financing requirements. In order to limit that risk and to enable businesses to have greater access to capital, many sole traders and partnerships 'incorporate' and become limited liability companies.

A company limited by shares is the most common type of incorporated business structure. Such companies are owned by their shareholders but managed by their directors. The identifying feature of a company limited by shares is that the liability of the shareholders for the debts of the company is limited to the amount, if any, unpaid on the shares held by them. Since shareholders normally pay fully for their shares when they are issued, shareholders are rarely held liable for the company's debts.

A company limited by shares has a separate legal personality from its shareholders or directors. As such, it can enter into contracts in its own name, it can sue and be sued, and it is liable to the tax authorities for tax on any profits earned. Because the company is a 'person' in its own right, the directors must manage it in the interests of the company, not themselves or individual shareholders.

Public and private companies

A company limited by shares can be a private company or a public company. A public company is one that is stated to be a public company, and is registered as such. A private company is defined in law as one that is not a public company.

The major features distinguishing a private company from a public company are that a private company is not allowed to offer shares in the company to the general public and a public company has minimum share capital requirements.

Public companies are subject to greater restrictions than private companies and, consequently, most companies limited by shares are private companies. Conversely, because of these restrictions, investors have greater confidence in public companies and therefore many large companies are public companies.

1.2 The need for regulation

BASIC

INTERMEDIATE

ADVANCED

Limited company financial statements, unlike those of sole traders and partnerships, are publicly available documents. As well as providing financial statements to their shareholders, limited companies are required to file accounts at Companies House, and these are available for all interested parties to see. The public availability of financial information about a company is a price that must be paid for the benefit of limited liability. With sole traders and partnerships, the owners of such a business can often glean considerable amounts of financial information from their day-to-day involvement in managing its affairs, and consequently do not depend solely on financial statements to provide them with this information. Indeed, many smaller businesses prepare accounts simply to satisfy the tax authorities and to determine their annual tax liabilities.

On the other hand, particularly with large limited companies where the shareholders have no direct involvement with the running of the business, the published financial statements will be all that such shareholders have with which to judge the performance of both the company and the directors. As a consequence of being publicly available, and to try to achieve uniformity so that meaningful comparison can be made between companies and over time, the form and content of these financial statements are subject to regulation by law, professional bodies and the stock exchange.

If the form and content of financial statements were not regulated it would be possible for dishonest or incompetent directors to provide shareholders and other users with misleading financial information.

Users and their information needs

The main users of financial statements are identified as follows.

- **Investors** need information to:
  - assess the stewardship of management, e.g. in safeguarding the entity's resources and using them properly, efficiently and profitably
  - take decisions about management, e.g. assessing the need for new management
  - take decisions about their investment or potential investment, e.g. deciding whether to hold, buy or sell shares, and assessing the ability to pay dividends.

- **Lenders** need information to:
  - determine whether their loans and interest will be paid on time
  - decide whether to lend and on what terms.
- **Suppliers** need information to:
  - decide whether to sell to the entity
  - determine whether they will be paid on time
  - determine longer-term stability if the company is a major customer.
- **Employees** need information to:
  - assess the stability and profitability of the company
  - assess the ability to provide remuneration, retirement benefits and employment opportunities.
- **Customers** need information to:
  - assess the probability of the continued existence of the company, taking account of their own degree of dependence on the company, e.g. for future provision of specialized replacement parts and servicing product warranties.
- **Government and other agencies** need information to:
  - be aware of the commercial activities of the company
  - regulate these activities
  - raise revenue
  - produce national statistics.
- **Public**: Members of the public need information to:
  - determine the effect on the local economy of the company's activities, e.g. employment opportunities, use of local suppliers
  - assess recent developments in the company's prosperity and changes in its activities.

Regulatory framework for financial accounting

The regulatory framework refers to the rules and regulations that apply to financial reporting. Accounting tends to be regulated in different ways in different countries; this is primarily due to the nature of the legal system prevailing in each country. This book deals with the position in the UK.

The system of accounting in the UK has been derived from statute, accounting standards and precedent. Collectively, these sources of reference give rise to the term 'Generally Accepted Accounting Practice' (GAAP), which is a widely used term that refers to rules that are followed in the preparation of financial statements. It is important to note that there are many different types of accounting entities and that the rules applying to each will differ. This book deals with financial reporting by companies; however, the international standards that are the subject of this book could be applied to any class of business entity. The regulatory framework that applies to financial reporting by companies consists of the following main components:

- legislation
- accounting standards
- stock exchange regulations.

Each of these is now considered in turn.

Legislation

The Companies Act 2006 contains rules and regulations relating to such matters as:

- record-keeping obligations
- the requirement to prepare annual accounts for each financial year
- the requirement that these accounts must show a 'true and fair' view

- the requirement that these accounts must be accompanied by a directors' report
- the requirement that the accounts must be prepared in accordance with either international standards or national standards
- the company's duty to circulate its accounts to shareholders and to make the accounts available for public inspection.

Some of these rules have arisen as a result of European Union (EU) Directives. For example, the European Commission adopted a regulation requiring all stock exchange-listed companies of EU member states to prepare their consolidated financial statements according to International Accounting Standards Board (IASB) standards.

Accounting standards

One of the most important principles in UK accounting is that the financial statements of a company must give a 'true and fair view' of its financial affairs. A similar principle applies in international accounting standards, which require 'fair presentation'. In most cases, compliance with accounting standards will ensure a true and fair view/fair presentation.

Accounting standards contain the detailed rules that govern the accounting treatment of transactions and other items shown in financial statements. Many countries have their own standard-setting bodies, which are responsible for devising and publishing accounting standards for use in the country concerned. In the UK this is the Accounting Standards Board (ASB), while the USA has the Financial Accounting Standards Board (FASB).

In recent years there has been a trend towards internationalization of business and this has led to calls for the internationalization of accounting rules to help both users and companies. The International Accounting Standards Board (IASB) has developed, and issues, International Financial Reporting Standards (IFRS) (formerly International Accounting Standards (IAS)).

International Financial Reporting Standards (IFRS)

The EU has, since 2005, required all listed companies to use IFRS. However, some EU countries, including the UK, still permit non-listed companies to use domestic standards. The UK is still considering whether or not it will stop issuing its own standards and require all companies to use international standards.

This book deals mainly with the international standards; however, comparisons are made in various chapters between UK and US standards in order to highlight the alternative accounting treatments available for transactions.

Stock exchange regulations

In addition to legislation and accounting standards, stock exchange listing rules also influence financial statements. These are regulations set out by the stock exchange, to which companies must adhere before their shares can be quoted on the stock exchange.

Progress Point 1.1

Explain the term 'regulatory framework' and why this framework is needed.

Solution

The term regulatory framework refers to the rules and regulations that govern financial reporting, and includes legislation, accounting standards and stock exchange regulations. This framework is needed so that shareholders and other users of financial statements can rely on their content.

1.3 Preparation of company annual accounts

The preparation of company annual accounts follows broadly the same principles as for sole traders and partnerships. The main differences are in relation to the presentation of figures and the inclusion of certain additional items that are not found in the accounts of sole traders and partnerships.

Perhaps one of the biggest challenges for the student new to company annual reports is the change in terminology. When preparing financial statements for sole traders and partnerships, the traditional statements which are prepared are the profit and loss account and the balance sheet. While these same statements are prepared for limited companies, under international standards these terminologies differ. Table 1.1 sets out the traditional 'unincorporated' terminologies and their international equivalents.

Although the international standard which governs the presentation of financial statements, IAS 1 Presentation of Financial Statements, recognizes that other titles for the statements exist and, indeed, permits their use (para 10), for the purposes of consistency with the standard and the following chapters, the international terminologies will be used from now on.

In relation to presentation, the statement of comprehensive income (profit and loss account) and statement of financial position of limited companies are required to be in a particular format. The additional items are necessary as a result of a limited company's separate legal persona. These additional items are considered first.

Share capital

In the case of sole trader and partnership accounts, capital represents the owners' interest in the net assets of the business. That is, capital represents the residual claim on the net assets of the business once all its liabilities have been accounted for. When net assets increase, capital increases; and where there is a decrease in net assets there will be a corresponding decrease in capital.

With a limited company the ownership interest is split between the original investment and the subsequent changes in net assets made through profits. The original investment is usually made in return for shares in the company, and the subsequent profits and gains are known as reserves. Shares represent the basic units of ownership of a business and each share has a named value, which is called its nominal or par value. This nominal value is simply the value that is attached to the divided units of total share capital.

Table1.1 **Unincorporated vs international terminologies**

Term used for unincorporated businesses	Term under international standards
Profit and loss account	Statement of comprehensive income
Balance sheet	Statement of financial position
Cash flow statement	Statement of cash flows
Balance sheet date	End of the reporting period
Fixed assets	Non-current assets
Long-term loans	Non-current liabilities
Company	Entity
Stocks	Inventories
Trade debtors	Receivables
Trade creditors	Payables

Example

Suppose a company has share capital of £100,000. This could comprise:

- 100,000 shares of £1
- 200,000 shares of £0.50
- 400,000 shares of £0.25.

In companies, share capital is shown in an account that is kept separate from retained earnings and dividends. In sole traders, profits are usually added to the figure for capital and drawings are deducted from capital.

Share premium

If a company issues shares at an amount greater than their par value, that excess is known as a share premium. For example, a company with shares having a par value of £1 decides to issue 20,000 new shares of £1 at a price of £5 per share. This would raise £100,000 and would be recorded as two separate items – ordinary share capital of £20,000 and share premium of £80,000.

Ordinary shares and preference shares

Ordinary shares are sometimes referred to as 'equity shares' because each one represents an equal interest in the ownership of the company. A company might also issue preference shares, which entitle the holders to a dividend out of profits before the ordinary shareholders are entitled to them. This gives the preference shareholder some 'preferential' treatment. In general terms, the preference dividend is usually a fixed percentage each year. Once the preference dividend has been paid, the profit remaining belongs to the ordinary shareholders.

It would not be very prudent for directors to pay out all the remaining profits to shareholders, so it is likely that some profits will be retained in the business. These profits remaining after the company has paid the dividends are referred to as retained earnings. Any dividends paid by a company are based on the nominal value of the issued share capital.

Example

A company has £100,000 ordinary share capital of £1 shares. The company pays a dividend of 10%. How much dividend will be paid?

The dividend to be paid is based on the nominal value of the share capital, in this case £100,000. So the dividend will be 10% of £100,000 = £10,000.

Reserves

Issued share capital is shown in the statement of financial position. Any other amounts attributable to ordinary shareholders are shown as reserves. A company may have a number of different reserves, each for a different purpose. The main reserves include:

- retained earnings
- revaluation reserve
- general (or other) reserves.

Retained earnings

These are the profits after tax (less any losses), which the company keeps within the business. These profits have not been paid out by way of dividend, nor transferred to any other reserve. Each year the opening balance on retained earnings will be increased by the profit earned for the year, and reduced by any dividend payment and any other transfers to reserves. At the end of a period the amount remaining in the retained earnings of a company is the total (accumulated) profits (and losses) the company has built up over time. A company can choose to use some of these retained earnings to pay any future dividends.

Revaluation reserve

Some non-current (fixed) assets may have been purchased several years ago and have risen in value over time. This means that the amount shown in the statement of financial position for such items is now out of date and no longer represents the current value of the asset. This is particularly true in the case of land and buildings. Land may have been purchased several years ago and may now be worth much more than was originally paid for it.

Certain non-current assets may therefore be revalued. If the asset value has increased then the company has made a revaluation gain. However, because such revaluation gains do not arise in the ordinary course of business they do not form part of the company's income from which dividends can be paid.

General reserve

A company may hold retained earnings that it has no intention of paying out to shareholders as a dividend in the future. In this case such earnings might be held in a general reserve, rather than in retained earnings.

Borrowing

A company may borrow directly from a bank, or it may borrow by issuing what is known as loan stock or debentures. The company is obliged to pay interest on this borrowing and will at some time in the future have to repay this loan. Any interest payment due on this borrowing is shown as a finance cost in the statement of comprehensive income.

Taxation

A limited company is a separate legal entity and is liable for tax on its profits. As such, limited companies will show in the statement of comprehensive income the amount of tax for the year and, in the statement of financial position, will record under current liabilities the tax due for the year. Taxation paid by sole traders or partners in a partnership is treated as a repayment of capital and is shown as a deduction in the capital account only.

Dividends

Shareholders receive a reward in the form of dividends for the capital they have invested. The equivalent payments to sole traders are called drawings.

Dividends on ordinary shares are accounted for only in the period in which they are declared as being payable by the directors. When directors declare that an ordinary dividend will be paid in respect of a particular accounting period, it is accounted for only at that time. Final ordinary dividends are usually declared only in the following period so they do not appear in the statement of financial position as a liability on the statement of financial position of the period to which they relate. Interim ordinary dividends are usually declared during the period to which they relate, and so are accounted for in the period to which they relate.

Dividends are not accounted for in the statement of comprehensive income but are treated as a reduction in retained earnings.

Shareholders' funds

In companies there is a heading for shareholders' funds, which can include a number of items such as share capital, share premium, revaluation reserve and retained earnings. In sole traders a single capital account usually includes all that the owners have invested in the business, capital and profits.

1.4 Preparing company financial statements for internal use

The preparation of the financial statements of limited companies does not present many new problems. Accruals, prepayments, provisions for bad and doubtful debts, and other similar adjustments are all prepared in the same way as for a sole trader, as is the statement of comprehensive income and statement of financial position. However, once the profit is calculated, the amount of tax payable to the government has to be determined.

As far as the statement of financial position is concerned, the main differences will be seen in the share capital and reserves section. The following simple example illustrates the financial statements of a company, prepared for internal use.

Example

The following trial balance is taken from the records of ST Ltd as at 31 December 2012.

	£000	£000
Ordinary share capital (£1 each)		300
Preference share capital (£1 each)		150
Share premium		25
Revaluation reserve		30
General reserve		20
Retained earnings at 1 January 2012		50
Long-term loan (debentures)		80
Land and buildings	550	
Patents	50	
Motor vehicles	50	
Opening inventory	10	
Accounts receivable	80	
Accounts payable		45
Bank	75	
Electricity expense	8	
Wages expense	50	
Telephone expense	7	
Sales revenue		350
Purchases	150	
Loan interest	8	
Other expenses	12	
	1,050	1,050

BASIC

INTERMEDIATE

ADVANCED

Additional information

1. Closing inventory is £25,000
2. Amounts payable:

Ordinary dividend	£6,000
Preference dividend	£3,000
Taxation	£26,000

3. Authorized share capital is as follows:

Ordinary share capital	£350,000
Preference share capital	£200,000

The statement of comprehensive income and the statement of financial position will be similar to that for a sole trader. The only difference, as was indicated above, is in the capital and reserves section of the statement of financial position.

BASIC

INTERMEDIATE

ADVANCED

Statement of comprehensive income
for the period ended 31 December 2012

	£000	£000
Sales revenue		350
Less cost of sales		
Opening inventory	10	
Add purchases	150	
	160	
Less closing inventory	25	135
Gross profit		215
Less expenses:		
Electricity	8	
Wages	50	
Telephone	7	
Loan interest	8	
Other expenses	12	85
Profit before tax		130
Less taxation		26
Profit after tax		104

Statement of financial position as at 31 December 2012

	£000	£000	£000
Non-current assets			
Intangible assets			
Patents			50
Tangible assets			
Land and buildings			550
Motor vehicles			50
Total non-current assets			650
Current assets			
Inventory	25		
Accounts receivable	80		
Bank	75	180	
Current liabilities: amounts falling due within one year			
Accounts payable	45		
Tax payable	26		
Dividends payable	9	80	
Net current assets			100
Total assets less current liabilities			750
Amounts falling due after more than one year:			
Debenture loan			80
			670
Capital and reserves			
Share capital		Authorized	Issued
Ordinary share capital		350	300
Preference share capital		200	150
		550	450
Reserves			
Share premium		25	
Revaluation reserve		30	
General reserve		20	
Retained earnings (£50 + £95 (retained profit))		145	220
			670

Retained profit = profit for year less dividends paid
= 104 – 6 – 3 = £95

It needs to be remembered that the above statements are prepared for *internal* use. However, these internal company accounts are not suitable for external users. In order to be suitable for external users, they need to be incorporated into the annual report of the company. The annual report of a company is governed by legal and professional requirements and has to be presented in a particular way.

BASIC

INTERMEDIATE

ADVANCED

Progress Point 1.2

The following balances have been taken from the books of ABC Ltd at 31 December 2012.

	£	£
Share capital:		
900,000 ordinary shares of £1		900,000
450,000 6% preference shares		450,000
Share premium		255,000
Retained earnings		720,000
10% debenture loan		900,000
Accounts receivable	365,000	
Accounts payable		585,000
Cash	25,000	
Property (at cost)	2,400,000	
Plant and machinery (at cost)	2,850,000	
Inventory (at end)	450,000	
Provision against bad debts		30,000
Accumulated depreciation:		
Property		600,000
Machinery		1,050,000
Directors' remuneration	260,000	
Audit fee	15,000	
Administration expenses	400,000	
Selling expenses	525,000	
Debenture interestw	90,000	
Sales		6,045,000
Cost of sales	4,155,000	
	11,535,000	11,535,000

The following information is to be taken into account.

1. Depreciation on plant and machinery is to be provided at 10% per annum on cost.
2. Provision for doubtful debts is to be adjusted to 2.5% of debtors.
3. Taxation on profit is estimated at £75,000. This amount will be paid next year.
4. The directors have decided to pay the preference dividend, payment to be made during 2013. In addition, the directors declare a dividend of 10p per share on the ordinary shares on 30 November. This was paid in January 2013.
5. At December 2012 the property was revalued at £3,000,000. This new value is to be brought into the statement of financial position.
6. Depreciation of 5% per annum is to be provided on buildings that were valued at £2,000,000.

Required
Prepare a statement of comprehensive income for the year ended 31 December 2012, together with a statement of financial position at that date for internal use.

BASIC

INTERMEDIATE

ADVANCED

Solution

Statement of comprehensive income for the year ended 31 December 2012

	£	£
Sales revenue (turnover)		6,045,000
Cost of sales		4,155,000
Gross profit		1,890,000
Reduction in bad debt provision		20,875
		1,910,875
Directors' fees	260,000	
Audit fee	15,000	
Admin expenses	400,000	
Selling	525,000	
Depreciation: buildings	100,000	
Depreciation: plant	285,000	
Debenture interest	90,000	1,675,000
Profit before tax		235,875
Taxation		75,000
Profit after taxation		160,875

Statement of financial position as at 31 December 2012

Non-current assets	Cost or valuation	Accumulated depreciation	
	£	£	£
Land and buildings	3,000,000	700,000	2,300,000
Plant	2,850,000	1,335,000	1,515,000
	5,850,000	2,035,000	3,815,000
Current assets			
Inventory		450,000	
Accounts receivable	365,000		
Less provision	9,125	355,875	
Cash		25,000	
	830,875		
Less current liabilities			
Accounts payable	585,000		
Dividends payable	117,000		
Tax payable	75,000	777,000	
Net current assets			53,875
Total net assets			3,868,875
Creditors: amounts falling due after more than one year:			
10% debentures			900,000
			2,968,875
Capital and reserves			
Share capital			
900,0000 ordinary shares of £1			900,000
450,000 preference shares of £1			450,000
Share premium			255,000
Revaluation reserve			600,000
Retained earnings (£720,000 + £43,875)			763,875
			2,968,875

BASIC

INTERMEDIATE

ADVANCED

Working notes:

Depreciation

Plant

	£	£
Cost	2,850,000	
Depreciation 10%	£285,000	
Depreciation for year		285,000
Accumulated to date		1,050,000
Total for statement of financial position		1,335,000

Property

	£	£
Total	2,400,000	
Buildings	2,000,000	
Therefore land	400,000	
Depreciation on buildings = 5% of £2,000,000 =		100,000
Depreciation for year		100,000
Accumulated depreciation		600,000
Statement of financial position total		700,000

Bad debts provision

	£
Accounts receivable (debtors)	365,000
Existing provision	30,000
Provision 2.5% =	9,125
Decrease in provision	20,875

(Note: a decrease in provision is accounted for by increasing the profit, i.e. is a credit to the statement of comprehensive income.)

Revaluation of asset

Property revalued upwards by £600,000 (£2,400,000 to £3,000,000)

Dividends

Preference 6% of £450,000	=	£27,000
Ordinary 10% of £900,000	=	90,000
		£117,000
Retained earnings	=	profit for year less preference and ordinary dividends
	=	£160,875 – 27,000 – 90,000
	=	£43,875

It is important to remember that this solution shows the financial statements for *internal* use and not for publication. Financial statements for publication are dealt with in the next section.

Section Summary

Limited company financial statements are publicly available documents. As such, their presentation and content is standardized and is prescribed by law. In addition, various regulatory bodies govern the content and the rules to be followed in the preparation of published financial statements. There are various stakeholders who may have an interest in financial statements, including investors, lenders, creditors and employees. As well as a statement of comprehensive income, statement of financial position, statement of changes in equity and a statement of cash flows, financial statements comprise additional narrative information to assist the user in the decision-making process.

Company financial statements follow the same accounting principles as those applied to other types of business organization. However, in the case of companies, the differences arise in terms of financing and in ownership. Companies are financed by issuing shares, to shareholders, and sometimes by long-term borrowing (debentures). Shareholders are rewarded by being paid a dividend, while debenture holders will receive an interest payment.

Section 2: Intermediate Issues

1.5 The regulatory framework for company financial statements

BASIC

INTERMEDIATE

ADVANCED

Company financial statements that are prepared for external use and for publication are regulated both by law and by accounting standards in order to provide protection for investors. Investors in general use the information provided in company financial statements as a basis to compare different companies. In order for comparison to be meaningful, published financial statements need to be prepared on a similar basis by all companies.

Contents of annual accounts

While the preparation of company annual accounts follows the same principles as for sole traders and partnerships, as would be expected given the wider audience using the financial statements, the content of published annual accounts is significantly greater than for sole traders and partnerships. Users may be seeking more detailed explanation of what is revealed in the accounts, and they may be looking for information about future prospects and performance.

Consequently, as well as the formats of the financial statements being prescribed by law, the content of published financial statements is also prescribed by law.

In addition to a statement of comprehensive income and statement of financial position, companies are required to produce a directors' report that contains a great deal of standardized formal information, including the following:

- principal activities of the company, and any changes
- business review of the activities during the year
- future developments
- research and development activities
- events after the reporting period – any important changes since the end of the reporting period
- value of land and buildings – significant differences between statement of financial position values and market values
- statement about employee involvement

- number of employees with disabilities
- donations to charities and to political parties, each disclosed separately
- purchase of own shares – number of shares purchased, amount paid and reasons for doing so
- information about directors – their names and the number of shares held by each at the beginning and end of the year
- creditor payment – the company's policy should be disclosed, and a calculation given of the average number of days taken to pay creditors.

Substantial information is also provided about directors' remuneration and how it is determined, and about corporate governance and how the directors run the company. There will be an auditor's report and a statement of directors' responsibilities, confirming that the financial statements are the responsibility of the directors and not the auditors. Finally, the financial statements themselves are followed by substantial notes to the financial statements, which provide additional detail to the summarized figures in the statement of comprehensive income and statement of financial position.

Smaller companies

Disclosure requirements are significantly reduced for small and medium-sized companies. Because financial statements have to be filed at Companies House it is not difficult to obtain them; however, the amount of information that can be gleaned from them is extremely limited.

The international accounting standard that deals with presentation of financial statements is IAS 1 *Presentation of Financial Statements*.

1.6 IAS 1 *Presentation of Financial Statements*

Objective of IAS 1

The objective of IAS 1 is to prescribe the basis for general presentation of general purpose financial statements to ensure comparability both with the entity's financial statements of previous periods and with the financial statements of other entities. IAS 1 sets out overall requirements for the presentation of financial statements, guidelines for their structure and minimum requirements for their content (para 1).

Scope

IAS 1 applies to all entities preparing and presenting general purpose financial statements in accordance with International Financial Reporting Standards (para 2).

IAS 1 goes on to define general purpose financial statements as those intended to serve users who are not in a position to require financial reports tailored to their particular information needs (para 7).

The objective of financial statements

Financial statements are a structured representation of the financial position and financial performance of an entity. The objective of financial statements is to provide information about the financial position, the financial performance and cash flows of an entity. This information should be useful to a wide range of users in making economic decisions. Financial statements also show the results of how well the resources of the entity have been managed. In order to meet this objective, financial statements should provide information about an entity's:

- assets
- liabilities
- equity
- income and expenses, including gains and losses
- contributions by owners to the business
- payments to owners
- cash flows.

IAS 1 states (para 9) that this information, along with other information in the notes, assists users of financial statements in predicting the entity's future cash flows and, in particular, their timing and certainty.

Components of financial statements

A complete set of financial statements comprises:

- a statement of financial position (formerly called a balance sheet) as at the end of the period
- a statement of comprehensive income (formerly called an income statement or profit and loss account) for the period
- a statement of changes in equity for the period
- a statement of cash flows for the period
- notes, comprising a summary of the significant accounting policies and other explanatory information.

As was noted in Section 1, IAS 1 permits an entity to use titles for the statements other than those used in the standard (para 10). It also recognizes that an entity may present other reports such as a financial review, environmental report or a value added statement but states that these other reports which are presented outside financial statements are outside the scope of IFRSs.

This chapter will concern itself with the first three. Statements of cash flow will be considered in more detail in Chapter 10. Notes to the accounts are dealt with in the chapters dealing with specific topics, e.g non-current assets. Accounting policies are dealt with in the advanced section of this chapter.

General features

IAS 1 sets out a number of rules relating to the presentation of financial statements under the heading of 'general features'. These are as follows:

(a) Fair presentation and compliance with IFRSs
(b) Going concern
(c) Accrual basis of accounting
(d) Materiality and aggregation
(e) Offsetting
(f) Frequency of reporting
(g) Comparative information
(h) Consistency of presentation.

Each of these is considered in turn.

Fair presentation and compliance with IFRSs

Financial statements must present fairly the financial position, financial performance and cash flows of an entity. Fair presentation requires the faithful representation of the effects of transactions, other events and conditions in accordance with the definitions and recognition criteria for assets, liabilities, income and expenses set out in the Conceptual Framework. (The Conceptual Framework for Financial Reporting is considered in detail in the advanced section of this chapter). It is assumed that the application of IFRSs, with additional disclosure where necessary, will result in financial statements that achieve a fair presentation.

IAS 1 requires that an entity whose financial statements comply with IFRSs make an explicit and unreserved statement of such compliance in the notes. Financial statements shall not be described as complying with IFRSs unless they comply with all the requirements of IFRSs.

IAS 1 states that in virtually all circumstances, an entity achieves a fair presentation by compliance with applicable IFRSs but that a fair presentation also requires an entity to:

(a) select and apply appropriate accounting policies in accordance with the requirements of IAS 8 *Accounting Policies, Changes in Accounting Estimates and Error*. IAS 8 sets out a hierarchy of authoritative guidance that management considers in the absence of an IFRS that specifically applies to an item

(b) present information in a manner that provides relevant, reliable, comparable and understandable information

(c) provide additional disclosures when compliance with the IFRSs is insufficient to enable users to understand the impact of particular transactions, other events and conditions on the entity's financial position and financial performance.

IAS 1 acknowledges (para 19) that in extremely rare circumstances, management may conclude that compliance with an IFRS requirement would be so misleading that it would conflict with the objective of financial statements. In these circumstances, the entity is required to depart from the IFRS requirement, with detailed disclosure of the nature, reasons and impact of the departure.

Going concern

An entity shall prepare financial statements on a going concern basis unless management either intends to cease trading or has no realistic alternative but to do so. If management has significant concerns about the entity's ability to continue as a going concern, those uncertainties must be disclosed. If financial statements are not prepared on a going concern basis, the entity should disclose that fact together with the basis on which it prepared the financial statements and the reason why the entity is not regarded as a going concern.

Accrual basis of accounting

IAS I requires that entity should prepare its financial statements, except for cash flow information, using the accrual basis of accounting.

Materiality and aggregation

Each material class of similar items must be presented separately in the financial statements. IAS 1 notes that financial statements result from processing large numbers of transactions or other events that are aggregated (totalled) into classes according to their nature or function. These aggregated classes then form line items in the financial statements. For example, purchases, carriage in and direct labour costs will be aggregated into a single cost of sales figure which will appear in the statement of comprehensive income.

Where there are items of a dissimilar nature or function these should be presented separately unless they are immaterial. If a line item is not individually material it may be aggregated with other line items.

Importantly, IAS 1 states (para 31) that 'an entity need not provide a specific disclosure required by an IFRS if the information is not material'. This means that compliance with IFRSs can still be achieved without having to disclose immaterial items either as line items in the financial statements or in the notes.

Offsetting

Assets and liabilities, and income and expenses, may not be offset unless required or permitted by an IFRS.

IAS 1 recognizes that unless offsetting reflects the substance of the transaction or other event, it detracts from the users' ability to understand these transactions and events and to assess the entity's future cash flows.

Figure 1.1◦ Marks & Spencer reporting on a 52 week basis		
	52 weeks ended 2 April 2011	53 weeks ended 3 April 2010
	£m	£m
Revenue	9,740.3	9,536.6
Operating profit	836.9	852.0
Finance income	42.3	12.9
Finance costs	(98.6)	(162.2)
Profit before tax	780.6	702.7
Income tax expense	(182.0)	(179.7)
Profit for the year	598.6	523.0

Source: Marks & Spencer (2011), p. 74

Frequency of reporting

An entity shall present a complete set of financial statements at least annually. If the annual reporting period changes and the financial statements are prepared for a different period the entity must disclose the reason for the change and that the amounts presented are not entirely comparable.

IAS 1 also notes that for practical reasons some entities prefer to report for a 52-week period, and that the Standard does not preclude this practice. Marks and Spencer plc, for example, adopts this practice (Figure 1.1).

Note that in the previous period Marks & Spencer reported for 53 weeks.

Comparative information

IAS 1 requires that comparative information shall be disclosed in respect of the previous period for all amounts reported in the current period's financial statements unless another standard requires otherwise. This requirement extends to narrative and descriptive information when it is relevant to an understanding of the current period's financial statements.

Consistency of presentation

The presentation and classification of items in the financial statements should be retained from one period to the next unless a change is justified either by a change in circumstances such that another presentation or classification would be more appropriate, or because an IFRS requires a change in presentation.

Structure and content

IAS 1 requires particular disclosures in the statement of financial position, the statement of comprehensive income and in the statement of changes in equity, and requires disclosure of other line items in those statements or in the notes. These disclosures are dealt with in IAS 1 under the following headings:

(a) Identification of the financial statements

(b) Statement of financial position

(c) Statement of comprehensive income

(d) Statement of changes in equity

(e) Statement of cash flows

(f) Notes.

Each of these is considered in turn.

Identification of financial statements

IFRSs apply only to financial statements and not necessarily to other information presented in an annual report, therefore it is important that the financial statements are clearly identified and distinguished from other information in the same published document. In addition, each financial statement should be clearly identified and the following information displayed prominently and repeated when necessary for the information presented to be understandable.

(a) the name of the reporting entity and any change in that information from the end of the preceding reporting period

(b) whether the financial statements are of an individual entity or a group of entities

(c) the date of the end of the reporting period or the period covered by the set of financial statements or notes

(d) the presentation currency, as defined in IAS 21 (see Chapter 12)

(e) the level of rounding used in presenting amounts in the financial statements (e.g. £000, £m etc)

Statement of financial position

Information to be presented in the statement of financial position

A statement of financial position shows an entity's assets, liabilities and equity at the end of the reporting period.

IAS 1 does not prescribe the specific format this statement should follow, but instead simply lists line items that are sufficiently different in nature or function to warrant separate presentation in the statement of financial position.

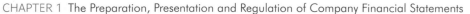

As a minimum the following information should be presented in the statement of financial position:

(a) property, plant and equipment
(b) investment property
(c) intangible assets
(d) financial assets
(e) investments accounted for using the equity method
(f) biological assets
(g) inventories
(h) trade and other receivables
(i) cash and cash equivalents
(j) assets classified as held for sale
(k) trade and other payables
(l) provisions
(m) financial liabilities
(n) liabilities and assets for current tax
(o) deferred tax liabilities and deferred tax assets
(p) liabilities classified as held for sale
(q) non-controlling interests presented within equity
(r) issued capital and reserves attributable to owners of the parent.

Additional line items, headings and subtotals should be presented on the face of the statement of financial position when such presentation is relevant to the understanding of the financial position of the business.

Current/non-current distinction

IAS 1 requires that current and non-current assets, and current and non-current liabilities, should be presented separately in the statement of financial position except when a presentation based on liquidity provides information that is reliable and more relevant.

The standard explains that when an entity supplies goods or services within a clearly identifiable operating cycle, this separate classification of current and non-current assets and liabilities provides useful information by distinguishing the net assets that are continuously circulating as working capital from those used in the entity's long-term operations. It also highlights assets that are expected to be realized within the current operating cycle, and liabilities that are due for settlement within the same period.

Current assets

An asset is classified as current if it satisfies *any* of the following criteria:

- it is expected to be realized, or is intended for sale or consumption, in the normal operating cycle of the business
- it is held primarily for the purpose of being traded
- it is expected to be realized within 12 months after the end of the reporting period
- it is cash, or a cash equivalent (e.g. receivables).

All other assets are non-current. Such assets will include tangible, intangible and financial assets.

The operating cycle of an entity is the time between the acquisition of assets for processing and their realization in cash or cash equivalents. When an entity's normal operating cycle is not clearly identifiable, it is assumed to be 12 months. Note, however, that current assets include items such as inventories and trade receivables that are realized as part of the normal operating cycle even when they are not expected to be realized within 12 months.

The standard uses the term non-current to describe assets of a long-term nature; however, it does not prohibit the use of alternative descriptions as long as the meaning is clear.

Current liabilities

A liability is classified as current if it satisfies *any* of the following criteria:

- it is expected to be settled in the normal operating cycle of the business
- it is held primarily for the purpose of being traded
- it is due to be settled within 12 months after the end of the reporting period
- the business does not have a right to defer settlement of the liability for at least 12 months after the end of the reporting period.

A liability that does not satisfy any of these criteria is a non-current liability. In a manner similar to current assets, current liabilities include items such as trade payables and accrued expenses that are expected to be settled during the operating cycle, even if they are not expected to be settled within 12 months. Current liabilities also include items such as bank overdrafts, dividends payable and income taxes which are not settled as part of the normal operating cycle but which are due to be settled within 12 months.

Information to be presented either in the statement of financial position or in the notes

It is important to note that some of the line items in the statement of financial position can contain a variety of different items and it may be useful to users to be aware of the make-up of such items. IAS 1 has a general requirement that, either on the face of the statement of financial position or in the notes, further sub-classifications should be provided as appropriate. Some sub-classifications are required by accounting standards, others are a matter of judgement. Examples given include:

- property, plant and equipment analysed into major classes (as required by IAS 16)
- receivables, analysed into, for example, trade receivables, prepayments and other amounts, receivables from other customers
- inventories analysed as required by IAS 2
- provisions analysed into provisions for employee benefits and others as required by IAS 37
- equity, analysed into share capital, share premium, and revaluation reserve.

The following disclosures are also required by IAS 1 in relation to share capital either in the statement of financial position or the statement of changes in equity (covered later in this chapter), or in the notes.

(a) For each class of share capital:
  (i) the number of shares authorized;
  (ii) the number of shares issued and fully paid, and issued but not fully paid;
  (iii) the par value per share;
  (iv) a reconciliation of the number of shares outstanding at the beginning and at the end of the period;
  (v) the rights, preferences and restrictions attaching to that class of share.
(b) A description of the nature and purpose of each reserve within equity.

Figure 1.2 is an illustrative presentation of a statement of financial position in accordance with IAS 1.

Statement of comprehensive income

Introduction

As noted in the introductory section to this chapter, the traditional profit and loss account is, under international standards, known as the statement of comprehensive income. More significant, however, is the distinction between what is traditionally included in the profit and loss account as income and what is included as comprehensive income in the statement of comprehensive income. Perhaps the most surprising of these items for the student new to IFRS is a revaluation gain on a non-current (fixed) asset. In the financial statements of an unincorporated business, such a revaluation gain would be credited directly to reserves; under IFRS, however, this gain will be presented in the statement of comprehensive income.

The statement is a financial performance statement which shows an entity's total income and expenses recognized for a period. Most income and expenses will be taken into account in arriving at an entity's profit or loss for the reporting period. However, some international standards require that certain types of income or expense should be disregarded when calculating an entity's profit and loss. Consequently, because the purpose of the statement is to show total comprehensive income, the statement also includes

Figure 1.2 Statement of financial position in accordance with IAS 1

XYZ Group
Statement of Financial Position as at 31 December 2012

ASSETS

Non-current assets	£
Property, plant and equipment	350,700
Goodwill	80,800
Other intangible assets	227,470
Investment in associates	100,150
Available for sale financial assets	142,500
	901,620
Current assets	
Inventories	135,230
Trade receivables	91,600
Other current assets	25,650
Cash and cash equivalents	312,400
	564,880
Total assets	1,466,500

EQUITY AND LIABILITIES

Equity attributable to owners of the parent	
Share capital	650,000
Revaluation reserve	240,000
Retained earnings	83,750
Total equity	973,750
Non-current liabilities	
Bank loans	100,000
Long-term borrowings	40,000
Deferred taxation	20,000
Obligations under a finance lease	10,000
Provisions	7,650
Total non-current liabilities	177,650
Current liabilities	
Trade and other payables	115,100
Bank overdrafts and loans	150,000
Current tax	45,000
Provisions	5,000
Total current liabilities	315,100
Total liabilities	492,750
Total equity and liabilities	1,466,500

BASIC

INTERMEDIATE

ADVANCED

those items of income and expense that are not recognized in profit or loss. Such items are known as 'other comprehensive income' and include:

(a) changes in revaluation surplus arising on tangible non-current assets

(b) changes in revaluation surplus arising on intangible assets

(c) gains and losses arising from translating the financial statements of a foreign operation.

In broad terms the effect of the statement is to disclose, as income, all profits and gains in the period, whether realized or unrealized. IAS 1 makes the distinction between owner changes in equity such as dividends paid and non-owner changes in equity such as revaluation gains. The statement of comprehensive income thus reports all non-owner changes in equity.

It should be noted that despite its name, the statement can also include expenses within 'other comprehensive income'. This means that other comprehensive income can be negative.

IAS 1 requires that an entity shall present all items of income and expense recognized in a period:

(a) in a single statement of comprehensive income, or

(b) in two statements: a statement displaying the components of profit or loss (i.e. a separate income statement) and a second statement beginning with the profit or loss, and showing other comprehensive income in a separate statement (statement of comprehensive income).

There has been some debate over the choice of methods permitted by IAS 1, and an exposure draft was issued which proposed eliminating this choice and requiring a single statement of comprehensive income in all cases. On 16 June 2011, however, the IASB published amendments to IAS 1 which retain the 'one or two statement' approach at the option of the entity.

Information to be presented in the statement of comprehensive income

Information to be presented in the statement of comprehensive income includes the following minimum information requirements:

(a) revenue

(b) finance costs

(c) share of profit (or loss) of associate and joint ventures (see Chapter 11)

(d) tax expense

(e) a single amount comprising the total of
   – the post-tax profit or loss of discontinued operations;
   – the post-tax gain or loss recognized on the measurement to fair value on the disposal of the assets constituting the discontinued operation;

(f) profit or loss

(g) each component of other comprehensive income

(h) share of other comprehensive income of associates and joint ventures

(i) total comprehensive income.

In addition to this information, the following items should be disclosed in the statement of comprehensive income as allocations of profit or loss for the period:

(a) profit (or loss) attributable to non-controlling interests (minority interest) (see Chapter 11)

(b) profit (or loss) attributable to owners of the parent (see Chapter 11).

Also total comprehensive income for the period attributable to:

(a) non-controlling interests, and

(b) owners of the parent.

A non-controlling interest is the proportion of a company that is owned by outside interests. This is often referred to as the minority interest. This is dealt with more fully in Chapter 11.

Example

During the year to 31 December 2012 Ermat plc writes off a debt due by Bartos plc of £76,500,000. This level of write-off is considered to be exceptional and unlikely to recur. Ermat plc would report this as follows:

Ermat statement of comprehensive income for the year ended 31 December 2012		
	2012	2011
	£000	£000
TURNOVER	903,690	704,820
Cost of sales	(565,622)	489,847
Gross profit	338,068	214,973
Administrative expenses – bad debt charge	(76,500)	–
Administrative expenses – other	(229,605)	198,541
Administrative expenses – total	(306,105)	(198,541)
Profit before tax	31,963	16,432

In a manner similar to the statement of financial position, an entity should present additional line items, headings and subtotals when such presentation is relevant to an understanding of the entity's financial performance.

An important additional requirement in IAS 1 is that an entity should not present any items of income or expense as extraordinary items either in the statement of comprehensive income or the separate income statement (if presented) or in the notes. This is an important point. The standard is not stating that extraordinary items cannot be disclosed separately – it is stating that they cannot be disclosed as extraordinary. Instead, such items should be allocated to an expense line item and disclosed under the general heading to which the expense belongs.

Profit or loss for the period

An entity shall recognize all items of income and expense in a period in profit or loss unless an IFRS requires or permits otherwise. As noted earlier, the requirements of specific standards such as IAS 16 *Property, Plant and Equipment* mean that surpluses arising on the revaluation of tangible non-current assets should be presented as other comprehensive income.

Other comprehensive income for the period

The amount of taxation relating to each component of other comprehensive income needs to be disclosed either in the statement of comprehensive income or in the notes. The components of other comprehensive income may be disclosed either net of taxation, or before taxation with one amount shown for the total amount of taxation relating to those components.

Information to be presented in the statement of comprehensive income or in the notes

When items of income or expense are material, an entity needs to disclose these separately. There are a number of circumstances that will give rise to separate disclosure of such items. These include:

(a) write-down of inventories to net realizable value or of property, plant and equipment to recoverable amount, as well as reversals of such write-downs

(b) restructuring of a business

(c) disposals of items of property, plant and equipment

(d) disposals of investments

Example 1
Analysis of expenses by nature of expense

Statement of comprehensive income

	£000
Revenue	25,000
Other income	700
Changes in inventories of finished goods and work in progress	(1,000)
Raw materials used	(10,200)
Employee benefit costs	(5,600)
Depreciation	(1,300)
Other expenses	(900)
Operating profit	6,700
Finance costs	(1,500)
Profit before tax	5,200
Taxation	(1,800)
Profit for the period	3,400

Example 2
Analysis of expenses by function of expense

Statement of comprehensive income

	£000
Revenue	25,000
Cost of sales	(14,800)
Gross profit	10,200
Other income	700
Distribution costs	(1,900)
Administration costs	(1,400)
Other expenses	(900)
Operating profit	6,700
Finance costs	(1,500)
Profit before tax	5,200
Taxation	(1,800)
Profit for the period	3,400

(e) discontinued operations

(f) legal settlements

(g) other reversals of provisions.

BASIC

INTERMEDIATE

ADVANCED

How are expenses to be shown?

Expenses should be analysed either by *nature* (e.g. raw materials, staffing costs, depreciation) or by *function* (e.g. cost of sales, administration, finance). The information must be shown either on the face of the statement of comprehensive income or in the notes. If a business classifies expenses by function, then additional information on the nature of expenses, such as depreciation and staff costs, must be disclosed. Both statements in the examples produce the same profit figure. The only difference is how the expenses are analysed. Companies that analyse expenses by function must disclose this information in the notes. This must include information on the nature of expenses, including depreciation and employee benefit expenses.

There is no definitive list of items that should appear under the functional headings. The following is a suggested list.

(a) *Cost of sales*

This relates to the cost of production or provision of goods, and services and will include:

- direct costs of production (raw materials, labour, components, direct expenses)
- production overheads – overheads should be classified by function and can include costs that vary with time as well as with output; depreciation, rent and costs associated with production would be included; the costs of general management as opposed to functional management would not be included as these are not related to current production.

(b) *Distribution costs*

This deals with the cost of the distribution of goods to customers. A delivery charge is part of the cost of obtaining the goods and so would be included in cost of sales. Distribution costs can include wages and salaries, freight charges, fuel and road tax. Distribution overheads can include depreciation of vehicles used in distribution.

(c) *Administrative expenses*

These deal with the general costs of running the business, such as salaries and related costs of general management. This would include administrative overheads.

Figure 1.3(a) is an illustration of comprehensive income presented in one statement with expenses classified within profit by *function*.

Any taxation relating to each component of comprehensive income should be disclosed in the notes to the accounts.

Alternatively this information could be presented in two statements as shown in Figures 1.3(b) and (c).

BASIC

INTERMEDIATE

ADVANCED

Figure 1.3(a) Comprehensive income in one statement

XYZ Statement of comprehensive income for the year ended
31 December 2012

	£
Revenue	390,000
Cost of sales	(245,000)
Gross profit	145,000
Other income	20,667
Distribution costs	(9,000)
Administrative expenses	(20,000)
Other expenses	(2,100)
Finance costs	(8,000)
Share of profit of associate	35,100
Profit before tax	161,667
Taxation	(40,417)
Profit for the year	121,250
Other comprehensive income	
Exchange differences on foreign operations	5,000
Gains on property revaluation	50,000
Other comprehensive income for the year	55,000
Total comprehensive income for the year	176,250

Figure 1.3(b) Comprehensive income statement in two parts: income statement

XYZ Income statement for the year ended 31 December 2012

	£
Revenue	390,000
Cost of sales	(245,000)
Gross profit	145,000
Other income	20,667
Distribution costs	(9,000)
Administrative expenses	(20,000)
Other expenses	(2,100)
Finance costs	(8,000)
Share of profit of associate	35,100
Profit before tax	161,667
Taxation	(40,417)
Profit for the year	121,250

Figure 1.3(c) Comprehensive income statement in two parts: other comprehensive income

Statement of comprehensive income for the year ended 31 December 2012

	£
Profit for the year	121,250
Other comprehensive income	
Exchange differences on foreign operations	5,000
Gains on property revaluation	50,000
Other comprehensive income for the year	55,000
Total comprehensive income for the year	176,250

BASIC

INTERMEDIATE

ADVANCED

In addition to the statement of comprehensive income (income statement) and statement of financial position (balance sheet), IAS 1 requires an additional primary financial statement: *statement of changes in equity*.

Statement of changes in equity
Information to be presented in the statement of changes in equity
IAS 1 requires a company to present a statement of changes in equity as a separate component of the financial statements. The statement reconciles the capital and reserves at the beginning of the period with those at the end.

A statement of changes in equity will show:

(a) total comprehensive income for the period, showing separately the total amount attributable to owners of the parent company and to non-controlling interests

(b) for each component of equity, a reconciliation between the carrying amount at the beginning and end of the period; changes resulting from the following should be disclosed separately

  (i) profit or loss

Progress Point 1.3

The following is an extract from the trial balance of H plc as at 30 November 2012.

	£	£
Purchase of raw materials	2,100,000	
Sales revenue		9,300,000
Wages and salaries	1,850,000	
Inventory at 1 December 2011	325,000	
Depreciation:		
Plant and machinery	185,000	
Motor vehicles	26,000	
Office equipment	10,400	
Buildings	28,000	
Employer's national insurance	190,000	
Rent received		12,500
Other external charges	2,620,000	
Company contribution to pension	160,000	

Additional information

1. Inventory at 30 November 2012 has been valued at £348,000. Inventory comprises the following:

	30.11.12	30.11.11
Raw materials	£65,000	£60,000
Work in progress	£34,000	£38,000
Finished goods	£249,000	£227,000
	£348,000	£325,000

2. It is estimated that employment costs and other external charges can be allocated as follows:

	%
Cost of sales	72
Distribution	18
Administration	10

3. Plant and machinery, motor vehicles and office equipment relate to cost of sales, distribution costs and administrative expenses, respectively. Buildings depreciation is 60% to cost of sales, 20% to distribution and 20% to administration.

Required

As far as the information given permits, prepare the statement of comprehensive income of H plc in accordance with IAS 1, using:

(a) analysis by function

(b) analysis by nature.

BASIC

INTERMEDIATE

ADVANCED

Solution

(a) Classification of expenses by function:

Statement of comprehensive income for the year ended 30 November 2012	
	£
Revenue	9,300,000
Cost of sales	(5,749,200)
Gross profit	3,550,800
Other income	12,500
Distribution costs	(899,200)
Administrative expenses	(498,000)
Operating profit	2,166,100

Working notes

	Cost of sales	Distribution	Administration
	£	£	£
Opening inventory	325,000	–	–
Purchases	2,100,000	–	–
Wages and salaries	1,332,000	333,000	185,000
Employer's NI	136,800	34,200	19,000
Pension contributions	115,200	28,800	16,000
Other charges	1,886,400	471,600	262,000
Depreciation			
P&M	185,000	–	–
Motor vehicles	–	26,000	–
Office equipment	–	–	10,400
Buildings	16,800	5,600	5,600
Closing inventory	(348,000)	–	–
	5,749,200	899,200	498,000

Each expense is allocated to the appropriate function, either directly or apportioned according to the information given.

(b) Classification by nature:

Statement of comprehensive income for the year ended 30 November 2012	
	£
Revenue	9,300,000
Other income	12,500
Change in inventories of finished goods and work in progress	18,000
Raw materials and consumables used	(2,095,000)
Employee benefits	(2,200,000)
Depreciation	(249,400)
Other expenses	(2,620,000)
Operating profit	2,166,100

BASIC

INTERMEDIATE

ADVANCED

Working notes

Change in inventory	£
Finished goods and work in progress at 30.11.12 (£34,000 + £249,000)	283,000
Finished goods and work in progress at 30.11.11 (£38,000 + £227,000)	265,000
Increase	18,000

An increase in closing inventory will have the effect of reducing the cost of sales and so will increase profit. It will be a credit in the statement of comprehensive income. The converse would be true of a reduction in closing inventory.

Raw materials	£
Opening inventory	60,000
Purchases	2,100,000
Less closing inventory	(65,000)
	2,095,000
Employee benefits	
Wages and salaries	1,850,000
Employer's NI	190,000
Pension contributions	160,000
	2,200,000
Depreciation	
Plant and machinery	185,000
Motor vehicles	26,000
Office equipment	10,400
Buildings	28,000
	249,400

   (ii) each item of other comprehensive income

   (iii) transactions with owners, e.g.

      – Contributions by owners

      – Distributions to owners (dividends).

Information to be presented in the statement of changes in equity or in the notes

Additional information must be provided either in the statement of changes in equity or in the notes namely:

(a) for each component of equity, an analysis of other comprehensive income by item

(b) the amount of dividends recognized as distributions to owners during the period and the related amount of dividends per share.

Figure 1.4 is an illustration of the statement of changes in equity.

Statement of cash flows

The standard notes that cash flow information provides users of financial statements with a basis to assess the ability of the entity to generate cash and the needs of the entity to utilize these cash flows. IAS 7 (Chapter 10) sets out requirements for the presentation and disclosure of cash flow information.

Figure 1.4 Statement of changes in equity

	Share capital	Retained earnings	Foreign currency	Revaluation surplus	Non-controlling interests	Total
	£	£	£	£	£	£
Balance at start	650,000	1,750	0	200,000	64,750	916,500
Total comp. income		97,000	4,000	40,000	35,250	176,250
Dividends		(15,000)				(15,000)
Balance at end	650,000	83,750	4,000	240,000	100,000	973,750

Progress Point 1.4

The following are the extracts from the accounts of ABC Ltd.

Statement of financial position extract		
As at	31 Dec 2012	31 Dec 2011
Capital and reserves	£000	£000
Share capital	8,000	7,000
Share premium	890	600
Revaluation reserve	870	400
Retained earnings	3,380	2,600
	13,140	10,600

Statement of comprehensive income extract	
For the year until	31 Dec 2012
	£000
Profit before tax	1,100
Taxation	(300)
Profit for the year	800

Additional information

1. The company issued 1 million ordinary shares of £1 at £1.29 per share. The issue was made during the year ended 31 December 2012.
2. Property revaluation at the year end gave a surplus of £350,000 and there was a revaluation gain of £250,000 on investments.
3. Additional depreciation on previous revalued assets was £40,000.
4. An asset previously revalued in 2007 was sold. The balance in the revaluation reserve relating to this asset at the date of disposal was £90,000.
5. Dividend payments of £150,000 were made during the year.

BASIC

INTERMEDIATE

ADVANCED

Required

Prepare the following for inclusion in the financial statements of ABC plc for the year ended 31 December 2012 in, accordance with IAS 1:

(a) statement of comprehensive income

(b) statement of changes in equity.

Solution

(a)

Statement of comprehensive income	
	£000
Profit for the year	800
Other comprehensive income	
Gain on revaluation of investments	250
Gain on property revaluation	350
Other comprehensive income for the year	600
Total comprehensive income for the year	1,400

(b)

	Ordinary share capital	Share premium	Revaluation reserve	Retained profits	Total
Statement of changes in equity					
	£000	£000	£000	£000	£000
At 31.12.11	7,000	600	400	2,600	10,600
Profit for the year				800	800
Dividends				(150)	(150)
Revaluation surplus			600		600
Revaluation gain realized (i)			(90)	90	
Additional depreciation (ii)			(40)	40	
Issue of shares	1,000	290	–	–	1,290
At 31.12.12	8,000	890	870	3,380	13,140

Notes:

(i) The amount in the revaluation reserve relating to the asset disposal of i.e. £90,000 is treated as realized and transferred to retained profits.

(ii) The additional depreciation charged on the revalued assets may be transferred from revaluation reserve to retained earnings.

Note that both of these transfers take place in the statement of changes in equity and have no effect on the statement of comprehensive income.

Progress Point 1.5

The following trial balance is taken from the books of Krystal, a publicly listed company.

Trial balance at 31 March 2013		
	£000	£000
Land and buildings at cost	270,000	
Plant and machinery at cost	156,000	
Investment properties at valuation	90,000	
Purchases	78,200	
Operating expenses	39,500	
Dividends paid	15,000	
Inventory at 1 April 2012	37,800	
Trade receivables	53,200	
Revenue		278,400
Income from investment property		4,500
Equity shares of £1 each		150,000
Retained earnings at 1 April 2012		119,500
Long-term loan (8%)		50,000
Accumulated depreciation at 1 April 2012		
Buildings		60,000
Plant and machinery		26,000
Trade payables		33,400
Deferred taxation		12,500
Bank		5,400
	739,700	739,700

The following notes are relevant.

1. The land and buildings were purchased on 1 April 1997. The cost of the land was £70 million. No land and building have been purchased since that date. On 1 April 2012 the company had its land and buildings professionally valued at £80 million and buildings valued at £175 million. The estimated life of the buildings was originally 50 years and the remaining life has not changed as a result of the valuation.

2. Plant is depreciated at 15% per annum using the reducing balance method. Depreciation on buildings and plant is charged to the cost of sales.

3. The long-term loan was raised on 1 April 2012. At the year end, interest had not yet been paid.

4. The provision for taxation for the year to 31 March 2013 has been estimated at £28.3 million.

5. Inventory at 31 March 2013 was valued at £43.2 million.

Required

Prepare the following financial statements for the year ended 31 March 2013 in accordance with IAS 1:

(a) statement of comprehensive income

(b) statement of changes in equity

(c) statement of financial position.

Solution

Working notes	£
Cost of sales:	
Opening inventory	37,800
Purchases	78,200
	116,000
Closing inventory	43,200
	72,800
Depreciation: plant	19,500
Depreciation: buildings	5,000
	97,300
Depreciation:	
Plant at cost:	156,000
Accumulated depreciation	26,000
Net book value	130,000
Depreciation rate	15%
Depreciation =	19,500

Land and buildings

	Land	Buildings	Total
	£000	£000	£000
Cost	70,000	200,000	270,000
Depreciation	0	60,000	60,000
Carrying amount	70,000	140,000	210,000
Revaluation	10,000	35,000	45,000
Carrying amount	80,000	175,000	255,000

Buildings have been depreciated from 1997 to 2012, a period of 15 years. Therefore, £60m represents depreciation of £4m each year. New carrying amount = £175m; remaining life = 35 years, therefore new depreciation = £5,000 per annum.

Carrying amounts for property, plant and equipment

	Cost	Depreciation	Net book value
Plant	£000	£000	£000
Costs	156,000	26,000	130,000
Depreciation for the year	–	19,500	–
	156,000	45,500	110,500
Property (land and buildings)			
Carrying amount	255,000	5,000	250,000
Total			360,500

(a) Statement of comprehensive income

	£000
Revenue	278,400
Cost of sales	(97,300)
Gross profit	181,100
Other income	4,500
Operating expenses	(39,500)
Finance costs	(4,000)
Profit before tax	142,100
Taxation	28,300
Profit for the year	113,800
Other comprehensive income	
Gains on property revaluation	45,000
Other comprehensive income for the year	45,000
Total comprehensive income for the year	158,800

If there was a minority share in the company, then both the profit for the year and total comprehensive income would be split into that portion which was attributable to the parent company and that which was attributable to the minority (non-controlling) interest.

(b) Statement of changes in equity

	Share capital	Revaluation reserve	Retained profits	Total
	£000	£000	£000	£000
At 1.04.2012	150,000	–	119,500	269,500
Profit for the year			113,800	113,800
Revaluation of property	–	45,000		45,000
Dividend paid	–	–	(15,000)	(15,000)
At 31.03.2013	150,000	45,000	218,300	413,300

(c) Statement of financial position as at 31 March 2013

Assets	
Non-current assets	£000
Property, plant and equipment	360,500
Investment property	90,000
	450,000
Current assets	
Inventory	43,200
Trade receivables	53,200
	96,400
Total assets	546,900

Equity and liabilities	
Equity attributable to owners	
Share capital	150,000
Retained earnings	218,300
Revaluation reserve	45,000
Total equity	413,300
Non-current liabilities	
Long-term borrowing	50,000
Deferred taxation	12,500
Total non-current liabilities	62,500
Current liabilities	
Trade payables	33,400
Accrued interest	4,000
Taxation	28,300
Bank overdraft	5,400
Total current liabilities	71,100
Total equity and liabilities	546,900

Notes

Structure

Throughout this review of IAS 1, reference has been made to the notes which accompany the financial statements. These notes are an integral part of the financial statements and consequently fall within the scope of IAS 1.

The notes should:

(a) present information about the basis of preparation of the financial statements and the specific accounting policies used including:

  (i) the measurement basis (or bases) used in preparing the financial statements, and

  (ii) the other accounting policies used that are relevant to an understanding of the financial statements

(b) disclose the information required by IFRSs that is not presented elsewhere in the financial statements

(c) provide any additional information which is relevant to an understanding of any of the financial statements.

The notes should be presented in a systematic manner and cross-referenced to the financial statements. The notes should normally be presented in the following order to assist users to understand the financial statements and to compare them with financial statements of other entities:

(a) a statement of compliance with IFRSs

(b) a summary of significant accounting policies applied

(c) supporting information for items presented in the financial statements in the order in which each statement and each line item is presented

(d) other disclosures including:

  (i) contingent liabilities (see Chapter 8) and unrecognized contractual commitments, and

  (ii) non-financial disclosures, such as the entity's financial risk management objectives and policies.

Disclosure of accounting policies

Accounting policies are the specific principles, bases, conventions, rules and practices applied by an entity in preparing and presenting financial statements. An example would be the use of the cost model rather than the revaluation model for measuring properties.

As noted above, an entity is required to disclose in the summary of significant accounting policies the measurement basis or bases used in the financial statements (e.g. historic cost, net realizable value etc.), as well as any other accounting policies that are relevant to an understanding of the financial statements. In addition, the judgements, apart from those involving estimations, that management have made in the process of applying the entity's accounting policies that have the most significant effect on the amounts recognized in the financial statements should also be disclosed. An example cited by IAS 1 is whether, in substance, particular sales of goods are financing arrangements and therefore do not give rise to revenue.

Sources of estimation uncertainty

It may be necessary for an entity to make estimations of uncertain future events when determining the amount at which assets or liabilities are carried in the financial statements. If there is a significant risk that these sources of estimation uncertainty may cause a material adjustment to the carrying amounts of assets or liabilities within the next financial year, IAS 1 requires that the notes to the financial statements should disclose details of the nature of the estimation uncertainty and details of the assumptions that have been made.

IAS 1 states that these disclosures do not involve disclosing budgeted information or forecasts.

Other disclosures

In addition to the distributions information in the statement of changes in equity, an entity must also disclose in the notes:

(a) the amount of dividends proposed or declared before the financial statements were authorized for issue but not recognized as a distribution during the period

(b) the amount of any cumulative preference dividends not recognized

(c) unless disclosed elsewhere in information published with the financial statements, the entity's domicile and legal form, its country of incorporation, the address of its registered office and a description of the nature of the entity's operations and its principal activities

(d) if the entity is part of a group, the name of its parent and the ultimate parent of the group.

Summary

IAS 1 sets out overall requirements for the presentation of financial statements, guidelines for their structure and minimum requirements for their content. Significant differences from the traditional profit and loss account and balance sheet for the student new to IFRS are the terminologies and the reporting of all non-owner changes in equity within the statement of comprehensive income. This brings, for example, revaluation surpluses on non-current assets to the user's attention more readily and helps to explain the change in net assets over a period. All owner changes in equity, for example dividends paid, are shown in the statement of changes in equity. The purpose of this is to provide information by aggregating items with shared characteristics and separating items with different characteristics.

IAS 1 also requires an entity to present a statement of financial position at the end of the reporting period together with a statement of cash flows. All four statements should be supplemented by disclosures in the notes to the financial statements. Some disclosures may be required by IFRSs while others may be relevant to an understanding of the financial statements.

As was noted earlier, an entity achieves a fair presentation by compliance with IFRSs. The next section considers the International Accounting Standards Board regulatory function in more detail, covering its structure, objectives, the standard setting process and the structure of an international standard.

Disclosure in practice

Throughout this book, real life examples of disclosure in practice are illustrated using extracts from the financial statements of Logica plc. It is indicative of the dynamic business environment in which companies operate today that Logica plc was acquired by another company, CGI, a leading business and technology services company in August 2012 and as such the Logica name and brand no longer exists. Prior to the acquisition in the notes to its financial statements, Logica provided this general information about the company:

General information

Logica [...] provides business consulting, systems integration and outsourcing services to clients around the world, including many of Europe's largest businesses. Logica creates value for clients by successfully integrating people, business and technology. It is committed to long-term collaboration, applying insight to create innovative answers to clients' business needs. The Company is a public limited company incorporated and domiciled in the UK.

Source: Logica (2011), p. 96

Companies are required to meet the specific disclosure requirements as laid down by legislation. Logica, which controls a number of companies, discloses information for Logica, the company, and for combined information of Logica and all the other companies it controls. This is referred to as the 'consolidated financial statements of the group'. This is covered in detail in Chapter 11, on business combinations.

The company statement of financial position is given in Figure 1.5. Note that information is given for the current and the previous year.

Figure 1.5 Logica: company statement of financial position

Company statement of financial position

31 December 2011

	2011 £'m	2010 £'m
Fixed assets		
Investments	1,417.2	1,379.5
Current assets		
Debtors: amounts due within one year	578.1	455.8
Cash at bank and in hand	1.6	0.7
	579.7	456.5
Creditors – amounts falling due within one year	(2.4)	(3.4)
Net current assets	577.3	453.1
Total assets less current liabilities	1,994.5	1,832.6
Creditors – amounts falling due after one year	(297.3)	(88.7)
Net assets	1,697.2	1,743.9
Capital and reserves		
Called-up equity share capital	161.2	160.2
Share premium account	1,110.6	1,107.4
Profit and loss account	393.7	444.6
Capital redemption reserve	8.4	8.4
Other reserves	23.3	23.3
Equity shareholders' funds	1,697.2	1,743.9

Source: Logica (2011), p. 144

Figure 1.6 Logica: consolidated statement of comprehensive income

Consolidated statement of comprehensive income
for the year ended 31 December 2011

	2011 £'m	2010 £'m
Revenue	3,921.3	3,696.8
Net operating costs	(3,866.8)	(3,486.2)
Operating profit	**54.5**	210.6
Analysed as:		
Operating profit before exceptional items	59.3	212.3
Exceptional items	(4.8)	(1.7)
Operating profit	54.5	210.6
Finance costs	(36.1)	(27.2)
Finance income	13.3	8.9
Share of post-tax profits from associates	1.0	0.6
Profit before tax	**32.7**	192.9
Taxation	(5.5)	(40.8)
Net profit for the year	27.2	152.1
Other comprehensive income/(expense)		
Actuarial gains/(losses) on retirement benefit schemes	26.7	(3.1)
Tax on items taken directly to equity	(7.3)	0.6
Cash flow hedges	(3.2)	–
Interest rate swaps fair value difference	0.1	(0.1)
Exchange differences on translation of foreign operations	(54.0)	11.4
Other comprehensive income/(expense) for the year, net of tax	(37.7)	8.8
Total comprehensive income/(expense) for the year	(10.5)	160.9

Source: Logica (2011), p. 92

1.7 The International Accounting Standards Board

The International Accounting Standards Board (IASB) was formed in 2001 having as its objectives a commitment to developing, in the public interest, a single set of high-quality, global accounting standards that require transparent and comparable information in general purpose financial statements.

The IASB consists of 16 members whose qualifications for membership are professional competence and practical experience. They are selected in such a way that a broad geographical balance is maintained on the board.

The IASB is selected, overseen and funded by the International Financial Reporting Standards Foundation. The IFRS Foundation receives financial support from the major accounting firms, private financial institutions and industrial companies throughout the world, central and development banks, and other international and professional organizations.

BASIC

INTERMEDIATE

ADVANCED

Figure 1.7 Logica: consolidated statement of changes in equity

Consolidated statement of changes in equity
for the year ended 31 December 2011

	Share capital £'m	Share premium £'m	Retained earnings £'m	Other reserves £'m	Total share-holders' equity £'m	Non-controlling interests £'m	Total equity £'m
At 1 January 2011	160.2	1,107.4	(239.1)	972.6	2,001.1	0.1	2,001.2
Net profit for the year	–	–	27.2	–	27.2	–	27.2
Other comprehensive income/(expense):							
Actuarial gains on retirement benefit schemes	–	–	26.7	–	26.7	–	26.7
Tax on items taken to equity	–	–	(7.3)	–	(7.3)	–	(7.3)
Cash flow hedges	–	–	–	(3.2)	(3.2)	–	(3.2)
Interest rate swaps fair value difference	–	–	0.1	–	0.1	–	0.1
Exchange differences	–	–	–	(54.0)	(54.0)	–	(54.0)
Total comprehensive income/(expense)	–	–	46.7	(57.2)	(10.5)	–	(10.5)
Transactions with owners:							
Dividends paid	–	–	(70.2)	–	(70.2)	–	(70.2)
Repurchase of non-controlling interests	–	–	–	–	–	(0.1)	(0.1)
Share-based payment	–	–	9.2	–	9.2	–	9.2
Shares allotted under share plans	1.0	3.2	(0.6)	–	3.6	–	3.6
Total transactions with owners	1.0	3.2	(61.6)	–	(57.4)	(0.1)	(57.5)
At 31 December 2011	161.2	1,110.6	(254.0)	915.4	1,933.2	–	1,933.2

At 1 January 2010	160.0	1,107.1	(331.1)	961.2	1,897.2	0.1	1,897.3
Net profit for the year	–	–	152.1	–	152.1	–	152.1
Other comprehensive income/(expense):							
Actuarial losses on retirement benefit schemes	–	–	(3.1)	–	(3.1)	–	(3.1)
Tax on items taken to equity	–	–	0.6	–	0.6	–	0.6
Interest rate swaps fair value difference	–	–	(0.1)	–	(0.1)	–	(0.1)
Exchange differences	–	–	–	11.4	11.4	–	11.4
Total comprehensive income	–	–	149.5	11.4	160.9	–	160.9
Transactions with owners:							
Dividends paid	–	–	(66.8)	–	(66.8)	–	(66.8)
Share-based payment	–	–	9.4	–	9.4	–	9.4
Shares allotted under share plans	0.2	0.3	(0.1)	–	0.4	–	0.4
Total transactions with owners	0.2	0.3	(57.5)	–	(57.0)	–	(57.0)
At 31 December 2010	160.2	1,107.4	(239.1)	972.6	2,001.1	0.1	2,001.2

Source: Logica (2011), p. 95

BASIC

INTERMEDIATE

ADVANCED

The IFRS Foundation

The IFRS Foundation sets out in its constitution that its objectives are:

(a) to develop, in the public interest, a single set of high-quality, understandable, enforceable and globally accepted financial reporting standards based upon clearly articulated principles. These standards should require high-quality, transparent and comparable information in financial statements and other financial reporting to help investors, participants in the world's capital markets and other users of financial information to make economic decisions;

(b) to promote the use and rigorous application of those standards;

(c) in fulfilling the objectives associated with (a) and (b), to take account of, as appropriate, the needs of a range of sizes and types of entities in diverse economic settings;

(d) to promote and facilitate adoption of International Financial Reporting Standards, being the standards and interpretations issued by the IASB, through the convergence of national accounting standards and IFRSs.

These objectives are echoed in the IASB's Preface to International Reporting Standards which sets out the IASB's mission and objectives, the scope of International Financial Reporting Standards, the due process for developing IFRSs and Interpretations, and policies on effective dates, format and language for IFRSs.

Twenty-two Trustees provide oversight of the operations of the IFRS Foundation and the IASB. Their responsibilities include the appointment of members of the IASB, the IFRS Advisory Council and the IFRS Interpretations Committee; monitoring the IASB's effectiveness and adherence to its due process and consultation procedures; establishing and maintaining appropriate financing arrangements; approval of the budget for the IFRS Foundation; and responsibility for constitutional changes. The Trustees comprise individuals who as a group provide an appropriate balance of professional backgrounds, including auditors, preparers, users, academics and other officials securing the public interest.

The IFRS Advisory Council

The IFRS Advisory Council provides a forum for participation by organizations and individuals with an interest in international financial reporting with the objective of:

(a) giving advice to the IASB on agenda discussions and priorities in the IASB's work

(b) informing the IASB of the views of the organizations and individuals on the Council on major standard-setting projects, and

(c) giving advice to the IASB or the Trustees.

The Advisory Council comprises 30 or more members drawn from diverse geographical and functional backgrounds who normally meet at least three times a year.

The IFRS Interpretations Committee

The purpose of the IFRS Interpretations Committee is to interpret the application of IFRSs and provide timely guidance on financial reporting issues not specifically addressed in IFRSs.

A diagrammatical overview of the IFRS Foundation is shown in Figure 1.8.

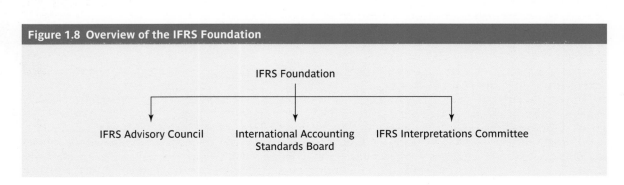

Figure 1.8 Overview of the IFRS Foundation

IFRS Foundation

IFRS Advisory Council   International Accounting Standards Board   IFRS Interpretations Committee

Scope and authority of International Financial Reporting Standards

The IASB achieves its objectives primarily by developing and publishing IFRSs and promoting the use of those standards in general purpose financial statements. IFRSs set out recognition, measurement, presentation and disclosure requirements dealing with transactions and events that are important in general purpose financial statements. IFRSs apply to all general purpose financial statements of profit-oriented entities. The standards refer to entities rather than companies as they apply whether the entities are in corporate or other forms. Such financial statements are directed towards the common information needs of a wide range of users about an entity's financial position, performance and cash flows. A complete set of financial statements includes a statement of financial position, a statement of comprehensive income, a statement of changes in equity, a statement of cash flows, and accounting policies and explanatory notes.

While some IFRSs permit different treatments for given transactions and events, the IASB's objective is to require like transactions and events to be accounted for and reported in a like way. Consequently, in developing standards the IASB intends not to permit choices in accounting treatment and furthermore intends to reconsider the choices in existing IFRSs with the objective of reducing the number of those choices.

Due process

IFRSs are developed through an international due process that involves accountants, financial analysts and other users of financial statements, the business community, stock exchanges, regulatory and legal authorities, academics and other interested individuals and organizations from around the world. The due process for projects normally involves the following steps.

(a) the identification and review of all the issues associated with the topic and consideration of the application of the Conceptual Framework (covered in the advanced aspects section of this chapter) to these issues

(b) a study of national accounting requirements and practice in relation to the topic and an exchange of views about the issues with national standard-setters

(c) consultation with the Trustees and the Advisory Council about the advisability of adding the topic to the IASB's agenda

(d) the publication of a discussion document for public comment

(e) the publication of an exposure draft for public comment

(f) consideration of all comments received with the comment period

(g) approval of a standard by at least nine votes of the IASB if there are fewer than 16 members or by ten of its members if there are 16 members

(h) publication of the standard.

Timing of application of International Financial Reporting Standards

IFRSs apply from a date specified in the document. New or revised IFRSs set out transitional provisions to be applied on their initial application.

1.8 The annual audit

It is generally accepted that compliance with accounting standards will ensure that financial statements will present a true and fair view. Another key protection for investors and other users of financial statements is the annual audit requirement. In an external audit, independent auditors examine the financial statements of an entity and express an opinion on them.

The annual accounts of all companies (with the exception of small companies) must be independently audited. An audit involves obtaining evidence about the amounts and disclosures in the financial statements sufficient to give reasonable assurance that the financial statements are free from material misstatement, whether caused by fraud or error. This includes an assessment of: whether the accounting policies are appropriate to the company's circumstances and have been consistently applied and adequately disclosed; the reasonableness of significant accounting estimates made by the directors; and the overall presentation of the financial statements.

It is worth pausing at this stage to consider the roles of the directors, accountants and auditors in the financial reporting process, and to clarify the responsibilities of each.

The directors

A company's financial statements are the responsibility of the directors. Directors are responsible for the preparation and fair presentation of these financial statements in accordance with International Financial Reporting Standards. This responsibility includes: designing, implementing and maintaining internal controls relevant to the preparation and fair presentation of financial statements that are free from material misstatement, whether due to fraud or error; selecting and applying appropriate accounting policies; and making accounting estimates that are reasonable in the circumstances.

The accountant

The role of the accountant very much depends upon the size of the entity. While the financial statements may well be the responsibility of the directors, in many small limited companies the directors themselves may not have the appropriate accounting and technical knowledge to prepare the financial statements, and consequently will employ accountants to carry out this work. The financial statements will remain the responsibility of the directors, even though they may not have prepared them.

In larger organizations, particularly plcs, it is likely that these will have their own 'in-house' accounting departments that will undertake to prepare the entity's accounts and ensure compliance with the appropriate rules and standards. Again, even though most of the directors may have little accounting expertise, nevertheless the directors will continue to remain responsible for the financial statements.

The auditor

Auditors are professionally qualified persons from the accounting field who are appointed by the shareholders. They are responsible for expressing an opinion on the financial statements. Auditors are required to report to the members whether, in their opinion, the financial statements give a true and fair view, and that the financial statements have been properly prepared in accordance with the Companies Act 2006 and International Financial Reporting Standards.

It is important to note that the auditor may also be the preparer of the financial statements. As noted above, in the case of large plcs, it is likely that there will be an in-house accounting department. In such instances, the role of the auditor will be to examine the financial statements that have been prepared by the company. In many smaller businesses that require an audit, it may well be the case that the auditor will prepare the accounts and then audit them. There is, therefore, a potential conflict of interest. It is not difficult to imagine that pressure could be placed upon auditors/accountants by directors in order to present information in a particular manner. It is for reasons such as this that auditors are subject to extensive and rigorous regulation to ensure their independence, and to ensure that users of financial statements may rely on the reported figures.

The audit report

The annual audit requirement is a further regulation that helps to ensure that publicly available financial statement information can be relied upon. Ultimately, however, the financial statements are the responsibility of the directors and therefore the quality of the reported information is very much dependent on them producing reliable accounting information. Clearly, there may be unscrupulous and dishonest directors who will seek to present misleading information; however, this ought to be identified at the audit stage and brought to the members' attention by means of the annual audit report.

Unqualified opinion

Where an auditor is satisfied of the correctness of the financial statements, an 'unqualified' audit opinion will be given, which states that:

> *the accounts give a true and fair view of the state of affairs of the company and that they have been properly prepared in accordance with all the relevant legislation and accounting standards.*

Qualified opinion

An opinion is referred to as 'qualified' when the directors state that, in their opinion, the accounts give a true and fair view except for certain material matters on which the auditors have reservations. A reservation is material if its omission or misstatement would reasonably influence the decisions of a user of the financial statements. The reservations must be fully explained either in the audit opinion or by reference to a note to the accounts.

Adverse opinion

An adverse opinion is issued when the effect of a disagreement between the auditor and the directors about the treatment or disclosure of a matter in the financial statements is so material and pervasive that the auditor feels that the financial statements are seriously misleading. In this instance, they are required to express the opinion that the 'financial statements do not give a true and fair view'.

Disclaimer of opinion

A disclaimer of opinion is expressed when there has been a limitation on the scope of the auditor's work, and the possible effect of that limitation is so material and pervasive that the auditor has 'not been able to obtain sufficient evidence to form an opinion'. The nature of the limitation should be explained in the audit report together with the fact that the auditor is unable to express an opinion on the financial statements.

Summary

Legislation governs the contents and presentation of financial statements; accounting standards provide mandatory guidance on the accounting treatment of items within the financial statements; directors are responsible for the financial statements; and auditors are responsible for expressing an opinion on the financial statements. Collectively, there is a system in place to ensure the publication of high-quality accounting information by companies. This system, by which companies are directed and controlled, is known as corporate governance. The next section looks in detail at corporate governance requirements and how such requirements have shaped the content of company financial statements.

1.9 Corporate governance

Introduction

In general terms, corporate governance refers to the way in which an organization is administered or controlled. This is usually done by means of a set of processes, policies, laws and institutions. Corporate governance also refers to the ways in which stakeholders in the company, such as shareholders, company management and the board of directors, interact with each other. One important theme of corporate governance is to ensure accountability. Since 2001 there has been a renewed interest in corporate governance practices mainly due to high-profile company failures, such as Enron Corporation and Worldcom, in the USA. Following these company failures, the US Federal Government passed the Sarbanes–Oxley Act, with the intention of restoring public confidence in corporate governance.

Principal/Agency issues

Both the US and UK capital markets have widely dispersed share ownership. This is in contrast to the concentrated shareholdings predominant in Europe and in many developing countries. In general terms, ownership patterns influence the way in which corporate governance is approached by policy makers, and how the potential conflicts of interest between ownership and control are managed. This potential conflict of interest between ownership and control is often referred to as the 'principal/agency' problem. The principals are the owners of the company (the shareholders) and the agents are the boards of directors who have effective control over the company. In countries with widely dispersed shareholdings, the conflict of interest arises between these two groups, in that the agents may allow self-interest to influence decision making.

In contrast, countries that have more concentrated ownership structures often have majority shareholders who have a significant influence on the board of directors. So, in this context a potential conflict can arise between the controlling 'majority' shareholders who may gain additional benefits at the expense of 'minority' owners.

The aim of corporate governance is to protect shareholder rights, improve disclosure of information, help provide an efficient legal framework and help the board of directors to function more effectively. The principal/agency problem is addressed through a mixture of company law, stock exchange requirements and self-regulatory codes.

It should be noted that there is no single approach to corporate governance and it is unlikely that 'one size will fit all'. Some countries in continental Europe have adopted an inclusive 'stakeholder' approach where companies are considered to have a wider remit than being accountable to shareholders. In these countries companies are considered to be 'social institutions' and as such are accountable, not just to shareholders, but to the wider community in general. This is in contrast to the US and UK approaches, where the emphasis is on wealth creation for shareholders.

Principles of good corporate governance

While the approaches to corporate governance may differ, it would be fair to say that most would adhere to the Organization for Economic Co-operation and Development (OECD's) generic corporate governance principles of responsibility, accountability, transparency and fairness:

- responsibility of directors, who take strategic decisions and who employ, monitor and reward management
- accountability of the board of directors to the shareholders, who have a right to receive information on the financial stewardship of their investment
- transparency of information, which is clear and from which some analysis of the company can be made
- fairness, so that all shareholders are treated equally.

Key elements of good corporate governance include honesty, trust, integrity, accountability and commitment to the organization. Senior executives of a company should be seen to be conducting themselves both honestly and ethically in terms of managing a potential conflict of interest and in disclosure of information in financial reports. Commonly accepted principles of corporate governance include those discussed below.

Equitable treatment of shareholders

Organizations should respect the rights of shareholders and also help shareholders exercise those rights though effective means of communication. This implies that information that is communicated to shareholders is both understandable and accessible. Shareholders should also be encouraged to participate in the annual general meeting of the company.

Other stakeholders

Other stakeholders include suppliers, customers, employees, creditors and the community at large. Organizations should recognize that they have obligations, both legal and otherwise, to all such stakeholders.

Board of directors

In order to deal with the various business issues that arise, the board of directors needs to have a range of skills and abilities. In addition, the board needs to have the ability to review and challenge management performance. The board therefore needs to be of sufficient size and have an appropriate level of commitment to fulfil its responsibilities and duties. The mix of executive and non-executive directors needs to be carefully considered. The key roles of chairperson of the board and chief executive officer (CEO) should not be carried out by the same person.

Ethical behaviour

Organizations need to develop a code of conduct that promotes ethical and responsible decision making by the directors.

Disclosure

Organizations should disclose the roles and responsibilities of the board of directors, and of management, so as to provide shareholders with a degree of accountability. Any material matters concerning the organization should be disclosed in good time so as to ensure that all investors have access to factual information, which is clear.

Specific issues involving corporate governance principles include:

- preparation of financial statements
- independence of auditors
- internal controls
- review of compensation arrangements for chief executive
- management of risk
- how individuals are appointed to the board of directors
- dividend policy.

Role of the accountant

For a corporate governance system to function effectively, financial reporting is very important. Accountants and auditors are, in essence, the main providers of information that helps investors and potential investors with their decision making. The directors of a company are entitled to expect that the management of a company conforms with both statutory and regulatory obligations when preparing financial statements.

Under current accounting standards, a degree of choice of method of accounting is possible. This may lead to management selecting an accounting choice to maximize reported profit. This is sometimes referred to as 'creative accounting' and, in extreme cases, this can lead to the non-disclosure of information.

Sometimes an accounting firm acts as both management consultant to an organization and as independent auditor. This may give rise to a conflict of interest in that, if an accounting firm is acting both as consultant and as auditor, there may be some pressure put upon the firm by the client to follow the wishes of management. It is also within the power of management to appoint and dismiss the auditors. This conflict of interest was addressed by the US government, after the collapse of Enron, through the Sarbanes–Oxley Act, which prohibits accounting firms from providing both auditing and management consulting services.

Corporate governance models

The corporate governance models that exist around the world tend to differ according to the variety of capitalism in which they are embedded. The model that is common in Anglo-American countries, often referred to as the 'liberal model', tends to give priority to the interests of shareholders. On the other hand, the model common in continental Europe and Japan, the 'coordinated' model, gives recognition to the interests of workers, managers, customers, suppliers and the community. The liberal model of corporate governance encourages radical innovation and cost competition, whereas the coordinated model favours step-by-step innovation and quality competition. However, that said, there are important differences between the USA and the UK in recent approaches to governance.

Codes and guidelines

Corporate governance principles and codes have been developed in different countries and issued from stock exchanges, companies and institutional investors with the support of governments. In general, compliance with such codes is not a legal requirement, although if a company does not follow stock exchange requirements then it will fail to get a listing. For example, companies quoted on the London Stock Exchange (and Toronto Stock Exchange) need not formally follow the recommendations of the national corporate governance codes. However, if they do not do so, explanations must be provided as to where adherence to the code is not undertaken and reasons why should be given. Such disclosure requirements do put significant pressure on listed companies to comply with the recommendations of the codes.

One of the most influential guidelines has been the OECD Principles of Corporate Governance, published in 1999. This code was revised in 2004 and remains a major focus for corporate governance principles throughout the world. Building on the work of the OECD, other international organizations and national corporate governance codes, the United Nations Intergovernmental Working Group of Experts on International Standards of Accounting and Reporting (ISAR) has produced a voluntary Guidance on Good Practices in Corporate Governance Disclosure. This internationally agreed benchmark consists of more than 50 distinct disclosure items across five broad categories. These categories are identified as:

1. board and management structure and process
2. ownership structure and exercise of control rights
3. financial transparency and information disclosure
4. auditing
5. corporate responsibility and compliance.

Corporate governance in the UK

Corporate governance developments in the UK began in the late 1980s and early 1990s in the wake of company scandals such as Polly Peck and Maxwell. Polly Peck reported very healthy profits one year while the following year filed for bankruptcy. The Maxwell group of companies had entered into a series of high-risk acquisitions, which resulted in a high level of debt being financed by diverting resources from the companies, pension funds. It emerged that one of Maxwell's companies (the Mirror Group) had debts greater than its level of assets, and £440 million was 'missing' from the pension fund.

It was such scandals that led to the formation of the Financial Aspects of Corporate Governance Committee, chaired by Adrian Cadbury. The report published by this committee in 1992 (the Cadbury Report) outlined a number of recommendations around the separation of the role of the chief executive and chairman, balanced composition of the board of directors, selection process for non-executive directors, transparency of financial reporting and the need for good internal controls.

The Cadbury Report included a Code of Best Practice, and its recommendations were incorporated into the listing requirements of the London Stock Exchange. The report's recommendations have been adopted in varying degrees by the European Union, the USA, the World Bank and others.

Following on from Cadbury, a Working Group on Internal Control was established. The remit of this group was to provide guidance to companies on how to comply with 'reporting on the effectiveness of the company's system of internal control', one of the principles of the Cadbury Report. The outcome of this was the publication in 1994 of the Rutteman Report on 'Internal Control and Financial Reporting'.

Following concerns about the level of directors' pay and share options, the Greenbury Report was published in 1995. Greenbury recommended extensive disclosure in annual reports of the remuneration of directors. The report called for the establishment of a remuneration committee comprising non-executive directors. The stock exchange listing rules were amended to incorporate the majority of the recommendations.

The extent to which the Cadbury and Greenbury Reports had been implemented and whether the objectives of these reports had been met was reviewed by the Hampel Committee. The report from this committee, the Hampel Report published in 1998, found there was no need for a revolution in the UK system of corporate governance. The Hampel Report led to the publication of the Combined Code of Corporate Governance.

Part of the Combined Code requires that companies provide a statement in their annual report on how they have applied the provisions of the code relating to internal control. The need for guidance led to the establishment of the Turnbull Committee in 1998 by the Institute of Chartered Accountants in England and Wales (ICAEW), which resulted in the publication of 'Internal Control: Guidance for Directors on the Combined Code'.

In 2001 the relationship between institutional investors and companies was addressed by the Myners Review, commissioned by the government. The resulting report, 'Institutional Investment in the UK', included suggestions for the improvement of communication between investors and companies, and encouraged institutional investors to consider their responsibilities as owners and how they should exercise their rights on behalf of beneficiaries.

The 'Directors' Remuneration Report Regulations' were introduced in 2002. These regulations were to further strengthen the powers of shareholders in relation to directors' pay. The regulations increased the amount of information shareholders are given on directors' remuneration.

A review of the Combined Code was carried out in 2002 at the request of the Department of Trade and Industry (DTI) and the Treasury. This resulted in the publication of the Higgs Report on 'The Role and

Effectiveness of Non-Executive Directors' in 2003. The Higgs Report made a number of recommendations, including the definition of 'independence' and the proportion of non-executive directors on the board and its committees. The role of the senior independent director was to be expanded to provide an alternative channel to shareholders and to lead evaluations on the performance of the chairman. There was also to be added emphasis on the process of nominations to the board of directors through a process that was to be both transparent and rigorous. The performance of the board, its committees and of individual directors was to be evaluated. Higgs strongly backed the existing non-prescriptive approach to corporate governance, yet advocated more provisions with more stringent criteria for board composition and evaluation of independent directors. Higgs wanted to remove some of the discretion of the Combined Code.

Around this time, the Financial Reporting Council published the Smith Report, 'Guidance on Audit Committees'. The UK government was concerned with the independence of auditors in the wake of the collapse of Arthur Andersen and the Enron scandal in the USA in 2002. The Higgs Report was substantially influenced by the views taken by the EU Commission. One important point was that an individual auditor should look at whether a company's corporate governance structure provides safeguards to preserve that individual's independence. The Higgs and Smith Reports were published in 2003, and were followed by the publication of the Tyson Report on the recruitment and development of non-executive directors (NEDs). The Tyson Report was commissioned by the DTI.

Recommendations from the Higgs and Smith Reports led to changes in the Combined Code of Corporate Governance, published in 2003.

The revised code was in sections, covering the following elements.

- *Directors:* this section sets out the requirements for non-executive directors (NEDs); the appointments committee should be run by NEDs and its independence needs to be assured.

- *Directors' remuneration:* this section sets out guidance for the committee that determines directors' remuneration; its focus is that of performance-related pay; the remuneration committee is meant to be composed of NEDs.

- *Accountability and audit:* in this section rules about the audit committee are discussed. The audit committee is meant to be composed only of NEDs; in the wake of the Enron scandal, more emphasis has been placed on high standards of integrity.

- *Relations with institutional shareholders:* this section sets out the best practice of maintaining good relationships with shareholders and keeping them well informed on company affairs.

- *Responsibilities of institutional shareholders:* these provisions deal with a unique part of UK financial market structure, which tends to have a high level of involvement and influence of institutional investors.

The Turnbull Review Group was established in 2004 by the Financial Reporting Council (FRC). The group was to consider the impact of 'Internal Control: Guidance for Directors on the Combined Code', and to determine the extent to which guidance needed to be updated. Revised guidance was published in 2005.

In 2005, following a Company Law Review, the statutory requirement to produce an Operating and Financial Review (OFR) was removed. At the beginning of 2008, the ASB issued a notice reminding companies of the need to follow the enhanced business review reporting requirements contained in the Companies Act 2006.

The European Union also significantly influences corporate governance in the UK. The European Commission's 'Corporate Governance and Company Law Action Plan (May 2003)' proposes a mix of legislative and regulatory measures that will affect all member states. Such measures relate to:

- disclosure requirements
- exercise of voting rights
- cross-border voting
- disclosure by institutional investors
- responsibilities of board members.

The UK has pioneered a flexible model of regulation of corporate governance, known as the 'comply or explain' code of governance. This is a principle-based code that lists a number of recommended practices, as indicated above.

Publicly listed companies in the UK have either to apply such principles or, if they choose not to, to explain in a designated part of their annual reports why they have decided not to comply. The shareholders are then in a position to monitor and judge such explanations. The tenet of the code is that one size does not fit all in matters of corporate governance. Some flexibility needs to be left to companies themselves to make choices appropriate to their particular circumstances. If companies have a good reason not to comply with a particular aspect, then they should be able to explain this to shareholders.

Disclosure in practice

Companies are taking this aspect of reporting very seriously. Consequently, a large part of company reports is devoted to corporate governance aspects. The following sections are given by Logica.

Corporate governance aspects

Corporate governance report

In keeping with our commitment to the highest standards of corporate governance, the Board supports the Financial Reporting Council's 2010 UK Corporate Governance Code (UK Code)

Leadership

What is the Board's composition?

The Group is led by a Board of three Executive and six Non-Executive Directors, two of whom are women. Overall, the Board has an extremely wide range of international, management, governance, commercial and financial expertise which is particularly well suited to our operational requirements.

Effectiveness

How did we assess Board effectiveness?

Following our 2010 external review of the Board's effectiveness, in 2011 the Board undertook more robust reviews of the Group's strategic plans and succession planning. An internal review of effectiveness was also carried out.

The next external review is scheduled for 2013.

Accountability

How did we mitigate risks and uncertainties?

The Board has overall responsibility for our system of internal control and risk management which is implemented by Group management through mandatory policies and procedures. The system is overseen by the Executive Committee and is subject to audit by the Group Internal Audit function.

The effectiveness of the system is kept under regular review by the Audit Committee.

Relations with shareholders

How did we communicate with our investors?

Communicating with shareholders was especially important in 2011. We undertook introductory meetings for shareholders with our new CFO and Executive Director Himanshu Raja, in addition to the normal programme of activities organised by Investor Relations for our Directors and other Executive Committee members. We also undertook to meet our larger shareholders to explain the actions we took in December 2011 to better position the business for 2012.

Note the reference by Logica to the Combined Code.

Source: Logica (2011), p. 58

Non-executive directors' independence

In terms of non-executive directors, and their independence, Logica makes the following disclosures.

Non-Executive Directors

The Non-Executive Directors bring a very broad level of experience to the Board and make a valuable contribution to achieving our objectives. Their primary aims are to maximise shareholder value and develop the Group in line with our strategic goals. All of the Non-Executive Directors together with the Executive Directors and other members of the Executive Committee attended a Board strategy conference during the year organised to discuss and develop the strategic plans for the Group.

Source: Logica (2011), p. 59

Logica also takes its responsibility regarding shareholders very seriously. Shareholders' views are sought, and the company claims these views are listened to. The company indicates that shareholders are welcome to attend the AGM, and provides information about the company on its website. Disclosure is given as outlined below.

Communications with shareholders

The way we communicate with our shareholders is a key priority for the Group. We encourage an active dialogue and ensure that opportunities for engagement, such as the AGM and meetings with institutional investors, are used effectively to provide a clear understanding of our objectives and performance. In 2011, the Chairman and the Chairman of the Remuneration Committee held meetings with a number of existing and prospective shareholders in order to understand their views more comprehensively. In addition, the Chief Executive Officer, Chief Financial Officer and the Head of Investor Relations held meetings with shareholders regarding the Group's normal course of business. In total, during the year, members of the Board and Investor Relations met with around 280 shareholders, or their representatives, at investor meetings and conferences.

The Board is made aware of shareholders' views through direct feedback from face-to-face meetings and presentations with institutional shareholders. As well as meetings with our existing and potential shareholders, Directors also attend meetings with brokers and analysts on a regular basis throughout the year. Institutional shareholders and investors are also offered the opportunity to meet our Senior Independent Director should they wish to discuss any views or concerns that they may have. In addition, Directors are regularly updated on shareholder and market issues through our Investor Relations department which provides summaries of external analysts' reports and direct internal briefings.

Source: Logica (2011), p. 64

The board is made aware of shareholders' views through feedback from face-to-face meetings and presentations with institutional shareholders.

As required by the codes, separation of the role of chairman and chief executive is followed by Logica.

Chairman and chief executive officer

Chairman

The Chairman is responsible for ensuring the effectiveness of the Board. He is also Chairman of the Nominations Committee and during 2011 led the successful recruitment exercise which resulted in the appointment of a new Chief Financial Officer. There is a clear division of responsibility between the role of the Chairman and that of the Chief Executive Officer, who is responsible for the overall management of the Group's operations. The Chairman liaises with the Chief Executive Officer on strategic and other issues.

Chief Executive Officer and Executive Directors

In addition to membership of the Board, the Chief Executive Officer and our other Executive Directors play a major role in driving the Executive Committee, the Group's most senior operational body, charged with recommending and implementing the Board's strategy worldwide.

Source: Logica (2011), p. 59

Again, in accordance with the Combined Code requirements and those of Smith, an audit committee has been established.

Audit committee

Composition

The composition of our Audit Committee and its terms of reference comply with the UK Code. It is made up of independent Non-Executive Directors and we consider Jan Babiak to have recent and relevant financial experience following her previous role as a managing partner at Ernst and Young.
The membership of the Committee and attendance at scheduled meetings in 2011 are set out above.

Terms of reference

The Committee's terms of reference were updated during the year to ensure that they remain in full compliance with the new Guidance on Audit Committees issued by the FRC in December 2010.

Activities

The Committee's activities include the review and approval of presentations and reports from senior management, consulting as necessary with the external auditors. In 2011, the Committee specifically reviewed and considered the following:

- the independence, objectivity and performance of PwC and recommended to the Board that they be re-elected
- the effectiveness of the 2010 and 2011 audit processes, including PwC's reports and updates which summarised their conclusions and contained feedback on the status of our control environment and management's responsiveness to the audit results
- PwC's proposed fee and audit strategy
- the appropriateness of our accounting policies
- our 2010 full year and 2011 interim announcements
- our 2010 annual report and auditor representation letter
- the effectiveness of our Group Internal Audit function
- reports and updates from Group Internal Audit including their audit plans for 2012, which also covered the management of our internal controls
- reports relating to our risk management process, including any specific key risks identified and the impact of changing legislation and regulations
- major contracts, including the introduction of the more detailed and rigorous reporting and review process over our top (by size and risk) contracts
- our tax and treasury strategies and policies
- our implementation of the UK Bribery Act and ethical training throughout the Group
- our data security arrangements
- an extensive goodwill evaluation which supported its carrying value with no impairment considered necessary
- our Going Concern statement.

Source: Logica (2011), p. 66

As required by the Combined Code, a remuneration committee is also necessary.

Remuneration committee

Composition

The Remuneration Committee comprises three independent Non-Executive Directors. During 2011 the membership of the Committee and attendance at scheduled meetings was as set out opposite.

Although the composition of the Committee does not meet the strict recommendations of the UK Code, due to the membership of the Company's Chairman, we believe that the wide range of knowledge and experience brought to the Committee by a membership which has executive and non-executive experience in the IT industry and other sectors, both in the UK and abroad, is particularly well suited to our current requirements.

Activities

The Remuneration Committee's principal activities are to determine our senior executive remuneration policy and levels of remuneration for the Executive Directors, Executive Committee, certain other members of senior management, the Company Secretary and the Head of Internal Audit. The Committee takes into consideration the pay and conditions of employment for employees when considering executives' remuneration. The Chief Executive Officer and the Group's Chief People Officer attend meetings on request.

The Committee has the right to appoint independent advisers and, if it is not satisfied with the advice received, seek further independent professional advice at the Company's expense.

The Directors' remuneration report, which describes the Committee's functions and its remuneration policies in more detail, is set out on pages 69 to 89.

The Committee believes that the skills, qualifications and commercial experience of its members are appropriate for them to perform their duties in accordance with its terms of reference.

Source: Logica (2011), p. 67

Section summary

This intermediate section has focused on the preparation and presentation of company financial statements. Basic understanding of how to prepare a set of financial statements was extended by introducing the requirements of company law and accounting standards. This knowledge was then applied in order to prepare financial statements that would be published and made available to shareholders and other users.

Company financial statements, as well as being required to show minimum amounts of information, must be presented in a specific way. The rules governing the presentation and preparation of company financial statements are specified in the law and in the accounting standards.

The law requires that companies, or more specifically those running the company, the directors:

- maintain proper accounting records
- prepare annual financial statements
- give a report on their (i.e. the directors') activities
- make sure the reports are available.

The regulations governing how the statements should be prepared are contained in the International Financial Reporting Standards, or IFRS. These were formerly known as International Accounting

Standards, or IAS. Specifically, the standard that applies to company financial statements is IAS 1 *Presentation of Financial Statements*. This standard sets out the structure and content of financial statements. Financial statements should comprise:

- a statement of financial position
- a statement of comprehensive income
- statement of changes in equity
- statement of cash flows
- notes containing a summary of the main accounting policies of the company and other information.

The annual audit requirement is a further regulatory function that helps to ensure the publication of high-quality accounting information by companies.

The section concludes with an overview of corporate governance. Corporate governance refers to the way in which a company is administered and controlled. It is becoming increasingly important for companies not only to act ethically, but be seen to be so doing. The principles of good corporate governance are outlined by the OECD as:

- responsibility
- accountability
- transparency
- fairness.

Common accepted principles of corporate governance tend to differ, depending on the variety of capitalism in which they are embedded. The two general models are the 'liberal' model, which gives priority to the interests of shareholders, and the 'coordinated' model, which gives priority to the interests of workers, managers, customers, suppliers and the wider community.

Codes and guidelines have been developed worldwide, the most influential coming from the OECD.

As far as the UK is concerned, corporate governance came into being with the formation of the Financial Aspects of Corporate Governance, leading to the publication of the Cadbury Report. Over time, various other reports and recommendations were issued, resulting in the Combined Code being published. This code has subsequently been updated.

Clearly corporate governance is seen to be a very important aspect of company reporting. In matters of corporate governance it is recognized that one specific set of rules will not necessarily work for every company. So, while there is no strict legal requirement to comply with the provisions of corporate governance codes, should a company choose not to, an explanation must be given as to the reasons for non-compliance. Shareholders and other users are then in a position to monitor and judge for themselves such explanations.

Section 3: Advanced Aspects

Introduction

As the previous sections of this chapter have illustrated, financial reports are constructed in accordance with generally accepted accounting principles. In reality, there is potentially an almost unlimited number of ways in which financial transactions could be recorded and accumulated to produce financial reports. Without any rules or guidelines as to how these reports should be prepared, accountants would be faced with an impossible task in preparation, and users would have little confidence in their content. The guidelines that govern financial reporting have evolved over time as being those that help in the achievement of overall objectives. Consequently, the overall objectives of financial reporting first need to be identified before the rules and guidelines can be formulated.

For a number of years, attempts have been made to develop an agreed conceptual framework for financial accounting and reporting. A conceptual framework consists of a set of agreed fundamental principles that underpin financial accounting, and consequently provide a sound theoretical basis for developing new financial reporting practices and for assessing existing ones. A conceptual framework addresses such issues as:

- what a set of financial statements should include
- which events should be included in a set of financial statements
- how these events should be measured
- how these events should be communicated to users.

The development of such a conceptual framework is not an easy task; as business becomes more and more complex, so too do the accounting transactions that serve as the monetary audit trail evidencing complicated contracts and events. Moreover, as the objectives of financial reporting may change over time, it is possible that the guidelines that helped the achievement of objectives in one time period will no longer be relevant in later time periods. In this sense, accountancy can be seen to be a continually evolving discipline. It is perhaps an indication of the complexity of the task that there is no currently agreed conceptual framework.

The first part of this section considers the IASB Conceptual Framework in detail.

The next part looks at fair value accounting and the requirements of IFRS 13.

Accounting policies have been referred to throughout this chapter. This advanced section concludes with a review of IAS 8 *Accounting Policies, Changes in Accounting Estimates and Errors*. IAS 8 sets out the criteria to be applied in the selection and change of accounting policies, how to account for changes in accounting policies, accounting estimates and errors, and how these should be disclosed.

1.10 The IASB Conceptual Framework

The IASB Conceptual Framework is termed the 'Conceptual Framework for Financial Reporting' (the 'Conceptual Framework'). It is being developed jointly with the US FASB in a series of eight phases and replaces the IASB Framework for the Preparation and Presentation of Financial Statements which was published in 1989. As each chapter is finalized, the relevant paragraphs in the original Framework will be replaced. When the project is completed, the IASB will have a 'complete, comprehensive and single document called the Conceptual Framework for Financial Reporting'.

The first version of the new Conceptual Framework was published in 2010 and contains the first two chapters that the Board published as a result of its first phase of the Conceptual Framework project, namely the objective of general purpose financial reporting and qualitative characteristics of useful financial information. The remainder of the Conceptual Framework (2010) consists of text transferred from the original 1989 Framework.

The Conceptual Framework itself is not an accounting standard and does not override any standards. Indeed, the Conceptual Framework specifically states that, where there is a conflict between the Framework and an International Accounting Standard, 'the requirements of the IFRS will prevail over those of the Conceptual Framework'.

Purpose

The main purposes of the IASB Conceptual Framework are stated as being to:

(a) assist in the development of future international standards and in the review of existing standards

(b) assist in the harmonization of regulations, accounting standards and procedures by providing a basis for reducing the number of alternative treatments permitted by international standards

(c) assist national standard-setting bodies in developing national standards

(d) assist preparers of financial statements in applying international standards and in dealing with topics that have yet to form the subject of an international standard

(e) assist auditors in forming an opinion as to whether financial statements conform with international standards

(f) assist users of financial statements in interpreting the information contained in financial statements prepared in accordance with international standards

(g) provide information about the formulation of international standards.

Scope

The Conceptual Framework deals with:

(a) the objective of financial reporting

(b) the qualitative characteristics of useful financial information

(c) the definition, recognition and measurement of the elements from which financial statements are constructed, and

(d) concepts of capital and capital maintenance.

The Conceptual Framework consists of four chapters, the main features of which are discussed below. It should be noted that the Conceptual Framework – and indeed all the IFRSs and IASs referred to in this book – run to many pages in length and a full understanding of their content can only be achieved by reading the standards themselves. This book highlights the main features of each standard, taking extracts from the standards and presenting these in as clear and concise a manner as possible to illustrate their meaning and effects.

Chapter 1: The objective of general purpose financial reporting
Objective, usefulness and limitations of general purpose financial reporting

BASIC

INTERMEDIATE

ADVANCED

The objective of general purpose financial reporting is to provide financial information about the reporting entity that is useful to existing and potential investors, lenders and other creditors in making decisions about providing resources to the entity. Those decisions involve buying, selling or holding equity (shares) and debt (loans) instruments, and providing or settling loans and other forms of credit.

The Conceptual Framework continues by stating that:

(a) Decisions by existing and potential investors depend upon the returns they expect from an investment e.g. dividends or market price increases. Decisions by lenders and other creditors depend upon the returns that they expect e.g. interest. Consequently, investors, lenders and other creditors need information to help them assess the prospects for future net cash inflows to an entity. Investors, lenders and creditors are the primary users to whom general purpose financial reports are directed and in order to assess an entity's prospects for future net cash inflows, they require information about the entity's resources and claims against the entity. They also require information about how efficiently and effectively management have used the entity's resources.

(b) General purpose financial reports do not and cannot provide all of the information that primary users need and they cannot require reporting entities to provide information directly to them. Consequently those users need to consider pertinent information from other sources such as general economic assessments, political climate, and industry and company outlooks.

(c) General purpose financial reports are not designed to show the value of a reporting entity but they provide information to help primary users to estimate the entity's value.

(d) Individual primary users may have different and possibly conflicting information needs. In developing IFRS, the Board seeks to provide the information that will meet the needs of the maximum number of primary users. This does not, however, prevent the entity from including additional information that is most useful to a particular subset of primary users.

(e) While the management of a reporting entity is also interested in financial information about that entity, it does not need to rely on general purpose financial reports because it is able to obtain the financial information it needs internally.

(f) In addition to the primary users, other parties may also find general purpose financial reports useful; however, those reports are not primarily intended for their benefit. These other parties include regulators, members of the public, employees, customers and suppliers.

(g) To a large extent, financial reports are based on estimates, judgements and models rather than exact depictions. The Conceptual Framework establishes the concepts that underline those estimates, judgements and models.

Information about a reporting entity's economic resources, claims, and changes in resource and claims

General purpose financial reports provide information about the financial position of an entity i.e. information about the entity's economic resources and claims against the entity. Financial reports also provide information about the effects of transactions and other events that change the entity's financial position. Both types of information provide useful input for decisions about providing resources to an entity.

Economic resources and claims

Information about the nature and amounts of an entity's financial position can help users to identify the entity's financial strengths and weaknesses; to assess its liquidity and solvency, and its need and ability to obtain financing.

A reporting entity's economic resources and claims are reported in the statement of financial position (IAS 1 1.54–80A).

Changes in economic resources and claims

Changes in a reporting entity's financial position may result from that entity's performance (i.e. the making of a profit) or from other events or transactions such as the issuing of debt or shares. Users need to be able to distinguish between both of these changes.

Information about an entity's financial performance helps users to understand the return that the entity has produced on its economic resources. This in turn provides an indication of how efficiently and effectively management has used the entity's resources. Information about the variability and components of that return helps assess the uncertainty of future cash flows while information about past performance may be helpful when predicting the entity's future returns on its economic resources.

The changes in an entity's economic resources and claims are presented in the statement of comprehensive income (IAS 1 1.81–105).

Financial performance reflected by accrual accounting

The use of accrual accounting depicts the effects of transactions and events on an entity's financial position in the periods in which those effects occur and not when the resulting cash receipts or payments occur. This provides a better basis for assessing the entity's past and future performance than information solely about cash receipts and payments during that period.

Information about a reporting entity's financial performance during a period, reflected by changes in its economic resources and claims other than those obtained directly from investors and creditors, is useful in assessing the entity's past and future ability to generate net cash inflows. That is, that information shows the extent to which the entity has generated cash through its own operations rather than by obtaining additional resources from investors and creditors. Such information may also indicate the extent to which general economic events have changed the entity's ability to generate future cash inflows.

Financial performance reflected by past cash flows

Information about an entity's cash flows during a period helps users assess the entity's ability to generate future cash flows. It indicates how the entity obtains and spends cash, including information about its borrowing and repayment of debt, cash dividends and distributions to shareholders.

The changes in the entity's cash flows are presented in the statement of cash flows (IAS 7).

Changes in economic resources and claims not resulting from financial performance

Information about changes in an entity's financial position resulting from events and transactions other than financial performance is necessary to give users a complete understanding of how and why the entity's financial position has changed. For example, changes caused by share issues.

The changes in an entity's economic resources and claims not resulting from financial performance is presented in the statement of changes in equity (IAS 1.106–110).

BASIC

INTERMEDIATE

ADVANCED

Chapter 2: The Reporting Entity

At time of writing this chapter has not yet been added to the Conceptual Framework. It will be inserted once the IASB has completed its re-deliberations following the Exposure Draft ED/2010/2 issued in March 2010 and which had a comment period that ended on 16 June 2010.

Chapter 3: Qualitative characteristics of useful financial information
Introduction

The qualitative characteristics of useful financial information identify the types of information that are likely to be most useful to the primary users for making decisions about the entity on the basis of information in its financial report. The qualitative characteristics apply equally to financial information in general purpose financial reports as well as to financial information provided in other ways.

Qualitative characteristics of useful financial information

Financial information is useful when it is relevant and represents faithfully what it purports to represent. The usefulness of financial information is enhanced if it is comparable, verifiable, timely and understandable.

The Conceptual Framework characterizes these qualities as being 'fundamental' and 'enhancing'.

Fundamental qualitative characteristics

Relevance and faithful representation are the fundamental qualitative characteristics of useful financial information.

Relevance

Financial information is relevant if it is capable of making a difference in the decisions made by users. Financial information is capable of making a difference in decisions if it has predictive value, confirmatory value or both. The predictive value and confirmatory value of financial information are interrelated.

Materiality

Information is material if omitting or misstating it could influence decisions that users make on the basis of financial information about a specific entity. Materiality is therefore an entity-specific aspect of relevance based on the nature or magnitude, or both, of the items to which the information relates in the context of an individual entity's financial report. Consequently the IASB cannot specify a uniform qualitative threshold as it is an entity-specific matter.

Faithful representation

The second fundamental qualitative characteristic of useful financial information is that it must faithfully represent the transactions and other events that it purports to represent. The Conceptual Framework states that to be a perfectly faithful representation, a depiction would have three characteristics. It would be complete, neutral and free from error. The objective of the IASB is to maximize these qualities to as great an extent as possible.

(a) Completeness. A complete depiction includes all information necessary for a user to understand the transactions and other events being depicted, including all necessary descriptions and explanations.

(b) Neutrality. A neutral depiction is without bias in the selection or presentation of financial information. A neutral depiction will not increase the probability that financial information will be received favourably or unfavourably by users.

(c) Freedom from error. Freedom from error does not mean perfectly accurate in all respects. It means that there are no errors or omissions in the description of the items being represented and that no errors have been made when selecting and applying the process used to produce the reported information. For example, a value may be an estimate, but that estimate may be regarded as being free from error as long as it is described clearly and accurately as being an estimate, the nature and limitations of the estimating process are explained, and no errors have been made in selecting and applying that process.

It is perhaps worth noting one particular item which has not been carried forward from the original 1989 Framework. The concept of prudence – one of the four fundamental accounting concepts studied at non-IFRS level – has been omitted from the IASB list of qualities.

Prudence involves the provision for all known liabilities while only recognizing revenue and profits when it is reasonably certain that they will be realized. This ensures that assets and revenues are not overstated and that liabilities and expenses are not understated.

The IASB now takes the view, however, that prudence is inconsistent with neutrality and that it is in effect biased towards a non-neutral depiction. As will be seen in the remainder of this book, many of the existing IFRS, adopt a prudent approach and it remains to be seen whether these standards will be amended to reflect this current thinking.

Applying the fundamental qualitative characteristics

Information must be both relevant and faithfully represented if it is to be useful. The most efficient and effective process for applying the fundamental qualitative characteristics would usually be as follows:

(i) The identification of a transaction or other event that has the potential to be useful to the users of the reporting entity's financial information.

(ii) The identification of the type of information about the transaction or other event that would be most relevant if it is available and can be faithfully represented.

(iii) The determination of whether that information is available and can be faithfully represented.

Enhancing qualitative characteristics

As noted earlier, the enhancing characteristics are comparability, verifiability, timeliness and understandability. These qualitative characteristics enhance the usefulness of information that is relevant and faithfully represented.

Comparability

Information about an entity is more useful if it can be compared with similar information about other entities and with similar information about the same entity for other periods. It should be noted that consistency is not the same as comparability. Consistency refers to the use of the same accounting treatments for the same items either from period to period by one entity or in a single period across entities. Consistency helps to achieve the goal of comparability. The Conceptual Framework concedes that while a single transaction can be faithfully represented in multiple ways, permitting alternative accounting methods for the same transaction diminishes comparability.

Verifiability

Verifiability helps to assure users that information represents faithfully the transactions and other events that it purports to represent. Verifiability means that different knowledgeable and independent observers could reach consensus, although not necessarily complete agreement, that a particular depiction is a faithful representation. Verification can be direct, such as counting cash, or indirect, such as checking the inputs to a cost model and recalculating the outputs using the same methodology. An example is verifying the carrying amount of inventory by checking the inputs (quantities and costs) and recalculating the ending inventory using the same cost flow assumption e.g. first in first out.

Timeliness

Timeliness means that information is available to decision-makers in time to be capable of influencing their decisions.

Understandability

Classifying, characterizing and presenting information clearly makes it understandable. Some items are, however, inherently complex and cannot be made easy to understand. Such items should not be excluded on those grounds as omitting this information would make financial reports incomplete and potentially misleading.

The Conceptual Framework states that financial reports are prepared for users who have a reasonable knowledge of business and economic activities and who review and analyse the information diligently.

BASIC

INTERMEDIATE

ADVANCED

The Conceptual Framework also acknowledges that, at times, even well-informed and diligent users may need to seek the aid of an adviser to understand information about complex transactions and other events.

Applying the enhancing qualitative characteristics
Enhancing qualitative characteristics should be maximized to the extent possible. It should be noted, however, that the enhancing qualitative characteristics, either individually or as a group, cannot make information useful if that information is irrelevant or not faithfully presented.

The cost constraint on useful financial reporting

The Conceptual Framework recognizes that cost is a pervasive constraint on the information that can be provided by financial reporting. Reporting such information imposes costs and those costs should be justified by the benefits of reporting that information. Although the costs of financial reporting are met initially by the providers of that information, ultimately the users bear these costs in the form of reduced returns. These users may also incur additional costs of analysing and interpreting the information in financial reports.

When developing a proposed financial reporting standard the IASB seeks information from providers of financial information, users, auditors, academics and others about the expected nature and quantity of the benefits and costs of that standard. The IASB assesses costs and benefits in relation to financial reporting generally and not just in relation to individual reporting entities. The IASB will also consider whether different sizes of entities and other factors justify different reporting requirements in certain situations.

BASIC

INTERMEDIATE

ADVANCED

Chapter 4: The 1989 Framework: The Remaining Text

As was noted at the beginning of this advanced section, the IASB is in the process of updating its Conceptual Framework. Chapter 4 contains the remaining text of the 1989 Framework. It is important to note that this text has not been amended to reflect the changes made by IAS 1 *Presentation of Financial Statements* (as revised in 2007). Consequently the text still uses the terms income statement and balance sheet rather than the statement of comprehensive income and statement of financial position. To be consistent with the wording of the Conceptual Framework, the terms of the 1989 Framework will be used for the remainder of this section.

Underlying assumption

Going concern

The financial statements are normally prepared on the assumption that the business is a going concern and will continue in operation for the foreseeable future. Under this assumption fixed assets, for example, are depreciated over their estimated useful life as it is assumed that the business will continue and use the asset in the future. If the company is not a going concern it would be more relevant to value the assets on a sales basis.

The elements of financial statements

Financial statements portray the financial effects of transactions and other events by grouping them into broad classes according to their economic characteristics. These broad classes are termed the elements of financial statements, and the Framework distinguishes between those elements that are directly related to the measurement of financial position in the balance sheet and those that are directly related to the measurement of performance in the income statement.

Financial position

The elements directly related to the measurement of financial position are assets, liabilities and equity. These are defined as follows.

■ *Assets:* an asset is a resource controlled by the entity as a result of past events and from which future economic benefits are expected to flow to the entity. In Chapter 2, this definition is examined in detail.
■ *Liabilities:* a liability is a present obligation of the entity arising from past events, the settlement of which is expected to result in an outflow from the entity of resources embodying economic benefits. This definition is examined in detail in Chapter 8.

- *Equity:* equity is the residual interest in the assets of the entity after deducting all its liabilities. This is examined in detail in Chapter 7.

Assets

The future economic benefit embodied in an asset is the potential to contribute to the flow of cash and cash equivalents to an entity. This flow of cash may be direct, as in the case of an asset that is part of the operating activities of an entity; or indirect, such as when an alternative manufacturing process lowers the cost of production.

Many assets, for example plant and equipment, have a physical form but this is not essential to the existence of as asset. Patents and copyrights, for example, are assets if future economic benefits are expected to flow from them to the entity and they are controlled by the entity.

In determining the existence of an asset, there is no requirement for the item to be legally owned by the entity. Consequently an item held on a lease is an asset providing the entity controls the benefits which are expected to flow from the item. This is an application of the principle of substance over form.

An asset can only arise as the result of a past transaction or other past event. Normally assets are purchased or manufactured. Transactions or events expected to occur in the future do not give rise to assets e.g. the intention to buy an asset does not, of itself, meet the definition of an asset.

Although an entity may incur expenditure on an item with a view to obtaining future economic benefits, this is not conclusive proof that an item satisfying the definition of an asset has been obtained; an item cannot be classed as an asset unless it is expected to generate future economic benefits for the entity.

Similarly, the absence of a related expenditure does not preclude an item from satisfying the definition of an asset – an item that has been donated to the entity may satisfy the definition of an asset.

Liabilities

An essential characteristic of a liability is that the entity has a present obligation. An obligation is a duty or responsibility to act or perform in a certain way. Obligations may be legally enforceable, for example, with amounts payable for goods and services received; however, obligations also arise from normal business practice, custom and a desire to maintain good business relations. For example, an entity may decide as a matter of policy to rectify faults in its products after the warranty period has expired. The amounts that are expected to be expended in respect of goods already sold will be liabilities. Such obligations are knows as 'constructive obligations'.

The distinction has to be made between a present obligation and a future commitment. A decision by management to acquire assets in the future does not, of itself, give rise to a present obligation, as that decision could be reversed.

A liability can only result from past transactions or other events such as the acquisition of goods giving rise to trade payables, or the receipt of a bank loan giving rise to an obligation to repay the loan.

A liability which can be measured only by using a substantial degree of estimation is referred to as a provision.

Equity

Although equity is defined as a residual amount, it may be subclassified in the balance sheet into funds contributed by shareholders, retained earnings, and reserves representing capital maintenance adjustments, and be shown separately. Such classifications can be relevant to users when they indicate legal or other restrictions on the ability of the entity to distribute that equity.

Performance

The Framework states that profit is frequently used as a measure of performance and that the elements directly related to the measurement of profit are income and expenses. These are defined as follows:

- **Income:** Income is increases in economic benefits during the accounting period in the form of inflows or enhancements of assets or decreases of liabilities that result in increases in equity, other than those relating to contributions from equity participants. The definition of income encompasses both revenue and gains. Revenue arises in the course of the ordinary activities of an entity (e.g. sales, fees, interest, dividends, royalties and rent). Gains represent other items that meet the definition of income, and may or may not arise in the course of the ordinary activities of an entity (e.g. gains arising on the disposal of fixed assets).

■ **Expenses:** Expenses are decreases in economic benefits during the accounting period in the form of outflows or depletions of assets or incurrence of liabilities that result in decreases in equity, other than those relating to distributions to equity participants. The definition of expenses encompasses losses as well as those expenses that arise in the course of the ordinary activities of the entity. Expenses that arise in the course of the ordinary activities of the entity include, for example, cost of sales, wages and depreciation. They usually take the form of an outflow or depletion of assets such as cash, inventory, plant and equipment. Losses represent other items that meet the definition of expenses, and may or may not arise in the course of the ordinary activities of the entity. Losses represent decreases in economic benefits and as such they are no different in nature from other expenses. The fact that income and expenses are defined in terms of increases or decreases in net assets has led to the suggestion that the IASB Framework takes a 'balance sheet approach' to defining the elements of financial statements.

Recognition of the elements of financial statements

Not all the items that meet the above definitions will be recognized in the financial statements. Recognition is the process of incorporating in the balance sheet or income statement an item that meets the definition of an element and satisfies the following criteria for recognition:

■ it is probable that any future economic benefit associated with the item will flow to or from the entity, and

■ the item has a cost or value that can be measured with reliability.

These criteria apply principally to the recognition of assets and liabilities, since equity is defined as the difference between an entity's total assets and total liabilities, and the other elements of the financial statements (income and expenses) are defined in terms of changes in the entity's assets and liabilities. That is, the recognition criteria for an asset, for example, automatically require the recognition of another element, for example income or a liability.

The probability of future economic benefit

The use of the word probable in the recognition criteria is simply to reflect the environment in which the entity operates. There will always be a degree of uncertainty surrounding particular transactions – no one, for example, can say for certain that a debtor will pay. However, if it is probable that the amount will be received then the recognition of this amount as an asset (and related revenue) will be justifiable.

Reliability of measurement

In some instances, it may not be possible to obtain a precise cost or value and therefore an estimate must be used. The Framework acknowledges that the use of estimates is an essential part of the preparation of financial statements and that this does not undermine their reliability. When, however, a reasonable estimate cannot be made, the item is not recognized in the balance sheet or income statement.

An item that possesses the essential characteristics of an element but fails to meet the recognition criteria may instead warrant disclosure in the notes to the financial statements.

Based on these general recognition criteria:

■ an *asset* is recognized in the balance sheet when it is probable that the future economic benefits will flow to the entity and the asset has a cost or value that can be measured reliably

■ a *liability* is recognized in the balance sheet when it is probable that an outflow of resources embodying economic benefits will result from the settlement of a present obligation and the amount at which the settlement will take place can be measured reliably

■ *income* is recognized in the income statement when an increase in future economic benefits related to an increase in an asset or a decrease of a liability has arisen that can be measured reliably; this means, in effect, that recognition of income occurs simultaneously with the recognition of increases in assets or decreases in liabilities

■ *expenses* are recognized when a decrease in future economic benefits related to a decrease in an asset or an increase of a liability has arisen that can be measured reliably; this means, in effect, that recognition of expenses occurs simultaneously with the recognition of an increase in liabilities or a decrease in assets.

Measurement of the elements of financial statements

Measurement is the process of determining the monetary amounts at which the elements of the financial statements are to be recognized and reported.

The Framework acknowledges that a variety of measurement bases are used today to different degrees and in varying combinations in financial statements. They include the following.

- **Historical cost:** assets are recorded at the amount paid to acquire them. Liabilities are recorded at the amount of proceeds received in exchange for the obligation, or in some circumstances (e.g. income taxes) at the amount expected to be paid to satisfy the liability in the normal course of business.

- **Current cost:** assets are carried at the amount that would have to be paid to acquire an asset currently (replacement cost). Liabilities are carried at the undiscounted amount that would be required to settle the obligation currently.

- **Realizable (settlement) value:** assets are carried at the amount that could currently be obtained by selling the asset in an orderly disposal. Liabilities are carried at the undiscounted amount expected to be paid to satisfy the obligation in the normal course of business.

- **Present value:** assets are carried at the present discounted value of the future cash inflows that the item is expected to generate in the normal course of business. Liabilities are carried at the present discounted value of the future net cash outflows that are expected to be required to settle the liabilities in the normal course of business.

The Conceptual Framework states that the measurement basis most commonly used is historical cost, but that it is usually combined with other measurement bases. For example, inventories are usually carried at the lower of cost and net realizable value. The Framework also states that some entities use the current cost basis to deal with the effects of changing prices of non-monetary assets (e.g. inflationary pressures on property). A particular criticism of the Conceptual Framework is that it does not include concepts or principles for selecting which measurement basis should be used for particular elements of financial statements or in particular circumstances. A conceptual framework ought to prescribe such measurement bases rather than simply describing the bases that tend to be adopted in practice. The qualitative characteristics noted earlier do, however, provide some guidance.

The concept of capital and capital maintenance

The final section of the Conceptual Framework is concerned with the concept of capital and capital maintenance. The Conceptual Framework states that a financial concept of capital is adopted by most entities in preparing their financial statements. Under a financial concept of capital, capital is synonymous with the net assets or equity of the entity. The Conceptual Framework offers an alternative view of capital, however: that of physical capital. Under a physical concept of capital, capital is regarded as the productive capacity of the entity based on, for example, units of output per day.

The selection of the appropriate concept of capital by an entity should be based on the needs of the users of its financial statements. The concept chosen indicates the goal to be attained in determining profit. For example, if the users of the financial statements are primarily concerned with the maintenance of invested capital then a financial concept of capital should be adopted. If, however, the main concern of users is with the operating capability of the entity, a physical concept of capital should be used.

The Conceptual Framework distinguishes between these two ways of comparing an entity's capital at the beginning and the end of the accounting period, and so determining the profit, as follows.

1. **Financial capital maintenance:** under this concept a profit is earned only if the financial amount of the net assets at the end of the period exceeds the financial amount of net assets at the beginning of the period after adjusting for any amounts distributed to or contributed by the owners during the period. Financial capital maintenance can be measured in either nominal monetary units or units of constant purchasing power, i.e. where purchasing power is determined in accordance with changes in an index of general prices.

2. **Physical capital maintenance:** under this concept a profit is earned only if the physical operating capability of the entity at the end of the period is greater than its physical operating capability at the start of the period after adjusting for any amounts distributed to or contributed by the owners during the period.

BASIC

INTERMEDIATE

ADVANCED

The Conceptual Framework states that the selection of measurement bases and concept of capital maintenance will determine the accounting model used in the preparation of the financial statements. The Conceptual Framework does not, however, prescribe a particular model other than in exceptional circumstances, such as those entities reporting in the currency of a hyperinflationary economy. Instead, the Framework merely points out that different accounting models exhibit different degrees of relevance and reliability, and states that an entity's management must seek a balance between relevance and reliability when choosing an appropriate model.

In the introduction to this section it was suggested that accountancy could be seen as a 'continually evolving' discipline. The final sentence of the Conceptual Framework concurs with this suggestion by concluding. 'This intention [to prescribe a particular model] will, however, be reviewed in light of world developments.'

Example

An entity sells a single product X. It carries out all its transactions on a cash basis. Initial investment by the owners is £10 which is sufficient to buy one unit of X. During year 1 the item of X is sold for £20. There were no other transactions.

(a) Calculate the profit for the period in nominal monetary terms.

(b) If the initial unit of X was acquired when the RPI stood at 100 and it was sold on the last day of the accounting year when the RPI stood at 140, calculate the profit for the period in terms of the general purchasing power of the business.

(c) If the cost of X at the beginning of year 2 was £15, calculate the profit for the year in terms of the power of the business to maintain its physical operating capability.

Solution

	Financial capital maintenance (nominal) £	Financial capital maintenance (purchasing power) £	Physical capital maintenance £
Assets at end of year 1	20	20	20
Cost (a)	10		
(b)		14	
(c)			15
Profit	10	6	5

Notes

(a) In normal monetary terms, the profit is £10.

(b) Under general purchasing power, the cost of the inventory is restated in line with the RPI so as to take account of the general increase in prices.

(c) Under physical capital maintenance, the replacement cost of the inventory is taken in arriving at the profit figure.

The point at issue is that during periods of rising prices, profits calculated on the basis of nominal financial capital (historical cost) will not be distributable to owners and still ensure the maintenance of the physical amount of capital invested. Even though profits are £10, no more than £6 could be withdrawn from the business without reducing its general purchasing power and no more than £5 could be withdrawn without reducing the power of the business to maintain its physical operating capability i.e. to replace its inventory. Consequently it is agreed that the conventionally calculated profit figure understated the amount which should have been set aside to provide for maintenance of business operations.

1.11 Fair value

As the above example highlights, in times of rising prices, the use of historical cost accounting can result in asset values being misleading in the statement of financial position and the statement of comprehensive income deficient in terms of profit measurement.

A significant recent concept has been the use of fair values and indeed, several standards which have been issued over the last 25 years have required the use of fair values for one or more classes of assets and liabilities.

Fair value is defined in IFRS 13 as 'the price that would be received to sell an asset or paid to transfer a liability in an orderly transaction between market participants at the measurement date'.

Fair value accounting

Fair value accounting involves the substitution of historical cost values with current fair values. In considering the merits or otherwise of using fair value instead of historical cost in a statement of financial position it is perhaps useful to consider the purpose of financial statements. The objective of general-purpose financial reporting is to provide information that is useful for decision making. As was seen in our examination of the statement of comprehensive income, that performance statement now reports all gains recognized in the period, regardless of whether or not they are realized. So, for example, if an entity adopts fair value accounting for an investment property, any increase (or decrease) in the fair value of that property will be reflected in other comprehensive income. Consequently, with fair value accounting, an increase in total comprehensive income is not necessarily as a result of an entity's economic activity but instead could be profit arising purely out of an increase in the fair value of assets. That is, changes in market values can lead to a change in the results reported in the statement of comprehensive income.

Opponents of fair value accounting argue that this can make it difficult to attribute performance changes to internal (management) or external (market) factors; however supporters of the concept argue that the purchase of assets that fall in value is indicative of poor stewardship and this should be recognized in the performance statement. Notwithstanding, the use of fair values undoubtedly results in reported annual income being more volatile and the recognition of unrealized gains goes against the traditional prudent approach to accounting – albeit this too is now being shunned by the IASB in favour of faithful representation.

Some concerns have also been raised about the reliability and comparability of fair value for certain assets. While defining the fair value in cases where there is a well-defined market is not an issue, for assets and liabilities where there is no market available, this would mean the use of an accounting model to derive the value e.g. one based on the present value of future cash flows. The reliability or otherwise of such valuations would likely be highly subjective, dependent upon the model's assumptions as to the discount rate, future cash flows etc. Moreover, this uncertainty has implications for auditors whose verification depends upon the acceptance of the logic of the underlying valuation model used.

Supporters of the use of fair values argue that even although there is a degree of potential unreliability to the values, they are more useful to decision making than historical cost because fair values represent economic reality as opposed to carrying values which are simply an intermediate stage in the cost allocation process. Indeed, if the statement of financial position is seen as more relevant for decision making, then fair values will result in a more faithful representation of the net worth of its components in a winding up. The counter argument is that financial statements are prepared on the going concern basis and because statements of financial position contain a mix of values e.g. current assets at lower of cost or net realizable value, then unless all assets and liabilities were based on fair values, that argument does not hold.

A further problem with fair value accounting is that it increases the risk of misunderstanding by existing or potential investors. While the fair value might be the realizable value, nevertheless the value of the company concerned is likely to be significantly higher due to the existence of internally generated goodwill. Consequently, while the fair value may bring a statement of financial position closer to the market value, it will never match it exactly unless non-purchased intangible assets are recognized in the statement of financial position.

The arguments for and against fair value accounting are numerous. There is, however, consensus amongst both sides in relation to the way it has been implemented. The term fair value is already referred to in several standards and has been so for a number of years. Their use has been as a response to needs rather than as a result of an amendment to the Conceptual Framework and this has resulted in inconsistent guidance found within the various standards. The IASB wanted to enhance disclosures for fair value so that users could better assess the valuation techniques and inputs used to measure it. Consequently, in a joint project with the US FASB, the IASB issued a new standard to try to deal with many of the measurement issues.

In May 2011, IFRS 13 *Fair Value Measurement* was issued to establish a single framework for measuring fair value when that is required by other standards. It defines fair value, provides guidance on how fair value should be measured, and introduces consistent requirements for disclosures regarding fair value measurements.

1.12 IFRS 13 *Fair Value Measurement*

Introduction

Prior to IFRS 13 being issued, guidance on how to measure fair value was included in the various standards that require or permit its use. Because these standards were developed over many years, the requirements for measuring fair value were dispersed and did not necessarily provide a clear measurement objective. Furthermore, the guidance in the previous standards was not always consistent. To address these issues IFRS 13 was developed to provide a single source of guidance on the measurement of fair value which clarifies the definition of fair value and provides a coherent framework for measuring fair value. Note, however, that IFRS 13 does not mandate *when* fair value measurements should be used – requirements regarding when it is appropriate to measure particular categories of assets, liabilities and an entity's own equity instruments continue to be dealt with in other standards.

Objective and scope

The objective of IFRS 13 is to:

(a) define fair value

(b) set out in a single IFRS a framework for measuring fair value

(c) require disclosures about fair value measurements.

IFRS 13 applies when another IFRS requires or permits fair value measurements or disclosures about fair value measurements except in limited specified circumstances.

Definition

IFRS 13 defines fair value as:

> *The price that would be received to sell an asset or transfer a liability in an orderly transaction between market participants at the measurement date.*

This definition is based on an exit price and it emphasizes that fair value is a market-based measurement, not an entity-specific measurement. When measuring fair value, an entity uses the assumptions that market participants would use when pricing the asset or a liability under current market conditions, including assumptions about risk. Consequently, it is not a relevant argument in the valuation process for an entity to insist that prices are too low relative to its own valuation of the asset and that it would be unwilling to sell at such low prices.

IFRS 13 explains that a fair value measurement requires an entity to determine the following:

(a) The particular asset or liability being measured. The asset or liability measured at fair value may be a stand-alone asset or liability, a group of assets and a group of liabilities, or a group of assets and liabilities (e.g. a cash-generating unit, see Chapter 3). The level at which fair value is measured will depend on the 'unit of account' specified in the individual standard. A 'unit of account'is the single asset or liability or a group of assets or liabilities. When measuring fair value, the characteristics of the asset or liability that market participants would consider when pricing that asset should be taken into account. Such characteristics include the condition and location of the asset and any restrictions on its sale or use.

(b) For a non-financial asset, the highest and best use of the asset and whether the asset is used in combination with other assets or on a stand-alone basis. The highest and best use is defined as 'the use of a non-financial asset by market participants that would maximize the value of the asset or the group of assets and liabilities (e.g. a business) within which the asset would be used'. The highest and best use takes into account the use of the non-financial asset that is physically possible, legally permissible, and financially feasible.

(c) The market in which an orderly transaction would take place for the asset or liability. The transaction to sell the asset or transfer the liability is assumed to take place in the principal market for the asset or liability or, in the absence of a principal market, in the most advantageous market for the asset or liability. The prices to be used are those in 'an orderly transaction'. That is, one that assumes exposure to the market for a period before the date of measurement to allow for normal marketing activities and to ensure that it is not a forced transaction. If the transaction is not orderly there will not have been enough time to create competition and this may reduce the price. Also, if a seller is forced to accept a price in a short period of time, then the price may not be representative. If there is a principal market for the asset or liability, the fair value measurement should reflect the price in that market, even if the price in a different market is potentially more advantageous at the measurement date.

(d) The appropriate valuation techniques to use when measuring fair value. The valuation techniques used should maximize the use of relevant observable inputs and minimize unobservable inputs. These inputs should be consistent with the inputs a market participant would use when pricing the asset or liability. In order to achieve this, the standard introduces a fair value hierarchy, which prioritizes the inputs into the fair value measurement process. Fair value measurements are categorized into a three-level hierarchy, based on the type of inputs to the valuation techniques used, as follows.

Fair value hierarchy

To increase consistency and comparability in fair value measurements and related disclosures, the IFRS establishes a fair value hierarchy that categorizes into three levels the inputs to valuation techniques used to measure fair value. The fair value hierarchy gives the highest priority to quoted prices (unadjusted) in active markets for identical assets or liabilities (Level 1 inputs) and the lowest priority to unobservable inputs (Level 3 inputs).

Level 1 inputs are unadjusted quoted prices in active markets for items identical to the asset or liability being measured. As with current standards, if there is a quoted price in an active market, an entity uses that price without adjustment when measuring fair value. An example of this would be prices quoted on a stock exchange. The entity needs to be able to access the market at the measurement date.

Active markets are ones where transactions take place with sufficient frequency and volume for pricing information to be provided.

Determining whether a fair value measurement is a Level 2 or Level 3 input depends on whether the inputs are observable or unobservable, and on their significance.

BASIC

INTERMEDIATE

ADVANCED

Level 2 inputs are inputs other than quoted prices in Level 1 that are observable for that asset or liability. They are quoted assets or liabilities for similar items in active markets or supported by market data. Adjustments may be needed to Level 2 inputs, and if these are significant, the fair value may need to be classified as Level 3.

Level 3 inputs are unobservable inputs, which should be used as a minimum. Where situations occur when relevant inputs are not observable, they must be developed to reflect the assumptions that market participants would use when determining an appropriate price for the asset or liability. Unobservable inputs are inputs for which market data are not available and that are developed using the best information available about the assumptions that market participants would use when pricing the asset or liability. They include the use of an entity's own data.

The entity should maximize the use of relevant observable inputs and minimize the use of unobservable ones.

Application to liabilities and an entity's own equity instruments

IFRS 13 sets out certain valuation concepts to assist in the determination of fair value. A fair value measurement assumes that a financial or non-financial liability or an entity's own equity is transferred to a market participant at the measurement date. Often there is no observable market to provide pricing information and the highest and best use is not applicable. In such circumstances the fair value is based on the perspective of a market participant who holds the identical instrument as an asset. If there is no corresponding asset, IFRS 13 lists a number of appropriate bases for measuring the fair value in descending order of preference, ending with the use of valuation techniques such as an income approach using present value techniques.

Disclosure

IFRS 13's disclosure requirements replace many of the fair value measurement disclosures previously required by other IFRSs.

The standard's general disclosure requirements are that the entity should disclose information that helps users of its financial statements to assess both of the following:

(a) for assets and liabilities that are measured at fair value on a recurring or non-recurring basis in the statement of financial position after initial recognition, the valuation techniques and inputs used to develop those measurements; and

(b) for recurring fair value measurements using significant unobservable inputs (Level 3), the effect of the measurements on profit or loss or other comprehensive income for the period.

More detailed disclosures, for which the standard should be read for a full explanation, include:

- information about the hierarchy level into which fair value measurements fall;
- transfers between Levels 1 and 2 and the reasons for those transfers;
- methods and inputs to the fair value measurements and changes in valuation techniques; and
- additional disclosures for Level 3 measurements that include a reconciliation of opening and closing balances, and quantitative information about unobservable inputs and assumptions used.

Summary

As has been noted, the issue of IFRS 13 has been as a result of a response to needs rather than as an amendment to the Conceptual Framework. More significant, however, is the shift away from a historic focus where financial statements were used to provide investors with the means to assess stewardship, to one which provides a current perspective on value where decision making is the primary aim. While the informational benefit of current values is clearly of benefit to investors, there remains the problem of the other non-financial assets, particularly internally generated goodwill, that are precluded from being recognized in a statement of financial position at all, let alone at current fair values. As a consequence, the statement of financial position will continue to contain assets and liabilities at a range of values – cost, net realizable value, fair value, and – in the case of internally generated goodwill – no value at all.

1.13 Accounting policies

The intermediate section to this chapter covered IAS 1 *Presentation of Financial Statements* in some detail. Reference was frequently made to the requirement for explanatory information which is necessary to assist in the understanding of the financial statements, to be reported in the notes to the financial statements. These notes were seen to require the presentation of information about the basis of preparation of the financial statements and the accounting policies which have been used, including:

(a) the measurement bases used in preparing the financial statements, and

(b) other accounting policies relevant to an understanding of the financial statements.

Moreover, the selection and application of accounting policies was seen to be an essential component in arriving at a set of financial statements which achieve a fair presentation.

It is worthwhile pausing at this stage to consider the distinction between measurement bases and accounting policies.

Measurement bases and accounting policies

Measurement bases are the methods that have been developed for applying fundamental accounting concepts to financial transactions for the purpose of the financial statements. They provide a framework for the reporting of the results of an entity and are intended to restrict subjectivity by identifying a range of acceptable methods. For example, assets may be valued according to historical cost, current cost, net realizable value, fair value or recoverable amount. Each of these is acceptable and each is used by different entities to suit their individual requirements.

When an entity chooses and consistently follows certain specific measurement bases they become the accounting policies of that entity. Accounting policies determine which facts about an entity are to be presented in the financial statements, and how those facts are to be presented.

The wording of IAS 1 which requires entities to select and apply accounting policies suggests that an entity has a choice in which policies it chooses to adopt. Some policies are, however, dictated by an international standard which does not permit a choice. Examples of such policies are:

- inventories being measured at the lower of cost and net realizable value as required by IAS 2 Inventories
- the prohibition of recognizing internally generated goodwill as prevented by IAS 38 Intangible Assets.

Some standards do, however, permit a choice. For example:

- IAS 2 Inventories allows the cost of interchangeable inventory items to be assigned by either the first in first out (FIFO) cost formula or the weighted average cost formula (Chapter 5).
- IAS 16 *Property, Plant and Equipment* allows items of property, plant and equipment to be measured using either the cost model or the revaluation model.

Other examples of accounting policies which an entity may adopt include policies on such matters as:

- the accounts being prepared under the historical cost convention
- the treatment of goodwill arising from acquisitions
- the definition of sales in the financial statements e.g. sales comprise the amount receivable in the ordinary course of business, net of value added tax and sales taxes
- the treatment of research and development expenditure
- the treatment of advertising expenditure
- the treatment and calculation of deferred tax (Chapter 9).

The accounting issue involved

The selection and application of accounting policies was seen, in IAS 1, to be an essential component of financial statements achieving fair presentation – it is necessary therefore to have guidance on the selection of such policies. Moreover, if the accounting policies which have been adopted by an entity are no longer considered by management to be appropriate, there needs to be a mechanism by which changes to these policies can be effected and the resulting effects on the financial statements reported. Furthermore, as comparability is a desirable characteristic of financial information and comparability is improved through consistency, then if there is a change in the accounting policies it would seem to be desirable for any changes in policy to be reflected in periods prior to the year of the policy change. These are matters which are dealt with in IAS 8 *Accounting Policies, Changes in Accounting Estimates and Errors.*

1.14 IAS 8 *Accounting Policies, Changes in Accounting Estimates and Errors*

Objective

IAS 8 states as its objective to prescribe the criteria for selecting and changing accounting policies, together with the accounting treatment and disclosure of changes in accounting policies, changes in accounting estimates and corrections of errors.

Scope

The standard should be applied in selecting and applying accounting policies, and accounting for changes in accounting policies, changes in accounting estimates and corrections of prior period errors.

Definitions

IAS 8 defines *accounting policies* as the specific principles, bases, conventions, rules and practices applied by an entity in preparing and presenting financial statements. The standard goes on to define a *change in accounting estimate* as being an adjustment of the carrying amount of an asset or liability or related expense, resulting from the reassessment of the expected future benefits and obligations associated with that asset or liability. It further states that changes in accounting estimates result from new information or new developments and, accordingly, are not corrections of errors. *Prior period errors* are omissions from, and misstatements in, an entity's financial statements for one or more prior periods arising from a failure to use, or misuse of, reliable information that was available and could reasonably be expected to have been obtained and taken into account in preparing those statements. Such errors are the result of mathematical mistakes, mistakes in applying accounting policies, oversights or misinterpretation of facts, and fraud.

Accounting policies
Selection and application of accounting policies

The standard provides the following guidance in selecting accounting policies:

(a) when a Standard or Interpretation specifically applies to a transaction, the accounting policy applied to that transaction should be determined by applying the relevant standard or interpretation and considering any relevant implementation guidance.

(b) in the absence of a standard that specifically applies to a transaction, management should use its judgement in developing and applying an accounting policy that results in information that is relevant and reliable. In making that judgement, management should refer to, and consider the applicability of, the following sources in descending order:

(1) the requirements and guidance in IASB standards and interpretations dealing with similar and related issues; and

(2) the definitions, recognition criteria and measurement concepts for assets, liabilities, income and expenses in the Conceptual Framework.

Management may also consider the most recent pronouncements of other standard-setting bodies that use a similar conceptual framework (e.g. the ASB in the UK), other accounting literature and accepted industry practice, as long as these do not conflict with international standards, interpretations or the Conceptual Framework.

Consistency of accounting policies

An entity should select and apply its accounting policies consistently for similar transactions and events unless a standard or interpretation specifically requires or permits categorization of items, for which different policies may be appropriate. For example, IAS 16 permits entities to revalue some, but not all, categories of fixed assets.

Changes in accounting policies

An entity is permitted to change an accounting policy only if the change:

(a) is required by an international standard or interpretation; or

(b) results in the financial statements providing reliable and more relevant information about the effects of transactions, other events or conditions on the entity's financial position, financial performance or cash flows.

Users of financial statements need to be able to compare an entity's financial statements over time to identify trends. Therefore, the same accounting policies should be applied within each period and from one period to the next unless the above conditions are satisfied.

IAS 8 clarifies that the following are not changes in accounting polices:

(a) the application of a policy to a transaction that differs in substance from those previously occurring; and

(b) the application of a new accounting policy for transactions that did not occur previously or were immaterial.

Applying changes in accounting policies

If a change in accounting policy results from the initial application of an international standard or interpretation, the change should be accounted for in accordance with the specific transitional provisions, if any, in that standard or interpretation.

If, however, there are no transitional provisions or if the change has been made voluntarily, IAS 8 requires that the change should be accounted for retrospectively.

Retrospective application is applying a new accounting policy to transactions as if that policy had always been applied. This means adjusting the opening balance of each affected component of equity for the earliest prior period presented and the other comparative amounts disclosed for each prior period presented as if the new accounting policy had always been applied. This maintains comparability between accounting periods in spite of the change to the policy. It also reduces the opportunity for management to confuse users by showing the effect of the change on both the previous year and the current year. However, if it is impracticable to determine either the period-specific effects or the cumulative effect of the change for one or more periods presented, the entity should apply the new accounting policy to the carrying amounts of assets and liabilities as at the beginning of the earliest period for which retrospective application is practicable, which may be the current period, and should made a corresponding adjustment to the opening balance of each affected component of equity for that period.

Also, if it is impracticable to determine the cumulative effect, at the beginning of the current period, of applying a new accounting policy to all prior periods, the entity should adjust the comparative information to apply the new accounting policy prospectively from the earliest date practicable.

Disclosure

IAS 8 naturally requires that certain disclosures should be made in the notes to the financial statements if an entity changes any of its accounting policies.

The disclosures relating to changes in accounting policy caused by a new standard or interpretation include:

■ the title of the standard or interpretation causing the change

■ when applicable, that the change in accounting policy is made in accordance with its transitional provisions and a description of these provisions.

The disclosures relating to voluntary changes in accounting policy include:

■ the reasons why applying the new accounting policy provides reliable and more relevant information

The additional disclosures required for both of the above changes include:

■ the nature of the change
■ for the current period and each prior period presented, to the extent practicable, the amount of the adjustment made to each affected line item in the financial statements and the effect of any adjustment to the entity's earnings per share
■ where retrospective application would be required but has not been done, why it is impracticable to apply retrospectively and a description of how and from when the changes have been applied.

Example – voluntary change in accounting policy

The following extracts have been taken from the statement of comprehensive income for a company for the year to 30 June 2012.

	2012	2011
	£000	£000
Profit before taxation	2,700	2,650
Taxation	810	795
Profit after taxation	1,890	1,855

The company began trading on 1 July 2009. At the year end of 30 June 2012, management reviewed its policy in relation to inventory valuation and adopted a revised policy which would provide reliable and more relevant information. If the new policy had been applied in the previous reporting periods, the company's inventory at 30 June 2010 would have been £150,000 higher than the amount originally recognized. At 30 June 2011 the inventory would have been £400,000 higher than originally reported. The closing inventory valuation at 30 June 2012 is in accordance with the new policy. Retained earnings at 30 June 2010 were originally reported at £750,000. It can be assumed that the company's taxation expense is equal to 30% of its profit before tax.

Required

(a) Prepare an extract from the company's amended statement of comprehensive income for the year to 30 June 2012, showing comparative figures for 2011, after adopting the new inventory valuation policy.
(b) Calculate the effect of the change in policy on the company's retained earnings at 30 June 2012 and the restricted retained earnings at 30 June 2010 and 30 June 2011.

Solution

(a) If the new policy had been adopted from the commencement of trading, the company's profits would have been £150,000 higher in the year to 30 June 2010. This would result in an additional taxation charge for that year of £45,000 (£150,000 × 30%). In the year to 30 June 2011, the increased opening inventory figure of £150,000 and the increased closing inventory figure of £400,000 would have resulted in an increase in profits in that year of £250,000 on which additional taxation of £75,000 (£250,000 × 30%) would be payable. The increased opening inventory figure of £400,000 in the year to 30 June 2012 has resulted in the profits being overstated by that amount. The closing inventory figure needs no adjustment as it has been calculated in accordance with the new policy.

The reduction in profits in the year to 30 June 2012 will reduce the taxation expense by £120,000 (£400,000 × 30%).

Extract statement of comprehensive income for the year to 30 June 2012		
		Restated
	2012	2011
	£000	£000
Profit before taxation	2,300	2,900
Taxation	690	870
Profit after taxation	1,610	2,030

Note the effect of the change in policy. In the unadjusted draft figures, the company was showing an increase in profit before taxation of £50,000 between 2011 and 2012. Following the change in policy, this has resulted in a decrease in reported pre-taxation profits of £600,000. The requirement to restate the comparative has highlighted the effects of the change. Had no such requirement existed, the decrease in profits would only have been £350,000 (£2,650,000 (original) – £2,300,000 (restated)).

(b) Retained earnings

	£000
Retained earnings at 30 June 2010, as previously reported	750
Change in accounting policy relating to inventories	105
Restated balance at 30 June 2010	855
Restated profit for the year to 30 June 2011	2,030
Restated balance at 30 June 2011	2,885
Profit for the year to 30 June 2012	1,610
Balance at 30 June 2012	4,495

Note that the retained profit figure at 30 June 2012 would still have been £4,495,000 if the change in accounting policy had not been applied retrospectively i.e. £750,000 + £1,855,000 + £1,890,000 = £4,495,000. However, the distribution of profits and the reported trend in earnings would have been very different and misleading.

Changes in accounting estimates

The nature of the principles underlying the preparation of financial statements means that estimates are inherent in the reported figures. Examples include bad debt provisions, useful life, pattern of benefits and residual value of non-current assets, and the net realizable value of inventories. The use of reasonable estimates is an essential part of the preparation process and does not undermine their reliability.

BASIC

INTERMEDIATE

ADVANCED

It is possible, however, that estimates may require revision as new information becomes available or more experience is gained. For example, new information may become available about the solvency of a debtor or experience may give evidence of how many products require repair under warranty. The point at issue here is that the revision of an estimate is necessitated by current information and does not relate to prior periods. The estimates used in those prior periods reflected the then currently available information. Moreover, a change in an estimate is not a correction of an error.

It is important, however, to distinguish between a change in an accounting estimate and a change in the measurement basis used. A change in the measurement basis used (e.g. from cost to fair value for non-current assets) is a change in accounting policy and not a change in an estimate.

Example

Explain whether the following items constitute changes in accounting policy.

(1) Change from straight line to reducing balance depreciation method
(2) Increase in bad debt provision from 5% of outstanding receivables to 10%
(3) Change of valuation of inventories of chemicals from weighted average historical cost to first in first out
(4) Overheads previously shown in 'cost of sales' are to be included in 'administrative expenses'.

Solution

(1) The policy is to depreciate and the method is a way of estimating the amount of depreciation. The measurement basis is unchanged – the historical cost measurement basis is still being used, therefore there is no change in accounting policy. It is only the estimation technique that has changed.

(2) The policy is to make a provision for bad debts. The measurement basis is unchanged, therefore there is no change in accounting policy. It is only the estimation technique that has changed.

(3) The measurement basis has changed as the valuation method now differs from the previous year. It therefore constitutes a change in accounting policy.

(4) The measurement basis is unchanged – it is only the classification that has changed, not the overall costing method. The way the information is presented has been changed as the overheads were previously part of the gross profit calculation. It therefore constitutes a change in accounting policy.

IAS 8 states that when it is difficult to distinguish a change in accounting policy from a change in an accounting estimate, the change is treated as a change in an accounting estimate.

A change in an accounting estimate should be dealt with prospectively by including it in profit or loss for the period of the change and, if applicable, future periods. Prospective application means applying a new accounting policy after the date at which the policy is changed and recognizing the effect of the change in accounting estimates in the current and future periods affected by the change. If the change affects assets and liabilities but has no effect on profit and loss or equity, only the assets and liabilities are changed.

Note the very important difference here. A change in an accounting estimate does not require the restatement of comparative figures for prior periods. This is totally different from the required treatment of changes in accounting policy.

Disclosure

IAS 8 requires disclosure of:

- the nature and amount of a change in an accounting estimate that has an effect in the current period or is expected to have an effect in future periods
- if the amount of the effect in future periods is not disclosed because estimating it is impracticable, an entity shall disclose that fact.

Errors

Errors can occur in the recognition, measurement, presentation and disclosure of elements of financial statements. For example, failure to recognize a liability or valuing inventory inaccurately. Financial statements do not comply with international standards if they contain material errors. Errors which are discovered during the period are corrected before the financial statements have been issued. Errors which

> 'omissions from, and misstatements in, the entity's financial statements for one or more periods arising from a failure to use, or misuse of, reliable information that:
>
> **(a)** was available when financial statements for those periods were authorised for issue; and
> **(b)** could reasonably be expected to have been obtained and taken into account in the preparation and presentation of those financial statements'.

are discovered after the financial statements have been issued are referred to as prior period errors. IAS 8 defines prior period errors as:

Such errors include the effects of mathematical mistakes, mistakes in applying accounting policies, oversights or misinterpretation of facts, and fraud.

The general principle in IAS 8 is that an entity must correct all material prior period errors retrospectively in the first set of financial statements authorised for issue after their discovery by:

(a) restating the comparative amounts for the prior period(s) presented in which the error occurred; or

(b) if the opening error occurred before the earliest period presented, restating the opening balances of assets, liabilities and equity for the earliest prior period presented.

However, if it is impracticable to determine the period-specific effects of an error on comparative information for one or more prior periods presented, the entity must restate the opening balances of assets, liabilities and equity for the earliest period for which retrospective restatement is practicable (which may be the current period).

Further, if it is impracticable to determine the cumulative effect, at the beginning of the current period, of an error an all prior periods, the entity must restate the comparative information to correct the error prospectively from the earliest date practicable.

Disclosure of prior period errors

The following should be disclosed:

(a) the nature of the prior period error;

(b) the amount of correction for each prior period presented:
   - for each financial line item affected; and
   - if applicable the amount of any correction to the entity's earnings per share

(c) the amount of the correction at the beginning of the earliest prior period presented; and

(d) if retrospective restatement is impracticable, why this is so and how and from when the error has been corrected.

BASIC

INTERMEDIATE

ADVANCED

Example – Prior period error

During the audit of a company's accounts for the year to 31 December 2012, an error in the invoicing system was discovered. The error led to sales of £950,000 in January 2013 being included in the December 2012 accounts. Further investigation revealed that a similar error occurred at the end of 2011 when sales of £800,000 in January 2012 were included as December 2011 income. There was no evidence of errors in earlier years. The directors believe that the errors are material. The only other effect on the statement of comprehensive income of these errors is on the taxation charge which requires to be adjusted by 30% of the error. An extract from the company's draft statement of comprehensive income for the year to 31 December 2012 (before the error was discovered) is shown below.

BASIC

INTERMEDIATE

ADVANCED

	Draft 2012 £000	2011 £000
Sales	13,000	12,000
Cost of goods sold	3,665	3,250
Gross profit	9,335	8,750
Other expenses	3,300	3,000
Profit before tax	6,035	5,750
Taxation expense	2,000	1,500
Profit after taxation	4,035	4,250

Required

(a) Calculate the effect of the error on the profits of the company for the year to 31 December 2012 and 2011; and

(b) prepare, with comparatives, the amended statement of comprehensive income for the year to 31 December 2012 and any related disclosure.

Solution

(a) Effect on profits

	2012 £000	2011 £000
Overstatement of income	950	800
Less: correction for previous year	(800)	–
Net overstatement	150	800
Reduction in taxation charge @ 30%	45	240

(b)

Statement of comprehensive income
Year ended 31 December 2012

	2012	Restated 2011
	£000	£000
Sales	12,850	11,200
Cost of goods sold	3,665	3,250
Gross profit	9,185	7,950
Other expenses	3,300	3,000
Profit before tax	5,885	4,950
Taxation expense	1,955	1,260
Profit after taxation	3,930	3,690

Error

During the audit of the current year's accounts a material error affecting 2011 was discovered. Sales in January 2012 had been included in the accounts for the year to 31 December 2011. The correction of this error has been accounted for retrospectively. The 2011 figures have been restated to reflect this. The error had no impact on earlier years' financial statements.

Effect on accounts of 2011

	£000
Sales – as previously reported	12,000
Less: overstatement error	800
Restated sales figure	11,200
Decrease in operating profit	800
Decrease in taxation expense	240
Decrease in profit after tax	560
Decrease in receivables and retained profit	560

Disclosure in practice

Logica has extensive accounting policies which have been applied in the preparation of the financial statements. As this extract shows, the fundamental principles noted in the Conceptual Framework have been adhered to.

BASIC

INTERMEDIATE

ADVANCED

2. Accounting policies

The principal accounting policies applied in the preparation of these consolidated financial statements are set out below. These policies have been consistently applied to all the years presented, unless otherwise stated.

Basis of preparation

These consolidated financial statements have been prepared in accordance with International Financial Reporting Standards (IFRSs) as adopted by the European Union (EU), IFRIC interpretations and those parts of the Companies Act 2006 (the Act) that are applicable to companies reporting under IFRSs.

The consolidated financial statements have been prepared on a going concern basis and under the historical cost convention, as modified by the revaluation of certain financial instruments, share based payments and pension scheme assets.

Source: Logica (2011), p. 98

Section summary

The IASB Conceptual Framework consists of a set of fundamental principles and definitions which underlie financial accounting.

Its purposes include assisting in the development of future international standards, promoting harmonization of accounting standards relating to the presentation of financial statements by reducing the number of alternative accounting treatments, and assisting standard-setting bodies in developing national standards. The objective of general purpose financial reporting forms the foundation of the Conceptual Framework, which is to provide financial information that is useful for decision making. There is a presumption that its objectives are achieved when financial statements are prepared in accordance with international standards. IAS 1 deals with the Presentation of Financial Statements and prescribes the basis for the presentation of general purpose financial statements to ensure comparability over time and between different entities. It also sets out guidelines for their structure and minimum requirements for their content.

Various standards over the years have required the use of fair values but there were inconsistencies between the standards in terms of their measurement requirements. IFRS 13 has been issued to prescribe the correct accounting treatment.

Finally, IAS 8 lays down criteria for the selection and change of accounting policies, and deals with changes in accounting estimates and corrections of prior period errors.

Chapter summary

IAS 1: *Presentation of Financial Statements*

- Financial statements should comprise a statement of financial position, a statement of comprehensive income, a statement of changes in equity, a statement of cash flows and notes containing a summary of the main accounting policies of the company and other information.
- Financial statements should be prepared on the accruals basis and on the going concern basis.
- The presentation and classification of items should be consistent from one accounting period to the next.
- Comparative information should be disclosed in respect of the previous period for all amounts reported in the financial statements.
- Current and non-current assets and current and non-current liabilities should be shown separately in the statement of financial position.

- IAS 1 lists the main line items that should be presented in the statement of financial position and in the statement of comprehensive income.
- The standard lists other disclosures and analyses that should be made in the statements or in the notes.
- The statement of changes in equity shows the changes in each component of equity during an accounting period.
- The notes to the financial statements are within the scope of international standards.

IFRS 13: *Fair Value Measurement*

- Fair value is the price that would be received to sell an asset or paid to transfer a liability in an orderly transaction between market participants at the measurement date.
- Fair value is based on an exit price.
- Fair value is a market-based measurement and not an entity specific value.
- The transaction to sell the asset or transfer the liability is assumed to take place either in the principal market for the asset or liability or, in the absence of a principal market, in the most advantageous market.
- The price at which a transaction is assumed to occur is the price in an orderly transaction and under current market conditions at the measurement date.
- A fair value measurement for a non-financial asset is based on its highest and best use.
- The fair value of a liability or an entity's own equity instrument is measured based on the assumption that the liability or equity instrument is transferred to a market participant at the measurement date.
- When the price of an asset or liability cannot be observed directly, it must be estimated using a valuation technique.
- Inputs to valuation techniques are categorized into 3 levels with Level 1 having the highest priority and Level 3 the lowest priority.
- Disclosures should be made of the valuation techniques and inputs used and the effects of the fair value measurements on the total comprehensive income for the period.

The Conceptual Framework for Financial Reporting

- The Framework is not an accounting standard.
- It provides fundamental principles and definitions that underpin the preparation of financial statements.
- One of its main purposes is to assist in the development and review of international standards
- The objective of general purpose financial reporting is to provide financial information that is useful to a wide range of users in making decisions about providing resources to the entity.
- The primary users of general purpose financial reports are investors, lenders and other creditors.
- Other users of financial reports include employees, customers, the government and the public.
- The financial statements are prepared on the accruals basis and the going concern basis.
- The fundamental qualitative characteristics of financial statement information are relevance and faithful representation. The enhancing characteristics are comparability, verifiability, timeliness and understandability.
- The main elements of financial statements are assets, liabilities, equity, income and expenses.
- An element is recognized in the financial statements when it is probable that any economic benefits associated with the element will flow to or from the entity, and that element has a cost or value that can be reliably measured.
- A number of measurement bases exist, including historical cost, current cost, realizable value and current value.
- Profits and losses can be measured in terms of financial or physical capital.

IAS 8: *Accounting Policies, Changes in Accounting Estimates and Errors*

- Accounting policies are the specific principles, bases, conventions, rules and practices applied by an entity in preparing and presenting financial statements.
- Accounting policies should be applied consistently and only changed if the change is required by an international standard, or if it results in reliable and more relevant information.
- A change in accounting policy should be accounted for retrospectively by restating comparative figures for each prior period presented.
- Full disclosure of the details of the change should be given in the notes to the financial statements.
- Changes in accounting estimates are not corrections of errors.
- Changes in accounting estimates should be accounted for prospectively and, if material, disclosed in the notes to the financial statements.
- Material prior period errors should be accounted for retrospectively and disclosed in the notes to the financial statements.

✓ Key terms for review

Definitions can be found in the glossary at the end of the book.

Accounting policies	Private company	Share premium
Audit	Public company	Shareholders
Conceptual framework	Regulatory framework	Statement of changes in equity
Dividend	Reserves	Statement of comprehensive income
Measurement	Retained earnings	
Ordinary shares	Revaluation reserve	Statement of financial position
Preference shares	Share capital	

? Review questions

1. What different types of business structure exist, and how are the preparation and presentation of their financial statements affected by that structure?

2. Explain the term 'generally accepted accounting practice' (GAAP).

3. (a) State the objectives of financial statements.

   (b) Identify the main users of financial statements and explain why each user group might be interested in the information provided in these statements.

4. IAS 1 lists seven 'general features' relating to the presentation of financial statements. List these 'general features' and explain their main requirements.

5. Explain why two companies carrying out identical transactions could produce different gross profit figures.

6. What are the functions of:

   (a) the IFRS Foundation

   (b) the International Accounting Standards Board

   (c) the IFRS Advisory Council

   (d) the IFRS Interpretations Committee?

7. Outline the roles of the directors, accountants and auditors in the financial reporting process and clarify the responsibilities of each.

8. Explain what is meant by corporate governance and list the OECD's principles of good corporate governance.

9. In relation to corporate governance, explain the differences between the 'liberal' model and the 'coordinated' model and why these differences exist.

10. Explain what is meant by a 'conceptual framework'.

11. The IASB Conceptual Framework for Financial Reporting refers to qualitative characteristics of useful financial information. Identify and explain the qualitative characteristics of useful financial information, distinguishing between fundamental characteristics and enhancing characteristics.

12. Explain what is meant by the term recognition and explain what criteria must be satisfied before an element can be recognized in the financial statements.

13. Explain the measurement bases identified in the Conceptual Framework.

14. Explain the capital maintenance concepts identified in the Conceptual Framework.

15. What criticisms can be levelled at the Conceptual Framework?

16. What are the arguments for and against fair value accounting?

17. With reference to IAS 8, distinguish between accounting policies and accounting estimates.

18. What should an entity do in relation to an item if there is no applicable international standard or interpretation?

 Exercises

Level I

1. The following summarized trial balance has been extracted from the books of Kendun Ltd at 31 December 2012.

	£000	£000
Administrative expenses	130	
Cash at bank	50	
Distribution costs	244	
Dividends paid	35	
Inventories as at 1 January 2012	45	
Other expenses	24	
Property, plant & equipment	700	
Property, plant & equipment (accumulated depreciation 31/12/12)		250
Purchases	490	
Retained earnings at 1 January 2012		48
Sales		1,000
Share capital		500
Trade payables		120
Trade receivables	200	
	1,918	1,918

Additional information:

(i) Inventories at 31 December 2012 amounted to £43,000

(ii) The corporation tax charge for the year has been calculated at £25,000

Required

Prepare the following financial statements for the year ended 31 December 2012 in accordance with IAS 1:

(a) statement of comprehensive income

(b) statement of financial position

(c) statement of changes in equity.

2. The following summarized trial balance has been taken from the books of Huntsman Ltd at 31 March 2013.

	£000	£000
Land, at cost	120	
Equipment at cost	196	
Equipment – accumulated depreciation (1/4/12)		76
Inventory at 1 April 2012	107	
Trade receivables	183	
Trade payables		67
Cash at bank	137	
Ordinary shares of £1 each (31/3/13)		400
Retained earnings at 1 April 2012		104
Sales		1,220
Purchases	640	
Distribution costs	203	
Administrative expenses	221	
Finance costs	20	
Dividend paid	40	
	1,867	1,867

Additional information:

(i) During the year the company issued 200,000 ordinary shares at par.

(ii) The company's non-depreciable land was valued at £300,000 on 31 March 2013 and this valuation is to be incorporated into the accounts for the year to 31 March 2013.

(iii) Equipment is to be depreciated at 25% on cost. This equipment is used solely in production.

(iv) Inventory at 31 March 2013 was valued at £119,000.

(v) The corporation tax charge for the year has been estimated at £45,000.

Required

Prepare the following financial statements for Huntsman Ltd for the year to 31 March 2013 in accordance with IAS 1:

(a) statement of comprehensive income

(b) statement of financial position

(c) statement of changes in equity.

Level II

3. Flofoam plc is a manufacturer and supplier of specialist seat padding for passenger aircraft. The following trial balance has been extracted from the financial records of Flofoam plc at 31 March 2013.

	Dr £000	Cr £000
Bank	14	
Trade payables		62
Other payables		77
Trade receivables	300	
Chairman's salary	50	
Electricity (factory)	33	
Insurance	17	
Workshop building at cost	200	
Machinery	420	
Accumulated depreciation (machinery)		152
Office expenses	25	
Share capital (£0.50 shares)		300
Retained earnings at 1 April 2012		132
Provision for bad debt and doubtful receivables		8
Purchases	1,314	
Rent of distribution depot	28	
Workshop rates	40	
Sales		2,350
Inventory at 1 April 2012	156	
Vehicles at cost	96	
Accumulated depreciation (vehicles)		56
Wages and salaries	448	
Royalties received		4
	3,141	3,141

Additional information:

 (i) Inventory at 31 March 2013 valued at cost amounted to £164,000.

 (ii) Depreciation is to be provided on machinery and vehicles at rates of 25% and 20%, respectively. Flofoam plc has adopted the reducing balance method of providing for depreciation. Machinery is used entirely for production and vehicles are used 75% in distribution and 25% in administration.

 (iii) The audit fee for the year to 31 March 2013 is estimated to be £12,000 and should be accrued in the 2013 financial statements.

 (iv) Insurance paid in advance at 31 March 2013 amounted to £3,000. Insurance should be allocated as follows:

 Production – 50%

 Administration – 50%

 (v) The provision for bad debts is to be set to 5% of the outstanding trade receivables at 31 March 2013.

 (vi) Corporation tax of £80,000 has been estimated in respect of the profit for the year.

 (vii) An ordinary dividend of 10p per share was declared on 1 March 2013 and paid on 15 April 2013.

8. The salaries expense can be analysed as follows:

	£000
Sales directors' salary	48
Production staff wages	150
Distribution depot staff	80
Administration wages	170
	448

Required

Prepare the following financial statements for the year ended 31 March 2013 in accordance with IAS 1:

(a) statement of comprehensive income

(b) statement of changes in equity

(c) statement of financial position.

4. Burnfoot Brickworks plc is a manufacturer and supplier of bricks to the construction industry. The following trial balance has been extracted from the financial records at 31 March 2013.v

	£000	£000
Accumulated depreciation – buildings		80
Accumulated depreciation – plant and machinery		160
Advertising	112	
Bank	214	
Bank interest received		17
Debenture loans – 10% (repayable 2020)		200
Electricity	80	
General administration expenses	128	
Insurance	93	
Interest paid on debentures	20	
Land and buildings	600	
Plant and machinery	840	
Purchases	1,427	
Purchases returns		35
Rents receivable		100
Sales		3,480
Sales returns	60	
Share capital (£1 ordinary shares)		600
Inventory at 1 April 2012	211	
Telephone	456	
Trade payables		296
Trade receivables	584	
Wages and salaries	740	
Retained earnings b/f		597
	5,565	5,565

Additional information:

(i) Depreciation for the year is to be calculated as follows:

   Buildings (cost £400,000) – 2% straight line

   Plant and machinery – 20% reducing balance

   Depreciation should be allocated as follows:

Production	50%
Distribution	25%
Administration	25%

(ii) Audit fees of £18,000 should be accrued for the year to 31 March 2013.

(iii) Closing inventory was valued at cost on 31 March 2013 at £223,000.

(iv) A dividend of 10p per share is declared.

(v) Insurance prepaid at 31 March 2013 amounted to £3,000. The insurance expense should be allocated as follows:

Production	$33\frac{1}{3}$%
Distribution	$33\frac{1}{3}$%
Administration	$33\frac{1}{3}$%

(vi) An electricity bill of £14,000 for the final quarter did not arrive until mid-April 2013. This should be accrued in full in the year to 31 March 2013.

   Electricity and telephone should be allocated as follows:

Production	20%
Distribution	50%
Administration	30%

(vii) Corporation tax on the profits for the year is estimated at £105,000.

(viii) The wages and salaries expense can be analysed as follows:

Factory salaries	150
Salesmen's salaries	370
Office staff	220
	740

Required

Pepare the following financial statements for the year ended 31 March 2013 in accordance with IAS 1:

(a) statement of comprehensive income

(b) statement of changes in equity

(c) statement of financial position.

5. Orangejuice plc is a manufacturer of soft drinks. At 30 June 2013, the following list of balances was extracted from the company's accounting records.

	£000
Warehouse rates	10
Wages and salaries	400
Cash and bank	275
Production costs	630
Vehicle repairs and petrol	125
General expenses	450
Trade payables	105
Trade receivables	210
Land and buildings at cost	2,000
Plant and machinery at cost	850
Fixtures and fittings at cost	340
Accumulated depreciation:	
Land and buildings	180
Plant and machinery	120
Fixtures and fittings	136
Share capital (£1 ordinary shares)	1,000
Loan stock (10%)	500
Heat and light	125
Sales	2,600
Closure costs	187
Other payables including taxation	355
Retained earnings at 1 July 2012	606

Notes:

(i) Depreciation for the year is to be calculated as follows:
    Buildings (cost £500,000) – 2% straight line
    Plant and machinery 20% – reducing balance
    Fixtures and fittings 10% – straight line
    Depreciation should be allocated as follows:
    Production – 30%
    Distribution – 40%
    Administration – 30%

(ii) Closing inventory on 30 June 2013 was £150,000. Opening inventory has already been accounted for.

(iii) The company declared a dividend of 5p per share on 15 June 2013. Interest payable to debenture holders is still outstanding.

(iv) The invoice for the audit fee arrived in the post on 2 July 2013. The amount was £35,000.

(v) Corporation tax on the profits for the year has been estimated at £110,000.

(vi) Wages and salaries expense should be allocated on the same basis as depreciation.

(vii) Vehicle repairs and petrol costs relate 100% to delivery lorries and sales representatives' cars.

(viii) Heat and light costs are to be allocated as follows:

Production – 50%

Distribution – 20%

Administration – 30%

(ix) One of the factories was closed during the year as part of a restructuring programme, incurring closure costs of £187,000. In relation to this, closure turnover was £185,000 and the operating loss was £2,000.

Required

Prepare the following financial statements for the year ended 31 March 2013 in accordance with IAS 1:

(a) statement of comprehensive income

(b) statement of changes in equity

(c) statement of financial position.

6. Oakwood plc manufactures kitchen furniture. The following trial balance has been extracted from Oakwood's accounting records at 31 March 2013.

	£000	£000
Accumulated depreciation:		
Land and buildings		720
Plant and machinery		480
Fixtures and fittings		544
Warehouse rates	40	
Wages and salaries	1,600	
Cash and bank	1,100	
Production costs	2,520	
Vehicle repairs and petrol	500	
General expenses	920	
Trade payables		420
Trade receivables	840	
Land and buildings at cost	8,000	
Plant and machinery at cost	3,400	
Fixtures and fittings at cost	1,360	
Share capital (£1 ordinary shares)		4,000
10% debenture loan stock		2,000
Corporation tax	880	
Heat and light	360	
Auditors' fees	140	
Sales		10,400
Closure costs	748	
Other creditors including taxation		1,420
Retained earnings at 1 April 2012		2,424
	22,408	22,408

Notes:

(i) Depreciation for the year is to be calculated as follows:

   Buildings (cost £1,500,000) – 2% straight line

   Plant and machinery – 20% reducing balance

   Fixtures and fittings – 10% straight line

   Depreciation should be allocated as follows:

   Production – 40%

   Distribution – 30%

   Administration – 30%

(ii) Wages and salaries expense should be allocated on the same basis as depreciation.

(iii) Vehicle repairs and petrol costs relate 100% to delivery lorries and sales representatives' cars.

(iv) Heat and light costs should be allocated as follows:

   Production – 50%

   Distribution – 20%

   Administration – 30%

(v) Closing inventory on 31 March 2013 was £150,000. Opening inventory has been accounted for in the trial balance.

(vi) A dividend of 5p per share was declared on 15 March 2013. Interest to debenture holders is outstanding.

Required

Prepare the following financial statements for the year ended 31 March 2013 in accordance with IAS 1:

(a) statement of comprehensive income

(b) statement of changes in equity

(c) statement of financial position.

7. The following is the trial balance of Cooper plc as at 31 March 2013.

	Debit	Credit
	£	£
Share capital: authorized and issued		
125,000 ordinary shares of £1 each		125,000
25,000 7% preference shares of £1 each		25,000
Property (at valuation)	140,000	
Plant and machinery (cost £80,000)	66,900	
Goodwill	30,000	
Vehicles (cost £25,000)	19,100	
Wages and salaries	25,000	
Inventory at 1 April 2012	9,400	
Receivables/Payables	11,200	8,300
Bank overdraft		7,800
Purchases/sales	49,700	160,250
Directors' salaries	22,000	
Office rates	4,650	

Light and heat	3,830	
Interest on debentures	1,200	
Vehicle repairs	1,270	
10% debentures		24,000
Provision for bad debts		910
Share premium		25,000
Retained earnings		2,580
General reserve		10,200
Interim dividend on ordinary shares	3,250	
Audit fees	3,350	
Revaluation reserve		9,860
Bad debts	700	
Listed investments	8,000	
Investment income		650
	399,550	399,550

The following additional information is available:
  (i)   Inventory at 31 March 2013 is valued at £13,480.
 (ii)   Rates include a payment of £2,300 for the six months from 1 January 2013.
(iii)   Depreciation is to be applied as follows:
          Plant and machinery – 15% per annum on cost
          Vehicles – 10% on cost.
        Depreciation is to be allocated: 50% cost of sales, 25% administration and 25% selling and distribution.
 (iv)   Wages and salaries expense should be allocated on the same basis as depreciation. Vehicle repair costs relate to delivery lorries and sales representatives' cars.
  (v)   Heat and light costs should be allocated as follows:
          Cost of sales – £2,000
          Distribution – £1,500
          Administration – £330
 (vi)   The provision for bad debts is to be adjusted to 10% of the receivables at the end of the year.
(vii)   The preference share dividends are outstanding at the end of the year and the last half year's interest on debentures has not been paid.
(viii) Corporation tax on this year's profit is £6,370.
 (ix)   The directors declare a final dividend on the ordinary shares of 5p per share.
  (x)   The balance on the revaluation reserve relates to the company's property and arose as follows:

Balance at 1 April 2012	£2,860
Revaluation during the year to 31 March 2013	£7,000
	£9,860

Required

Prepare the following financial statements for the year ended 31 March 2013 in accordance with IAS 1:

(a) statement of comprehensive income

(b) statement of changes in equity

(c) statement of financial position.

8. The following draft figures have been prepared for Engel Ltd for the year to 30 June 2012. The published figures for 2011 are also shown.

Statement of comprehensive income for the year ended 30 June 2012		
	2012	2011
	£000	£000
Sales	1,050	900
Cost of goods sold	860	650
Gross profit	190	250
Administrative expenses	120	110
Profit before taxation	70	140
Taxation	21	42
Profit for the year	49	98

After completion of the draft accounts, it was discovered that an arithmetic error during the compilation of the inventory sheets resulted in the inventory at 30 June 2011 being overstated by £50,000. This is considered to be a material amount.

Engel Ltd had retained earnings at 30 June 2010 of £260,000.

Required

(a) Prepare an extract from the company's statement of comprehensive income for the year to 30 June 2012, showing restated comparatives for 2011.

(b) Calculate the company's retained earnings at 30 June 2012 and the restated retained earnings at 30 June 2011.

(Note: it can be assumed that the company's tax expense is equal to 30% of its profit before tax.)

References

Companies Act 2006.

IAS 1 *Presentation of Financial Statements*. IASB, revised 2007.

IAS 8 *Accounting Policies,Changes in Accounting Estimates and Errors*. IASB, revised 2005.

IFRS 13 *Fair Value Measurement*. IASB, FABS, 2011.

IASB (2010) *The Conceptual Framework for Financial Reporting*.

Logica (2011) *Annual Report and Accounts*.

Marks & Spencer (2011) *Annual Report and Financial Statements*.

Further Reading

Belkaoui, A. (2000) *Accounting Theory* (4th edn). Thomson Learning.

Black, G. (2003) *Students' Guide to Accounting and Financial Reporting Standards* (9th edn). FT/PrenticeHall.

Companies Act 1985.

FASB (1974) *Conceptual Framework for Accounting and Reporting: Consideration of the Report of the Study Group on the Objectives of Financial Statements*. FASB.

Framework for the Presentation and Preparation of Financial Statements. IASB, 1989.

IAS 1 *Presentation of Financial Statements*. IASB, revised 2004.

Objectives of Financial Reporting by Business Enterprises, Statement of Financial Accounting Concepts no. 1, 1978.

Objectives of Financial Statements, Report of the Study Group on the Objectives of Financial Statements. AICPA, 1973.

OECD (2004) *Principles of Corporate Governance*. OECD.

Statement of Principles for Financial Reporting. ASB, 1995.

Wilson, A., Davies, M., Curtis, M. and Wilkinson-Riddle, G. (2001) *UK and International GAAP* (7th edn). Ernst & Young, Butterworths Tolley.

When you have read this chapter, log on to the Online Learning Centre website at *www.mcgraw-hill.co.uk/textbooks/mckeith* to explore chapter-by-chapter test questions, further reading and more online study tools.

Chapter 2

Tangible Non-current Assets

Learning Outcomes

After studying this chapter you should be able to:

- ✓ Define a non-current asset
- ✓ Explain under what conditions non-current assets are recognized
- ✓ Explain the nature of depreciation
- ✓ Explain the requirements of IAS 20 on how government grants are treated
- ✓ Explain how borrowing costs are treated under IAS 23 relating to borrowing costs
- ✓ Explain and apply the principles of IAS 16 *Property, Plant and Equipment*
- ✓ Evaluate the alternative treatments for investment properties
- ✓ explain and evaluate the requirements of IAS 40 relating to investment properties.

Introduction

This chapter considers the nature of tangible non-current assets – that is, those assets that can be seen and touched. Remember that the IASB uses the term 'non-current assets' rather than fixed assets. The accounting standard which deals with tangible non-current assets is IAS 16 Property, Plant and Equipment; however, certain issues relating to the measurement of these non-current assets are dealt with by IAS 20 Accounting for Government Grants and Disclosure of Government Assistance and IAS 23 Borrowing Costs. The chapter also introduces the impairment of assets. An asset is said to be impaired when the amount that can be expected to be recovered from its use or sale falls below its carrying amount. Finally IAS 40 Investment Property deals with accounting for properties that are not held for use by an entity but for investment purposes.

Section 1: Basic Principles

2.1 What are non-current assets?

Of all the items contained in a company's statement of financial position, non-current assets are probably considered by many to be the most straightforward and understandable of figures. Tangible non-current assets are the 'resources' a company uses to generate revenue. The 'value' of those assets in the statement of financial position is often seen as a reflection of the financial strength of a company, and also the extent to which a company can offer security to lenders and investors.

Unfortunately, tangible non-current assets can also be the most misinterpreted and contentious items within a company's statement of financial position. Although the term 'non-current asset' is used frequently in accounting literature, there is no precise definition of what constitutes a non-current asset. In order to define a non-current asset we need first of all to define an asset.

2.2 Definition of assets

An asset is defined as:

> *a resource controlled by the entity as a result of past events and from which future economic benefits are expected to flow to the entity. (Conceptual Framework, para. 4.4(a))*

This definition is deliberately wide so that it encompasses all possible assets and not simply the more obvious tangible assets.

To understand this definition fully, each phrase must be considered separately.

- **Controlled by the entity:** Control can be used in the positive sense in that the company has access to the economic benefits derived from using an asset, but it can also be used in the negative sense of preventing others from accessing such benefits. From this perspective, an asset such as skilled employees cannot be included on the statement of financial position. While there is no doubt that having a skilled workforce will benefit a company, there is no way a company could exercise control over the workforce.

  It is important to note that the definition does not make any reference to ownership. While ownership is likely to be the strongest form of control available to a company, the right to use an item may, in practice, be very similar to the right of ownership. Such rights may be conferred by legal arrangements such as an agreement to lease or rent a resource, or a licence allowing exclusive use of a resource.

- **A result of past events:** A resource cannot simply appear and be recognized. Something must have happened for a resource to have been identified and there must be objective evidence to prove that the entity has some entitlement to the resource. A past event provides objective evidence that an entity has done something to create a resource or has purchased it. The evidence provided by a past transaction is, therefore, an objective starting point. A transaction is an agreement between two parties which usually involves exchanging goods or services for cash or a future right to cash. Sometimes, however, there may be no transaction as such but there is an event that is sufficient to give this objective evidence. The event could be the performance of a service that, once completed, gives the right to demand payment.

- **Future economic benefits:** An entity may use up many resources in the expectation that they will provide future cash. Some resources generate cash more quickly than others. For example, stocks of goods purchased for resale carry a future economic benefit in terms of the expectation of sale. Such a benefit comes to the entity relatively quickly. The entity may also own a warehouse where goods are stored before being sold. The warehouse also provides future economic benefits since it helps create the cash flow from the sale of goods (by having them available for sale).

BASIC

INTERMEDIATE

ADVANCED

In addition, the warehouse itself could be sold at some point in the future, which again would generate cash.

It is important to note that the future economic benefits may be direct, as in the case of inventories purchased for resale, or indirect, as in the case of the warehouse that assists in the generation of those directly identifiable benefits.

In addition, there may be uncertainty surrounding the amount of future economic benefits. Inventories purchased for resale may or may not be sold at a profit; inventories sold on credit to a customer may or may not be paid for, i.e. bad debts. This uncertainty does not prevent the resource being recognized as an asset, but it may impact on how the asset is measured in money terms.

Table 2.1 gives examples of assets commonly found in company statements of financial position and illustrates the test aspects of the definition being satisfied.

It is conventional practice to divide assets into current assets and non-current assets. An asset should be classified as a current asset when it:

- is expected to be realized in, or is held for sale or consumption in, the normal course of the entity's operating cycle,
- is held primarily for trading purposes or for the short term, and expected to be realized within 12 months of the end of the reporting period, or
- is cash or a cash equivalent asset that is not restricted in its use (IAS 1 para 66).

All other assets should be classified as non-current assets.

The classification between current and non-current is the intention to which the asset is to be put, and not the length of the life of the asset. If the intention is to use the asset over an extended period then it will be classified as a non-current asset. In contrast, if the asset is likely to undergo some transaction

Table 2.1 How test aspects of the definition of assets are met

Asset	Controlled by the entity by means of	Past event	Future economic benefits
Land and buildings owned by the company	Outright ownership	Signing the contract as evidence of purchase of land and buildings	Used in continuing operations of the business; possible future sale of items
Plant and machinery owned by the company	Outright ownership	The receiving of the goods and a supplier's invoice	Used in continuing operations of the business
Equipment used under a finance lease	Contract for exclusive use	Signing lease agreeing rental terms	Used in continuing operations of the business
Goods purchased for resale	Ownership	The receiving of the goods and a supplier's invoice	Expectation of sale
Amounts due from customers (trade receivables)	Contract for payment	Delivery of goods to customer; issue of sales invoice and creation of obligation to pay for goods at future date	Expectation that the customer will settle the obligation and pay cash
Work in progress (partly finished goods)	Ownership	Costs incurred to date and evaluation of the state of completion of works as evidenced by work records	Expectation of completion and sale
Prepaid insurance premiums	Contract for insurance cover for a specific period	Paying insurance premiums in advance; cheque payment	Expectation of continuing insurance cover

within 12 months, then it should be classified as current. Note that this definition does not include assets that are held for resale in the normal course of business.

In this context, while a motor trader will classify cars for resale as a current asset (inventory), a furniture dealer will treat cars as a non-current (fixed) asset. In other words, motor cars will be classified according to the use to which they will be put, and according to how long they will be used in the business.

2.3 Recognition and non-recognition of assets

Recognition

Although an item may have satisfied the criteria to be defined as an asset, this in itself does not qualify the item as an asset for inclusion in the statement of financial position. There are further tests of recognition that must be met.

Recognition means reporting an item by means of words and amounts within the main financial statements in such a way that the item is included in the arithmetic totals. An item that is reported in the notes to the accounts is said to be disclosed but not recognized.

An asset is recognised in the statement of financial position when:

- it is probable that future economic benefits associated with the item will flow to the entity, and
- the cost of the item to the entity can be measured reliably.

In order to satisfy the first criterion for recognition, an entity needs evidence that the future benefit will flow to it – proof of ownership (e.g. vehicle registration documents, title deeds of property, invoices from suppliers of machinery). Existence of such evidence suggests that an entity can be reasonably certain that it will receive the rewards attaching to the asset.

The second criterion is usually satisfied by the exchange transaction that gave rise to the expenditure in the first instance (i.e. the purchase of the asset identified its cost). As we discovered in the first section of this chapter, the purchase price of the asset will not always necessarily be equal to the asset's cost and, indeed, as we will see later on in this section, there are other factors that may affect the calculation of an asset's cost.

Non-recognition

It is worth pausing to consider the following items that pass the definition tests of assets but fail the recognition tests:

- a skilled workforce
- a quality product
- a strong customer base.

All the above meet the conditions of rights or other access to future economic benefits, control (to an extent) and a past transaction or event.

In addition, however, they all have some degree of uncertainty attached to them and, as a result, fail one or both of the recognition tests.

A skilled workforce may, as a result of unforeseen circumstances, become unreliable or problematic; a product may have a reputation for quality but as fashions and tastes change, that reputation may not carry the value it once did; customers may well be loyal but they could change their allegiance at a moment's notice.

These items, then, cannot be recognized in the financial statements. Should they, however, be disclosed in the notes to the financial statements?

The answer is that because of the level of uncertainty attaching to the future benefits, the prudent approach is to avoid being over-optimistic and consequently not to disclose such items as assets in the notes.

2.4 The accounting issue involved: depreciation

Having established whether or not an item of expenditure qualifies as a non-current asset, the main accounting issue is how to deal with that expenditure in the financial statements.

When a company acquires a non-current asset it will be shown in the statement of financial position and recorded initially at cost. However, since non-current assets are 'acquired for use within the business' this means that these non-current assets will be used in generating revenue for the business–either directly in the form of, for example, machinery, or indirectly in the form of, perhaps, delivery vehicles. The key point to note is that the use of the non-current assets is an expense in generating revenues. Revenue generation is important in that revenues generated contribute to the measure of profit. In order to measure profit it is necessary to match the revenue generated with the costs associated with generating those revenues. Consequently, as a result of non-current assets being recorded in the statement of financial position and the measure of profit being made in the statement of comprehensive income, an adjustment requires to be made to reflect the usage of those non-current assets within the statement of comprehensive income. The accounting issue involved is how to measure this usage.

The solution is that an estimate of how much of the non-current asset has been used in generating revenues requires to be made and a portion of the asset's original cost allocated to the statement of comprehensive income to be shown as an expense in generating those revenues. The cost of the non-current assets used up in generating revenue, in accounting terms, is known as depreciation.

What is depreciation?

Depreciation is an accounting estimate of how much of an asset has been used up in generating revenue. If the matching concept is adhered to, it follows that the measure of the amount of asset used up – and resulting allocation of costs–should be based on the pattern of benefits expected to be derived from using the particular asset. In order to calculate the depreciation the following information is required:

- cost of the asset
- residual value, i.e. the value at the end of the asset's life
- useful life of the asset.

Given that depreciation is an estimate of the cost of an asset used up in generating revenue, this depreciation charge will be shown in the statement of comprehensive income as an expense, and so will be matched against the revenues generated for the period.

There are a number of ways of calculating this depreciation charge; the most common ones are:

- straight line method
- reducing balance method.

Straight line method of depreciation

This method of depreciation allocates an equal amount of depreciation over the life of the asset. It is calculated by dividing the net cost of the asset by its useful life. Net cost is the cost of the asset less the residual value. This net cost is also known as 'depreciable amount' and is the cost of an asset less its residual value.

Example

A company buys an asset costing £7,000 that is expected to last for three years. At the end of the three-year period the scrap value is estimated to be £1,000. The depreciation charge can be calculated as follows:

$$\text{Depreciation charge} = \frac{\text{cost} - \text{residual value}}{\text{useful life}}$$

$$= \frac{£7,000 - £1,000}{3}$$

$$= £2,000$$

This means that the net cost of the asset, £6,000, is spread over the life of the asset. The depreciation charge is recorded in the statement of comprehensive income in each of the three years at £2,000 each year.

Statement of comprehensive income (for Year 1)	
Depreciation	£2,000
Statement of financial position (for Year 1)	
Non-current asset	£7,000
Less depreciation	£2,000
Net book value	£5,000

The statement of comprehensive income shows the charge for depreciation, while the statement of financial position shows the cost of the asset minus the total depreciation allocated to the asset.

In Year 2, the financial statements will show:

Statement of comprehensive income (for Year 2)		
Depreciation	£2,000	
Statement of financial position (for Year 2)		
Non-current asset (cost)	£7,000	
Less total depreciation	£4,000	(for two years)
Net book value	£3,000	
And in Year 3		
Statement of comprehensive income (for Year 3)		
Depreciation	£2,000	
Statement of financial position (for Year 3)		
Non-current asset (cost)	£7,000	
Less total depreciation	£6,000	(for three years)
Net book value	£1,000	

This shows that the asset is now reduced to its residual i.e. scrap value, at the end of the three-year period.

It is worth pausing at this stage to look more closely at the above figures in the preceding example.

The statement of comprehensive income entries are readily understandable. This shows that the asset is expected to make an even contribution to revenues over the three years. The cost of the asset used up in generating these revenues is £2,000 each year.

The information disclosed by the statement of financial position entries is perhaps less obvious. In Year 1 the original cost of £7,000 is recorded and the first allocation of depreciation of £2,000 is deducted from that cost to give what accountants call 'net book value' or 'carrying value'. The net book value is £5,000.

BASIC

INTERMEDIATE

ADVANCED

What does the term 'net book value' mean?

This term is rather unfortunate, since the figure of £5,000 has nothing to do with value. It does not represent what the company could sell the asset for – that is, its market value – nor is it the amount the company would have to pay to replace the asset – that is, its replacement cost. As was noted in the introduction to this chapter, non-current assets can be the most misinterpreted and contentious items within a company's statement of financial position. This example clearly illustrates why. Far from being a market value, all net book value represents is the cost of that asset which has still to be allocated to the statement of comprehensive income as an expense. A better description of the £5,000 net book value would be 'unallocated cost'.

Progress Point 2.1

What does depreciation do and why is it necessary?

Solution

Depreciation spreads the cost of an asset over its useful life in appropriate proportion to the benefit gained from its use.

It is necessary to adhere to the matching principle – allocating expense against corresponding benefit, as part of the profit calculation.

Reducing balance method

This method of depreciation applies a higher depreciation charge in the earlier years of an asset's life and a lower charge in the later years. The same three basic pieces of information are used: asset cost, residual value and asset life. The reducing balance method calculates a rate of depreciation that, when applied to the net book value of the asset, will reduce the cost of the asset to the residual value over the life of the asset.

As with the straight line method of depreciation, part of the asset's cost is allocated to the statement of comprehensive income each year, while the statement of financial position entries show the unallocated cost of the asset.

It could be argued that the reducing balance method reflects the efficiency and maintenance costs of the asset. When it is new, the asset will be operating at maximum efficiency with few repair costs, especially if under guarantee. As the asset gets older, repair costs are more likely to occur and these will tend to offset the lower depreciation charge.

The formula for calculating the appropriate percentage to make the net book value equal to the residual value is as follows:

$$r = 1 - \sqrt[n]{\text{(residual value/cost)}}$$

Where:

r is the required rate and n is the number of years.

In practice, this formula is rarely used and instead a standard 'round' figure is usually taken as a satisfactory rate for the type of asset under consideration (e.g. motor vehicles 25%). This formula will not work if the residual value is zero. In this case residual value has to be imputed as 1.

Example

An asset with an initial cost of £10,000 is expected to be used for three years and to have a residual value at the end of the three years of £7,290.

$$\text{Depreciation rate} = 1 - \sqrt[3]{(7,290/10,000)}$$
$$= 1 - \sqrt[3]{(0.729)}$$
$$= 1 - 0.9$$
$$= 0.1 \text{ or } 10\%$$

The depreciation would be calculated as follows:

Asset cost	£10,000
Depreciation in Year 1 (10% of £10,000)	£1,000
Net book value	£9,000
Depreciation in Year 2 (10% of £9,000)	£900
Net book value	£8,100
Depreciation in Year 3 (10% of £8,100)	£810
Net book value	£7,290

This means that the cost of the asset has been reduced to its residual value of £7,290 at the end of three years. The accounting entries are identical to those given for the straight line method, except of course the amount of depreciation is different.

Statement of comprehensive income (for Year 1)	
Depreciation	£1,000
Statement of financial position (for Year 1)	
Non-current asset	£10,000
Less depreciation	£1,000
Net book value	£9,000

As before, the statement of comprehensive income shows the charge for depreciation, while the statement of financial position shows the cost of the asset minus the total depreciation allocated to the asset. In Year 2 the financial statements will show:

Statement of comprehensive income (for Year 2)		
Depreciation	£900	
Statement of financial position (for Year 2)		
Non-current asset (cost)	£10,000	
Less total depreciation	£1,900	(for two years)
Net book value	£8,100	

And in Year 3:

Statement of comprehensive income (for Year 3)		
Depreciation	£810	
Statement of financial position (for Year 3)		
Non-current asset (cost)	£10,000	
Less total depreciation	£2,710	(for three years)
Net book value	£7,290	

BASIC

INTERMEDIATE

ADVANCED

Progress Point 2.2

Explain how the straight line and reducing balance methods of depreciation work. What different assumptions does each method make?

Solution

The straight line method charges a constant percentage of the cost of the asset each year as depreciation; the reducing balance method charges a constant percentage of the net book value (i.e. cost less accumulated depreciation brought forward), as depreciation each year.

The straight line method therefore results in a constant charge, while the reducing balance method has a charge reducing each year of the asset's life. The two methods, therefore, make different assumptions about the usefulness, the trend or pattern of benefits of the non-current asset concerned.

The straight line method assumes that the asset will give a constant return over its useful life, while the reducing balance method assumes that the benefits will be higher in the early years and diminish as the asset tends towards the end of its useful life.

Other methods of calculating depreciation

In addition to the methods of calculating depreciation indicated above, there are another two methods, which are described below.

Sum of the digits method

This method, while popular in the USA, is not all that common in the UK. Under this method, the depreciation rate is calculated by relating the remaining life of an asset to its initial expected life. The asset's initial expected life is expressed in digits and the digits are then summed.

Example

An asset costing £12,000 has an estimated useful life of four years and a residual value at the end of Year 4 of £2,000.

$$\text{Depreciation rate} = \frac{\text{No. of remaining years of asset's life}}{\text{Asset's initial expected life, expressed in digits and summed}}$$

Depreciation charge in Year t = Depreciation amount × depreciable rate in Year t

$$\text{Charge} - \text{Year 1} = \frac{4}{(4 + 3 + 2 + 1)} \times (£12,000 - £2,000) = £4,000$$

$$\text{Charge} - \text{Year 2} = \frac{3}{10} \times £10,000 = £3,000$$

$$\text{Charge} - \text{Year 3} = \frac{2}{10} \times £10,000 = £2,000$$

$$\text{Charge} - \text{Year 4} = \frac{1}{10} \times £10,000 = £1,000$$

The sum of the digits method has the advantage that, unlike the reducing balance method, it can use a residual value of zero. In addition, the pattern of depreciation is similar to that of the reducing balance method, giving a higher depreciation charge in the earlier years of an asset's life.

Output or usage method

The depreciation rate is the ratio of the asset's output or usage in a period to its total expected output or usage.

$$\text{Depreciation rate in the year} = \frac{\text{Output or usage in the year}}{\text{Total expected output or usage}}$$

$$\text{Depreciation charge} = \text{Depreciable amount} \times \text{Depreciation rate in year}$$

This method of depreciation results in a depreciation charge that fluctuates with the output or asset's use. This method is commonly employed in the aviation industry, where aircraft are depreciated on the basis of flying hours.

As far as the accounting is concerned, in each case the statement of comprehensive income will show the annual charge for depreciation. This will be recorded as an expense and so will reduce the profit for the year.

In the statement of financial position the non-current asset will be recorded at cost less the total (accumulated) depreciation to date.

Progress Point 2.3

The Pizza Company has just opened a pizza restaurant in Glasgow. The restaurant contains a new pizza oven that cost £110,000 to buy and install. The oven has an expected life of ten years with a residual value of zero. The total expected output of the oven over ten years is 600,000 standard-size pizzas. The forecast output for Years 1 to 5 is as follows:

Year 1	30,000 pizzas
Year 2	48,000 pizzas
Year 3	66,000 pizzas
Year 4	78,000 pizzas
Year 5	84,000 pizzas

(a) Calculate the depreciation charge in each of the five years using:
  (i) the straight line method
  (ii) the reducing balance method (assume a rate of 15%)
  (iii) sum of years digits
  (iv) units of production.
(b) Show the net book value of the oven at the end of each of Years 1 to 5.

Solution

(a) (i) Straight line method of depreciation:

$$\text{Depreciation charge} = \frac{\text{cost} - \text{residual value}}{\text{life}}$$

$$= \frac{£110,000 - £0}{10}$$

$$= \underline{£11,000} \text{ per annum for each of year 1 to 5}$$

(ii) Reducing balance:

Cost of asset	£110,000
Depreciation Year 1 (15%)	£16,500
	£93,500
Depreciation Year 2	£14,025
	£79,475
Depreciation Year 3	£11,921
	£67,554
Depreciation Year 4	£10,133
	£57,421
Depreciation Year 5	£8,613
	£48,808

(iii) Sum of years digits:

Digits = 1 + 2 + 3 + 4 + 5 + 6 + 7 + 8 + 9 + 10 = 55

Cost	£110,000
Depreciation Year 1 = 10/55	£20,000
	£90,000
Depreciation Year 2 = 9/55	£18,000
	£72,000
Depreciation Year 3 = 8/55	£16,000
	£56,000
Depreciation Year 4 = 7/55	£14,000
	£42,000
Depreciation Year 5 = 6/55	£12,000
	£30,000

(iv) Units of production:

Depreciation rate is calculated as follows:

Year 1	(30,000/600,000) =	5%
Year 2	(48,000/600,000) =	8%
Year 3	(66,000/600,000) =	11%
Year 4	(78,000/600,000) =	13%
Year 5	(84,000/600,000) =	14%
Cost	£110,000	
Depreciation Year 1 (5%)	£5,500	
	£104,500	
Depreciation Year 2 (8%)	£8,800	
	£95,700	
Depreciation Year 3 (11%)	£12,100	
	£83,600	
Depreciation Year 4 (13%)	£14,300	
	£69,300	
Depreciation Year 5 (14%)	£15,400	
	£53,900	

BASIC

INTERMEDIATE

ADVANCED

(b) Net book values of assets:

Year	Straight line	Reducing balance	Sum of years digits	Units of production
	£	£	£	£
1	89,000	93,500	90,000	104,500
2	78,000	79,475	72,000	95,700
3	67,000	67,554	56,000	83,600
4	56,000	57,421	42,000	69,300
5	45,000	48,808	30,000	53,900

Regardless of the method chosen, the issue with respect to depreciation is that the cost of using the asset is being allocated to the statement of comprehensive income as an expense over the period the asset is being used. This allocation process is matching the cost of using the asset with the benefits being derived from the asset.

An alternative way of describing an asset's value is as an unallocated cost. This cost will be allocated, that is, spread over the life of the asset in the form of a depreciation expense in the statement of comprehensive income. So what has been described as the 'net book value' of an asset has, in reality, nothing to do with the 'value' of the asset, but is the cost of the asset that has still to be allocated over the life of the asset.

What depreciation is not

As noted above, the depreciation calculation is not performed to produce measurements of value in the statement of financial position that are particularly meaningful or useful. The statement of financial position figures are measurements of unallocated costs.

A common misconception regarding depreciation is that it ensures that an entity will have sufficient funds to replace the particular asset at the end of its useful life. Depreciation, however, does not involve a flow of cash and does not increase the amount of any asset, cash or otherwise. What depreciation does do is to reduce the level of profit available for distribution and so help 'increase' the cash retained in the business. Note, however, that there is nothing to prevent an entity from spending that retained cash on some purpose other than the replacement of non-current assets.

A further issue arising is that the replacement asset is likely to cost more than the asset being depreciated due to inflationary pressures. Indeed, it may not be possible to replace the depreciated asset with a similar asset if it has been superseded by a technologically more efficient asset.

At best, therefore, it can be said that the cash not distributed *may* be used to replace assets at the end of their useful lives.

2.5 Asset cost

As was noted earlier, in order to calculate the depreciation charge, the cost of the asset has to be determined. On the face of it, this would seem to be a straightforward figure to identify. Surely the cost of an asset is the amount paid for it (i.e. its invoice cost)? While in some cases this is true, there are situations where determining the cost of an asset is less clear. Consider the following example.

Example 1

A company buys a machine costing £20,000. This machine is in a warehouse in London and has to be installed in the company's factory in Edinburgh. The cost of transporting the machine from London to Edinburgh is estimated to be £500. In order to get the machine operational and ready for use, the company has to pay installation costs of £1,000. What is the cost of the machine?

Clearly the purchase price of £20,000 is part of the cost of the asset. The question is, however, how are the costs of transport and installation to be treated? Without the machine being delivered to the factory and then subsequently installed, it would not be able to be used. The additional costs of transport and of installation are, therefore, necessary. It could be argued, then, that these additional costs should be added to the cost of the asset. Indeed, without them, the machine would be of no benefit to the company at all.

In Example 1, above, while the purchase price of the machine is £20,000, as far as the company is concerned, the *cost* of the machine is £21,500 (i.e. the purchase price, plus transportation and installation costs).

Example 2

Instead of buying a new machine, suppose the company buys a second-hand machine for £10,000. Transportation costs and installation costs remain the same at £500 and £1,000 respectively. When the machine was installed it was found that it was not working properly and had to be repaired at a cost of £800. After two months' production the machine broke down again and was repaired at a cost of £300.

As before, the purchase price of the machine is £10,000. In addition, the transportation and installation costs will also form part of the cost of the machine. However, before the machine could be used, further repairs were necessary. Without those further repairs the machine would not work properly. It could be argued therefore that this cost, too, should be added to the cost of the asset. Indeed, without these essential repairs, the machine would not be of any benefit to the company.

The accounting treatment of the other repairs that were carried out after two months' production is less clear cut.

It could be argued that these repairs are simply due to normal wear and tear, and consequently should be treated as simply being part of the cost of running the machine. This is similar to the cost of car repairs, which can be viewed as part of a maintenance programme to keep the car working properly. The cost of the machine would be recorded at £12,300 (i.e. £10,000 + £500 + £1,000 + £800).

The above examples illustrate that there can often be problems in determining the cost of an asset. Each case needs to be judged on its merits, but, as a general rule, the cost of an asset will include all the costs incurred in bringing the asset to its location and making it ready for use. Such costs would include acquisition cost, delivery costs and installation costs. A feature of such costs is that they are generally non-recurring.

Problems can arise with repair costs, however, but again, as a general rule, if the cost is necessary in order to bring the asset into use for the first time it should be capitalized; if it is being incurred after the asset is brought into use and is simply maintaining the asset at its current operating levels, then it should be treated as an expense.

Progress Point 2.4

A company purchased a second-hand machine which had cost £150,000 when new from London at an invoice price of £100,000. Transportation costs to Liverpool were £5,000 and costs of installation amounted to £4,000. Once installed it was found that it was not working properly and had to be repaired at a cost of £3,000. At the same time a modification was made to the machine to improve output at a cost of £4,500. After two months production the machine broke down again and was repaired at a cost of £2,000.

Required

Calculate and explain the cost figure that the company would recognize in its financial statements for the machine.

Solution

The starting point is the invoice price of the machine which was £100,000. The fact that it had cost £150,000 when new is not relevant. As the transportation costs of £5,000 and initial installation costs of £4,000 were incurred in bringing the asset to its location and in a position to make it ready for use, then these too would be added to the cost of the asset. As the machine required initial repairs costing £3,000 to make it work properly then, again, these should be capitalized. The modifications costing £4,500 have increased the output of the machine and this will ensure that the company derives greater future benefits from its use. These costs should therefore be capitalized.

The repair costs incurred after two months' production would be treated as revenue expenditure. The capitalized cost of the asset would be:

	£
Invoice price	100,000
Transportation costs	5,000
Installation costs	4,000
Initial repairs	3,000
Modifications	4,500
Total cost	116,500

2.6 Residual value

The residual value is the amount received by a business for the sale of an asset at the end of its expected useful life. This is highly subjective and usually involves estimating the future disposal value. It is not an easy task to estimate a residual value, which involves an attempt at forecasting what might be expected from the sale of an asset at some point in the future. Such an estimate involves many variables, including:

- when the asset will be disposed of
- the expected condition of the asset at the end of its useful life
- the possible technological advances that may have occurred over the years
- the amount that the company would currently obtain from selling the asset (assuming the asset was already of the age and condition expected at the end of its useful life).

Estimated useful life

The useful life of an asset is its economic life and not its physical life. Many assets become less efficient, both economically and technologically, as they grow older. While careful maintenance can extend the economic life of an asset, it is likely that the effects of technological progress, the cost and availability of replacements and repair costs will render the economic life of an asset much shorter than the working life – for example, a computer may have a physical life of eight years and an economic life of only three years.

In addition to estimating the length of the useful life, an estimate needs to be made of the expected pattern of benefit or usefulness to be derived from the asset – all highly subjective.

Disposal of assets

The calculation of a depreciation charge involves an estimate of the expected useful life, the pattern of the expected benefits and the expected residual value.

The depreciation charge is a positive calculation (i.e. it is a positive movement from the statement of financial position to the statement of comprehensive income). It cannot be found by comparing statement of financial position values from one accounting period to the next. At the outset, however, the charge can only ever be at best an estimate. There is subjectivity involved in this calculation and, consequently, at the end of the asset's useful economic life, a company may realize more or less for the asset than it had anticipated.

If a company sells an asset for more than the net book value, it will have made a gain on disposal. The converse is also true: if a company sells an asset for less than the net book value, there will be a loss on disposal.

Example

A company buys an asset costing £10,000 with an estimated useful life of four years and no anticipated residual value. It expects a constant flow of benefits from the asset and adopts the straight line method to calculate its depreciation charge. At the end of Year 2, however, the company decides to sell the asset and receives £6,500.

At the end of Year 2 the asset will have a net book value of:

Cost	£10,000
Depreciation Year 1 (£10,000/4)	£2,500
Depreciation Year 2 (£10,000/4)	£2,500
Net book value	£5,000
Selling price	£6,500
The company will have made a gain on disposal of £6,500 − £5,000 =	£1,500

The accounting issue involved

The accounting issue involved is what the gain (or loss) on disposal actually represents. The gain (or loss) on disposal is calculated by comparing the sales proceeds with the net book value. The net book value of an asset is the amount of the original cost of an asset not yet allocated to the statement of comprehensive income – that is, the opening carrying value less the accumulated depreciation. It follows therefore that a gain or loss on disposal arises because of an 'incorrect' depreciation charge in earlier years. In other words, had the company known that it would keep the asset for only two years and be able to sell it for £6,500, it would have depreciated the asset as follows:

$$\text{Year 1} \quad = \quad \frac{(10{,}000 - 6{,}500)}{2} \quad = \quad £1{,}750$$

$$\text{Year 2} \quad = \quad \frac{(10{,}000 - 6{,}500)}{2} \quad = \quad £1{,}750$$

Total depreciation charged	£3,500

These facts were not, however, available at the outset and consequently the depreciation was calculated as shown below.

$$\text{Year 1} \quad = \quad \frac{(10{,}000 - 0)}{4} \quad = \quad £2{,}500$$

$$\text{Year 2} \quad = \quad \frac{(10{,}000 - 0)}{4} \quad = \quad £2{,}500$$

Gain on disposal	(£1,500)
Total depreciation/gain on disposal	£3,500

Note that, overall, the total amount charged to the statement of comprehensive income in respect of the use of the asset is still the same: £3,500. It is the pattern of the charges that differs.

Note also that it is the depreciation expense that is being positively calculated and not the reduction in the asset figure. It is only when the asset is ultimately disposed of that the net book value is used to positively calculate any gain or loss on disposal. At that point the exact amount of the asset used in generating economic benefits is determined.

Land

So far in this chapter the analysis has been concerned with assets whose useful economic life is limited. Moreover, the contention that assets held on a company's statement of financial position are simply costs yet to be allocated to the company's statement of comprehensive income further emphasizes the limited life span of the assets and their ultimate usage in generating income. Whichever valuation base is placed on such non-current assets, there can be no doubt that the 'value' of such assets will reduce over time as the asset is used.

The position regarding land is somewhat different. Land itself will tend to have an infinite life unless it is held for the extraction of minerals (e.g. a diamond mine). As such, land will not tend to be 'used up' in the course of generating income, and consequently it does not require to be depreciated.

2.7 Revaluation of non-current assets

As noted above, land that is not held for the extraction of minerals does not require to be depreciated. In reality, the price of land tends to increase virtually every year, and its inclusion in the statement of financial position at historic cost is likely to seriously understate its value, particularly if looked at over a long period of time.

In order to remove such distortions, a company may choose to bring the asset value up to date, and so may choose to revalue the asset.

In order to account for an increase in value, the asset account is increased by the amount of the revaluation. The corresponding credit entry is made to a revaluation reserve. In other words, the asset account will be debited and the revaluation reserve credited.

An increase in value of an asset will also be shown as 'other comprehensive income' in the statement of comprehensive income (see Chapter 1).

Example

A business has its land valued at £100,000. The directors wish this value to be reflected in the accounts. The statement of financial position before the revaluation showed land at cost of £70,000.

The revaluation will be recorded as follows:

Dr	Non-current assets – land	£30,000	
	Cr Revaluation reserve		£30,000
Being revaluation of land.			

Extract statement of financial position entries will show:

Non-current assets	
Land	£70,000
Revaluation	£30,000
At valuation	£100,000
Financed by:	
Revaluation reserve	£30,000

Extract statement of comprehensive income entries will show:

Profit for the year	xx
Other comprehensive income	
Gain on property revaluation	£30,000
Total comprehensive income	

BASIC

INTERMEDIATE

ADVANCED

Section summary

This chapter started with the widely held perception that non-current assets are one of the most reliable, robust figures in a company's statement of financial position. However, the determination of the cost of an asset can be difficult to measure and may involve subjective judgement. Moreover, the subsequent depreciation calculation based on that cost figure involves even more uncertainty and subjectivity.

This section has considered in detail the IAS definition of an asset. The definition clearly indicates that it is not the physical existence of the asset itself which qualifies it to be classified as an asset, but rather the rights to income which are embodied within the asset. Indeed a company may well own a piece of equipment but if it is not, or cannot, be used in generating future benefits then it would not be included as an asset on that company's statement of financial position. The definition also makes it clear that an entity need not necessarily own the asset to recognize it in the financial statements as long as it can control the benefits embodied in that asset.

The recognition criteria of assets have been explained. While an item may pass the definition tests of an asset, in order for it to be included as an asset within a statement of financial position it also has to satisfy strict recognition tests.

In addition, the section shows that the non-current asset value in the statement of financial position represents the cost of that asset which has still to be allocated to the statement of comprehensive income as an expense. A company can also show non-current assets at their up-to-date value by revaluing them.

Section 2: Intermediate Issues

This section extends and develops some of the ideas from Section 1. In particular, it will focus on specific measurement issues and identify the detailed reporting requirements of the international standards relating to the measurement and presentation of non-current assets.

2.8 More on cost

In the first section of this chapter the cost of an asset was shown to include all the costs incurred in bringing the asset to its present location and in a condition ready for use. Cost therefore can include cost of acquisition, delivery and handling costs, installation costs and professional fees.

Accounting policies in relation to government grants receivable and to capitalization of borrowing costs may also have a bearing on the calculation of the capitalized cost figure. Both are subjects of separate international standards and it is helpful to look briefly at their requirements before moving on to examine the requirements of IAS 16 *Property, Plant and Equipment* in detail.

Government grants

Government grants are broadly defined as assistance in the form of cash to an entity in return for past or future compliance with certain conditions relating to the operations of the entity.

Government grants may be either revenue-based grants or capital-based grants. Revenue-based grants, as their name suggests, are intended to be a contribution towards revenue expenditure, and capital-based grants are a contribution towards capital expenditure.

Common to both types of grant, however, is the accruals concept, which requires the matching of cost and revenue so as to recognize both in the statements of comprehensive income of the periods to which they relate. This treatment should, of course, also take account of any potential clawbacks of the grants. Prudence requires that revenue is not anticipated and, consequently, credit should never be taken until the receipt of the grant is relatively certain. Indeed, failure to comply with the grant covenants may mean that the grant has to be repaid.

IAS 20 *Accounting for Government Grants and Disclosure of Government Assistance* sets out two acceptable methods of dealing with grants relating to assets in the statement of financial position.

The first is to set up the grant as a deferred credit in the statement of financial position and to release a portion of it annually to revenue over the useful life of the asset.

Example

A government grant is paid to an entity under the strict condition that the entity purchases a piece of manufacturing equipment.

The relevant details are:

Purchase price	£60,000
Expected useful life	4 years
Expected residual value	0
Grant received	£20,000
Depreciation method	straight line

This 'deferred income method' would give the following statement of comprehensive income and statement of financial position extracts for the four years.

Statement of comprehensive income extracts

	Year 1 £	Year 2 £	Year 3 £	Year 4 £
Depreciation	(15,000)	(15,000)	(15,000)	(15,000)
Grant released	5,000	5,000	5,000	5,000
Net effect on profit	(10,000)	(10,000)	(10,000)	(10,000)

Statement of financial position extracts

Assets	Year 1 £	Year 2 £	Year 3 £	Year 4 £
Non-current assets at cost	60,000	60,000	60,000	60,000
Accumulated depreciation	15,000	30,000	45,000	60,000
Net book value	45,000	30,000	15,000	0
Liabilities	£	£	£	£
Deferred credit	20,000	15,000	10,000	5,000
Less: grant released	5,000	5,000	5,000	5,000
	15,000	10,000	5,000	0
Net effect on net assets	30,000	20,000	10,000	0

There would be an initial carrying amount for the asset of £60,000 and a deferred income credit of £20,000. In the first year of use there would be a straight line depreciation charge of £15,000 (£60,000/4). A similar rate of release will be applied to the grant in order to recognize both in the statement of comprehensive income of the period to which it relates, i.e. £5,000 (£20,000/4).

The net charge to the statement of comprehensive income in Year 1 would therefore be £10,000 (£15,000 – £5,000) and, as a straight line policy for the depreciation charge and grant release has been adopted, there would be a net £10,000 charge in Year 2 through to Year 4.

The statement of financial position extracts show the asset being depreciated down to its residual value of nil and the grant being reduced to nil as it is released to income over the four years.

The second method deducts the grant in arriving at the carrying amount of the relevant asset. This 'netting method' would give the following statement of comprehensive income and statement of financial position extracts using the example figures above.

Example

Statement of comprehensive income

	Year 1	Year 2	Year 3	Year 4
	£	£	£	£
Depreciation	(10,000)	(10,000)	(10,000)	(10,000)
Net effect on profit	(10,000)	(10,000)	(10,000)	(10,000)
Statement of financial position				
Non-current asset at net cost	40,000	40,000	40,000	40,000
Accumulated depreciation	10,000	20,000	30,000	40,000
Net book value	30,000	20,000	10,000	0
Net effect on net assets	30,000	20,000	10,000	0

Using this 'netting method' there would be an initial carrying amount of the asset at its net cost after deducting the grant of £40,000 (£60,000 – £20,000). The straight line depreciation charge for each of the four years would be £10,000 (£40,000/4). As can be seen from the above, the net effects on profit and net assets are exactly the same for each of the years using both methods. The only difference is in presentation in the statement of comprehensive income and statement of financial position.

Progress Point 2.5

A government grant is paid to an enterprise under the strict condition that it purchases a piece of manufacturing equipment.

The relevant details are:

Purchase price	£90,000
Expected useful life	3 years
Expected residual value	0
Grant received	£30,000
Depreciation method	straight line

(a) Show the statement of comprehensive income entries for each of the Years 1 to 3 using:
   (i) deferred income method
   (ii) netting method.
(b) Show the statement of comprehensive income extracts for each of the years 1 to 3.

Solution

Deferred income method			
Statement of comprehensive income	Year 1	Year 2	Year 3
	£	£	£
Depreciation	(30,000)	(30,000)	(30,000)
Grant released	10,000	10,000	10,000
Net effect on profit	(20,000)	(20,000)	(20,000)
Statement of financial position extracts:			
Assets	Year 1	Year 2	Year 3
	£	£	£
Non-current assets at cost	90,000	90,000	90,000
Accumulated depreciation	30,000	60,000	90,000
Net book value	60,000	30,000	0
Liabilities			
Deferred credit	30,000	20,000	10,000
Less: grant released	10,000	10,000	10,000
	20,000	10,000	0
Net effect on net assets	40,000	20,000	0

There would be an initial carrying amount for the asset of £90,000 and a deferred income credit of £30,000. In the first year of use there would be a straight line depreciation charge of £30,000 (£90,000/3). A similar rate of release will be applied to the grant in order to recognize both in the statement of comprehensive income of the period to which it relates, i.e. £10,000 (£30,000/3).

The net charge to the statement of comprehensive income in Year 1 would therefore be £20,000 (£30,000 – £10,000) and, as a straight line policy for the depreciation charge and grant release has been adopted, there would be a net £20,000 charge in Years 2 and 3.

The statement of financial position extracts show the asset being depreciated down to its residual value of nil and the grant being reduced to nil as it is released to income over the four years.
Netting method:

Statement of comprehensive income			
	Year 1	Year 2	Year 3
	£	£	£
Depreciation	(20,000)	(20,000)	(20,000)
Net effect on profit	(20,000)	(20,000)	(20,000)
Statement of financial position			
Non-current asset at net cost	90,000	90,000	90,000
Accumulated depreciation	30,000	60,000	90,000
Net book value	60,000	30,000	0
Net effect on net assets	40,000	20,000	0

Using this 'netting method' there would be an initial carrying amount of the asset at its net cost of £60,000 after deducting the grant (£90,000 – £30,000). The straight line depreciation charge for each of the four years would be £30,000 (£90,000/3). As can be seen from the above, the net effects on profit and net assets are exactly the same for each of the years using both methods.

Asset disposal

In a situation where the company disposes of an asset on which a deferred income balance remains, and where the grant has to be repaid, this should be accounted for by first reducing the balance on the deferred income account, with any additional charge being directed to the statement of comprehensive income.

Where the grant itself does not need to be repaid, then the balance on the deferred income account should be considered in calculating the profit or loss on disposal.

Example

A company received grant assistance of £18,000 for the purchase of a non-current asset costing £43,200 on 1 January 2011. The net book value of the asset at 31 December 2012 is £24,000 and the amount of the grant deferred at that date was £10,000. Assuming the company was to sell the asset on 31 December 2012 for £20,000, show what the statement of comprehensive income entries would be at that date if:

(a) the terms of the grant are such that if the asset is sold the grant must be repaid in full

(b) the terms of the grant are such that it does not need to be repaid if the asset is sold

Solution

(a) If the asset is sold then the grant must be repaid in full. The sale proceeds would first of all go to reduce the balance on the deferred income account of £10,000 with the balance of the grant repayable charged to the statement of comprehensive income i.e. £8,000. There will be a loss on disposal of £4,000 (i.e. £24,000 – £20,000)

Statement of comprehensive income extract
Year ended 31 December 2012

	£
Loss on disposal	4,000
Grant repayable	8,000

Note that the effect on retained profits is to restore them to the position that would have existed had the grant never been received. That is, there is a clawback of the £8,000 that had been released to the statement of comprehensive income in the first two years. The total charges to the statement of comprehensive income would be:

Depreciation (Yrs 1 & 2) £43,200 – £24,000	£19,200
Grant released (Yrs 1 & 2) £18,000 – £10,000	(8,000)
Loss on disposal	4,000
Grant repayable	8,000
Total charges	23,200

This represents the initial cost of the asset less the sale proceeds i.e. £43,200 – £20,000 = £23,200.

(b) If the asset is sold and the grant is not repaid then it forms part of the calculation of profit on disposal i.e. proceeds + grant retained less net book value. The gain on disposal is £20,000 + £10,000 – £24,000 = £6,000.

Statement of comprehensive income extract
Year ended 31 December 2012

	£
Gain on disposal	6,000

In this scenario, the total charges to the statement of comprehensive income would be:

Depreciation (Yrs 1 & 2) £43,200 – £24,000	£19,200
Grant released (Yrs 1 & 2) £18,000 – £10,000	(8,000)
Gain on disposal	(6,000)
	5,200

This represents the initial cost of the asset, less the sale proceeds and total grant receivable, i.e. £43,200 – £20,000 – £18,000 = £5,200.

Borrowing costs

Borrowing costs are another expense that may have an impact on the cost of an asset. If cost is to include *all* the costs incurred in bringing the asset to its location and in a position to make it ready for use then under the accruals basis of accounting it could be argued that such costs should be included in that asset's cost.

This would be particularly relevant to an asset that takes a substantial period of time to get ready for its intended use or sale (for example, the construction of a cruise ship).

There are convincing arguments for and against capitalization of finance costs.

Arguments for capitalization

1. If finance costs are incurred as a result of a decision to acquire an asset, then these costs are no different from other costs that are commonly capitalized, e.g. transportation or installation costs. Moreover, if the asset takes a substantial period of time to bring it to the condition and location necessary for its intended use, the finance costs incurred during that period as a result of expenditures on the asset are a part of the cost of acquiring the asset.

2. This treatment better adheres to the matching principle in that the interest incurred with a view to future benefit (i.e. the asset) is carried forward to be expensed in the periods expected to benefit; if, on the other hand, the interest is immediately expensed, this will reduce current earnings and distort reported profits – all as a consequence of the acquisition of assets.

3. This method allows better comparison between companies constructing assets and other companies buying similar completed assets. This is because the purchase price of completed assets acquired will normally include interest as the seller will require to take account of all his costs, including interest, in pricing the asset. By treating the interest cost as an expense, this could artificially reduce the cost of the self-constructed asset and result in an incorrect make or buy decision.

Arguments against capitalization

1. The treatment of the interest expense should be consistent. It does not make sense to treat finance costs as a period expense in normal circumstances, then to treat them as a direct cost of an asset during its period of construction, and then to revert to treating them as a period expense once the asset is complete. The nature of the interest cost does not change because of the use to which the funds are put. Interest cost is a period cost incurred in financing the business and its treatment should not change merely as a result of the completion of a non-current asset.

2. Because finance costs are incurred for the whole of the activities of the entity, it can be difficult to identify specific borrowings with specific projects. Where funds are raised centrally, any attempt to allocate finance costs with a particular asset will necessarily be arbitrary.

3. It is inappropriate that the same type of asset would have a different carrying amount depending on whether its construction was financed by borrowings or by equity. By limiting capitalized interest to interest on borrowings this would preclude the equity-funded enterprise from capitalizing interest – even though it incurs an economic cost of the same order as an enterprise that has borrowed funds.

It is inconsistent to allow debt-funded entities to include interest costs in the cost of an asset while prohibiting equity-funded entities from reflecting similarly the cost of capital in the cost of an asset.

IAS 23 *Borrowing Costs* sets out the prescribed accounting treatment for borrowing costs.

Borrowing costs that are directly attributable to the acquisition, construction and production of a qualifying asset should be treated as part of the cost of that asset.

A qualifying asset is an asset that takes a substantial period of time to get ready for its intended use (e.g. ships, aircraft, long-term construction contracts, wine and spirits being aged).

The foregoing reflects revisions to IAS 23 adopted by the IASB in March 2007, which prohibit immediate expensing of borrowing costs. Prior to the revision, the previous version of IAS 23 permitted, as an accounting option, the 'immediate expensing model'. Under that model, all borrowing costs could be expensed in the period in which they were incurred.

The IASB believes that application of the revised standard will improve financial reporting in three ways. First, the cost of an asset will include all costs incurred in getting it ready for use or sale. Second, comparability is enhanced because one of the two accounting treatments that previously existed for those borrowing costs is removed. Third, the revision to IAS 23 achieves convergence in principle with US GAAP.

Where funds are borrowed specifically for obtaining a qualifying asset, the amount of borrowing costs eligible for capitalization as part of the cost of that asset is the actual costs incurred less any income earned on the temporary investment of such borrowings.

Where funds are borrowed generally and used for the purpose of obtaining a qualifying asset, then the enterprise should use a capitalization rate to determine the borrowing costs that may be capitalized. The capitalization rate will be the weighted average of the borrowing costs applicable to the enterprise.

Capitalization should commence (IAS 23 para 17) when:

- expenditures for the asset are being incurred
- borrowing costs are being incurred
- activities that are necessary to prepare the asset for its intended use or sale are in progress.

Capitalization should be suspended (IAS 23 para 20):

- during extended periods in which active development of a qualifying asset is interrupted.

Capitalization should cease (IAS 23 para 22) when:

- substantially all of the activities necessary to prepare the asset for its intended use or sale are complete.

An enterprise should disclose in its financial statements:

- the accounting policy adopted
- the amount of borrowing cost capitalized during the accounting period
- the capitalization rate used.

Example

On 1 April 2012 a company engages in the development of a property that is expected to take five years to complete, at a cost of £6,000,000. The statements of financial position of the company at 31 December 2011 and 31 December 2012, prior to capitalization of interest, are as follows:

Statements of financial position as at	31/12/11	31/12/12
	£	£
Development property		1,200,000
Other assets	6,000,000	6,800,000
	6,000,000	8,000,000

Loans:	£	£
8% debenture stock	2,500,000	2,500,000
Bank loan (10% per annum)		2,000,000
Bank loan (12% per annum)	1,000,000	1,000,000
	3,500,000	5,500,000
Shareholders' equity	2,500,000	2,500,000

The bank loan at 10% was taken out on 31 March 2012 and the total interest charge for the year ended 31 December 2012 was as follows:

	£	
Debenture stock £2,500,000 × 8%	200,000	
Bank loan £2,000,000 × 10% × 9/12	150,000	(9 months only)
Bank loan £1,000,000 × 12%	120,000	
	470,000	

Expenditure was incurred on the development as follows:

	£
1 April 2012	600,000
1 July 2012	400,000
1 October 2012	200,000
	1,200,000

(i) If the bank loan at 10% p.a. is a new borrowing taken out specifically to finance the development, then the amount of interest to be capitalized is as follows:

	£
£600,000 × 10% × 9/12 =	45,000
£400,000 × 10% × 6/12 =	20,000
£200,000 × 10% × 3/12 =	5,000
	70,000

That is, the amount of the loan interest that can be specifically attached to the project expenditure as it progresses should be capitalized.

(ii) If all the borrowings would have been avoided but for the development then the amount of interest to be capitalized would be found as follows.

(a) First, determine the weighted average of the borrowing costs applicable to the company.

$$\text{i.e.} \quad \frac{\text{Total interest expense}}{\text{Weighted average total borrowings}} \times 100\%$$

$$\frac{470,000}{(3,500,000 + (2,000,000 \times 9/12))} = 9.4\%$$

(b) Next, apply the capitalization rate to the expenditure as incurred.

		£
i.e.	£600,000 × 9.4% × 9/12 =	42,300
	£400,000 × 9.4% × 6/12 =	18,800
	£200,000 × 9.4% × 3/12 =	4,700
		65,800

Note that had the 8% debenture stock been irredeemable, then as the borrowings could not have been avoided, the calculation would be done using the figures for the bank loans and their related interest costs only. The debenture interest and debenture itself would not form part of the calculation.

2.9 IAS 16 *Property, Plant and Equipment*

The objective of IAS 16 is to prescribe the accounting treatment for property, plant and equipment. The principal issues are the timing of recognition of assets, the determination of their carrying amounts, and the depreciation charges to be recognized in relation to them.

Scope
IAS 16 notes that the general definition and recognition criteria for an asset given in the Conceptual Framework for Financial Reporting must be satisfied before IAS 16 applies. While IAS 16 does not apply to biological assets related to agricultural activity (IAS 41), or mineral rights and mineral reserves such as oil, natural gas and similar non-regenerative resources, it does apply to property, plant and equipment used to develop or maintain such assets.

Definition
IAS 16 defines property, plant and equipment as tangible items that:

- are held for use in the production or supply of goods or services, for rental to others, or for administrative purposes, and
- are expected to be used during more than one period.

Recognition and initial cost
Items of property, plant and equipment should be recognized as assets when it is probable that (IAS 16.7):

(i) the future economic benefits associated with the asset will flow to the enterprise, and

(ii) the cost of the asset can be measured reliably.

The recognition principle is applied to all property, plant and equipment costs at the time they are incurred. These costs include costs incurred initially to acquire or construct an item of property, plant and equipment and costs incurred subsequently to add to, replace part of, or service it.

The normal point of recognition is delivery to the company. It is not usual to recognize the item on order as the company does not control the item at this point, does not have access to most of the future benefits and is not exposed to most of the risks.

Cost can usually be measured reliably as it is normally evidenced by purchases from third parties. This also applies to self-constructed assets where purchase of materials, labour, etc., will indicate the cost.

IAS 16 does not prescribe the unit of measure for recognition of what constitutes an item of property, plant and equipment.

Judgement is required in applying the recognition criteria to an entity's specific circumstances – that is, what may be recognized as an asset by one entity may not necessarily be recognized as an asset by another.

IAS 16 allows for the aggregation of items that may, individually, be insignificant (e.g. moulds, tools, dies). The aggregation is then treated as an asset if the recognition criteria are met.

Conversely, although an asset may initially be acquired as a whole, each part of the asset with a cost that is significant in relation to the total cost of the asset should be accounted for and depreciated separately. The standard cites an aircraft and its engines as a likely example. This separation allows the depreciation figures to more accurately reflect the different consumption patterns of the various components (e.g. the aircraft body will probably last significantly longer than its engines).

Non-current assets acquired for safety or environmental reasons should be capitalized even though they do not directly generate benefits in themselves. Indirectly they allow the entity to secure benefits from its other assets.

Subsequent costs

Note that the recognition principle applies to costs incurred subsequently to add to, replace part of, or service an item of property, plant and equipment.

Ongoing maintenance costs – often described as 'repairs and maintenance' – are revenue expenses and not additions to costs. Such expenses, as we have covered earlier in this chapter, simply maintain an asset at its current operating level.

IAS 16 recognizes, however, that major parts of some items of property, plant and equipment may require replacement at regular intervals, e.g. the seats and galleys of an aircraft may require replacement several times during the life of the airframe.

Under the recognition principle, an entity will include the cost of replacing the part of such an item in the carrying amount of the item. The carrying amount of those parts that are replaced is derecognized in accordance with the derecognition provisions of the standard.

Note that, in order to facilitate this, the component parts of the original example need to have been accounted for separately in the first place.

Example

An aircraft is purchased for £15,000,000. Past experience has shown that the useful life of the seats is five years and that the cost of replacing these is £2,000,000.

The carrying amount of the aircraft would be recorded in the financial statements as follows:

Airframe	£13,000,000
Seats	£2,000,000
Total	£15,000,000

In a similar vein, the continued operation of an item of property, plant and equipment may require regular major inspections for faults regardless of whether parts of the item are replaced.

When each major inspection is performed, its cost is recognized in the carrying amount of the item of property, plant and equipment as a replacement if the recognition criteria are satisfied. Any remaining carrying amount of the cost of the previous inspection (as distinct from the physical parts) is derecognized. This occurs regardless of whether the cost of the previous inspection was identified in the transaction in which the item was acquired or constructed.

If necessary, the estimated cost of a future similar inspection may be used as an indication of what the cost of the existing inspection component was when the item was acquired or constructed.

Example

A company buys a new helicopter for £750,000. The helicopter requires a major inspection every two years at a cost of £100,000. Two years after purchase the helicopter undergoes its first major inspection.
    The costs of the inspection amount to £110,000.
The original carrying amount would have been allocated as follows:

Helicopter	£650,000
Inspection cost	£100,000
	£750,000

The original inspection costs will be derecognized and the new inspection costs will be recognized in the carrying amount of the asset.

Helicopter	£650,000
Inspection costs (original)	(£100,000)
Inspection costs (new)	£110,000
Carrying value	£760,000

That is, the new inspection costs are accounted for as an asset addition and the original inspection costs accounted for as an asset disposal.

Once the criteria for recognition have been met, the next issue to be considered is that of measurement. IAS 16 deals with this in two stages: initial measurement and measurement subsequent to initial recognition.

Measurement at recognition

An item that qualifies for recognition as an asset should be initially recorded at cost.

Elements of cost

Cost includes all costs necessary to bring the asset to working condition for its intended use. These can include:

(a) purchase price (including import duties, stamp duty, etc., after deducting any trade discounts and rebates, but not early settlement discounts)

(b) directly attributable costs in bringing the asset to the location and condition necessary for its intended use, including

- cost of site preparation
- delivery and handling
- installation
- professional fees for architects and engineers
- costs of testing whether the asset is functioning properly after deducting the net proceeds from selling any items while bringing the asset to that location and condition
- dismantling and removing the asset and restoring the site.

Example

Pecant Ltd completed construction of a chemical plant at a cost of £25m in early 2008. As part of the planning permission, Pecant Ltd agreed to dismantle the plant at the end of its useful life. The present value of dismantling is £2m.

Pecant Ltd should capitalize the construction costs of £25m as well as the estimated costs of dismantling of £2m as it has an obligation under the terms of the planning permission.

The journal entries to record this would be as follows:

Dr	Plant	£25m	
	Cr Bank		£25m
Being purchase of plant.			
Dr	Plant	£2m	
	Cr Provision for dismantling		£2m
Being provision for dismantling costs.			

The standard also identifies items of expenditure that would not be included in the cost:

(a) costs of opening a new facility

(b) costs of introducing a new product or service (including costs of advertising and promotional activities)

(c) costs of conducting a new business in a new location (including staff training costs), and

(d) administration and other general overhead costs.

Progress Point 2.6

A German engineering company decides to replace an older machine with a new one because of efficiency concerns and higher quality requirements. The machine was bought in Canada and transported by plane to Germany. This new machine replaces an old one, which was dismantled.

Which of the following items of expenditure will be included in the initial cost of the new machine?

1. Air transportation costs

2. 7% trade discount on the purchase price

3. Production losses in the start-up phase of operations

4. Installation costs paid to installing company

5. Personnel costs of employees involved with testing the machine before bringing it into production

6. Training costs of the personnel required to operate the machine

7. Insurance cost of transport from Canada to Germany.

Solution

The items to be included in the initial cost of the machine are: 1, 2, 4, 5 and 7.

Measurement of cost

Where payment for an item of property, plant and equipment is deferred, the defined or imputed interest must be removed from the total of the payments, thus reducing the cost to the cash purchase price equivalent i.e. the interest would be shown as a finance cost.

If an asset is acquired in exchange for another asset, the cost will be measured at the fair value unless:

- the exchange transaction lacks commercial substance, or
- the fair value of neither the asset received nor the asset given up is reliably measurable.

If the acquired item is not measured at fair value, its cost is measured at the carrying amount of the asset given up.

The recognition of costs in the carrying amount of an item ceases when the item is in the location and condition necessary for it to be capable of operating in the manner intended by management.

Example

Portelux buys a new non-current asset and makes the following payments in relation to it:

	£	£
Cost – as per brochure	15,000	
Less: discount received	2,000	13,000
Delivery charge		200
Erection charge		100
Maintenance charge		300
Replacement parts		150
Additional components to increase capacity		400

The costs that Portelux should recognize in relation to the non-current asset are as follows:

		£
(i)	The purchase price of the asset	13,000
(ii)	Delivery charge	200
(iii)	Erection charge	100
(iv)	Additional components	400
		13,700

Costs (i), (ii) and (iii) are all incurred in bringing the asset to working condition for its intended use.

The additional component (iv) is included in the cost of the machine as it enhances the revenue-earning capacity of the asset.

The maintenance costs and replacement parts are a cost of usage and are not included in the cost. These items will be expensed as incurred through the statement of comprehensive income.

Progress Point 2.7

Morkirk Ltd purchased an asset from abroad at invoice price £450,000. Import duties were an additional £25,000. Installation costs totalled £28,000. The company was granted a discount of £10,000 by the supplier for early payment. Testing the asset cost £40,000 but goods produced during testing were sold for a net profit of £15,000.

Calculate the cost of the asset to be recognized in the financial statements of Morkirk Ltd.

Solution

Cost comprises all costs necessary to bring the asset to working condition for its intended use:

	£
Invoice price	450,000
Installation costs	28,000
Import duties	25,000
Testing (£40,000 – £15,000)	25,000
	528,000

The discount for early settlement should not be deducted as it relates to financial settlement rather than the purchase of the asset.

Measurement after recognition

Choice of models

IAS 16 permits two accounting models – the cost model and the revaluation model – and an entity decides which model to choose as its accounting policy for an entire class of property, plant and equipment. A class of property, plant and equipment is a grouping of assets of a similar nature (e.g. land, land and buildings, machinery, motor vehicles, furniture and fixtures, office equipment).

Cost model

The cost model (which is the most common) results in an asset being carried at cost less accumulated depreciation and any accumulated impairment losses.

Revaluation model

Under the revaluation model the asset is carried at a revalued amount, being its fair value at the date of revaluation less subsequent accumulated depreciation and subsequent accumulated impairment losses.

The fair value of an asset is defined in IAS 16 as 'the amount for which an asset could be exchanged between knowledgeable and willing parties in an arm's length transaction' – in effect, the asset's market value.

If a market value is unavailable because of the specialized nature of the plant and equipment, and because these items are rarely sold, IAS 16 requires that the revaluation be based on depreciated replacement cost.

Example: revaluation model – no fair value

A company purchased an item of plant for £12,000 on 1 January 2011. The estimated useful life of the plant was six years and the straight line basis of depreciation was adopted. On 1 January 2013, management took the decision to revalue its plant.

There was no fair value available for the item of plant which had cost £12,000 on 1 January 2011; however, the replacement cost of the plant at 1 January 2013 was £21,000.

The carrying value of the plant immediately before the revaluation would have been:

Cost		£12,000		
Annual depreciation charge	=	$\dfrac{£12,000}{6}$	=	£2,000
Written down value	=	£12,000	–	(£2,000 × 2)
	=	£8,000		

Under the principles of IAS 16, the revaluation would be based on depreciated replacement cost. The revalued amount would therefore be:

Replacement cost		£21,000		
Annual depreciation charge	=	$\dfrac{£21,000}{6}$	=	£3,500
Written down value	=	£21,000	−	(£3,500 × 2)
	=	£14,000		

i.e. the written down value would be increased to that amount that would have arisen had the asset cost been £21,000 at the outset and the depreciation charge based upon that figure.

Accumulated depreciation

IAS 16 (paragraph 35) discusses the treatment of accumulated depreciation, as follows.

When an item of property, plant and equipment is revalued, any accumulated depreciation at the date of revaluation is treated in one of the following ways:

(i) restated proportionately with the change in the gross carrying amount of the asset so that the carrying amount of the asset equals its revalued amount; this method is often used when an asset is revalued by means of an index to its depreciated replacement cost, or

(ii) eliminated against the gross carrying amount of the asset and the net amount restated to the revalued amount of the asset; this method is often used for buildings.

Example: treatment of accumulated depreciation

Continuing with our example – revaluation model, no fair value – this would give the following results.

(a) Restated proportionately:

Non-current assets	£
Cost	12,000
Change after valuation	9,000
Revised value	21,000

	£
Accumulated depreciation	
At 1 January 2013	4,000
Change on revaluation	3,000
	7,000
Net book value	14,000

i.e. the gross figure and the accumulated depreciation would both be restated by the proportionate increase in replacement cost:

$$\text{Valuation} = \pounds 12,000 \times \frac{21,000}{12,000} = \pounds 21,000$$

$$\text{Accumulated depreciation} = \pounds 4,000 \times \frac{21,000}{12,000} = \pounds 7,000$$

(b) Revised gross figure:

Non-current assets	£
Cost	12,000
Change after valuation	2,000
Revised value	14,000

	£
Accumulated depreciation	
At 1 January 2013	4,000
Written back on revaluation	(4,000)
	-
Net book value	14,000

i.e. the gross figure is revised to £14,000 and the accumulated depreciation charged to date is reversed out so as to give a carrying value at £14,000.

BASIC

INTERMEDIATE

ADVANCED

Requirements regarding revaluations

Under the revaluation model, revaluations should be carried out regularly, so that the carrying amount of an asset does not differ materially from its fair value at the end of the reporting period.

If an item is revalued, the entire class of assets to which that asset belongs should be revalued. Examples would include:

- land
- land and buildings
- machinery.

This provision is important because it prevents companies from 'cherry picking' their best assets for revaluation.

Revalued assets are depreciated in the same way as under the cost model (see below).

The accounting issue involved

The accounting issue with regard to revaluations – upward or downward – is where to recognize the increase or decrease in valuation. The statement of comprehensive income (Chapter 1) shows an entity's income and expenses, most of which are taken into account when calculating the entity's profit or loss for the reporting period. Income comprises not only revenue but gains as well. For an income gain to be taken into account in calculating an entity's profits, it needs to be a realized gain – for example a gain on the disposal of a non-current asset.

If, however, a gain arises as a result of a revaluation, then such gains are not realized and are not taken into account in arriving at profit or loss. They are instead shown as 'other comprehensive income'. The distinction is important as unrealized gains cannot be distributed to equity holders. The potential for confusion arises here as all revaluations will need to be shown in the statement of comprehensive income; however, the nature of the revaluation will determine whether it is taken into account 'above the line' and included in arriving at profit or loss for the year, or 'below the line' and included as 'other comprehensive income' – the 'line' being the profit for the year. Where a revaluation affects the profit or loss for the year this is referred to as being 'recognized in profit or loss', and where a revaluation does not affect the calculation of profit, it is referred to as being recognized in 'other comprehensive income'. Note that both realized and unrealized gains will show in the calculation of 'total comprehensive income'.

Note also that any resulting revaluation reserves will still be recognized in the statement of financial position under the heading of equity. The double entry for a revaluation still results in a credit to a revaluation reserve – it is simply that this increase is recognized in the statement of comprehensive income to show the total of an entity's recognized income in a period whether realized or unrealized. The statement of changes in equity links the movements on the revaluation reserve in the year between the statement of comprehensive income and the statement of financial position.

The specific requirements of IAS 16 in relation to revaluations are that:

(a) if an asset's carrying amount is increased as a result of a revaluation, the increase should be credited to a revaluation reserve and shown as 'other comprehensive income' in the statement of comprehensive income. However, a revaluation increase must be recognized as income when calculating the entity's profit or loss to the extent that it reverses any revaluation decrease in respect of the same item that was previously recognized as an expense.

(b) If an asset's carrying amount is decreased as a result of a revaluation, the decrease should be recognized as an expense in calculating the entity's profit or loss. However, the decrease should be debited to the revaluation reserve and shown as a negative figure in other comprehensive income to the extent of any previously existing credit balance in the revaluation reserve in respect of that same asset.

When a revalued asset is disposed of, any revaluation surplus may be transferred directly to retained earnings or it may be left in equity under the heading revaluation surplus. This transfer takes account of the fact that a previously unrealized gain has now been realized. The transfer is recorded in the statement of changes in equity and not through profit or loss.

Accounting for revaluations

The adjustments that require to be made to the revaluation reserve and accumulated depreciation will now be illustrated for the following scenarios:

1. a first revaluation gain after initial recognition
2. a first revaluation decrease after initial recognition
3. revaluation gain followed by revaluation loss
4. revaluation loss followed by revaluation gain
5. sale of revalued asset and the transfer of any revaluation surplus to realized reserves.
6. sale of revalued asset – proceeds greater than revalued amount.

Example 1: revaluation gain after initial recognition

An entity has a tangible non-current asset that cost £15,000 at the start of Year 1; it has a useful economic life of ten years, a residual value of £3,000 and is being depreciated on a straight line basis. At the end of Year 1, the asset was revalued upwards to £17,500.

Accounting treatment: Year 1	£
Cost of asset	15,000
Residual value	3,000
Useful life	10 years

BASIC

INTERMEDIATE

ADVANCED

$$\text{Annual depreciation charge } \frac{£15,000 - 3,000}{10} = £1,200 \text{ per annum}$$

	£
∴ Cost of asset	15,000
Depreciation charge	1,200
Adjusted book amount	13,800
Gain on revaluation	3,700
Closing book amount	17,500

Notes

(a) The initial depreciation charge is recognized in profit or loss in the statement of comprehensive income

Dr	Depreciation	1,200	
	Cr Accumulated depreciation		1,200
Being depreciation charge.			

(b) The gain on revaluation of £3,700 should be credited to reserves.

(c) The corresponding debit entries are as follows:

(1) the initial depreciation charge that was credited to accumulated depreciation – non-current assets will be removed, i.e.:

Dr	Accumulated depreciation	1,200	
	Cr Revaluation reserve		1,200
Being removal of accumulated depreciation on revaluation.			

(2) The balance (3,700 – 1,200) will be dealt with as follows:

Dr	Non-current assets	2,500	
	Cr Revaluation reserve		2,500
Being revaluation of non-current asset.			

(d) The asset will be depreciated over its remaining useful life:

$$\text{i.e. } \frac{17,500 - 3,000}{9}$$

$$= \underline{£1,611} \text{ per annum}$$

The relevant statement of comprehensive income, statement of changes in equity and statement of financial position extracts are as follows:

Statement of comprehensive income

Expenses

	£
Depreciation	1,200

Other comprehensive income

Surplus on revaluation	3,700

Statement of financial position			Statement of changes in equity	
Non-current assets:			Revaluation reserve	
Cost or valuation	£			£
At beginning	15,000		At beginning	0
Surplus on revaluation	2,500		Surplus on revaluation	3,700
At end of year	17,500		At end of year	3,700
Depreciation	£			
Charge for year	1,200			
Written back on revaluation	1,200			
	0			
Net book value	17,500			
Equity:				
Revaluation reserve	3,700			

Note that the closing value under 'Cost or valuation' is the revalued amount. The balance on revaluation reserve will be shown in the statement of financial position under equity.

Example 2: revaluation decrease after initial recognition

An asset has a cost of £1,000,000 and a life of ten years. At the end of Year 3, the asset is revalued downwards to £350,000.

Accounting treatment: Years 1 and 2

Cost of asset	£1,000,000
Residual value	0
Useful life	10 years

$$\text{Annual depreciation charge } \frac{1,000,000 - 0}{10 \text{ years}} = £100,000 \text{ p.a.}$$

	Year 1	Year 2
	£	£
Opening book amount	1,000,000	900,000
Depreciation	100,000	100,000
Closing book amount	900,000	800,000
Accounting treatment: Year 3		
Opening book amount	800,000	
Depreciation	100,000	
Adjusted book amount	700,000	
Loss on revaluation	350,000	
Closing book amount	350,000	

Notes

(1) The depreciation charge for Years 1, 2 and 3 is £100,000, recognized in profit or loss as follows:

Dr	Depreciation	100,000	
	Cr Accumulated depreciation		100,000
Being depreciation charge.			

(2) The loss on revaluation is recognized in profit or loss:

Dr	Loss on revaluation	350,000	
	Cr Non-current assets – revaluation deficit		350,000
Being loss on revaluation.			

(3) A transfer between accumulated depreciation and non-current assets is required in order to reflect the new valuation for the asset:

Dr	Accumulated depn – write back on revaluation	300,000	
	Cr Non-current assets – deficit on revaluation		300,000
Being write back of depreciation on revaluation.			

(4) The asset will be depreciated over its remaining useful life at:

$$\frac{350,000}{7 \text{ years}} = £50,000 \text{ per annum.}$$

The relevant statement of comprehensive income and statement of financial position extracts for Year 3 are as follows:

BASIC

INTERMEDIATE

ADVANCED

Statement of comprehensive income

Expenses

	£
Depreciation	100,000
Loss on revaluation	350,000

Statement of financial position

Non-current assets:		
Cost or valuation	£	
At beginning	1,000,000	
Deficit on revaluation	650,000	(350,000 + 300,000)
At end	350,000	
Accumulated depreciation	£	
At beginning	(200,000)	
Charge for year	(100,000)	
Written back on revaluation	300,000	
	0	
Net book value	350,000	

Note that the closing value under cost or revaluation is the revalued amount.

Example 3: revaluation gain followed by revaluation loss

A company buys freehold land for £100,000 in Year 1. The land is revalued to £150,000 in Year 3 and £90,000 in Year 5. The land is not depreciated.

In Year 3, a surplus of £50,000 (£150,000 – £100,000) is credited to equity under revaluation surplus and recognized as 'other comprehensive income' in the statement of comprehensive income.

The relevant statement of comprehensive income, statement of financial position and statement of changes in equity extracts are as follows:

Statement of comprehensive income

	£
Other comprehensive income	
Surplus on revaluation	50,000

Statement of financial position Year 3

Non-current asset	
Cost or valuation:	£
At beginning	100,000
Surplus on revaluation	50,000
At end	150,000
Equity	
Revaluation reserve	50,000

Statement of changes in equity

Revaluation reserve	
	£
At beginning	0
Surplus on revaluation	50,000
At end	50,000

The balance on the revaluation reserve will be shown in the statement of financial position under equity. In Year 5 a deficit arises of £60,000 (£90,000 – £150,000) on the second revaluation. This deficit is dealt with as follows:

- the amount previously credited to reserves is reduced, i.e. £50,000
- the excess, i.e. £60,000 – £50,000 = £10,000, is recognized as an expense in arriving at profit or loss.

The relevant statement of comprehensive income, statement of changes in equity and statement of financial position extracts are as follows:

Statement of comprehensive income Year 5

Expenses	
Loss on revaluation	£10,000
Other comprehensive income	
Deficit on revaluation	£50,000

Statement of financial position Year 5		Statement of changes in equity	
Non-current assets			
Cost or valuation:		Revaluation reserve	
	£		£
At beginning	150,000	At beginning	50,000
Deficit on revaluation	60,000	Deficit on revaluation	50,000
At end	90,000		0
Equity			
Revaluation reserve	0		

Note that the only effect on profit or loss in the statement of comprehensive income is when the carrying amount of the land falls below its original cost. That is, the £10,000 is the amount by which the Year 5 carrying amount is lower than the cost of the land (£100,000 – £90,000 = £10,000).

Example 4: revaluation loss followed by revaluation gain

An asset costs £15,000 at the start of Year 1; it has a useful economic life of ten years, a residual value of £3,000 and is being depreciated on a straight line basis. At the end of Year 1 the asset was revalued downwards to £10,500. At the end of Year 2 the asset is revalued upwards to £17,500.

Accounting treatment: Year 1

$$\text{Depreciation charge} = \frac{15,000 - 3,000}{10 \text{ yrs}} = £1,200 \text{ per annum.}$$

		£
∴	Cost of asset	15,000
	Depreciation charge	1,200
	Adjusted book amount	13,800
	Loss on revaluation	3,300
	Closing book amount	10,500

Notes

(1) The initial depreciation charge is recognized in profit or loss in the statement of comprehensive income

Dr	Depreciation	1,200
	Cr Accumulated depreciation	1,200
Being depreciation charge.		

(2) The revaluation loss of £3,300 should also be recognized in profit or loss because it represents the fall in value below depreciated historical cost (i.e. that depreciated historical cost that would have arisen had no revaluation taken place):

Dr	Loss on revaluation	3,300
	Cr Non-current assets – deficit on revaluation	3,300
Being deficit on revaluation.		

(3) Finally a transfer between accumulated depreciation and non-current assets is required to reflect the new valuation for the asset.

Dr	Accumulated depreciation – write back on revaluation	1,200
	Cr Non-current assets – deficit on revaluation	1,200
Being write back of accumulated depreciation on revaluation.		

The relevant statement of comprehensive income and statement of financial position extracts are as follows:

Statement of comprehensive income

Expenses	£
Depreciation	1,200
Loss on revaluation	3,300

Statement of financial position

Non-current assets:		
Cost or valuation	£	
At beginning	15,000	
Deficit on revaluation	4,500	(3,300 + 1,200)
At end	10,500	

Depreciation	£
At beginning	–
Charge for year	(1,200)
Write back on revaluation	1,200
At end	0
Net book value	10,500

At the end of Year 2, the asset is revalued upwards to £17,500.
Accounting treatment: Year 2

$$\text{Depreciation charge} = \frac{10,500 - 3,000}{9} = £833$$

		£
∴	Valuation b/f	10,500
	Depreciation charge	833
	Adjusted book amount	9,667
	Gain on revaluation	7,833
	Closing book amount	17,500

Notes

(1) The depreciation charge (Year 2) is recognized in profit or loss in the statement of comprehensive income:

Dr	Depreciation	833	
	Cr Accumulated depreciation		833

Being depreciation charge.

(2) The revaluation gain of £7,833 should be accounted for as follows.

First, a portion of the loss on revaluation made in Year 1 can be reversed. The amount that can be reversed is the amount of the loss less that sum that, had the original downward revaluation not been carried out, would have been charged as additional depreciation.

Had the downward revaluation not been made, then the depreciation charge in Year 2 would have been £1,200. As a result of the downward revaluation to £10,500, the actual depreciation charge was only £833 (i.e. it was reduced by £367). The standard allows us to reverse out the previously posted loss, but net of the amount of depreciation that would have been charged had the loss not been recognized, i.e. £3,300 – £367 = £2,933.

The balance of £4,900 (£7,833 – 2,933) should be credited to reserves:

Dr	Non-current assets	7,833	
	Cr Reversal of revaluation loss (P&L)		2,933
	Cr Surplus on revaluation (OCI)	4,900	

Being revaluation of asset.

(3) Finally, a transfer between accumulated depreciation and non-current assets is required to reflect, in cost or valuation, the new valuation for the asset:

i.e.	Dr	Accumulated depreciation – write back on revaluation	833	
		Cr Non-current assets – surplus on revaluation		833

Being write back of accumulated depreciation on revaluation.

Note: the credit entry to non-current assets is required to reduce the carrying amount for cost or valuation to £17,500.

The relevant statement of comprehensive income, statement of changes in equity and statement of financial position extracts are as follows:

Statement of comprehensive income

Expenses	£
Depreciation	833
Revaluation loss reversal	(2,933)

Other comprehensive income

Surplus on revaluation	4,900

Statement of financial position

Non-current assets		
Cost or valuation	£	
At beginning	10,500	
Surplus on revaluation	7,000	(7,833 – 833)
At end	17,500	

Depreciation	£
At beginning	0
Charge for year	(833)
Write back on revaluation	833
At end	0
Net book value	17,500
Equity	
Revaluation reserve	4,900

Statement of changes in equity

Revaluation reserve	£
At beginning	0
Surplus on revaluation	4,900
At end	4,900

Note that the asset would now be depreciated as follows:

$$\frac{17,500 - 3,000}{8 \text{ yrs}} = £1,813 \text{ p.a.}$$

Example 5: sale of revalued asset and the transfer of any revaluation surplus to realized reserves

An asset is purchased for £12,000 on 1 January 2009. It was depreciated on a straight line basis over its useful economic life, which was estimated at six years. On 1 January 2011 the asset was revalued at £14,000. The asset was finally sold on 1 January 2013 for £5,000.

Accounting treatment: Year 1 and Year 2

		Year 1	Year 2
Cost of asset	£12,000		
Useful life	6 years		
Annual depreciation charge : $\frac{£12,000}{6 \text{ yrs}} = £2,000$ per annum			
		£	£
Opening book amount		12,000	10,000
Depreciation		2,000	2,000
Closing book amount		10,000	8,000

On 1 January 2011 the asset is revalued to £14,000. The revaluation surplus of £6,000 will be credited to a revaluation reserve; the accumulated depreciation of £4,000 reversed out and the gross carrying value increased by £2,000 to give a carrying value of £14,000.

Accounting treatment: Year 3 and Year 4

Revised carrying amount   £14,000
Useful life   4 years (remaining useful life)

Annual depreciation charge : $\frac{£14,000}{4 \text{ yrs}} = £3,500$ per annum

	Year 3	Year 4
Opening book amount	£14,000	£10,500
Depreciation	£3,500	£3,500
Closing book amount	£10,500	£7,000

On 1 January 2013, the asset is sold for £5,000.

i.e.	Book amount	£7,000
	Sales proceeds	£5,000
	Loss on sale	£2,000

The loss on sale would be recognized in profit or loss, and the revaluation surplus would be transferred directly to retained earnings in the statement of changes in equity.

The statement of changes in equity extract would show

	Retained earnings £	Revaluation reserve £
At beginning	X	6,000
Revaluation surplus transferred	6,000	(6,000)
At end	XX	0

It is worth summarizing the above to see the effects on the statement of comprehensive income and the statement of changes in equity.

The total charges recognized in profit or loss were:

		£
Year 1	Depn	2,000
Year 2	Depn	2,000
Year 3	Depn	3,500
Year 4	Depn	3,500
Year 5	Loss	2,000
		13,000

On the disposal of the asset a transfer of £6,000 from the revaluation reserve to retained earnings was made. The net effect on retained earnings was £13,000 – £6,000 = charge £7,000. Note that this equals the original cost less the sales proceeds, i.e. £12,000 – £5,000 = £7,000.

It is important to note, however, that the revaluation surplus was transferred directly to retained earnings; it was not recognized as income in arriving at profit or loss and, consequently, as a result of the revaluation – and the increased depreciation charges – the actual amounts charged as expenses are significantly greater than if no revaluation had been made.

Had the revaluation not taken place then the charges recognized in profit or loss would have been as follows:

		£	
Year 1	Depn	2,000	
Year 2	Depn	2,000	
Year 3	Depn	2,000	
Year 4	Depn	2,000	
Year 5	Gain on sale	(1,000)	(NBV £4,000 – proceeds £5,000)
		7,000	

i.e. £13,000 compared with £7,000 if no revaluation. The end result on retained earnings is the same – it is just that profits have been reduced in the statement of comprehensive income up to the point of disposal.

Total comprehensive income was increased in the year of revaluation and that increase – the revaluation – clawed back over the remaining life of the asset by virtue of the increased depreciation charges.

Alternative treatment

IAS 16 allows for the revaluation surplus to be transferred to retained earnings as the asset is depreciated.

Continuing with our example, the annual depreciation charge increased from £2,000 to £3,500 following the revaluation; IAS 16 allows an amount equivalent to the 'excess depreciation' to be transferred from the revaluation surplus to retained earnings as the asset is depreciated. This transfer takes place in the statement of changes in equity and does not affect the statement of comprehensive income. This would lead to a transfer of £1,500 (£3,500 – £2,000) to be made in Years 3 and 4. In Year 5, the remaining revaluation surplus of £3,000 (£6,000 – (2 × £1,500)) would be transferred to retained earnings.

Statement of comprehensive income (Year 3)

Expenses	
Depreciation	3,500

Statement of changes in equity (Year 3)

	Retained earnings £	Revaluation reserve £
At beginning	X	6,000
Revaluation surplus transferred	1,500	(1,500)
At end	XX	4,500

Note that there is no effect on profit or loss either with this alternative treatment. The statement of comprehensive income will be charged in full in arriving at profit or loss with the increased depreciation expense.

Example 6: sale of revalued asset – proceeds greater than revaluation

Teranga acquired freehold premises in 2010 for £120,000. These premises were revalued in 2012 at £150,000, recognizing a gain of £30,000 in other comprehensive income. In 2013 the freehold premises were sold for £225,000. Teranga does not depreciate freehold premises.

Accounting treatment: 2012

The initial revaluation of £30,000 will be credited to the revaluation reserve:

i.e.	Dr	Freehold premises – revaluation	30,000	
		Cr Revaluation reserve		30,000
Being revaluation of freehold premises.				

The freehold premises will then be carried at their revalued amount of £150,000.

Accounting treatment: 2013

The freehold premises are sold for £225,000.

The gain on disposal is calculated as follows:

Sales proceeds	225,000
Less: Carrying value	150,000
Gain on disposal	75,000

The gain on disposal of £75,000 will be recognized in arriving at profit or loss in the statement of comprehensive income.

The original revaluation gain of £30,000, which was recognized in the revaluation reserve, will be transferred directly to retained earnings in the statement of changes in equity.

The overall gain between the original cost of £120,000 and the sales proceeds of £225,000, i.e. £105,000, has been dealt with as follows.

(1) £30,000 of the gain was recognized on the first revaluation. It was not a realized gain and therefore was recognized in other comprehensive income and shown as revaluation surplus in the statement of financial position.

(2) On disposal, the remaining gain of £75,000 was realized and was recognized in arriving at profit or loss. The earlier recognized gain was transferred directly to retained earnings in the statement of changes in equity.

(3) The realized gain is therefore the difference between the sales proceeds and the original cost less any previous recognized gains. In this example the total gain made was £105,000 (£225,000 − £120,000); however, as £30,000 had previously been recognized, only £75,000 was recorded as a realized gain.

Progress Point 2.8

Mallit buys plant and machinery for £1,800,000. It has an estimated useful life of ten years, no residual value and company policy is to depreciate such assets on the straight line basis. A full year's depreciation is charged in the year of purchase.

At the beginning of its fourth year of using the plant and machinery, Mallit decides to report the plant and machinery at open market value, which is £1,960,000. Company policy when dealing with revaluations is to show the revalued amount at cost/revaluation and to reverse out the accumulated depreciation charges.

Required
Calculate what the revised annual depreciation charge will be following the revaluation.

Solution
When the plant and machinery are purchased the initial depreciation charge will be:

$$\frac{1,800,000}{10 \text{ yrs}} = 180,000 \text{ p.a.}$$

Following the revaluation, the depreciation charge will be based on the revalued amount and depreciated over the remaining useful life:

$$\text{Revalued amount} = 1,960,000$$
$$\text{Remaining useful life} = 10 - 3 = 7 \text{ yrs}$$
$$\therefore \text{Revised depreciation charge} = \frac{1,960,000}{7 \text{ yrs}} = 280,000 \text{ per annum.}$$

Depreciation
Definitions

IAS 16 defines depreciation as the systematic allocation of the depreciable amount of an asset over its useful life.

IAS 16 also defines a number of other terms which are used in the standard as follows:

(a) Depreciable amount is the cost of an asset, or other amount substituted for cost, less its residual value.

(b) The residual value of an asset is the estimated amount that an entity would currently obtain from disposal of the asset, after deducting the costs of disposal, if the asset were already of the age and in the condition expected at the end of its useful life.

(c) Useful life is the period over which an asset is expected to be available for use by an entity; or the number of production or similar units expected to be obtained from the asset by an entity.

Depreciation: amount, period and methods

IAS 16 makes the following requirements with regard to the depreciation of property, plant and equipment:

(a) Each part of an item of property, plant and equipment with a cost that is significant in relation to the total cost of the item should be depreciated separately. For example, it may be appropriate to depreciate separately the airframe and engines of an aircraft. However, parts may be grouped in determining the depreciation charge where they have the same useful life and if the same depreciation method is applicable to each part.

(b) The depreciation charge for each period should be recognized in profit or loss unless is it included in the carrying amount of another asset. For example, the depreciation of manufacturing plant and equipment may be included in the cost of inventories.

(c) The residual value and the useful life of an asset should be reviewed at least at each financial year end and, if expectations differ from previous estimates, any change is accounted for as a change in accounting estimate under IAS 8 *Accounting Policies, Changes in Accounting Estimates and Errors*. The asset's remaining depreciable amount should be amended to reflect any change in residual value and then this amount should be allocated as depreciation over the remainder of the asset's expected useful life.

(d) A number of factors should be considered in determining the useful life of an asset. These include expected usage of the asset by reference to its expected capacity or physical output, expected physical wear and tear and the likelihood of technical or commercial obsolescence. The useful life is defined in terms of the asset's expected usefulness to the entity and this may be shorter than its economic life. For example, management may have a policy of disposal after a specific time period.

(e) The depreciation method used should reflect the pattern in which the asset's economic benefits are consumed by the entity. The standard mentions three depreciation methods by name – straight line, reducing (diminishing) balance and the units of production method – although this list is neither exhaustive nor in order of preference. Once the method has been chosen, it should be applied consistently from period to period.

(f) The depreciation method should be reviewed at least annually and, if the pattern of consumption of benefits has changed, the depreciation method should be changed and accounted for as a change in estimate under IAS 8.

(g) Depreciation begins when the asset is available for use, and continues until the asset is derecognized (derecognition is covered in the next section of this chapter), even if it is idle. Note, however, that under the units of production method of depreciation, the depreciation charge can be zero while there is no production.

(h) Depreciation is recognized even if the fair value of the asset exceeds its carrying amount, as long as the asset's residual value does not exceed its carrying amount.

This requirement is designed to forestall the arguments that some companies have made in the past to justify non-depreciation of certain properties. It is sometimes argued, in the case of licensed premises, that depreciation of the building is not necessary, on the grounds that the fair value is being maintained by incurring maintenance costs that are being charged as expenses. Such premises require to be maintained to high standards in order to attract and maintain custom, and it is argued that to charge depreciation as well would appear to be double counting.

Repair and maintenance of an asset does not, however, negate the need to depreciate. The basic requirement of IAS 16 is that the depreciable amount should be allocated over the useful life of an asset using a method that reflects as fairly as possible the pattern in which its economic benefits are being consumed.

This is done in order to charge the statement of comprehensive income with the consumption of the asset, i.e. the purpose of the depreciation charge is to allocate an expense between accounting periods and depreciation must be charged whether or not the asset has declined in value in the period.

(i) The depreciable amount of an asset is determined after deducting its residual value. In practice, the residual value of an asset is likely to be insignificant and therefore immaterial in the calculation of the depreciable amount.

(j) The residual value may increase to an amount equal to or greater than the asset's carrying amount. In such circumstances, the asset's depreciation charge is nil unless and until its residual value subsequently decreases to an amount below the asset's carrying amount. This may happen in the case of licensed premises.

It is worth pausing at this point to consider the implications of this.

IAS 16 recognizes and confirms that while a depreciation charge is required for all items of property, plant and equipment, the correctly calculated charge may well be zero.

(k) Land and buildings are separate assets with different accounting characteristics and should be considered separately, even if acquired as a single purchase. Freehold land is considered to have an infinite life, unless it is held simply for the extraction of minerals, etc., and is not therefore depreciated. Note, however, that IAS 16 stresses that an increase in the value of the land on which the building stands does not affect the determination of the depreciable amount of the building. Buildings have a useful life and therefore are depreciable assets.

Impairment: recoverability of the carrying amount

It is necessary to determine whether or not an item of property, plant and equipment has become impaired. An asset is said to be impaired when its recoverable amount falls below its carrying amount. Recoverable amount is the higher of net selling price or value in use, with value in use being the present value of estimated future cash flows generated by the asset. Impairment is covered by IAS 36 *Impairment of Assets* and is covered in detail in Chapter 3. For the purposes of this section, however, if there is an indication that impairment may have occurred then non-current assets will be required to be reviewed for impairment (e.g. slump in property market or expected future losses).

The objective of IAS 36 is to ensure that relevant assets are recorded at no more than their recoverable amount.

This objective may impact on the depreciation charge, and paragraph 17 of IAS 36 states:

If there is an indication that an asset may be impaired this may indicate that the remaining useful life, the depreciation method or the residual value for the asset need to be reviewed and adjusted under the IAS applicable to the asset, even if no impairment loss is recognized for the asset.

Example

Ion is a machinery company producing specialist automotive engine parts for high-performance cars. A change in technology means that one of its machinery tools, which was being depreciated over five years, will become obsolete in two years.

Ion, faced with this indication of impairment, would revise its depreciation method to take account of the revised estimated useful life, and depreciate the machine over its remaining useful life of two years.

Where there is evidence of impairment and that level of impairment has been quantified, the impairment loss should be recognized immediately as an expense in profit or loss and the carrying amount of the related asset reduced to its recoverable amount.

Example

Hambald plc has a piece of very sensitive laboratory equipment costing £35,000. It has a useful life of five years and is being depreciated at £7,000 per annum. The residual value is expected to be zero.

At the beginning of its third year of operations, a technician accidentally spills a cup of coffee over the equipment. Although the equipment can still be used, it is estimated that its value has been impaired by £3,000. The effect this has on the financial statements and on the annual depreciation charge is as follows:

At the beginning of Year 3, the asset will have been written down as follows:

$$35,000 - (2 \times 7,000) = 21,000$$

Following the impairment the asset will be further written down:

	£
Carrying value	21,000
Less impairment	3,000
Revised carrying value	18,000

The depreciation charge for Years 3 to 5 will now be based on the asset's written-down value, i.e. 18,000 ÷ 3 years = £6,000 per annum.

The impairment loss of £3,000 will be charged in the statement of comprehensive income for Year 3 as an expense.

Any claim for compensation from third parties for impairment is included in profit or loss when the claim becomes receivable.

The cost of items of property, plant and equipment restored, purchased or constructed as replacements is determined in accordance with IAS 16.

Derecognition (retirements and disposals)

An asset should be removed from the statement of financial position on disposal or when it is withdrawn from use and no future economic benefits are expected from its disposal.

The gain or loss arising from the derecognition of an item of property, plant and equipment is the difference between the net disposal proceeds, if any, and the carrying amount of the item, and should be included in profit or loss. Gains shall not be classified as revenue and any element of revaluation reserve relating to the item will not pass through the statement of comprehensive income (i.e. it will transfer directly to retained earnings in the statement of changes in equity).

Disclosure

For each class of property, plant and equipment the following should be disclosed:

- basis for measuring carrying amount
- depreciation method(s) used
- useful lives or depreciation rates
- gross carrying amount, and accumulated depreciation and impairment losses
- reconciliation of the carrying amount at the beginning and the end of the period, showing:
  - additions
  - disposals
  - acquisitions through business combinations
  - revaluation increases
  - impairment losses
  - reversals of impairment losses
  - depreciation
  - net foreign exchange differences on translation
  - other movements.

In addition, disclosure should be made of:

- restrictions on title
- the existence and amounts of property, plant and equipment pledged as security for liabilities
- expenditures to construct property, plant and equipment during the period
- commitments to acquire property, plant and equipment
- compensation from third parties for items of property, plant and equipment that were impaired, lost or given up that is included in profit or loss.

If property, plant and equipment is stated at revalued amounts, certain additional disclosures are required:

- the effective date of the revaluation
- whether an independent valuer was involved
- the methods and significant assumptions used in estimating fair values
- the carrying amount that would have been recognized had the assets been carried under the cost model
- the revaluation surplus, including changes during the period and distribution restrictions.

2.10 Disclosure in practice

In practice, the required disclosures of IAS 16 *Property, Plant and Equipment* are given in distinct sections. The accounting policies note is normally used to disclose the entity's policy on measurement bases and depreciation rates while the statement of financial position discloses the total figure for Property, Plant and Equipment (PPE) and the notes provide the detail.

Property, plant and equipment

Property, plant and equipment are stated at cost less accumulated depreciation and any accumulated impairment losses. The cost of an item of property, plant and equipment comprises its purchase price and any costs directly attributable to bringing the asset into use.

Depreciation is calculated on a straight-line basis to write down the assets to their estimated residual value over their useful economic lives:

Equipment and plant	3–10 years
Freehold land and buildings	50 years
Leasehold property and improvements	Life of lease

The residual values and useful economic lives of property, plant and equipment are reviewed annually. Freehold land and properties under construction are not depreciated.

Gains and losses on disposals are determined by comparing the proceeds with the carrying amount and are recognised within 'Operating profit' in the consolidated statement of comprehensive income.

Source: Logica Annual Report (2011), p. 97

Logica's policy note on PPE shows the measurement base used, together with the rates of depreciation used to depreciate its various classes of PPE. The note also states that residual values and useful economic lives are reviewed annually.

The extract from Logica's statement of financial position in Figure 2.2 shows property, plant and equipment in the non-current assets section as expected. The current year carrying value of £139.7 million and comparative balance of £138.5 million are detailed further in Note 18 to the financial statements.

The notes to the statement of financial position in Figure 2.2 disclose the movements in cost and accumulated depreciation over the year for the classes of non-current assets identified within the accounting

Figure 2.1 Logica: carrying values of property, plant and equipment

	Note	2011 £'m	2010 £'m
Non-current assets			
Goodwill	16	1,883.4	1,906.5
Other intangible assets	17	174.0	200.7
Property, plant and equipment	18	139.7	138.5
Investments in associates	19	2.6	2.7
Financial assets	20	41.5	12.5
Retirement benefit assets	36	52.4	38.7
Deferred tax assets	28	84.0	70.3
		2,377.6	2,369.9

Source: Logica (2011), p. 93

policies note. Logica has grouped together all classes of non-current assets with the exception of freehold land and buildings, and leasehold property and improvements. Note the way that Logica deals with disclosing comparative balances. It adopts a columnar approach beginning at 1 January 2010 and shows vertically the various movements in cost, accumulated depreciation and, ultimately, net carrying amount (net book value).

Section summary

This section has considered the detailed accounting and reporting requirements of IAS 16, IAS 20 and IAS 23 in relation to the treatment of non-current assets. In particular, the issues of cost determination and the measurement of property, plant and equipment have been examined in detail. The issue of impairment of non-current assets was introduced and the accounting implications of an impairment explained.

Progress Point 2.9

A company acquired an asset for £75,000 that had an estimated useful life of 10 years, and a residual value of nil. If, after two years of depreciation using the straight line method, the useful life of the asset is reassessed as being only another four years (i.e. six years in total), what effect would this have on the annual depreciation charge?

Solution

It is first of all necessary to calculate the net book value of the asset at the time the estimated useful life is reassessed. The depreciation charge for the first two years would be £75,000/10 years = £7,500 per annum.

	£	
Cost	75,000	
Depreciation to date	15,000	(2 years × £75,000/10 years)
Balance to be depreciated	60,000	
Revised remaining useful life	4 years	
Revised depreciation charge is £60,000/4 years = £15,000 per annum		

Figure 2.2 Logica: summary of property, plant and equipment

	Freehold land and buildings	Leasehold property and improvements	Equipment and plant	Total
	£'m	£'m	£'m	£'m
Cost				
At 1 January 2010	28.4	49.3	235.2	312.9
Additions	0.3	2.7	44.1	47.1
Acquisition of subsidiaries/businesses	–	0.6	1.2	1.8
Disposals	–	(1.7)	(14.3)	(16.0)
Exchange differences	(0.2)	1.1	1.0	1.9
At 1 January 2011	28.5	52.0	267.2	347.7
Additions	0.7	5.9	43.7	50.3
Acquisition of subsidiaries/businesses	0.1	1.5	0.7	2.3
Disposals	–	(1.0)	(18.3)	(19.3)
Exchange differences	(0.4)	(1.8)	(10.2)	(12.4)
At 31 December 2011	**28.9**	**56.6**	**283.1**	**368.6**
Accumulated depreciation				
At 1 January 2010	8.7	23.3	148.1	180.1
Charge for the year	1.0	4.4	37.3	42.7
Disposals	–	(1.1)	(12.8)	(13.9)
Exchange differences	(0.2)	0.6	(0.1)	0.3
At 1 January 2011	9.5	27.2	172.5	209.2
Charge for the year	0.8	4.2	41.6	46.6
Disposals	–	(0.7)	(17.9)	(18.6)
Exchange differences	(0.2)	(1.0)	(7.1)	(8.3)
At 31 December 2011	**10.1**	**29.7**	**189.1**	**228.9**
Net carrying amount **At 31 December 2011**	**18.8**	**26.9**	**94.0**	**139.7**
At 31 December 2010	19.0	24.8	94.7	138.5

Equipment and plant included assets held under finance leases with a net book value of £2.0 million (2010: £3.1 million). Additions to equipment and plant during the year amounting to £0.6 million (2010: £1.3 million) were financed by new finance leases.

Source: Logica (2011), p. 115

Section 3: Advanced Aspects

This section considers problems faced by the accountant in practice, and the accounting treatment required where properties are purchased not for use within the business, but for investment purposes.

Finally, the section concludes with a critical appraisal of IAS 16 and once more considers the implications of reporting property, plant and equipment in accordance with IAS 16 for the user of the financial statements.

2.11 Problems in practice

Notwithstanding the definitions and guidance given in the Conceptual Framework and IAS 16, in practice there can be some difficulty in deciding when an item should be classified as a non-current asset. For example, a kit of hand tools may well be shown as property, plant and equipment in the financial statements of a self-employed carpenter, while, in the financial statements of a large company, a similar kit of tools will generally be written off as an expense.

In practice, items of expenditure may not always be so obvious and often there may be as much compelling evidence to treat the expenditure as revenue as there is to treat it as capital. Each case must be judged on its own merits with consideration given to both the Conceptual Framework definition and the IAS recognition criteria. What would almost certainly be classified as a non-current asset in one enterprise may not necessarily be classified as such in another.

Materiality is another useful indicator of recognition. An item is said to be material if it is likely to influence decisions or provide useful information to decision makers. Accordingly, many firms treat smaller items as an expense even although they fulfil all the theoretical requirements of non-current assets. This is done because it is easier and because the amounts involved are not material.

The issue of taxation is another problem faced by the reporting accountant in practice. Expenditure on non-current assets tends to attract tax relief over a number of accounting periods, whereas revenue expenditure normally attracts tax relief in the accounting period in which it is incurred. An item of expenditure that falls into the 'middle ground' may well be written off for tax purposes while meeting all the theoretical requirements to be treated as a non-current asset.

Having decided to treat an item of expenditure as a non-current asset, the next problem faced by the accountant in practice is how, and over what period, that asset should be depreciated. Accountants understand that the inclusion of depreciation in the profit statement is designed to show a fair charge for the use of assets. This means the statement will show a true and fair view. Many company directors, particularly those in owner-managed businesses, leave the choice of depreciation method up to the accountant.

Assets are conventionally grouped into classes or categories. A class of property, plant and equipment is a grouping of assets of a similar nature and use in an enterprise's operations, e.g. land and buildings, machinery, motor vehicles. Depreciation is normally calculated on the class of assets as a whole with reference taken from the rates used for similar types of assets used in similar businesses. However, this is not necessarily appropriate as the level of activity demanded by different users may vary. For example, consider two motor cars owned by a business: one is used by the national sales manager covering 100,000 miles per annum visiting clients; the other is used by the finance director to drive from home to work and covering perhaps 10,000 miles per annum.

Self-constructed assets

Occasionally, an enterprise may construct, rather than purchase, an item of property, plant and equipment. The cost of a self-constructed asset is determined using the same principles as for a bought asset. The cost is the total of all costs incurred in bringing the asset to its location and in a condition for use. If the constructed asset is one the enterprise would construct in the normal course of business then the cost of the asset is usually the same as the cost of producing the asset for sale; it would be determined under the principles of IAS 2 *Inventories*.

Note that the normal profit the enterprise would make if the asset were sold to a third party is not recognized in cost. This means that identical assets may be carried at different values depending on whether they were self-constructed or purchased.

Example

Buildwell plc, a construction company, began construction of an asset for its own use in April 2012 and this is scheduled to be complete in August 2013. Payments for materials were:

	£
30 September 2012	200,000
31 December 2012	214,500
28 February 2013	210,000

A further £75,100 was outstanding at the year end. A firm of architects was paid £51,000 at the end of January 2013 and consulting engineers were paid £67,900 at the end of November 2012.

The company's own staff were used to clear and prepare the site at an additional direct cost of £96,000. Buildwell plc would normally expect to charge £288,000 for this labour. Based on this figure, an additional allocation of general overheads of £36,200 has been calculated.

What is the cost of the asset as at 31 March 2013?

		£
Materials costs	– paid	624,500
	– accrued	75,100
Professional fees	– architects	51,000
	– engineers	67,900
Own staff		96,000
Total cost		914,500

The normal profit that Buildwell would make on the labour is not recognized in cost. The general overhead allocation is not directly attributable to the construction and should be excluded.

Non-current assets held for sale

It may be that an enterprise decides to cease a particular area of operations and dispose of the constituent components making up the operation. IFRS 5 deals with *Non-current Assets Held for Sale and Discontinued Operations*.

IFRS 5 classifies a non-current asset as 'held for sale' if its carrying amount will be recovered principally through a sale transaction rather than through continuing use.

The IFRS requires that assets 'held for sale' should:

- be measured at the lower of carrying amount and fair value less costs to sell,
- not continue to be depreciated, and
- be presented separately on the face of the statement of financial position.

In addition, disclosure needs to be made of the circumstances surrounding the sale, including the expected manner and timing of the sale and the gain or loss if not separately presented on the face of the statement of comprehensive income.

Renewals accounting

Infrastructure assets of certain public utilities (e.g. water companies) require special consideration. It has been argued, in a manner similar to the arguments put forward by hoteliers and brewers, that the amount spent on maintenance removes the necessity to depreciate.

Renewals accounting is a solution to this problem. Under renewals accounting, the level of the annual expenditure required to maintain an infrastructure asset is deemed to be the depreciation charge. This amount is charged to profit or loss as an expense and deducted from the carrying value. The *actual* expenditure on maintaining the system is capitalized as part of the cost of the asset and added to the carrying value. The carrying value of that part of the infrastructure asset that is replaced or restored by the subsequent expenditure should be eliminated.

Example

A water company spends £5,000,000 maintaining its infrastructure in the year to 31 March 2013. The statement of financial position extract for the company is as follows:

Infrastructure assets

	£m
Cost	
Balance b/f	10,000
Additions	5
Disposals	(5)
	10,000
Accumulated depreciation	
Balance b/f	0
Charge for year	5
On disposals	(5)
	0
Net book value	10,000

The journal entries help to explain the treatment.

Dr	Asset additions	£5,000,000	
	Cr Bank		£5,000,000
Being annual expenditure on maintenance.			

Dr	Depreciation	£5,000,000	
	Cr Accumulated depreciation		£5,000,000
Being notional depreciation charge based on annual maintenance expenditure.			

Dr	Accumulated depreciation	£5,000,000	
	Cr Asset disposals		£5,000,000
Being carrying value of restored asset eliminated.			

2.12 Accounting for investment properties

An **investment property** is property, land or a building, or part of a building, or both, held by the owner (or by the lessee under a **finance lease**) to earn rentals or for capital appreciation, or both.

The accounting issues involved

As we have seen from IAS 16, the purpose of the annual depreciation charge is to reflect the general wearing out of assets used in generating revenues. Such assets are necessary to support the day-to-day operations of the business, and are used in production, distribution and administration. They are an integral part of the enterprise's activities, and the depreciation charge recognizes and reflects the systematic allocation of these assets' costs over their useful lives.

Investments, on the other hand, are not an integral part of an enterprise's activities. An investment is held to earn positive returns in the form of interest, dividends or rent, or through capital appreciation. Moreover, an investment is not normally 'consumed' while delivering its returns; the main issue is the investment's positive or negative changes in value. Depreciation, therefore, would not appear to be appropriate or indeed necessary.

The accounting issue involved is that where a property is held for its investment potential, should the provisions of IAS 16 apply and the property be subject to an annual depreciation charge; or is there some other means of accounting for such a property, which gives a more accurate reflection of its purpose and value?

2.13 IAS 40 *Investment Property*

Accounting for investment properties is dealt with in IAS 40 *Investment Property*. The need for a standard arises from the specific problem with properties in that they can be held for either usage or investment purposes or for both purposes, at different times. Moreover, given the tendency over time for property prices to rise significantly, the distinction in practice is correspondingly significant.

It follows from the definition of an investment property that it will generate cash flows 'largely independently' of other assets held by an enterprise. It is this that distinguishes investment property from owner-occupied property – the latter only generating cash flows in conjunction with other operating assets necessary for the production or supply process.

Examples of investment property include:

- land held for long-term capital appreciation
- land held for undecided future use
- building leased out under an operating lease
- vacant building held to be leased out under an operating lease
- property that is being constructed or developed for use as an investment property.

The following are not investment properties and, therefore, are outside the scope of IAS 40:

- property held for use in the production or supply of goods or services, or for administrative purposes – normal IAS 16 treatment would apply
- property held for sale in the ordinary course of business, or in the process of construction or development for such sale – dealt with by IAS 2 *Inventories*
- property being constructed or developed on behalf of third parties – dealt with by IAS 11 *Construction Contracts*
- owner-occupied property, i.e. held by the owner or by the lessee under a finance lease for use in the production or supply of goods or services, or for administrative purposes
- property held for future use as owner-occupied property
- property held for future development and subsequent use as owner-occupied property
- property occupied by employees
- owner-occupied property awaiting disposal
- property leased to another entity under a finance lease.

In some cases, judgement may be required in distinguishing investment properties from owner-occupied properties.

Partial own use

It may be that part of a property is used by the owner and part let out to earn rentals or for capital appreciation. If the portions can be sold or leased out separately, they are accounted for separately. The part that is rented out is investment property. If the portions cannot be sold or leased out separately, the property can be classified as investment property only if the owner-occupied portion is insignificant.

Ancillary services

The level of ancillary services provided to the occupants of a property held by an enterprise will also help determine the appropriateness of classification as investment property. If the ancillary services provided are a relatively insignificant component of the arrangement as a whole, then the enterprise may treat the property as investment property. For example, the building owner supplies security and maintenance services to the lessees. If, however, the services provided are more significant – for example, in the case of an owner-managed hotel – the property should be classified as owner-occupied.

Note, however, that the owner of a building that is managed as a hotel by a third party is deemed to be holding an investment. That is, the cash flows arising from the rental are 'largely independent' from the cash flows arising from the hotel operation.

Intracompany rentals

Property that is rented to a parent, subsidiary or fellow subsidiary is not investment property in the consolidated financial statements that include both the lessor and the lessee. This is because, from a group perspective, the property is owner (group) occupied. Note, however, that the property could qualify as investment property in the separate financial statements of the lessor if the definition of investment property is otherwise met.

Property held under an operating lease

A property interest that is held by a lessee under an operating lease may be classified and accounted for as an investment property provided that:

- the rest of the definition of an investment property is met (i.e. held for rentals)
- the operating lease is accounted for as if it were a finance lease in accordance with IAS 17 *Leases*, and
- the lessee uses the fair value model (see below) set out in IAS 40 for the asset recognized.

IAS 40 allows this classification to be made on a property-by-property basis. If, however, this classification alternative is selected for one such property held under an operating lease, *all* property classified as investment property should be accounted for using the fair value model. This is because, if adopted, the fair value model applies to all investment property whether owned outright or leased, as in the case above. Note, however, that this is an option, not a requirement, and it would therefore be possible to treat the operating lease payments as operating lease payments and expense them, and not account for them as if they were a finance lease. In this case, the fair value model would not require to be adopted and consequently the remaining investment properties could be accounted for using the cost model or fair value model.

Recognition

An investment property within the definition should be recognized as an asset when, and only when:

- it is probable that the future economic benefits that are associated with the investment property will flow to the enterprise, and
- the cost of the investment property can reliably be measured.

Initial measurement

Investment property is initially measured at cost including any directly attributable expenditure such as professional fees for legal services and property transfer taxes.

Measurement subsequent to initial recognition

IAS 40 permits enterprises to choose between either:

- a fair value model, or
- a cost model.

An enterprise must apply the model chosen for all of its investment property. A change from one model to the other is permitted only if this will result in a more appropriate presentation; however, IAS 40 notes that this is highly unlikely to be the case for a change from the fair value model to the cost model.

Fair value model

Under the fair value model, investment property should be measured at fair value and changes in fair value should be recognized in the profit or loss for the period in which it arises. The standard makes it absolutely explicit that changes in fair value are to be taken directly to earnings and not taken to or from reserves.

Fair value is the amount for which the property could be exchanged between knowledgeable, willing parties in an arm's-length transaction. Fair value should reflect the actual market state and circumstances at the end of the reporting period – not as of either a past or future date.

The best evidence of fair value is normally given by current prices on an active market for similar property in the same location and condition, and subject to similar lease and other contracts. In the absence of current prices on an active market, the entity may consider current prices for properties of a different nature or subject to different conditions, recent prices on less active markets with adjustments to reflect changes in economic conditions, and discounted cash flow projections based on reliable estimates of future cash flows.

There is a rebuttable presumption that an enterprise will be able to determine the fair value of an investment property reliably on a continuing basis. However, in the rare situations in which fair value measurement proves impossible for a particular property, the property should be accounted for in accordance with the benchmark treatment in IAS 16 (i.e. using the cost model). The residual value of the investment property should be assumed to be zero and IAS 16 should be applied until the disposal of the investment property.

Where a property has previously been measured at fair value, it should continue to be measured at fair value until disposal, even if comparable market transactions become less frequent or market prices become less readily available.

Although not specifically mentioned in the standard, a consequence of the fair value model is that no depreciation is charged.

Cost model

After initial recognition, an enterprise that chooses the cost model should measure all its investment property using the benchmark treatment in IAS 16 – that is, at cost less accumulated depreciation and less accumulated impairment losses.

It should be noted, however, that IAS 40 requires an enterprise that has chosen the cost model to disclose the fair value of its investment properties in the notes to the accounts. Fair value, therefore, has to be determined in *all* cases.

Subsequent expenditure

When an investment property has already been recognized, subsequent expenditure on that property should be recognized as an expense when it is incurred unless it is probable that this expenditure will enable the asset to generate future economic benefits in excess of its originally assessed standard of performance, and the expenditure can be measured and attributed to the asset reliably.

Example

A company has three properties at 31 December 2013.

Property A

This has been an investment property for a number of years. It had a fair value of £7.5m at 31 December 2012 and £8.7m at 31 December 2013. Maintenance of the property cost £200,000 during 2013.

Property B

This was bought for £5.1m on 1 August 2013. Legal fees and stamp duty amounted to £300,000. The property was rented to a third party from 1 August 2013 and had a fair value of £5.9m at 31 December 2013.

Property C

This is in the process of being constructed by the company. At 31 December 2013 a total of £7.9m had been spent. The property is expected to be completed in early 2014. A tenant has already been found and the level of rent indicates the property will have a market value of £9.0m.

The policy of the company is to value investment properties at fair value, and property, plant and equipment at cost.

Required

Explain how each of the properties should be treated in the accounts of the company for the year to 31 December 2013.

Property A

Property A should be stated in the statement of financial position at £8.7m. The gain in value of £1.2m in the year should be recognized in the calculation of profit or loss.

The maintenance expenditure should be written off as an expense to the statement of comprehensive income as it does not improve the property.

Property B

The initial cost of the property, which would be recorded when it was purchased, is £5.4m (i.e. purchase price plus legal fees on acquisition). It would immediately be classified as an investment property on 1 August 2013. At 31 December 2013, the property would be stated at market value of £5.9m with the gain over the initial cost, £0.5m (£5.9m – £5.4m) being recognized in profit or loss.

Property C

At 31 December 2013 the property is in the course of construction and should be accounted for under IAS 40. The property would be included at cost of £7.9m.

Property held under a finance lease

The initial cost of an investment property held under a finance lease shall be as prescribed for a finance lease by paragraph 20 of IAS 17. That is, the asset shall be recognized at the lower of the fair value of the property and the present value of the minimum lease payments. A corresponding amount shall be recognized as a liability in accordance with that same paragraph.

Transfers and disposals

Almost inevitably, an enterprise may decide to change the use to which its properties are being put, resulting in a transfer to or from investment property classification to or from owner-occupied classification. Under IAS 40, transfers to or from investment property should be made only when there is a change in use, evidenced by:

- commencement of owner occupation, i.e. a transfer from investment property to owner-occupied property
- commencement of development with a view to sale, i.e. a transfer from investment property to inventories
- end of owner occupation, i.e. a transfer from owner-occupied property to investment property
- commencement of an operating lease to another party, i.e. a transfer from inventories to investment property.

Note that when an enterprise decides to sell an investment property without development, the property is not reclassified but is dealt with as investment property until it is disposed of. The requirement to transfer a property from investment property to inventories is when, and only when, there is a change of use, evidenced by commencement of development with a view to sale.

Accounting for transfers between categories

When an enterprise uses the cost model for investment property, transfers between investment property, owner-occupied property and inventories do not change the carrying amount of the property transferred, and they do not change the cost of the property for measurement or disclosure purposes. It should be remembered, however, that the fair value of investment properties accounted for using the cost model needs to be disclosed in the notes to the accounts. No such requirement exists in respect of properties held as owner occupied or inventories.

A transfer to or from investment properties that are being carried at fair value has the potential to have very significant effects on the measurement process and the carrying amount of an asset.

The following rules apply for accounting for transfers between categories:

- For a transfer from investment property being carried at fair value to:
  (i) owner-occupied property, or
  (ii) inventories
  the fair value at the date of the change of use is the 'cost' of the property under its new classification.

- For a transfer from owner-occupied property to investment property carried at fair value, IAS 16 should be applied up to the date of reclassification; any difference arising between the carrying amount under IAS 16 at that date and the fair value is dealt with in the same way as a revaluation under IAS 16; that is, if the fair value is greater than the carrying amount, the increase will be recognized in other comprehensive income and credited to a revaluation reserve. Note that, once classified as an investment property, subsequent changes in fair value will be recognized in profit or loss.

- For a transfer from inventories to investment property at fair value, any difference between the fair value at the date of transfer and its previous carrying amount should be recognized in profit or loss for the period; that is, the treatment is consistent with that of a sale of inventory under IAS 2.

- When an entity completes the construction or development of a self-constructed investment property that will be carried at fair value, any difference between the fair value at the date of transfer and the previous (cost-based) carrying amount should be recognized as part of the profit or loss for the period; again, the treatment is consistent with that of a sale of inventory under IAS 2.

It is worth pausing at this point to consider the implications of the last two requirements under IAS 40, i.e. the transfers from inventory and self-constructed property to investment property carried at fair value.

This requirement to recognize as income what is effectively an unrealized gain would appear to contradict the requirements in IAS 1 to be prudent. What we have is an entity 'selling' an item to itself and recognizing a gain.

This is, however, the whole point of the fair value concept. Because there is reliable evidence to determine fair value by reference to current prices in active markets, it follows logically and consistently with what is in effect a true sale, i.e. that a gain relating to operating processes has been 'made'. It is as if the property has been sold at fair value and immediately reacquired at that same value. Those who argue against fair value accounting are of the view that only a completed transaction provides adequate evidence of fair value.

Disposal

An investment property should be derecognized on disposal or when the investment property is permanently withdrawn from use and no future economic benefits are expected from its disposal.

The gain or loss on disposal should be calculated as the difference between the net disposal proceeds and the carrying amount of the asset, and should be recognized in profit or loss in the statement of comprehensive income. This treatment is, of course, consistent with the treatment of annual changes in fair value of a retained investment property, which are likewise recognized in profit or loss.

Disclosure

The disclosure requirements of IAS 40 are extensive and detailed, and the standard itself should be consulted for a full description. In general, full details and reconciliations of movements concerning additions, disposals, depreciation, impairments, fair value adjustments, transfers to and from inventories and owner-occupied property, and other changes are required.

Given the potential for significant effects in reported figures, the standard requires that disclosure be made of the methods and assumptions applied in determining the fair value of investment property and the extent to which the fair value is based on a valuation by a qualified independent valuer; if there has been no such valuation, that fact must be disclosed. Crucially, the point to note is that if the cost model is being used, then disclosure by way of note is still required of the fair values.

International divergence

In the UK, non-listed companies have instead to use SSAP 19. This requires investment property be carried at open market value (fair value). The standard specifically prohibits, however, the recognition at depreciated historical cost and in this respect is very different from IAS 40. Furthermore, there is a major difference between SSAP 19 and IAS 40 when it comes to the treatment of gains or losses.

SSAP 19 requires that changes in the market value of investment properties should be taken to the statement of total recognized gains and losses (being a movement on an investment revaluation reserve) unless a deficit (or its reversal) on an individual property is expected to be permanent, in which case it should be charged (or credited) in the profit and loss account of the period. This is in marked contrast to the IAS 40 requirements, which require such changes in market value to be taken directly to annual reported earnings in the statement of comprehensive income. The UK requirements are, therefore, significantly more prudent than the requirements of the fair value alternative in IAS 40.

US GAAP, under ARB 43 and APB 6, currently requires that investment properties be treated in the same way as any other properties; US GAAP is, therefore, totally inconsistent with the original IAS E64 proposals for recognition at fair value, and the UK proposals which do not permit the depreciation of investment properties.

BASIC

INTERMEDIATE

ADVANCED

Example

Roget plc has the following details regarding the investment property it purchased on 1 January 2009.

Purchase price (01/01/2009)	£400,000
Expected useful life	25 yrs
Residual value	£150,000
Open market (fair) value (01/01/2012)	£600,000
Open market (fair) value (31/12/2012)	£680,000

Roget plc adopts the straight line method for providing for depreciation.

The major differences that would arise between applying UK GAAP, US GAAP and IAS 40 are as follows.

UK GAAP

Under SSAP 19, investment properties are carried at open market (fair) value and must not be depreciated. Changes in open market value between the end of one reporting period and the next are taken directly to revaluation reserve.

US GAAP

Under US GAAP, the investment property would be treated the same as any property and would be carried at depreciated historical cost.

IAS 40 Cost Model

Using the cost model under IAS 40, the property would be carried at depreciated historical cost and the fair value would be disclosed in a note to the accounts.

IAS 40 Fair Value Model

Using the fair value model under IAS 40, the property would be carried at fair value and changes in fair value between the end of one reporting period and the next would be recognized in profit or loss.

The statement of financial position and statement of comprehensive income extracts shown in Figures 2.3(a) and (b) show the position at 31 December 2012 under each of the four different sets of rules.

Figure 2.3(a) Statement of financial position

Statement of Financial Position

Investment properties:	UK GAAP	US GAAP	IAS 40 Cost Model	IAS 40 Fair Value Model
	£	£	£	£
Cost or valuation	–	–	–	–
At 01/01/12	600,000	400,000	400,000	600,000
Revaluation	80,000	–	–	80,000
At 31/12/12	680,000	400,000	400,000	680,000
Depreciation				
At 01/01/12	N/A	30,000	30,000	N/A
Charge for period	N/A	(i) 10,000	(i) 10,000	N/A
At 31/12/12	N/A	40,000	40,000	N/A
NET BOOK VALUE	680,000	360,000	360,000	680,000
Fair value disclosure	N/A	N/A	680,000	N/A
Revaluation reserve				
At 01/01/12	200,000	N/A	N/A	N/A
Surplus	80,000	N/A	N/A	N/A
At 31/12/12	280,000	N/A	N/A	N/A

Figure 2.3(b) Statement of comprehensive income

Statement of comprehensive income

	UK GAAP	US GAAP	IAS 40 Cost Model	IAS 40 Fair Value Model
Depreciation	N/A	(£10,000)	(£10,000)	N/A
Surplus on revaluation	N/A			£80,000

(i) Depreciation $= \dfrac{400,000 - 150,000}{25 \text{ years}} = £10,000 \text{ p.a.}$

As can be seen, under UK GAAP and the IAS 40 *Fair Value* model, the net book values of the property are the same. Note, however, that the revaluation surplus in the year of £80,000 is taken directly to the statement of financial position under UK GAAP, while IAS 40 deals with this through the statement of comprehensive income in arriving at profit or loss for the period.

Under IAS 40, if the cost model is used then the position is very similar to the US GAAP situation – the main difference being that, under IAS 40, the fair value needs to be disclosed.

It goes without saying that, overall, there are very significant differences.

2.14 Property, plant and equipment: a critical appraisal

At the beginning of this chapter it was suggested that, far from being the most straightforward and understandable of figures, non-current assets were possibly the most misunderstood and contentious items within an enterprise's statement of financial position.

This becomes all the more apparent when the effects of the accounting policy adopted for property, plant and equipment are considered when interpreting financial statements.

Although the provisions of IAS 16 go some way towards making accounting information more consistent and comparable, i.e. by requiring companies to provide for depreciation, and, where a policy of revaluation exists, to keep such valuations current and applied to all assets within a class, nevertheless different management policies on the method of depreciation can have a major impact on the profit for the year. Moreover, the very nature of the depreciation calculation itself is fraught with difficulties. The amount of depreciation charged depends on the estimate of the economic life of assets, which is affected not only by internal factors such as the workload to which the asset is subjected, but also by external factors outwith the control of management. Technological, commercial and economic factors may all have a bearing on an asset's useful economic life and, hence, the depreciation charged on that asset.

This means that the interpreter of the accounts must pay particular attention to the depreciation policies of an enterprise, and pay attention also to the market in which the enterprise operates.

The effects of inflation are also a limiting factor in terms of ensuring comparability both between companies and with the same company over time.

Two companies following the historical cost convention may own identical assets, but, as they were purchased at different times, may well appear as dramatically different figures in the accounts. This problem is particularly relevant in respect of purchases of land and buildings. While IAS 16 allows revaluation of assets it is not compulsory and consequently the depreciation charged on non-revalued assets may well be significantly less than on revalued assets. IAS 16 is concerned to ensure that the earnings of an enterprise reflect a fair charge for the use of the assets by the enterprise. Unless revaluations are made to reflect increases in asset values, depreciation will be based on historic cost. A further issue arising from this is the calculation of the return on capital employed. To make a fair assessment of return on capital it is essential to know the current replacement cost of the underlying assets. It is only the provisions of IAS 40 in relation to investment properties that require such up-to-date valuations.

At a more simplistic level, perhaps the biggest difficulty facing the user of accounting information is the multitude of valuation bases used in a statement of financial position. The net book value of non-current assets is the, as yet, unallocated cost or valuation. Net book value is not intended to be (although many non-accountants assume it is) an estimate of the value of the underlying assets.

Monetary current assets are valued at current values; non-monetary current assets at the lower of cost or net realizable value. With such a variety of valuation methods, it would take a particularly skilled investor to establish the valuation of a business from a statement of financial position.

Finally, consider whether the objectives of IAS 16 meet the needs of the user. For the business owner, the supplier, the creditor, the unsophisticated investor, it is likely that IAS 16 adds little to their understanding of non-current assets. Unless specifically studied, it is unrealistic to expect such users to know that net book values have no relevance to current values; nor to know that the depreciation charge is a subjective, arithmetical calculation that will not wholly provide the finance to replace assets or ensure maintenance of the business's operational base.

Indeed, even for sophisticated users, fund managers, directors, accountants, these problems still exist. To deal with the effects of lost purchasing power through inflation, to compensate and adjust for the effect of changes in supply and demand on replacement prices, and external factors such as technological change and competition, requires not only a very high level of skill, but also far more information than is available in a set of financial statements.

One further point, which indicates clearly at which user groups the standard setters are aiming with IAS 16, is that property, plant and equipment deals with non-current assets. This assumes that users will know what current assets are. It would seem that the level of complexity now inherent in both the definitions and the standard itself has effectively determined its intended audience. IAS 16 is a standard by accountants for accountants.

Section summary

As their name suggests, investment properties are held for their investment potential and not for use within the business. As such, it could be argued that it is not appropriate to depreciate them in the same manner as property which is used in the course of generating profits. However, the approach taken by IAS 40 is to allow an entity a choice of treatments: the cost model, which effectively follows the requirement of IAS 16 with properties measured at cost less accumulated depreciation; and the fair value model with properties measured at their fair values at the end of the reporting periods with any changes in value taken to profit or loss. If the cost model is adopted IAS 40 requires the disclosure of fair value by way of a note. The trend towards fair value reporting is very much evident and is no doubt an indication that, in the future, the fair value model will become mandatory. This is exactly what the IASB wanted when they issued their exposure draft E64 in July 1999.

Chapter summary

IAS 16 *Property, Plant and Equipment*

- Property, plant and equipment (PPE) consists of items that are held for use in the production or supply of goods or services, or for rental to others or for administrative purposes.
- Property, plant and equipment should be recognized when it is:
  - (i) probable that future benefits will flow from it, and
  - (ii) its cost can be measured reliably.
- Initial measurement should be at cost.
- Subsequently, IAS 16 permits two accounting models:
  - cost model – the asset is carried at cost less accumulated depreciation and impairment
  - revaluation model – each class of asset is carried at a revalued amount, being its fair value at the date of revaluation less subsequent depreciation provided that fair value can be measured reliably.
- Revaluations should be credited to reserves and recognized as other comprehensive income in the statement of comprehensive income unless reversing a previous charge to profit or loss.
- Decreases in valuation should be charged to profit or loss unless reversing a previous credit to other comprehensive income.
- The depreciable amount of an asset shall be allocated on a systematic basis over its useful life.
- The depreciation method used shall reflect the pattern in which the asset's future economic benefits are expected to be consumed by the entity.
- Depreciation begins when the asset is available for use and continues until the asset is derecognized, even if it is idle.
- Gains or losses on retirement or disposal of an asset should be calculated by reference to the carrying amount.

IAS 20 *Government Grants*

- Grants related to assets should be deducted from the cost or treated as deferred income.

IAS 23 *Borrowing Costs*

- Borrowing costs that are directly attributable to the acquisition, construction and production of a qualifying asset form part of the cost of that asset and, therefore, should be capitalized.

- Other borrowing costs should be recognized as an expense.
- Where funds are specifically borrowed, the borrowing costs should be calculated after any investment income on temporary investment of the borrowings. If funds are borrowed generally, then a capitalization rate should be used based on the weighted average of borrowing costs for general borrowings outstanding during the period.
- Capitalization should commence when expenditures and borrowing costs are being incurred and activities are in progress to prepare the asset for use or sale.
- Suspension should occur when active development is suspended for extended periods.
- Cessation of capitalization should occur when all activities are substantially complete.

IAS 40 *Investment Property*

- Investment property is held to earn rentals or for capital appreciation, rather than being owner occupied.
- Initial measurement should be at cost, and there should be subsequent capitalization of expenditure that improves the originally assessed standard of performance.
- Subsequently, IAS 40 permits an enterprise-wide choice between:
  - the fair value model, and
  - the cost model.
- Under the fair value model, gains and losses are recognized in profit or loss in the statement of comprehensive income. If fair value is not determinable at the beginning then cost should be used.
- Under the cost model, investment property is accounted for in accordance with the cost model as set out in IAS 16 *Property, Plant and Equipment* – cost less accumulated depreciation and less accumulated impairment losses.
- Under the cost model, fair value should be disclosed.
- Transfers to owner-occupied property or inventory should take place at fair value.
- Transfers to investment property should treat the initial change to fair value as a revaluation under IAS 16.

✓ Key terms for review

Definitions can be found in the glossary at the end of the book.

Asset	Fair value	Recognition of an asset
Borrowing costs	Finance lease	Recognized
Carrying amount	Grants related to assets	Recoverable amount
Cash	Impairment loss	Residual value
Cost	Investment property	Tangible non-current asset
Current asset	Non-current (fixed) asset	Useful life
Depreciable amount	Property, plant and equipment	
Depreciation	Qualifying asset	

? Review Questions

1. What is the definition of a non-current (fixed) asset?
2. Define the term 'property, plant and equipment'.

3. When should an item of property, plant and equipment be recognized in the financial statements?

4. Define cost in relation to property, plant and equipment.

5. 'Depreciation is a process of allocation not of valuation.' Say whether you agree with this statement, and explain why, or why not.

6. What factors need to be taken into account in determining the useful life of an asset?

7. How should grants received towards the cost of buying property, plant and equipment be treated?

8. Outline general guidelines for determining whether expenditure on repairs should be treated as capital rather than revenue expenditure.

9. Define the term 'borrowing costs' and explain the required accounting treatment of the revised standard IAS 23.

10. Define an investment property and explain the required accounting treatment of IAS 40.

 Exercises

Level I

1. Silver Tours plc buys a motor vehicle with a useful economic life of five years, costing £25,000 and with a residual value of £5,000.

Required

(a) Calculate the depreciation charge in each of the five years using the following methods of providing for depreciation:

(i) straight line

(ii) reducing balance (assuming a rate of 27.5% per annum)

(iii) sum of years digits.

(b) Show the net book value of the vehicle at the end of each of the Years 1 to 5 under each of the above methods.

Level II

2. Thomson plc has acquired a new piece of specialized, very sensitive laboratory equipment. Its invoice price was £26,000. Installation costs amounted to £8,000, of which £4,000 related to the cost of labour supplied by Thomson's own staff. The equipment's residual value is expected to be £2,500. Its useful life was estimated as being three years; however, immediately on installation one of Thomson's experienced technicians made changes to the equipment, at a cost of £4,000, which will extend its life by a further two years. Thomson adopts the straight line method of providing for depreciation.

Required

(a) (i) At what cost will Thomson plc recognize the equipment in its financial statements? Explain your answer.

(ii) Calculate the annual depreciation expense. Explain your answer.

(b) At the beginning of Year 3 of operations, a technician accidentally spills a cup of coffee over the equipment, causing £5,800 of damage.

(i) How should the costs to restore the equipment be accounted for? Explain your answer.

(c) Assuming the equipment cannot be restored and its value has been impaired by £5,800, what is the effect on the carrying value and on the annual depreciation charge?

3. The financial statements for Leith plc for the year ending 31 March 2013 are currently being drafted. Below is information relating to the non-current assets table, which is to appear in the notes to the financial statements.

Non-current assets (£)				
	Land and buildings	Plant and equipment	Motor vehicles	Total
Cost or valuation				
Cost as at 01/04/12	684,200	447,900	123,400	1,255,500
Additions during year				
Disposals during year				
Cost as at 31/03/13				
Accumulated depreciation				
Acc. depn as at 01/04/12	161,500	268,300	85,000	514,800
Provided in year				
Disposals				
Acc. depn as at 31/03/13				
Net book value				
NBV as at 01/04/12	522,700	179,600	38,400	740,700
NBV as at 31/03/13				

Further information: additions during the year, at cost, were land and buildings, £46,700; plant and equipment, £34,500; motor vehicles, £66,800.

The company's policy is to provide a full year's depreciation in the year of acquisition and none in the year of disposal. The depreciation charge for the year for buildings is £5,800. Land is not depreciated. Depreciation for plant and equipment is calculated on a straight line basis at 10% (residual value is assumed to be negligible). Motor vehicles are depreciated at 25% reducing (declining) balance.

The only disposal during the year was a building that had cost £90,000. Leith plc received £120,000 cash for this building. The gain on disposal was £34,600.

Required

(a) Complete the non-current assets table.

(b) What is the total for tangible non-current assets to appear in the statement of financial position?

4. At 1 January 2012, the non-current asset balances of Sunnyside Greenhouse Supplies plc, comprised the following:

	Original cost	Accumulated depreciation
	£	£
Freehold land and buildings	1,165,000	119,000
Leasehold improvements	890,000	89,000
Plant and equipment	456,000	101,000

The company's policy is to charge depreciation at the following rates:

Buildings: 2% straight line
Plant and equipment: 15% reducing (declining) balance

The leasehold taken on the property and to which improvements had been made in 2010 was 20 years, and company policy is to depreciate such improvements over the period of the lease. A full year's depreciation is charged in the year of acquisition for all assets; however, no depreciation is charged in the year of sale. The following additional information is relevant to the calculation of depreciation for the year to 31 December 2012.

(i) The amount of the original cost relating to buildings is £850,000, and these were purchased in June 2005.

(ii) The company traded in a forklift during the year and acquired a new one costing £50,000. A cheque for £25,000 was written by the finance director of Sunnyside Greenhouse Supplies plc, being the balance due for the new forklift. The forklift traded in had originally cost £40,000 in May 2010 and had a net book value of £28,900 at 1 January 2012.

(iii) Additional leasehold improvements were carried out during the year, costing £190,000. Legal and architect's fees in relation to the improvements were also incurred, amounting to £8,000.

(iv) A second-hand loader was purchased during the year for £30,000. Sunnyside Greenhouse Supplies incurred additional expenditure on the loader amounting to £5,000 without which it could not have been used. Mr Burleigh, the workshop foreman declared the machine to be 'like new'.

Required

(a) Prepare a schedule of non-current assets for inclusion in the company's notes to the financial statements for the year to 31 December 2012.

(b) Show all the relevant statement of comprehensive income entries that would result.

(c) Briefly explain the differences between the straight line and the reducing (declining) balance methods of depreciation, outlining the different assumptions the use of each method makes.

5. Mawrill plc buys an asset for £100,000. It receives an investment grant of 30% towards the cost of purchase. The asset is depreciated on a straight line basis over ten years, assuming no residual value.

Required

(a) Calculate the statement of comprehensive income charges/credits for each year using:
   (i) the deferred income method
   (ii) the netting method.

(b) Show the statement of financial position extracts for Years 1 to 3 under both methods.

6. Park Transport Ltd sells for £8,000 an asset originally purchased for £45,000. Depreciation of £30,000 has been charged on the asset, which had an estimated useful life of 15 years. Park Transport Ltd was awarded a government grant of £22,500 to help fund the purchase and adopted the deferred income method to release the grant over the useful life of the asset (15 years). The asset was subsequently sold after Year 10 and Park Transport was not required to repay the outstanding grant.

Required

Calculate the gain or loss on disposal of the asset.

7. DialM plc undertook a major construction project during the year to build a new petrochemical processing plant for its own use. Work started on 1 July 2012 and the plant is scheduled to be ready for operation by early 2014.

You are preparing the accounts for the year to 31 March 2013. The following information relates to the project.

(i) Analysis of payments made in the year to 31 March 2013:

Date	Details	Amount
		£
01/08/12	Purchase of land and site clearance costs	3,800,000
01/10/12	First payment to construction company	4,000,000
01/12/12	Second payment to construction company	4,500,000
01/01/13	Professional fees – surveyor	200,000
01/02/13	Purchase of chemical distillation machinery	1,300,000

(ii) Year end accruals

At 31 March 2013, DialM plc owed £2,400,000 to the construction company and the architects have advised that their fee will amount to £700,000.

(iii) Financing arrangements

DialM plc arranged a loan facility of £25m to cover the payments to the construction company. Appropriate amounts were drawn down when the payments were made. Interest is charged at 7% per annum from the date of draw down.

All other costs are being financed by the company's overdraft facility. The average overdraft interest rate was 8.5% for the year to 31 March 2013.

(iv) Accounting policy

The policy of the company is to capitalize borrowing costs.

Required

Calculate the cost of the plant as at 31 March 2013.

Level III

8. Denlar plc acquired a hotel on 1 January 2005 for £12m. Depreciation is charged at 2% per annum straight line. The estimated residual value was £4m.
Denlar Plc incorporated the following revaluations relating to the hotel into its financial statements:

31/12/09	£14m
31/12/11	£9m

The estimated useful life and estimated residual value have remained the same throughout. Denlar plc makes transfers between revaluation reserve and retained earnings in the statement of changes in equity equivalent to the difference in depreciation on the historical cost and revalued amount of the asset.

Required

Show extracts from the statements of comprehensive income and statement of changes in equity for the years from 31 December 2008 to 31 December 2012.

9. Invercraft plc purchased freehold property costing £440,000 on 1 February 2009. The property is depreciated on a straight line basis over 50 years, in accordance with the company's accounting policy. Company policy is to charge a full year's depreciation in the year of purchase and none in the year of sale.
At 30 June 2012, the company's year end, the property was valued at £520,000. The property was estimated to have a remaining useful life of 46 years as of that date. Invercraft has a policy of eliminating accumulated depreciation on revaluations. In addition, it is company policy to transfer an amount from revaluation surplus to retained earnings each year equal to the difference between depreciation on the revalued carrying amount and the asset's original cost. The property was sold in August 2013 for £596,000.

Required

(a) Record the revaluation of the property as at 30 June 2012.

(b) Record the depreciation charge and movements on reserves for the year ended 30 June 2013.

(c) Prepare the journal entries to incorporate the sale of the property in August 2013.

10. Marros plc has a policy of depreciating assets using the straight line method, with the following average estimated useful lives:

Buildings	20–50 years
Plant	6–10 years
Vehicles	4–8 years

Marros charges a full year's depreciation in the year of acquisition and none in the year of disposal.

The accountant of Marros plc, Mr Walker, would like advice relating to depreciation on the following transactions and events in the year to 30 June 2013.

(i) A factory building that cost £5m in July 2003 and was being depreciated over 40 years has had its total estimated life reduced to 25 years.

(ii) A piece of equipment was purchased in January 2011 for £120,000 and is being depreciated over six years with an estimated residual value of £30,000. Recent information indicates that a revised residual value of £20,000 as at 1 July 2012 is more appropriate.

(iii) Office buildings with a cost of £10m, a net book value of £8m at 1 July 2012 and total estimated useful life of 50 years were revalued on 1 July 2012 to £20m. The total estimated useful life is still 50 years and the residual value is now estimated to be £4m.

(iv) A production line was refurbished during the year at a cost of £2.6m. It had originally cost £1.8m in December 2007 and was depreciated to zero over five years. The refurbishment has led to the restoration of the asset's productive capacity, and the production line is expected to be useful for another four years and then have an immaterial scrap value.

(v) The company spent £250,000 on the maintenance of its fleet of vehicles.

Required

Draft a letter to Mr Walker, the accountant of Marros plc, explaining how the above matters should be treated in the accounts of Marros plc for the year to 30 June 2013 so far as they affect depreciation.

11. Bilmont Properties plc has a number of investment properties at 31 January 2013. Details of certain properties are as follows.

Property A

Acquired for £4.5m in December 2012. Stamp duty and legal fees on acquisition totalled £250,000. The fair value of the property at 31 January 2013 was £4.9m. The estimated useful life is 25 years.

Property B

Acquired in 2005 for £2.6m (with an estimated useful life of 40 years) and included at fair value of £6.3m as at 31 January 2012. The fair value at 31 January 2013 is estimated to be £6.1m.

Property C

Acquired in 2007 for £3.4m and included at fair value of £5.1m as at 31 January 2012. During the year to 31 January 2013, £3.1m was spent upgrading and refurbishing the property. This has led to increases in the rent for the property and, as a result, its estimated fair value at 31 January 2013 is £9.4m. Had the additional expenditure not been incurred it is estimated that the value of the property would have been £5.2m. The property has an estimated useful life of 35 years.

Property D

Purchased on 1 June 2012 for £4.2m with an estimated useful life of 40 years. The property is specialized and the directors are of the opinion that it will not be possible to obtain reliable fair values on a continuing basis.

Property E

Held under an operating lease commencing on 1 March 2012. Annual rentals of £1.6m are payable. The fair value of the property on 1 March 2012 is estimated at £20m. The present value of the minimum lease payments is £22m. The fair value at 31 January 2013 is estimated at £21.2m.

Accounting policy

(i) Investment properties, including those held under operating leases, are measured at fair value.

(ii) Where no reliable fair values can be obtained on a continuing basis, properties are carried at cost and amortized over their estimated useful life on a monthly basis.

Required

Explain how the properties should be dealt with in the accounts of Bilmont Properties plc for the year to 31 January 2013.

12. Archfield plc has a number of investment properties, which it carries at fair value. Other assets are held at cost. The following information is relevant.

(i) At 31 December 2011 investment properties had a fair value of £100m.

(ii) During the year to 31 December 2012, four new investment properties were bought from another company for a total of £17m. Legal fees and other acquisition costs amounted to an additional £0.4m.

(iii) On 1 August 2012, Archfield occupied for its own use a property that up until then had been rented out as an investment property. Its fair value at 1 August 2012 was £5.2m (£5.1m at 31 December 2011). The property had an estimated remaining useful life of 20 years. Archfield's policy is to depreciate buildings straight line on a monthly basis. The land element of the property is £1.2m at 1 August 2012.

(iv) On 1 December 2012, Archfield decided that two investment properties should be sold as soon as possible:

Property A (fair value of £3m at 31/12/11 and £2.8m at 01/12/12) is to be sold after redevelopment. Redevelopment work started on 1 December 2012.

Property B (fair value of £4m at 31/12/11 and £4.1m at 01/12/12) is to be sold without redevelopment.

(v) The fair value of investment properties, which were investment properties as at 31 December 2012, equals £125m.

Required

(a) Explain how the situations in notes (ii) to (iv) should be dealt with in the financial statements of Archfield for the year to 31 December 2012.

(b) Calculate the credit/charge to be taken to the statement of comprehensive income of Archfield for the year to 31 December 2012 in respect of investment properties.

References

IAS 1 *Presentation of Financial Statements*. IASB, revised 2004.
IAS 1 *Presentation of Financial Statements*. IASB, revised 2007.
IAS 8 *Accounting Policies, Changes in Accounting Estimates and Errors*.

IAS 11 *Construction Contracts*. IASB, 1993.
IAS 16 *Property, Plant and Equipment*. IASB, revised 2004.
IAS 20 *Accounting for Government Grants and Disclosure of Government Assistance*. IASB, 1983.
IAS 23 *Borrowing Costs*. IASB, revised 2004.
IAS 36 *Impairment of Assets*. IASB, amended 2009.
IAS 40 *Investment Property*. IASB, 2004.
Logica (2011) *Annual Report and Accounts*.
SSAP 19 *Accounting for Investment Properties*. ASB, July 1994.

Further reading

FAS 58 *Capitalization of Interest Cost in Financial Statements*.
FASB Framework for the Presentation and Preparation of Financial Statements. IASB, 1989.
IAS 2 *Inventories*. IASB, revised 2003.
IAS 17 *Leases*. IASB, amended 2009.
IAS 41 *Agriculture*. IASB, amended 2008.
'Avoiding depreciation'. Company Reporting, No. 134, August 2001.
Baxter W.T. (2000) 'Depreciation and interest'. *Accountancy*, October.

When you have read this chapter, log on to the Online Learning Centre website at *www.mcgraw-hill.co.uk/textbooks/mckeith* to explore chapter-by-chapter test questions, further reading and more online study tools.

Chapter 3

Intangible Assets and Impairment of Assets

Learning Outcomes

After studying this chapter you should be able to:

- [✓] define and distinguish intangible assets and goodwill
- [✓] explain and apply the recognition requirements of IAS 38 to intangible assets
- [✓] explain and appraise alternative treatments for purchased goodwill
- [✓] explain and apply the recognition requirements of IFRS 3 relating to purchased goodwill
- [✓] explain and apply the requirements of IAS 36 relating to impairment of assets
- [✓] critically appraise the effectiveness of IAS 38, IAS 36 and IFRS 3 in achieving their stated objectives.

Introduction

This chapter will outline the key characteristics of intangible assets. Intangible assets are those long-term assets that lack physical substance. However, these assets are important to a company since they represent the right to future economic benefits. After introducing the main characteristics of intangible assets, this chapter will examine the reporting requirements of the international accounting standards relating to intangible assets.

Section 1: Basic Principles

When considering what constitutes an asset, the tendency is to think of physical, tangible items such as land and buildings, machinery, vehicles, and other such readily identifiable and definable items. These items are normally classified as tangible non-current assets – that is, assets of a business having a physical substance that are expected to benefit accounting periods extending more than one year.

However, in terms of the definition of what constitutes an asset, an asset need not necessarily be physical or tangible. Indeed, as was covered in Chapter 2, an asset is defined as a resource, controlled by an enterprise, as a result of past events, from which future benefits are expected to flow to the enterprise. There is no reference to the asset having physical substance.

This section examines the non-physical resources that satisfy the accounting criteria for classification as an asset, together with related accounting issues. Such non-physical resources are commonly referred to as intangible assets.

3.1 The accounting issue involved

Accounting standards and procedures have developed to help convey to the user of the financial statements a clearer picture of the economic reality surrounding a particular business. The problem of how to account for intangible assets is perhaps one of the best examples, which demonstrates how accounting information can be shown in dramatically different forms, with each form claiming to be the economic reality.

A number of intangible assets will be dealt with. However, at this stage, the two main ones outlined are research and development expenditure, and goodwill.

Research and development expenditure

This is expenditure undertaken by a company to develop a new product or process – for example, developing a new piece of computer software. As noted above, the traditional view of what constitutes an asset tends to involve the asset having physical substance. Consider the example of a company undertaking expansion and constructing a new factory. The costs of the factory will be readily identifiable, and there will be little argument that such costs should be capitalized and shown as non-current assets. The factory building will be the new asset that will give benefit to the company in future accounting periods.

A problem arises, however, when a company spends money with a view to obtaining a future economic benefit – not on physical assets, but on intangible assets. This problem is best explained using a simple example.

Example

A computer software company currently manufactures and sells its software product. The statement of comprehensive income relating to the company for the year is as follows:

Statement of comprehensive income		
Sales		£200,000
Wages and salaries	£200,000	
Direct overheads	£100,000	
		£300,000
Loss for period		(£100,000)

The company is now developing a new product: a new piece of software. A team of specialist software engineers is being employed to write and develop the new software and, in order to have the product finished at an early stage, all available resources are being utilized to ensure speedy completion. Of the overall costs, approximately £150,000 of the wages and salaries costs and £90,000 of the direct overheads relate entirely to the development of the new product. The approximate costs relating to the development of the company's existing product are wages and salaries £50,000 and direct overheads £10,000.

While the cost information shows all the revenues and expenses for the period, the figures do not show the underlying reality of the situation.

The company is developing a new product – an asset – which in essence will be the same as any other asset yielding future economic benefits. The only difference will be that this asset does not have physical substance. Unless some adjustment or reclassification is made to the figures, it would appear that no asset exists.

If, however, the definition of an asset is considered in terms of its constituent parts, it becomes apparent that an asset, albeit intangible, could be created from the expenditure incurred by the company.

That is:

- the product is expected to yield future benefits
- it is controlled by the company
- the company has spent large sums by way of wages and other overhead expenses (the result of a past transaction).

By applying the above criteria to the expenditure, it becomes possible to restate the statement of comprehensive income as follows:

Statement of comprehensive income (restated)		
Sales (old product)		£200,000
Wages and salaries (old product)	£50,000	
Direct overheads (old product)	£10,000	
		£60,000
Profit for period		£140,000

The statement of financial position would show:

Statement of financial position	
Intangible assets	
Software	£240,000

The costs relating to the development of the new product, wages and salaries of £150,000 and direct overheads of £90,000 have been reclassified as intangible assets, and reallocated from the statement of comprehensive income to the statement of financial position. Moreover, the statement of comprehensive income once more adheres to the matching principle whereby the expenditure relating to sales of the old product is matched with the revenue generated from sales of that product.

This example illustrates clearly the accounting issue involved. The picture being portrayed by simply classifying the expenditure as expenses is that a substantial loss is being made. The economic reality is that a new asset is being developed.

3.2 The position in practice

The problem of how to account for research and development expenditure is perhaps one of the best examples of how accounting information can be shown in two dramatically different forms, with each purporting to be the economic reality.

A real-life example will illustrate the problem.

Example

As a newly qualified accountant, I was sent to do the audit of a software development company. In my earlier years as a trainee I had often assisted the audit senior with the job and in that time had established that this was a particularly profitable company.

BASIC
INTERMEDIATE
ADVANCED

On my arrival at the firm's premises, however, I found the MD to be in a particularly sad state. 'I don't know what to do,' he said. 'We have been developing new software, which I know will sell, but because of the decision to concentrate on the new product, sales of our old software have fallen dramatically. Our existing customers will buy the new product but only if we can keep going long enough to complete it. Our accounts are showing a substantial loss, the bank is threatening to foreclose and my family fear that we will lose our house. I would give the company away if I could.'

Taking all that the MD said on board, I asked to see the latest management accounts. They looked exactly as he had portrayed – a substantial loss caused by falling sales and large wages costs paid to the software developers:

Sales		£100,000
Wages and salaries	£100,000	
Other overheads	£50,000	
		£150,000
Loss for period		£50,000

I quizzed the MD about the future potential of the new software and, although despondent about the current situation, he felt that it would be a better seller than the existing software had been at the peak of its popularity. It would be very profitable.

I then asked him roughly what percentage of the overhead expenses related to the development of the new software. He advised that it was approximately 75%.

I quickly took the figures and reworked them as follows:

Sales	£100,000
Expenses	£25,000
Net profit	£75,000

'How would you feel if these figures were presented to you?' I asked. 'I'd be delighted,' he said. 'Indeed – that's roughly the profit I would expect to make on the remaining sales of the old software. How did you manage that?'

The principal issue here was that the company was developing a new product – an asset – no different from any other income-generating asset, other than that it had no physical substance. The problem was that, on the face of it, no assets actually existed but rather all the costs were expenses and had been classified as such.

If the definition of an asset is considered in terms of its constituent parts, however, it becomes apparent that an asset could be created from the expenditure incurred by the firm.

An asset is defined as 'an economic resource expected to yield future benefits, which is controlled by the firm and acquired as a result of a past transaction'.

(i) A probable future benefit exists:
   ■ the MD was in no doubt the new software would sell.
(ii) Controlled by the firm:
   ■ the company had applied for licences to limit usage of the software to licence holders only.
(iii) Past transaction:
   ■ the company had paid large sums by way of wages and other overhead expenses.

By applying the above criteria to the expenditure it became possible to reclassify it as an asset and therefore reallocate it from the statement of comprehensive income, where it was causing a substantial loss, to the statement of financial position, where it would increase net assets and, in the case of this company, return it to a solvent position. The reality of the picture portrayed by simply looking at the expenses incurred for the year was that a loss had been made. The economic reality was that a new asset was being developed. When the accounts were eventually finalized they did show a completely different picture from the management accounts shown to me. The bank suddenly became supportive and the MD regained the enthusiasm he had always shown in the past. The project was eventually completed and this proved to be extremely successful – so successful, in fact, that the MD received an offer for the sale of his company, which he accepted.

3.3 Goodwill

Another example of an intangible asset is goodwill. Goodwill is the excess of purchase price of a business acquired over the fair value of the net assets. Purchased goodwill is the additional sum paid for a business over and above what would normally be expected for a similar business with equivalent net assets. The additional sum is therefore related to the expected stream of additional income, and its inherent definition effectively qualifies purchased goodwill as an asset.

Goodwill can also be generated internally. This non-purchased goodwill can arise when the reputation of the business, or its skilled workforce or management team, enables the business to achieve a greater income than would be obtainable without the goodwill.

If a company with non-purchased goodwill were to be sold, the amount of the non-purchased goodwill would be determined and recognized by the acquiring company. The actual price paid would reflect the additional earning potential of the business over and above the fair value of the net assets. That premium would then become purchased goodwill.

Why it matters

Two types of intangible asset have been considered: research and development expenditure, and goodwill. Both satisfy the accounting definition of an asset. Why, then, should these intangible assets be treated any differently from tangible non-current assets?

The first reason is that a greater uncertainty surrounds the likely stream of future benefits obtainable from intangible assets. For example, the computer software example given above may not reach its expected sales level; with the goodwill example, the skilled workforce may resent a change in owners. Consequently, because of this uncertainty, the allocation of the intangibles cost to accounting periods can be problematic. Prudence would suggest an immediate write-off.

The second reason is that, in addition to the uncertainty surrounding the likelihood of future benefits, a further element of uncertainty is the actual cost of acquisition. This is particularly true in the case of research and development expenditure, where the cost of a product not only includes direct costs but also an allocation of overheads from other areas of the business.

Concepts in conflict

As a result of this, a conflict arises between the prudence concept, which holds that all such expenditure should be written off, and the matching concept, which holds that expenditure should be matched against the income that it has generated.

BASIC

INTERMEDIATE

ADVANCED

Progress Point 3.1

A pharmaceutical company spends £500,000 on labour costs developing a new drug to combat hair loss.

Explain, with reference to the prudence and matching concepts, how this expenditure could be treated. Why would it be necessary to have an accounting standard governing the accounting treatment of such expenditure?

Solution

Labour costs are traditionally period expenses and, as such, are expensed in the period in which they are incurred. In this instance, there are labour costs that have been incurred developing a new product that, if successful, could yield future economic benefits. The prudence concept would dictate that the costs should be expensed as incurred, as, unless there was reasonable certainty of future economic benefits, it would be imprudent to defer the expenditure to a future accounting period. This would, however, result in expenses being £500,000 greater than they would have been had the development not taken place. The matching concept, on the other hand, would suggest that the expenditure should be deferred and then written off in the accounting periods in which the new drug generated sales revenues. This treatment would more accurately reflect the company's intention in incurring the expenditure in the first instance (i.e. to develop a new drug). This would result in an intangible asset being created, of £500,000.

An accounting standard is necessary to govern the accounting treatment of such expenditure as a result of the significant differences in reported earnings between the two methods. Moreover, given these differences, companies could, if not adequately regulated, argue the case for capitalization/non-capitalization of such expenditure to manipulate reported earnings to suit their needs (i.e. to reduce profits or to boost profits).

Section summary

Assets can be classified as tangible or intangible. Intangible assets are created, as in the case of research and development, when costs that are normally expensed in the statement of comprehensive income are reclassified and capitalized as assets. Goodwill is another intangible asset, which can be purchased or internally generated.

The rationale for carrying such items as assets comes from the supposition that they will provide positive cash flows to the business in future accounting periods. The accounting problems arise in measuring the amount of the expenses to be capitalized and taking care not to overstate the future economic benefits expected to be derived from the asset.

It can be demonstrated, however, that to ignore the fact that the expenditure satisfies the criteria for classification as an asset can result in a misleading presentation of reported figures with understated profits and understated net assets.

Section 2: Intermediate Issues

This section looks in more detail at the measurement and classification issues faced in accounting for intangible assets, the problems surrounding internally generated intangible assets and, in particular, the important distinction and differences between capitalized research and development expenditure and internally generated goodwill.

3.4 Internally generated intangible assets

Many businesses will have ongoing staff development programmes. Depending on the type of business, this may involve staff training to ensure that individuals' knowledge is kept up to date, or performance is kept at a particular level. There may be ongoing product testing and evaluation, or research into new products or production methods.

The accounting issues arise when development goes beyond maintaining performance at a particular level, to a situation where there is enhancement of performance. In this way a business effectively creates the ability to earn future cash flows above their current levels. In such cases, it may be that a new asset has been created. Unless additional accounting information relating to this expenditure on this development is disclosed, valuable information on the performance of the company may not be disclosed.

When might an asset be created?

As noted above, many businesses will have some type of ongoing development programme, not necessarily causing any accounting problems. Consider, for example, a travel agency. Travel agencies provide personal service, and it is likely that staff training will be extensive and continuous. The importance placed on good customer relations will be at the forefront of the travel agency's training aims, and will ensure that customers' enquiries are dealt with courteously, efficiently and knowledgeably.

The question arises whether such staff training costs constitute the creation of an asset and so require disclosure in the financial statements of the travel agency. There is no doubt that such qualities in a workforce create goodwill – the problem is how to quantify it.

One way of dealing with these training costs is to capitalize them as goodwill. However, this would result in an ever-increasing goodwill figure. Moreover, the reality is that the expenditure is more than likely to maintain good customer relations and hence maintain goodwill at its current level. Is it possible therefore to measure the level of goodwill?

If the goodwill has been purchased as part of a business acquisition then the answer is undoubtedly yes. The goodwill will be the excess of the price paid over the fair value of the net assets of the business acquired. If no such purchase has taken place then the valuation of goodwill becomes more problematic. It may be possible to have an external valuation made of the business; however, such valuations tend to be very subjective. Moreover, if the desirable characteristics of accounting information are considered, then objectivity and reliability cast doubt on the acceptance of such a proposal.

Because non-purchased goodwill has been created but has not arisen as a result of a past transaction, it is not recorded in the books of account. Consequently, according to the accounting records it has zero value. It may, however, have a very real value to the business itself.

Now consider a company in the pharmaceutical industry employing scientists to research alternative drug therapies. The work carried out by the scientists could be on a variety of levels. For example, it may involve continuous testing of drugs currently on sale and monitoring any adverse reactions to them. Such tests and trials are an essential part of any ongoing analysis and it will be generally agreed that the costs associated with drug testing should be expensed.

The work may involve the creation of a new drug. At the initial stages of such a project, there may be a high level of uncertainty as to its outcome. Any costs incurred at this early stage ought, according to the prudence concept, to be written off. As the research continues, the project may reach the point where the outcome becomes more certain and the likelihood of a marketable, income-generating final product arises.

It is at this point that any costs incurred could be considered as creating an intangible asset – development expenditure, and consequently capitalized. Note, however, that an element of uncertainty may still exist. It would only be once all the clinical trials of the new drug had been carried out successfully that there would be any certainty of income. Note also that the certainty of income does not necessarily mean the certainty of profits.

BASIC

INTERMEDIATE

ADVANCED

3.5 Internally generated goodwill vs internally generated intangible assets

The above analysis has demonstrated that goodwill is something that is attached to a business, inherently present and subject to many variables. It may have arisen through a determined course of action by management or simply by the determined efforts of staff to provide a quality service. One thing that is clear, however, is that the inherent goodwill of a business could not in itself be sold. Goodwill cannot therefore be separately identified. It is this difficulty in identifying and therefore valuing goodwill that sets it apart from other internally generated intangible assets.

Compare and contrast this with the illustration of a development programme within a pharmaceutical company. The expenditure relating to the development of a product will have been part of a conscious management decision, and it will be identifiable and capable of measurement. It may also, on completion, be possible to sell the product or even the rights to sell the product.

It is this distinction between the two that determines the appropriate accounting treatment of intangible assets.

Intangible assets are dealt with by IAS 38 *Intangible Assets*. The next part of this chapter examines the IAS definition of intangible assets and goodwill, and looks in detail at the conditions that must be satisfied before expenditure can be capitalized and intangible assets created. The chapter also considers the subsequent treatment of intangible assets following their initial recognition.

3.6 IAS 38 *Intangible Assets*

Objective

The objective of IAS 38 is to prescribe the accounting treatment for intangible assets that are not dealt with specifically in another IAS. The standard requires an enterprise to recognize an intangible asset if, and only if, certain criteria are met. The standard also specifies how to measure the carrying amount of intangible assets and requires certain disclosures regarding intangible assets.

Scope

IAS 38 applies to all intangible assets other than:

- financial assets
- mineral rights, and exploration and development costs incurred by mining and oil and gas companies
- intangible assets arising from insurance contracts issued by insurance companies
- intangible assets covered by another IAS, such as intangibles held for sale, deferred tax assets, lease assets, assets arising from employee benefits, and goodwill (goodwill is covered by IFRS 3).

Definitions

IAS 38 defines an intangible asset as: 'an identifiable non-monetary asset without physical substance'.

An asset is a resource that is controlled by the enterprise as a result of past events and from which future economic benefits are expected. Note that the past events need not necessarily relate to an actual purchase – self-creation is possible, and the future economic benefits can be reduced future costs as well as revenues.

Identifiability

The importance of the IAS definition of intangible assets is the word 'identifiable'. An intangible asset is identifiable when it:

- is separable, i.e. it is capable of being separated and sold, transferred, licensed, rented or exchanged, either individually or as part of a package, or
- arises from contracted or other legal rights, regardless of whether those rights are transferable or separable from the entity or from other rights and obligations.

It is important to note that this definition of intangible assets *excludes* goodwill. Goodwill is the difference between the value of a business as a whole and the aggregate of the fair values of its separable net assets.

Example

Purchase price	£1,000,000
Fair value of net assets acquired	£800,000
Goodwill	£200,000

The goodwill figure as calculated above is the amount that is left over after applying valuation rules to the *identifiable* assets and liabilities. The goodwill figure is a residual amount and cannot be identified separately. That is, the fair value of the net assets can be identified; the purchase price can be identified; the goodwill, however, cannot be identified in the absence of the purchase price and the net fair value. Goodwill can be calculated only once the other two components of the calculation are known. Consequently, the provisions of IAS 38 do not extend to goodwill. Goodwill is covered instead by IFRS 3. Note, however, that goodwill is still an intangible asset. It is just that it is dealt with in a different manner from other intangible assets.

Examples of possible intangible assets include:

- computer software
- patents
- copyrights
- motion picture films
- customer lists
- brands
- licences
- import quotas
- franchises

- marketing rights
- trade marks
- costs of research and development.

The purpose of IAS 38 is to distinguish between those items that qualify as assets and those that do not. For example, IAS 38 mentions items of expenditure that it refers to as intangible resources and that do not meet its asset recognition criteria. Such items of expenditure include:

- internally generated goodwill
- start-up costs
- training costs
- advertising costs.

Recognition under IAS 38

The three critical attributes that apply in the recognition of an intangible asset are as follows:

1. *Identifiability:* this is necessary to distinguish an intangible asset from goodwill.
2. *Control:* control is exercised by an enterprise over an asset if the enterprise:
   (a) has the power to obtain the future economic benefits flowing from the underlying resource
   (b) can restrict the access of others to such benefits; this generally results from legal rights.
3. *Reliable measurement:* an intangible asset should be recognized only if its cost can be measured reliably. The asset should then be recorded at that cost.

IAS 38 requires an enterprise to recognize an intangible asset, whether purchased or self-created (at cost), if, and only if:

- it is probable that the future economic benefits that are attributable to the asset will flow to the enterprise, and
- the cost of the asset can be measured reliably.

This requirement applies whether an intangible asset is acquired externally (i.e. through purchase) or generated internally. Additional recognition criteria apply to internally generated intangible assets, and this is covered later in this section.

The probability that future economic benefits will flow to the enterprise must be based on reasonable and supportable assumptions about conditions that will exist over the life of the asset. Where a company acquires an intangible asset, whether separately or through a business combination, this usually means that future economic benefits will flow to the enterprise.

In other words, where intangible assets have been paid for by an enterprise, it is assumed that these intangible assets will give future economic benefits. The rationale behind this is that such assets would be acquired only if they were going to provide future economic benefits.

Recognition criteria not met

If an intangible item does not meet *both* the definition of *and* the criteria for recognition as an intangible asset, IAS 38 requires the expenditure on this item to be recognized as an expense in the period in which it is incurred.

The guidance in IAS 38 on the recognition and initial measurement of intangibles takes account of the way in which an entity obtained the asset. Separate rules for recognition and initial measurement exist for intangible assets depending on whether they were:

- acquired by separate acquisition
- acquired as part of a business combination
- acquired by way of a government grant
- obtained in exchange for assets
- generated internally i.e. self-creation.

Each of these is looked at in turn.

Separate acquisition

Where an entity acquires an intangible asset in a separate transaction, the price paid will reflect expectations that the probable future economic benefits will flow to the entity. Consequently, when an entity acquires separately an intangible asset, the probability criterion noted above is always considered to be satisfied. Moreover, the cost of a separately acquired intangible asset can usually be measured reliably – particularly when the purchase consideration is in the form of cash.

The cost of a separately acquired intangible asset comprises:

(a) its purchase price, including import duties and non-refundable purchase taxes, after deducting trade discounts and rebates, and

(b) any directly attributable costs of preparing the asset for its intended use such as costs of employee benefits, professional fees and testing costs.

The following costs are not considered to be part of the cost of a separately acquired intangible asset:

(a) costs of introducing a new product or service (including costs of advertising and promotional activities);

(b) costs of conducting business in a new location or with a new class of customer including costs of staff training; and

(c) administrative and other general overhead costs.

Generally the same rules for tangible non-current assets apply to intangibles.

Acquisition as part of a business combination

As well as separate acquisition, an intangible asset may be acquired in a business combination (Chapter 11). A business combination is defined in IFRS 3 Business Combinations as 'a transaction or other event in which an acquirer obtains control of one or more businesses'.

IAS 38 permits the recognition of an intangible asset acquired in a business combination if it meets the definition of an intangible asset and its fair value can be measured reliably. The standard indicates that the fair value reflects the probability that the future economic benefits will flow to the entity and this therefore satisfies the probability recognition criterion.

The cost will therefore be the fair value of the intangible asset.

This approach by IAS 38 of recognizing separately an intangible asset of the acquiree leads to the possibility of the recognition of intangible assets on a business combination that may not have been recognized in the accounts of the acquired company. An example quoted in the standard is that of in-process research and development. This may not have met the criteria for recognition in the accounts of the acquired company but will do so in a takeover if it meets the definition of an asset and is identifiable.

Acquisition by way of a government grant

An intangible asset may sometimes be acquired free of charge, or for nominal consideration, by way of a government grant. Examples of intangible assets that governments frequently allocate to entities include airport landing rights, licences to operate radio or television stations, import licences or quotas or rights to access other restricted resources.

Government grants should be accounted for in accordance with IAS 20 *Accounting for Government Grants and Disclosure of Government Assistance* which permits an entity to recognize both the intangible asset and the grant initially at fair value. If an entity chooses not to recognize the asset initially at fair value, the entity should recognize the asset at a nominal amount plus any expenditure that is directly attributable to preparing the asset for its intended use.

Exchanges of assets

IAS 38 requires all acquisitions of intangible assets in exchange for non-monetary assets, or a combination of monetary and non-monetary assets, to be measured at fair value. The cost of such an intangible asset is measured at fair value unless:

(a) the exchange transaction lacks commercial substance; or

(b) the fair value of neither the asset received nor the asset given up is reliably measureable

Example

Probelt Ltd is a long-established supplier of specialist seat belts to the aviation industry. Elqual Ltd, a manufacturer of oxygen masks, has developed a product for use in aircraft in emergency situations and requires contacts in the aviation industry in order to market its new product. Probelt Ltd has agreed to sell its customer list to Elqual for £100,000. Will the purchase of the customer list qualify as an asset in the books of Elqual?

In order to answer this question, the constituent elements of the definition of and criteria for recognition as an intangible asset need to be considered.

The purchase of the customer list by Elqual Ltd is:

- identifiable – a distinct item has been purchased
- measurable – an amount of money, £100,000, has been paid
- likely to result in future economic benefits – IAS 38 considers the probability recognition criteria to be satisfied for intangible assets that are acquired separately
- as a result of a past transaction – the customer list has been purchased by Elqual, not self-created.

The final recognition criterion to be satisfied that would enable Elqual to recognize the customer list as an asset is control. As Elqual will have purchased the list it will have control of as well as access to the customer base in order to derive benefits from it. The customer list will therefore be recognized as an intangible asset at cost £100,000.

Progress Point 3.2

The accountant of Antar Holdings plc, a transport company, is considering whether the following meet the definition of an intangible asset.

1. Recruitment and training of the workforce: Antar Holdings has been using television advertising to recruit new employees and has spent considerable amounts on training.
2. Bus licence: the licence gives Antar Holdings the right to operate a bus route in the south-east of England. The licence was granted by the government to Antar Holdings after satisfying rigorous safety and reliability tests. The licence is not transferable.
3. Domain name: the company registered ' imyourbus.com' as its domain name.
4. Advertising: Antar Holdings plc advertises heavily to promote its services.
5. Brand 'Country-wide Cruisers': this was purchased from a competitor.
6. Investment: Antar Holdings plc owns the entire share capital of Kyles & Isles plc.

Required

Explain to the accountant whether the above meet the definition of an intangible asset.

Solution

1. Recruitment and training: in order for an item to be recognized as an intangible asset, a company must be able to exercise control over the asset. It is unlikely that Antar Holdings has sufficient control over the workforce to give access to future economic benefits. The staff could leave. This, therefore, does not meet the definition of an intangible asset.
2. Bus licence: although the licence is not transferable, it confers a legal right to access the future economic benefits and therefore meets the definition of an intangible asset. It may or may not be separable, but that is not relevant owing to the existence of legal rights.
3. Domain name: the domain name is registered and therefore Antar Holdings has the legal rights to it. It may or may not be separable from Antar Holdings itself. Nevertheless, it meets the definition of an intangible asset.
4. Advertising: although it would be expected that advertising would yield future economic benefits (i.e. sales), there is insufficient control to give rise to an asset. Even if there were, advertising

would fail the identifiability test as it is neither separable nor does it arise from contractual or other legal rights.

5. Brand: as this brand was purchased it is separable and meets the definition of an asset. It can, therefore, be regarded as an intangible asset.

6. Investment: this meets the definition of an asset, albeit a financial asset. Financial assets are outwith the scope of IAS 38.

IAS 38 and internally generated intangible assets

Inherent goodwill and research and development costs are the most common internally generated intangible resources. Inherent goodwill, as has already been explained, does not meet the IAS 38 criteria of an intangible asset and so cannot be capitalized. There are no such restrictions on research and development expenditure, which can, if certain criteria are met, be capitalized.

Before considering in detail the IAS requirements, it is worth revisiting the accounting issue involved.

If a company undertakes research and development expenditure, if no adjustments are made, there will be charges to the statement of comprehensive income in respect of such expenditure. These charges will reduce profits and reduce the net assets in the statement of financial position. This may be advantageous for some companies since low profits may reduce shareholder pressure for dividends and make the company less attractive to a potential takeover bid.

If, on the other hand, the directors are being put under pressure by the shareholders or other financiers to show profits then the directors will wish to show a profitable statement of comprehensive income and strong net asset position. This impact could be achieved by capitalizing some or all of this research and development expenditure. As has been seen, the decision whether or not to capitalize research and development expenditure can have a dramatic effect on the financial statements, and unscrupulous directors may attempt to mislead users by adopting a policy of capitalizing expenditure to suit their own ends.

The problems identified

Notwithstanding the issues noted above, IAS 38 states that it is sometimes difficult to assess whether an internally generated intangible asset qualifies for recognition because of problems in:

(a) identifying whether and when there is an intangible asset that will generate expected future economic benefits; and

(b) determining the cost of the asset reliably. In some cases, the cost of generating an intangible asset internally cannot be distinguished from the cost of maintaining or enhancing the entity's internally generated goodwill or of running day-to-day operations.

IAS 38 attempts to remove these ambiguities by setting out a methodology to assess whether or not an internally generated intangible resource meets the criteria for recognition as an asset.

Research and development costs

IAS 38 requires any internal project resulting in the generation of a resource to the business to be classified into two phases:

1. a research phase, and
2. a development phase.

If the distinction cannot be made, then the entire project should be considered as a research phase and all research costs charged as expenses.

Research phase

Research is original and planned investigation undertaken with the prospect of gaining new scientific or technical knowledge and understanding. It is highly speculative and, at this early stage, there is no certainty that any benefits will flow to the enterprise. Given this inability to demonstrate future benefits, IAS 38 takes a prudent approach and requires that such research expenditure be charged as an expense when incurred and not capitalized.

Examples of research activities include:

- activities aimed at obtaining new knowledge
- the search for, evaluation and final selection of applications of research findings or other knowledge
- the search for alternatives for materials, devices, products, processes, systems and services
- the formulation, design, evaluation and final selection of possible alternatives for new or improved materials, devices, products, processes, systems or services.

Development phase

Development is the application of research findings to a plan or design for the production of new or substantially improved materials, devices, products, processes, systems or services before the start of commercial production or use.

Examples of development activities include:

- the design, construction and testing of preproduction and pre-use prototyping and models
- the design of tools, jigs, moulds and dies involving new technology
- the design, construction and operation of a pilot plant that is not of a scale economically feasible for commercial production
- the design, construction and testing of a chosen alternative for new or improved materials, devices, products, processes, systems or services.

Development expenditure is less speculative than research expenditure and, as the production and sale of the product comes nearer, it becomes more predictable to forecast its future outcome. As such, the matching concept argues that such development expenditure should be capitalized and then expensed at some future date against the resulting benefits.

IAS 38 requires (note the compulsion of the standard) that an intangible asset be recognized in respect of such development expenditure if the enterprise can demonstrate *all* of the following:

- the technical feasibility of completing the intangible asset so that it will be available for use or sale
- its intention to complete the intangible asset and use or sell it
- its ability to use or sell the intangible asset
- how the intangible asset will generate probable future economic benefits, i.e. the existence of a market for the intangible asset or, if it is to be used internally, its usefulness to the enterprise
- the availability of adequate technical, financial and other resources to complete the development and to use or sell the intangible asset; this may be demonstrated by the use of a business plan
- the enterprise's ability to measure reliably the expenditure attributable to the intangible asset through its development, e.g. by means of its costing system.

If all the above conditions are met then IAS 38 *requires* that the development costs be capitalized.

Internally generated brands, mastheads, titles and lists

Brands, mastheads, publishing titles, customer lists and items similar in substance that are internally generated should not be recognized as intangible assets. IAS 38 states that expenditure on these items cannot be distinguished from the cost of developing the business as a whole.

Cost of an internally generated intangible asset

The costs that are capitalized are the sum of the expenditure incurred from the date when the intangible asset first meets the recognition criteria.

Cost includes all expenditure that is either directly attributable to generating the asset or that has been allocated, on a reasonable basis, to the activity that gave rise to it. Expenditure that is not part of the cost includes expenditure on selling, administration and training staff to operate the asset.

Expenditure on an intangible resource that was initially recognized as an expense in previous financial statements (i.e. expenditure during the 'research' phase) should not be recognized as part of the cost at a later date.

Finally, any expenditure that is not part of the cost of an intangible asset is to be recognized as an expense when incurred. These points can be illustrated as follows.

Example

Bizant is a computer software developer. As part of the company's research into ways of improving software, the directors have identified a product that, they believe, will dramatically improve computer processing times and, consequently, will generate significant sales and profits for the company.

Bizant maintains a detailed costing system, which indicates that expenditure incurred on the project to date is £200,000. The directors have decided that the new product is both technically feasible and commercially viable, and that Bizant can finance the development through to the product's launch.

From this point up to the launch date, development costs can be capitalized as the relevant tests have been met. The £200,000 expenditure on development costs prior to this point should have been expensed and IAS 38 does not allow the reinstatement and capitalization of such costs.

Subsequent expenditure

The nature of intangible assets is such that, in many cases, there are no additions to such an asset or replacements of part of it. Accordingly, most subsequent expenditures are likely to simply maintain the expected future benefits embodied in the asset rather than meet the criteria within the standard to enable the recognition of a new intangible asset. Moreover, it is often difficult to attribute subsequent expenditure directly to a particular asset rather than to the business as a whole.

Consequently, expenditure incurred after the initial recognition of a purchased intangible asset or after the completion of an internally generated intangible asset should be recognized as an expense, except in the rare cases where:

- it can be demonstrated that probable enhancement of the economic benefits will flow from the asset
- the expenditure can be measured and attributed to the asset reliably.

Progress Point 3.3

Cornton plc entered into the following transactions in the year ending 31 December Year 6:

1. The company had developed a new invention and has now applied for a patent. Development work incurred a cost of £400,000 and the application for the patent cost £20,000. At the present time the invention has no commercial market, but the company is hopeful of finding one.
2. The company bought a patented design for a product. The patent cost £300,000.
3. A new company was acquired for £6 million. This new company has a special brand, but the directors of Cornton were unable to place a value on it.
4. Staff training costs amounted to £120,000.
5. Cornton spent £2 million developing a new brand.

Explain how each of the above should be treated in the accounts of Cornton for the year ended 31 December Year 6.

Solution

1. Invention and patent. This is an internally developed intangible. As no market has been identified it fails at least one of the criteria for recognition as an intangible. This expenditure should be written off as an expense.
2. This is a purchased intangible. Cost is known and therefore can be measured reliably. By paying £300,000 it is assumed that benefits will be generated by the asset.
3. No reliable value can be placed on the brand so it should not be separately recognized.
4. Staff training does not meet the definition of an intangible asset. There is insufficient control, and such expenditure is specifically required to be written off as an expense.
5. Internal brand being developed. The standard prohibits internally generated brands from being recognized.

Progress Point 3.4

During the year to 31 December Year 4, a company spent £400,000 researching and developing a new product. At 31 December Year 4 not all the criteria were met for recognizing an intangible asset. During Year 5 all the intangible asset recognition criteria were met and a further £620,000 was spent on the product by the end of the year.

How should the expenditure be treated in the accounts for the year ended December Year 4 and Year 5?

Solution
December Year 4

The expenditure should be written off as an expense as the criteria has not been met.

December Year 5

The expenditure of £620,000 should be capitalized as the criteria are now met. The £400,000 written off in Year 4 remains written off, and is not added to the cost of the intangible asset.

Measurement after recognition

IAS 38 allows an entity to choose between the cost model and the revaluation model for the measurement of intangible assets subsequent to initial recognition.

Cost

An intangible asset should be carried at cost less any accumulated depreciation and (if any) accumulated impairment losses (the concept of impairment will be dealt with more fully later in this chapter). Generally speaking, an asset is impaired when an entity cannot recover the statement of financial position carrying value of the asset, either through using it or selling it.

Revaluation model

IAS 38 allows a revaluation model to be adopted and to carry the intangible asset at a revalued amount based on fair value less any subsequent amortization and impairment losses.

An entity can only apply the revaluation model for assets for which there is an active market. If an active market is not available, the revaluation model cannot be used.

An active market is a market in which all the following conditions exist:

(a) the items traded in the market are homogeneous;

(b) willing buyers and sellers can normally be found at any time; and

(c) prices are available to the public.

To prevent an entity from circumventing the recognition rules of the standard, the revaluation model does not allow:

(a) the revaluation of intangible assets that have not previously been recognized as assets; or

(b) the initial recognition of intangible assets at amounts other than cost.

IAS 38 does, however, allow an entity to apply the revaluation model to the whole of an intangible asset even if only part of its cost is recognized as an asset because it did not meet the criteria for recognition until part of the way through the process.

Example

A company spent £20,000 in preparing its application for a number of taxi licences which was written off as an expense due to the uncertain outcome of the process. The company was granted a number of freely transferable taxi licences and paid a nominal registration fee of £100 which it recognized as an asset. There is an active and liquid market in these taxi licences.

BASIC

INTERMEDIATE

ADVANCED

Solution

The company can apply the revaluation model under IAS 38 to the taxi licences because it previously recognized the licences (even although it only recognized part of the cost as an asset) and there is an active market in these licences.

The strict application of these rules would, however, prohibit the revaluation of quotas and permits allocated by governments. These are amongst the few intangible assets that do have an active market. Consequently, the standard does permit the revaluation model to be applied to an intangible asset that was received by government grant and recognized at a nominal amount.

Example

A company obtained a number of freely transferable taxi licences free of charge from a local authority which it recognized at a nominal amount. There is an active market in taxi licences.

Solution

The company can apply the revaluation model under IAS 38 to these taxi licences, because it previously recognized them (even if it only recognized them at a nominal amount) and there is an active market in these licences.

An entity can only apply the revaluation model if the fair value can be determined by reference to an active market for the intangible asset. The standard concedes that it is uncommon for an active market to exist for an intangible asset as each is unique in nature, although this may happen. For example, in some jurisdictions, an active market may exist for freely transferable taxi licences, fishing licences or production quotas. IAS 38 notes, however, that an active market cannot exist for brands, newspaper mastheads, music and film publishing rights, patents or trademarks, because each such asset is unique. Moreover, although intangible assets are bought and sold, contracts are negotiated between individual buyers and sellers and transactions are relatively infrequent. Consequently, even if a market price exists for one intangible asset, the standard does not consider this to provide sufficient evidence of the fair value of another. Finally, if prices are not available to the public, this is taken as evidence that an active market does not exist. Few intangible assets will therefore be revalued.

If an intangible asset is revalued, a revaluation of all other assets in the same class should also be carried out, except for those assets for which there is no active market. In this case, these intangibles for which there is no active market should be shown at cost less accumulated depreciation and impairment losses.

Valuations should be carried out regularly to ensure that the carrying amount of the asset is not materially different from the current fair value.

Recognition of revaluation gains and losses

The specific requirements of IAS 38 in relation to revaluations are:

(a) If an asset's carrying amount is increased as a result of a revaluation, the increase should be credited to a revaluation reserve and shown as 'other comprehensive income' in the statement of comprehensive income. However, a revaluation increase must be recognized as income when calculating the entity's profit or loss to the extent that it reverses any revaluation decrease in respect of the same item that was previously recognized as an expense.

(b) If an asset's carrying amount is decreased as a result of a revaluation, the decrease should be recognized as an expense in calculating the entity's profit or loss. However, the decrease should be debited to the revaluation reserve and shown as a negative figure in other comprehensive income to the extent of any previously existing credit balance in the revaluation reserve in respect of that same asset.

These rules are identical to the corresponding rules in IAS 16 with regard to the revaluation of property, plant and equipment (Chapter 2).

The cumulative revaluation surplus may be transferred directly to retained earnings when the surplus is realized. Realization may occur through retirement or disposal of the asset or through the process of using up the asset. In the latter case the amount of the surplus realized is the difference between amortization based on the revalued carrying amount of the asset and amortization that would have been recognized based on the asset's historical cost. Note, however, that the transfer is made in the statement of changes in equity and does not affect the statement of comprehensive income. The transfer does not affect reported earnings in the year the transfer is made.

If an intangible asset is revalued, the standard allows an entity to account for any accumulated amortization at the date of the revaluation by either:

(a) restating it proportionately with the change in the gross carrying amount of the asset so that the carrying amount of the asset after revaluation equals its revalued amount; or

(b) eliminating it against the gross carrying amount of the asset and the net amount restated to the revalued amount of the asset.

Example : Restatement of accumulated amortization after a revaluation

A company revalued an intangible asset from its carrying amount of £120 to its fair value of £150. The position before and after revaluation using the two approaches is as follows:

| | | After revaluation | |
	Before revaluation	Proportionate restatement	Eliminating amortization
	£	£	£
Gross carrying amount	300	375	150
Accumulated amortization	(180)	(225)	–
Net carrying amount	120	150	150

The proportionate restatement approach leads to the grossing up of both the gross carrying amount i.e. $300 \times 150/120$ and the accumulated amortization i.e. $180 \times 150/120$. The elimination approach results in elimination of the accumulated amortization.

Measurement: a critical appraisal

The standard sets out rigorous tests that require to be satisfied before intangible resources can be classified as intangible assets. The standard also prohibits the inclusion as intangible assets of internally generated brands, customer lists, publishing titles and other items similar in substance. It does, however, allow the revaluation of intangible assets to fair value if an active market exists.

On the face of it, this seems to be reasonable. It would be imprudent and perhaps misleading to have items disclosed as assets that did not yield any future benefits to the company. It would also seem reasonable to reflect the fair value of intangible assets within the statement of financial position so as to convey the true value of those intangible assets to the user of financial statements. The standard's prohibition on capitalizing certain items as intangibles can, however, give rise to some problems. Consider the following example.

Example

JAR Ltd has been trading for a number of years and, over that time, has accumulated a substantial customer list of businesses to which it sells its product. JAR Ltd has been approached by a company, Brinley Ltd, which has a product that will complement that which JAR Ltd currently sells. JAR Ltd has followed the requirements of IAS 38 and has not capitalized the value of its customer lists. Brinley Ltd, however, is prepared to pay JAR Ltd £50,000 for its customer lists.

Two questions arise from this:

1. If JAR Ltd accepts the £50,000 from Brinley Ltd, how should this income be classified?
2. Given that the customer list has a 'value', should JAR not be allowed to capitalize it?

There is no asset in JAR Ltd's records so there is no asset disposal. Nor can it be classified as sales revenue. The 'sale' must therefore be classified as either sundry income or as gain on disposal of an asset with no value!

The strict application of the standard may prevent a true picture being presented. By adhering to the standard, JAR Ltd has an unrecognized intangible asset, which means its 'value' is unrecognized. The non-recognition of this intangible asset results in a substantial asset being omitted from the statement of financial position, and so results in the loss of valuable information about the business.

While the requirements of the standard in relation to what items may or may not be capitalized are effective in deterring inappropriate expenditure from being classified as intangible assets, strict adherence to the standard in certain self-created intangibles can, it seems, be counter-productive.

Amortization and depreciation

The main argument for the creation of intangible assets is that, although lacking physical substance, they share all the same characteristics of tangible assets. As such, intangible assets are expected to yield future benefits to the enterprise over the period of their useful lives. Consequently, the net carrying amount of an intangible asset requires to be allocated to the statement of comprehensive income in a systematic way over the useful life of the asset. Such an allocation is known as amortization. The residual value should be assumed to be zero unless:

- there is a commitment by a third party to purchase the asset at the end of its estimated useful life, or
- there is an active market for the asset such that the asset's residual value can be determined by reference to that market.

Useful life

Intangible assets are classified as having either an indefinite life or a finite life, and the accounting treatment is applied accordingly.

An intangible asset with an indefinite life (i.e. no foreseeable limit to the period over which the asset is expected to generate net cash in flows for the entity) should not be amortized.

An intangible asset with a finite life (i.e. a limited period of benefit to the entity) should be amortized.

Intangible assets with finite lives

The cost less residual value of such an intangible asset should be amortized over the life of the asset.

The amortization should start when the asset first becomes available for use – that is, when it is in the location and condition necessary for it to be capable of operating in the manner intended by management.

The amortization method chosen should reflect the pattern of benefits derived from using the asset; however, if the pattern of benefits cannot be determined reliably, the straight line method must be used.

The amortization charge for each period is recognized in profit or loss as an expense (unless another standard requires that it be included in the cost of another asset).

The amortization shall cease at the earlier of the date that the asset is classified as held for sale and the date that the asset is derecognized.

An intangible asset shall cease to be recognized:

- on disposal, or
- when no future economic benefits are expected from its use.

The amortization period and method should be reviewed at least annually. If the expected useful life of the asset is significantly different from previous estimates, then the amortization period should be changed accordingly. If the expected time pattern of economic benefits has changed, then the amortization method, too, should be changed.

In addition to all the above, the requirements of IAS 36 *Impairment of Assets* (covered later in this chapter) will apply.

Example

A manufacturing company acquires a patent with a remaining legal life of ten years for the manufacture of a particular product. Technological advances suggest that the product is likely to become obsolete in five years.

The patent would be amortized over its five-year estimated useful life. The patent would also be reviewed for impairment in accordance with IAS 36 by assessing at each reporting date whether there is any indication that it may be impaired.

Intangible assets with indefinite useful lives

Note that the term indefinite does not mean infinite. An infinite life would imply that, once purchased or self-created, the intangible asset would yield economic benefits continuously. The term indefinite is intended to reflect the fact that, providing the asset is properly maintained, it will continue to yield economic benefits.

However, the asset should not be classified as having an indefinite life if planned future expenditure is greater than that required to maintain the asset at its standard of performance at the time of estimating its useful life. In other words, if the intangible asset will require to be 'improved' with subsequent expenditure, then it should not be classified as having an indefinite life.

An intangible asset with an indefinite useful life should not be amortized.

Instead, a review of the asset's useful life should be carried out annually. If the findings do not support an indefinite useful life assessment for the asset then the change in the useful life assessment from indefinite to finite should be accounted for as a change in an accounting estimate in accordance with the requirements of IAS 8 (Chapter 1).

In addition, an impairment test should be carried out annually and whenever there is an indication that the intangible asset may be impaired. If the findings suggest impairment, this will lead to reductions in carrying value to the recoverable amount at the date of the impairment test.

Example

A radio station acquires a broadcasting licence, renewable every five years. The licence is renewed at little cost as long as the radio station provides at least an average level of service to its customers and complies with the relevant legislative requirements. The licence had been renewed twice before the most recent acquisition. The radio station intends to renew the licence indefinitely and evidence supports its ability to do so. Historically, there has been no challenge to the licence renewal and the technology used in broadcasting is not expected to be superseded in the foreseeable future. The licence is, therefore, expected to contribute to the radio station's net cash inflows indefinitely.

The broadcasting licence would be treated as having an indefinite useful life because it is expected to contribute to the radio station's net cash inflows indefinitely. Therefore, the licence would not be amortized until its useful life is determined to be finite. The licence would be tested for impairment in accordance with IAS 36 annually and whenever there is an indication that it may be impaired.

Derecognition
Retirements and disposals

The gain or loss arising from the derecognition of an intangible asset should be the difference between the net disposal proceeds (if any) and the carrying amount of the asset. This gain or loss should be recognized in profit or loss when the asset is derecognized.

3.7 Disclosure

The disclosure requirements in IAS 38 are long and detailed, and require full information in relation to balances, useful lives, amortization rates and methods, any changes over the year, and any revaluations or impairment losses.

Disclosure in practice

The required disclosures of IAS 38 *Intangible Assets* are usually contained in the accounting policies note, the statement of financial position and the notes.

Intangible assets

All intangible assets, except goodwill, are stated at cost less accumulated amortisation and any accumulated impairment losses. Goodwill is not amortised and is stated at cost less any accumulated impairment losses.

Goodwill

Goodwill represents the excess of the cost of acquisition over the fair value of the Group's interest in the identifiable assets, liabilities and contingent liabilities acquired in a business combination.

Other intangible assets

Expenditure incurred in the development of software products or enhancements, and their related intellectual property rights, is capitalised as an intangible asset only when the future economic benefits expected to arise are deemed probable and the costs can be reliably measured. Development costs not meeting these criteria, and all research costs, are expensed in the statement of comprehensive income as incurred. Once the related software product or enhancement is available for use, capitalised development costs are amortised on a straight-line basis over their useful economic lives which does not exceed four years.

Intangible assets purchased separately, such as software licences that do not form an integral part of related hardware, are capitalised at cost and amortised on a straight-line basis over their useful economic life. Intangible assets acquired through a business combination are initially measured at fair value and amortised on a straight line basis over their useful economic lives.

The useful economic lives of the other intangible assets are as follows:

Brand names	3–5 years
Software products recognised on acquisition	3–7 years
Purchased computer software	3 years

Customer contracts and relationships are amortised on a straight-line basis over their useful economic life which are between five and eight years, except for one contract in the International category which has a useful life of 10 years.

Source: Logica (2011), p. 97

This extract from Logica's accounting policies note discloses the measurement base adopted for intangible assets together with the types of intangible assets contained within the financial statements and the amortization period adopted for each of the classes identified.

Figure 3.1 Logica: consolidated statement of financial position

	2011 £'m	2010 £'m
Non-current assets		
Goodwill	1,883.4	1,906.5
Other intangible assets	174.0	200.7
Property, plant and equipment	139.7	138.5
Investments in associates	2.6	2.7
Financial assets	41.5	12.5
Retirement benefit assets	52.4	38.7
Deferred tax assets	84.0	70.3
	2,377.6	2,369.9

Source: Logica (2011), p. 93

Figure 3.2 Logica: other intangible assets

	Purchased computer software	Development costs	Brand names	Customer contracts/ relationships	Software Products	Total
	£'m	£'m	£'m	£'m	£'m	£'m
Cost						
At 1 January 2010	36.0	41.2	124.3	359.1	40.9	601.5
Additions	7.6	21.2	–	–	–	28.8
Acquisition of subsidiaries/businesses						
Disposals	–	–	–	0.3	–	0.3
Exchange differences	(1.7)	(3.3)	–	–	–	(5.0)
	0.8	0.3	1.8	6.4	0.3	9.6
At 1 January 2011	42.7	59.4	126.1	365.8	41.2	635.2
Additions	7.2	22.0	–	–	–	29.2
Transfers	–	8.0	–			8.0
Acquisition of subsidiaries/businesses						
Disposals	–	–	1.4	10.0	–	11.4
Exchange differences	(10.8)	(0.9)	–	–	–	(11.7)
	(1.3)	(0.5)	(2.5)	(7.3)	(0.9)	(12.5)
At 31 December 2011	**37.8**	**88.0**	**125.0**	**368.5**	**40.3**	**659.6**
Accumulated amortisation						
At 1 January 2010	18.5	16.0	120.4	180.0	23.2	358.1
Charge for the year	6.2	9.1	3.4	50.3	5.9	74.9
Disposals	(1.1)	(3.3)	–	–	–	(4.4)
Exchange differences	0.7	(0.1)	1.9	3.2	0.2	5.9
At 1 January 2011	24.3	21.7	125.7	233.5	29.3	434.5
Charge for the year	8.3	10.0	0.3	48.5	5.7	72.8
Disposals	(10.4)	(0.9)	–	–	–	(11.3)
Exchange differences	(0.9)	(0.2)	(2.4)	(6.1)	(0.8)	(10.4)
At 31 December 2011	**21.3**	**30.6**	**123.6**	**275.9**	**34.2**	**485.6**
Net carrying amount						
At 31 December 2011	**16.5**	**57.4**	**1.4**	**92.6**	**6.1**	**174.0**
At 31 December 2010	18.4	37.7	0.4	132.3	11.9	200.7

Purchased computer software represented assets bought from third parties, whilst development costs represented internally generated intangible assets. Brand names, customer contracts/relationships and software products represented assets recognised as part of a business combination.

Individual intangible assets considered material to the Group related to customer contracts/relationships in Sweden with a net book value of £45.3 million (2010: £65.5 million) which had a remaining useful life of between two and three years (2010: three and four years). These assets related to the WM-data acquisition.

Source: Logica (2011), p. 114

Intangible assets are contained within the non-current assets section of Logica's statement of financial position (Figure 3.1). The carrying value at 2011 is £174 million with a comparative 2010 balance amounting to £200.7 million. Analysis of both these balances is given in note 18 to the financial statements.

This note to Logica's statement of financial position discloses the movements in the various classes of intangible assets held at the end of each reporting period (Figure 3.2). A columnar approach is used to assist in the disclosure of comparative balances beginning at 1 January 2010 and showing vertically the various additions, disposals and exchange differences in cost, accumulated amortization and net carrying amount (net book value).

International differences

The position for UK unlisted companies

Research and development expenditure is regulated by SSAP 13. This standard is very similar to IAS 38 but does not require that expenditure be capitalized if all criteria are met. Instead, it states that the expenditure may be capitalized.

The US position

With the exception of certain software development costs, which are required to be capitalized in accordance with FAS 86, US GAAP (FAS 2) requires all research and development costs to be immediately expensed. In addition, while International GAAP permits the reinstatement of intangible assets to their fair values where an active market for that type of asset exists, this treatment is not permitted by US GAAP. US GAAP permits useful lives of identified intangibles to have a duration of up to 40 years.

3.8 Goodwill

Goodwill can be self-generated or purchased. IAS 38 *Intangible Assets* deals with self-generated goodwill and prohibits its recognition as an intangible asset within the financial statements.

The reason for this is the potential to alter reported figures. If companies were permitted to include self-generated goodwill in their financial statements:

- they could boost assets and produce a stronger balance sheet (e.g. by reducing gearing)
- if the credit entry was to a capital reserve in the statement of financial position, there would be no effect on reported profits, but
- if the credit entry was recognized in profit or loss in the statement of comprehensive income, this would boost the profit for the year, which would allow the manipulation of reported profit.

IFRS 3 *Business Combinations* deals with purchased goodwill. As already noted, goodwill is a residual amount and is defined as: 'an asset representing the future economic benefits arising from assets acquired in a business combination that are not capable of being individually identified and separately recognized'.

Goodwill is the amount remaining after applying valuation rules to the *identifiable* assets and liabilities.

Example

	£
Purchase price	1,000,000
Net fair value of assets acquired	800,000
Goodwill	200,000

Goodwill is not therefore an identifiable asset in itself, but is instead a residual amount.

Why does goodwill arise?

As noted earlier in this chapter, goodwill can arise when a skilled workforce, an efficient production process or an established customer base results in an enterprise returning greater profits than could be generated by another company utilizing the same net assets. The cost of this self-generated goodwill is the cost of the training, production reviews and advertising incurred in developing the business to this particular level.

Purchased goodwill arises when one company acquires another company in a business combination and the purchase price paid reflects the ability of the acquiring company to earn these future super-profits.

From the acquiring company's point of view, this excess amount paid over the fair value of the net assets acquired is expected to yield future benefits. The anticipation of expected future benefits effectively constitutes goodwill as an asset in the same way as any other tangible asset that would be expected to yield future benefits.

It is important to remember that in arriving at the purchase price of an acquisition in a business combination, the value placed on the net assets will be the fair values and the excess is likely to have been based upon an estimate of the future maintainable earnings of the acquiring company.

Accounting treatment of purchased goodwill: the options

There are a number of possible approaches to accounting for purchased goodwill.

(i)   *Carry the purchased goodwill as an asset and amortize it over its estimated useful life through profit or loss in the statement of comprehensive income.* It could be argued, however, that to charge amortization of the goodwill figure is effectively a double charge to profit or loss if the goodwill itself is being 'maintained' by other revenue expenditure (i.e. training, advertising, quality controls).

(ii) *Carry the purchased goodwill as an asset and amortize it over its estimated useful life by writing off directly against reserves.* The problem here is that, as amortization is an expense, it ought to be treated as such and charged to profit or loss, not against reserves.

(iii) *Eliminate purchased goodwill against reserves immediately on acquisition.* This would effectively treat purchased goodwill in the same way as non-purchased goodwill (i.e. it solves the problem as if the goodwill had never existed in the first place).

(iv) *Retain purchased goodwill in the accounts indefinitely unless a permanent reduction in its value becomes evident.* This is acceptable if the view is taken that goodwill can be maintained, as, for example, a building can. The costs of maintaining the goodwill are being expended as they occur and to charge amortization as well would be double counting. As we have seen, however, goodwill is a variable figure and it could be argued that, over time, the purchased goodwill is being replaced by self-generated non-purchased goodwill.

(v)   *Charge purchased goodwill as an expense against profits in the period when it is acquired.* This seems to suggest that the goodwill on acquisition will have suffered an immediate reduction in value. This is clearly not the case as a loss in value, if at all, will take place over a longer period of time. Moreover, the write-off is not related to the results of the year in which the acquisition was made.

(vi) *Show purchased goodwill as a deduction from shareholders' equity (and either amortize it or carry it indefinitely).* This 'moves' the goodwill down the statement of financial position, reducing both net assets and, correspondingly, shareholders' funds. The figure is shown as a debit but not on the net asset side. Instead it is shown as a deduction from shareholders' equity. It is the same as writing off purchased goodwill against reserves while implying that the goodwill remains available as a form of asset. Ultimately, however, this treatment can be rejected as it represents the offset of a liability against an asset, which, under certain countries' legislation, is not permitted.

(vii) *Revalue it annually to incorporate later non-purchased goodwill.* This would be consistent with the trend towards fair value, but is highly subjective. Moreover, if self-generated (i.e. non-purchased) goodwill is not recognized as an asset, this treatment would, it could be argued, be inconsistent with the international accounting standard, particularly if, over time, purchased goodwill is replaced by non-purchased goodwill. This treatment would also be particularly susceptible to manipulation.

Goodwill and IFRS 3

The excess of purchase cost over the fair value of the identified net assets is the goodwill on acquisition figure. This is positive goodwill.

Positive goodwill should be:

- recognized in a business combination as an asset
- initially measured as the excess of the cost of the business combination over the proportion of the fair value of the identifiable net assets acquired.

Goodwill acquired in a business combination should not be amortized. Instead it should be tested annually for impairment. The impairment test may be applied more frequently in accordance with IAS 36 if events or circumstances indicate that the asset might be impaired. Note that this treatment is exactly consistent with the requirements for identifiable intangible assets with indefinite lives.

Negative goodwill

So far the examples given have all assumed that the calculated goodwill is a positive figure. In other words, that the payment made is greater than the fair value of the net assets acquired. It is, of course, possible for the goodwill figure to be negative. This could happen if the price paid by the acquiring company was less than the fair value of the tangible net assets acquired.

How can this happen?

In order to determine the purchase price, accountants will restate the individual assets and liabilities at their fair values. These new values will then become the historical cost to the new owners of the individual assets and liabilities recognized at the date of acquisition. Consequently, negative goodwill or, to put another it way, a 'bargain' purchase, should not be possible if correct valuation procedures have been followed. This is certainly the case if one is concerned only with the cost of the investment. The cost of the individually identified assets and liabilities cannot exceed the cost of the business purchased.

If, however, in the assessment of the purchase price, *future* reorganization costs are anticipated, then this can give rise to the negative goodwill phenomenon. Why might it be that these future liabilities have not been taken into account in the net fair value calculation? The reason for this is that, although clearly quantifiable, they do not satisfy the criteria for recognition as provisions at the date of acquisition and consequently cannot be included in the net fair value calculation. They can, however, be included in the calculation of what the acquirer is prepared to pay for the investment.

Accounting treatment of negative goodwill: the options

In the same way that there are several methods of dealing with positive goodwill, negative goodwill could also be accounted for in a number of different ways.

(i) If the negative goodwill arises as a result of the future expectation of losses and expenses identified by the acquirer in the assessment of the value of the acquisition, and can be measured reliably, then the negative goodwill could be included as income in the periods when the future losses and expenses are identified. This would certainly adhere to the matching principle; however, the measurement of future losses is likely to be problematic.

(ii) If negative goodwill arises, the acquirer could reassess the identification and measurement of the acquiree's identifiable assets, liabilities and contingent liabilities, and the measurement of the cost of the combination. In this assessment there will be two types of assets and liabilities: monetary and non-monetary. Monetary assets and liabilities are those assets and liabilities whose amounts are contractually fixed and as such can be excluded from the computation. This is because, in any reassessment, these values will, by definition, be fixed. Any negative goodwill and hence any uncertainty must therefore relate to the non-monetary items.

A possible method of dealing with the negative goodwill would be to recognize it in profit or loss in the periods over which the non-monetary assets are recovered, either through depreciation or disposal. Any negative goodwill in excess of fair values of the non-monetary assets acquired could be recognized in profit or loss for the period expected to benefit.

Example

Lanbell plc acquired its investment in Prion plc in the year ended 31 December 2012. The goodwill on acquisition was calculated as follows:

	£000	£000
Cost of investment		250
Fair value of net non-monetary assets (remaining useful life 4 years)	400	
Stock (non-monetary asset)	50	
Net monetary assets	100	
		550
Negative goodwill		300

The negative goodwill could be accounted for as follows.

Allocated, first, against the non-monetary assets recognized through profit or loss for the year ended 31 December 2012:

	£000
Stock (on the assumption it is all sold)	50
Depreciation (£400,000/4 years)	100
	150
Total non-monetary assets at acquisition (400,000 + 50,000)	450
Proportion recognized in year to 31 December 2012 is $\frac{150}{450}$ i.e. $\frac{1}{3}$	
Credit to profit or loss is $\frac{1}{3} \times £300,000 =$	100,000

The statement of financial position will show negative goodwill of £300,000 − £100,000 = £200,000.

This negative goodwill will be released to profit or loss over the remainder of the net assets' useful lives, i.e. 3 years (4 years − 1 year):

$$= \frac{1}{3} \times £200,000 = £66,667$$

If the negative goodwill had been greater than the fair values of the non-monetary assets acquired (£450,000) this could have been written off over the periods expected to benefit.

(iii) Any negative goodwill arising could be credited to profit or loss immediately.

(iv) A combination of (i), (ii) and (iii).

There are a number of ways that negative goodwill could be accounted for, each with its own merits and problems.

IFRS 3 and negative goodwill

IFRS 3 requires that negative goodwill should be recognized immediately as income and included in profit or loss.

However, before concluding that 'negative goodwill' has arisen, IFRS 3 requires that there should be a reassessment of the fair value of the consideration and the fair values of identifiable assets and liabilities acquired.

Example

Horatio plc acquires its investment in Denlon plc in the year ended 31 December 2012. The goodwill on acquisition was calculated as follows:

	£000
Cost of investment	700
Fair value of net assets	900
Negative goodwill	(200)

The negative goodwill figure of £200,000 is recognized as a gain in arriving at profit or loss in the statement of comprehensive income for the year ended 31 December 2012.

International differences

The UK position

Goodwill and intangible assets are regulated by FRS 10. FRS 10 does not allow the inclusion of internally generated goodwill in accounting statements. FRS 10 permits the non-amortization of goodwill if it is expected to be maintained indefinitely. If the goodwill is not amortized, then FRS 10 requires that an annual impairment review be carried out. Where positive purchased goodwill is not expected to be maintained indefinitely it should be amortized over a period not exceeding 20 years.

Negative goodwill up to the fair value of the non-monetary assets acquired should be recognized in profit or loss for the periods in which the non-monetary assets are recovered, either by depreciation or disposal. Any negative goodwill should be recognized in profit or loss for the period expected to benefit.

The US position

US GAAP now requires annual impairment reviews and prohibits amortization.

BASIC

INTERMEDIATE

ADVANCED

3.9 IAS 36 *Impairment of Assets*

Reference to impairment of assets has been made in this and earlier chapters.

If an asset is regarded as being an unallocated expense (or deferred charge) then the principle of deferring charges to future periods means that such deferred charges appear as assets in statements of financial position. The going concern convention assumes that there will be future accounting periods in which such assets can be allocated to profit or loss as expenses. At an intermediate stage in this allocation process, assets will have a carrying amount equal to the unallocated cost. This unallocated cost is more usually referred to as the 'book value' and, in accounting terms, represents the value of the non-monetary benefit yet to be derived from the asset.

If, however, the carrying amount of an asset is greater than the amount that will be gained from the asset's use or from its sale, then to continue carrying the asset at its book value would be imprudent. Where the carrying amount of an asset is greater than this recoverable amount (i.e. the value in use or the asset's fair value less costs to sell), the asset is said to be impaired. If such a situation arises, and if no action is taken, then this would conflict with the prudence convention and could be potentially misleading to users of the accounting statements. IAS 36 *Impairment of Assets* deals with this issue.

Objective

The objective of IAS 36 is to ensure that assets are carried at no more than their recoverable amount. Where the recoverable amount is lower than the carrying value, an impairment loss must be recognized immediately.

Scope of IAS 36

IAS 36 applies to all assets except those that are covered in detail by other international accounting standards. The scope of IAS 36 includes land, buildings, machinery and equipment, investment property carried at cost, intangible assets, goodwill, investments in subsidiaries, associates and joint ventures, and assets carried at revalued amounts under IAS 16 and IAS 38.

IAS 36 does not apply to inventories (IAS 2), assets arising from construction contracts (IAS 11), deferred tax assets (IAS 12), assets arising from employee benefits (IAS 19), financial assets (IAS 39), investment property carried at fair value (IAS 40), certain agricultural assets carried at fair value (IAS 41), insurance contracts assets (IFRS 4) and assets held for resale (IFRS 5).

Key definitions

IAS 36 gives a number of key definitions – many of them interrelated and contained within the definition of other key terms.

(i) *Impairment*: an asset is impaired when its carrying amount exceeds its recoverable amount.

(ii) *Carrying amount:* the amount at which an asset is recognized in the balance sheet after deducting accumulated depreciation (amortization) and accumulated impairment losses.

(iii) *Recoverable amount:* the higher of an asset's fair value less costs to sell (sometimes called net selling price) and its value in use.

(iv) *Fair value:* the amount obtainable from the sale of an asset in an arm's length transaction between knowledgeable, willing parties.

(v) *Value in use:* the discounted present value of estimated future cash flows expected to arise from the continuing use of an asset and from its disposal at the end of its useful life.

Identifying an asset that may be impaired

A review of all assets should be made at the end of each reporting period to look for any indication that an asset may be impaired. This does not mean that the recoverable amount must be determined annually in order to test for impairment. This would involve a great deal of effort and in normal circumstances it is unlikely that many of an entity's assets will actually be impaired. In general therefore, IAS 36 requires entities to determine the recoverable amount of an asset only if there is some indication that the asset might be impaired. IAS 36 has a list of external and internal indicators of impairment. If there is an indication that an asset may be impaired, the recoverable amount of the asset must be calculated.

This is done using a two-stage process:

1. assess at the end of each reporting period (annually) whether there is any *indication* that an asset may be impaired

2. estimate the recoverable amount of the asset if any such indication exists.

Notwithstanding, the recoverable amounts of the following types of intangible asset should be measured annually whether or not there is any indication that they may be impaired:

- an intangible asset with an indefinite useful life
- an intangible asset not yet available for use
- goodwill acquired in a business combination.

Progress Point 3.5

Describe what is meant by impairment. When would an impairment review be carried out?

Solution

Impairment refers to the loss of value of an asset below its book value (i.e. generally, its depreciated cost). It is found by comparing the book value with the recoverable amount. The recoverable amount is the higher of an asset's fair value less costs to sell and its value in use.

An impairment review would be carried out when there is an indication that assets might be impaired. If there are no such indications, there may be no reason to suspect that assets might be impaired.

Indications of impairment (stage 1)

IAS 36 suggests that when assessing whether or not there is any indication that an asset may be impaired, as a *minimum* the following indications should be considered.

External sources

- Where the market value of an asset has declined significantly more than would be expected as a result of either the passage of time or of normal use.
- Where significant technological, market, economic or legal changes have occurred, having an adverse effect on the entity.
- Where market interest rate increases have a bearing on the discount rate used in calculating the value in use of an asset, thereby decreasing its recoverable amount.
- Where the company's stock price is lower than the book value of the net assets.

Internal sources

- Evidence of obsolescence or physical damage of an asset.
- The asset is part of a restructuring or held for disposal.
- Evidence that the economic performance of an asset will be worse than expected.

If any indication of impairment exists then the asset concerned must be tested for impairment by estimating the recoverable amount of the asset and comparing this with the carrying amount. Note that the move to the second stage is necessary only *if* an indication of likely impairment exists.

Determining recoverable amount (stage 2)

The 'recoverable amount' of an asset is the higher of an asset's fair value less costs to sell and its value in use. It follows that *if either* fair value less costs to sell or value in use is greater than the asset's carrying amount, the asset is not impaired.

Also, if the fair value less costs to sell is not obtainable because there is no active market for the asset, then the recoverable amount can be taken as equal to value in use. Conversely, the recoverable amount may be taken as the fair value less costs to sell if the value in use is unlikely to differ materially from the fair value less costs to sell. It is necessary to calculate value in use only if the carrying amount is greater than fair value less costs to sell.

Fair value less costs to sell

The fair value less costs to sell is defined as being the amount obtainable from the sale of an asset in an arm's length transaction between knowledgeable, willing parties, less the costs of disposal. If there is a binding sale agreement, the price under that agreement less costs of disposal should be used as fair value less costs to sell.

If there is an active market for the asset, the market price should be used less costs of disposal. If there is no active market, the best estimate of the asset's fair value less costs of disposal should be used.

Costs of disposal are the direct added costs only. Examples of such costs are legal costs, stamp duty and costs of removing the asset.

Value in use

The value in use of an asset is defined as the present value of estimated future cash flows expected to arise from the continuing use of an asset and from its disposal at the end of its useful life.

The calculation of value in use is therefore likely to be more difficult. However, a detailed calculation of value in use will not be necessary if:

- the fair value less costs to sell is greater than the carrying amount, or
- a simple estimate is sufficient to show that value in use is higher than the carrying amount, or
- value in use is lower than fair value less costs to sell, in which case impairment is measured by reference to fair value less costs to sell.

If value in use does have to be calculated, that calculation should reflect the following elements:

- an estimate of the future cash flows the entity expects to derive from the asset in an arm's length transaction,
- expectations about possible variations in the amount or timing of those future cash flows,
- the time value of money, represented by the current market risk-free rate of interest,
- the price for bearing the uncertainty inherent in the asset, and
- other factors, such as illiquidity, that market participants would reflect in pricing the future cash flows the entity expects to derive from the asset.

Cash flow projections should be based on reasonable and supportable assumptions, and should include projections of cash inflows from the continuing use of the asset, net of projections of cash outflows that are necessarily incurred to generate the cash inflows and that can be directly attributed to the asset. The net cash flows, if any, to be received for the asset at the end of its useful life should also be included. The most recent budgets and forecasts should be used but they must not go beyond five years.

Cash flow projections should relate to the asset in its current condition – future restructurings to which the entity is not committed and expenditure to improve or enhance the asset's performance should not be anticipated.

Discount rate

The discount rate should be the pre-tax rate that reflects current market assessments of the time value of money and the risks specific to the asset.

The discount rate should not reflect risks for which future cash flows have been adjusted, as this would involve double counting.

For impairment of an individual asset or portfolio of assets, the discount rate is the rate the company would pay in a current market transaction to borrow money to buy that specific asset or portfolio.

If a market-determined asset-specific rate is not available, a surrogate must be used that reflects the time value of money over the asset's life as well as country risk, currency risk, price risk and cash flow risk. The following would normally be considered:

- the enterprise's own weighted average cost of capital,
- the enterprise's incremental borrowing rate, and
- other market borrowing rates.

The effect of all of the above considerations means that the appropriate discount rate may be different for different types of asset or different circumstances within the same entity.

Example

KPA is carrying out an impairment review of a piece of production machinery at 31 December 2012. Budgeted information concerning net cash flows for the next three years has been provided by the marketing department as follows:

2013	£35,000
2014	£30,000
2015	£15,000

The production director has estimated that the scrap value of the machinery would be £10,000 in 2015. KPA currently borrows at a rate of 10%.

Value in use is calculated as follows:

	2013	2014	2015	Total
	£	£	£	£
Net cash inflows	35,000	30,000	15,000	
Scrap proceeds	–	–	10,000	
Cash flows	35,000	30,000	25,000	
Discount rate[1]	0.909	0.826	0.751	
Present value	31,815	24,780	18,775	75,370

[1]From tables: present value of £1

i.e. the value in use of the production machinery is £75,370.

Recognition and measurement of impairment losses

After all the complexities of the previous section it is perhaps worth remembering at this point what the objectives of IAS 36 are. They are to ensure that assets are carried at no more than their recoverable amount. In the event the recoverable amount of an asset is less than its carrying amount, the carrying amount of the asset should be reduced to its recoverable amount. That reduction is an impairment loss.

When impairment occurs, a revised carrying amount is calculated as shown in Figure 3.3.

Example 1

As part of the annual review for impairment, a company identifies a machine that, as a result of technological advances, gives concern as to possible impairment. The machine is currently held in the financial statements at £80,000. It is estimated that the machine could be sold for scrap for £50,000. Its value in use has been calculated at £110,000. What value should the asset be carried at in the financial statements?

Impairment occurs when the recoverable amount is less than the carrying amount.

The recoverable amount is the higher of an asset's fair value less costs to sell and its value in use. In this illustration the recoverable amount is £110,000 (i.e. the higher of value in use and net selling price).

The recoverable amount is greater than the carrying amount of £80,000 and therefore no impairment has arisen. The asset will continue to be carried in the financial statements at £80,000.

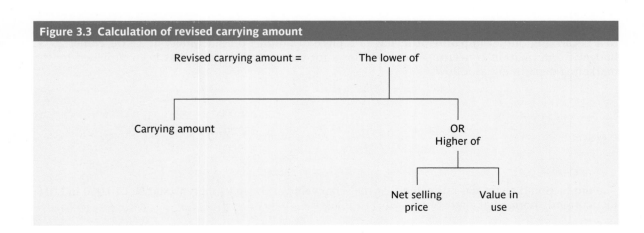

Figure 3.3 Calculation of revised carrying amount

Example 2

Suppose the asset in Example 1 had a value in use of £40,000. What value should the asset be carried at now in the financial statements?

The recoverable amount is now £50,000 – that is, the higher of fair value less costs to sell (£50,000) and value in use (£40,000).

The recoverable amount is now less than the carrying amount and consequently the carrying amount requires to be reduced to the recoverable amount:

	£
Carrying amount	80,000
Recoverable amount	50,000
Impairment loss	30,000

The new carrying amount of the asset will be £50,000 (£80,000 – 30,000).

Progress Point 3.6

Sherton plc purchased a non-current asset for £200,000 in January 2010. Sherton depreciates non-current assets at 15% using the straight line method with a nil residual value. A full year's depreciation is charged in the year of acquisition. At 31 December 2012 the net selling price of the asset is £98,000 and the value in use is estimated at £85,000.

Required

Has an impairment occurred and, if so, how much?

Solution

The net book value (carrying amount) of the asset at 31 December 2012 is:

Cost		£200,000
Less: accumulated depn		
Y/e 31/12/10 (15% × £200,000)	£30,000	
Y/e 31/12/11 (15% × £200,000)	£30,000	
Y/e 31/12/12 (15% × £200,000)	£30,000	
		£90,000
Net book value at 31/12/12		£110,000
Recoverable amount is higher of:		
Net selling price	£98,000	
and		
Value in use	£85,000	
i.e. Net selling price		£98,000
Revised carrying amount is lower of:		
Carrying amount	£110,000	
and		
Recoverable amount	£98,000	
i.e. Recoverable amount		£98,000

As the recoverable amount is £98,000, there has been an impairment of £12,000 (i.e. carrying amount of £110,000 less £98,000).

Recognizing and measuring an impairment loss

An impairment loss should be recognized immediately as an expense in profit or loss unless it relates to a revalued asset where the value changes are recognized as a revaluation decrease.

If the impaired asset has been revalued, the impairment loss is debited to the revaluation reserve and shown as a negative figure in other comprehensive income to the extent of any credit balance previously existing in the revaluation reserve in respect of that same asset. Any excess is then recognized as an expense.

The standard requires that impairment losses should be included in the appropriate line item in the statement of comprehensive income. For example, an impairment loss relating to an item of production machinery would be included within cost of sales. The notes to the statement of comprehensive income would provide the appropriate disclosure. An example of which would be 'Impairment of owned non-current tangible assets'.

It is important to note that the impairment loss should not be included within the depreciation expense. IAS 16 defines depreciation as the systematic allocation of the depreciable amount of an asset over its useful life. The recognition of an impairment loss is as a result of a valuation exercise, rather than an allocation exercise, and should not therefore be presented in such a manner that might encourage the belief that it is part of that allocation i.e. the depreciation expense.

The corresponding credit entries depend on how the carrying amount at which the asset subject to the impairment is determined. This will affect the presentation of the amounts in the non-current assets note.

(a) If the asset is carried on a historical cost basis, the impairment should be included within accumulated depreciation.

BASIC

INTERMEDIATE

ADVANCED

Example
Extract non-current asset note

Accumulated depreciation	
At beginning	X
Charge for year	XX
Impairment charge	YY
At end	XXX

(b) If the asset is carried at market value, the impairment should be included within the revalued carrying amount.

Example
Extract non-current asset note

Cost or Revaluation	
At beginning	X
Additions	XX
Disposals	(XXX)
Impairment adjustment to Revaluation	(YY)
At end	YYY

After an impairment loss has been recognized, the depreciation charge for the asset should be adjusted to allocate the revised carrying amount, net of any expected residual value, over its remaining useful life.

Cash generating units

Wherever possible, individual non-current assets should be tested for impairment. In practice, however, it is rare to be able to identify cash flows arising from a single asset. Often, several assets are interrelated in their usage in a way that makes it impossible to attribute cash inflows to each individual asset. In such cases, cash flows can be seen to be attributable to a collection of assets. Such a collection of assets is called a cash-generating unit (CGU) and is defined as being the smallest identifiable group of assets that generates cash inflows that are largely independent of the cash inflows from other assets or groups of assets.

An example will help to illustrate CGUs.

Example

A company has a three-stage production process:

1. acquisition of raw materials
2. conversion of materials into components
3. assembly of components into finished products.

The company also sells raw materials, but there is no market for components.

The first stage (acquisition of raw materials) is independent of the second and third stages. Moreover, there is an external market for the raw materials and this price can be used for the internal transfers. It is therefore a CGU.

The second stage is dependent upon the products being sold at the third stage because there is no market for the components. The second- and third-stage processes should therefore be combined into a single CGU.

The company has two CGUs: stage 1, and stages 2 and 3 combined. Once the CGU has been identified, the recoverable amount should be calculated and compared with the carrying amount.

Allocation of impairment losses

Where an impairment loss arises, the loss should ideally be set against the specific asset to which it relates. Where the loss cannot be identified as relating to a specific asset, it should be apportioned within the CGU to reduce the most subjective assets first, as follows:

- first, to reduce any goodwill within the CGU
- then, to the other assets of the unit on a pro-rata basis based on the carrying amount of each asset in the unit
- however, no individual asset should be reduced below the highest of
  - its fair value less costs to sell
  - its value in use
  - zero.

The amount of impairment loss that would otherwise have been allocated to the asset should be allocated to the other assets of the unit on a pro rata basis. The effect of this is to:

- eliminate goodwill, but
- to ensure that the carrying amount of any individual asset is not reduced to the extent that it produces an amount not economically relevant to that asset.

Example 1

An impairment review has revealed that a CGU has a value in use of £25 million and a fair value less costs to sell of £23 million.

The carrying values of the net assets comprising the CGU are as follows:

	£000
Goodwill	5,000
Property, plant and equipment	18,000
Net current assets	4,000
	27,000

The review also indicated that an item of plant (included within the figure of £18 million) with a carrying value of £1 million had been severely damaged and was virtually worthless. There was no other evidence of obvious impairment to specific assets.

Calculate the impairment loss and show how it should be dealt with in the accounts.

The impairment loss is the difference between the recoverable amount and the carrying amount.

The recoverable amount is the higher of the fair value less costs to sell and value in use:

Value in use (£25 million) > fair value less costs to sell (£23 million)

∴ recoverable amount is (value in use) £25 million

The recoverable amount (£25 million) is less than the carrying amount (£27 million), therefore impairment exists:

	£000
Carrying value	27,000
Recoverable amount	25,000
Impairment loss	2,000

The impairment loss should be allocated as follows:

- first, against the item of plant specifically identified as being worthless, which has a carrying value of £1 million
- then against the goodwill.

	Carrying value £000	Impairment £000	Revised carrying value £000
Goodwill	5,000	(1,000)	4,000
Property, plant and equipment	18,000	(1,000)	17,000
Net current assets	4,000		4,000
	27,000	(2,000)	25,000

Example 2

A CGU has a carrying value of £190 million. An impairment review shows that the recoverable amount is £130 million and that the intangible assets have a fair value less costs to sell of £20 million.

The assets making up the CGU are as follows:

	£m
Goodwill	25
Intangible assets	45
Tangible assets	120
	190

Calculate the impairment loss and show how this would be allocated.

	£m
Carrying value	190
Recoverable amount	130
Impairment loss	60

	Carrying value £m	Impairment £m	Revised carrying value £m
Goodwill	25	(25)	–
Intangible asset	45	(9.5)	35.5
Tangible assets	120	(25.5)	94.5
	190	(60)	130

The impairment loss of £60m is allocated:

- first to goodwill – £25m
- then to the other assets of the unit on a pro rata basis, based on the carrying amount of each asset in the unit.

$$\text{Intangible assets} \quad \frac{45}{(120 + 45)} \times (60 - 25) = 9.5\text{m}$$

$$\text{Tangible assets} \quad \frac{120}{(120 + 45)} \times 35 = 25.5\text{m}$$

International perspective

The requirements of the UK's FRS 11 are very similar to those of IAS 36, and compliance with the FRS will ensure conformity with IAS 36 in all material respects. However, under FRS 11 an impairment loss is written off in the order:

- first to goodwill,
- then to intangible assets, and
- finally to tangible non-current assets.

In IAS 36, intangible and tangible assets are grouped together.

Under FRS 11, which aims to write down the assets with the most subjective valuations first, no intangible asset with a readily ascertainable market value should be written down below its net realizable value.

Continuing with Example 2, this gives:

	Carrying value £m	Impairment £m	Revised carrying value £m
Goodwill	25	(25)	–
Intangible asset	45	(25)	20
Tangible assets	120	(10)	110
	190	(60)	130

The impairment loss of £60m is allocated:

- first to goodwill
- then to intangible assets – but only so as to reduce them to their net realizable value
- then the remainder to the tangible non-current assets.

That is, the most subjective valuation first, then the next subjective, then, finally, the tangible non-current assets.

Impairment of goodwill

Goodwill is the amount that is left over after applying valuation rules to identifiable assets and liabilities, and comparing this value with the acquisition cost. Goodwill cannot be identified separately, so, by definition, does not generate cash flows independently from other assets or groups of assets. It follows that the recoverable amount of goodwill cannot be determined. Consequently, if there is an indication that goodwill may be impaired, the recoverable amount is determined for the cash generating unit (CGU) to which the goodwill belongs. This recoverable amount is then compared to the carrying amount of this CGU and any impairment loss is recognized.

The allocation of goodwill to CGUs

As the preceding paragraph explains, goodwill is not separately identifiable but instead forms an integral part of CGUs.

IAS 36 requires that the goodwill on acquisition should be allocated to each of the acquirer's CGUs, or group of CGUs, that are expected to benefit from the synergies of the business combination, irrespective of whether other assets of liabilities of the acquiree are assigned to those units or groups of units.

Each unit or group of units to which the goodwill is allocated should:

(a) represent the lowest level within an entity at which the goodwill is monitored for internal management purposes

(b) not be larger than a segment based on either the entity's primary or the entity's secondary reporting format determined in accordance with IAS 14 *Segment Reporting*.

Where goodwill cannot be allocated to individual CGUs:

- calculate any impairment of the assets (excluding goodwill) of individual CGUs,
- identify the smallest group or groups of CGUs (which may be the whole company) to which goodwill can be allocated on a reasonable basis (the 'larger' CGU), and
- then compare the recoverable amount of the larger CGU to its carrying amount (including the carrying amount of allocated goodwill) and recognize any impairment loss.

Example

Robren pays £1,000,000 for the net assets of Henon, which at acquisition has a fair value of £900,000. Henon has two identifiable CGUs and their relative net asset values are £500,000 for CGU A and £400,000 for CGU B. The relative benefits expected from the CGUs are assumed to be in proportion to their net asset values.

The goodwill of £100,000 (£1,000,000 – £900,000) would be allocated as follows:

$$\text{CGU A} \quad \frac{500,000}{900,000} \times £100,000 = 55,555$$

$$\text{CGU B} \qquad \frac{400,000}{900,000} \times £100,000 = 44,445$$

The carrying values of the two CGUs would therefore be the net asset value together with the appropriate allocation of the goodwill on acquisition. That is:

$$\text{CGU A} \qquad £500,000 + £55,555 \quad = £555,55$$

$$\text{CGU B} \qquad £400,000 + £44,445 \quad = £444,44$$

Progress Point 3.7

Malafed plc operates three department stores, which it purchased from a competitor several years ago when goodwill of £2m arose. Each department store is a separate cash generating unit (CGU).

As part of the company's annual impairment review process, the following information at 31 March 2012 is available.

	Store 1	Store 2	Store 3
	£m	£m	£m
Carrying amount	4.1	5.6	3.8
Fair value less costs to sell	3.8	6.0	2.9
Value in use	4.3	5.8	3.2

It has not been possible to allocate goodwill to individual stores. The three stores form the smallest CGU to which the goodwill can be allocated and management monitors goodwill at this combined level.

The recoverable amount of the three stores together is estimated at £13.8m.

Required
What impairments arise?

Solution
As the goodwill cannot be directly allocated, impairment of each individual store (CGU) is calculated excluding goodwill.

	Store 1	Store 2	Store 3
	£m	£m	£m
Carrying amount	4.1	5.6	3.8
Recoverable amount	4.3	6.0	3.2
(Higher of fair value less costs to sell and value-in-use)			
Impairment	–	–	(0.6)

The smallest group of CGUs to which goodwill can be allocated on a reasonable basis is the three stores combined (i.e. the larger CGU).

	£m
Carrying amount (£4.1m + £5.6m + £3.8m)	13.5
Less: impairment	(0.6)
Add: goodwill	2.0
Total carrying amount	14.9
Recoverable amount of three stores combined	13.8
Impairment	1.1

Consequently, goodwill should be reduced by £1.1m (i.e. to £0.9m).

Testing for impairment

IAS 36 requires that goodwill be tested for impairment annually. A cash-generating unit to which goodwill has been allocated shall be tested for impairment at least annually by comparing the carrying amount of the unit, including the goodwill, with the recoverable amount of the unit.

If the recoverable amount of the unit exceeds the carrying amount of the unit, the unit and the goodwill allocated to that unit are not impaired.

If the carrying amount of the unit exceeds the recoverable amount of the unit, the entity must recognize an impairment loss.

The impairment loss should be allocated to reduce the carrying amount of the assets of the unit in the following order:

- first, to goodwill allocated to cash-generating unit
- then to the other assets of the unit on a pro rata basis, based on the carrying amount of each asset in the unit.

The carrying amount of an asset should not be reduced below the *highest* of:

- its fair value less costs to sell (if determinable)
- its value in use (if determinable)
- zero.

The amount of the impairment loss that would otherwise have been allocated to the asset should be allocated to the other assets of the unit on a pro rata basis. The effect of this is to initially eliminate goodwill, but then to ensure that the carrying amount of any individual asset is not reduced to the extent that any amount arrived at is not economically relevant to that asset.

Example

Dupover has identified an indication of impairment and is conducting an impairment review.

Its summarized statement of financial position is:

	£000
Goodwill	600
Property	820
Plant	730
Net current assets	265
	2,415
Share capital and reserves	2,415

The whole of the company is considered to be a cash-generating unit.

The present value of the future cash flows is estimated at £1.2 million and can be taken as being the recoverable amount.

Assuming that the net current assets are at the lower of cost and net realizable value, and that the net realizable value of the property is £900,000, calculate the impairment loss and prepare a revised statement of financial position for Dupover.

Carrying value	£2,415,000
Recoverable amount (present values)	£1,200,000
Impairment loss	£1,215,000

The impairment loss is allocated as follows:

	Carrying value	Impairment	Revised carrying value
	£000	£000	£000
Goodwill	600	(600)	–
Property	820	–	820
Plant	730	(615)	115
Net current assets	265	–	265
	2,415	(1,215)	1,200

The allocation of the loss has been made:

- first to goodwill – £600,000
- then the balance to plant – £615,000.

No allocation of the loss has been made against the property as it has a net realizable value higher than its carrying value.

Similarly, no allocation of the loss has been made against the net current assets as these are already being carried at the lower of cost and net realizable value.

Corporate assets

Corporate assets are defined in IAS 36 as 'assets other than goodwill that contribute to the future cash flows of both the cash generating unit under review and other cash generating units'. Corporate assets include such items as head office buildings, central computing facilities etc. that serve more one CGU. Like goodwill, corporate assets do not generate cash inflows independently of other assets and so must be allocated to CGUs (or groups of CGUs) for impairment testing purposes. In testing a CGU for impairment, an entity should identify all the corporate assets that relate to the CGU under review and allocate on a reasonable and consistent basis, to that unit, a portion of the carrying amounts of these corporate assets.

Example

A graphic design company owns a head office building with a carrying value of £4,000,000. Two distinct CGUs can be identified within the company – production and distribution. It is estimated that the production CGU utilizes 75% of these head office facilities while the distribution CGU uses 25%.

In allocating the corporate asset i.e. head office building to the two CGUs it would seem reasonable, based upon each CGU's usage of the facilities, to allocate 75% of the carrying amount of the head office building (£3,000,000) to the production CGU, and 25% (£1,000,000) to the distribution CGU.

If it becomes necessary to test a CGU (or group of CGUs) for impairment, the procedure is as follows:

(a) An individual CGU to which a portion of corporate assets has been allocated should be tested for impairment by comparing its carrying amount (including the portion of corporate assets allocated to that unit) with its recoverable amount.

(b) A group of CGUs to which a portion of corporate assets has been allocated should be tested for impairment by comparing the carrying amount of the group (including the portion of corporate assets allocated to that group) with the group's recoverable amount.

(c) An individual CGU to which no portion of corporate assets has been allocated should be tested by comparing the CGUs carrying amount (excluding the corporate assets) with its recoverable amount in the usual way.

Progress Point 3.8

Jackson Ltd acquired 100% of the ordinary share capital of James Ltd for £10 million on 1 January Year 1. This figure included £960,000 for goodwill. Jackson Ltd is preparing group accounts for the year to 31 December Year 5 and, due to a decline in the market conditions, has decided to carry out an impairment review of the non-current assets and goodwill of James Ltd.

James operates in two distinct business areas, which are largely independent, one is services to the oil industry and the other is the operation of a rail franchise. The following assets have been attributed to these activities as follows:

	Oil services £000	Rail franchise £000
Non-current assets:		
Tangible	10,000	6,900
Intangible	0	1,200

All assets are held at depreciated cost. The following items have still to be allocated:

- head office property with a net book value of £3,200,000; it is estimated that this can be split 60:40 between oil and rail
- goodwill – it is estimated that 75% of this relates to the rail franchise and the remainder to oil.

The directors estimate that the rail franchise has a fair value less costs to sell of £7,500,000 and oil services a fair value less costs to sell of £9,600,000.

The intangible asset in the rail franchise relates to the net book value of the operating licence associated with the franchise. The following pre-tax cash flows have been estimated for each CGU:

Year	Oil services £000	Rail franchise £000
6	3,000	4,200
7	2,800	3,400
8	2,800	3,400*
9	4,800*	

* The rail franchise expires at the end of Year 9 and the oil services division will be wound up in Year 9. The pre-tax market rate of return for oil services is estimated at 15% and 20% for the rail franchise.

Required

(i) Calculate the total net assets for each CGU.

(ii) Calculate the value in use for each CGU.

(iii) Calculate the impairment (if any) for each CGU.

Solution

(i) Total net assets:

	Oil services £000	Rail franchise £000
As allocated	10,000	8,100
Head office (60 : 40)	1,920	1,280
Goodwill (25 : 75)	240	720
Total net assets	12,160	10,100

(ii) Value in use:

Workings

Oil services	Discount factor (15%)	Cash flow £000	PV £000
Year 6	0.870	3,000	2,610
Year 7	0.756	2,800	2,117
Year 8	0.658	2,800	1,842
Year 9	0.572	4,800	2,746
			9,315

Rail franchise	Discount factor (20%)	Cash flow £000	PV £000
Year 6	0.833	4,200	3,499
Year 7	0.694	3,400	2,360
Year 8	0.579	3,400	1,969
			7,828

(iii) Impairment:

	Oil services	Rail franchise
	£000	£000
Carrying amount of net assets	12,160	10,100
Fair value less costs to sell	9,600	7,500
Value in use	9,315	7,828
Impairment (£12,160 – £9,600)	2,560	
Impairment (£10,100 – £7,828)		2,272

BASIC

INTERMEDIATE

ADVANCED

Progress Point 3.9

Using the same information as in Progress Point 3.8, show how the impairment of the assets would be recorded at 31 December Year 5.

Solution

There is no indication that any specific assets are impaired. The assets are held at cost, therefore losses are recognized in profit or loss in the statement of comprehensive income. The amount of write-down should be included within accumulated depreciation.

Oil services

The impairment loss of £2,560,000 would first be allocated to the goodwill (£240,000) and the balance to tangible non-current assets £2,320,000. Each tangible non-current asset would be written down by 19.46% (2,320/(10,000 + 1,920):

	£000	£000
Dr Impairment loss (S.O.C.I.)	2,560	
Cr Goodwill		240
Cr Tangible non-current assets: accumulated Depreciation		2,320
Being recognition of impairment loss.		

Rail franchise

The impairment should first be allocated to goodwill, then to the other assets. No distinction is made between intangible and tangible assets.

	£000	£000
Dr Impairment loss (S.O.C.I.)	2,272	
Cr Goodwill		720
Cr Intangible assets		199
Cr Tangible non-current assets: accumulated depreciation		1,353
Being recognition of impairment loss.		

Working notes

Total impairment loss to be allocated:	£2,272,000
Less: allocated to goodwill	720,000
Remaining loss	1,552,000

Remaining loss allocated on a pro rata basis based on the carrying amount of each asset in the unit.
  Carrying amount of:

Tangible non-current assets	
As given	6,900
Head office allocation	1,280
	8,180
Intangible assets	1,200

Loss allocated as follows:

	NBV		Remaining loss allocated
Tangible non-current assets	8,180	8,180 × 1,552	1,353
		(8,180 + 1,200)	
Intangible assets	1,200	1,200 × 1,552	
		(8,180 + 1,200)	199
	9,380		1,552

Reversal of an impairment loss

The objective of testing for impairment is to ensure that assets are carried at no more than their recoverable amount in the financial statements. It may be the case, however, that the indicators that gave cause for the original impairment tests – and subsequent impairment losses – now indicate that the reasons for the impairment no longer exist. IAS 36 requires the entity to assess at the end of each reporting period whether there are any indications that these impairment losses have now decreased or no longer exist.

In such a situation, IAS 36 requires that the original impairment loss must be reversed – except where the original impairment loss relates to goodwill.

As with impairment losses, there is a two-stage process to consider:

1. whether there is any indication that an impairment loss recognized in earlier years may have decreased significantly
2. if so, the recoverable amount requires to be calculated.

In assessing whether there is any indication that an impairment loss may no longer exist or has decreased, the entity should consider the following indications:

(a) External sources of information

    (1) The asset's market value has increased significantly during the period.

    (2) Significant and favourable changes have taken place (or will take place in the near future) in the technological market, economic or legal environment in which the entity operates or in the market to which the asset is dedicated.

    (3) Interest rates have decreased during the period which are likely to affect the discount rate used in calculating the asset's value in use and materially increase the asset's recoverable amount.

(b) Internal sources of information

    (1) Significant and favourable changes have taken place (or are expected to take place in the near future) in the extent to which or the manner in which an asset is used.

    (2) Evidence is available that indicates that the economic performance of the asset is, or will be, better than expected.

These indications apply to previously impaired individual assets and to previously impaired CGUs. If any of these indications exist, the recoverable amount of the asset or CGU must be determined once again, with a view to reversing all or part of the previously recognized impairment loss. Note, however, as the standard frequently repeats, that an impairment loss recognized for goodwill shall not be reversed in a subsequent period.

Note also that the impairment loss recognized for an asset can be reversed only where there has been a change in the estimates used to determine the recoverable amount of the asset since the last impairment loss was recognized. In other words, the unusual or extraneous factors that gave rise to the 'extra' drop in accounting value over and above the 'normal' consumption that would have been recorded following that asset's regular accounting treatment, no longer exist.

A reversal of an impairment loss reflects an increase in the estimated service potential of an asset (or CGU), either from use or sale. Examples of such changes in estimates include:

(a) a change in the basis for recoverable amount (i.e. whether recoverable amount is based on fair value less costs to sell or value in use);

(b) if recoverable amount was based on value in use, a change in the amount or timing of estimated future cash flows or in the discount rate; or

(c) if recoverable amount was based on fair value less costs to sell, a change in estimate of the components of fair value less costs of disposal.

If this is the case, the carrying amount of the asset should be increased to its recoverable amount. That increase is the reversal of an impairment loss. It is not simply that the recoverable amount is higher than the carrying amount. The value of an asset in use may become greater than the asset's carrying amount simply because the present values of future cash flows increase as they become closer. There is no change to the service potential of the asset. Consequently, such an impairment loss would not be reversed.

Reversing an impairment loss for an individual asset

The reversal of an impairment loss should not increase the carrying value of an asset above what it would have been if no impairment loss had previously been recognized (i.e. after taking account of normal depreciation that would have been charged had no impairment occurred). It follows that any reversals of impairment losses will not tend to be as large as the original impairment loss. The new carrying value will form the basis for the systematic depreciation of the asset over its remaining useful life.

A reversal of an impairment loss should be recognized immediately in profit or loss unless the asset is carried at a revalued amount under another International Accounting Standard.

Any reversal of an impairment loss of a revalued asset should be treated as a revaluation increase.

Reversing an impairment loss for a cash-generating unit

The required process for allocating the reversal of impairment losses by cash-generating units is the reverse of the sequence required for allocating the original impairment loss.

In allocating the reversal of impairment loss for a cash generating unit, the carrying amount of an asset should not be increased above the lower of:

■ the recoverable amount

■ the carrying amount that would have been determined (net of amortization or depreciation) had no impairment loss been recognized for the asset in prior years.

The amount of the reversal that would otherwise have been allocated to the asset should be allocated to the other assets of the unit, except goodwill, on a pro-rata basis.

Example: reversal of impairment loss

A CGU consists of a production unit with non-current assets, as shown below:

	Carrying amount before impairment £m
Goodwill	40
Intangible assets	20
Tangible non-current assets	80
	140

As a result of the product the production unit makes becoming obsolete, the recoverable amount of the CGU falls to £60m.

The impairment loss is calculated and allocated as follows:

	£m
Carrying value	140
Recoverable amount	60
Impairment loss	80

	Carrying amount before impairment £m	Impairment £m	Revised carrying amount £m
Goodwill	40	(40)	–
Intangible assets	20	(18)	12
Tangible non-current assets	80	(32)	48
	140	(80)	60

The impairment loss would be allocated as follows:

■ first, against goodwill

■ then to the other assets of the CGU, in proportion to their carrying amounts.

Suppose there is a reversal of these economic circumstances because the company makes its own technological advance and the recoverable amount of the CGU is now estimated at £90m. Had the original impairment review not taken place, the tangible non-current assets would have been written down to £70m (i.e. £80m less £10m depreciation). The intangible assets have an indefinite life and have not been amortized.

The value of the CGU after the reversal of the impairment loss would be as follows:

	Carrying amount before reversal of impairment loss £m	Reversal £m	Carrying amount after reversal of impairment loss £m
Goodwill	–	–	–
Intangible assets	–	20	20
Tangible non-current assets	60	10	70
	60	30	90

Notes

1. Goodwill is not restated as this is not permitted by IAS 36.
2. The reversal is allocated to the assets of the unit (except goodwill), pro rata with the carrying amount of those assets.

$$\text{i.e. Intangible assets } 12/60 \times £30m = £6m$$
$$\text{Non-current assets } 48/60 \times £30m = £24m$$

This allocation would, however, result in the carrying amount of the non-current assets being increased to £84m (i.e. £60m + £24m). IAS 36 does not permit the carrying amount of the asset to be increased above the carrying amount that would have been determined (net of depreciation) had no impairment loss been recognized in prior years i.e. £70m. Consequently the reversal is restricted to £10m.

3. The amount of the reversal of the impairment loss that would otherwise have been allocated to the non-current assets is allocated, pro rata, to the other assets of the unit. In this case the remainder of the loss (£20m) is allocated to the intangible assets to restore them to their original carrying amount. Note that because these intangible assets were deemed to have an indefinite life, they were not subject to amortization.

BASIC

INTERMEDIATE

ADVANCED

Progress Point 3.10

A CGU comprising the whole of Kidd Products Ltd became impaired because its products became out of date and unattractive compared to those of competitors. The recoverable amount fell to £25m resulting in an impairment loss of £15m, allocated as follows:

	Carrying amount before impairment based on historic cost £m	Carrying amount after impairment £m
Goodwill	10	–
Tangible non-current assets	30	25
	40	25

The impairment loss of £15m was recognized in profit or loss as the assets were at historic cost.

After two years, the company improves its product range substantially by adding new models and the recoverable amount of the CGU (and company) increases to £35m. The carrying amount of the tangible non-current assets is now £23.5m. The carrying amount of these tangible non-current assets had the impairment not occurred would have been £27m (i.e. they would have continued to have been depreciated).

Required

How should the reversal of the impairment loss be accounted for?

Solution

The reversal of the impairment loss is recognized to the extent that it increases the carrying amount of the tangible non-current assets to what it would have been had the impairment not taken place – that is, a reversal of £3.5m of the impairment loss is recognized in profit or loss, which comprises the difference between the carrying amount of the assets following impairment and the carrying amount of the assets had no impairment taken place (i.e. £27m – £23.5m). The tangible non-current assets will be written back to £27m. Any uplift beyond £27m is a revaluation. If the company wishes to recognize the remainder of the uplift in its statement of financial position, this would be possible if it decides to adopt the revaluation model. Reversal of the impairment in relation to the goodwill is not permitted.

The goodwill issue arising

The rationale for prohibiting the reversal of impairment losses for goodwill can be found with reference to IAS 38 *Intangible Assets*. IAS 38 prohibits the recognition of internally generated goodwill. Given this prohibition, in theory it would be acceptable to reverse an impairment loss relating to previously *purchased* goodwill if the circumstances surrounding the impairment had reversed. In practice, however, there is a practical problem in distinguishing between a reversal of a previous impairment to previously purchased goodwill, and the self-creation of new internally generated goodwill – which cannot be recognized. It is because of this danger of capitalizing internally generated goodwill that the outright prohibition of the recognition of a reversal of an impairment loss for goodwill has been introduced.

Disclosure

The disclosure requirements of IAS 36, although extensive, are quite straightforward and require detailed disclosure by class of assets and by segment: numerical, explanatory and background information.

Disclosure in practice

The required disclosures of IAS 36 Impairment of Assets are normally included in the accounting policies note, the statement of comprehensive income and the notes to the statement of financial position.

Impairment of non-current assets

Goodwill is allocated to cash-generating units for the purpose of impairment testing. The recoverable amount of the cash-generating unit to which the goodwill relates is tested annually for impairment or when events or changes in circumstances indicate that it might be impaired. The carrying values of property, plant and equipment, investments measured using a cost basis and intangible assets other than goodwill are reviewed for impairment only when events indicate the carrying value may be impaired.

In an impairment test, the recoverable amount of the cash-generating unit or asset is estimated to determine the extent of any impairment loss. The recoverable amount is the higher of fair value less costs to sell and the value in use (VIU) to the Group. An impairment loss is recognized to the extent that the carrying value exceeds the recoverable amount and is not subsequently reversed.

In determining a cash-generating unit's or asset's value in use, estimated future cash flows are discounted to their present value using a pre-tax discount rate that reflects current market assessments of the time value of money and risks specific to the cash-generating unit or asset that have not already been included in the estimate of future cash flows.

Source: Logica (2011), pp. 97

Logica's policy on impairment testing is to allocate goodwill to cash-generating units. In addition, the note explains how and when impairment reviews are carried out for both tangible and intangible assets.

Section summary

As with other assets, intangible assets are expected to bring future benefits to the enterprise. Internally generated intangible assets such as employee skills and product design can bring such benefits to the enterprise. The difficulties in quantifying the future benefits – and indeed claiming rights to the benefits – however, prevents them from being classified as non-current assets under the Conceptual Framework's definition. Research expenditure must be written off as incurred; however, under certain circumstances, internally generated development expenditure must be capitalized as an intangible asset.

The IAS 38 definition of intangible assets excludes goodwill. Intangible assets are classified as having indefinite lives or finite lives. Intangible assets with finite lives should be amortized over that life. Intangible assets with indefinite lives should not be amortized but should be assessed for impairment in accordance with IAS 36.

Internally generated goodwill should not be capitalized. Purchased goodwill should be capitalized and not amortized. Instead it should be tested for impairment at least annually in accordance with IAS 36.

The objective of IAS 36 *Impairment of Assets* is to ensure that assets are carried at no more than their recoverable amount. The recoverable amount of an asset is the higher of the fair value less costs to sell or the asset's value in use.

The accounting treatment of goodwill and intangibles has been – and continues to be – the subject of great debate. The next section considers what problems practitioners come up against in practice and some of the other accounting methodologies put forward for dealing with these issues over the years.

Section 3: Advanced Aspects

This section looks in more detail at the measurement and classification issues faced in accounting for intangible assets, the problems surrounding internally generated intangible assets and, in particular, the important distinction and differences between capitalized research and development expenditure, and internally generated goodwill. It will examine in more detail some of the accounting issues and dilemmas arising from intangible assets and goodwill.

3.10 Research and development: problems in practice

In an ideal world it would theoretically be possible to clearly distinguish between the research and development stages of particular projects; to accurately quantify the costs attributable to each stage and therefore the amounts to be capitalized; to accurately determine the future benefits; and to accurately forecast the related pattern of benefits expected to flow from the capitalized expenditure.

The reality of the situation could not be more different.

In practice, the first hurdle of uncertainty to overcome is in respect of the viability of the project itself. Inventors, developers and researchers tend to be notoriously optimistic about their ideas. By their very nature, these individuals are enthusiastic about their projects and often have no real idea as to what the ultimate development costs are likely to be. They are not accountants nor do they understand fully the information that accountants require. Furthermore, accountants are not inventors and consequently have to rely on inventors' assertions for estimates, timescales and future expected benefits. There is therefore the potential for a gulf to develop between the quality of information required by accountants to prepare meaningful figures, and the quality of the information provided by the developers.

Whenever an accountant is faced with uncertainties, a prudent approach needs to be adopted. This can result in those costs attributable to and classified as research costs being expensed for longer into the project than the benefit of hindsight would more accurately determine. This means that the development project will probably be approaching completion before future development costs can be estimated reliably.

BASIC

INTERMEDIATE

ADVANCED

Once the development project has been completed, the next problem is in determining whether sales of the product will be profitable. In many cases, the product is likely to be highly innovative and consequently there will not be a great deal of market data available to assess its profitability. In addition, it is possible that similar products have been developed at the same time, spelling potential competition in the market. As the development in computers has demonstrated, high-technology products command a high price for only a relatively short period of time, as competitive firms develop their own technology and drive the market price down.

Given these uncertainties, the unambiguous, prudent approach would be to write off all research and development expenditure as it occurred. This would remove all doubt as to its accuracy and correctness of classification within the financial statements. This approach could also be potentially very misleading. As has been pointed out, such development expenditure can meet the Conceptual Framework's definition of an asset and therefore to not be classified as an asset can be very misleading indeed.

The difference between expensing such costs and capitalizing them may mean the difference between losses and profits, and an insolvent statement of financial position and a solvent statement of financial position. This potential to vary reported figures adds a further problem for the reporting accountant. As noted above, the accountant may have to rely very heavily on the representations made by the developers of products in his assessment of the appropriate accounting treatment to be adopted. Desperate times may result in desperate measures and, unfortunately, projects may be credited with greater probabilities of success than they should be.

Do the requirements of the standard in relation to research and development expenditure satisfy user needs? As ever, the answer to this depends on the user. The detailed disclosure requirements of IAS 38 in relation to R&D are comprehensive and if adequate detail is provided then there ought to be sufficient information to enable a wide range of users to make economic decisions. From an enterprise's perspective, however, it perhaps, more importantly, allows it to present a more accurate statement of affairs – and a more realistic reflection of its activities.

Research and development in the pharmaceutical industry

Of all the different industries, perhaps the one most synonymous with research and development is the pharmaceutical industry. Companies within the pharmaceutical industry spend considerable amounts on research and development every year and consequently, it would be expected that these companies would carry significant internally generated intangible assets – development assets – in their statements of financial position. However, a review of the financial statements of pharmaceutical companies shows that they consider the uncertainties surrounding the development of pharmaceuticals to be too great to meet the requirements of IAS 38 regarding the capitalization of development costs. The following extracts illustrate this point.

Extract 1: Syngenta International AG
Research and development

Research expenses are charged to the consolidated income statement when incurred. Internal development costs are capitalized as intangible assets only when there is an identifiable asset that can be completed and is expected to generate future economic benefits and when the cost of such an asset can be measured reliably. Due to regulatory and other uncertainties inherent in the development of its key new products, Syngenta currently has no development costs that meet the criteria for recognition.

Costs of purchasing distribution rights, patent rights and licences to use or sell products, or technology or registration data are capitalized as intangible assets. Costs of applying for patents for internally developed products, costs of defending existing patents and costs of challenging patents held by third parties where these are considered invalid, are considered part of development expense and expensed as incurred.

Source: Syngenta International AG (2011), p. 35

Extract 2: Bayer Group
Research and development expenses

A substantial proportion of the Bayer Group's financial resources is invested in research and development. In addition to in-house research and development activities, especially in HealthCare, various research and development collaborations and alliances are maintained with third parties. For accounting purposes, research expenses are defined as costs incurred for current or planned investigations undertaken with the prospect of gaining new scientific or technical knowledge and understanding. Development expenses are defined as costs incurred for the application of research findings or specialist knowledge to production, production methods, services or goods prior to the commencement of commercial production or use. Research costs cannot be capitalized. The conditions for capitalization of development costs are closely defined: an intangible asset must be recognized if, and only if, there is a reasonable certainty of receiving future cash flows that will cover an asset's carrying amount. Since our own development projects are often subject to regulatory approval procedures and other uncertainties, the conditions for the capitalization of costs incurred before receipt of approvals are not normally satisfied.

Research and development expenses mainly comprise the costs for active ingredient discovery, clinical studies, and research and development activities in the areas of application technology and engineering. They also include non-allocable costs for regulatory approvals, approval extensions and field trials.

Source: Bayer Group (2010), p. 157

As can be seen from the above, neither company is in a position to capitalize its development expenditure. This is due to the nature of the research and development activities being undertaken in the pharmaceutical industry. In the case of true 'development' activities the relative lengths of the research and development phases of a project are likely to be very different. It is likely that the technical and economic feasibility criteria will be established very late in the development phase resulting in only a small proportion of the development costs ever being capitalized. Indeed, many drugs require approval by a regulator before they can be put on the market and until that time there may be great uncertainty surrounding their success. Following approval, there is likely to be very little expenditure other than advertising, and companies are precluded by IAS 38 from capitalizing this as part of the asset. The following extract from GSK provides a good example of these issues faced by companies.

Extract 3: GlaxoSmithKline
Research and development

Research and development expenditure is charged to the income statement in the period in which it is incurred. Development expenditure is capitalised when the criteria for recognising an asset are met, usually when a regulatory filing has been made in a major market and approval is considered highly probable. Property, plant and equipment used for research and development is capitalised and depreciated in accordance with the Group's policy.

Source: GlaxoSmithKline (2011), p. 143

Intangible assets – other innovative industries

Although IAS 38 stresses research and development, the standard applies to all intangible assets that are created internally for use by a company itself. Many companies in diverse industries produce intangible assets as a matter of course. For example, software companies produce software, television production companies produce television programmes and newspapers produce newspaper content. Many of these meet the recognition criteria in the standard but no specific guidance is available to help such companies in dealing with the practical problems that arise in dealing with them. As the following extract from Sage Group's accounting policy note shows, the policy simply states the requirements of IAS 38. Note also that the only intangible asset referred to is research and development expenditure.

Extract 4: Sage Group
Internally generated intangible assets – research and development expenditure

Expenditure on research activities is recognized as an expense in the period in which it is incurred. An internally generated intangible asset arising from the development of software is recognized only if all of the following conditions are met:

- It is probable that the asset will create future economic benefits;
- The development costs can be measured reliably;
- Technical feasibility of completing the intangible asset can be demonstrated;
- There is the intention to complete the asset and use or sell it;
- There is the ability to use or sell the asset; and
- Adequate technical, financial and other resources to complete the development and to use or sell the asset are available.

Internally generated intangible assets are amortized over their estimated useful lives which is between three to six years on a straight-line basis. Where no internally generated intangible asset can be recognised, development expenditure is charged to the income statement in the period in which it is incurred.

Source: Sage Group (2011), p. 74

3.11 Intangible assets : a critical appraisal

IAS 38 requires the recognition as an intangible asset of costs arising from the development phase of an internal project. The standard also imposes stringent conditions that restrict recognition. In the Basis for Conclusions section of IAS 38, BCZ40, the IASB concluded that there should be no difference between the requirements for:

(a) intangible assets that are acquired externally; and

(b) internally generated intangible assets whether they arise from development activities or other types of activities.

The IASB have also concluded that the recognition criteria are met implicitly for acquired intangible assets and, therefore, it is for the company to demonstrate explicitly that they are met in the case of the internally generated intangible assets.

There is, however, an inconsistency inherent in IAS 38 that results in a different treatment of acquired versus internally generated intangible assets. The cost of an acquired intangible asset will reflect its total costs – research, development and advertising and other costs which were incurred by the vendor – some of which may or may not have been capitalized in the vendor's own financial statements. Internally developed intangible assets can only be recognized when they meet the strict – and indeed subjective – recognition criteria in IAS 38. A key enhancing qualitative characteristic of useful accounting information is comparability. It is clear that, under IAS 38, it would be possible to have two companies with identical intangible assets being carried at very different amounts depending on whether the intangible asset had been purchased or self-created. Furthermore, it would be possible to have disparity between two companies who self-created identical intangible assets depending on when each company concluded that the recognition criteria for the intangible asset had been met. Ultimately these are subjective decisions which depend upon many variables.

A solution to this problem is, of course, to require companies to carry their intangible assets at fair value. At present, IAS 38 permits the revaluation of an intangible asset only when an active market for that intangible asset exists. The problem therefore arises not from any underlying doubt of the value attaching to internally generated intangibles, but more simply from our inability to value these intangibles reliably. The challenge therefore will be to find an acceptable, logical and consistent method that can be used to value all intangibles that have worth, without excluding those whose valuations present too many difficulties. As it currently stands, while IAS 38 has been drafted as unambiguously as may reasonably be expected, it does not provide a logically consistent treatment of intangible assets.

Internally generated goodwill vs purchased goodwill: a critical appraisal

IAS 38 prohibits the recognition of internally generated goodwill. Purchased goodwill is dealt with under IFRS 3, which states that it must not be amortized but instead requires to be subject to an annual impairment review.

It is worth considering what purchased goodwill actually represents. IFRS 3 defines goodwill as 'future economic benefits arising from assets that are not capable of being individually identified and separately recognized'. Purchased goodwill is therefore the amount paid for these future economic benefits.

As far as the acquiring company is concerned, it will be acquiring, and indeed disclosing as an intangible asset, the purchased goodwill. As far as the acquiree company is concerned, this 'goodwill' is not something that has simply arisen as a result of its sale. The goodwill may have been in existence for a long time, the terms of the accounting standards prohibiting its recognition. What this gives rise to is effectively the same asset, but because of the terms of the IAS, the asset is unrecognized in one set of financial statements yet recognized in the other.

There is, as a consequence, an inconsistent treatment for the same 'asset' (i.e. the goodwill). While the reasons for not allowing the recognition of internally generated goodwill are numerous, nevertheless its non-recognition is undoubtedly leaving a very important asset off many companies' statements of financial position – an asset that will be recognized only when a business combination occurs.

If the internally generated goodwill cannot be capitalized, in order to achieve consistency, any purchased goodwill could be written off immediately. By doing this, however, we are in exactly the same situation. Valuable information will not be being disclosed.

The IFRS 3 requirement not to amortize goodwill also makes the treatment of goodwill inconsistent with the treatment of other assets. Under IFRS 3, a charge is made to profit or loss only when the goodwill becomes impaired. This 'balance sheet' approach concurs with the Conceptual Framework's assertion that 'Expenses are recognized in profit or loss when a decrease in future economic benefits related to a decrease in an asset has arisen.'

This balance sheet approach can itself be open to criticism. An income statement approach would suggest that the goodwill be written off over the period it is expected to produce benefits (i.e. it would be depreciated). Adopting a balance sheet approach to non-current assets would mean that, instead of depreciation being charged, the assets would be written down to their residual values immediately after they come into use.

Adopting a balance sheet approach – and the IFRS 3 requirement not to amortize goodwill – means that the timing of any charge to profit or loss will be incorrect. A charge to profit or loss will be made when the goodwill becomes impaired (i.e. when its recoverable amount falls below its original cost). This effectively means that when profits are being generated, and the recoverable amount exceeds the carrying amount, no element of the original cost will be charged to profit or loss. Conversely, as soon as the goodwill, having been tested for impairment, falls below the carrying amount, a charge will be made to profit or loss to reflect the level of impairment. This treatment results in a charge being made not when profits are being made (and the goodwill being consumed) but instead when profits are not being made (and the goodwill *has* been consumed). The treatment is therefore in conflict with the matching principle.

Is there a solution?

From what appears to be, on first consideration, an impossible task, the solution to the problems of the inconsistency of treatment between internally generated goodwill and purchased goodwill, and the subsequent problem of measurement after initial recognition, may actually be quite simple.

In arriving at the solution, the objectives of financial statements need to be considered. The objectives of financial statements are to provide information about a firm that is useful to a wide range of people making economic decisions. 'Useful information' is information on a company's financial position, performance and liquidity.

The constraints imposed by the standards on what information is presented within traditional financial statements results in the problems detailed above. What is required therefore is an extension to traditional financial statements to allow additional information to be presented in a manner that will remove the lack of comparability caused by the prohibition of capitalizing internally generated goodwill and the subjective problem of its subsequent write-off.

A possible solution

Given the difficulty – indeed the impossibility – of arriving at a meaningful figure for goodwill in the traditional financial statements (i.e. statement of financial position), all goodwill should be written off immediately. Then, in a new separate statement, companies could summarize the current values of the individual assets and liabilities recognized in the statement of financial position and, in addition, provide an estimate of the valuation of the business as a whole – perhaps based on its market capitalization. In other words, companies could use the IFRS 3 definition of goodwill to actually try to disclose it – that goodwill figure being the difference between the market capitalization and the current values of net assets.

The benefits of such an approach are numerous and varied. It removes the problem of distinguishing between purchased and self-generated goodwill, particularly over time. If an efficient market exists then a company's share price will reflect all information relevant to it. This will effectively discount the total goodwill. The fact that no distinction is made between purchased and self-generated goodwill is arguably not relevant. Indeed, a year-on-year comparison would show any changes and deeper investigation made at that point. This treatment also addresses the fungible nature of goodwill – that is, it is not a constant, the constituent 'parts' will vary and the level of purchased/self-generated goodwill will fluctuate over time.

More importantly, however, it addresses many of the issues arising in respect of providing useful information. At the moment there are two extremes: companies with inherent goodwill that is not being disclosed and companies with purchased goodwill that may or may not be carried at the correct amount. This treatment allows a greater level of analysis to be made and arguably discloses a greater wealth of information about a company. For example, if using market capitalization as a benchmark results in a company displaying a high level of goodwill, this could be an indicator of high efficiency. Changes over time could indicate improvements or highlight potential problems. Conversely, low levels of goodwill could be indicators of poor efficiency and under-utilization of resources.

This is not a perfect solution to the goodwill issue. Depending on the size of the company, market capitalization data may not be available. Indeed, for smaller companies whose shares are not actively traded, there will be no such data at all. The method of calculation would, however, be apparent and the resulting information presented would be no more misleading than that which is currently being disclosed by following existing standards' requirements.

3.12 Brand accounting

A **brand** is the registered trade mark of a particular product. Some examples of companies whose names are brands are Mercedes-Benz, Coca-Cola and Microsoft. Brand accounting refers to the practice of including, as separate intangible assets, the amount attributable to brands, including them with the fair values of other identifiable assets acquired, and typically not amortizing them but subjecting them to impairment reviews.

Prior to IAS 38, brand accounting emerged for two main reasons.

First, if brand values were included with the fair values of other identifiable assets acquired, this would mean that the amount of the purchase price attributable to goodwill (i.e. the premium over the fair value of net assets) would be reduced:

Goodwill = purchase price – fair value of net assets acquired including brands

Reducing the goodwill figure had a twofold effect:

1. it reduced the charge to the profit or loss in respect of the amortization of the goodwill, and
2. there was no charge to profit or loss in respect of the brand, as brands were not usually amortized.

Second, non-acquisitive companies that created self-generated brands argued that their statements of financial position would be strengthened if they were permitted to include a valuation of these brands.

The first argument was effectively dealt with in IFRS 3 and IAS 38. That is, goodwill should not be amortized but should instead be subject to an impairment review; intangible assets with indefinite useful lives should not be amortized but should also be subject to an impairment review. The second argument is more familiar. As with other intangible assets, the accounting issues which arise with brands are in relation to their reliable measurement; no one doubts that brand names have significant economic values – and in certain industry sectors they are of overwhelming importance to the success of the company. The debate is not on that issue; it is once more on whether it is within the ability of the current Conceptual Framework to capture and convey useful information about such assets.

In relation to internally generated brands, IAS 38 maintains that some internally generated items, such as brands, are not capable of being distinguished from the cost of developing the business as a whole and are therefore prohibited from being capitalized as internally generated intangible assets. If, however, brands are purchased either individually, or as part of a business combination, they may meet the recognition criteria and therefore may be recognized. Indeed, IAS 38 was amended in 2008 so as to be clear that it should always be possible to reach a reliable measure of the fair value of an intangible asset acquired in a business combination. The effect of this amendment was to remove the possibility of arguing for the non-recognition of such intangible assets on the basis that their value cannot be measured reliably.

Section summary

The current requirements of IAS 38 and IFRS 3 can result in valuable information being omitted from company statements of financial position. The failure to recognize internally generated goodwill and other intangible assets means that the value of those assets is excluded from the traditional financial statements.

A solution to this problem has been put forward in the form of an extension to the traditional accounting statements to include an attempt at an objective goodwill calculation with reference to market capitalization and valuations of current net assets in the statement of financial position.

The provision of useful information to a wide range of users, to enable economic decisions to be made, is not being achieved by following the current standards' requirements. As historical analysis shows, over the years, firms have been aware of the values of their intangible assets. Brand accounting developed as a mechanism to detach the value of brands from goodwill, and hence strengthen statements of financial position and reduce charges to profit or loss.

Chapter summary

IAS 38 *Intangible Assets*

- An intangible asset is an identifiable, non-monetary asset without physical substance.
- Intangible assets should be recognized where it is:
  (i) probable that future economic benefits will flow to the enterprise, and
  (ii) cost can be measured reliably.
- All research costs should be charged as expenses.
- Development costs are capitalized only after the technical and commercial feasibility of the asset for sale or use has been established.
- Costs treated as expenses cannot subsequently be capitalized.
- Brands, mastheads, publishing titles, customer lists and items similar in substance that are internally generated should not be recognized as assets.
- Internally generated goodwill must not be capitalized.
- Initial measurement should be at cost.
- Subsequently, IAS 38 permits two accounting models:
  - cost model – intangible assets should be carried at cost less any amortization and impairment losses
  - revaluation model – intangible assets for which there is an active market can be carried at fair value.
- Revaluation increases are credited to reserves and recognized as other comprehensive income unless reversing a previous charge to profit or loss.
- Decreases in valuation should be charged to profit or loss unless reversing a previous credit to reserves.

- Intangible assets are classified as having a:
  - (i) finite life – a limited period of benefit to the entity, or an
  - (ii) indefinite life – no foreseeable limit to the period over which the asset is expected to generate net cash inflows for the entity.

- Intangible assets with finite lives should be amortized over the life of the asset:
  - the amortization period and amortization method should be reviewed at least annually
  - the asset should also be assessed for impairment in accordance with IAS 36.

- An intangible asset with an indefinite useful life should not be amortized:
  - a review of the asset's useful life should be carried out annually
  - the asset should also be assessed for impairment in accordance with IAS 36.

IAS 36 *Impairment of Assets*

- An impairment loss is the amount by which the carrying amount of an asset or cash-generating unit (CGU) exceeds its recoverable amount.
- Enterprises are required to check at the end of each reporting period whether there are any indications of impairment.
- If an indication, external or internal, of impairment exists, the asset's recoverable amount must be calculated.
- The recoverable amount of an asset or CGU is the higher of its fair value less costs to sell and its value in use.
- The recoverable amounts of the following types of intangible assets should be measured annually:
  - an intangible asset with an indefinite useful life
  - an intangible asset not yet available for use
  - goodwill acquired in a business combination.

- The recoverable amount should be determined for the individual asset if possible.
- If it is not possible to determine the recoverable amount for the individual asset, the recoverable amount for the asset's cash-generating unit (CGU) should be determined.
- An impairment loss should be recognized whenever recoverable amount is below carrying amount.
- The impairment loss should be recognized immediately as an expense in profit or loss unless it relates to a revalued asset where the value changes are recognized as a revaluation decrease.
- Where an impairment loss arises, the loss should ideally be set against the specific asset to which it relates.
- Where the loss cannot be identified as relating to a specific asset, it should be allocated to reduce the carrying amount of the assets of the CGU in the following order:
  - first to reduce any goodwill within the CGU
  - then, to the other assets of the unit on a pro rata basis, based on the carrying amount of each asset in the unit.

- The carrying amount of an asset should not be reduced below the highest of:
  - its fair value less costs to sell
  - its value in use
  - zero.

- If the preceding rule is applied, further allocation of the impairment loss is made pro rata to the other assets of the unit.
- Impairment losses should be reversed under certain circumstances. Enterprises should assess at the end of each reporting period whether there is an indication that an impairment loss may have decreased. If so, the recoverable amount should be calculated.

- The increased carrying amount due to reversal should not be more than the depreciated historical cost would have been had the impairment not been recognized.
- Reversal of an impairment loss is recognized as income in profit or loss unless the asset is carried at a revalued amount, in which case it should be treated as a revaluation increase.
- Reversal of an impairment loss for goodwill is prohibited.

✓ Key terms for review

Definitions can be found in the glossary at the end of the book.

Amortization	Costs of disposal	Intangible asset
Brand	Development	Research
Cash-generating unit	Fair value less costs to sell	Value in use

? Review questions

1. Define the term intangible asset and explain the main features of this definition.
2. How should an intangible asset be measured at initial recognition if it is acquired in a separate transaction?
3. In connection with IAS 38 *Intangible Assets*:
   (a) distinguish between *research* expenditure and *development* expenditure
   (b) explain the accounting treatment required by IAS 38 in relation to each of these types of expenditure.
4. Give some examples of intangible asset that are unlikely to be included in financial statements, and the reason for their exclusion.
5. Explain the effects of using the cost model and the revaluation model for the measurement of intangible assets subsequent to their initial recognition.
6. What is goodwill, and how does it arise?
7. Explain the requirements of IFRS 3 in relation to goodwill.
8. Define the term *impairment loss*.
9. List the main indications which would suggest that an asset might be impaired.
10. Which assets must always be tested for impairment even though there are no indications that impairment has occurred?
11. What is the *recoverable amount* of an asset?

✏ Exercises

Level II

1. The following information relates to Entrepreneurial Enterprises plc.
   (i) Purchased a brand in 1995 for £2 million. The directors believe the brand is now worth £7 million.
   (ii) Acquired a patent in January 2007, with ten years left to run, for £350,000.
   (iii) Bought a fishing quota to catch 1,000 tonnes of fish for £1,000 per tonne on 1 January 2012. The market value for the quota, for which there is an active market, was £1,400 per tonne on 31 December 2012.

(iv) Acquired a bus operating licence on 30 June 2012 to operate routes for the next eight years. The initial price paid was £480,000. A further £120,000 is payable on 1 January 2013. In addition, the company directors and senior management spent time (costed at £80,000) in developing the bid.

(v) A major advertising campaign was carried out in the autumn of 2012. The directors believe the main benefits of this will arise in 2013.

(vi) The accounting policy of the company in respect of intangible assets is as follows.

(a) Amortization:

On a straight-line basis over:	
Quota	20 years
Brands	20 years
Patents, licences, etc.	remaining legal life when acquired

(b) Valuation:

- Intangible assets for which there is an active market are revalued annually.

Required

Explain how each of the above items should be dealt with in the accounts of Entrepreneurial Enterprises plc for the year to 31 December 2012, and prepare the journal entries to show the adjustments for each of the items in preparing the accounts to 31 December 2012.

2. During the course of a year Venture Forth Ltd incurred expenditure on many research and development activities. Details of two of them are given below.

Project 3

To develop a new compound in view of the anticipated shortage of raw material currently being used in one of the company's processes. Sufficient progress has been made to suggest that the new company can be produced at a cost comparable to that of the existing raw material.

Project 4

To improve the yield of an important manufacturing operation of the company. At present, material input with a cost of £100,000 p.a. becomes contaminated in the operation and half is wasted. Sufficient progress has been made for the scientists to predict an improvement so that only 20% will be wasted.

The directors of Venture Forth Ltd consider that both projects will be successful. In addition, the company has enough finances to complete both projects and enough capacity to see both projects through to a successful conclusion.

Costs incurred during the year were:

Project	3	4
	£	£
Staff salaries	5,000	10,000
Overheads (direct)	6,000	12,000
Plant at cost (life 10 years)	10,000	20,000

Required

In relation to IAS 38 *Intangible Assets*,

(a) define

(i) research, and

(ii) development

(b) say under what circumstances it would be appropriate to defer development expenditure to future periods

(c) show how the expenditure on Projects 3 and 4 would be dealt with in the statement of financial position and statement of comprehensive income in accordance with IAS 38 *Intangible Assets*.

3. Wyse Associates Limited has recently embarked on several projects designed to expand its business in the future. During the year to 30 June 2013, the following information is available regarding two of the projects.

Project A

Cost of £80,000 was incurred in substantially improving an existing product with a view to making it safer and with fewer side effects. Tests were still ongoing at 30 June, but it was hoped to market the product in time for Christmas 2013. In addition to the above £80,000, a special analysis machine has been purchased costing £50,000, which has a useful life of four years with a residual value of £10,000. This will be used to carry out a range of research activities over its useful life.

Project B

The company has spent £60,000 investigating possible alternative raw materials with similar properties that it could use instead of asbestos. It also purchased a machine to assist in analysing the properties of various alternative materials, for £30,000. It is the company's intention to spend another two years researching into this field. At the end of this time, if the search for an alternative to asbestos has not proved fruitful, it will research into making asbestos safer to use.

Required

Discuss how the expenditure on Projects A and B would be dealt with in the company's accounts for the year to 30 June 2013, and justify your decisions.

4. Montezemolo Engineering produces highly sensitive thermostatic switchgear for use in aeronautic and satellite production. As chief accountant at Montezemolo, you have been given the following information by the director of research in respect of the year ended 30 September 2012.

Project F550

This project commenced on 1 October 2011. By December 2011, the viability of the project was confirmed and it was agreed that the final product would be produced for sale. Costs incurred to 30 September 2012 amounted to £200,000, of which 25% relate to research expenditure and 75% to development expenditure.

Additional further costs to complete the development are £350,000 and these will be incurred in the year to 30 September 2013. The first sales are expected on 1 October 2013.

It was necessary to purchase a highly specialized electronic analyser, which was to be used initially to test production prototypes, then, when production commences, the analyser will be used to ensure the correct operation of the completed thermostatic switchgear. Given the highly specialist nature of the analyser it would be used only on Project F550. The analyser was purchased on 1 January 2012 at a cost of £2,500,000, has an estimated useful life of six years and a forecast residual value of £100,000. Montezemolo Engineering charges a full year's depreciation in the year of purchase.

The board of directors considers that this project will be similar to the other projects the company undertakes and is confident of a successful outcome. Sales forecasts have been prepared following completion as shown:

	£000
Year to 30 September 2014	1,000
Year to 30 September 2015	1,000
Year to 30 September 2016	1,000
Year to 30 September 2017	1,000

It is estimated that the final product would have a sales life of four years.

The company has sufficient finance to complete the development and enough capacity to produce the new product.

Required

Show how the expenditure on Project F550 would be dealt with in the statement of comprehensive income and statement of financial position of Montezemolo Engineering for each of the years ending 30 September 2012 to 30 September 2017 inclusive. Extract entries only are required.

5. Main Enterprises Ltd ('Main') is a farm management company operating in central Scotland. An innovative management approach by the directors has seen the diversification of the business into a number of new areas.
The following information is available in respect of the year ended 31 December 2012.

   (i) Main purchased a suckler cow quota for 100 cows for £250 per cow on 1 January 2012. There is an active market for suckler cow quotas, which must be owned to enable an application for subsidy income to be made. On 31 December 2012, the market value of the quota was £300 per cow.

   (ii) On 1 April 2009, Main acquired an operator's licence for a fleet of 20 heavy goods vehicles to set up a haulage division. Main had rented out several of its farm sheds to manufacturing companies and it had identified a further source of revenue by offering a haulage service to the tenants. The price paid for the licence, which is for five years, was £3,000 per vehicle. In addition to the initial price, Main spends £4,000 each year advertising the haulage division. Main received the invoice for the year ended 31 December 2012 from the advertising agency in January 2013.

   (iii) On 1 July 2010, Main purchased for £28,000 shooting rights which entitle the company to seven years' shooting on a nearby estate. The managing director uses this primarily for corporate entertaining. The rights are non-transferable during the seven-year period and therefore there is no active market.

   (iv) During the year to 31 December 2012, Main began the development of a new type of organic crop spray. The costs incurred on this project in the year amounted to £40,000. The book-keeper, who was unsure how to classify this expenditure, has posted it to a suspense account. The research manager believes that the product will be both technically feasible and commercially viable. However, the product is still at an early stage and it is not certain how long it will be before it can be marketed.

The accounting policy of the company in respect of intangible assets is:

   ■ intangible assets with an active market are revalued on an annual basis
   ■ intangible assets are amortized on a straight line basis over 20 years or their estimated useful lives, whichever is the lower, on a monthly basis.

Required

   (a) Explain how each of the items 1 to 4 should be dealt with in the accounts of Main for the year ended 31 December 2012, and prepare the journal entries required.

   (b) Prepare the disclosure note in respect of 'intangible assets' for inclusion in Main's financial statements for the year ended 31 December 2012.

6. Bartpart plc has 800 hectares of agricultural land among its non-current assets at cost of £4,400,000 as at 30 June 2013.
Owing to the general downturn in the agricultural sector, the directors have carried out an impairment review.
The land has been rented out at an annual rent of £400 per hectare with five-yearly rental reviews. The rent has recently been renegotiated for the five years commencing 1 July 2013 at an annual rent of £350 per hectare.
Agricultural valuers have estimated that the land would realize £4,000 per hectare on a sale at 1 July 2013. The required rate of return for Bartpart plc is 7%.

Required

Advise the directors if an impairment has occurred and, if so, provide the accounting entry required to reflect the impairment in the accounts for the year to 30 June 2013.

Note: Land is assumed to have an indefinite life. The rental income should also be indefinite.

7. Ernon plc has identified an indication of impairment and is conducting an impairment review. Its summarized statement of financial position at 31 March 2013 is as follows:

	£000
Goodwill	600
Property	820
Plant and equipment	730
Net current assets	265
	2,415
Share capital and reserves	2,415

The whole of the company is considered to be a single cash-generating unit (CGU). The net current assets have been valued at the lower of cost and net realizable value, and the net realizable value of the property is £900,000. The plant and equipment is estimated to have a sale value of £115,000. The value in use is estimated to be £1.4 million.

Required

Calculate whether an impairment loss has occurred and, if so, prepare a revised statement of financial position for Ernon plc as at 31 March 2013. Explain your workings fully.

8. Shankers Ltd has carried out an impairment review of its telecommunications division. The assets allocated to the division were as follows:

	£000
Property, plant and equipment	15,100
Intangible assets	2,300
Goodwill	1,100
	18,500

The net selling price has been estimated at £14m and value in use calculated at £14.4m.

Required

Compare the allocation of any impairment loss in the telecommunications division of Shankers Ltd under IAS 36 with that under FRS 11.

9. JAJ Industries plc operates a number of businesses. Evidence suggests that one of these may have impaired assets. The following information has been obtained:

CGU	Construction	Haulage	Maintenance
	£m	£m	£m
Carrying amount	3.1	2.6	1.8
Net selling price	2.5	2.1	2.0
Value in use	2.7	1.7	1.9

In addition to the carrying amount of the assets allocated to the above cash generating units there is goodwill of £2.3m. The goodwill relates to construction and haulage, but it is not possible to allocate it between the two. It is estimated that the combined recoverable amount of construction and haulage is £5.0m.

None of the assets has previously been revalued.

Required

Calculate, and prepare journal entries, for any impairment of:

(a) the individual cash generating units, and

(b) the goodwill relating to construction and haulage.

Level III

10. CMG Exporting Ltd revalued a tangible non-current asset from net book value £1m (cost £2m, depreciation £1m) to £2.5m on 31 December 2009. The asset's remaining useful life is ten years from the date of revaluation. It is company policy to make reserve transfers annually in respect of the difference between the depreciation charge on revalued and historical cost amounts. Owing to a downturn in economic conditions, the asset suffered an impairment loss of £1.15m at 31 December 2012.

Required

How should the above be treated in the accounts for the four years from 31 December 2009 to 31 December 2012?

11. Elimax plc has recently been acquired by a new owner, who has installed a new management team. Elimax has faced difficult trading activities in the past few years and the new finance director has doubts about the value of some of the assets in the statement of financial position. Elimax consists of two divisions, which currently employ the following net assets:

	Estate agency division £000	Public relations division £000
Non-current assets		
Tangible	16,750	15,900
Intangible	400	–
Goodwill	–	620
	17,150	16,520

In addition the company has central tangible non-current assets of £4,500,000. These are estimated to be equally related to the two divisions. None of the assets has been revalued in the past.

The intangible asset of the estate agency division relates to the cost of a trade mark acquired from a competitor several years ago. It is estimated that the trade mark has a net selling price of £380,000.

Both divisions have suffered from under-investment in recent years.

The net fair value of the estate agency division is estimated to be £13,500,000, and £12,000,000 for the public relations division.

Budgeted pre-tax cash flows for the next four years are as follows:

	Estate agency £000	Public relations £000
Year 1	3,800	4,700
Year 2	3,900	4,750
Year 3	5,500	5,300
Year 4	5,200	6,000

The required rate of return is 14% for both divisions. The significant increases in cash flow will arise from the impact of the new management team. There will be no significant cash flows from the assets employed in each division after Year 4.

Required

(a) Calculate the extent of any impairment in either division.

(b) Prepare a schedule of adjustments to the net assets of each division.

Discount factors at 14% are:

Year	Factor
1	0.877
2	0.769
3	0.675
4	0.592

References

Bayer Group (2010) *Annual Report*.
FAS 86 *Accounting for the Costs of Computer Software to be Sold, Leased or Otherwise Marketed*. FASB Framework for the Presentation and Preparation of Financial Statements. IASB, 1989.
GlaxoSmithKline (2011) *Annual Report*.
IAS 36 *Impairment of Assets*. IASB, 2009.
IAS 38 *Intangible Assets*. IASB, 2009.
IFRS 3 *Business Combinations*. IASB, 2008.
Logica (2011) *Annual Report and Accounts*.
Sage Group (2011) *Annual Report and Accounts*.
Syngenta International AG (2011) *Financial Report*.

Further reading

Baker C.R. (2001) *Impairment tests for goodwill instead of amortization: the potential impact on British Companies*. Colchester, University of Essex Department of Accounting, Finance and Management.
Barwise P., Higson C., Likierman A. and Marsh P. (1989) *Accounting for Brands*. ICAEW, June.
Finance directors say yes to brand valuation. *Accountancy*, January 1990.
Goodacre A. and McGrath J. (1997) An experimental study of analysts' reactions to corporate R & D expenditure. *British Accounting Review*.
IAS 8 *Accounting Policies, Change in Accounting Estimates and Errors*, IASB, revised 2003.
IAS 14 *Segment Reporting*. IASB, 1997. Superseded by IFRS 8 *Operating Segments*, IASB, 2006.
IAS 16 *Property, Plant and Equipment*. IASB, amended 2012.
IAS 20 *Accounting for Government Grants and Disclosure of Government Assistance*. IASB, amended 2008.

Chapter 4

Leases

Introduction

The decision by companies to invest in new equipment can often be very complex. Once a company has identified a need for a particular asset there are a number of options open to the company on how to acquire the asset.

If the company has enough cash available then the asset could be bought for cash. If not, the company may obtain a bank loan to finance the purchase of the asset, or perhaps buy it on hire purchase. Another alternative is for the company to rent the asset for a period of time. Such rentals are commonly known as leases.

Section 1: Basic Principles

A lease is a contract between two parties: a *lessor* and a *lessee*. The lessor is the legal owner of the asset and the lessee rents the asset from the lessor. The lessor keeps the ownership of the asset and agrees to rent the asset to the lessee for an agreed period of time in return for a rental payment. Examples of assets that can be the subject of a lease agreement include motor vehicles, aeroplanes, ships, machines and computer equipment.

4.1 Why might a company choose to lease an asset?

There are several reasons why a company may choose to lease a particular asset rather than buy it and these include those discussed below.

- It permits flexibility.

An asset may be leased for a specific period of time. A company that needs a particular asset for a specific time period can lease the asset for that specific time period. This avoids the company having to buy the asset and then having to sell it at the end of its period of use. By tailoring the lease agreement to its specific needs, a company can have the use of the asset for the optimum length of time.

- It avoids obsolescence.

Many assets become obsolete in relatively short time periods. This problem is particularly relevant to computers and computer equipment. By leasing computer equipment rather than buying it, companies will have up-to-date equipment and can avoid the problem of outdated technology.

- It gives tax advantages.

Certain tax advantages are available when assets are leased rather than purchased. In the UK, for example, tax allowances are granted at 18% of the asset's costs per annum on a reducing balance basis. Lease rentals can attract 100% relief of payments made against tax.

- It improves cash flow.

Although a company may buy an asset for cash, such a decision very often would put a strain on the company's cash resources. Many companies would not have sufficient cash reserves to finance asset purchases this way. Indeed, even if the purchase of the asset was financed by borrowing, there is usually a deposit to be paid. Leasing avoids the need for companies to find relatively large sums of cash either to buy the asset outright or for deposits, and so helps the cash position of the company.

Progress Point 4.1

Outline four different ways in which a business may obtain the use of an asset.

Solution

A business may obtain the use of an asset by: (i) outright purchase if it has cash funds available; (ii) purchase using a bank loan; (iii) hire purchase; or (iv) entering into a lease agreement whereby the asset is rented for a specific period of time.

4.2 The accounting issues involved

Where a company acquires assets outright, or through bank loans or hire purchase arrangements, then the assets belong to the company and are therefore disclosed in that company's statement of financial position. Where assets are leased, then these assets belong to the lessor and their use is simply being granted to the lessee in return for a rental payment.

The accounting problems that arise with leases are in the definition of assets and what is disclosed in a company's financial statements.

As noted above, a lease is a rental and, as such, rental payments are expensed through profit or loss. If, however, the terms of the lease agreement are of sufficient length and obligation such that it permits the lessee to use the item as if it had bought the item, then the financial statements will omit valuable information if the lease payments are simply treated as expenses.

The financial statements will not show that the company is using the particular asset, nor will they show that the company has an obligation to make future lease payments.

Example

Company A and Company B are firms producing the same manufactured product. The policy of Company A is to buy equipment, whereas the policy of Company B is to lease equipment. Company A borrows £50,000 from its bank to finance the purchase of a machine, while Company B leases the identical machine on a long-term lease from Company C.

The statement of financial position of Company A will be as follows:

Company A Statement of financial position			
Non-current assets: machine	£50,000	Loan	£50,000

That is, there will be an asset and a corresponding loan.

Company B, because it is leasing the asset, and because the ownership of the asset will remain with the lessor (Company C), will not record any information regarding the leased asset in its statement of financial position. There will be no evidence that Company B is using this particular asset, other than the fact that lease rentals are shown as expenses in the statement of comprehensive income.

It could be argued that in order to provide users with information to help them make correct and meaningful decisions, Company B should disclose in its statement of financial position the facts that:

- it is using this particular machine, and
- it has an obligation to make lease payments in the future.

If so, then a more informative statement of financial position for Company B could be produced as follows:

Company B Statement of financial position			
Leased assets	£50,000	Lease creditor	£50,000

By adopting this treatment a fairer comparison can be made between Company A and Company B. Indeed, unless such a treatment is adopted, any comparison between Company A and Company B using financial ratios – for example, return on capital employed (ROCE) – will be distorted. In addition, the liabilities of a company leasing the equipment will be understated.

4.3 Accounting for leases

We have seen in Chapter 2 that non-current assets have been defined as resources controlled by an entity as a result of past events and from which future economic benefits are expected to flow to the entity. Note that there is no reference to ownership.

It follows from this that where a lease agreement allows the lessee company to use the item for most of its useful life, requires the lessee company to pay the full cost (possibly more than the purchase price of the item) and to look after the item as though it had been purchased by the lessee, then in terms of the *substance* of the transaction, it is clear that the lessee company would be in the same position in terms of deriving benefit from the usage of the asset as if it actually *owned* the asset.

Moreover, the requirement to make lease payments greater than the normal purchase price of the asset means that the lessee company is effectively in the same economic position *as if* it had taken out a loan to purchase the asset at an agreed rate of interest.

In such circumstances, the economic substance of the transaction is that the lessee company has both:

- an asset, *and*
- a liability to make future payments.

However, the legal ownership, by virtue of the legal form of the lease agreement, remains with the lessor.

In order to take account of the substance of the leasing arrangement, rather than the legal form, it could be argued that the lessee company ought to record both the leased asset and the obligation to pay the future rentals in its statement of financial position. The lessor company will record the asset as sales revenue and as a receivable in its statement of financial position.

This treatment will allow greater comparability between companies who purchase assets and those companies leasing identical assets. The statements of financial position will show:

- the underlying assets in use by the lessee company (whether owned or not), and
- the liabilities associated with such leasing contracts.

The 'value' of the leased asset can be measured. The purchase price of the asset will be available (i.e. fair value) and the lease payments will be quantified by reference to the lease agreement. Any lease payments made in excess of the purchase price of the asset will represent the cost of leasing the asset. This cost is effectively the same charge as a bank or other lender would impose in lending to finance the purchase of an asset – in other words, interest.

Given that such information is available within the financial statements, it seems reasonable to proceed on the basis that where a lease agreement essentially conveys all the risks and rewards of ownership of an asset to the lessee company, then from an accounting point of view, the asset should be treated as a 'legal purchase'. This would imply that the leased item would be included in the statement of financial position of the lessee company as an asset, while the obligation to pay the lease rentals would be recorded as a liability.

Progress Point 4.2

Explain why the substance of a leasing transaction rather than its legal form should determine the accounting treatment used to record it in the financial statements.

Solution

If the terms of a lease are such that the lessee has effective ownership of the asset, then although out-right ownership does not transfer, it is as if the lessee has acquired the asset. In such circumstances, by following the substance of the transaction it could be argued that valuable information is being disclosed by showing the leased item as an asset with a corresponding lease creditor (i.e. the financial statements will disclose the assets in use by the business together with details of its current and future lease obligations). If the legal form were adopted then no such asset would be shown and therefore it could be argued that valuable information is being omitted from the financial statements with regard to assets in use and future lease obligations.

Example

A machine is leased for a period of four years at a rate of £1,000 per year payable in advance. The machine could have been purchased outright for £3,486.

The machine is recorded in the financial statements as:

- an asset (at cost) – £3,486
- an obligation to pay – £3,486.

Over the period of the lease, the total lease payments will amount to £4,000 (4 × £1,000). The difference between these total lease payments (£4,000) and the cost of the machine (£3,486) is the interest charge of £514. This interest charge is essentially a charge for the deferred credit being extended by the company.

Each lease payment of £1,000 would consist of two elements:

1. a capital element that will go towards reducing the lease obligation, and
2. an interest element, charged to profit or loss, reflecting the finance charge payable on the outstanding lease obligation.

Allocating the interest

Having calculated the interest charge, this amount now requires to be allocated to profit or loss according to the matching principle. This would allocate the interest charge over the period being financed. One method of doing this is by the straight line method.

Straight line method

Continuing with the above example, the annual interest charge to profit or loss would be calculated as follows:

$$\frac{£514}{3 \text{ years}} = £171 \text{ per year}$$

Note that because the first lease payment is in advance, the number of periods being financed is only three (i.e. the final lease payment will fall just after the end of the third period). Had payments been made in arrears, the number of periods financed would have equalled the number of payments.

The annual rentals would be apportioned as follows:

Period	Total rental	Finance charge	Capital repayment
	£	£	£
1	1,000	171	829
2	1,000	171	829
3	1,000	172	828
4	1,000	–	1,000
	4,000	514	3,486

Note that the total capital repayment corresponds to the originating lease obligation. The above transactions would be reflected in the financial statements as follows:

Statement of comprehensive income	
Period	Finance charge
	£
1	171
2	171
3	172
4	–

BASIC

INTERMEDIATE

ADVANCED

Statement of financial position	
End of period	Lease obligation
	£
1	2,657
2	1,828
3	1,000
4	–

Sum of digits method

This is an alternative method of allocating the interest. The annual allocation of the interest charge is calculated by relating the remaining number of periods being financed to the total number of periods being financed.

As before, the number of periods being financed is three and the sum of the digits is therefore 6, i.e. (3 + 2 + 1).

The following formula can be used to establish the sum of the digits.

$$S = \frac{n(n + 1)}{2}$$

Where n = number of periods being financed.

The finance charge is found by applying the 'relevant digit' to the finance charge.

In this example the allocation would be:

Period	Relevant digit	Finance charge	Workings
		£	
1	3/6	257	(3/6 × 514)
2	2/6	171	(2/6 × 514)
3	1/6	86	(1/6 × 514)
4	–	–	

Using the sum of digits method, the annual rentals of £1,000 would be apportioned as follows:

Period	Total rental	Finance charge	Capital repayment
	£	£	£
1	1,000	257	743
2	1,000	171	829
3	1,000	86	914
4	1,000	–	1,000
	4,000	514	3,486

Note again that the total capital repayment corresponds to the originating lease obligation, and these would be reflected in the financial statements as follows:

Statement of comprehensive income	
Period	Finance charge
	£
1	257
2	171
3	86
4	–

Statement of financial position		
End of period	Lease obligation	
	£	
1	2,743	(3,486 – 743) i.e. originating creditor less capital repayment
2	1,914	(2,743 – 829) b/f creditor less capital repayment
3	1,000	(1,914 – 914) b/f creditor less capital repayment
4	–	

Actuarial method

Another alternative allocation method that could be used is the actuarial method. The actuarial method allocates the interest charge to the accounting periods so as to produce a constant periodic rate of charge on the remaining balance of the lease obligation.

Continuing with the example:

(i) the cash price of our asset is £3,486

(ii) this represents the present value at an implied interest rate of four annual rentals payable in advance, of £1,000

(iii) the present value of the first rental is £1,000 (i.e. it is payable now)

(iv) it follows that £2,486 (£3,486 – £1,000) = the present value at implied interest rate of three rentals of £1,000

(v) therefore 2,486/1,000 = 0.248 = present value at implied interest rate of three rentals of £1.00

(vi) using present value of annuity of £1 tables, the interest rate is 10%.

The total interest charge of £514 will be allocated as follows:

Period	Capital sum at start of period	Rental Paid	Capital sum during period	Finance charge (10%)	Capital sum at end of period
	£	£	£	£	£
1	3,486	1,000	2,486	249	2,735
2	2,735	1,000	1,735	174	1,909
3	1,909	1,000	909	91	1,000
4	1,000	1,000	–	–	–
				514	

The interest charge of 10% is applied to the capital sum outstanding during each period. Because the first instalment is paid immediately, interest only accrues on the balance of £2,486 which is repaid with 3 instalments of £1,000 each. As the capital sum reduces, so too does the interest charged on that capital sum.

The finance charges will be shown in the statement of comprehensive income while the capital sums at the end of each reporting period will be shown in the statement of financial position.

Discounting and present value

It is perhaps worth pausing at this point to consider further what is meant by present value. The IASB refers to discounting and present value in a number of standards, and therefore an understanding of present value calculations is necessary to fully understand the requirement of those standards.

The concept of present value is concerned with the fact that money has a 'time value'. In other words, an amount of money received today will be worth more than the same amount of money in, for example, a year's time. This is because it is possible to invest money and it will therefore grow. For example, if money can be invested at 10% p.a., each £1 invested will grow to become £1.10 in one year's time. If the money is invested for a further year, it will become £1.21 in two year's time, and so on [£1.10 + (£1.10 × 10%)]. It can be said, therefore, that in present value terms, £1.21 to be received two years from now is worth £1.00 in today's terms (assuming a rate of interest of 10%).

The process of determining the present value of an amount to be received (or paid) in the future is known as 'discounting' and involves multiplying the amount concerned by a discount factor. Discount factors can either be calculated or found within present value tables.

Comparison of leasing methods

The interest/capital split is different under each method because different assumptions have been made about how interest is incurred (see Table 4.1). Both the actuarial method and sum of digits method allocate the interest in relation to the capital amount outstanding during the period. As this is in effect how a bank would charge interest on a loan then these methods would seem to be the preferred methods. The straight line method, although simpler to use, does not make any reference to the capital amount outstanding and therefore does not produce as comparable a result.

Depreciating a leased asset

In addition to the interest cost, the other item that requires to be recorded in the financial statements is depreciation. As the asset in the example is being leased over four years, if a straight line depreciation policy is adopted the annual charge will be:

$$\frac{£3,486}{4 \text{ years}} = £871 \text{ p.a.}$$

Table 4.1 Comparison of statement of comprehensive income charges under each method

Period	Actuarial			Sum of digits			Straight line		
	Depn	Finance	Total charge	Depn	Finance	Total Charge	Depn	Finance	Total charge
	£	£	£	£	£	£	£	£	£
1	871	249	1,120	871	257	1,128	871	171	1,042
2	871	174	1,045	871	171	1,042	871	171	1,042
3	871	91	962	871	86	957	871	172	1,043
4	873	–	873	873	–	873	873	–	873
	3,486	514	4,000	3,486	514	4,000	3,486	514	4,000

Note that the total lease payments of £4,000 (i.e. 4 × £1,000) have been charged to profit or loss, regardless of the method used, in a combination of depreciation (reflecting the usage of the asset) and the finance charge (reflecting the interest payable on the outstanding lease obligation).

4.4 The accounting issue revisited

It is worth recapping the reasons for adopting the substance over form treatment of leases – that is, capitalizing the leased assets and including as liabilities the obligations to make future lease payments. Comparing the total charges to profit or loss (depreciation and interest charges under the actuarial method) with the actual lease payments made gives the following result:

Period	Depreciation + finance charge	Lease payment	Difference
	£	£	£
1	1,120	1,000	+ 120
2	1,045	1,000	+ 45
3	962	1,000	– 38
4	873	1,000	– 127
	4,000	4,000	0

The differences are not significant although the higher depreciation and finance charges compared to the lease payments in the earlier periods tend to concur with the concept of the asset providing a greater benefit to the company when the asset is new, and that benefit diminishing as the asset ages.

It is the statement of financial position, however, that provides the user with the otherwise 'hidden' information. From an informational point of view the user can now see the assets the company is using to generate income. If accounting ratios are to be calculated using total assets then it is clear that, without capitalizing leased assets, comparison with similar companies that purchase assets would not be possible. Similarly, without adopting the substance over form approach, the obligations to make such lease payments would not be disclosed either. It should also be noted that the amounts disclosed as lease obligations are not the actual amounts payable but rather the present value of the future amounts payable, discounted at the interest rate implicit in the lease. In the actuarial example given above, the obligations under finance leases at the end of period 1 are £2,735. The actual payments still to be made at that point are £3,000 (three payments of £1,000).

So why the fuss?

The informational value of capitalizing leases is clear: both assets in use and future obligations to pay are disclosed. Such informational value is not, however, always welcomed. A traditional attraction of leasing assets, and indeed one of the perceived benefits, is that of 'off balance sheet' financing. Off balance sheet financing is the use of assets and related obligations not being disclosed within the financial statements.

The analysis thus far has been based upon the lease agreement conveying benefits to the lessee to such an extent that it is as if the lessee actually owns the asset. Clearly not all leases convey the risks and rewards to such an extent. Where this is not the case it may be that an alternative accounting treatment is required.

In such cases, it may be appropriate to treat the rental payments as costs, and charge them as expenses in arriving at profit or loss. The problem is identifying at which particular point the lease ought to be capitalized rather than expensed. If such a point is made too prescriptive then companies may well attempt to

Progress Point 4.3

A company enters into a lease on 1 January 2012. The following information is available regarding the lease and the asset that is the subject of the lease. Show the effect of this lease on the financial statements.

Company's reporting period end	31 December
Date of lease	1 January 2012
Value of leased asset if purchased (fair value)	£12,500
Term of lease	3 years
Rentals half-yearly in advance	£2,500
Implied interest rate (given)	7.93%
Depreciation policy	straight line

(a) Identify the capital value.

(b) Calculate the total rentals.

(c) Calculate the total finance charge.

(d) Calculate the periodic finance charge.

(e) Show the rentals apportioned between capital and revenue.

(f) Calculate the depreciation.

(g) Show the effect on the statement of comprehensive income and the statement of financial position

Solution

(a) Capital value in this case is the fair value: £12,500.

(b) Total rentals are £2,500 × 6 = £15,000.

(c) Total finance charge is total rentals, £15,000, less capital value: £12,500 = £2,500.

(d) Periodic finance charge is calculated as follows:

Period	Capital sum at start £	Rental paid £	Capital sum during period £	Finance charge (7.93%) £	Capital sum at end of period £
1/1/12	12,500	2,500	10,000	793	10,793
1/7/12	10,793	2,500	8,293	658	8,951
				1,451	
1/1/13	8,951	2,500	6,451	511	6,962
1/7/13	6,962	2,500	4,462	354	4,816
				865	
1/1/14	4,816	2,500	2,316	184	2,500
1/7/14	2,500	2,500	–	–	–
				184	
				2,500	

Note that, in this example, the rentals are paid in advance.

(e) Rentals are apportioned between capital and interest (finance charge) as follows:

	Capital £	Interest £	Total £
2012	3,549	1,451	5,000
2013	4,135	865	5,000
2014	4,816	184	5,000

(f) Depreciation is calculated as follows:

Lease term 3 years

Annual depreciation (straight line) $\dfrac{12,500}{3} = £4,167$ p.a.

(g) Effect on reported figures in annual accounts:

Statement of comprehensive income		
	Depreciation £	Finance charge £
Y/e 31/12/12	4,167	1,451
Y/e 31/12/13	4,167	865
Y/e 31/12/14	4,166	184

Statement of financial position			
Non-current assets	Cost	Accumulated depreciation	NBV
	£	£	£
Y/e 31/12/12	12,500	4,167	8,333
Y/e 31/12/13	12,500	8,334	4,166
Y/e 31/12/14	12,500	12,500	–
Obligations under leases	£		
Y/e 31/12/12	8,951		
Y/e 31/12/13	4,816		
Y/e 31/12/14	nil		

Section summary

The issue of accounting for leases can be summarized very simply. If a lease agreement essentially conveys all the risks and rewards of ownership to the lessee then the accounting treatment proceeds as if it were an actual 'legal' purchase. This ensures that the assets in use by a company are disclosed and that the associated obligations inherent within leasing agreements are also adequately disclosed.

'push the boundaries' to be able to disclose lease obligations in such a way as to provide maximum benefit for the company. This issue is considered at length in the next section.

Section 2: Intermediate Issues

This section develops some of the ideas from Section 1. In particular, it examines how leases may be classified. The section also explains the requirements of IAS 17 *Leases*. The section concludes with an overview of the treatment of leases, and examines the distinction of operating and finance leases from the point of view of the IASB.

4.5 Classification of leases

When leases are disclosed as assets together with the corresponding liability to pay the obligations under a lease, such information is of more value to a user of financial statements. Such leases are referred to as finance leases. Leases that do not convey such ownership rights, and are therefore not disclosed as assets in the statement of financial position, are referred to as operating leases. In the case of operating leases, payments made for lease rentals are expensed in arriving at profit or loss for the period under review.

Example

AWF plc is a manufacturing company that prepares accounts to 31 December each year. The company negotiates a lease to begin on 1 January 2012 with the following terms:

Terms of lease	4 years
Annual payments	£4,000
Useful life of machine	10 years
Age of machine on 1 January 2012	3 years
Purchase price of new machine	£35,000

In this example the lease applies to only part of the asset's useful life. Such a lease is classed as an operating lease. The lessor will be able to lease the asset again at the end of the lease term agreed with AWF plc.

The statement of comprehensive income entry for AWF plc is as follows:

Statement of comprehensive income	
Operating lease rentals	£4,000

Operating lease rentals should be charged to profit or loss on a straight line basis over the term of the lease unless another systematic basis is more representative of the time pattern of the user's benefit. If the charge for the period does not equal the payments made, accruals and prepayments can arise.

No asset or lease obligation will be recorded in the statement of financial position. This is an example of 'off balance sheet' financing. In this case there is a debt that is not shown as a liability on the face of the statement of financial position.

Because the classification of a lease as an operating lease will often present a better picture of financial gearing, lessees will often prefer to have a lease classified as an operating lease rather than as a finance lease. Consequently, many leasing companies will structure the specific conditions of their contracts in an attempt to ensure that a lease would not fall to be classified as a finance lease. The classification of a lease is based on an analysis of those terms of the lease agreement that are likely to have commercial effect, and ignores those terms that are not likely to have commercial effect.

Progress Point 4.4

Explain how the accounting treatment for operating leases differs from the accounting treatment for finance leases.

Solution

The accounting treatment of leases classified as finance leases results in an asset being capitalized in the financial statements with a corresponding lease creditor.

In the case of a lease that is classified as an operating lease, the payments made for the lease rentals will be expensed in arriving at profit or loss in the statement of comprehensive income, and no asset or liability will be recognized.

In practice all leases transfer some of the risks and rewards of ownership to the lessee, and the distinction between a finance lease and an operating lease is essentially one of degree.

The question that must now be considered is where exactly the dividing line is between a finance lease and an operating lease. Unfortunately, the dividing line is not always clear cut. The key test, which is applied in practice, is whether or not the lessee faces the same risks and rewards as an owner. If the answer is yes, the lease is judged to be a finance lease.

4.6 IAS 17 *Leases*

Objective

The objective of IAS 17 is to prescribe, for lessees and lessors, the appropriate accounting policies and disclosure to apply in relation to leases.

Definitions

From an accounting perspective the distinction between operating and finance leases is particularly important. Under international accounting rules the two types of lease are accounted for very differently. Appendix 4.1, at the end of this chapter, contains detailed provisions from IAS 17:

- a lease is an agreement whereby the lessor conveys to the lessee in return for a payment or series of payments the right to use an asset for an agreed period of time
- a finance lease is a lease that transfers *substantially all* the risks and rewards incidental to ownership of an asset; title may or may not be transferred
- an operating lease is a lease other than a finance lease.

Classification of leases

The classification of leases adopted in IAS 17 is based on the extent to which risks and rewards incidental to ownership of a leased asset lie with the lessor or the lessee. The risks of ownership can be identified as:

- losses from idle capacity or technological obsolescence
- asset breakdown
- repairs
- theft.

The rewards of ownership are those benefits derived from the asset while in use by the lessee.

Unfortunately, IAS 17 does not define 'substantially all', however, it does give a number of situations that 'would normally' point to a lease being classified as a finance lease:

(i) ownership of asset transferred to lessee by end of lease

(ii) bargain purchase option at end of lease

(iii) lease term is a major part of economic life of asset

(iv) present value of the minimum lease payments amounts to substantially all of asset fair value (see below)

(v) leased asset of a specialized nature (specific to lessee).

IAS 17 also provides situations that 'could' point to a lease being classified as a finance lease:

(i) if lessee cancels lease, lessee bears lessor's losses associated with cancellation

(ii) gains/losses in residual value fall to lessee

(iii) lessee can continue lease for secondary period at low rent (bargain rental option).

It is worth noting that some national GAAPs take a more numerical approach. For instance, the USA and Germany require that at the inception (start) of the lease, the present value of the minimum lease payments must be 90% or more of the fair value of the asset. The UK suggests that 90% or more gives the 'presumption' of a finance lease but that the determining factor is 'substantially all' and not 90%.

The attractions of a numerical approach are clear. It is an objective benchmark and one that auditors can calculate exactly. Unfortunately, a cleverly worded lease could be drawn up such that the present value of the minimum lease payments falls just short of the benchmark and a company could argue that the lease did not therefore require to be capitalized.

It is for reasons like this that a definition based on an ownership concept is perhaps more beneficial.

Finance leases: minimum lease payments

One of the major criteria for deciding whether or not a lease is a finance lease is the total minimum amounts payable under the lease contract. In the substance over form approach, a contractual requirement to make payments greater than the cost of the leased asset effectively places the lessee in the same economic position as if the asset had been acquired at arm's length through a loan under agreed repayment and interest terms. This 'arm's length' value is known as the 'fair value' and the excess paid over the fair value is the interest.

There are instances, however, where the minimum lease payments are less than the fair value of the asset and, as has been noted, some national GAAPs take a numerical approach to lease classification.

An example of such a situation would be where a lessor company has, by virtue of perhaps bulk ordering, been able to negotiate substantial discounts on the purchase of assets and some of this discount is being passed on to the lessee by way of a favourable lease rental.

Another example may be where the lessor, at the end of the lease, has a market for the asset and effectively 'discounts' the lease for the future sales proceeds.

Progress Point 4.5

(a) Explain the difference between a finance lease and an operating lease.

(b) Petter acquires three identical pieces of machinery for use in his factory on the same day.

    (i) Machine 1 is rented from Busco at a cost of £250 per month payable in advance and terminable at any time by either party.

    (ii) Machine 2 is rented from CB Dobco at a cost of eight half-yearly payments in advance of £1,500.

    (iii) Machine 3 is rented from Adenco at a cost of six half-yearly payments in advance of £1,200.

The cash price of this type of machine is £8,000 and its estimated life is four years.

    Explain how the leases would be classified.

Solution

(a) A finance lease is a lease that transfers substantially all the risks and rewards of ownership of an asset to the lessee. Such a transfer is normally assumed to have taken place when at the inception of the lease the present value of the minimum lease payments amounts to substantially all (90% or more) of the fair value of the leased asset. Present value is computed using the interest rate implicit in the lease. This assumption may be refuted by other evidence. An operating lease is any lease other than a finance lease (i.e. one that fails to meet the above conditions).

(b)

    (i) Machine 1 is held on an operating lease – the contract is terminable at any time and so there is no transfer of the risks or rewards of ownership.

    (ii) Machine 2 involves total lease payments of £12,000. Although we have not been given details of the interest rate implicit in the lease, the present value of the lease payments will almost certainly be more than the £8,000 fair value of the asset. Machine 2 is therefore held on a finance lease.

    (iii) Machine 3 involves a total payment of £7,200. Again, although we have not been given details of the interest rate, the present value will be significantly lower than £8,000 and certainly less than 90% of the fair value (i.e. £8,000 × 90% = £7,200). This would mean that Machine 3 is held on an operating lease.

Leases in the financial statements of lessees

Finance leases

Initial recognition

IAS 17 requires that lessees should recognize finance leases as assets and liabilities in their statements of financial position at amounts equal at the inception of the lease to:

- the fair value of the leased property or, if lower
- at the present value of the minimum lease payments.

Fair value is the amount for which an asset could be exchanged, or a liability settled, between knowledge-able, willing parties in an arm's length transaction. In calculating the present value of the minimum lease payments, the discount rate is the interest rate implicit in the lease, if this is practicable to determine.

Example

A machine is leased for four years at a rental of £1,000 per year payable in advance. The fair value (i.e. cash price) of the machine is £3,828. The interest rate implicit in the lease is 10%.

Fair value = £3,828.

Present value of minimum lease payments (£1,000 + (1,000 × 2.486)) = £3,486 (from present value tables). The machine would be capitalized in the financial statements at the lower of the two values (i.e. £3,486).

Implicit interest rate

It may be the case that the implicit interest rate is not practicable to determine, in which case the lessee's incremental borrowing rate should be used.

This situation is not uncommon. Remember that the interest rate is determined by the lessor and not the lessee. Moreover, the terms that are set by the lessor will be determined by many factors, including the lessor's own tax position, the price the lessor paid for the asset, the expected residual value of the asset and the lessor's own expected profits on the transaction.

Any initial direct costs of the lessee should also be added to the amount of the asset. Initial direct costs are incremental costs that are directly attributable to negotiating and arranging a lease, and include costs such as legal costs and professional fees.

Subsequent measurement

Minimum lease payments should be apportioned between the finance charge and the reduction of the outstanding liability. IAS 17 requires that this finance charge should be allocated to each period during the lease term so as to produce a constant periodic rate of interest or the remaining balance of the liability i.e. the actuarial method. In practice, however, IAS 17 allows a lessee to use some form of approximation to simplify the calculation e.g. sum-of-the-digits method.

Depreciating a finance lease asset

A leased asset, if capitalized, requires to be depreciated.

The period over which the asset should be depreciated will depend upon the expected useful life of the asset and the terms of the lease itself. For example, if an asset has an expected useful life of five years but is being leased for only four years, it would not be appropriate to depreciate the asset over the longer term. This would understate the depreciation charge reflecting the usage of the asset.

The length of term of the lease can, in practice, be more complicated to determine. Many leases consist of two distinct parts:

1. the primary term, which is usually non-cancellable, and
2. the secondary term for which the lessee has the option to continue to lease the asset with or without payment.

When calculating the length of term of the lease at the outset, a company will require to make a judgement as to what its intentions are likely to be at the end of the primary term. Unless it is reasonably certain that the option to continue leasing the asset beyond the primary term will be exercised, the secondary period should be ignored.

As a general rule the asset should be depreciated over the shorter of the lease term and the asset's useful life.

Example

(i) A company enters into a finance lease for a machine with a useful life of five years. The primary term of the lease is three years and the company expects to return the asset at the end of that primary term.

The company should depreciate the asset over three years (i.e. the shorter of the lease term and the asset's useful life).

(ii) Suppose at the outset of the lease the company had the option to continue leasing the asset for a further two years after the primary term and thought it highly likely that it would do so.

The company would depreciate the asset over five years (i.e. in this instance the lease term and the useful life are the same and so the capitalized cost would be written off over the longer term). To be prudent the secondary term should be included only when it is reasonably certain at the commencement of the lease that it will be taken up.

(iii) Suppose that at the outset of the lease the company planned to take full advantage of the secondary term and lease the asset for an indefinite period until the asset wears out.

The company would depreciate the asset over five years. Although the secondary term is indefinite, the asset's useful life is five years. The asset is expected to be used, therefore, for five years.

Note from the above example that the useful life relates to the expected situation for the lessee. The useful life can exceed the lease term. This is because the current lessee may or may not be the only user.

Residual values

It is not uncommon at the end of a lease, for the lessor to sell the leased asset, and to pass back to the lessee some or all of the sales proceeds. This is known as the lessee having an interest in the residual value and can vary between 0% and 100%. Where a lessee has a 100% interest in the residual value, this means that it will receive back from the lessor 100% of the sales proceeds of the asset.

At the outset of a lease, therefore, where it is anticipated that the lessee will return the asset to the lessor and will share in the sales proceeds, the depreciation charge should reflect this in the same way as if the lessee company were disposing of an owned asset (i.e. it would take account of any expected residual values at disposal).

Example

Cost of asset	£50,000
Primary lease term	8 years
Expected residual value at end of primary term	£2,000
Lessee's interest in residual value	100%
Secondary lease term	Indefinite
Residual value at end of secondary term	Nil
Estimated useful life of asset	10 years

Situation 1

At the outset of the lease the lessee intends to use the asset for the period of the primary lease term only. The depreciation will be calculated as follows:

$$\frac{£50,000 - £2,000}{8 \text{ years}} = £6,000 \text{ per annum}$$

Situation 2

The lessee intends to use the asset for an indefinite period until the asset wears out. The secondary term is indefinite but the useful life is ten years. The asset is expected to be used therefore for ten years. The depreciation charge would be:

$$\frac{£50,000 - £0}{10 \text{ years}} = £5,000 \text{ per annum}$$

Remember that the secondary term is included only when at the commencement of the lease it is reasonably certain that it will be taken up; and remember also that the asset will be depreciated over the *shorter* of the lease term and the asset's useful life.

BASIC

INTERMEDIATE

ADVANCED

Progress Point 4.6

Statco acquires a loader with a fair value of £45,000 on a finance lease from Demenco, a specialist supplier of lifting machinery. Lease payments are £10,000 per annum for five years payable in advance (i.e. the first payment is made on taking delivery of the asset). The interest rate implicit in the lease is 10%. Demenco, being a specialist supplier, is able to obtain bulk discounts on machinery and its policy is to pass such discounts on to the lessee. In addition, at the end of the lease, the loader is expected to have a residual value of £2,500, which will be passed to the lessee as a refund of rentals.

At what value should Statco capitalize the loader in its financial statements, and what will be the depreciable amount?

Solution

IAS 17 requires that lessees should capitalize leased assets at the lower of

- the fair value of the leased asset, or
- the present value of the minimum lease payments.

The present value of the minimum lease payments discounted at 10% can be calculated using the present value of £1 in n years' time.

Payment date	Present value of £1	Present value of £10,000 payment
On delivery	1.000	£10,000
In 1 year	0.909	£9,090
In 2 years	0.826	£8,260
In 3 years	0.751	£7,510
In 4 years	0.683	£6,830
Present value of minimum lease payments		£41,690

The fair value of the loader is £45,000. The present value of the minimum lease payments is £41,690. Statco is required to capitalize the loader at the lower of these amounts (i.e. £41,690).

> The depreciable amount is calculated as being the capitalized cost less residual value (i.e. £41,690 – £2,500 = £39,190).
>
> Note that the expected residual of £2,500 does not affect the value at which the asset is capitalized. The expected residual affects the depreciation policy of the lessee only as regards the capitalized asset. Statco will depreciate the loader to an expected residual of £2,500, and any difference between this net book value figure and the amount received by the lessee will give rise to a gain or loss on disposal of the asset.

Classification of land and buildings

Land and buildings can be the subject of leases and are classified as operating and finance leases in the same way as other leased assets. This means that, depending upon the terms of the lease, land and buildings could be shown as assets in a company's statement of financial position.

Under the terms of a 'true' lease, ownership never passes to the lessee, although many lease arrangements are such that the title of the asset subject to the lease is transferred to the lessee at the end of the lease term. This is likely to be the case when the present value of the minimum lease payments has effectively 'paid' the lessor for the asset and satisfied the lessor's profit objective. Moreover, the useful life of the leased asset at the end of the lease term is likely to be very limited and perhaps may even have expired.

A characteristic of land, however, is that it normally has an indefinite economic useful life. Therefore, if legal title is not due to pass to the lessee by the end of the lease term, then substantially all of the risks and rewards of ownership have not been transferred. The lease of land would therefore be classified as an operating lease.

This means, therefore, that where a lessee enters into a land and buildings lease, and title is not due to pass to the lessee, the lease should be classified into two leases: a land lease, which is an operating lease, and a buildings lease, which could be an operating or finance lease.

Where the lease of land is classified as an operating lease and the lease of buildings as a finance lease, the minimum lease payments should be allocated between land and buildings in proportion to the fair values of each at the inception of the lease.

Land and buildings: from a user's perspective

Of all the assets a company may disclose in its statement of financial position, none provides more information to a user than land and buildings. They are the most tangible of assets, usually the greatest value and, from the point of view of a user of financial statements, the assets that indicate the wealth of a business.

It has been suggested that incorporating leased assets in a company's statement of financial position adds to the informational value provided by the financial statements. This is undoubtedly true when plant and equipment, vehicles and machinery are concerned – such capitalization is essential when comparison between companies that lease and companies that buy assets is attempted. Moreover, the disclosure of the related lease obligations is invaluable information to the user of the financial statements whether the user is an investor, a supplier or a lender.

The distinction made, therefore, between land and buildings, and the subsequent classification between operating leases and finance leases, is extremely important. When reviewing sets of accounts – and in particular the statement of financial position – the non-current asset note is often the schedule on which time is spent.

If accurate classification has not been made, nor adequate disclosure given in the notes that clearly emphasizes the legal form of the transaction, then the information provided, regardless of whether it conforms to the substance of the transaction or not, could be very misleading. The distinction has to be made very clear between a company using land and buildings and a company *owning* land and buildings.

4.7 The impact of capitalization

Prior to IAS 17, one of the major attractions of leasing was the 'off balance sheet' nature of the transaction. A company could have the use of – and generate income from – an asset that was not disclosed in its statement of financial position. Moreover, the related lease obligations – which could be substantial – were also not disclosed.

The capitalization of finance leases effectively means that key accounting ratios such as gearing, return on assets and return on investment are substantially affected.

Example

Satnav Logistics, a delivery company, currently leases its fleet of delivery vehicles. Cleverly worded lease agreements have ensured that the leases all qualify as operating leases and all lease payments have been treated as revenue expenditure. The managing director asks you to show the impact of capitalizing the leases on the financial statements and on key ratios.

The annual lease payments are £120,000 per annum.

The fair value of the leased vehicles is £309,250, and you have calculated that in the current year the depreciation charge on the vehicles would be £103,083 and that, if capitalized, the leases would give rise to a finance interest charge of £24,740. At the end of the year the obligations under leases were £102,881 due within one year, and £111,109 due after one year.

The financial statements before and after capitalization are as follows:

Statement of comprehensive income

BEFORE	£	AFTER	£
Turnover	3,000,000	Turnover	3,000,000
Operating profit	100,000	Operating profit	100,000
Interest charge	5,000	Add: lease rentals[1]	120,000
	95,000		220,000
		Less: extra depn[2]	103,083
		Adjusted operating profit	116,917
		Interest charge	5,000
		Lease interest[3]	24,740
			87,177
Taxation	17,000	Taxation	17,000
Retained profit	78,000	Retained profit	70,177

Statement of financial position

	£		£
Non-current assets	200,000	Non-current assets	200,000
		Leased assets (309,250 − 103,083)[4]	206,167
			406,167
Net current assets	220,000	Net current assets	220,000
		Lease due < 1 year[5]	102,881
	420,000		523,286
Long-term loans	100,000	Long-term loans	100,000
		Leases due > 1 year	111,109
	320,000		312,177
Share capital	100,000	Share capital	100,000
Retained earnings	220,000	Retained earnings	220,000
		Change in p&l a/c (78,000 − 70,177)	(7,823)
	320,000		312,177

Notes

1. The annual lease payments of £120,000 will have been deducted in arriving at the operating profit of £100,000. This lease payment requires to be added back as it will instead be going to (a) partly reduce the lease creditor and (b) lease interest.

2. The depreciation on the leased assets will require to be deducted in arriving at the adjusted operating profit.

3. The lease interest will be shown as a finance charge.

4. The statement of financial position will include the leased asset at net book value.

5. The lease obligations will be included and disclosed as appropriate between amounts falling due less than and greater than one year.

The difference in retained profit is relatively small. Note, however, that the operating profit has increased under capitalization. This is due to the lease rental payments of £120,000 being substituted with the lower depreciation charge of £103,083.

The ratio of operating profit/sales is therefore 3.33% before capitalization and 3.89% after.

It is the statement of financial position that shows a dramatic difference following lease capitalization.

If the return on capital employed is considered, the following changes demonstrate this point:

$$\text{Before} \quad \frac{£100,000}{£200,000} = 50\% \qquad \text{After} \quad \frac{£116,917}{£311,109} = 37.5\%$$

This is because the leased asset now forms part of the capital employed.

Of even greater significance is the worsening in reported gearing:

$$\text{Gearing} : \frac{\text{Long-term debt}}{\text{Shareholders' funds}}$$

$$\text{Before} \quad \frac{£100,000}{£320,000} = 31.25\% \qquad \text{After} \quad \frac{£211,109}{£312,177} = 67.6\%$$

This is because the commitment to long-term lease rentals has been recognized in the financial statements.

Operating leases are not required to be capitalized, and they remain therefore a form of off balance sheet financing. Consequently they remain popular with lessees, and many leasing agreements are structured specifically to be classified as operating leases.

BASIC

INTERMEDIATE

ADVANCED

Progress Point 4.7

(a) Summarize the effect on the financial statements of a lessee treating a lease as an operating lease as opposed to a finance lease; and explain the importance of the categorization of the lease transactions into operating lease or finance lease decisions when carrying out financial ratio analysis. What ratios are particularly affected?

(b) Midson plc, a haulage company, leases a truck on 1 January 2012 under the following terms:

- annual rental of £10,000 for four years, first payment on 31 December 2012
- cash price of truck is £28,550
- Midson plc adopts the straight line method of providing for depreciation.

(i) Calculate and state the charges to profit or loss for 2012 if the lease is treated as an operating lease.

(ii) Calculate and state the charges to profit or loss for 2012 if the lease is treated as a finance lease and capitalized, using the sum of digits method for the finance charges.

(iii) Show how the truck would be incorporated in the statement of financial position at 31 December 2012 if capitalized.

(iv) Comment on your findings.

Solution

(a) The accounting treatment for the lessee of an operating lease is that the statement of comprehensive income is simply charged with the periodic rentals and there is no effect on the statement of financial position. By contrast, the accounting treatment for a finance lease takes a substance over form approach – as if the lessee had taken out a loan to purchase an asset. This means that both the asset and the obligations under the lease are shown in the statement of financial position.

The impact on the statement of comprehensive income of treating a finance lease as an operating lease is minimal; over the lifetime of the lease, substantially the same amount of depreciation and interest (finance lease) will be charged to profit or loss as would operating lease rentals.

The impact on the statement of financial position is more dramatic and highlights the importance of the correct categorization between operating lease and finance lease. Treatment as an operating lease means that neither the asset nor the liability is included in the lessee's statement of financial position. This will hide the true level of assets employed in the business and will result in an artificially high return on capital employed figure.

The absence of the lease obligation from the statement of financial position will also mask the true level of gearing (i.e. the level of interest bearing liabilities to shareholders' funds).

(b) Midson plc:

(i) Statement of comprehensive income extract:

Year Ended 31 December 2012	
	2012
	£
Operating lease	10,000

As an operating lease each annual payment is simply rent.

(ii) Working notes: finance lease treatment

Total lease payments = 4 × £10,000 =	£40,000
Cash price	£28,550
Finance charge	£11,450

Period of lease = 4 years
Sum of the digits = 4 + 3 + 2 + 1 = 10
∴ Charge to 2012 = 4/10 × 11,450 = £4,580
Depreciation charge = 28,550 ÷ 4 = £7,138 p.a.

Statement of comprehensive income extract:

Year to 31 December 2012	
	£
Finance charge	4,580
Depreciation	7,138
	11,718

(iii) Working notes

Lease creditor: At 1 January 2012	£28,550
Less: payment	10,000
	18,550
Add: finance charge	4,580
Lease creditor at 31 December 2012	23,130

Statement of financial position extract:

As at 31 December 2012	Cost	Acc. depn	NBV
Non-current assets	£	£	£
Leased truck	28,550	7,138	21,412
Creditors			
Leases			23,130

(iv) The statement of comprehensive income is not greatly affected by treating a finance lease as an operating lease; however, the effect of capitalizing the lease on the statement of financial position more realistically states the assets employed by Midson plc. In addition, the lease obligations are shown on the face of the statement of financial position.

Operating leases

Lease payments under an operating lease should be recognized as an expense on a straight line basis over the lease term unless another systematic basis is more representative of the time pattern of the user's benefit.

4.8 Disclosure requirements

The disclosure requirements of IAS 17 are considerable and aim to highlight to users of financial statements the various risks faced by companies that lease assets. The main disclosures are in paragraph 31 for finance leases and paragraph 35 for operating leases.

Finance leases

Lessees should make the following disclosures for finance leases:

(a) for each class of asset, the net carrying amount at the end of the reporting period

(b) a reconciliation between the total of future minimum lease payments at the end of the reporting period, and their present value. In addition, disclosure must be made of the total of future minimum lease payments at the end of the reporting period and their present value for each of the following periods:

- not later than one year
- later than one year and not later than five years
- later than five years.

Total minimum lease payments are the minimum payments that the lessee is obliged to make to the lessor over the remaining part of the lease term.

This means, therefore, that at the end of the reporting period a reconciliation is required between the lessee's future payments in total and that recognized as the lease liability in the statement of financial position. Usually the only reconciling item is unallocated interest (i.e. interest to be charged in future periods).

Example

Finance lease creditor	Minimum Lease Payments	Present value of minimum lease payments
	£	£
Due within 1 year	10,000	6,756
Due in 2 to 5 years	40,000	32,998
Due in more than 5 years	10,000	10,000
	60,000	49,754
Less: finance charges allocated to future periods	(10,246)	
Present value of minimum lease payments	49,754	

(c) Any contingent rent payments that have been made during the period must be separately disclosed in the notes to the financial statements. A contingent rent payment is not fixed in amount and occurs when the lessee has been charged on a basis other than the passage of time (e.g. charge per mile for a leased car).

IAS 32 *Financial Instruments: Presentation* requires that a company should disclose the total interest expense for the reporting period. This will include finance lease interest.

(d) A general description of the significant leasing arrangements that have been entered into should be disclosed. This should include detail of any renewal or purchase options, any escalation clauses and the basis on which contingent rent payments are calculated.

If any restrictions have been imposed on the lessee by the finance lease agreement then these should be disclosed. These restrictions include limits on dividend payments, any further debt and any other lease obligations.

Operating leases

IAS 17 requires the following disclosures for operating leases:

(a) the amount of operating lease payments recognized as an expense in the period

(b) the total of future minimum lease payments under non-cancellable operating leases for each of the following periods:

- not later than one year
- later than one year and not later than five years
- later than five years.

This disclosure allows users of the accounts to anticipate future cash outflows that are not reflected anywhere else in the accounts. With operating leases, although they are normally non-cancellable, there is no liability reflected in the statement of financial position. This is, therefore, a very important disclosure and is made in the notes to the accounts.

(c) A general description of the significant leasing arrangements that have been entered into should be disclosed. This should include detail of any renewal or purchase options, any escalation clauses and the basis on which contingent rent payments are calculated.

 If any restrictions have been imposed on the lessee by the lease agreement then these should be disclosed. These restrictions include limits on dividend payments, any further debt and any other lease obligations.

Disclosure in practice

As noted earlier, the disclosure requirements of IAS 17 are considerable, and the relevant disclosures can be found within the accounting policies, statement of comprehensive income, statement of financial position, and the notes.

Leases

Leases are classified as finance leases whenever the terms of the lease transfer substantially all the risks and rewards of ownership to the lessee. All other leases are classified as operating leases.

 Assets held under finance leases are initially recognised as property, plant and equipment at an amount equal to the fair value of the leased assets or, if lower, the present value of minimum lease payments at the inception of the lease, and then depreciated over their useful economic lives or term of the lease, whichever is shorter. Lease payments are apportioned between repayment of capital and interest. The capital element of future lease payments is included in the statement of financial position as a liability. Interest is charged to the statement of comprehensive income so as to achieve a constant rate of interest on the remaining balance of the liability.

 Rentals payable under operating leases are charged to the statement of comprehensive income on a straight-line basis over the lease term. Operating lease incentives are recognised as a reduction in the rental expense over the lease term.

Source: Logica (2011), p. 97

Figure 4.1 Logica: property, plant and equipment (showing leased assets)

	Freehold land and buildings £'m	Leasehold property and improvements £'m	Equipment and plant £'m	Total £'m
Cost				
At 1 January 2010	28.4	49.3	235.2	312.9
Additions	0.3	2.7	44.1	47.1
Acquisition of subsidiaries/businesses	–	0.6	1.2	1.8
Disposals	–	(1.7)	(14.3)	(16.0)
Exchange differences	(0.2)	1.1	1.0	1.9
At 1 January 2011	28.5	52.0	267.2	347.7
Additions	0.7	5.9	43.7	50.3
Acquisition of subsidiaries/businesses	0.1	1.5	0.7	2.3
Disposals	–	(1.0)	(18.3)	(19.3)
Exchange differences	(0.4)	(1.8)	(10.2)	(12.4)
At 31 December 2011	28.9	56.6	283.1	368.6

Accumulated depreciation				
At 1 January 2010	8.7	23.3	148.1	180.1
Charge for the year	1.0	4.4	37.3	42.7
Disposals	–	(1.1)	(12.8)	(13.9)
Exchange differences	(0.2)	0.6	(0.1)	0.3
At 1 January 2011	9.5	27.2	172.5	209.2
Charge for the year	0.8	4.2	41.6	46.6
Disposals	–	(0.7)	(17.9)	(18.6)
Exchange differences	(0.2)	(1.0)	(7.1)	(8.3)
At 31 December 2011	10.1	29.7	189.1	228.9
Net carrying amount				
At 31 December 2011	18.8	26.9	94.0	139.7
At 31 December 2010	19.0	24.8	94.7	138.5

Source: Logica (2011), p. 115

Logica's policy note on leases echoes the requirements of IAS 17 in relation to initial measurement and measurement subsequent to initial recognition: the policy note also discloses that Logica uses the actuarial method to allocate finance charges (i.e. interest is charged so as to achieve a constant rate of interest on the remaining lease liability balance).

The following extract from Logica's note to the financial statements on property, plant and equipment discloses the net book value of assets held under finance leases of £2.0 million included within the overall net book value of assets in use of £139.7 million:

Equipment and plant included assets held under finance leases with a net book value of £2.0 million (2010: £3.1 million). Additions to equipment and plant during the year amounting to £0.6 million (2010: £1.3 million) were financed by new finance leases.

Source: Logica (2011), p.115

This disclosure allows the user to determine the return on all the assets in use by the company and not simply those that are owned. This disclosure also aids the user in determining the financial strength of the company by providing important information about those assets that are used but not owned, and that would not be available for distribution in, for example, a winding up.

Figure 4.2 Logica: borrowings showing finance lease obligations

	2011 £'m	2010 £'m
Current		
Bank overdrafts	33.0	25.8
Bank loans	0.2	175.2
Finance lease obligations	1.5	2.7
Other borrowings	0.4	0.6
	35.1	204.3

Presented as:		
Other borrowings	35.1	204.3
	35.1	204.3
Non-current		
Bank loans	71.8	41.1
Private placement debt notes	297.3	88.7
Finance lease obligations	1.6	1.5
Other borrowings	5.4	1.0
	376.1	132.3

Source: Logica (2011), p. 119

At 31 December, the Group had commitments under non-cancellable operating leases, principally for offices, cars and computer equipment, as follows:

Figure 4.3 Logica: operating lease commitments

Future minimum lease payments payable	2011 Land and buildings £'m	Other £'m	2010 Land and buildings £'m	Other £'m
Within one year	86.4	58.2	90.9	48.0
Between two and five years	233.3	69.2	256.3	52.5
After five years	108.5	1.0	110.7	–
	428.2	128.4	457.9	100.5

The expense recognised in the statement of comprehensive income for payments under non-cancellable operating leases fors the year ended 31 December 2011 was £146.1 million (2010: £147.9 million). At 31 December 2011, the total future minimum sub-lease payments expected to be received under non-cancellable sub-leases were £33.7 million (2010: £31.1 million).

Figure 4.4 Logica: capital expenditure commitments

	2011 Group £'m	Associates £'m	2010 Group £'m	Associates £'m
Contracted at the end of the reporting period	0.5	–	–	–

Source: Logica (2011), p. 142

In accordance with the requirements of the standard, Logica discloses its obligations under both finance lease and operating lease arrangements. In addition, disclosure is made of the lessor's security over finance lease assets and, in respect of operating leases, that these are principally for offices and computer equipment.

4.9 Change in accounting focus

Capitalization of finance leases has for a long time been mandatory in countries with an Anglo-Saxon accounting tradition (e.g. the UK, USA and Commonwealth countries). In countries with a continental European accounting tradition, the distinction between operating and finance leases is relatively new. Until recently, all leases in these countries were treated as rentals.

An international group has questioned this distinction between finance and operating leases. Standard setters from the UK, Australia, Canada, New Zealand, the USA and the IASC issued a Special Report, *Accounting For Leases – A New Approach*, which concluded that non-cancellable operating leases should be treated in the same way as finance leases. Regardless of the length of the lease, the lessee has:

- an asset – the lessee can *control* the future economic benefits embodied within the leased asset for the period of the lease term
- a liability – the lease contract establishes an obligation on the lessee to make future lease payments.

This approach firmly addresses the problems with the current approach and removes the ambiguity that can exist between finance leases and operating leases. Moreover, it removes the potential for creatively manipulating a finance lease as an operating lease to avoid having to capitalize the leased asset in the lessee's statement of financial position.

A further position paper was issued by the G4 + 1 group in 1999.

This paper followed on in a similar vein to the previous report, and further argued the reasons for capitalizing all operating leases.

It was argued that capitalization would result in 'fair value' statement of financial position disclosure – that is, the assets and liabilities resulting from the capitalization of operating leases would be reported at the fair value of the rights and obligations in the lease (e.g. where a lease is only for a small part of an asset's economic life, only that part would be reflected in the lessee's statement of financial position).

Moreover, assuming that in an arm's length transaction, the present value of the lease payments will correspond to the fair value of the asset, then the assets and liabilities referred to in the proposals appear to be able to be calculated. A further possibility would, however, be to include the leased asset at its full value, in which case the liability would be the present value of the minimum lease payments plus the obligation to return the asset at the end of the rental period.

Improving lease accounting has been a long-term goal of both the IASB and the FASB. The major criticism of the existing lease standards is that lessees do not recognize all lease obligations on their statements of financial position – based on what some consider to be arbitrary distinctions between operating and finance leases. The Boards issued a joint exposure draft on lease accounting in August 2010 addressing many of the criticisms but attracting great controversy in the process.

ED leases

The ED proposes a 'right-of-use' accounting model which would effectively remove the distinction between finance leases and operating leases. All leases would be dealt with in broadly the same way as is currently required by IAS 17 for finance leases, meaning that lessees would recognize assets and liabilities for all leases.

The lessee would be required to record a liability for the present value of the obligation to make lease payments and an intangible asset representing the right to use the leased item for the lease term (the right-of-use asset). The lease asset and liability to be recorded for each lease would be based on the expected payments to be made over the lease term.

The initial lease liability would be measured based upon estimates of the lease term, contingent rentals, term option penalties and residual value guarantees, using the lessees' incremental borrowing rate to discount future payments to present value. These estimates would be reassessed at each reporting date. Changes to the estimated lease term would adjust the related right-of-use asset and lease liability; changes due to contingent rentals and expected payments under term option penalties and residual value guarantees would be reflected in profit or loss if they relate to past or current periods, and to the right-of-use asset if they relate to future periods, with a corresponding adjustment to the lease liability.

The right-of-use asset would be amortized over the shorter of its useful life or the lease term.

Lease payments would be allocated between interest expense and a reduction of the lease liability under the effective interest method (rather than be recognized as a rental expense under the straight line method).

As was noted in Chapter 1, part of the standard setting process is to subject the exposure draft to public comment. The response to the exposure draft was huge and has attracted nearly 800 comment letters.

While many respondents were supportive of the IASB's and FASB's efforts to develop a single, principles-based, converged and less complex lease accounting standard, almost all expressed significant concerns over the technical content and complexities of the proposals in the exposure draft. Many of these concerns related to the definition of a lease, lease term, variable lease payments, profit or loss recognition pattern and lessor accounting models.

One such criticism was that the proposed classification of leases was not consistent with the principles established in the Conceptual Framework. The new classification of leases is very much based on the argument that leases are predominately financing transactions and the proposed new measures are designed to ensure that no 'off balance sheet' opportunities arise for masking the future lease obligations. Many respondents took objection to this and in particular made reference to the Conceptual Framework and two of the characteristics of useful financial information as detailed in the Conceptual Framework, namely relevance and faithful representation.

The respondents argued that the Boards, in suggesting that all leases were financing transactions, were not applying the principles of the Conceptual Framework correctly. Moreover, by not responding appropriately to the different economic circumstances of different leasing arrangements, such leases would not be faithfully represented in the financial statements. Many entities, it was argued, enter into leases, not for financing reasons, but to benefit from flexibility in the event of temporary decrease or increase in business, and also to avoid considerations linked to ownership such as maintenance, disposal, obsolescence and insurance. Leasing also ensures that entities can benefit from the latest technologies. Several other arguments were put forward against the new proposals and included the additional costs that would be involved in accumulating the necessary information with which to calculate the right-of-use asset and liability values.

Of more fundamental concern to many respondents was the fact that one of the roles of the Conceptual Framework is to set down definitions of assets and liabilities and their criteria of recognition. By incorporating variable lease payments and payments under options in the measurement of right of use and of the liability, the Boards were not respecting the Conceptual Framework definitions. Indeed, variable lease payments, by their very nature, cannot be measured reliably and so cannot meet the recognition criteria; payments under options do not meet the definition of a liability as there is no present obligation.

Many respondents concluded that while it was necessary to develop distinct accounting principles for the two types of leases, it was also necessary to develop an accounting model for both types of leases that represented faithfully the substance of the lease transactions as stated by the Conceptual Framework. As it stands, the right-of-use model is not appropriate for arrangements that are not financing transactions, and those arrangements should be dealt with as operating leases are being dealt with currently i.e. off balance sheet.

Having considered the feedback the Boards have indicated that the proposed new standard might classify leases into:

(a) *Finance leases*, and

(b) *Other-than-finance leases*. These are leases that are similar to a rental transaction and would be accounted for in a way similar to that which IAS 17 currently requires for operating leases.

Such was the level of feedback, the Boards' original intention to have a final new leases standard in place by 2011 has not been possible. Indeed, given the number of issues to be resolved, it may be some time yet before a final revised standard is issued.

4.10 The accounting issues revisited: a critical appraisal

So far in this chapter the positive aspects of capitalizing leases have been clearly demonstrated. Comparison between companies is made easier, the underlying assets in use by a company are disclosed and the associated obligations related to leased assets are also disclosed. Indeed the current view is that all leases – whether they be finance or operating – should be capitalized to show the assets in use by companies and the related lease obligations.

Care must be taken, however, with the extent to which the substance over form approach is taken. That there are advantages to capitalizing leases is not being disputed. There are unfortunately disadvantages, however, and some of these are considered below.

Disadvantages

Sophistication of the user

The informational benefit of capitalizing leases will depend upon the sophistication of the user. A professional accountant will appreciate the need to look at the financial statements as a whole and will be able to put figures in context. The accountant will look at an asset schedule knowing that the notes pertaining to the schedule contain relevant information, and will be able to identify the associated obligations relating to any leased assets within the liabilities section of the statement of financial position.

Contrast this, however, with an unsophisticated user – for example, a potential supplier to a company who has no accounting background. As far as the supplier is concerned, an asset is an asset. The supplier will have no concept of the accountant's definition of an asset being 'a right to future economic benefits embodied within the leased asset' and may not fully appreciate the information provided in the notes to the accounts, or even realize that it is relevant.

The danger is that some users may look at the figures in isolation when forming their opinion of a particular company. As has been noted earlier, many users focus on the non-current assets in a statement of financial position when determining that company's wealth, and unless adequate disclosure is made and sufficient information given to draw the user's attention to the fact that the assets may not be assets as such, then capitalizing leases could be very misleading indeed.

Company financial statements can run to several pages and it must be questioned whether it is reasonable to expect users to be able to refer to all the relevant sections.

Reliance on the notes

As noted above, the extent to which the benefit of capitalizing leases is appreciated by the user depends upon the sophistication of the particular user. There is only a benefit where the financial statements are read as a whole and constituent parts not looked at in isolation. It could perhaps be suggested therefore that the legal form of the transaction should take precedent and all the information regarding the leases be given in the notes to the financial statements instead. No leased 'assets' would be in the statement of financial position; however, the payments due under the leases would be shown in the notes. While comparability between companies would suffer, the sophisticated user could – if sufficient information was given in the notes – make appropriate adjustments to the figures to make comparison possible. The unsophisticated user would have the benefit of not being misled.

To what extent should future liabilities be disclosed?

A further issue worthy of consideration is the position regarding the associated costs of leasing particular assets. Land and buildings provides a useful illustration of this particular point. Where a lease is taken on land and buildings then it depends on whether the lease on the buildings element is determined as being a finance lease or an operating lease whether the building is capitalized and the corresponding lease creditor shown, or treated as revenue expenditure and the future lease obligations disclosed in the notes to the accounts.

There will also be associated costs of leasing the building, however, such as rates, insurance and upkeep, and these will continue for as long as the lease is in place. Should disclosure of the likely future payments due on these expenses be noted also? After all, they will most certainly become due, and if the aim of the financial statements is to disclose information to enable decisions about future performance to be made then this could be argued to be very relevant also.

Section summary

The use of a substance over form approach ensures that important omissions in respect of leased assets do not occur. Care must be taken, however, to ensure that information is presented in such a way so that leased assets are easily identifiable and not mistaken for assets actually owned by a company.

Section 3: Advanced Aspects

This section identifies some of the more advanced aspects of leasing. In particular, it addresses sale and leaseback agreements, under both operating and finance leases. It concludes by examining leases from the point of view of the lessor.

4.11 Sale and leaseback agreements

It is not uncommon for companies to enter into sale and leaseback agreements whereby a company (the owner) sells an asset and immediately reacquires the right to use the asset by entering into a lease with the purchaser (Figure 4.5).

Such arrangements can involve the sale of a major asset and are often done as a way of raising funds while retaining use of the asset.

Such transactions can often be very attractive to companies as typically, if trying to raise funds from a bank, a company may only be able to raise 75% to 80% of the value of the asset; with a sale and leaseback transaction the company may be able to 'borrow' 100% of the asset's value.

A further benefit to a company of this means of raising finance is that the associated lease rentals will be fully deductible for tax purposes, while with a mortgage, only the interest element of the repayments can be offset against tax.

IAS 17 deals with the accounting treatment of sale and leaseback transactions in paragraphs 58 to 66. In order to determine the correct accounting treatment for such transactions, it must be established whether the leaseback is a finance lease or an operating lease.

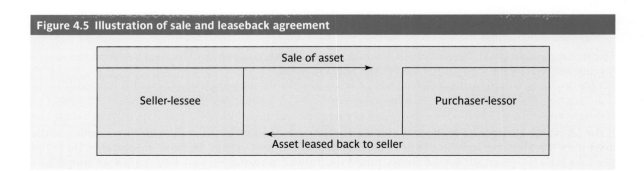

Figure 4.5 Illustration of sale and leaseback agreement

Leaseback under a finance lease

If the lessee, following the transaction, is still the economic owner of the asset then the leaseback is judged to be a finance lease and the seller-lessee has, in effect, borrowed funds against the asset. The position before and after the transaction is relatively unchanged: the seller may have disposed of the legal title of the asset but has not disposed of the ownership interest in the asset.

Further, when the substance of the transaction is considered, it is as if there has been no sale at all, the substance of the transaction being to raise finance and not to dispose of an asset. It would not be appropriate, therefore, to recognize a gain or loss on disposal as, in substance, there has been no disposal. The lease is effectively a mechanism for raising a loan with the asset as security.

If the sale proceeds exceed the carrying amount then the 'gain' needs to be treated as deferred income and released to profit or loss over the period of the lease. The asset is retained in the statement of financial position but at its fair value at the date the lease is entered into, with the corresponding sale proceeds treated as the initial lease creditor. The asset will be depreciated over the shorter of the remaining useful life and the term of the lease, and the lease payments will be treated partly as a repayment of the lease creditor and partly as a finance charge recognized in arriving at profit or loss.

Example

A company has a building with a net book value of £5m at 1 January 2012. The remaining useful economic life is 28 years. On 1 January 2012, the company enters into a sale and leaseback transaction with a finance house and sells the building at its market value of £8.5m. The building is immediately leased back for 25 years at an annual lease payment of £1m payable in arrears.

A lease creditor of £8.5m would be set on 1 January 2012 and the accounting entries would be as follows:

			£	£
Dr	Bank		8.5m	
	Cr	Finance lease creditor		8.5m

Being proceeds from sale and leaseback of asset.

The excess of the fair value (sale proceeds) over the carrying amount (£5m) would be recorded as deferred income and amortized over the lease term.

			£	£
Dr	Non-current asset – building		3.5m	
	Cr	Deferred income		3.5m

Being deferred income recognized at start of lease.

The rental payable on 31 December 2012 would be split between capital and interest based on the rate of interest implicit in the lease or the sum of the digits method.

The building would be depreciated over 25 years (the shorter of lease term and useful economic life).

If the fair value at the time of the sale and leaseback transaction is less than the carrying amount of the asset then the apparent loss should not be taken to profit or loss – again, because in substance there has been no sale. However, such a difference might indicate an impairment and may require an immediate write-down in the statement of comprehensive income.

Example

A company has a property with a net book value of £13m on 1 January 2012. On that date it enters into a sale and leaseback arrangement for £9m. The property is immediately leased back for £0.8m per annum.
  In this instance, a lease creditor would be set up on 1 January 2012 as follows:

			£	£
Dr	Bank		9m	
	Cr	Finance lease creditor		9m

Being proceeds from sale and leaseback of asset.

The property would continue to be carried in the financial statements at £13m and depreciated over the shorter of the lease term and the useful economic life. The difference between the fair value (sales proceeds) and carrying value would give an indication that an impairment review would be required and, if impairment was necessary, any impairment loss would be recognized immediately in profit or loss.

Leaseback under an operating lease

If the leaseback following the transaction is an operating lease, and the lease payments and sale price are established at fair value, the seller has in fact disposed of substantially all the risks and rewards of ownership. There has been a normal sale transaction and any profit or loss on sale can be recognized immediately. Consequently, if the fair value is less than the carrying amount of the asset, a loss equal to the amount of the difference between the carrying amount and fair value should be recognized immediately. A gain would be recognized immediately where the fair value is greater than the carrying amount.

  It may be the case, however, that the sale price is less than the fair value and the seller will be compensated by future lease payments at below market price. In this case, the loss as calculated between the difference of the carrying value and fair value should be recognized immediately, and the additional loss as calculated between the fair value and sales value should be deferred and written off over the period for which the asset is to be used.

Example

RJL Ltd enters into a sale and leaseback transaction with a finance house in respect of a ship. The carrying value in the financial statements of RJL Ltd is £5m and the fair value of the ship is £4m. RJL Ltd agrees to sell the ship for £3.5m following an agreement with the finance house to lease back the ship for a period of five years at £0.5m per year. A fair market rental for such a lease would normally be £0.6m.
  RJL Ltd will record in its financial statements the disposal of the ship as follows:

$$\text{Loss on disposal of ship} = \text{carrying value} - \text{fair value}$$

$$= £5m - £4m = £1m$$

The additional 'loss' on disposal between the fair value and the sale price (i.e. £4m – £3.5m = £0.5m) will be deferred and written off to profit or loss over the period for which the asset is expected to be used (i.e. five years). The additional loss will therefore be charged to profit or loss at £0.1m per annum.

The effect of this treatment is that the total charges going through profit or loss in respect of this leasing transaction (i.e. the operating lease payments and the deferred additional loss), should equate to a fair market value lease payment for a similar asset had the leasing payments not been artificially lowered by the sale of the asset at less than fair value.

There are a number of possibilities where the transaction is not based on the fair value of the asset. The following schedule identifies the various permutations that may arise and explains the appropriate accounting treatment. The following amounts are used.

1. CV = carrying value of the asset prior to its sale by the seller/lessee.
2. SV = sales value at which the asset is sold to the buyer/lessor.
3. FV = fair value of the asset (i.e. value if a sale at arm's length).

Possible permutations

1. SV < CV < FV: loss (CV – SV) recognized immediately unless lease rentals are below normal levels, when it should be deferred and amortized.
2. SV < FV < CV: loss based on fair value (CV – FV) recognized immediately. Balance (FV – SV) should also be recognized immediately unless lease rentals are below normal levels, when it should be deferred and amortized.
3. CV < SV < FV: gain (SV – CV) recognized immediately.
4. CV < FV < SV: profit based on fair value (FV – CV) recognized immediately. Balance (SV – FV) deferred and amortized.
5. FV < CV < SV: loss based on fair value (CV – FV) recognized immediately. Profit (SV – FV) deferred and amortized.
6. FV < SV < CV: loss based on fair value (CV – FV) recognized immediately. Profit (SV – FV) deferred and amortized.

The rationale behind the above treatments is that if the sales value is not based on fair values then it is likely that the normal market rents would have been adjusted to compensate. The effect of the treatment is to record the transaction as if it had been based on fair values.

It should be noted, however, that fair disclosure will not always result. For example, where the fair value is greater than the carrying value, the seller may arrange to have the sale value anywhere within that range and report a gain in the year of sale based on that sales value. Any compensation that the seller/lessee obtains by way of reduced rentals will be reflected in later years.

However, there may also be perfectly legitimate reasons why the sale value is less than the fair value. If the seller has had to raise cash quickly (i.e. a forced sale) then the sale value may be less than the fair value. In these cases, though, as the rentals are unlikely to have been reduced to compensate, the profit or loss should be based on the sales value.

4.12 Operating leases: incentives to customers

Many leasing companies offer incentives to attract potential customers and to encourage existing customers to renew leases, and these include rent-free periods and cash-back offers. IAS 17 does not deal specifically with such matters, but the Standing Interpretations Committee has clarified the position in SIC 15 *Incentives in an Operating Lease*. Such incentives should be recognized by the lessee as a reduction of the rental expense over the lease term on a straight line basis unless another systematic basis is more representative of the time pattern in which benefit is derived from the leased asset.

Rent-free periods

As noted earlier in the chapter, operating lease rentals should be charged to profit or loss on a straight line (or other systematic) basis, irrespective of the timing of the payments. Incentives also require to be recognized on the same basis.

Example

Obelisk leases a second-hand machine for a five-year period on 1 January 2012. Annual rentals of £4,000 are payable from 1 January 2013 to 2016. Obelisk was given the first year's rental free of charge as an incentive to take out the lease. What entries are required in Obelisk's financial statements assuming a 31 December year end?

Although Obelisk has not paid anything to the leasing company in the year to 31 December 2012, nevertheless it has had the use of the leased asset to generate income. In order to match the appropriate expense with the benefits generated we need to:

1. establish the total amount of lease payments made i.e. $4 \times £5,000 = £20,000$
2. allocate the total over the period of the lease on a straight line basis (i.e. £20,000/5 = £4,000 per annum).

£4,000 will therefore be charged to each accounting period in respect of the operating lease.
Note that the lease charge does not correspond with the relevant cash payments.

In the year to 31 December 2012, there will need to be an accrual to record the lease charge for that year, which will be reduced in subsequent years. That is:

Year 1			
Dr	Operating lease rentals	£4,000	
	Cr Accrual		£4,000
Being recording of lease charges.			

Years 2–5			
Dr	Operating lease rentals	£4,000	
	Accrual	£1,000	
	Cr Bank		£5,000
Being payment and recording of lease charges.			

Cash-back incentives

A similar approach is adopted where a company is offered cash back or reverse premium deals. These are treated as being a reduction of the rental expense over the lease term, and are recognized in profit or loss on a straight line (or other systematic) basis. The initial receipt of cash back is treated as deferred income and subsequently released to profit or loss.

Example

Carpetbag leases a machine for five years and under the terms of the lease is required to make payments of £4,000 at the end of each year. As an incentive to take out the lease, Carpetbag was given an immediate cash-back of £2,000 on signing the lease agreement.

In this example, the cash-back is effectively a reduction in the net cost of the lease. The total lease payments are therefore:

$$(5 \text{ years} \times £4,000 \text{ per year}) - \text{cash-back } £2,000 = £18,000$$

As the lease is over 5 years, the annual charge to profit or loss will be £18,000/5 = £3,600.

In order to achieve this charge in profit or loss, the following entries will be recorded:

Year 1

Dr	Bank	£2,000	
	Cr Deferred income		£2,000

Being cash back received.

This £2,000 will be released to profit or loss over the lease term at (£2,000/5) = £400 per annum.

The annual adjustments will therefore be:

Dr	Operating lease rentals	£4,000	
	Cr Bank		£4,000

Being lease payments made.

Dr	Deferred income	£400	
	Cr Operating lease rentals		£400

Being annual release of cash back.

The effect of the adjustments is that the annual charge in profit or loss in respect of operating lease charges is £3,600 (i.e. £4,000 – £400).

4.13 Accounting for leases by lessors

This chapter has so far considered leases from the lessee's standpoint only. We now consider the position from the lessor's point of view.

Although the detailed accounting treatment for lessors can be relatively difficult, broadly speaking, the approach that requires to be adopted in determining the accounting treatment for lessors is very similar to that which requires to be adopted for lessees – that is, the substance of the transaction requires to be determined and the appropriate accounting treatment followed from there.

As was the situation for lessees, the substance of a lease transaction for lessors can essentially fall into one of two categories.

The lease of an asset by a lessor could, if the terms are considered, have all the characteristics of an asset disposal – that is, the ownership risks and rewards are effectively transferred to the lessee (finance lease). Conversely, the nature of the lease may be more like a short-term rental, whereby the lessor may lease the particular asset to a number of parties (operating lease).

Where a lease is classified as a finance lease – that is, where the ownership rights have effectively been transferred – then the accounting follows that form. The substance of such a transaction is that the lessor does not control the asset subject to the lease and consequently should not include in its statement of financial position the assets subject to the lease agreement. Instead, the amounts owed by the lessee under the lease contract should be recorded as a receivable.

On the other hand, where the terms of the lease agreement are such that an operating lease exists, the asset should be recorded as a non-current asset and depreciated in the normal way. Rentals received are treated as income.

Finance lease: accounting requirements

The amount due from the lessee under a finance lease should be shown as a receivable in the statement of financial position. At the commencement of the lease term, the lessor should record a finance lease as a receivable at an amount equal to the net investment in the lease.

The net investment at any point in time comprises:

- gross investment, i.e. the total of the minimum lease payments *less*
- gross earnings allocated to future periods, i.e. the lessor's gross finance income over the lease term.

Example

Forhire plc leases an asset to Jigsaw Joiners for a period of three years. The cost of the asset after negotiating bulk discounts was £12,500. The terms of the lease are six rentals of £2,500 payable in advance and these payments are sufficient to achieve Forhire plc's return on investment of 7.93%. At the commencement of the lease, Forhire plc will record the following:

	£
Gross value of minimum lease payments (6 × £2,500)	15,000
Less: finance income over the lease term	2,500
Net investment	12,500

At the commencement of the lease, the net investment equals the cost of the asset.

The finance income should be allocated to accounting periods to give a constant periodic rate of return on the lessor's net investment outstanding in respect of the finance lease.

The rentals received each year will be as follows:

Period	Gross investment at start	Rental received	Net investment	Finance income (7.93%)	Gross investment at end
	£	£	£	£	£
1/1/Yr1	12,500	2,500	10,000	793	10,793
1/7/Yr1	10,793	2,500	8,293	658	8,951
				1,451	
1/1/Yr2	8,951	2,500	6,451	511	6,962
1/7/Yr2	6,962	2,500	4,462	354	4,816
				865	
1/1/Yr3	4,816	2,500	2,316	184	2,500
1/7/Yr3	2,500	2,500	–	–	–
				184	
				2,500	

The statement of comprehensive income and statement of financial position extracts would be as follows:

Statement of comprehensive income			
	Yr 1	Yr 2	Yr 3
	£	£	£
Gross earnings under finance leases	1,451	865	184

BASIC

INTERMEDIATE

ADVANCED

Statement of financial position			
	£	£	£
Net investment in finance leases	8,951	4,816	–

The important thing is to note that, under a finance lease, no non-current asset is reported in the financial statements but, instead, the amounts owed by the lessees under the lease contract are recorded, as a receivable. The interest element of the lease is the lessor's income and this is allocated to the accounting periods so as to give a constant periodic rate of return on the lessor's net investment in the lease.

Operating leases: accounting requirements

Assets held for operating leases should be presented in the statement of financial position of the lessor according to the nature of the asset, and depreciated in the normal way. The rentals received should be recognized over the lease term on a straight line basis unless another systematic basis is more representative of the time pattern in which use benefit derived from the leased asset is diminished.

Example

MAF plc leases a machine to AWF plc on the following terms:

Period of lease	4 years
Annual payments	£4,000

MAF purchased the machine for £35,000 and the expected useful life is ten years. MAF depreciates all its equipment using the straight line method.

The statement of comprehensive income extracts will be as follows:

	Yr 1	Yr 2	Yr 3	Yr 4
	£	£	£	£
Lease income	4,000	4,000	4,000	4,000
Depreciation	3,500	3,500	3,500	3,500

The statement of financial position would contain the net book value of the machine. Assuming the machine was purchased at the start of Year 1, the statement of financial position entries would show the following:

	Yr 1	Yr 2	Yr 3	Yr 4
	£	£	£	£
Non-current assets	31,500	28,000	24,500	21,000

Section summary

The accounting provisions for some of the more common leasing arrangements have been set out from both the lessee's and the lessor's perspective. The main arguments for capitalizing leases and the substance over form approach have also been put forward. It is now perhaps worth looking again at what adoption of IAS 17 prescribed accounting treatment achieves and whether this does meet the needs of the user.

This question instantly reverts to one of not whether a particular accounting treatment meets the needs of the user, but rather, what *are* the needs of the user. Moreover, are not the needs of the user determined by that user's expectations and what information is available to meet those expectations?

The question has perhaps therefore altered to one of identifying the user's expectations.

Accounting practices have evolved differently in different countries according to the cultural, economic, legal and political environments prevailing in those countries. Accordingly, if a legal bias is an overriding condition of 'fair view' reporting, then adoption of IAS 17 and capitalization of leases will not meet the needs of those users. Such users expect to receive accounting information detailing total lease payments made in a year, not manipulated reconstructions of non-existent purchase agreements.

In such environments, IAS 17 will not meet its objectives. Consequently, while IAS 17 fulfils expectations of reporting for many cultures, it should be remembered that it fulfils those expectations only because the users *have* those expectations of what accounting information should provide. That is, in these cultures and environments, the prerequisite expectation is a true and fair view, and the disclosure of the relevant information to provide that – for example, a substance over form approach allowing users to determine the assets in use by a reporting entity.

Equally convincing arguments could be put forward that show such treatments to be misleading. The values at which companies carry non-current assets are often a cause for criticism (i.e. historic cost). The capitalizing of assets subject to lease agreements, it could be argued, simply adds to users' confusion as to what those values actually represent.

The final question must be therefore whether or not capitalizing leases is desirable.

The answer to this is a resounding 'it depends': it depends on the user's needs, expectations, culture and legal background. In other words, 'yes' and 'no'.

Chapter summary

IAS 17 *Leases*

In the books of the lessee:

- accounting treatment depends on whether an operating or finance lease
- a finance lease is a lease that is, in substance, the purchase of an asset with debt
- an operating lease is any lease other than a finance lease; such a lease is treated as a rental transaction for accounting purposes
- finance leases should initially be recorded as an asset and a liability at the lower of the fair value of the asset and the present value of the minimum lease payments (discounted at the interest rate implicit in the lease)
- finance lease payments should be apportioned between the finance charge and the reduction of the outstanding liability (the finance charge to be allocated so as to produce a constant periodic rate of interest on the remaining balance of the liability)

- the asset should be depreciated over the shorter of the lease term and its useful life
- for operating leases, the lease payments should be recognized as an expense in profit or loss over the lease term on a straight line basis.

In the books of the lessor:

- accounting treatment depends on whether an operating or finance lease
- finance leases should initially be recorded in the statement of financial position as a receivable at an amount equal to the net investment in the lease
- finance income should be recognized in profit or loss based on a pattern reflecting a constant periodic rate of return on the lessor's net investment outstanding in respect of the finance lease
- assets held for operating leases should be shown as assets and depreciated
- lease income from operating leases should be recognized in profit or loss over the lease term on a straight line basis.

✓ Key terms for review

Definitions can be found in a glossary at the end of the book.

Gross investment (in the lease)	Lease	Off balance sheet finance
Initial recognition (of finance lease)	Lease term	Operating leases (lease payments)
	Minimum lease payments	
Interest rate implicit in the lease	Net investment (in the lease)	

? Review questions

1. Explain why a company might choose to lease an asset.
2. Explain the difference between a finance lease and an operating lease.
3. What are the advantages of capitalizing leases in financial statements?
4. What ratios are particularly affected by the categorization of a lease as an operating lease as opposed to a finance lease.
5. Explain the accounting treatment of a finance lease in the books of a lessee under IAS 17.
6. Explain the accounting treatment of an operating lease in the books of a lessee under IAS 17.
7. At the inception of a lease, at what value should lessees recognize finance leases as assets in their statements of financial position?
8. Explain how an asset held under a finance lease should be depreciated.
9. Explain the accounting treatment of a finance lease in the books of a lessor under IAS 17.
10. Explain whether the legal form of all leases should take precedence over their substance.

✎ Exercises

Level I

1. On 1 January 2012, Rednax Ltd acquires an item of equipment with a fair value of £20,000 on a finance lease. The terms of the lease require the company to make 4 annual payments of £6,654 annually in arrears i.e. on 31 December 2012, 2013, 2014 and 2015. The rate of interest implicit in the lease is 12.5% per annum.

Required

Assuming that the actuarial method is used, show the effects of this lease on the statement of comprehensive income and the statement of financial position at the end of each year of the lease. Show how the liability outstanding at the end of each year would be split between current and non-current liabilities. Extract entries only are required.

2. On 1 January 2012, Ofbal Ltd took delivery of a new machine from Equipment Solutions Ltd on a finance lease. The terms of the lease are as follows:

Fair value of leased asset	£31,700
Primary period of lease	4 years
Rentals payable annually in arrears	£10,000
First payment	31/12/12
Implied interest rate	10%

The estimated useful life of the machine is five years, with a nil residual value.

At the end of the primary lease term the expected residual value is £5,000 and Ofbal Ltd can retain all of these proceeds.

Ofbal Ltd provides for depreciation on a straight line basis.

Required

Show the effect of this lease on the statements of comprehensive income and statements of financial position of Ofbal Ltd for the four years to 31 December 2015, under the following headings:

(a) lease creditor

(b) finance charge

(c) depreciation charge, and

(d) net book value of assets.

3. Capital Hearing Ltd acquired a specialist audiometer on 1 April 2012 by means of a finance lease. The fair value of the asset on that date was £40,000 and the terms of the lease are that Capital Hearing Ltd is required to make six half-year payments in advance of £7,674. The rate of interest implicit in the lease is 6% per half-year.

Required

Assuming that the actuarial method is used to allocate the finance charge over the lease term, show the effects of this lease on the statement of comprehensive income and statement of financial position of Capital Hearing Ltd for each of the years to 31 March 2013, 2014 and 2015. Extract entries only are required.

Level II

4. On 1 January 2012, Main Contractors Ltd leased a new machine from the Solvitol Finance Company. The following details were obtained from the lease agreement.

The capital cost of the machine at 1 January 2012 was £50,000.

Six half-yearly payments of £11,000 each are payable in advance, commencing 1 January 2012 in the primary term.

Three annual payments of £100 are payable in the secondary term. Main Contractors Ltd has not yet decided if it will take advantage of the secondary term.

The estimated useful life of the machine is five years, with a nil residual value. The estimated residual value after three years is £10,000 and, of this, 95% is accountable to Main Contractors Ltd. It is the policy of Main Contractors Ltd to use the straight line method of providing for depreciation.

Required

Calculate the effect of this rental on the annual accounts of Main Contractors Ltd to 31 December for the relevant years using the sum of the digits method to allocate finance charges under the following headings:

(a) lease creditor

(b) finance charge

(c) depreciation, and

(d) net book value of asset.

5. Easygrow Ltd has leased an asset from the Lendalot Finance Co. Details are as follows:

  (i) Easygrow is responsible for insurance and maintenance, and is required to make five annual payments of £3,000, all payable in advance beginning on 1 January 2012, the date of commencement of the lease.

 (ii) After the primary lease period, Easygrow Ltd has the right to continue leasing the asset for an indefinite period for a nominal rental, which may be ignored.

(iii) The asset may be bought outright for £10,620, which, it can be assumed, provides an acceptable approximation to the present value of the minimum lease payments discounted at the rate of interest implicit in the lease of 21%.

(iv) Residual values may be ignored. The anticipated useful life of the asset is ten years and Easygrow intends to use the asset for this period. Easygrow uses the straight line method of providing for depreciation.

Required

Show the effect of this lease on the annual accounts of Easygrow Ltd for the years ended 31 December 2012 to 2016 under the following headings:

(a) lease creditor

(b) finance charge

(c) depreciation charge, and

(d) net book value of assets.

6. On 1 January 2012, Osprey Fish Processing Company Ltd took delivery of a new fish filleting machine from the JLA finance company, on a finance lease.

The terms of the lease are as follows:

Primary period of lease	3 years
Frequency of rental payments	6 monthly in arrears
Amount of each rental	£5,000
First payment	30 June 2012

The cost of the machine was £25,379, which is thought to be fair value. The implied rate of interest applied half yearly is 5%.

The estimated useful life of the machine is three years, with a nil residual value.

It is the policy of the Osprey Fish Processing Company to depreciate assets on the straight line basis.

Required

(a) Show the effect of this lease on the statements of comprehensive income and statements of financial position of Osprey Fish Processing Company Ltd for each of the three years to 31 December 2014.

(b) Discuss the arguments for and against the capitalization of finance leases in the accounts of the lessee.

7. In November 2012, the directors of Shockers Ltd, a manufacturer of electrical generators, were successful in their tender for a contract to supply generators to an international mining operator. An additional machine is now required to cope with the increased production levels resulting from the new contract and the directors have decided to lease, rather than buy the required machine. On 1 January 2013, the company took delivery of the new machine, which was leased through the Phoenix Finance Co Ltd. The terms of this lease are as follows:

Primary period of lease	4 years
Frequency of rental payments	Annually in advance
Amount of each rental	£10,000
First payment	1 January 2013

The cost to buy the machine is £34,868. The rate of interest implicit in the lease is 10% per annum. The estimated useful life of the machine is four years and Shockers Ltd provides for depreciation on the straight line basis.

Required

(a) Show the effect of this lease on the statements of comprehensive income and statements of financial position of Shockers Ltd in each of the four years from 31 December 2013 to 31 December 2016 in accordance with the requirements of IAS 17.

(b) With reference to IA7 17 *Leases*, explain the difference between a finance lease and an operating lease, and discuss briefly the merits of capitalizing a finance lease in the financial statements.

Level III

8. You have recently been appointed as finance director to a manufacturing company and are about to attend a board meeting to discuss the draft management accounts to 31 December 2012.

A change in company policy during the previous year saw a change from buying manufacturing equipment to leasing equipment. The book-keeper who prepares monthly management accounts for discussion at board meetings is unaware of the contents of IAS 17, and has treated all lease payments as expenses in the statement of comprehensive income. A memorandum issued by the chairman to you and the other directors in response to the draft accounts detailed below advises of 'a substantial improvement in the company's performance. Our decision to lease rather than purchase outright our manufacturing equipment has had the desired effect on our financial statements. Our return on capital employed is now equal to the industry average and our gearing ratio is one of the lowest around. This is a clear indication of the success of our new strategy and our share price will no doubt reflect this once the statutory financial statements are made public.'

Draft statement of comprehensive income for year ended 31 December 2012

	£
Turnover	3,500
Operating profit	1,500
Interest	25
Profit before tax	1,475
Tax	475
Profit after tax	1,000

Draft statement of financial position at 31 December 2012

	£
Non-current assets	500
Net current assets	1,500
	2,000
Bank loans due > 1 year	200
	1,800
Share capital	500
Retained earnings	1,300
	1,800

You are reviewing the draft financial statements with the senior book-keeper who provides the following information regarding two leases that were entered into on 1 January 2012.

Machine 1

Four annual instalments of £100,000 each, the first payment being made 1 January 2012. The cost of the machine were it to have been purchased was £348,680, and the finance cost implicit in the lease is 10% per year. The machine is expected to last five years.

Machine 2

A total of 24 monthly instalments of £1,000 per month payable in advance and terminable at any time by either party. The cash price of this machine would be £100,000 and its estimated useful life is ten years.

Company policy is to depreciate assets on the straight line basis. The effects on taxation can be ignored.

Required

(a) Explain, with reference to the two leases described above, the difference between a finance lease and an operating lease.

(b) Show the effect on the financial statements for the year ended 31 December 2012 of capitalizing the company's finance lease in accordance with IAS 17. (Note: only leases that qualify as finance leases should be capitalized.)

(c) Calculate the following key ratios before and after capitalizing the finance lease.

(i) $\dfrac{\text{Operating profit}}{\text{Sales}}$

(ii) Return on capital employed : $\dfrac{\text{earnings before interest and tax}}{\text{total assets less current libilities}}$

(iii) Gearing : $\dfrac{\text{long-term debt}}{\text{shareholders' funds}}$

Draft a memorandum to the chairman explaining the impact of capitalizing the finance lease on the ratios.

Appendix 4.1: Definitions in IAS 17

A lease is an agreement whereby the lessor conveys to the lessee, in return for a payment or series of payments, the right to use an asset for an agreed period of time.

A finance lease is a lease that transfers substantially all the risks and rewards incidental to ownership of an asset. Title may or may not eventually be transferred.

An operating lease is a lease other than a finance lease.

Economic life is either:

- the period over which an asset is expected to be economically usable by one or more users, or
- the number of production or similar units expected to be obtained from the asset by one or more users.

Useful life is the estimated remaining period, from the commencement of the lease term, without limitation by the lease term, over which the economic benefits embodied in the asset are expected to be consumed by the entity.

The lease term is the non-cancellable period for which the lessee has contracted to lease the asset, together with any further terms for which the lessee has the option to continue to lease the asset, with or without further payment, when, at the inception of the lease, it is reasonably certain that the lessee will exercise the option.

A non-cancellable lease is a lease that is cancellable in only one of the following four circumstances:

1. on the occurrence of some remote contingency
2. with the permission of the lessor
3. if the lessee enters into a new lease for the same or an equivalent asset with the same lessor
4. on payment by the lessee of an additional amount such that, at inception, continuation of the lease is reasonably certain.

The inception of the lease is the earlier of the date of the lease agreement and the date of commitment by the parties to the principal provisions of the lease. As at this date:

- a lease is classified as either an operating or a finance lease, and
- in the case of a finance lease, the amounts to be recognized at the commencement of the lease term are determined.

The commencement of the lease term is the date from which the lessee is entitled to exercise its right to use the leased asset. It is the date of initial recognition of the lease (i.e. the recognition of the assets, liabilities, income or expenses resulting from the lease, as appropriate).

Minimum lease payments are the payments over the lease term that the lessee is, or can be, required to make, excluding contingent rent, costs for services, and taxes to be paid by and reimbursed to the lessor, together with:

- in the case of the lessee, any amounts guaranteed by the lessee or by a party related to the lessee, or
- in the case of the lessor, any residual value guaranteed to the lessor by either:
  (a) the lessee
  (b) a party related to the lessee, or
  (c) a third party unrelated to the lessor that is financially capable of discharging the obligations under the guarantee.

Fair value is the amount for which an asset could be exchanged or a liability settled, between knowledgeable, willing parties in an arm's length transaction.

From the viewpoint of the lessee, the guaranteed residual value that is part of the residual value that is guaranteed by the lessee or by a party related to the lessee (the amount of the guarantee) being the maximum amount that could, in any event, become payable.

From the viewpoint of the lessor, the guaranteed residual value is that part of the residual value that is guaranteed by the lessee or by a third party unrelated to the lessor who, is financially capable of discharging the obligations under the guarantee.

Unguaranteed residual value is that portion of the residual value of the leased asset, the realization of which by the lessor is not assured or is guaranteed solely by a party related to the lessor.

The lessor's gross investment in the lease is the aggregate of the minimum lease payments receivable by the lessor under a finance lease and any unguaranteed residual value accruing to the lessor.

Net investment in the lease is the gross investment in the lease discounted at the interest rate implicit in the lease.

Unearned finance income is the difference between:

- the gross investment in the lease, and
- the net investment in the lease.

The interest rate implicit in the lease is the discount rate that, at the inception of the lease, causes the aggregate present value of (a) the minimum lease payments, and (b) the unguaranteed residual value to be equal to the sum of fair value of the leased asset and any initial direct cost of the lessor.

The lessee's incremental borrowing rate of interest is the rate of interest the lessee would have to pay on a similar lease or, if that is not determinable, the rate that, at the inception of the lease, the lessee would incur to borrow over a similar term, and with a similar security, the funds necessary to purchase the asset.

Contingent rent is that portion of the lease payments that is not fixed in amount but is based on the future amount of a factor that changes other than with the passage of time (e.g. percentage of sales, amount of usage, future price indices, future market rates of interest).

References

G4 + 1 *Accounting for Leases – A New Approach*. July 1996.
IAS 17 *Leases*. IASB, revised 2003.
Logica (2011) *Annual Report and Accounts*.

Further reading

Goodacre, A. (2003a) Assessing the potential impact of lease accounting reform: a review of the empirical evidence. *Journal of Property Research*, 20, 1, 49–66.
Goodacre, A. (2003b) Operating lease finance in the UK retail sector. *International Review of Retail, Distribution and Consumer Research*, 13, 1, 99–125.
IAS 32 *Financial Instruments: Presentation*. IASB, amended 2012
IFRS: www.ifrs.org
McGregor, W. (1996) Lease accounting: righting the wrongs. *Accountancy*, September, 96.

When you have read this chapter, log on to the Online Learning Centre website at *www.mcgraw-hill.co.uk/textbooks/mckeith* to explore chapter-by-chapter test questions, further reading and more online study tools.

Chapter 5

Inventories

Learning Outcomes

After studying this chapter you should be able to:

- [✓] explain the different types of inventories
- [✓] explain the different approaches to measurement of inventories
- [✓] show the effect that different cost flow assumptions have on reported profits
- [✓] demonstrate the accounting entries required to account for inventories
- [✓] value and account for inventories in accordance with IAS 2
- [✓] disclose all elements of inventories in accordance with IAS 2

Introduction

Inventories – also known as stocks – represent goods on hand at the year end that will be carried forward for sale in the next accounting period.

Section 1: Basic Principles

In the case of retail businesses, inventories are likely to consist of stocks of goods acquired for resale, while in the case of a manufacturing company these inventories may well comprise:

- raw materials (i.e. materials that will be subject to some manufacturing process prior to sale)
- work in progress (i.e. partially completed goods)
- finished goods (i.e. inventories that have been through the manufacturing process and are available for sale).

Some companies – particularly construction companies – have a further classification of year-end 'inventory'. Such companies are often involved in projects that may last for more than one accounting period. Moreover, as these companies are normally hired to complete specific contracts (e.g. the construction of a bridge), they are unlikely ever to carry stocks of 'finished goods'. It is likely, however, that they will, at the end of at least one accounting period, have a contract in progress and will, therefore, need to make appropriate accounting entries to reflect the work carried out to date. Furthermore, it may also be appropriate to recognize an element of the overall profit on the contract on an annual basis. This is dealt with in Chapter 6.

This chapter begins with an explanation of inventories, and in particular their accounting entries as far as double entry book-keeping is concerned, together with a review of inventory valuation methods.

The detailed requirements of IAS 2 *Inventories* are then covered in the second section and, finally, the advanced section deals with some of the problems encountered by accountants in practice when dealing with inventories.

5.1 Inventories

Depending on the type of organization, there may be a perpetual record kept of inventory items – updated continually – or it may be that inventories are determined by means of a year-end inventory count.

Whichever method is adopted, as far as financial reporting is concerned, a valuation will need to be made at the end of each reporting period.

Progress Point 5.1

What main categories of inventory are likely to be held by a manufacturing business?

Solution

A manufacturing business is likely to have the following categories of inventory:

- raw materials (i.e. materials used in the manufacture of the particular product)
- work in progress (i.e. materials that have started but not completed the manufacturing process)
- finished goods (i.e. goods that are complete and available for sale).

5.2 The accounting issue involved

Inventories are a unique item within an organization's financial statements as they appear in both the statement of comprehensive income, within cost of sales, and the statement of financial position, within current assets. The profit for the year is calculated after charging appropriate costs against turnover. Any products that are unsold at the end of the year will be included within closing inventory and carried forward to be charged against future years' turnover.

Example

Statement of comprehensive income (extract)		**Statement of financial position (extract)**	
Cost of sales:		Current assets	
Opening inventory	100	Inventory	80
Purchases	150		
Accumulated depreciation	250		
Net book value	80		
Net effect on net assets	170		

Moreover, closing inventory has a direct effect on profit and net assets as:

- an increase in closing inventory will reduce cost of sales and increase profit, and result in an increase in net assets, and
- a decrease in closing inventory will increase cost of sales and reduce profit, and result in a decrease in net assets.

Consequently, inventory provides a rich area for the creative accountant. An increase in inventory value will result in an increase in profit, and vice versa.

Example

Dean commences in business selling fireplaces. In his first year of trading he buys 50 fireplaces costing £2,000 each (i.e. £100,000) and sells 45 of these for £3,000 each (i.e. £135,000). Five fireplaces remain in inventory at the year end.

If the sales proceeds are simply compared with purchase costs (i.e. £135,000 – £100,000) it would appear that Dean has made a profit of £35,000. This is not the complete picture, however, as if the number of units bought is compared with number of units sold, it can be seen that Dean still has five fireplaces in inventory at the year end, which he hopes to sell in the next accounting period.

If the matching concept is to be adhered to, then rather than comparing sales proceeds with absolute purchase costs, sales proceeds need to be compared with the comparative costs of the fireplaces that were sold (i.e. the cost of goods sold). This results in Dean's profit increasing to £45,000 (i.e. $45 \times £3,000 - 45 \times £2,000$). The cost of goods sold is therefore the purchases made in the year – that is, 50 less the amount in inventory at the year end (i.e. 5: (50 – 5 = 45)), giving a cost of goods sold of $45 \times £2,000 - £90,000$.

5.3 Accounting for inventory

Double entry book-keeping

As noted above, many organizations determine year-end inventories by means of an annual inventory count. This means that inventories will not automatically be included in the organization's double entry system or, consequently, trial balance. To continue the example above, Dean will have inventory on hand at the year end with a cost of £10,000 (5 × £2,000). As far as Dean's trial balance is concerned it will simply show the sales value of the fireplaces sold and the purchase price of *all* fireplaces purchased, e.g.

Extract trial balance	Dr	Cr
Sales		£135,000
Purchases	£100,000	

In order to account for the unsold items, an inventory adjustment needs to be prepared to show the value of the inventories on hand at the year end – i.e. £10,000 (5 × £2,000). The journal entry to account for this is as follows:

Dr	Closing inventory (statement of financial position)	£10,000
	Cr Closing inventory (statement of comprehensive income)	£10,000
Being closing inventory.		

It has the effect of crediting the statement of comprehensive income (and thus reducing costs) with the value of the unsold fireplaces. It also has the effect of deferring the expenditure on those fireplaces to the statement of financial position, where it will be expensed in the next accounting period. Dean's statement of comprehensive income and statement of financial position extracts will show the following:

Statement of comprehensive income (extract)
for Year 1

		£	£
Sales			135,000
Less:	Cost of sales		
	Purchases	100,000	
	Less: closing inventory	10,000	
			90,000
Gross profit			45,000

Statement of financial position (extract)
as at Year 1

Current assets	£
Inventory	10,000

Suppose that, in the next accounting period, Dean purchases a further 60 fireplaces but that the cost of these has now increased to £2,100 each (i.e. £126,000). He sells 53 fireplaces in the year for £3,200 each (i.e. £169,600), 12 fireplaces remain in inventory at the year end, all at a cost of £2,100 each (i.e. £25,200).

In order to calculate the profit made in the second accounting period, it is once more necessary to match the cost of the fireplaces sold with their purchase cost.

Dean has sold 53 fireplaces: five fireplaces from the purchases made in the first year and 48 from the purchases made in the second year. His profit is therefore:

	£	£
Sales 53 × £3,200		169,600
Less: costs		
5 × £2,000	10,000	
48 × £2,100	100,800	
		110,800
Profit		58,800

In this example, it has been possible to match sales exactly with the cost of the items sold. In practice, however, this may not be possible and, as noted above, inventories are often measured annually by means of an inventory count. This brings in valuation issues and these will be covered in the next section. Continuing with this example, if the opening and closing inventory figures are inserted within the cost of sales calculation, Dean's statement of comprehensive income and statement of financial position extracts will show the following:

Statement of comprehensive income (extract) for Year 2

		£	£
Sales			169,600
Less :	Cost of sales		
	Opening inventory	10,000	
	Add: purchases	126,000	
		136,000	
	Less: closing inventory	25,200	
			110,800
Gross profit			58,800

Statement of financial position (extract) as at Year 2

Current Assets	£
Inventory	25,200

The journal entries required to account for the inventory adjustments through cost of sales are as follows.

First, the closing inventory at the end of Year 1 will require to be transferred to the statement of comprehensive income as an expense in Year 2 (i.e. these inventories have been sold in Year 2 and will therefore form part of the cost of sales calculation):

BASIC

INTERMEDIATE

ADVANCED

Dr	Opening inventory (Statement of comprehensive income)	£10,000	
	Cr Inventory (Statement of financial position)		£10,000
Being transfer to cost of sales.			

Second, the inventory on hand at the end of Year 2 needs to be accounted for as follows:

Dr	Closing inventory (Statement of financial position)	£25,200	
	Cr Closing inventory (Statement of comprehensive income)		£25,200
Being closing inventory.			

It can be seen that, because of the matching process, the cost of the unsold items at each year end is deferred to the next accounting period. Moreover, because of the cost of sales calculation, the higher the closing inventory figure at the year end, the higher will be the reported gross profit, and vice versa.

Progress Point 5.2

What are the effects of omitting goods costing £1,000 from the year-end inventory figure?

Solution
If inventories are omitted, this would increase cost of sales by £1,000 and consequently reduce profit by £1,000. Net assets would also be reduced by £1,000.

Valuation methods
The application of the matching principle requires the identification of the cost of goods sold to be charged against revenues received. The cost of goods sold calculation itself results in two complementary aspects of this problem: the first involves the identification of the cost of goods sold during each accounting period; the second involves the identification of the value (or cost) of goods unsold at the end of a period. The cost of goods unsold at the end of one period must be carried forward and allocated as expenses in the future periods in which revenues will be received from the ultimate sale of the goods.

It is worth noting at this stage that only those inventories that are expected to yield future economic benefits should be carried forward. Consequently, if any of the fireplaces in the previous example were, for instance, so badly damaged that a future sale would be impossible, then their cost would immediately be recognized in profit or loss as an expense of that period. It should also be noted that increases in the value of closing inventory are not recognized as it is not prudent to do so. This would be anticipating income in the hope of a future sale, which would conflict with the prudence concept.

Inventory cost recognition
In the earlier example, Dean was able to calculate the cost of sales by reference to the unit cost of the specific fireplaces sold. This is clearly the ideal situation where the costs of goods sold are specifically identified and matched with the goods physically sold. In practice this will be relatively rare as the

administrative effort involved in recording the inventory items bought and sold will inevitably be substantial unless there are relatively few high-value items being produced or purchased. Consequently, this would normally be found only where the inventory does comprise high-value items such as car dealers, jewellery dealers and antiques. In many cases, however, inventories may be indistinguishable from one another and, if costs have altered over an accounting period, the accountant is faced with a problem of cost recognition. In such circumstances, where it is physically impossible to identify which units were purchased at which cost, it is necessary to introduce a systematic method of cost recognition that will identify the order in which costs are to be allocated or expensed.

Cost flow assumptions based on the physical flow of goods

Specific identification/actual cost
As noted above, the allocation of costs based upon the physical flow of goods is the ideal.

FIFO (First In, First Out)
In the majority of businesses it will not be practicable to keep track of inventory cost on an individual unit basis. The First In First Out (FIFO) method of cost recognition assumes that when inventories are sold or used in a production process, it is the oldest that are sold or used first. This is best illustrated by reference to a business that deals in perishable goods; such a business will attempt to sell the earliest goods received before fresher goods adopting an inventory rotation basis to ensure the oldest goods are at the front of any displays. Therefore, by allocating the earliest costs incurred against revenue, actual cost flows are being matched with the physical flow of goods with reasonable accuracy. Consequently, where it is not possible to value inventory items individually, the FIFO method is most likely to approximate to the physical flow of goods sold resulting in the most accurate measurement of cost flows.

Cost flow assumptions which disregard the physical flow of goods

LIFO (Last In, First Out)
This method is the opposite of FIFO and assumes that the most recent purchases are disposed of first. It should be noted that in some circumstances this could represent the physical flow of stock – particularly if, for example, a tank is filled and emptied from the top. The rationale behind the LIFO method is that it matches current costs with current revenues even although the physical flow of inventory items would suggest that the earliest costs should be being matched. i.e. the earliest physical inventories may be being consumed but at are being valued at their current i.e. last in values.

Weighted average cost (AVCO)
This method is suitable where inventory items are identical or near identical and involves the computation of an average cost by dividing the total cost of the units by the number of units. This computation would be reworked whenever there was a receipt of inventory or alternatively, at the end of predetermined periods. The rationale behind this approach is that it is illogical to distinguish between similar inventory items simply because different levels of cost existed at the time they were purchased or produced.

Base inventory
Under this method a fixed quantity of inventory is stated at a fixed price and any amount over the fixed quantity is valued using more usual methods e.g. FIFO. The rationale behind this method is that any ongoing business must hold a minimum amount of inventory at all times and consequently this base inventory is more like a non-current asset, rather than inventory to be sold or consumed. The fixed quantity is that level of inventory which must always be held to maintain normal operating levels.

The following example illustrates the different methods – and the different values that can result from their use.

Example

Uno Retailing Ltd sells a single product line. Purchases and sales during the month of November 2012 were as follows:

Opening inventory		Nil
Purchases	(i) 10 units @ £5 each	£50
	(ii) 25 units @ £6 each	£150
		£200
Sales: 25 units at a price of £10 each		£250

The retailer is therefore faced with two problems:

1. identifying which costs to set against revenues for the month of November, and
2. identifying which costs to assign to the closing inventory of unsold goods.

First in first out (FIFO) method

The method that appeals intuitively is to recognize costs in the order in which they actually occur. That is, the costs of goods acquired first should be expensed first (i.e. first in first out); the units remaining will therefore be regarded as representing the latest units purchased. The FIFO method probably also gives the closest approximation to actual cost flows i.e. it is assumed that when inventories are used in the production process, the oldest are sold or used first and that, therefore, the balance of inventory on hand at any point represents the most recent purchases. In times of rising prices, however, FIFO tends to overstate profits as earlier and lower unit costs are matched with current prices in the statement of comprehensive income, while the period end inventories in the statement of financial position are the more up-to-date values. Calculation of gross profit for Uno Retailing Ltd using the FIFO basis of cost recognition is as follows:

	£
Sales revenue	250
Cost of goods sold:	
10 units @ £5	50
15 units @ £6	90
	140
Gross profit	110
Closing inventory: 10 units @ £6	£60

Last in first out (LIFO) method

Here, the order of cost recognition is reversed so that the last costs incurred will be recognized first. It is argued that, in times of rising prices, this method produces a cost of goods sold figure that reflects a close approximation to replacement cost, while still retaining the historic cost system of valuation, and thus gives a more realistic profit figure. It should be noted, however, that this will produce a relatively lower closing inventory figure. Calculation of gross profit for Uno Retailing Ltd using the LIFO basis of cost recognition is as follows:

	£
Sales revenue	250
Cost of goods sold	
25 units @ £6	150
Gross profit	100
Closing inventory: 10 units @ £5 each	50

Weighted average cost (AVCO) method

Using this method, the average cost is applied and weighted, according to the different proportions at the different cost levels, to the items in inventory. Weighted average unit cost is calculated by dividing the total cost of units acquired during an accounting period by the number of units acquired.

The weighted average cost of goods purchased by Uno Retailing Ltd for the month of November 2012 is as follows:

$$\frac{(10 \times £5) + (£25 \times £6)}{35 \text{ units}}$$
$$= \frac{£200}{35 \text{ units}}$$
$$= £5.71$$

Calculation of gross profit for Uno Retailing Ltd using a weighted average system of cost recognition is as follows:

	£
Sales revenue	250.00
Cost of goods sold	
25 units @ £5.71	142.75
Gross profit	107.25
Closing inventory: 10 units @ £5.71 each	57.10

Base inventory method

This final method is based on the argument that a certain minimum level of inventories is necessary in order to remain in business at all. It is argued therefore that some of the inventories viewed in the aggregate are not really available for sale and should instead be regarded as a fixed asset. This minimum level – defined by management – remains at its original cost and the remainder of the inventory above this level is treated, as inventory, by one of the other methods. Assume for Uno Retailing Ltd that the minimum level is five units. Calculation of gross profit for Uno Retailing Ltd based on a minimum stock level of five units and using FIFO is as follows:

	£
Sales revenue	250
Cost of goods sold	
5 units @ £5[1]	25
20 units @ £6	120
	145
Gross profit	105
Closing inventory: base inventory	
5 units @ £5 each	25
5 units @ £6 each	30
	55

[1] Of the original purchase of ten units, five are being treated as base inventory.

Which method should be used?

The method chosen should provide the fairest practicable approximation to cost. Neither IAS 2 nor SSAP 9 in the UK permit the use of LIFO or base inventory as these methods often result in inventories being stated in the statement of financial position at amounts that bear little relationship to recent cost levels. When this happens, not only can the presentation of current assets be misleading, but subsequent periods' profits may also be distorted if inventory levels reduce and out-of-date costs are transferred into cost of sales in the statement of comprehensive income.

FIFO and weighted average cost are both permitted methods under IAS 2 and SSAP 9.

Progress Point 5.3

(a) Name three methods of inventory valuation. Describe the differences between them, and the effects of those differences in terms of rising prices.

(b) Bedrock Supplies commenced trading on 1 April, supplying tarmac. During this month, the following transactions took place:

		Tonnes	Cost per ton
1 April	Purchased	10,000	£10
9 April	Purchased	20,000	£13
17 April	Sold	10,000	

Required

Calculate cost of sales and closing inventories for Bedrock Supplies using the FIFO, LIFO and AVCO methods of inventory valuation.

Solution

(a) The three methods of inventory valuation are as follows.

First in first out (FIFO)

Under this method, the costs of inventories that were acquired first are expensed first. In times of rising prices, this means that inventories in the statement of financial position are carried at higher (up-to-date) values and this therefore gives a higher profit in the statement of comprehensive income as cost of sales is based on lower (out-of-date) values.

Last in first out (LIFO)

Under this method, the costs of inventory that are acquired last are expensed first. In times of rising prices this will give a lower profit figure as sales will be matched against up-to-date costs and the statement of financial position will have a correspondingly lower inventory figure as it will be valued at lower (out-of-date) values.

Average cost (AVCO)

Under this method, the cost of goods sold and closing inventory figures are based upon a weighted average unit cost. In times of rising prices this would result in a profit and inventory figure that is between the two identified under FIFO and LIFO. The statement of financial position would therefore

BASIC

INTERMEDIATE

ADVANCED

carry inventories at an understated value, and the correspondingly lower closing inventory figure in the statement of comprehensive income would result in an understated profit figure.

(b) The cost of sales and closing inventories under the three methods would be as follows.

FIFO

Under the FIFO method, it is the first 10,000 tonnes that are assumed to be sold first. The remainder – which are the later purchases – will comprise the closing inventories.

$$\text{Cost of sales} = 10,000 \text{ tonnes} \times £10 = £100,000$$

$$\text{Closing inventory} = 20,000 \text{ tonnes} \times £13 = £260,000$$

LIFO

Under the LIFO method, it is the later purchases that are assumed to be the first sold and so it will be the remainder of the later purchases plus the earlier purchases that will comprise the closing inventories.

$$\text{Cost of sales} = 10,000 \times £13 = £130,000$$

$$\text{Closing inventory} = (20,000 - 10,000) \times £13 + 10,000 \times £10 = £230,000$$

AVCO

Under the AVCO method, the weighted average of the inventories purchased during the period will be used to determine a unit cost to be applied to the number of units sold in cost of sales and the number of units held in closing inventory.

$$\text{Average cost per unit} = \frac{10,000 \times £10) + (20,000 \times £13)}{(10,000 + 20,000)}$$

$$= £12 \text{ per tonne}$$

$$\text{Cost of sales} = 10,000 \times £12 = £120,000$$

$$\text{Closing inventory} = 20,000 \times £12 = £240,000$$

BASIC

INTERMEDIATE

ADVANCED

Perpetual and periodic inventory valuation

As was noted earlier, depending on the type of the organization, there may be a perpetual record kept of inventory items, maintained and updated continuously as items are purchased and sold. This has the advantage of providing inventory information on a timely basis but requires the maintenance of a full set of inventory records. In contrast, with a periodic system of inventory valuation, inventories are determined by a physical count at a specific date. The inventory shown in the statement of financial position is determined by the physical count and is priced in accordance with the cost recognition method used. The net change between opening and closing inventory enters into the computation of cost of goods sold. The examples above all use periodic valuations. The journal entries required to record cost of purchases and goods sold are as shown within the Dean's Fireplaces example (page 268).

With the perpetual method of cost recognition and inventory valuation, cost of goods sold will be identified immediately each sale has been made. Transfers from the inventory account to cost of goods sold expense account will be made following a sale, with the result that the inventory account will be continuously adjusted to the actual level of inventories held.

As the above comparisons show, under the FIFO method of cost recognition, the same figures for cost of goods sold and closing inventory are produced whether calculated on a periodic or perpetual basis. The LIFO and weighted average (AVCO) methods, however, produce different results according to whether they are applied on a perpetual or periodic basis. This is because under these methods, the identification of the

Example: periodic vs perpetual inventory valuation

Purchases and sales made by Handy Stores for the first seven days of June 2013 are as follows:

Day		
1 Purchases	20 units @ £5 each	
3 Sales		15 units
5 Purchases	30 units @ £6 each	
7 Sales		10 units

The effect of the application of different approaches is illustrated below. FIFO, LIFO and weighted average are compared using a periodic basis and perpetual basis of cost recognition and inventory valuation.

FIFO: periodic inventory valuation

Cost of goods sold		£	Closing inventory	£
20 units @ £5		100		
5 units @ £6		30	25 units @ £6	150
		130		150

FIFO: perpetual inventory valuation

	Day	Units	Unit price £	Inventory balance £	Cost of goods sold £	
Goods in	1	20	5	100		
Goods out	3	(15)	5	75	75	(15 @ £5)
		5		25		
Goods in	5	30	6	180		
		35		205		
Goods out	7	(10)		(55)	25	(5 @ £5)
					30	(5 @ £6)
Balance		25	6	150	130	

LIFO: periodic inventory valuations

Cost of goods sold			Closing inventory	£
25 units @ £6	150	20 units @ £5		100
		5 units @ £6		30
				130

LIFO: perpetual inventory valuation

	Day	Units	Unit price	Inventory balance	Cost of goods sold
			£	£	£
Goods in	1	20	5	100	
Goods out	3	(15)	5	(75)	75 (15 @ £5)
		5		25	
Goods in	5	30	6	180	
		35		205	
Goods out	7	(10)	6	(60)	60 (10 × £6)
Balance		25		145	135
		Comprising 5 @ £5		25	
		20 @ £6		120	
				145	

Weighted average: periodic inventory valuation

Cost of goods sold		Closing inventory	
			£
25 units @ £5.60	£140	25 units @ £5.60	140

$$\text{Weighted average cost} = \frac{(20 \times £5) + (30 \times £6)}{(20 + 50)}$$

$$= £5.60 \text{ per unit}$$

Weighted average: perpetual inventory valuation

	Day	Units	Unit price	Inventory balance	Cost of goods sold	
			£	£	£	
Goods in	1	20	5	100		
Goods out	3	(15)	5	(75)	75	(15 × £5)
		5		25		
Goods in	5	30	6	180		
Averaged to:		35	5.86	205		
Goods out	7	10	5.86	(58.60)	58.60	(10 × £5.86)
Balance		25		£146.40	£133.60	

cost of the items sold changes depending on whether a perpetual or periodic valuation system is adopted. That is, under a periodic system, the significant items and values are those at the beginning an end of the accounting period; under a perpetual system, every inventory and price change will have an immediate effect on the valuation of the inventory and cost of sales. With FIFO, it will always be the same costs which are expensed first regardless of whether a periodic or perpetual system is adopted. Under LIFO, the 'last in', items will be different as every time there is a change to the inventory – and because it is being perpetually updated, there will be a change to the 'last in' items. The same applies to the weighted average method.

Note that if prices remained stable, there would be no differences between any of the three methods, regardless of whether a perpetual or periodic valuation system was used. The extent of the divergence is a function of the rate of price changes.

Progress Point 5.4

If a company maintains a perpetual inventory control system, is it necessary to have an annual inventory count?

Solution

With an efficient and accurate perpetual inventory system, in theory an annual inventory count would not be necessary as closing inventory figures at any date can be taken from the inventory records. An annual inventory count does provide, however – albeit at a cost – a useful independent check on the accuracy of the perpetual inventory system. This may highlight and bring to the attention of management irregularities, such as theft, that could otherwise go undetected.

The problems identified

Under the historical cost framework, accounting for inventory is merely a cost allocation process and the inventory disclosed in the statement of financial position is no more than a deferred cost. As the above examples have illustrated, however, the calculation of cost of goods sold and closing inventory is by no means clear cut. The use of different cost recognition methods results in different values and those differences are further compounded depending upon whether a periodic or perpetual inventory system is maintained. The examples given above deal with finished goods. In reality, the problems will be much greater. It will not only be finished goods that will require valuation. In manufacturing businesses not only will the raw materials need to be valued but also the cost of converting raw materials into products and services for sale. This brings cost of purchase and cost of conversion into the valuation requirements. Cost of conversion brings the need to consider both direct and indirect overhead costs. Although direct costs ought to be easily identified, indirect overheads, by definition, will need to be assigned to particular units of product or service according to some reasonable allocation basis. This necessarily introduces assumptions and approximations to the equation – for example, the derivation of normal level of activity and the calculation of a reasonable overhead cost rate. As can be seen, therefore, the valuation of inventories is by no means straightforward, and it requires management to make several judgements.

Section summary

It is a fundamental accounting principle that revenues earned are matched with the related costs incurred in earning them. In determining the profit or loss for a particular period, the costs of the goods sold need to be calculated; in determining the profit or loss for future periods the cost of unsold inventories at the end of one financial year needs to be carried forward to the next accounting period so that they can be matched with the revenue recognized on their future sale. The inventory value is therefore a crucial element not only in the computation of profit, but also in the valuation of assets for statement of financial position purposes. In the next section, the requirements of IAS 2 *Inventories* are reviewed in detail, together with how IAS 2 seeks to narrow the differences and variations that result from the array of valuation methods available.

Section 2: Intermediate Issues

5.4 IAS 2 *Inventories*

Objective

The objective of IAS 2 is to prescribe the accounting treatment for inventories. It provides guidance for determining the cost of inventories and for subsequently recognizing an expense, including any write-down to net realizable value. It also provides guidance on the cost formulas that are used to assign costs to inventories.

Scope

IAS 2 defines (para. 6) inventories as assets that:

(a) are held for sale in the ordinary course of business (i.e. finished goods)

(b) are in the process of production for such sale (i.e. work in process), or

(c) are in the form of materials or supplies to be consumed in the production process or in the rendering of services.

However, IAS 2 excludes certain inventories from its scope (para. 2):

- work in progress arising under construction contracts (covered by IAS 11 *Construction Contracts*)
- financial instruments (covered by IFRS 9 *Financial Instruments*)
- biological assets related to agricultural activity and agricultural produce at the point of harvest (covered by IAS 41 *Agriculture*).

In addition, while the following are within the scope of the standard, IAS 2 does not apply to the measurement of inventories held by:

- producers of agricultural and forest products, agricultural produce after harvest, and minerals and mineral products to the extent that they are measured at net realizable value (above or below cost) in accordance with well-established practices in those industries; when such inventories are measured at net realizable value, changes in that value are recognized in profit or loss in the period of the change
- commodity brokers and dealers who measure their inventories at fair value less costs to sell; when such inventories are measured at fair value less costs to sell, changes in fair value less costs to sell are recognized in profit or loss in the period of the change.

Fundamental principle of IAS 2

The standard accounting practice set out in paragraph 9 of IAS 2 is as follows:

> *Inventories shall be measured at the lower of cost and net realizable value.*

This basic principle therefore requires that, in order to make such a comparison of cost and net realizable value, for each separate item of inventory the following needs to be determined:

- cost
- net realizable value (NRV).

The separate item point is significant, and para. 29 requires that inventories be written down to net realizible value on an item-by-item basis. It is allowable, however, for a group of similar items to be accounted for together – for example, items coming from the same product line (e.g. 500 g and 1 kg bags of flour). Returning to the separate item point, if the total cost was compared to the total net realizable value – without regard to the individual items making up the total – there could be an imprudent set-off of losses against unrealized profits. The following example illustrates this point.

Example

An enterprise has four products in its inventory with values as follows:

Product	Cost	NRV
	£	£
A	100	140
B	200	250
C	300	210
D	400	600
	£1,000	£1,200

At what value should the inventory be stated in the statement of financial position in accordance with IAS 2?

Solution

The correct value is:

Product	Lower of cost and NRV	
	£	
A	100	(cost)
B	200	(cost)
C	210	(NRV)
D	400	(cost)
	£910	

If the inventory is not separated into each type it would be valued at the lower of cost of £1,000 and NRV £1,200 (i.e. £1,000). However, IAS 2 requires each type of inventory to be valued separately and therefore the correct value is £910.

Progress Point 5.5

IAS 2 requires that inventories should be measured at the lower of cost and net realizable value. Why is this necessary?

Solution

It is necessary to value inventories in this way to adhere to the prudence and realization concepts. If net realizable value is less than cost, then to use cost would be to overstate the future benefits expected from the sale of the inventory item. This would go against prudence. On the other hand, if net realizable value is higher than cost, to include the higher figure would mean that unrealized profits were being recognized and this would be contrary to the prudence concept.

In order to be able to correctly account for the value of inventory, an understanding of the definitions of cost and net realizable value is necessary.

5.5 Cost of inventories

The cost of inventories is defined in IAS 2 (para. 10) as comprising all costs of purchase, costs of conversion and other costs incurred in bringing the inventories to their present location and condition.

Costs of purchase

Paragraph 11 further extends the costs of purchase to include:

- the purchase price
- import duties and other taxes (other than those subsequently recoverable by the enterprise from the taxing authority)
- transport costs (to the current location)
- handling costs, and
- other costs directly attributable to the acquisition of finished goods, materials and services.

And to deduct:

- trade discounts (but not settlement discount for early payment, which should be taken directly to profit or loss)
- rebates, and
- other similar items (e.g. subsidies).

Costs of conversion (para. 12)

These include:

- direct costs (e.g. direct materials and direct labour found from manufacturing or costing records)
- the systematic allocation of fixed production overheads (e.g. depreciation, maintenance charges)
- the systematic allocation of variable production overheads (e.g. indirect materials and labour).

Production overheads can be based on a number of methods and can include a wide range of overheads. Fixed production overheads are those indirect costs of production that remain relatively constant regardless of volume of production over a defined period of time, such as depreciation and maintenance of factory buildings and the cost of factory management and administration. Variable production overheads are those indirect costs of production that vary directly with changes in volume over a defined period of time such as indirect materials and indirect labour.

IAS 2, by stating that fixed costs should be included, therefore requires absorption costing for dealing with overheads. Absorption costing absorbs all production costs into products and the unsold inventory is valued at total cost of production. With marginal (or variable) costing, only variable costs of production are absorbed into products and the unsold inventory is valued at variable cost of production. With marginal costing, fixed costs of production are treated as a cost of the period in which they are incurred.

The allocation of fixed production overheads, however, must be based only on the normal capacity of the production facilities, taking into account the loss of capacity resulting from planned maintenance. Normal capacity is the production expected to be achieved on average over a number of periods. If production is below normal, fixed production overhead per unit should not be increased as a result of the low production or idle plant. The reason for this is straightforward. A primary issue in accounting for inventories is the amount of cost to be recognized as an asset and carried forward until the related revenues are recognized. If the increased cost per unit resulting from under-capacity or idle plant were to be absorbed into inventory, the cost of such inefficiencies would be effectively masked and deferred to be recognized in some future accounting period.

The same principle does not, however, apply to abnormally high levels of production. Inventory is never valued above the actual cost incurred.

The following examples illustrate these points.

Example: under-recovery of overheads

A company has variable production costs of £200 per unit and total fixed production costs of £800,000. Normal capacity of production is 10,200 units but this is reduced by 200 units for planned maintenance.

During the year to 31 December 2012, actual production was 8,000 units, of which 550 were in closing inventory. What is the cost of the closing inventory?

Solution

	£
Variable cost per unit	200
Fixed cost per unit (£800,000/10,000)	80
Total cost per unit	280
Inventory cost 550 units × £280	154,000

Note that the fixed overheads have been allocated based on normal production levels after taking account of planned maintenance (i.e. 10,200 – 200 = 10,000 units). The under-recovered overheads are an expense of the period. That is, the overheads which would have been deferred had the fixed costs been allocated according to the *actual* level of production: £800,000/8000 = £100 × 550 = £55,000.

Example: abnormally high production levels

Continuing with the above example, what would the cost of closing inventory be if actual production was 11,200 units?

Solution

	£
Variable cost per unit	200
Fixed cost per unit (£800,000/11,200)	271
Total cost per unit	271
Inventory cost 550 units × £271	149,050

Note that when production is abnormally high, fixed costs per unit is based on actual production – resulting in a lower cost per unit figure. This ensures that the cost of closing inventory is never higher than the actual cost incurred. Had a cost per unit based on normal production levels been used, this would, if all units remained in inventory at the period end, result in the fixed costs being absorbed into the inventory cost being higher than the actual fixed production costs incurred, i.e. (£800,000/10,000) × 11,200 = £896,000.

Other costs (para. 15)

Other costs should be included only if they are incurred in bringing the inventory to its present location and condition. It may be appropriate to include certain non-production overheads.

Administration overheads

Administration overheads are in respect of the whole business so only that portion that is easily identifiable to production should form part of the valuation. For example, the costs of the personnel or payroll department could be apportioned to production on a head-count basis and that element would be included in the inventory valuation. In addition, any production-specific administration costs (e.g. welfare costs, canteen costs) would also be included in the inventory valuation. Design costs related to a specific item of inventory is another example. If the expense cannot be identified as forming part of the production process, it will not form part of the inventory valuation.

Selling and distribution overheads

These costs will not normally be included in the inventory valuation as they are incurred after production has taken place. An exception to this rule exists, however, if the goods are on a 'sale or return' basis and are on the premises of the customer – but still belong to the supplier. In such circumstances the delivery and packing costs will be included in the inventory value of goods held on a customer's premises.

Interest costs

It may be possible to include interest on borrowings under IAS 23, as interest may be capitalized on a qualifying asset.

A qualifying asset is an asset that necessarily takes a substantial period of time to get ready for its intended use or sale (IAS 23, para. 4). Most inventories do not take a substantial period. An exception is maturing whisky, which takes several years to get to a sellable condition.

Progress Point 5.6

The following cost, overhead and expenses data relate to Hogden Company for the year ended 31 December 2012.

	£
Direct material cost of trowel per unit	1
Direct labour cost of trowel per unit	1
Direct expenses cost of trowel per unit	1
Production overheads per year	600,000
Administration overheads per year	200,000
Selling overheads per year	300,000
Interest payments per year	100,000

At the year end there were 250,000 trowels in finished goods inventory. You may assume that there were no finished goods at the start of the year and that there was no work in progress. The normal annual level of production is 750,000 trowels, but in the year ended 31 December 2012, only 450,000 were produced because of a labour dispute.

Calculate the cost of the inventory of trowels at 31 December 2012.

Suggested solution

The direct costs of the inventory are straightforward to identify and calculate:

	£
250,000 trowels at £1 direct material cost	250,000
250,000 trowels at £1 direct labour cost	250,000
250,000 trowels at £1 direct expenses cost	250,000
	750,000

The production overheads of £600,000 will be allocated according to normal levels of production (i.e. £600,000/750,000 = £0.80 per unit). The administrative overheads are not included as they are not incurred in bringing the inventory to its present location and condition. No account will be taken of the selling overheads or the interest payments as these are not incurred in respect of a qualifying asset. Closing inventory will therefore be valued at:

	£
Direct costs	750,000
Production overheads 250,000 × £0.80	200,000
	950,000

The abnormal costs associated with the labour dispute (i.e. £600,000 − (450,000 × £0.8) = £240,000) will be charged as an expense in the period they are incurred. Note that this is not an additional expense. The production overheads of £600,000 will remain. It is just that they will be allocated as follows:

	£
Cost of sales (200,000 units @ £0.80)	160,000
Closing stock (250,000 units @ £0.80)	200,000
Abnormal costs (300,000 units @ £0.80)	240,000
	600,000

IAS 2 (para. 16) gives examples of items that should not be included in the cost of inventory. These are:

■ abnormal amounts of wasted materials, labour or other production costs

■ storage costs (unless necessary in the production process prior to a further production stage, e.g. drying of wood before being made into furniture)

■ administrative overheads that do not contribute to bringing inventories to their current location and condition

■ selling costs (because the items are in inventory and have not yet been sold unless, as noted earlier, these inventories are sale or return items held on a customer's premises), and

■ interest cost when inventories are purchased with deferred settlement terms; when the transaction effectively contains a financing element, any difference between the purchase price on normal credit terms and the amount paid, is recognized as a finance cost over the period of the financing (para. 18).

Progress Point 5.7

Which of the following costs can be included in the cost of inventory under IAS 2?

■ Discounts on purchase price
■ Import duties
■ Transport insurance
■ Commission and brokerage costs
■ Storage costs after receiving materials that are necessary in the production process
■ Salaries of sales department
■ Warranty cost
■ Research for new products
■ Audit fees

Suggested solution

■ Discounts on purchase price	Yes
■ Import duties	Yes
■ Transport insurance	Yes
■ Commission on brokerage costs	Yes
■ Storage costs after receiving materials that are necessary in the production process	Yes
■ Salaries of sales department	No
■ Warranty cost	No
■ Research for new products	No
■ Audit fees	No

It is worth pausing for a moment here to recap on the accounting issues at hand. In endeavouring to adhere to the matching concept, only those costs that are incurred in bringing the inventories to their present location and condition should be included. Abnormal amounts of wasted materials, labour or other production costs should not be included in the cost of inventory. With this in mind, try working through Progress Point 5.8, which illustrates many of the issues covered so far in this chapter.

Progress Point 5.8

The following information relates to the actual production of vodka for the month of November.

	£
Cost of grain and other materials	30,000
Direct wages	4,000
Indirect production costs	6,000
Power	1,000
Administration – production	1,200
– general	1,350
Selling and marketing costs	3,400
Discount received for early payment	500
Depreciation	3,500

Notes

1. All administration costs and 40% of indirect production costs are fixed.
2. Included in depreciation is £1,850 relating to the distilling process. Depreciation is based on output.
3. 95% of the power relates to production.
4. Normal capacity is 300,000 litres per month.

Calculate the cost per litre of vodka in accordance with the requirements of IAS 2 assuming actual production in November was 240,000 litres.

Suggested solution

In tackling a problem such as this, a good approach is to 'simplify' the data by discounting any information that is not relevant. By following the requirements of IAS 2 (para. 16), the following details can immediately be eliminated:

	£
Administration – general	1,350
Selling and marketing costs	3,400
Discounts received for early payment	500

That is, general administration costs will not form part of the production process; selling and marketing costs will be incurred *after* production of the vodka has taken place; discounts received for early payment are treated as other income and do not affect the purchase price.

After taking account of the proportions of costs that are variable as given in the additional information notes, this leaves the following allowable costs that need to be allocated between fixed and variable costs:

	£
Costs of grain and other materials	30,000
Direct wages	4,000
Variable indirect production costs (60% × 6,000)	3,600
Power (95% × 1,000)	950
Depreciation	1,850
Total variable production costs	40,400
Fixed indirect production costs (40% × 6,000)	2,400
Fixed production administration	1,200
Total fixed production costs	3,600

The variable cost per litre can be calculated as follows:

Total variable costs/actual production = 40,400 ÷ 240,000 = £0.1683 per litre.

The allocation of fixed costs is more complex.

First, actual production needs to be compared with normal production, to determine whether or not there is an over- or under-recovery. In this instance, production is below normal and consequently the allocation of fixed overhead must be based on the level of normal capacity (i.e. 300,000 litres). (Remember that if actual production was greater than normal, we would have used the actual production volume.)

The fixed cost per litre can, therefore, be calculated as follows:

Total fixed production costs/normal production = 3,600/300,000 = £0.012.

The total cost per litre for November is as follows:

	£	
Variable cost	0.1683	
Fixed cost	0.012	
	£0.1803	i.e. 18.03 pence

Techniques for the measurement of cost

IAS 2 permits techniques for the measurement of inventories to be used for convenience if the results approximate cost. IAS 2 mentions the standard cost method, where normal levels of materials, supplies, labour, efficiency and capacity utilization are used to calculate a standard cost. A standard cost is a target cost that should be attained under specified operating conditions. In many cases this may be the only way to value manufactured goods in a high-volume/high-turnover environment.

The standard also permits the use of the retail method. Under the retail method the cost of inventory is determined by reducing the sales value of the inventory by the appropriate gross profit margin. Problems can occur where a retailer deals in products of widely differing profit margins, or discounts slow-moving items.

Use of standard costs (para. 21)

The standard cost method may be used for the measurement of cost, provided that the results approximate to actual cost. Standard costs have to be reviewed regularly if this method is used. Adjustments will need to be made for significant variances. Variances that relate to abnormal events of the period should not be adjusted for as they relate to the period and should be written off in the period. They should not be carried forward in inventory as this would simply defer the abnormality to a future accounting period.

Example: standard cost method

Allandale Ltd estimated the following standard cost for product X at 1 January 2012, the beginning of its accounting year.

	£ per unit
Direct labour	50
Direct materials	200
Direct expenses	40
Production overheads	60
Selling and distribution	20
	370

The following variances (i.e. differences between the planned standard cost and actual cost), occurred during the year. (Note: an adverse variance arises when the actual cost is greater than the standard cost; a favourable variance arises when the actual cost is less than the standard cost.)

- Labour – £120,000 favourable: this resulted from a more efficient use of labour throughout the year.
- Material – £20,000 adverse: this was caused by an undetected machine fault leading to materials being damaged and scrapped.
- Direct expenses – £60,000 favourable: a new subcontractor was used from 1 September 2012 onwards, resulting in reduced subcontracting costs.

At 31 December 2012, 2,000 units of product X were in stock. Total production for the year was 12,000 units. Allandale uses the FIFO method for stock valuation purposes.

Required

Calculate the cost of the closing stock of product X.

Solution

As explained earlier, decide which of the information given is relevant. While selling and distribution costs may well be relevant to Allandale for internal control purposes, they are not permitted, under IAS 2, to be included in the inventory valuation and so should be excluded from the calculation of closing inventory.

Having decided which information is relevant, decide whether adjustments need to be made for the variances. If so, these will add to, or reduce, the standard cost.

	£
Cost of inventory at standard cost	
2,000 units × (£370 − £20 selling and distribution)	700,000
Labour variance (favourable)	
Adjustment should be made as standard was inaccurate	
Units in inventory equal 1/6 of production (2,000/12,000)	
∴ 1/6 of variance = 1/6 × 120,000	(20,000)
Material variance (adverse)	
This was due to an abnormal event and no adjustment should be made.	
Expenses variance (favourable)	
This should be adjusted for as it is a normal event – it is just that it was	
not anticipated when the original standard was set.	
As the variance occurred over the last four months of the year and closing	
inventory equals the last two months of production the adjustment is:	
(2,000/4,000) × £60,000	(30,000)
Closing inventory of product X	650,000

Consider in detail the adjustments made, as described below.

(i) Selling and distribution costs, while no doubt invaluable information for internal control purposes, are not permitted to be included in closing inventories and so are removed from the initial unitary standard cost valuation (i.e. £370 − £20 = £350 per unit).

(ii) The favourable labour variance needs to be deducted from the standard cost as calculated. This is because the reduction in costs is due to greater efficiency. If no adjustment was made and the standard cost of £50 per unit was maintained there would be, by default, an element of inefficiency being included in the closing inventory valuation.

(iii) The unfavourable material variance will not be adjusted for. It will already be included in the materials purchased expense within cost of sales. It does not, therefore, require any further adjustment. The standard cost of £200 per unit for direct materials will continue to be used in the closing inventory valuation.

(iv) Similar to the favourable labour variance, the use of the new subcontractor has resulted in a reduction in costs. This will result in a new standard cost being calculated for this particular element of production, which presumably will be incorporated in the next year's standard cost calculation. For the current year, this requires to be adjusted for as, otherwise, direct expenses would be being carried forward that are in excess of those that ought to be being accounted for in inventory (i.e. subcontractor costs based on the standard would be in excess of the actual subcontractor costs incurred).

Progress Point 5.9

DRT Ltd manufactures a single product. It operates a standard costing system and updates these standards at the start of each financial year. At 1 January 2012, the following standard costs per unit were set:

	£ per unit
Direct materials	125
Direct labour	40
Direct expenses	30
Production overhead	35
Selling & distribution	10
	240

Information taken from the management accounts shows the following variances for the year to 31 December 2012.

	Price/cost increases £		Usage £		Efficiency £		Total £	
Direct materials	30,000	A	90,000	F			60,000	F
Direct labour	100,000	A			60,000	F	40,000	A
Production overhead					120,000	F	120,000	F
	130,000	A	90,000	F	180,000	F	140,000	F

A: adverse

F: favourable

Consultation with management has identified that the variances were caused by the following factors.

- Direct materials: a new production process was introduced from 1 September 2012. This required higher-quality and more expensive materials but led to reduced wastage.
- Direct labour: a higher than anticipated wage increase was made halfway through the year. This was partly offset by agreed new working practices, which led to efficiency savings.
- Production overhead: greater throughput in the year increased cost recovery.

At 31 December 2012, there were 2,000 units of finished goods in inventory. The units in inventory are equivalent to December production. Production arises evenly throughout the year. DRT Ltd uses the FIFO method in valuing inventory.

Required

Calculate the closing inventory value of DRT Ltd.

Solution

The use of standard costs is acceptable providing they reflect current conditions. As DRT Ltd sets its costs at the start of its accounting year, certain variances may require to be adjusted for in the inventory valuation.

	£
Standard cost	240
Less: selling and distribution costs	10
	230
∴ Inventories at standard cost = 2,000 × £230	460,000
Adjustments for variances:	
Direct material	(15,000)
Direct labour	6,667
Production overhead	(10,000)
Closing inventory value	441,667

Workings

Selling and distribution

As these costs are not related to bringing the inventory to its current location and condition they should be omitted from the inventory valuation.

Direct materials

A net £60,000 favourable variance arose in the last four months following the introduction of a new production process. The existing standard would therefore overstate cost per unit. A reduction is therefore required of:

£60,000/4 mths = £15,000

That is, as production arises evenly throughout the year, the adjustment reflects one month's production (i.e. 2,000 units).

Direct labour

A net £40,000 adverse variance arose over the last six months following a higher than expected wage increase. The existing standard would therefore understate cost per unit. An increase is therefore required of:

£40,000/6 mths = £6,667

Production overhead

The favourable increase of £120,000 arises from additional production and the existing standard would overstate inventories. A reduction is therefore required of:

£120,000/12 mths = £10,000

Retail price (para. 22)

As with the standard cost method, the retail method may be used provided that the results approximate to actual cost. The retail method, as its name would suggest, is used in the retail trade for dealing with inventory valuations of businesses that have high volumes of various line items of inventory, and where similar mark-ups are applied to all inventory items or groups of items. Under the retail method a conventional inventory count is carried out and the selling price is used to determine the cost of the inventory by reducing the sales value by the appropriate gross profit margin.

Example

Retco, a supermarket chain, achieves average mark-ups on goods sold of 50%.

At 31 December 2012, following its annual inventory count, inventories with a retail price of £750,000 were identified.

Under the retail method, the cost of these inventories may be approximated by converting it to cost by removing the normal mark-up. That is:

$$\text{Cost} + (50\% \text{ cost}) = \text{retail price}$$

$$\text{Cost} = \frac{\text{retail price}}{1\%_0}$$

$$= \frac{750,000}{1\%_0}$$

$$= £500,000$$

Clearly, the problem in applying the retail method is in determining the margin to be applied to the inventory at selling price to convert it back to cost. Because different lines and different departments may have widely different margins, it is normally necessary to subdivide inventory and apply the appropriate margins to each subdivision. An additional problem can arise where inventories have been marked down to below original selling price. In such a situation, adjustments have to be made to eliminate the effect of these mark-downs so as to prevent any item of inventory being valued at less than both its cost and its net realizable value.

Example

Beachwear Plus uses the retail method for inventory valuation. During December 2012, it marked down its swimwear lines to 75% of its normal selling price. At its year end of 31 December, it has inventories of swimwear amounting to a sale (after mark-down) price of £120,000. Beachwear Plus normally achieves a mark-up of 60% on cost. Assuming that all swimwear is expected to be sold following the winter mark-down, at what value should Beachwear Plus value the inventory at 31 December 2012?

Solution

The mark-down adjusted selling price is £120,000. The sales price prior to the mark-down would therefore have been as follows:

$$\text{Full sales price} = \frac{120,000}{75\%} = £160,000$$

Assuming a normal mark-up of 60% on cost, this would equate to a cost of:

$$\frac{160,000}{160\%} = 100,000$$

Beachwear Plus would therefore value its swimwear lines at £100,000.

The position in practice

In practice, companies that use the retail method tend to apply a gross profit margin computed on an average basis rather than apply specific mark-up percentages. This practice is acknowledged by IAS 2, which states that 'an average percentage for each retail department is often used'.

Cost formulas (paras 23 – 27)

The standard requires (para. 23) that for specific items that are not interchangeable, specific costs should be attributed to the specific items of inventory. In other words, costs should be identified for specific items of inventory where each item can be separately identified and separately costed.

Where items are made to a particular specification, it is appropriate to cost each individually. In practice, this method is rarely used owing to the complexity of most manufacturing and retailing businesses and the interchangeability of many items. IAS 2 recognizes this and allows the use of FIFO or weighted average cost formulas to value items that are interchangeable. The LIFO formula, which had been allowed prior to the 2003 version of IAS 2, is no longer permitted.

Para. 25 requires that the same cost formula should be used for all inventories having a similar nature or use to the enterprise. For other inventory items with a different nature or use, an alternative cost formula may be justified.

Prohibition of LIFO as a cost formula

The standard does not permit the use of the last-in, first-out (LIFO) formula to measure the cost of inventories. Under this method, the inventory items remaining at the end of a period are the oldest. The IASB objected to the use of the LIFO formula for a number of reasons:

(i) The use of LIFO is not representative of the actual flows of inventory in a business. Sound management policy would suggest that the oldest inventory items would be used first.

(ii) In times of rising prices, the use of the LIFO formula results in higher (later costs) being charged to profit or loss while leaving lower out-of-date inventory values in the statement of financial position. This results in lower reported profits which suited companies for tax purposes. It is the view of the IASB, however, that fiscal considerations unique to particular countries do not provide an adequate conceptual basis for selecting accounting treatments.

(iii) The use of LIFO results in inventories being shown in the financial statements at values that bear little relation to recent cost levels.

Cost of inventories of a service provider

Thus far in this chapter, the analysis has concentrated on the valuations of physical items of inventory (i.e. goods). IAS 2 defines inventories as including assets that are in the form of the rendering of services. The situation where an enterprise is involved not with the sale or manufacture of goods, but with the provision of services, needs to be considered.

Providers of professional services, such as accountants, solicitors and architects, may have commenced work for a client prior to the year end but may not be in a position at the year end to issue an invoice for the work carried out thus far and hence recognize the related revenue. This gives rise to service provider inventory and the same principles require to be applied to it as for physical inventory items. To the extent that service providers have inventories, they measure them at the costs of their production.

The costs that will need to be identified and carried forward as inventory to the next accounting period will be:

- labour costs of personnel directly engaged in providing the service
- other directly related costs (e.g. travelling costs)
- an appropriate allocation of supervisory costs and overheads, but not general administrative overheads.

The cost of inventories of a service provider does not include profit margins or non-attributable overheads that are often factored into prices charged by service providers.

5.6 Net realizable value (NRV)

Net realizable value (NRV) is defined as the estimated selling price in the ordinary course of business less the:

- estimated costs of completion, and
- the estimated costs necessary to make the sale.

The cost of inventories may not be recoverable if those inventories:

(a) are damaged;

(b) have become wholly or partially obsolete, or

(c) their selling price has declined, or

(d) if the estimated costs of completion or the estimated costs to be incurred to make the sale have increased.

IAS 2 requires that inventories should be measured at the lower of cost and net realizable value. This requirement is consistent with the view that assets should not be carried in excess of amounts expected to be realized from their sale or use.

When cost is higher than NRV, not all the cost incurred can be recovered and therefore inventory should be valued at the lower amount. The effect of this is to recognize the write-down immediately, and the 'loss' is recognized as an expense in the period in which the write-down occurs. Any reversal should be recognized as a reduction in the amount of inventories recognized as an expense in the period in which the reversal occurs. Inventories are usually written down to net realizable value item by item.

The mechanics of a write-down of inventory from cost to NRV are best illustrated with a numerical example.

Example: write-down of inventories from cost to NRV

Norbank carried out its annual inventory count at 31 March 2013, which showed inventories at cost of £120,000. Included in that sum, however, were £40,000 of items that, because of technical advances, were effectively obsolete. These items would, however, be able to be sold as spare parts at an estimated net realizable value of £15,000.

Norbank will, therefore, need to value its inventory at 31 March 2013 as follows:

	£
Inventories at cost as counted	120,000
Less: write-down to NRV of obsolete inventories	
(£40,000 – £15,000)	25,000
Revised inventory value	95,000

The cost of sales calculation (i.e. opening inventory + purchases-closing inventory) effectively ensures that the write-down is immediately recognized within cost of sales. In other words, cost of sales is reduced by the value of closing inventory. In this instance, it is being reduced by a lesser amount (i.e. £95,000) than it would have been had the inventory continued to be valued at cost (i.e. £120,000). Furthermore, the inventory value being carried forward to the next accounting period will more accurately match the revenues generated from its sale as spare parts.

Estimates of NRV should be based on the most reliable evidence at the time the estimates are made as to the amounts the inventories are expected to realize.

The estimates are made at the end of the reporting period but should take into account events after the end of the reporting period if these confirm conditions existing at the end of the reporting period (e.g. sales after the year end).

It must be remembered that net realizable value is the amount the business receives for its inventory from the market. It may be the case that additional expenses are incurred in getting the inventory to the market (e.g. packaging, advertising, delivery and even repair of damaged inventory). These additional costs must be deducted from the realizable value to arrive at the net realizable value.

Where inventories are held to service firm sales or service contracts, the NRV is based on the contract price. If additional inventory is held over and above that required to service the agreed sales or contracts, this additional inventory should be based on general selling prices.

Example: net realizable value

A company has the following items in inventory at 31 December 2012:

Item	Units	Cost	Sales price
		£	£
No. 876	1,200	415	580
No. 997	610	148	150
No. 1822	200	720	810
No. 2076	416	500	430
No. 4732	508	930	1,400

All sales prices are stated before 6% commission paid to sales staff on the sale of an item.

The company has received and accepted an order for all 416 units of item no. 2076. The goods would need to be reworked to the customer's specification, however, at a cost of £215 per unit. The sales price, before sales commission, would be £820 each for the completed units.

Required

Calculate the inventory value at 31 December 2012.

Solution

Item	Units	Cost	NRV1	Lower of cost and NRV	Value
		£	£	£	£
No. 876	1,200	415	545	415	498,000
No. 997	610	148	141	141	86,010
No. 1822	200	720	761	720	144,000
No. 2076	416	500	556[2]	500	208,000
No. 4732	508	930	1,316	930	472,440
					1,408,450

1. Inventory is valued on a line-by-line basis.
2. Costs to complete an item are deducted from sales price in arriving at NRV – they are not added to cost. Remember that these costs have not yet been incurred and so cannot be included in inventory at the end of the reporting period. They are of relevance in determining the net realizable value so that this may be compared to cost at the end of the reporting period. Only if there has been an error should the costs figures be changed.

Workings

(i) All sales prices have been reduced by the 6% sales commissions to arrive at net realizable value.

(ii) Item no. 2076: as the company has accepted the order for all the units, the NRV needs to be calculated on the revised selling price, taking account of the additional reworking costs:

	£
Selling price	820
Less: commission (6%)	49
Less: reworking costs	215
Net realizable value	556

Note that item no. 2076 is now profitable. Prior to the reworking, the NRV would have been as follows:

	£
Selling price	430
Less: commission (6%)	26
Net realizable value	404

Had the inventory of item no. 2076 been sold at these amounts this would have resulted in a loss per unit of:

	£
Net realizable value	404
Cost	500
Loss per unit	96

The inventory would have been valued at the lower of cost and NRV (i.e. £404).

Following the reworking, however, a profit will be made on the sale and it is therefore appropriate to value the inventory of item no. 2076 at cost:

	£
Revised net realizable value (820 – 49 – 215) =	556
Less: cost	500
Profit per unit	56

Progress Point 5.10

The closing inventory of Horne Products includes the following items:

Product A	£
5 units – costs incurred to date	140
Estimated sales revenue – 5 units	160
Selling and distribution expenses – 5 units	30
Product B	
10 units – costs incurred to date	230
Estimated sales revenue – 10 units	280
Selling and distribution expenses – units	20

Required
Calculate the inventory value to be included in Horne Products' financial statements.

Solution

IAS 2 requires that individual types of inventories be valued separately. Therefore, for each product, the cost and net realizable value require to be calculated and each product will be valued at the lower of the two amounts:

		£
Product A –	Sales revenue	160
	Less : selling and distribution expenses	30
	Net realizable value	130
	Costs incurred to date	140

∴ as NRV is lower than cost, Product A will be valued at £130.

Product B –	Sales revenue	280
	Less: selling and distribution expenses	20
	Net realizable value	260
	Costs incurred to date	230

∴ as cost is lower than NRV, Product B will be valued at £230.

Recognition as an expense

Although much of this section has been concerned with the valuation of inventories and the amount of cost to be recognized as an asset, there is the corresponding expense to be considered as and when those inventories are sold.

When inventories are sold, the carrying amount of those inventories should be recognized as an expense in the period in which the related revenue is recognized. The amount of any write-down of inventories to net realizable value and all losses of inventories should be recognized as an expense in the period the write-down or loss occurs. The amount of any reversal of any write-downs of inventories, arising from an increase in net realizable value, should be recognized as a reduction in the amount of inventories recognized as an expense in the period in which the reversal occurs.

The adjustments will be made within the cost of sales expense so that the amount of inventories recognized as an expense in the period will be:

- the carrying amount of any inventories sold in the period; plus
- the amount of any write-down of inventories to net realizable value and all losses of inventories in the period; less
- the amount of any reversal in the period of any write-down of inventories, arising from an increase in net realizable value.

IAS 2 acknowledges that inventories may be used by the entity rather than sold; in such circumstances, their cost may be capitalized as part of the cost of another asset e.g. property, plant and equipment. Their cost is then recognized as an expense through depreciation of that asset.

5.7 Work in progress

Issues examined so far in this chapter have related to a single production process and inventories of finished goods. Also included within the IAS 2 definition of inventories are assets in the production process for sale in the ordinary course of business. Such inventories are classified as work in progress (W-I-P) and are mainly found in manufacturing organizations. Work in progress is simply the cost of partly completed goods or services at the end of the accounting period.

The valuation of W-I-P follows the rules laid out in IAS 2, and consequently must be valued at the lower of cost and net realizable value.

The accounting issue involved

The accounting issue with work in progress is, as with inventory, deciding what to include in cost. Once more an allocation of total costs will need to be made to those goods and services that are at an intermediate stage of completion (i.e. direct materials, direct labour and appropriate overhead). Directly attributable costs can be assigned directly, after which indirect costs will be allocated by reference to one or more factors (e.g. direct labour cost, labour hours worked). Whichever method is chosen for the allocation procedure, it should attempt to relate the indirect costs as precisely as possible to the process that has given rise to them.

Direct materials

It is necessary to identify what proportion of direct materials has been used in work in progress.

The amount contained within work in progress will vary with different types of organization, as the following examples illustrate.

- If the item is complex or materially significant (e.g. a custom-made car), the W-I-P calculation will be based on actual materials and components that have been booked to the job to date.
- If, however, there is a mass-production process, it may not be possible to identify each individual item within W-I-P. In such circumstances, the accountant will make a judgement and define the W-I-P as being a particular percentage complete in respect of raw materials and components. For example, a bolt manufacturer with 5 million bolts per week in W-I-P may decide that, in respect of raw materials, they are 100% complete. The W-I-P valuation would therefore proceed on that basis and include the full materials cost for the 5 million bolts.

However work in progress is valued, consistency is essential and the same method should therefore be applied consistently.

Direct labour

As with direct materials, it is necessary to identify how much direct labour has been consumed into W-I-P. Again, there are two broad approaches.

1. If the item of W-I-P is complex or materially significant, the actual time booked to the job will form part of the W-I-P valuation.
2. In a mass production situation, it may not be possible to assign costs with such precision and an accounting judgement may have to be made as to the average percentage completion in respect of direct labour. In the example of the bolt manufacturer, it could be that, on average, W-I-P is 80% complete in respect of direct labour.

Appropriate overhead

The same two approaches as for direct labour can be adopted.

1. With a complex or materially significant item, it should be possible to allocate the overhead actually incurred. This could be an actual charge – for example, subcontract work – or an application of the appropriate overhead recovery rate (ORR). The ORR is the overhead cost divided by a measure of activity, such as direct labour hours, to give a cost per unit of activity. For example, if a direct labour recovery rate is used and the ORR is £20 per direct labour hour, and the recorded labour time on the W-I-P is ten hours, then the overhead charge for W-I-P purposes is £200.
2. With mass-production items, the accountant must either use an overhead recovery rate approach or, as with direct costs, adopt a percentage completion approach (e.g. in respect of overheads, W-I-P is 75% complete).

Whichever method is chosen, the company's auditors will check to ensure that application of the particular allocation process results in a true and fair view being achieved. In practice this can pose problems for the company accountant as well as the auditors. The responsibility for determining the percentage completion of W-I-P will often fall to a process engineer or a manager with technical knowledge of the product, rather than the accountant. The accountant may not have the technical expertise himself and so reliance on these other employees will be essential.

The following examples illustrate the allocation of total costs referred to above.

Example

Parkinson Products is a manufacturer of briefcases. The costs of a completed briefcase are:

	£	
Direct materials	12.00	
Direct labour	6.00	
Appropriate overhead	10.00	
Total cost	28.00	(for finished goods inventory value purposes)

After consultation with the production manager, the company accountant takes the view that, for W-I-P, the following applies:

Direct materials	100% complete
Direct labour	80% complete
Appropriate overhead	60% complete

Therefore, for one briefcase in W-I-P, the following values will be assigned:

		£
Direct materials	£12.00 × 100%	12.00
Direct labour	£6.00 × 80%	4.80
Appropriate overhead	£10.00 × 60%	6.00
W-I-P value		22.80

If the company has 10,000 briefcases in work in progress, the value will be: $10,000 \times £22.80 = £228,000$.

This technique is particularly useful in processing industries such as petroleum, brewing, dairy products or paint manufacture, where it may be impossible to identify W-I-P items precisely. In such circumstances, the role of the auditor in verifying such practices is essential.

Example

A custom chopper company making customized motorcycles has the following costs in respect of Project 907, an unfinished motorcycle, at the end of the month:

	£
Materials charged to Project 907	2,500
Labour: 100 hours at £25 per hour	2,500
Overheads: £22/DLH x 100 hours	2,200
W-I-P value of Project 907	7,200

BASIC

INTERMEDIATE

ADVANCED

This is an accurate work in progress value provided all the costs have been accurately recorded and an accurate overhead recovery rate established. The level of accounting work is not excessive as the information is required by a normal job costing system from inventory records, timesheets, etc. An added advantage is that, for audit purposes, the work in progress figure can be verified and proven.

The net realizable value of work in progress

It is important not to forget the underlying principle of IAS 2 that inventories should be measured at the lower of cost and net realizable value. It follows therefore that, in order to make a comparison of cost and NRV, the NRV of work in progress needs to be considered.

This poses the accountant some additional problems. It is highly unlikely that there will be a market for partly completed goods, and consequently the NRV calculation will need to be made taking account of costs to completion and ultimate selling price. Given the assumptions made, however, in arriving at cost for W-I-P, such calculations would be at best cumbersome and in many instances, unnecessary. The enterprise will be producing the inventory item with a view to making a profit and so the NRV is likely to be in excess of cost in any event. Consequently, in such circumstances, it is more appropriate to consider the NRV of the inventory item in its finished state. Then, if any of the conditions apply to suggest that NRV might be less than cost – for example, an increase in costs or a fall in selling price, physical deterioration of inventories, obsolescence of products, a decision as part of a company's marketing strategy to manufacture and sell products at a loss – the carrying value of the related raw materials and work in progress must also be reviewed and a provision made if required.

5.8 Raw materials

The net realizable value of raw materials

Again, it would be easy to forget the underlying valuation principles of IAS 2 in respect of raw materials. Raw materials, by definition, are subjected to some form of process by an enterprise in becoming finished goods. Consequently, it is normally not possible to arrive at a particular NRV for each item of raw material based on selling price. In such circumstances, current replacement cost might be the best guide to NRV. If current replacement cost is less than historic cost, however, a provision is required to be made only if the finished goods into which they will be made are expected to be sold at a loss. No provision should be made just because the anticipated profit will be less than normal. Where inventories of spares are held for resale, it may be possible to predict obsolescence – and identify the need for a provision – by reference to the number of units sold to which the spares are applicable. In forecasting net realizable value, events occurring between the end of the reporting period and completion of the accounts need to be considered.

Progress Point 5.11

Oscar Industries manufactures one standard product. The following information is available in respect of inventories and work in progress at the year end.

1. The inventory sheets at the year end show the following items:

Raw materials:

   100 tonnes of steel at cost £140 per ton

   Present price is £130 per tonne

Finished goods:

   100 finished units:

   Cost of materials £50 per unit

Labour cost £150 per unit

Selling price £500 per unit

Partly finished goods:

40 partly finished goods

For work in progress, the company accountant has advised the following:

Materials 100% complete

Labour $66\frac{2}{3}$% complete

Damaged finished units:

10 damaged finished units

Costs to rectify the damage – £200 per unit

Selling price when rectified   £500 per unit

2. Manufacturing overheads are   100% of labour costs
3. Selling and distribution costs are   £60 per unit

Required

From the information given, calculate the amounts to be included in the statement of financial position of Oscar Industries Ltd in respect of inventories and work in progress. State also the principles applied in arriving at the valuations.

Solution

1. Principles applied: inventories are valued at the lower of cost and net realizable value. Cost includes those overheads that have been incurred in bringing the inventories to their existing condition (i.e. manufacturing overheads).
2. Valuation method:

Raw materials

Inventory value = 100 tonnes @ £140 = £14,000

Note: as there is no indication that the finished goods will be sold at a loss it is appropriate to value the raw materials at £140 per tonne. Only if there had been such an indication would it have been appropriate to value the raw materials at the lower amount – that lower amount being the best guide to net realizable value.

Finished goods: 100 units		£
Cost	Direct materials: cost per unit	50
	Direct labour: cost per unit	150
	Manufacturing overheads: 100% of labour	150
	Cost per unit	350
NRV	Selling price per unit	500
	Less: selling and distribution costs	60
	Net realizable value per unit	440

The inventories of finished goods will, therefore, be valued at the lower of cost and net realizable value, i.e. £35,000 (100 units × £350).

Partly finished goods: 40 units	
	£
Cost (based on percentage complete)	
Direct materials 100% × £50	50
Direct labour 66⅔% × £150	100
Manufacturing overheads 100% of labour	100
Cost per unit	250
No. of units: 40 × £250	10,000

NRV (based on percentage method):

	£
Selling price	500
Less : selling and distribution costs	60
	440
Less: costs to complete:	
Direct labour 33⅓% × £150	50
Manufacturing overheads 100% of labour	50
	340
Less: costs incurred so far	250
Expected profit per unit	90

As the partly finished goods are expected to be sold at a profit, they should be valued at cost (i.e. 40 units × £250 = £10,000).

Damaged finished goods: 10 units.

In order to value the damaged finished goods, we need to determine the net realizable value. The net realizable value is:

	£
Selling price	500
Less: selling and distribution costs	60
Less: costs to rectify	200
NRV per unit	240

The cost of these damaged units would have been the same as the finished units, i.e.:

	£
Direct materials	50
Direct labour	150
Manufacturing overhead	150
	350

The damaged units should therefore be valued at the lower of cost and net realizable value, i.e.:

10 units × £240 = £2,400

Statement of financial position extract:

	£	
Inventories: raw materials	14,000	
Work in progress	10,000	
finished goods	37,400	(35,000 + 2,400)
	61,400	

5.9 Disclosure requirements

IAS 2 (para. 36) requires disclosure of:

(a) the accounting policy adopted in measuring inventories, including the cost formula used
(b) total inventory, analysed into appropriate categories
(c) the amount of inventory carried at net realizable value
(d) the amount of inventory recognized as an expense in the period (this will normally be part or all of cost of sales)
(e) the amount of any write-down of inventories recognized as an expense during the period
(f) the carrying amount of inventories pledged as security for liabilities
(g) the amount of any reversal of any write-down that is recognized as a reduction in the amount of inventories recognized as an expense in the period.

Disclosure in practice

In practice, the required disclosures of IAS 2 *Inventories* are dealt with in distinct sections. The accounting policies note is normally used to explain in narrative form the policies adopted by an enterprise in measuring inventories, the types of inventories held, and the cost formula used, while the statement of financial position discloses the total inventories, and the notes to the financial statements detail the classification and numerical elements of the required disclosures.

Inventories

The following extract from the accounting policy note of Logica identifies the nature of its inventories held (computer equipment and materials), and states its compliance to IAS 2 in its declaration that inventories are stated at the lower of cost and net realizable value.

Inventories

Inventories represent computer equipment that, at the end of the reporting period, had not yet been allocated to a specific customer contract and materials, including work-in-progress, used in document printing and finishing.

Inventories are stated at the lower of cost and net realisable value. Cost comprises direct materials and, where applicable, direct labour costs and those overheads that have been incurred in bringing the inventories to their present location and condition. Cost is calculated using the first-in-first-out (FIFO) method. Net realisable value represents the estimated selling price less costs to be incurred in marketing, distribution and sale.

Source: Logica (2011), p. 98

The extract from the accounting policy of Logica identifies the nature of its inventories held (computer equipment and materials) and states its compliance to IAS 2 in its declaration that inventories are stated at the lower of cost and net realizable value. The note then defines both cost and net realizable value.

Current assets

Inventories are included within the current assets section of Logica's statement of financial position (see Figure 5.1) and have a total carrying amount of £0.8 million at 31 December 2011, with a comparative balance at 31 December 2010 of £1.0 million. Further information regarding inventories is given in note 21 to the financial statements.

Figure 5.1 Current assets note of Logica plc

Current assets			
Inventories	21	0.8	1.0
Trade and other receivables	22	1,262.0	1,252.3
Current tax assets		24.8	11.4
Cash and cash equivalents	24	89.6	56.4

Source: Logica (2011), p. 93

Inventories

The note to the financial statements provides further analysis of the total inventories figure in the statement of financial position of £0.8 million (see Figure 5.2). Here, the carrying amounts of the different types of inventories referred to in the accounting policy note are disclosed, together with a statement from the directors that the carrying values of inventories approximated their fair value less cost to sell.

Figure 5.2 Logica: detailed analysis of inventory items

	2011 £'m	2010 £'m
Computer equipment not allocated to a customer contract	0.4	0.6
Materials used in document printing and finishing	0.4	0.4
	0.8	1.0

The Directors estimate that the carrying value of inventories approximated their fair value less cost to sell.
Source: Logica (2011), P. 93

BASIC

INTERMEDIATE

ADVANCED

Section summary

The objective of IAS 2 is to prescribe the accounting treatment for inventories, and to provide guidance for determining their cost and for subsequently recognizing an expense including any write-down to net realizable value.

The fundamental principle of IAS 2 is that inventories shall be measured at the lower of cost and net realizable value.

The calculation of unit cost is fraught with difficulties. IAS 2 allows expenses incidental to the acquisition or production cost of an asset to be included in its cost. This includes not only directly attributable production overheads but also those overheads that are indirectly attributable to production. Although IAS 2 provides guidelines on the classification of overheads to achieve an appropriate allocation, in practice it is difficult to make these distinctions, and the complexity of some manufacturing processes will result in auditors finding it difficult to challenge management on such matters. Moreover, if management is intent on fraud, then inventories are an ideal figure to manipulate.

Consequently, although the fundamental principle is straightforward, the valuation of inventories is by no means so. Furthermore, while the reporting requirements of IAS 2 no doubt go some way to defining practices, narrowing differences and variations in those practices, and ensuring adequate disclosure in the accounts, the valuation of inventory is still a subjective process relying heavily on the expertise and judgement of management. Unfortunately, this subjective judgement can have substantial effects on the reporting of financial information: financial information that may be manipulated to suit management's desired objectives.

Section 3: Advanced Aspects

5.10 Problems in practice

Establishing an accurate inventory valuation can be extremely difficult. The calculation of unit cost is fraught with difficulties and is often an exercise in judgement, which, however expert, is essentially subjective in nature. For example, the separation of direct and indirect costs, the basis for allocation of indirect overheads, the level of activity for which standard costs are calculated, the measurement of the degree of completion of work in progress – all these decisions involve an element of judgement, and the resulting costs will only be as accurate as the judgements on which they are based.

Unfortunately, no area of accounting provides more opportunities for subjectivity and creative accounting than the valuation of inventory. Furthermore, because inventories feature on both the statement of comprehensive income and statement of financial position, and because they can dramatically alter an enterprise's financial position, inventories are particularly susceptible to fraudulent manipulation. The practising accountant is faced with many problems relating to inventory valuation, and some of these are considered below.

While, in many instances, an auditor will attend a company's inventory count, there will be far more instances when the accountant will not attend – and instead, be provided with inventory valuations by the client companies themselves. This is particularly the case with sole traders and partnerships, as well as small to medium-sized limited companies. Such entities, if below a certain level of turnover limits, do not require an audit. It might well be the case that an inventory valuation is simply provided to the reporting accountant for inclusion within the financial statements. The accountant is then faced with the dilemma of accepting a figure that he has little means of checking. Moreover, depending on the business's circumstances, this figure may well have been 'chosen' to fulfil that business's 'needs'. For example, a company which knows that it has had a successful trading year may deliberately value inventory on the low side in order to reduce profits and consequently its income tax liability. On the other hand, a company having had a mediocre year may try to boost profits to keep its lenders happy or indeed, if there are external shareholders, to satisfy them that an efficient return is being made on their investment.

The question that naturally arises is, therefore, 'How can the accountant guard against such manipulations?'

First, the accountant should be aware of the pressures that are surrounding the particular business. If there has been a profitable year then it is likely that the company will wish to reduce the inventory valuation; if the company has been under pressure from its lenders then the tendency will be for the company to value higher than normal.

Second, the accountant can calculate ratios such as gross profit percentage and rate of inventory turnover, to help verify the cost of sales figures. Such ratios are considered in depth in Chapter 12 and help to highlight any possible discrepancies by comparing one year's results against previous year's ratios or industry norms.

Third, at a more detailed level, the accountant may look at the purchase and sales invoices in the last few months of the company's year to ascertain the level of inventory purchases and sales, and confirm that the relationship between them is consistent with the closing inventory level.

In larger organizations – particularly those where an audit opinion is required – there can be even more difficulties. An inventory count may last many days and it is essential to determine the 'cut-off' date (i.e. the date when the trading year effectively ceases and the line is drawn after which any profits will be allocated to the next accounting year). In practice, the matching of sales with cost of sales can be problematic – particularly if the inventory count does not happen on the year-end date and there continue to be physical flows of inventory between the year-end date and the date of the actual inventory count. This is particularly problematic for companies with year-end dates of 31 December – not many auditors would wish to be attending inventory counts on 1 January! The practical solution to this problem relies on having an accurate record of inventory movements between the date of the inventory count and the year-end date. An adjusted inventory figure can then be calculated:

	£
Inventories at 7 January 2013	156,123
Less: purchases (1 January 2013 – 7 January 2013)	(4,897)
Add: sales (1 January 2013 – 7 January 2013)	2,156
Inventories at 31 December 2012	153,382

Also related to the problems in determining the 'cut-off' date is linking physical inventories with the recorded flows of inventories in the company's financial records. The auditor must be aware that the recording of accounting transactions may not coincide with the physical flows of inventory. Inventories may have been sold, a sale recorded in the financial records but the related items may be in the warehouse awaiting dispatch. It would be essential therefore to exclude any such inventory from the closing inventory valuation; similarly, a purchase of inventory may have been recorded in the financial records but the related item may not have been delivered by the date of the inventory count. It will be essential therefore to include the value of that as yet undelivered inventory in the year-end valuation.

Further problems arise where goods are held on a sale or return basis – that is, goods may be on the company's premises but title still lies with the supplier – the purchase from the supplier not being required until the inventories have been sold. This happens frequently in the motor trade where a manufacturer will supply a dealership with several vehicles on a sale or return basis to assist the dealership by reducing stocking costs (i.e. the dealership would not have to fund the cost of stocking what might be hundreds of thousands of pounds' worth of vehicles). In such instances, this consignment inventory would require to be excluded from the dealer's year-end inventory valuation.

The company itself may operate a sale or return system for its goods (i.e. the company may have inventories that it has supplied to its customers on a sale or return basis). Such inventories have not been sold and consequently they require to be included in the year-end valuation at the lower of cost and net realizable value. This can pose significant problems for the auditor if these inventories are held at several different locations over a wide geographical area.

The auditor must be aware of all these possibilities and design appropriate procedures to test that controls are in place to ensure that inventories are dealt with correctly. In particular, the auditor will wish to be able to trace a sample of each inventory entry through the accounting records so that:

- if a purchase is recorded, but no sale, then the item must be in inventory
- if a sale is recorded, a purchase must also have been recorded, and the item should not be in inventory.

Physical condition of inventories

The auditor will need to satisfy himself of the physical condition of the inventories. Damaged inventories will have a lower value than inventories in first-class condition. The auditor must ensure that the

Table 5.1 **Illustration of the various possibilities and the required accounting treatment**

Treatment of inventory items	Inventory	Warehouse
Sales		
If invoiced to customer	Remove from inventory	Inventory not counted
If returned from customer	Include in inventory	Include
If not invoiced/returned	Include in inventory	Include
Purchases		
If invoiced to company	Include in inventory	Include
If returned by company	Remove from inventory	Inventory not counted
If invoiced/credited	Include	Include

condition of the inventory is recorded at the inventory count so that the correct value is assigned to it. Damaged items and items that have been in inventory for a long period will require to be written down to net realizable value.

Identification of high-value items

Clearly, inventory items with a higher value will have a more significant effect on the valuation of inventories overall. It is important, therefore, that the auditor familiarizes himself with the production process and has appreciation of the materials used, and their relative importance and their relative values. Distinguishing between two similar items can be crucial when there are large differences in value. For example, steel-coated brass rods look identical to steel rods but their relative values will be very different. It is important, therefore, that they are recorded correctly at the inventory count so that the correct values may be assigned to them.

Valuation of complex items

Some inventory counts will consist of the measurement of large vats of chemicals. While the auditor may be able to calculate the volume of a cylinder, he may not have the expertise to confirm what stage in the production process the particular chemical has reached. Again, knowledge of the industry is essential to ensure that an appropriate valuation is assigned.

Detailed audit trails

Tracing an item through an accounting system can often be time consuming and may require a great deal of effort (i.e. checking the order, the authority for the order, the purchase invoice, the pricing of the invoice, identifying the sale/identifying the item in inventory). If the particular item is messy and indistinguishable, the auditor may not have the expertise – or indeed the will – to verify the measurements taken by the client's own employees. Frequently, the more tedious audit tests are given to audit juniors – it is not surprising how many positive audit conclusions are arrived at by such staff.

The problems noted above are all inherent problems (i.e. they are problems that exist simply as a result of the particular processes or nature of the companies concerned). What if, as may be the case, management sets out to deliberately manipulate the inventory figures? The following sections give consideration to the types of manipulation management may try to implement.

Manipulating cut-off procedures

Determining the cut-off point is essential to ensure that purchases, sales and inventories are dealt with in the correct accounting period. One way of boosting closing inventory, and hence profit and net assets, is to take goods into inventory but not record the related purchase invoice.

Fictitious transfers

Again relating to cut-off, year-end inventories may be inflated by recording fictitious transfers of non-existing inventory (i.e. by declaring that goods are 'in transit' between different depots of the same company, a physical count becomes very difficult). Moreover, if the transfer is between depots in different countries, verification would be extremely costly.

Incorrect valuations

It may be the case that management attaches an unrealistic value to obsolete inventory. Knowledge of the business on the part of the auditor should prevent such manipulations, but the auditor may lack sufficient expertise to challenge management's assertions.

Inaccurate inventory records

If inventory records are poorly maintained, this may mask theft from within the organization. Such poor record-keeping may be deliberate and designed to 'hide' theft, or it may be that opportunistic employees have become aware of the shortcomings of the inventory recording system and are using them to their advantage.

Downright dishonesty!

Within auditing literature is the example of the audit assistant who was sent to audit coal at a coal yard. The audit assistant was shown various inventory piles of coal and so, equipped with the formula for determining the volume of a cone, the audit assistant set about measuring the diameter and height of the various conical piles of coal. What the audit assistant had not appreciated was that 'hidden' underneath one of the piles was a concrete shed! The volume of coal had therefore been inflated by the volume of the concrete shed.

Creative accounting

As the above shows, where there is a will to manipulate, inventories are the ideal items with which to be creative. In fairness to the auditor, even the most diligent of individuals may fail to uncover such fraudulent activities if management is determined enough to mislead and misrepresent the reality of the situation.

Section summary

The fundamental principle of IAS 2 is straightforward. Unfortunately the valuation of inventories is often not.

The complexity of some manufacturing processes results in auditors having to rely on management's assertions. Moreover, if management is intent on fraud, then inventories are an ideal figure to manipulate.

Consequently, although the fundamental principle is straightforward, the valuation of inventories is by no means so. Furthermore, while the reporting requirements of IAS 2 no doubt go some way to defining practices, narrowing differences and variations in those practices, and ensuring adequate disclosure in the accounts, the valuation of inventory is still a subjective process relying heavily on the expertise and judgement of management. Unfortunately, this subjective judgement can have substantial effects on the reporting of financial information: financial information that may be manipulated to suit management's desired objectives.

Chapter summary

IAS 2 *Inventories*

- Inventories should be valued at the lower of cost and net realizable value.
- Cost includes all costs to bring the inventories to their present condition and location.
- Where specific cost is not appropriate, the benchmark treatment is to use FIFO or weighted average.
- The standard cost and retail methods may be used for the measurement of cost, provided that the results approximate actual cost.
- The same cost formula should be used for all inventories with similar characteristics as to their nature and use to the enterprise.
- For inventories with a different nature or use, different cost formulas may be justified.
- When inventories are sold, the carrying amount of those inventories should be recognized as an expense in the period in which the related revenue is realized.

✓ Key terms for review

Definitions can be found in the glossary at the end of the book.

Cost of goods sold
Net realizable value
Inventories

? Review questions

1. Identify which costs should be included in the cost of inventories and which should be excluded from the cost of inventories.
2. Explain the effect an increase or decrease in the value of closing inventory will have on the reported profit of a company.
3. Briefly outline each of the following methods of stock valuation:
   (a) first in, first out (FIFO)
   (b) last in, first out (LIFO)
   (c) weighted average cost (AVCO).
4. Explain the difference between *perpetual* and *periodic* bases of inventory valuations.
5. What is the IAS 2 definition of *inventories*?
6. Explain how inventories should be measured to comply with IAS 2.
7. Explain how an under-recovery of overheads should be accounted for in arriving at a figure for closing inventory.
8. Explain how an over-recovery of overheads should be accounted for in arriving at a figure for closing inventory.
9. Identify the items that IAS 2 specifically excludes from the cost of inventory.
10. How should the inventory of a service provider be accounted for?

Exercises

Level I

1. BD Joiners inventory transactions for the three months ended 31 March 2013 were as follows:

	Units	Unit cost	Unit selling price
		£	£
Inventory on hand: 1/1/13	60	30	
January purchases	90	34	
January sales	(40)		60

February purchases	55	60	
February sales	(45)		100
March purchases	60	75	
March sales	(75)		130
Inventory on hand 31/3/13	105		

BD Joiners maintains its inventory records on the perpetual system, and all purchases are made on the first day of the month.

Required

(a) Calculate cost of goods sold, gross profit and closing inventory for the three months ended 31 March 2013 under FIFO and LIFO cost flow assumptions.

(b) With reference to your findings in (i) above, explain the effect each of the cost flow assumptions has on the statement of comprehensive income and statement of financial position in times of rising prices.

2. Purchases and sales of a certain product for the first seven days of June 2013 are as follows:

Day	1	Purchases	20 units @ £5 each
	3	Sales	15 units
	5	Purchases	30 units @ £6 each
	7	Sales	10 units

Required

(a) Determine the cost of goods sold for the week and closing inventory at the end of the week under the FIFO, LIFO and weighted average methods of inventory valuation, assuming a *periodic* system of inventory control.

(b) Determine the cost of goods sold for the week and closing inventory at the end of the week under the FIFO, LIFO and weighted average methods of inventory valuation, assuming a *perpetual* system of inventory control.

(c) Discuss the advantages and/or disadvantages of FIFO, LIFO and the weighted average method.

(d) If a company maintains a perpetual inventory control system, is it necessary to have an annual stock take?

3. Arch Racing Supplies has inventories which include the following four items.

Description	Purchase cost £	Selling price £	Cost of selling £
Engine	6,500	8,250	350
Chassis	2,000	1,800	200
Frame	4,800	4,900	300
Gearbox	1,200	1,500	100

Required

What amount should be reported as total inventory in respect of these items in the statement of financial position of Arch Racing Supplies?

Level II

4. Mod Transport Ltd manufacture four types of scooter: Models A, B, C and D. The following information relates to the value of finished goods and work in progress in inventories on 31 December 2012 (the company's financial year end):

Model	Number of items in inventory	Production cost to date £	Estimated further costs required to complete each item £	Expected selling price per item £
A	10	150	–	140
B	15	70	–	110
C	23	65	20	100
D	7	110	30	150

It is estimated that further costs will necessarily be incurred in selling the scooters. These additional costs are estimated at 5% of each item's total cost (production and completion).

Required

Calculate the value at which inventories will be stated in the statement of financial position at 31 December 2012.

5. D & C Stores is a food retailer that values inventory at a retail price less a margin. Inventory at 30 November 2012 has been counted and categorized as follows:

Category	Units	Retail price per unit £	Average gross margin %
Perishable goods	800	1.20	40
Drinks	1,850	2.90	20
Household, cleaning	550	2.10	18
Tinned goods	6,300	0.65	15
Packaged dry goods	4,100	1.40	24

It is company policy to create a provision of 50% of the cost of perishable goods.

Required

Calculate the closing inventory value to be included in the accounts of D & C stores at 30 November 2012.

Level III

6. Flofoam is a manufacturer of specialist lightweight padding for seating in passenger aircraft. As a result of the particular machinery required, Flofoam manufactures and sells only this one product. Raw materials are purchased in lots of 1,000 tonnes at the commencement of each week throughout the year ended 31 March 2013. The price per tonne was £100 for the first nine months and £130 thereafter. Transport costs to the factory amount to £20 per tonne and customs duty of £4 per tonne was paid throughout the year. Due to the volume of purchases, the supplier of raw materials gave a discount of £8 per tonne from 1 October 2012 onwards.

 Direct costs of processing amount to £30 per tonne and fixed production overheads have been calculated at £27 per tonne on the basis of normal levels of activity.

 Each tonne of raw material produces one tonne of finished goods.

 Company general administration overheads amount to £5,000 per week and selling costs are estimated at £18 per tonne.

 At the end of the year there were £4,000 tonnes of raw material and 1,500 tonnes of finished goods.

 The selling price to customers per tonne was £300 throughout the year. Opening inventory equalled £640,000 in total, made up of 3,000 tonnes of raw materials and 500 tonnes of finished goods.

 Required

 (a) Calculate the inventory value of raw materials and finished goods as at 31 March 2013. Assume the FIFO method is used.

 (b) Calculate the gross profit for the year to 31 March 2013 assuming an operational year of 52 weeks.

7. Bennett Building Supplies Ltd ('BBS') is a building supply company. At 31 December 2012, a stock count was carried out of the eight main categories of inventory held by the company. Relevant information is as follows:

Category	Units in inventory	Cost per unit	NRV per unit
		£	£
A	500	110	140
B	2,100	75	70
C	350	170	150
D	4,100	42	55
E	1,500	210	220

The calculation of NRV does not take into account a price cut equivalent to 5% of cost that will be applied from 1 January 2012 onwards.

 All building supply materials are finished goods.

BBS has received a firm order for 100 of the category C items at a price of £220 per unit. Selling costs would be £8 per unit. The customer requires these to be modified to meet its specification. BBS estimates this will cost £32 per unit.

Required

Calculate the total value of the closing inventory of BBS at 31 December 2012.

8. MCL has manufactured summerhouses for a number of years and has a well-developed costing system. In anticipation of the forthcoming year's budgeted demand for its prestige model, the Postcode Penthouse,

MCL has concentrated production on this one particular summerhouse. The standard costing information for the year ended 31 December 2012, which had been set on 1 January 2012, was as follows:

	Cost per summerhouse £
Raw materials	800
Direct labour	1,000
Production overheads	1,200
Distribution costs	100

The costing department has supplied the following information regarding variances.

(i) A production fault occurred during August 2012, which resulted in a batch of doors being scrapped.

(ii) The price of raw materials increased on 1 November 2012.

(iii) A changed in working practices took effect from 1 October 2012, which increased direct labour pay rates.

(iv) The variances recorded for the Postcode Penthouse for the year ended 31 December 2012 are as follows:

	Production fault £		Price rise £		Change in working practices £		Total £	
Raw materials	200,000	A	600,000	A	–		800,000	A
Direct labour	50,000	A	–		540,000	A	590,000	A
Production o/hds	50,000	A	–		480,000	F	430,000	F
	300,000	A	600,000	A	60,000	A	960,000	A

Note
A: adverse variance
F: favourable variance

Futher information

(1) Information regarding inventories of the Postcode Penthouse and work in progress at 31 December 2012 was as follows:

Finished goods   2,000 units
Work in progress   1,000 units

Work in progress was 100% complete as to raw materials, and 50% complete as to direct labour and production overheads.

(2) The normal monthly level of production of 4,000 units was achieved throughout the year ended 31 December 2012. Completed summerhouses were sold on the first in first out basis.

(3) Since the year end, the finished goods have all been sold to retailers at £3,800 each, and the work in progress has all been completed and sold at a special price of £3,000 each.

Required
Prepare the inventory valuations at 31 December 2012 for inventories and work in progress, in accordance with IAS 2 *Inventories*.

References

IAS 2 *Inventories*. IASB, 2003.
IAS 11 *Construction Contracts*. IASB, 1993.
Logica (2011) *Annual Report and Accounts*.

Further reading

IAS 23 *Borrowing Costs*. IASB, amended 2008.
IAS 41 *Agriculture*. IASB, amended 2008.
IFRS 9 *Financial Instruments*. IFRS 2009.
Woolf, E. (1976a) Auditing the stocks – part I. *Accountancy*, April.
Woolf, E. (1976b) Auditing the stocks – part II. *Accountancy*, May.
Perry, M. (2001) Valuation problems force FD to quit. *Accountancy Age*, 15 March.

When you have read this chapter, log on to the Online Learning Centre website at *www.mcgraw-hill.co.uk/textbooks/mckeith* to explore chapter-by-chapter test questions, further reading and more online study tools.

Chapter 6

Revenue Recognition and Construction Contracts

Learning Outcomes

After studying this chapter you should be able to:

- ✓ define revenue and what type of transactions it arises from
- ✓ determine when it should be recognized by an entity
- ✓ determine the amount of revenue to appear in an entity's statement of comprehensive income
- ✓ identify different types of revenue and explain the appropriate revenue recognition criteria in IAS 18
- ✓ prepare a disclosure note for revenue
- ✓ explain the reasoning why a new standard on revenue recognition is deemed necessary
- ✓ define construction contracts
- ✓ calculate amounts to be disclosed in financial statements relating to construction contracts
- ✓ disclose contract balances in accordance with IAS 11.

Introduction

The sale of goods or the rendering of services generates revenue for most businesses. Revenue is often referred to as sales or turnover. The term revenue can also be applied to rents received from letting out property or income from receipt of interest, royalties or dividends. It is important to establish principles to determine when revenue should be recognized in the accounts and how it should be measured. This chapter deals with this topic and considers the requirements of IAS 18 Revenue. The advanced section looks at a specific application of the revenue recognition issue – that of construction contracts and examines in detail the accounting and reporting requirements of IAS 11 *Construction Contracts*.

Section 1: Basic Principles

The statement of comprehensive income is used to report a profit of an entity by matching income with expenses. In order to carry out this matching process it is necessary to define income and expenses and determine at what point these should be recognized.

The IASB Conceptual Framework defines income as:

> *increases in economic benefits during the accounting period in the form of inflows or enhancements of assets or the decreases of liabilities that result in increases in equity, other than those relating to contributions from equity participants.*

This definition of income encompasses both revenue and gains. Revenue arises in the course of the ordinary activities of an entity and is referred to by a variety of different names, including sales, fees, interest, dividends, royalties and rent.

Gains arise from other items that meet the definition of income and which may, or may not arise in the course of an entity's ordinary activities. Gains arise from, inter alia, revaluation of assets, sale of non-current assets and pension surpluses.

This section covers revenue only – gains are dealt with by the appropriate IAS in the relevant chapters of this book.

6.1 What is revenue?

Revenue, often referred to as sales or turnover, is often regarded as being the value of all goods or services provided to customers, whether for cash or on credit. In a cash sale the customer pays cash immediately and in a credit sale situation, the customer takes the goods or services and becomes a debtor – agreeing to pay at some future date. In both cases, the sale would, if the goods or services are sold at a profit, result in an increase in recorded net assets. The cash sale would result in an increase in cash while the credit sale would result in an increase in trade receivables. Consider, however, the situation where goods are sold on credit but the customer does not come to collect them, or where, if services are supplied, doubt exists as to the amount the customer is prepared to pay for those services.

The actual time when revenues may be said to be earned can often be difficult to determine. For example, consider a company which manufactures and distributes goods. Should revenues be recognized when the goods are manufactured or when the goods are sold? Strictly speaking, the revenues are earned by both activities but to recognize revenue before a sale takes place would conflict with the prudence concept i.e. recognition of realizable values of inventories of goods available for sale would result in the recognition of unrealized gains which may never be realized if the goods remain unsold. Historically the normal procedure has been to recognize revenue only when a sale has been made i.e. when the ownership of goods passes to the customers. There are now a variety of forms of revenue-earning transactions, however, that include services as well as goods, and the application of this general procedure can be difficult. Traditionally the approach which has been adopted is to determine the 'critical event'. The critical event is that point in the production or sales process that is critical to providing sufficient reassurance that the revenue has been earned by the entity. In the case of sales of goods this is usually the point of delivery to the customer; for a contract of services, the critical event is the production of the service.

The problem is that these 'critical events' will be different for different types of business and are likely to be subjective. For example, while a supplier of stationery to professional businesses will recognize a sale when the goods are delivered to the customer, a market trader will only recognize a sale once he has received his money.

The accounting issue involved

The main issue involved with accounting for revenue is determining when it should be recognized. Assets are recognized at a point in time but revenue might be created over a period of time. Moreover, in the case

BASIC

INTERMEDIATE

ADVANCED

of a civil engineering contract, the service may extend over a number of accounting periods and it will therefore be necessary to try to match a portion of the overall revenue against the costs of each period so as to report a portion of the overall profit to each accounting period.

The next section of this chapter considers IAS 18 *Revenue* which deals with revenue recognition and measurement, while the advanced section examines IAS 11 *Construction Contracts* which prescribes the accounting treatment of revenue and costs associated with construction contracts.

> ### Section summary
> Revenue is key to the determination of the profit of an entity. Revenue is distinguished from income, which includes gains as well as revenues. Revenues are also classified as arising in the course of the ordinary activities of an entity, while gains are seen as those items that result from activities outside of those ordinary activities. The accounting issue involved with accounting for revenue is when it should be recognized.

Section 2: Intermediate Issues

6.2 Revenue recognition

As was explained in the preceding section, the IASB Conceptual Framework definition of income encompasses both revenue and gains. Revenue is income that arises in the course of an entity's ordinary activities and includes such things as sales, fees, interest, dividends and royalties.

6.3 IAS 18 *Revenue*

Objective and scope
The objective of IAS 18 is to prescribe the accounting treatment of revenue arising from the following transactions and events:

(a) the sale of goods;

(b) the rendering of services; and

(c) the use by others of entity assets yielding interest, royalties and dividends.

Definitions
Revenue is defined in IAS 18 as 'the gross inflow of economic benefits during the period arising in the course of the ordinary activities of an entity when those inflows result in increases in equity, other than increases relating to contributions from equity participants'.

This definition therefore excludes from revenue, increases in equity arising from contributions by shareholders.

IAS 18 also states that revenue includes only amounts collected by an entity on its own account. Amounts collected on behalf of third parties, such as sales taxes, VAT etc. are not to be included as revenue; these are not economic benefits which flow to the entity and do not result in increases in equity. Similarly, amounts collected by an agent on behalf of a principal are not revenue for the agent. Instead, revenue is the amount of the commission.

Progress Point 6.1

Identify the amount of revenue arising from the following transactions.

(i) A company sells goods for £2,500 plus VAT at 20% and receives £3,000 from the customer.

(ii) A company sells a factory block surplus to its requirements for £200,000. The block had been acquired 5 years earlier at a cost of £150,000.

(iii) A company issues 50,000 ordinary shares of £1 each at par.

(iv) A company sells an item of inventory on behalf of an agent for £100 and for which it retains a 10% commission charge on sale price.

Solution

(i) Although £3,000 is received, £500 of this relates to VAT which is paid over to the tax authorities. The revenue which would be recognized is £2,500. This would increase equity by £2,500.

(ii) The sale of the factory block is not part of the ordinary activities of the company. The gain on disposal would be dealt with in accordance with the requirements of IAS 16 *Property, Plant and Equipment*. Revenue is nil.

(iii) Although equity would be increased by £50,000, IAS 18 excludes from revenue, increases in equity arising from contributions by shareholders. Revenue is nil.

(iv) The revenue is the amount of the commission i.e. £10 (£100 × 10%). The other £90 is collected on behalf of the agent.

Measurement of revenue

Revenue should be measured at the fair value of the consideration received or receivable. IAS 18 defines fair value as the amount for which an asset could be exchanged, or a liability settled, between knowledgeable, willing parties in an arm's length transaction.

In most cases, the consideration is in the form of cash and the amount of revenue is the amount of cash received or receivable.

If, however, the inflow of cash is deferred and the fair value of the consideration is less than the nominal value of the cash received or receivable, the fair value should be determined by discounting all future receipts using an imputed rate of interest i.e. fair value is based on the present value of the consideration. The difference between the fair value and the nominal amount of the consideration is recognized as interest revenue over the period of finance.

Example

Planet Plasma Ltd offers a wide-screen television for sale at £1,000 with nothing to pay by the customer for 2 years. Alternatively, the television can be bought for cash at £890. The rate of interest is 6%.

A sale is made on 1 January 2012 with the customer paying on 31 December 2013.

Required

Show how the sale should be recorded in the financial statements of Planet Plasma Ltd for the years to 31 December 2012 and 31 December 2013.

Solution

Year to 31 December 2012

The sale should be recorded at the present value of the amount receivable in two years' time.

i.e. $£1,000/(1.06)^2 = £890$. Interest at 6% on the capital sum should be recognized as interest revenue in the year

i.e. $6\% \times £890 = £53$

The accounting entries are:

Dr	Receivables	£890	
	Cr Sales		£890
Being sale of television			
Dr	Debtor	£53	
	Cr Interest income		£53
Being interest earned on sale of television.			

Year to 31 December 2013

Interest at 6% of the new capital sum i.e. $(£890 + £53) \times 6\% = £57$ should be recognized as interest revenue during the year. The payment by the customer should also be recorded.

Dr	Receivables	£57	
	Cr Interest income		£57
Being interest earned on sale of the television.			
Dr	Bank	£1,000	
	Dr Receivables		£1,000
Being receipt from customer.			

Notes

The effect of adding the interest to the amount outstanding results in the receivables balance rising to £1,000 by 31 December 2013 i.e. $£890 + £53 + £57 = £1,000$.

The imputed rate of interest is the more clearly determinable of either:

(a) the prevailing rate for a similar instrument of an issuer with a similar credit rating; or

(b) a rate of interest that discounts the nominal amount of the transaction to the current cash sales price of the goods or services.

When goods or services are exchanged or swapped for goods or services which are of a similar nature and value, no sale is recognized as the entity has not in substance changed its position. IAS 18 cites the example of commodities such as oil or milk where suppliers exchange or swap inventories in various locations to fulfil demand on a timely basis in a particular location. When goods or services are exchanged for goods or services of a dissimilar nature, the transaction is regarded as a sale with revenue measured as the fair value of the goods or services received, adjusted for any cash element. Where the fair value of the goods or services received cannot be measured reliably, the revenue is measured at the fair value of the goods or services given up.

Identification of the transaction

The recognition criteria are usually applied separately to each transaction. In some cases, however, it may be necessary to apply the recognition criteria to the separately identifiable components of a single transaction in order to reflect the substance of the transaction e.g. where the sales prices includes a commitment to future servicing of the asset, that amount is deferred and recognized as revenue over the period during which the service is performed. In other cases a series of transactions may have to be looked at as a whole to understand the overall effect e.g. a sales and repurchase commitment negates the sale and so no sale should be recognized.

Sale of goods

Revenue arising from the sale of goods should be recognized when all of the following conditions have been satisfied:

(a) the entity has transferred to the buyer the significant risks and rewards of ownership of the goods;

(b) the entity retains neither continuing managerial involvement to the degree usually associated with ownership nor effective control over the goods sold;

(c) the amount of revenue can be measured reliably;

(d) it is probable that the economic benefits associated with the transaction will flow to the entity; and

(e) the costs incurred or to be incurred in respect of the transaction can be measured reliably

Example

A company sells goods costing £280,000 for £320,000 to B plc on 1 July 2012. The company has an option to repurchase the goods at any time within the next two years. The repurchase price will be £320,000 plus interest charged at 10% per annum from the date of sale to the date of repurchase. B plc has an option to require the company to repurchase the goods at the end of the two-year period for a price of £387,200.

Required

How should this be dealt with in the company's financial statements for the year to 31 December 2012?

Solution

Although the agreement is worded as a sale, the company has the option to repurchase the goods.

IAS 18 states that revenue from the sale of goods should be recognized when a number of conditions have been satisfied, including the transfer of the significant risks and rewards of ownership.

In this example, the company has not transferred these risks and rewards. If the market value of the goods rises sufficiently, the company will exercise the option, repurchase the goods and sell them on for a profit. If the market value of the goods falls, B plc will exercise its option and the company will be required to repurchase the goods even though they will be sold on at a loss.

Conclusion

In substance this is a secured loan.

The goods should remain in the statement of financial position as inventory and the 'sales proceeds' treated as a loan. An appropriate amount of interest should be charged to the statement of comprehensive income as finance costs i.e. $£320,000 \times 10\% \times 6/12 = £16,000$.

Normally the transfer of risks and rewards happens with the transfer of legal title or possession of the goods to the buyer. Sometimes only an insignificant risk is retained. For example, an invoice may state that 'legal title to the goods will not pass until they have been paid for'. This is solely to protect the collectability of the amount due. In such a case, if the entity has transferred the significant risks and rewards of ownership, the transaction is a sale and revenue is recognized. If, however, an uncertainty arises about the collectability of an amount already included in revenue, the uncollectible amount is recognized as an expense (e.g. bad debt) rather than as an adjustment of the amount of revenue originally recognized.

As stated above, revenue is recognized only when it is probable that the economic benefits associated with the transaction will flow to the entity. In some cases, this may not be certain. IAS 18 cites the example of goods being sold to an overseas customer but where there may be doubt that the foreign governmental authority will grant permission for the sale consideration to be remitted to the seller. If a significant uncertainty exists, revenue should not be recognized until the uncertainty is removed.

Revenue and expenses that relate to the same transaction are recognized simultaneously i.e. they are matched. Expenses, including warranties and other costs incurred after the shipment of the goods, can normally be measured reliably. If costs cannot be reliably measured any consideration already received for the sale of the goods should be recognized as a liability (deferred income).

The assessment of when an entity has transferred the significant risks and rewards of ownership requires an examination of the circumstances of the transaction. If the entity retains significant risks of ownership, the transaction is not a sale and revenue should not be recognized. There are a number of situations in which the seller may retain significant risks or rewards of ownership even after legal title has passed, such as:

(a) when the entity retains an obligation for unsatisfactory performance not covered by normal warranty provisions;

(b) when the receipt of the revenue from a particular sale is contingent on the derivation of revenue by the buyer from its sale of the goods;

(c) when the goods are shipped subject to installation by the seller and the installation is a significant part of the contract which has yet to be completed; and

(d) when the buyer has the right to rescind the purchase and the entity is uncertain about the probability of return.

6.4 Rendering of services

For revenue arising from the rendering of services, provided that all of the following criteria are met, revenue should be recognized by reference to the stage of completion of the transaction at the end of the reporting period:

(a) the amount of revenue can be measured reliably;

(b) it is probable that the economic benefits associated with the transaction will flow to the entity;

(c) the stage of completion of the transaction at the end of the reporting period can be measured reliably; and

(d) the costs incurred for the transaction and the costs to complete the transaction can be measured reliably.

This treatment permits revenue to be recognized before completion of the transaction provided there is sufficient reliability. This is reasonable, and indeed sensible, as many service contracts can last for a considerable length of time and may be incomplete at the end of the reporting period. To wait until the contract was completed before recognizing revenue would distort the results.

The recognition of revenue by reference to the stage of completion of a transaction is often referred to as the percentage of completion method. The stage of completion of a transaction may be determined by a variety of methods; however, the method chosen should be the one that reliably measures the services which have been performed by the end of the reporting period. Depending on the nature of the transaction, the methods may include:

(a) surveys of work performed;

(b) services performed to date as a percentage of total services to be performed; or

(c) the proportion that costs incurred to date bear to the estimated total costs of the transaction. Only costs that reflect services performed to date are included in costs incurred to date.

For practical purposes, if a contract for the rendering of services specifies that the services should be performed over a specific period of time, revenue is recognized on a straight line basis over that period unless some other method better represents the stage of completion.

When the outcome of the transaction cannot be estimated reliably, revenue should be recognized only to the extent of the expenses recognized that are recoverable. This ensures that no profit is recognized until the outcome can be estimated reliably. Furthermore, when the outcome of a transaction cannot be estimated reliably and it is not probable that the costs incurred will be recovered, revenue is not recognized and the costs incurred are recognized as an expense.

Example

A firm of Registered Auditors has provided a client with an estimated audit fee based on the following time allocation:

Staff	Hours	Charge out rate	Total
		£	£
Junior	200	50	10,000
Senior	100	90	9,000
Manager	10	110	1,100
Partner	5	245	1,225
			21,325

The fee has been discussed with the client who has raised no objections.

At 31 August 2012, the auditing firm's year end, the following hours had been spent on the audit which is not due to be completed until 30 November 2012.

Staff	Hours
Junior	60
Senior	50
Manager	3
Partner	2

These amounts are all in line with budget. None of the work to date has yet been invoiced.

Required

Calculate the amount of revenue the auditing firm should recognize in its statement of comprehensive income for the year to 31 August 2012. Costs incurred and to complete the work can be measured reliably.

Solution

The charge-out rate can be used to measure revenue reliably. The stage of completion can be estimated by reference to the hours spent to date as they are in line with budget. The client has raised no objections to the fee and it is therefore probable that they will pay. Costs can be measured reliably. As all the criteria to estimate the outcome of the transaction reliably are met, the revenue to be recognized would be calculated as follows:

Staff	Hours	Charge out rate	Total
		£	£
Junior	60	50	3,000
Senior	50	90	4,500
Manager	3	110	330
Partner	2	245	490
			8,320

As no invoice has been raised the revenue would be recorded as:

Dr	Receivables – accrued income	£8,320
	Cr Fees (SOCI)	£8,320

6.5 Interest, royalties and dividends

Revenue arising from the use by others of an entity's assets yielding interest, royalties and dividends should only be recognized when:

(a) it is probable that economic benefits will flow to the entity; and

(b) the amount of the revenue can be measured reliably.

Assuming that those criteria are met, revenue consisting of interest, royalties or dividends should be recognized as follows:

(a) Interest should be recognized using the effective interest method (Chapter 7). This is the interest rate that exactly discounts all future cash flows. The interest should be recognized on the accruals basis.

(b) Royalties should be recognized on an accruals basis in accordance with the substance of the relevant agreement.

(c) Dividends should be recognized where the shareholder's right to receive payment is established. This is usually when the dividend is declared.

Example

An entity places £5m on six-month deposit with a bank on 1 February 2012 at an interest rate of 4.5% per annum. Interest is payable at the end of the six-month period.

Required

Explain and calculate what revenue the entity should recognize in the year to 31 March 2012.

Solution

It is probable that the interest will be received and the amount can be measured reliably. Interest should be accrued for the two months to 31 March 2012 i.e.

$$£5m \times 4.5\% \times 2/12 = £37,500$$

This would be recorded as follows:

Dr	Receivables – interest receivable	£37,500
	Cr Interest (SOCI)	£37,500
Being accrued interest on six month bank deposit.		

Revenue is recognized only when it is probable that the economic benefits associated with the transaction will flow to the entity. Consequently, the ability of the other party to pay should always be considered. For example, money may be lent to a supplier or customer with interest being charged. If the borrower is facing financial difficulties and it is probable that no interest will be paid, then no revenue should be recognized until the situation becomes clearer.

Progress Point 6.2

A company has licensed another company to produce and sell one of its products in return for a 5% royalty on sales value. The licence was issued on 1 January 2013 and the royalty is payable at the end of each quarter. Sales of the product were £16m and £24m in the quarters ending 31 March and 30 June 2013. The amount due on 31 March was received on the due date.

Required

What revenue should the company recognize in the year to 30 April 2013? Explain your answer.

Solution

As the first royalty payment has been received it seems probable that future payments will be received. The licence agreement gives a method of calculating the royalties i.e. they can be measured reliably.

IAS 18 states that royalty income should be recognized on the accruals basis. The amounts due are as follows:

1 January 2013 – 31 March 2013 £16m × 5% = £800,000 (received)

1 April 2013 – 30 April 2013 £24m × 1/3 × 5% = £400,000 (accrued)

This would be recorded as follows:

Dr	Bank	£800,000	
	Receivables – royalty receivable	£400,000	
	Cr Royalty income (SOCI)		£1,200,000
Being royalty income for year to 30 April 2013.			

6.6 Appendix to IAS 18

An appendix accompanies, but is not part of, IAS 18. It contains a number of useful illustrations and explanations. The examples generally assume that the amount of revenue can be measured reliably, it is probable that the economic benefits will flow to the entity and the costs incurred or to be incurred can be measured reliably.

Sale of goods

(i) *Bill and hold sales.* These are sales in which delivery is delayed at the buyer's request but the buyer takes title and accepts billing. In such cases, revenue is recognized when the buyer takes title provided that:

(a) it is probable that delivery will be made;

(b) the item is on hand, identified and ready for delivery to the buyer at the time the sale is recognized;

(c) the buyer acknowledges the deferred delivery instructions; and

(d) the usual payment terms apply.

Revenue should not be recognized when there is simply an intention to acquire or manufacture the goods in time for delivery.

(ii) *Goods shipped subject to conditions:*

   (a) *Installation and inspection.* Revenue is normally recognized when the buyer accepts delivery and installation and inspection are complete. However, revenue is recognized immediately upon the buyer's acceptance of delivery when:

      – the installation process is simple in nature e.g. the unpacking and connection of a factory-tested television receiver

      – the inspection is performed only for price-determination purposes.

   (b) *On approval when the buyer has negotiated a limited right of return.* Revenue should not be recognized until either the goods have been formally accepted by the buyer, or the goods have been delivered and the time period for rejection has elapsed.

   (c) *Consignment sales under which the recipient (buyer) undertakes to sell the goods on behalf of the shipper (seller).* Revenue is recognized by the shipper when the goods are sold by the recipient to a third party.

   (d) *Cash-on-delivery sales.* Revenue is recognized when delivery is made and cash is received by the seller or its agent.

(iii) *Lay away sales under which the goods are delivered only where the buyer makes the final payment in a series of instalments.* Revenue should not usually be recognized until the goods are delivered; however, if a significant deposit is received and the goods are on hand, identified and ready for delivery to the buyer, and experience indicates that most such sales do go ahead, then revenue may be recognized.

(iv) *Sale and repurchase agreements where the seller has agreed (or has the right) to repurchase the goods at a later date or where the buyer can require such repurchase.* In these circumstances it is necessary to consider the substance of the agreement to determine whether the seller has transferred the risks and rewards of ownership to the buyer and hence revenue should be recognized. When the seller has retained the risks and rewards of ownership, even though legal title has transferred, the transaction is a financing arrangement and does not give rise to revenue.

(v) *Sales to intermediate parties, such as distributors, dealers or others for resale.* Revenue from such sales is generally recognized when the risks and rewards of ownership have passed. However, when the buyer is acting, in substance, as an agent, the sale is treated as a consignment sale.

(vi) *Subscriptions to publications and similar items.* Where the items involved are of a similar value in each time period, revenue is recognized on a straight line basis over the period in which the items are despatched. However, if the items vary in value from period to period, revenue is recognized on the basis of the sales value of the item despatched in relation to the total estimated sales value of all items covered by the subscription.

Example

On 1 September 2012, a publishing company received subscriptions in advance of £240,000. The subscriptions are for 24 monthly publications of an accounting magazine produced by the company. At its year end of 31 December 2012, the company had produced and despatched three of the 24 publications. The cost of producing each edition of the magazine is broadly similar.

Required

How would this be treated in the company's accounts to 31 December 2012?

Solution

IAS 18 states that where the items are of a similar value in each time period, the revenue should be recognized on a straight line basis over the period in which the items are dispatched. Accordingly, revenue of

$$£30,000 \quad \frac{(£240,000 \times 3)}{24}$$

should be recognized as revenue in the statement of comprehensive income.

    The remaining £210,000 should be recorded as deferred income in the statement of financial position.

(vii) *Instalment sales, under which the consideration is receivable in instalments.* Revenue equal to the sales price (excluding interest) should be recognized at the date of sale. The sale price is equal to the present value of the instalments to be received. The interest element is recognized as revenue as it is earned.

Rendering of services

(i) *Installation fees.* Installation fees are usually recognized by reference to the stage of completion of the installation work, unless they are incidental to the sale of a product, in which case they are recognized when the goods are sold.

(ii) *Servicing fees included in the price of the product.* When the selling price of a product includes an identifiable amount for subsequent servicing and support, that amount is deferred and recognized as revenue over the period during which the service is performed. The amount deferred is that which will cover the expected costs of the services under the agreement together with a reasonable profit on those services.

(iii) *Admission fees.* Revenue from an artistic performance or similar event is recognized when the event takes place. When a subscription to a number of events is sold, the fee is allocated to each event on a basis which reflects the extent to which services are performed at each event.

(iv) *Tuition fees.* Revenue is recognized over the period of instruction.

(v) *Initiation, entrance and membership fees.* If a fee permits only membership and all other services or products are paid for separately, or if there is a separate annual subscription, the fee is recognized as revenue when it is received or when there is no significant doubt as to its collectability. However, if the fee entitles the member to services, it should be recognized on a basis that reflects the timing and value of those services.

(vi) *Franchise fees.* Franchise fees may cover the supply of initial or subsequent services, equipment, know-how etc. and should be recognized as revenue on a basis that reflects the purpose for which the fees were charged. If the fees charged for the provision of subsequent services do not cover the cost of providing those services together with a reasonable profit, part of the initial franchise fee should be deferred and recognized as revenue as the subsequent services are provided. The amount deferred should be sufficient to cover the cost of the subsequent services and give a reasonable profit.

Progress Point 6.3

Clean 4 U Ltd owns the rights to a cleaning franchise. On 1 January 2012 it sold the rights to trade in a new area to Flashpans Ltd. The franchise is for a period of four years. The company received an initial fee of £400,000 from Flashpans Ltd on 1 January 2012 and the first annual fee of £40,000 on 31 December 2012. Clean 4 U Ltd has continuing service obligations on its franchise for maintaining its specialist cleaning equipment and for advertising that amount to £66,667 per annum per franchised area inclusive of a profit margin on the provision of the continuing services.

Required
How should this be dealt with in the financial statements of Clean 4 U Ltd for the year to 31 December 2012?

Solution
The fees cover the supply of initial and subsequent services. According to IAS 18, the fees should be recognized as revenue on a basis that reflects the purpose for which the fees were charged.

In addition to the initial fee, Clean 4 U Ltd is also charging an annual fee of £40,000 but this does not cover the costs of continuing service plus a profit margin i.e. £66,667.

In these circumstances, IAS 18 requires that a part of the initial fee should be deferred and recognized over the period that the services are provided to the franchisee.

The amount deferred should cover the cost of providing the services plus a reasonable profit margin i.e.

$$£66,667 - £40,000 = £26,667 \times 4 \text{ years} = £106,668$$

Therefore, the revenue to be recognized in the year to 31 December 2012 is:

	£
Initial fee (£400,000 − £106,668) =	293,332
Continuing fee	66,667
	359,999

The statement of financial position will include deferred income of £80,001 (£440,000 less £359,999). The deferred income will be reduced over the next 3 years at £26,667 per annum. This, when added to the annual fees of £40,000, covers the cost of the servicing obligations and the profit margin.

6.7 Disclosure requirements

IAS 18 requires disclosure of:

(a) the accounting policies adopted for the recognition of revenue, including the methods adopted to determine the state of completion of transactions involving the rendering of services:

(b) the amount of each significant category of income recognized during the period, including revenue arising from:

    (1) the sale of goods;

    (2) the rendering of services;

    (3) interest;

    (4) royalties; and

    (5) dividends;

(c) the amount of revenue arising from exchanges of goods or services included in each significant category of revenue.

Disclosure in practice

Logica's policy note on revenue and profit recognition covers all of the points noted above.

Revenue and profit recognition

Revenue represents the fair value of consideration received or receivable from customers for goods and services provided by the Group, net of discounts, VAT and other sales related taxes. Where the time value of money is material, revenue is recognised as the present value of the cash inflows expected to be received from the customer in settlement.

The Group generates revenue from the supply of outsourcing, consulting and professional services, software and hardware products. The Group will supply consulting and professional services to customers in connection with the design, building, implementation and testing of IT solutions. The Group may also source software and hardware products as part of these contracts, some of which may be developed in house.

In the case of outsourcing contracts the Group may also provide professional services in connection with the ongoing support and operation of systems and processes.

The main components within the Group's contracts are product sales and contracts to supply professional services. The revenue recognition approach to each is set out below:

Product sales

Revenue from the sale of software products or hardware with no significant service obligation is recognised 100% on delivery. Revenue from the sale of software products or hardware requiring significant modification, integration or customisation is recognised using the percentage of completion method.

Source: Logica (2011), p. 100

Proposed new standard

As was seen above, the appendix to IAS 18 provides a number of illustrative examples which relate to revenue recognition. It is perhaps indicative of the importance, and the infinite number of possible sale/purchase permutations, that the IASB provided this guidance to the implementation of the standard. Unfortunately, as business has become more and more complex, so too have the variety of forms of revenue-earning transactions which were never anticipated when the point of sale was established many years ago as the general rule for revenue recognition. Indeed, it has been argued that due to its 'principles base', IAS 18 leaves substantial scope for interpretation with the result that there has been a lack of clarity and comparability as new types of business have emerged. Furthermore, for several industrial sectors, neither the standard nor its appendices include any specific examples e.g. telecoms, software. Consequently, in June 2010, the IASB together with the US FASB jointly issued for public comment an exposure draft ED/2010/6 Revenue from Contracts with Customers. If adopted, the proposals would supersede not only IAS 18 but also IAS 11 *Construction Contracts* which is dealt with in the advanced section of this chapter.

The core principle proposed in the ED would require an entity to recognize revenue to depict the transfer of goods or services to customers in an amount that reflects the consideration that it expects to receive in exchange for those goods or services. For example, if an entity entered into contracts with customers and expected that a proportion of these customers would default, the amount of revenue to be recognized would be reduced to the amount which the entity expected to receive; if a product was sold with a warranty, part of the transaction price might be allocated to the warranty and recognized as revenue only when the warranty service was performed.

The ED contained a great deal of detailed guidance, much of which is not reflected in IAS 18 or IAS 11.

There was a substantial response to the June 2010 ED with nearly 1,000 comment letters received, which has resulted in the IASB redeliberating their proposals. Consequently, on 14 November 2011, a revised draft standard was issued which retained the core principles of the original ED but which clarified or simplified the application of these principles.

In particular, they:

- added guidance on how to determine when a good or service is transferred over time;
- simplified the proposals on warranties;
- simplified how an entity would determine a transaction price (including collectability, time value of money, and variable consideration);
- modified the scope of the onerous test to apply to long-term services only; and
- added a practical expedient that permits an entity to recognize as an expense, costs of obtaining a contract (if one year or less).

The comment period for this revised exposure draft closed on 13 March 2012 and further information on the progress of this standard can be found on the IASB website.

Given the importance of the revenue project and the volume of changes proposed, the expected IFRS will not be effective until at least 1 January 2015.

Section summary

There are problems in revenue recognition that continue to be debated. IAS 18 takes a 'principles based' approach to revenue recognition which is reliable and prudent; however, as new types of business have emerged, this approach may no longer be appropriate. The IASB in conjunction with the US FASB issued an exposure draft ED/2010/6 Revenue from Contracts with Customers which attempted to deal with many of the criticisms of the standard. A revised draft has been issued which will focus on seeking comments from constituents on the understandability, clarity, operationality, interaction of paragraphs and wording of the overall re-exposure draft.

Section 3: Advanced Aspects

6.8 Construction contracts

In the previous chapter, a particular type of 'inventory' was referred to that typically occurs within construction companies. Such companies are often involved in construction contracts that start in one accounting period and end in another. Consequently, at the end of an accounting period, a valuation must be made of the work carried out to date so that appropriate entries may be made in both the statement of comprehensive income and statement of financial position in respect of this 'work in progress'. As was covered in Chapter 5, under IAS 2, inventories are required to be valued at the lower of cost and net realizable value. This method concurs with both the prudence and realization concepts in prohibiting income or profit to be recognized until it is realized. In the case of construction contracts, however, a strict adherence to this policy would mean that profit could not be recognized until the contract was completed and accepted by the customer. Moreover, since contracts could continue for several years, it is clear that companies would not show a true and fair view of their activities or performance during the period of the contract by adopting this principle.

6.9 The accounting issue involved

The accounting issue is the allocation of profit over the various accounting periods during which the construction contract is in progress. The realization concept would argue against recognizing profits before the contract was completed. However, this will not give a 'fair representation' of the results for each period. Moreover, it could be argued that, if it was 'reasonably certain' during the contract of at least some profit, then it would be of far more informational benefit to recognize this profit as the contract progresses. It follows, then, that an alternative method of accounting for such contracts must be considered. This results in the need to exercise professional judgement and expertise in determining what amounts should be reported in the accounts. At its simplest level, it could be assumed that profits are accrued evenly as the contract progresses. While in practice this is unlikely to be the case, nevertheless it will enable a simple example to illustrate the accounting issues involved.

As the above example illustrates, the amount of profit allocated to each accounting period is based on the percentage level of completeness of the overall contract. This is known as the 'percentage-of-completion'

Example

Shamac is contracted to build a motorway flyover for £15m. The following data are available in relation to the contract:

	2012	2013	2014
Percentage complete	45%	80%	100%
Contract costs £10m			
Estimated profits £5m (i.e. £15m – £10m)			

If profits are not recognized until the contract is completed, Shamac would not recognize the profit of £5m (£15m – £10m) until 2014. This is known as the completed contract method.

Assuming profits are accrued in direct proportion to the percentage completion, the statements of comprehensive income would show the following:

	2012 £000	2013 £000	2014 £000	Total £000
Turnover	6,750	5,250	3,000	15,000
Contract costs	4,500	3,500	2,000	10,000
Profit	2,250	1,750	1,000	5,000

Notes

1. Turnover, contract costs and profit in 2012 are calculated by multiplying the total figures by 45%.
2. In 2013, the totals are multiplied by the incremental level of completion (i.e. 80% − 45% = 35%).
3. In 2014, the totals are multiplied by the incremental level of completion (i.e. 100% − 80% = 20%).

method, and requires allocation over accounting periods of the total profit on the contract. In this example, the turnover and contract costs are being recognized in proportion to the percentage completion. In practice, the actual invoices that are issued and expenses that are incurred as the contract progresses may not equate to the turnover and expenses being recognized. By their nature, contracts may take a considerable period to complete and will often be for considerable amounts. The contractor will not wish to bear the full cost of financing the contract, and the contract agreement will require that the customer will be invoiced for work done as the contract progresses. These amounts are referred to as 'progress billings'. These progress billings are normally ascertained by an external expert (e.g. engineer, architect or surveyor) who will confirm that the contract has reached a particular stage of completion.

These progress billings will normally be invoiced during the contract after work has been done, and may be after deduction of retentions. Retentions are usually held back by the customer as a safeguard to ensure that the work is completed and is up to standard. Retentions are usually a percentage of the amount billed (often 5%, but occasionally higher) that, under the terms of the contract, the customer does not pay until the contract is completed.

As these billings – also known as progress payments – are not for the completed project, they are not credited directly to sales or turnover, as would happen with a completed sale, but are recorded for each invoice raised as:

```
Dr   Receivables
        Cr   Contract account
```

Being progress billings invoiced.

When cash is received from the customer it is recorded in the normal way:

```
Dr   Bank
        Cr   Receivables
```

Being cash received from customer.

Example: retention

Works carried out by a contractor give rise to progress billings of £100,000. It is accepted practice that the customer will hold back a 5% retention. The progress billing and related receipt will be dealt with as follows:

```
Dr   Receivables              £100,000
        Cr   Contract account              £100,000
Being progress billing invoiced.
```

Dr	Bank		£95,000	
	Cr	Receivables		£95,000

Being cash received from customer.

Note that the amount of the retention (i.e. $5\% \times £100,000$) will remain as a debtor until it is ultimately received – usually on satisfactory completion of the contract.

6.10 Contract accounts

The contract account is a form of trading account for each contract. Each construction contract should have its own separate contract account. All expenditure traceable to the contract will be charged to the contract account. In practice, this is far easier than ascertaining direct expenses in a factory, as any expenditure on the contract will be treated as direct. Typical costs include:

- wages and salaries
- materials
- hire of equipment
- depreciation charge
- subcontractor costs
- allocation of overheads.

At the year end, this will include accrual and prepayment adjustments.

The contract account is essentially a holding account in the statement of financial position to which all invoices relating to the contract are posted during the year. At the year end, relevant amounts are transferred out to the statement of comprehensive income.

Progress billings can be thought of as potential sales or turnover to be recognized. As we will see, however, progress billings invoiced are not necessarily the same as turnover, as the following example illustrates.

Example

The following information relates to a contract in progress at the end of Year 1 by SBS Enterprises. An independent architect has been used to determine the level of completion of the contract, which has been agreed at 40%.

	£
Total contract revenue	1,300,000
Total contract expenses	1,125,000
Actual contract costs incurred (Year 1)	510,000
Progress billings (i.e. invoices issued)	400,000

Required

Calculate the turnover and cost of sales to be included in the statement of comprehensive income, and show the relevant statement of financial position extracts.

Solution

The amounts to be shown in the statement of comprehensive income in respect of turnover and cost of sales will be determined by the level of completion, and will therefore be as follows:

	£
Turnover (1,300,000 × 40%)	520,000
Cost of sales (1,125,000 × 40%)	450,000
Gross profit	70,000

Note: the proportion of net income that is attributable to the work performed to date as ascertained by the architect has been credited to the statement of comprehensive income. The actual costs so far incurred on this contract, however, amount to £510,000. There is therefore a difference between the actual costs and the costs recognized of £60,000 (i.e. £510,000 − £450,000). This is because the amount of costs recognized has been calculated as a percentage of the total contract costs to reflect the percentage level of completion, and not the actual costs incurred. An additional statement of financial position entry requires to be made, therefore, to deal with this difference:

	£
Costs incurred to date	510,000
Contact expenses	450,000
Amounts due from customers	60,000

The difference is treated as a receivable – amounts due from customers – and will be shown in current assets.

A further difference exists between the value of contract revenue recognized as turnover and the amount of progress billings made (i.e. invoices issued):

	£
Contract revenue	520,000
Progress billings	400,000
Amounts due from customers	120,000

Again, this difference has arisen because the amount of revenue recognized has been calculated as a percentage of the total contract revenue and not the actual invoices issued. This difference is also treated as a receivable – amounts due from customers – and will be shown in current assets. The appropriate statement of financial position extract will be:

	£
Current assets	
Amounts due from customers	180,000

Note that this figure can also be calculated as :

costs incurred £510,000 + recognized profits £70,000 less progress billings £400,000 = £180,000

BASIC

INTERMEDIATE

ADVANCED

To summarize the above example, the amounts to be included in the statement of comprehensive income in respect of long-term contracts should reflect the proportion of the contract completed during the accounting period. The differences between the actual progress billings made and contract revenues recognized, and actual expenses incurred and contract expenses recognized, are dealt with in the statement of financial position, and shown as amounts due from (or to) customers.

This simple example assumes that, over the contract, the actual costs would be equal to the budgeted costs and that no unforeseen expenses are likely to arise in the future relating to work already completed or work not yet started. Neither assumption will necessarily be realized in practice.

Let us now consider what complications can arise in practice and look in detail at the requirements of IAS 11 *Construction Contracts*.

6.11 IAS 11 *Construction Contracts*

Objective
The objective of IAS 11 is to prescribe the accounting treatment of revenue and costs associated with construction contracts and in particular the allocation of contract revenue and contract costs to the accounting periods in which construction work is performed.

Definitions
IAS 11 (para. 3) defines a construction contract as 'a contract specifically negotiated for the construction of an asset or a combination of assets that are closely interrelated or interdependent in terms of their design, technology and function or their ultimate purpose or use'.

Examples of a single asset would be a bridge, tunnel, building or ship. Examples of closely interrelated combinations of assets would be oil refineries, power plants or chemical works.

A contract may extend to more than one year but this is not an essential feature. Some contracts with a shorter duration should be accounted for as long term if they are so material that exclusion of their turnover and results would result in the accounts not giving a fair representation of the results for that period. A contract to develop software would also be covered by the IAS, although contracts for services are covered by IAS 18 *Revenue*.

The standard identifies (para. 3) two types of contract.

1. A fixed price contract: a fixed price contract is a construction contract in which the contractor agrees to a fixed contract price or a fixed rate per unit of output, which may be subject to cost escalation clauses (e.g. to allow for inflation).

2. A cost plus contract: a cost plus contract is a construction contract in which the contractor is reimbursed for allowable or otherwise defined costs, plus a percentage of these costs or a fixed fee.

Although the definitions would suggest that there are two types of contract, fixed price or cost plus, in practice the type of contract is not always so clear cut and many have characteristics of both types.

Combining and segmenting construction contracts
The standard also covers a separability issue. Under IAS 11, if a contract covers two or more assets, the construction of each asset should be accounted for separately if:

(a) separate proposals were submitted for each asset,

(b) each asset has been subject to separate negotiations, and the contractor and customer have been able to accept or reject that part of the contract relating to each asset, and

(c) the costs and revenue of each asset can be measured.

However, in certain circumstances, a group of contracts may in substance be a single construction contract and required to be treated as such when:

(a) the group of contracts is negotiated as a single package

(b) the contracts are so clearly interrelated that they are in effect part of a single project with an overall profit margin

(c) the contracts are performed concurrently or in a continuous sequence.

If a contract gives the customer an option to order one or more additional assets, construction of each additional asset should be accounted for as a separate contract if either:

(a) the additional asset differs significantly from the original asset(s), or

(b) the price of the additional assets is separately negotiated.

Progress Point 6.4

Explain what is meant by the term construction contract.

Solution

A construction contract is defined in IAS 11 as a contract specifically negotiated for the construction of an asset or a combination of assets that are closely interrelated or interdependent in terms of their design, technology and function, or their ultimate purpose or use, where the time taken to complete the contract is such that the contract actively falls into different accounting periods. A construction contract may extend to more than one year but this is not an essential feature. Some contracts with a shorter duration should be accounted for as long term if they are so material that exclusion of their turnover and results would result in the accounts not giving a fair representation of the results for that period; such a policy must be applied consistently.

Contract revenue

Contract revenue (para. 11) should comprise:

(a) the initial amount of revenue agreed in the contract, and

(b) variations in contract work, claims and incentive payments

   (i) to the extent that it is probable that they will result in revenue, and

   (ii) they are capable of being reliably measured.

In other words, all the revenues that are expected to be received from the contract providing the basic criteria of probable receipt and measurability are satisfied.

A variation (para. 13) is an instruction from the customer for a change in the scope of work (e.g. change in design). This may result in an increase or decrease in revenue. Variations should be included as part of total revenue when it is probable that the customers will approve both the variation and the monetary value.

A claim (para. 14) occurs when the contractor seeks recompense from the customer for costs not included in the contract price arising from, for example, delays caused by the customer or errors in specification. Because of their contentious nature claims are included as part of revenue only when negotiations have reached an advanced stage, such that it is probable that the customer will accept the claim.

Incentive payments (para. 15) are additional amounts paid to the contractor if specified performance standards are met or exceeded (e.g. early completion). These should be included only when the contract is sufficiently advanced that it is probable that the specified standard will be met and the amount of the incentive payment can be measured reliably.

Possible penalties through failure to meet performance standards should also be considered and included if they can be measured reliably. Note that penalties are viewed as a reduction in turnover and not as additional costs. Penalties should be deducted from revenue when it is probable they will be incurred.

Contract costs

Contract costs (para. 16) include the following.

(a) Costs that relate directly to the specific contract (e.g. site labour costs, costs of materials, depreciation of assets used on construction, costs of moving assets and materials to and from the contract site, hire charges, costs of design and technical assistance that are directly related to the contract, the estimated costs of rectification and guarantee work, including warranty costs, claims from third parties).

(b) Costs that are attributable to contract activity and can be allocated to specific contracts, such as insurance, costs of design and technical assistance that are not directly related to a specific contract, construction overheads; costs of this nature need to be allocated on a systematic and rational basis, based on the normal level of construction activity.

(c) Such other costs as are specifically chargeable to the customer under the terms of the contract: examples of these would be general administration and development costs for which reimbursement is specified in the terms of the contract. Permissible costs follow the same rules as in IAS 2.

Specifically, however, IAS 11 excludes the following costs (para. 20):

(a) general administration costs not specified in the contract

(b) selling costs

(c) research and development costs not specified

(d) depreciation of idle assets not used on a specific contract.

Contract costs normally include relevant costs from the date the contract is secured to the date the contract is finally completed. Costs incurred in securing a contract are also included if they can be separately identified and measured reliably and it is probable that the contract will be obtained (para. 21). However, where such costs were previously written off as an expense in the period in which they were incurred, they are not included in contract costs when the contract is obtained in a subsequent period (i.e. once these costs have been written off they stay written off).

6.12 Recognition of contract revenue and expenses

Reliable estimate of contract outcome

IAS 11 requires that, where the outcome of a construction contract can be estimated reliably, revenue and costs should be recognized in proportion to the stage of completion of contract activity. Under this process the proportion of revenue, expenses and profit that is attributable to the work performed to date will be reported in the statement of comprehensive income. This is known as the percentage of completion method of accounting.

To be able to estimate the outcome of a contract reliably, the enterprise must be able to make a:

- reliable estimate of total contract revenue, and assess that it is probable that the related economic benefits will flow to the enterprise
- reliable measurement of the total contract costs (both those incurred to date and those expected to be incurred in the future)
- reliable estimate of the stage of completion of the contract.

The stage of completion of a contract can be determined in a variety of ways. IAS 11 does not identify a single method that may be used to identify the stage of completion; however, whichever method is chosen, it should measure reliably the work performed. For many contracts this may involve an external expert (e.g. architect, quantity surveyor) confirming that the contract has reached a particular stage of completion. However, alternative methods that might be appropriate include:

- the proportion that costs incurred for work performed to date bear to the total estimated costs
- completion of a physical proportion of the contract work.

No reliable estimate of contract outcome

If the outcome cannot be measured reliably, no profit should be recognized. This could be the case where, for example, the contract is at too early a stage for an accurate prediction of the overall result. In such circumstances, provided there is no reason to expect that the contract will make an overall loss, the revenue that is recognized should be restricted to the costs incurred during the year that relate to the contract to the extent that they are expected to be recoverable. These contract costs should be expensed as incurred. In such circumstances, the net income recognized will be nil. Contract costs that are not likely to be recovered are recognized as an expense immediately. No revenue is recognized in respect of these items. Indications of doubt over recoverability include doubts over whether the customer will be able to pay, and costs on a contract that is subject to the outcome of pending litigation. IAS 11 (para. 34) gives further examples.

Recognition of expected losses

An expected loss on a construction contract should be recognized as an expense immediately on the grounds of prudence. The expected loss should be provided for immediately, irrespective of:

- whether or not work has started on the contract,
- the stage of completion of the contract, or
- the amount of profits expected to arise on other contracts.

Example: retention

The following data are available in respect of a construction contract:

Costs to date	£3m
Total contract revenue expected	£3m
Further costs to completion	£0.7m

How should this contract be shown in the accounts?

From the information given, the contract is forecast to make a loss of £0.7m. This expected loss is required to be recognised immediately as a expense on the grounds of prudence.

6.13 Accounting for construction contracts

Statement of comprehensive income entries

Having considered the recognition criteria for contract revenue and contract expenses, the following worked example will illustrate the accounting requirements of the standard and the related journal entry adjustments. It is perhaps worth pausing at this stage to remind ourselves of the overall objectives of the standard.

The standard prescribes the accounting treatment of revenue and costs associated with construction contracts.

It is necessary first of all to ascertain that a construction contract exists. Having confirmed that, it is then necessary to take a decision on the expected outcome based on available evidence at the time of estimated total revenue and estimated total costs. This will indicate whether the contract is estimated to make a profit or a loss. If that outcome is:

- profitable and the outcome can be estimated reliably, revenue, costs and profit should be recognized in line with the stage of completion of the contract
- profitable but the outcome cannot be estimated reliably, revenue and costs should be recognized but no profit
- loss making, then the full amount of the loss should be recognized immediately; an expected loss should be provided for immediately, irrespective of the stage of completion of the contract, whether or not work has started on the contract, or the amount of profits expected to arise on other contracts.

There are, therefore, three categories of contracts, and the accounting requirements will vary accordingly.

Example

Clarkstruction has three contracts in progress at 31 December 2012: Project A, Project B and Project C. All three contracts commenced during the year and the following information is currently available. Owing to the nature of the contracts, Clarkstruction can usually determine the outcome of the contract reliably when the contract is 40% complete. All costs are considered recoverable.

Contract	Project A	Project B	Project C
	£000	£000	£000
Total contract value	800	400	700
Costs incurred to date	500	30	400
Estimated further costs to completion	70	300	390
%age completion	80%	10%	50%

What are the turnover and cost of sales figures to be included in the statement of comprehensive income of Clarkstruction for the year to 31 December 2012?

Step 1: calculate whether the contract will make an overall profit or loss

In order to determine the appropriate accounting treatment, the expected outcome of each contract needs to be determined. Using the available information, the expected profit or loss can be calculated as follows:

	Project A	Project B	Project C
	£000	£000	£000
Contract value	800	400	700
Less: costs incurred to date	(500)	(30)	400
costs to complete	(70)	(300)	390
Estimated profit/(loss)	230	70	(90)

Projects A and B are profit making and Project C is loss making.

When a project is 40% complete, Clarkstruction can reliably estimate the outcome. Consequently, while Project A is profitable and 80% complete, and therefore its outcome can be measured reliably, Project B, although profitable, is only 10% complete and therefore at such an early stage there is no certainty as to the project's overall outcome.

Step 2: calculate turnover

Having determined the expected outcomes of each of the projects, the appropriate accounting treatments can now be applied.

Project A

Project A is a profitable contract where the outcome can be estimated reliably.

$$\text{Turnover} = \text{estimated total revenue} \times \text{stage of completion}$$
$$= 800,000 \times 80\%$$
$$= £640,000$$

Project B

Project B is a profitable contract where the outcome cannot be estimated reliably.

As the outcome cannot be estimated reliably, no profit is recognized. Turnover is restricted to the extent of contract costs incurred that it is probable will be recoverable. Therefore:

$$\text{Turnover} = \text{costs incurred that are expected to be recovered}$$
$$= £30,000$$

Project C

Project C is a loss-making contract.

Turnover is calculated as a percentage of the stage of completion.

$$\text{Turnover} = \text{extimated total revenue} \times \text{stage of completion}$$
$$= 700,000 \times 50\%$$
$$= \underline{\underline{£350,000}}$$

The journal entry required to account for these contracts will be:

		£	£
Dr	Contract account – Project A	640,000	
Dr	Contract account – Project B	30,000	
Dr	Contract account – Project C	350,000	
	Cr Turnover		1,020,000

Being turnover recognized on contracts.

Step 3: calculate cost of sales

Project A

Project A is a profitable contract where the outcome can be estimated reliably.

$$\text{Cost of sales} = \text{total estimated costs} \times \text{stage of completion}$$
$$= 570,000 \times 80\%$$
$$= \underline{\underline{£456,000}}$$

Project B

Project B is a profitable contract where the outcome cannot be estimated reliably.

$$\text{Cost of sales} = \text{costs expensed as incurred}$$
$$= \underline{\underline{£30,000}}$$

Project C

Project C is loss-making.

Project C is expected to make an overall loss of £90,000. As turnover of £350,000 based on percentage of completion has been recognized, the cost of sales figure requires to be set at a level that will give rise to a loss of £90,000, i.e.:

$$\text{Cost of sales} = \text{turnover} + \text{expected loss}$$
$$= 350,000 + 90,000$$
$$= \underline{\underline{£440,000}}$$

The journal entry required to account for these contracts would be:

		£	£
Dr	Cost of sales	926,000	
	Cr Contract account – Project A		456,000
	Cr Contract account – Project B		30,000
	Cr Contract account – Project C		440,000

Being cost of sales recognized on contracts.

Clarkstruction's statement of comprehensive income extract for the year ended 31 December 2012 will be as follows:

	£
Turnover	1,020,000
Cost of sales	926,000
Gross profit	94,000

Let us recap on the transactions thus far. The original expenses incurred on each contract were posted throughout the year to the individual contract accounts and then, at the end of the reporting period, the appropriate revenues and expenses that were recognized were transferred to the statement of comprehensive income. Earlier in this section it was noted that a contract account was essentially a holding account in the statement of financial position. With the information available to us thus far, the contract accounts for Projects A, B and C would be as follows:

Project A				
Costs incurred	£500,000	Cost of sales	£456,000
Contract revenue recognized	£640,000		

Project B				
Costs incurred	£30,000	Cost of sales	£30,000
Contract revenue recognized	£30,000		

Project C				
Costs incurred	£400,000	Cost of sales	£440,000
Contract revenue recognized	£350,000		

As has been noted, the invoices issued as the contract progresses may not equate to the turnover being recognized. In addition, if these 'progress billings' remain unpaid at the end of the reporting period, this too will give rise to an outstanding amount. Let us now consider the statement of financial position entries relating to construction contracts.

Statement of financial position entries

At the end of the reporting period, there may be two balances left relating to construction contracts:

1. trade receivables, i.e. progress billings invoiced – progress billings received
2. the balance on the 'contract account'.

If the balance on the 'contract account' is a debit, IAS 11 requires that this be shown as an asset and presented as:

Gross amount due from customers

If the balance is a credit, this would be shown as a liability and presented as:

Gross amount due to customers

The gross amount due from customers comprises:

costs incurred (i.e. the customer owes us for costs incurred on their behalf)	X
add recognized profits (i.e. we will be charging the customer a mark-up), or	X
less recognized losses (i.e. we cannot recoup all costs)	(X)
less progress billings invoiced (i.e. when we bill the customer it reduces what they owe us on the contract and becomes a debtor)	(X)
	X

This will be the case for all contracts in progress for which costs incurred plus recognized profits (less recognized losses) exceed progress billings. In other words, the customer still owes the company for costs incurred and/or work completed but not invoiced. It is, therefore, an asset.

The gross amount due to customers comprises:

Costs incurred	X
add recognized profits	X
less recognized losses	(X)
less progress billings invoiced	(X)
	(X)

This will be the case for all contracts in progress for which progress billings exceed costs incurred plus recognized profits (less recognized losses). In other words, the customer has been invoiced too much and is owed money back and/or the company is unable to recover all costs incurred. It is, therefore, a liability.

Example

Continuing with the earlier example, Clarkstruction Ltd, suppose the following additional information is available regarding progress billings invoiced and received:

	Project A	Project B	Project C
	£000	£000	£000
Total contract value	800	400	700
Costs incurred to date	500	30	400
Estimated costs to complete	70	300	390
Progress billings invoiced	600	35	330
Progress billings received	510	–	270
%age completion	80%	10%	50%

What amounts should appear in the statement of financial position of Clarkstruction at 31 December 2012?

Step 4: calculate the resultant statement of financial position amounts

In journal entry form, progress billings invoiced will be entered as follows:

Dr	Trade receivables – progress billings
Cr	Contract account

The journal entry required to account for these contracts would be:

		£	£
Dr	Trade receivables	965,000	
	Cr Contract account – Project A		600,000
	Cr Contract account – Project B		35,000
	Cr Contract account – Project C		330,000
Being progress billings invoiced.			

Progress billings received will be accounted for like any other debtor, i.e.:

Dr	Bank	
	Cr Trade receivables	
Being cash received from customer.		

The journal entry required to account for these contracts would be:

		£	£
Dr	Bank	780,000	
	Cr Trade receivables (510,000 + 270,000)		780,000
Being cash received from customers.			

The individual contract accounts for Projects A, B and C incorporating the progress billings invoiced will now be as follows:

Project A			
Costs incurred	£500,000	Cost of sales	£456,000
Contract revenue recognized	£640,000	Progress billings	£600,000
		Balance c/d	£84,000
	£1,140,000		£1,140,000
Balance b/d	£84,000		

This is a debit balance and will be presented as gross amount due from customers.

Project B			
Costs incurred	£30,000	Cost of sales	£30,000
Contract revenue recognized	£30,000	Progress billings	£35,000
Balance c/d	£5,000		
	£65,000		£65,000
		Balance b/d	£5,000

BASIC

INTERMEDIATE

ADVANCED

This is a credit balance and will be presented as gross amount due to customers.

Project C			
Costs incurred	£400,000	Cost of sales	£440,000
Contract revenue recognized	£350,000	Progress billings	£330,000
Balance c/d	£20,000		
	£770,000		£770,000
		Balance b/d	£20,000

This is a credit balance and will be presented as gross amount due to customers.

The summary debtor account will be as follows:

Trade receivables			
Project A – progress billings	£600,000	Bank (Project A)	£510,000
Project B – progress billings	£35,000	Bank (Project C)	£270,000
Project C – progress billings	£330,000		
		Balance c/d	£185,000
	£965,000		£965,000
Balance b/d	£185,000		

Alternatively, a columnar approach could have been adopted to determine the statement of financial position amounts:

	Project A £000	Project B £000	Project C £000
Progress billings invoiced	600	35	330
Progress billings received	510	–	270
Trade receivables	90	35	60
Costs incurred	500	30	400
Profit/(loss) recognized	184	–	(90)
Progress billings invoiced	(600)	(35)	(330)
Amounts due from/(to) customers	84	(5)	(20)

Clarkstruction's extract statement of financial position at 31 December 2012 would be as follows:

	£000
Current assets	
Trade receivables	185
Gross amounts due from customers	84
Current liabilities	
Gross amounts due to customers	(25)

Notes

The gross amounts due to customers on Projects B and C have been added together. This is the correct presentation.

Amounts due to and from customers must be presented as current asset and liability, respectively. They must never be netted off to give a single amount.

The journals to account for construction contracts and the steps to follow in arriving at the appropriate statement of comprehensive income and statement of financial position entries are summarised in Appendices 6.1 and 6.2, at the end of this chapter. Check your understanding by working through the example in Progress Point 6.5.

Progress Point 6.5

DSM Ltd is a construction company. In the year to 31 December 2012, it started work on the following two contracts. Relevant details are:

	Contract 1	Contract 2
	£000	£000
Contract value (total)	5,000	16,000
Costs incurred	3,050	7,300
Estimated costs to complete	1,150	9,100
Progress billings – invoiced	3,600	5,200
– received	3,100	4,800
%age completion	70%	40%

Relevant amounts are all regarded as recoverable and the outcomes of both contracts can be reliably estimated once they are 30% complete.

Required

(i) Prepare all necessary journal entries to record transactions relating to the contracts.
(ii) Prepare extracts of the statement of comprehensive income and statement of financial position of DSM Ltd for the year to 31 December 2012.

Suggested solution

(i)

Step 1: Calculate whether each contract will make an overall profit or loss

	Contract 1	Contract 2
	£000	£000
Contract value	5,000	16,000
Costs incurred	3,050	7,300
Estimated costs to complete	1,150	9,100
Estimated profit/(loss)	800	(400)

As both contracts are more than 30% complete the outcomes can be estimated reliably, i.e. Contract 1 is profitable while Contract 2 is loss-making.

Step 2: Calculate turnover

Contract 1: Turnover = estimated total revenue × stage of completion

$$= 5{,}000{,}000 \times 70\%$$

$$= \underline{3{,}500{,}000}$$

Contract 12: Turnover

$$= 16{,}000{,}000 \times 40\%$$

$$= \underline{6{,}400{,}000}$$

Journal entry to record turnover:

Dr	Contract account – Contract 1	£3,500,000	
Dr	Contract account – Contract 2	£6,400,000	
	Cr Turnover		£9,900,000
Being turnover recognized on contracts.			

Step 3: Calculate cost of sales

Contract 1: Cost of sales = total estimated costs × stage of completion

$$= (3{,}050{,}000 + 1{,}150{,}000) \times 70\%$$

$$= \underline{2{,}940{,}000}$$

Contract 2: Contract 2 is expected to make an overall loss of £400,000. As turnover of £6,400,000 has been recognized, the cost of sales figure is calculated as:

$$= \text{turnover} + \text{expected loss}$$

$$= 6{,}400{,}000 + 400{,}000$$

$$= \underline{6{,}800{,}000}$$

Journal entry to record cost of sales:

Dr	Cost of sales	£9,740,000	
	Cr Contract account – Contract 1		£2,940,000
	Cr Contract account – Contract 2		£6,800,000
Being cost of sales recognized on contracts.			

Step 4: Calculate the resultant statement of financial position amounts

In respect of progress billings invoiced:

Dr	Trade receivables – progress billings	£8,800,000	
	Cr Contract account – Contract 1		£3,600,000
	Cr Contract account – Contract 2		£5,200,000
Being progress billings invoiced.			

BASIC

INTERMEDIATE

ADVANCED

In respect of progress billings received:

Dr	Bank (3,100,000 + 4,800,000)	£7,900,000	
	Cr Trade receivables		£7,900,000
Being cash received from customers.			

	Contract 1	Contract 2	Total
	£000	£000	£000
Costs incurred	3,050	7,300	
Profit/(loss) recognized	560	(400)	
Progress billings invoiced	(3,600)	(5,200)	
Gross amounts due from customers	10	1,700	1,710
Progress billings invoiced	3,600	5,200	
Progress billings received	3,100	4,800	
Trade receivables	500	400	900

(ii)

DSM statement of comprehensive income (extract) for the year ended 31 December 2012	
	£000
Turnover	9,900
Cost of sales	9,740
Gross profit	160

Statement of financial position (extract) at 31 December 2012	
	£000
Current assets	
Trade receivables	900
Gross amounts due from customers	1,710

Reliable estimates

Contracts where the outcome can reliably be estimated have been dealt with. The question that does arise is how to decide whether an estimate is reliable or not. IAS 11 gives the following guidance.

The outcome can be estimated reliably (para. 23) when:

(a) total contract revenue can be assessed reliably

(b) it is probable that the economic benefits will flow to the company (i.e. the customer will pay)

(c) both contract costs to complete and stage of completion can be measured reliably, and

(d) contract costs can be clearly identified and measured reliably.

For a contract in its early stages or where there are significant risks remaining (e.g. on a contract using new technology or techniques) it will probably not be possible to meet criteria (c) above and the overall outcome cannot be estimated reliably. Such a contract will fall into the profitable not reliable category (i.e. the revenue that is recognized would be restricted to the costs incurred).

Contracts lasting several years

The examples thus far in this chapter have been concerned with contracts in their first year of construction. In practice, contracts may last for several years and the contract price and estimated total costs will undoubtedly be changing over the duration of the particular contract. In such circumstances it is important to keep track of the cumulative position.

Example

Stadium Structures entered into a contract to build a sports stadium in 2011, which is due to be completed by 2013. Relevant information is:

	2011	2012	2013
	£000	£000	£000
Contract price	15,000	15,000	15,000
Variations	–	200	400
Penalty	–	–	(100)
%age completion	35%	80%	100%

The variations and the penalty can be assumed to have been agreed, and have been measured reliably at the end of each reporting period. Assume that the contract is profitable overall and the outcome can be estimated reliably at the end of each reporting period.

What amounts should be recognized as turnover in 2011 to 2013?

	2011	2012	2013	Total
	£000	£000	£000	£000
Total contract revenue	15,000	15,200	15,300	
Percentage completion	35%	80%	100%	
Total revenue to be recognized	5,250	12,160	15,300	
Less: already recognized	–	5,250	12,160	
Turnover recognized	5,250	6,910	3,140	15,300

Notes

Variations should be included as part of total revenue only when it is probable that the customer will approve both the variation and the monetary value; penalties are viewed as a reduction in turnover and not as additional costs.

The approach adopted is therefore to: ascertain the total contract revenue at the end of each reporting period; determine the percentage completion to ascertain the cumulative contract revenue recognizable at the end of each reporting period; isolate the contract revenue to be recognized in each reporting period by deducting the previously recognized cumulative turnover from the total revenue to be recognized at each the end of each reporting period. As far as the statement of financial position is concerned, the figures presented will be based on the cumulative amounts.

Advances and retentions

Earlier in this section the accounting requirements in respect of retentions were explained and demonstrated. IAS 11 provides a formal definition of retentions as 'amounts of progress billings which are not paid until the satisfaction of conditions specified in the contract for the payment of such amounts or until defects have been rectified' (para. 41).

Advances received are amounts received by the contractor before the related work is performed. Advances are shown separately as payments on account. They are not offset against amounts due from customers until the relevant work is performed.

Progress Point 6.6

Show how the following information for construction contract Project 430 should be recorded in the financial statements.

	Project 430
	£
Contract revenue recognized	500
Contract expenses recognized	450
Progress billings	500
Progress billings received plus advance	525
Contract costs incurred	600

Project 430 is reliably estimated to be profitable.

Solution

Given the information provided, the statement of comprehensive income entries are straightforward (i.e. the contract revenue and contract expenses to be recognized have been given and so no further adjustments are required).

Therefore, the statement of comprehensive income entries will be:

	£
	£
Contract revenue	500
Contract expenses	450
Gross profit	50

The statement of financial position entries will have to be calculated to determine the position in respect to amounts due/from customers.

Using the steps detailed in Appendix 6.2 (at the end of this chapter) relating to the statement of financial position gives:

	£
Costs incurred to date	600
Add: recognized profits	50
Less: progress billings invoiced	(500)
Gross amounts due from customers	150

This is a debit balance and will therefore be disclosed under current assets.

In respect of the advance received of £25, this will be disclosed under current liabilities.

The statement of financial position extract entries will be:

Current assets	
Gross amounts due from customers	150
Current liabilities	
Advances received	25

6.14 Examination issues

As the examples in this section will have illustrated, there are a range of questions that may be asked in relation to construction contracts. Although there are two standard types of question, the situation and requirement in each can vary.

The two basic types of question are as follows.

1. One or more contracts started in the current year: here you will normally be tested to ensure you follow the correct steps to determine whether each contract is profitable, profitable but not reliable, or loss making, and apply the appropriate accounting treatment to each. Remember that in an exam it is likely that you would be given one of each. If, therefore, you are given three contracts and you think all are profitable, check again – this is an unlikely situation.

2. One contract that lasts for several years: here you will normally be asked to calculate the position for each year of the contract, or perhaps two or three years into the contract. Remember to keep track of the cumulative position, and remember also that the contract price and estimated contract cost are likely to alter over the duration of the contract.

Situation

The situation you are placed in, in the question, may also vary. You may have to do all the recording in some, but in many questions, the contract costs, payments on account invoiced and received will have been recorded but you will have to work out the amounts to be included in the statement of comprehensive income and statement of financial position. In some the figures to be transferred to the statement of comprehensive income will also be given and the emphasis will be on the statement of financial position.

Requirement

The requirement may also vary. Some questions may require full journals for initial recording, year-end adjustments through to producing extracts from the statement of financial position and statement of comprehensive income. Others may ask only for figures for the statement of comprehensive income and statement of financial position.

6.15 Disclosure requirements

These are detailed at paras 39–45, and are as follows:

(a) amount of contract revenue recognized in the period (para. 39(a))

(b) method used to determine revenue (para. 39(b))

(c) method used to determine stage of completion (para. 39(c))

(d) for contracts in progress at the end of each reporting period (para. 40)

- the aggregate amount of costs incurred and recognized profits (less recognized losses) to date
- the amount of advances received (if any)
- the amount of retentions (if any)

(e) the gross amount due from customers for contract work should be shown as an asset (para. 42)

(f) the gross amount due to customers for contract work should be shown as a liability (para. 42).

Disclosure in practice

In a similar manner to the disclosure of inventories, the disclosure requirements of IAS 11 *Construction Contracts* are satisfied in distinct sections.

Amounts recoverable on contracts

Incorporated along with the trade receivables note, Logica includes its accounting policy on construction contracts. This extract from the policy note of Logica explains amounts recoverable on contracts and refers to the group's policy on revenue recognition:

> Amounts recoverable on contracts represent revenue which has not yet been invoiced to customers on fixed price contracts. Such amounts are separately disclosed within trade and other receivables. The valuation of amounts recoverable on contracts is adjusted to take up profit to date or foreseeable losses in accordance with the Group's accounting policy for profit recognition.
>
> *Source: Logica (2011), p. 98*

Revenue and profit recognition

The group's policy on revenue recognition is disclosed, together with the method used (percentage of completion) to determine the contract revenue recognized in the period. As the note states, Logica uses a level of completion of 50% to determine reliably the outcome of a contract:

Outsourcing, Consulting and Professional Services

The revenue and profit of contracts for the supply of outsourcing, consulting and professional services ('services') at predetermined rates is recognised as and when the work is performed, irrespective of the duration of the contract.

The revenue and profit on fixed price contracts for the supply of services at predetermined rates is recognised on a percentage of completion basis when the outcome of a contract can be estimated reliably. A contract's outcome is deemed to be capable of reliable estimation at either the earlier of six months from contract commencement or the date at which the contract is 50% complete. If a contract outcome cannot be estimated reliably, revenues are recognised equal to costs incurred, to the extent that costs are expected to be recovered.

The stage of contract completion is determined by reference to the costs of services incurred to date as a proportion of the total estimated costs of services, except in rare circumstances when measuring the stage of contract completion using total contract costs is more representative of the work performed, in which case total contract costs are used (Note 4).

Contracts for the supply of both product sales and services

The majority of the Group's contracts are for the supply of both product and services and are accounted for as construction contracts. In accordance with IAS 11 'Construction Contracts', when a contract covers a number of different components the revenue and profits are recognized on each component separately where: there is a separate proposal for each component of a contract, each component is negotiated separately and the costs and revenues of each component can be identified.

When it is required to separate the product sales and professional services components in a contract and account for the revenue and profits on each component separately then the revenue recognition policies for the individual components outlined above will be followed.

Where a contract contains multiple components that do not meet the conditions for separation set out above, as in the majority of cases, then the contract will be treated as having one revenue component and will be treated as a fixed priced services contract with revenues for the contract recognized in line with the supply of services as outlined above. Generally where such contracts arise professional service costs will form the bulk of costs on the contract. If this is not the case then total costs are used as a basis for determining the percentage of completion.

Loss making contracts

Provision is made for all foreseeable future losses in the period in which the loss is identified.

Source: Logica (2011), p. 98

Figure 6.1 Logica: amounts recoverable on contracts note

	2011	2010
	£'m	£'m
Trade receivables	690.2	687.3
Less: provision for impairment	(7.2)	(6.1)
Trade receivables – net	683.0	681.2
Amounts recoverable on contracts	368.1	374.4
Accrued income	95.3	91.4
Prepayments	79.9	71.1
Derivative financial instruments (Note 26)	3.5	8.7
Other receivables	32.2	25.5
	1,262.2	1,252.3

Source: Logica (2011), p. 116

The notes to the statement of financial position detail the amounts recognized in the financial statements in respect of construction contracts. Note that the amounts due to and from customers is disclosed separately, the standard not allowing such balances to be netted off.

Figure 6.2 Logica: detailed contracts in progress disclosure note

Contracts accounted for under the percentage-of-completion method

Contracts in progress at the end of the reporting period:	2011	2010
	£'m	£'m
Contract costs incurred plus recognised profits less recognised losses to date	5,541.3	5,579.4
Less: progress billings to date	(5,298.1)	(5,335.2)
	243.2	244.2
Recognised as:		
Amounts due from contract customers included in trade and other receivables	368.1	374.4
Amounts due to contract customers included in trade and other payables	(124.9)	(130.2)
	243.2	244.2

The Group's credit risk on trade and other receivables is primarily attributable to trade receivables and amounts recoverable on contracts. The Group has no significant concentrations of credit risk since the risk is spread over a large number of unrelated counterparties. The majority of trade receivables and amounts recoverable on contracts represent amounts due from government bodies and large corporate internationals, spread across the following geographies:

BASIC

INTERMEDIATE

ADVANCED

	2011		2010	
	Trade receivables	Amounts recoverable on contracts	Trade receivables	Amounts recoverable contracts
	£'m	£'m	£'m	£'m
France	209.6	113.9	205.9	95.9
Northern and Central Europe	145.7	27..0	140.3	31.8
United Kingdom	72.0	175.8	65.0	187.2
Sweden	121.2	11.9	128.2	7.5
Benelux	61.6	12.4	72.8	30.6
International	72.9	27.1	69.0	21.4
	683.0	368.1	681.2	374.4

The Directors estimate that the carrying value of financial assets within trade and other receivables approximated their fair value.

Source: Logica (2011), p. 117

Progress Point 6.7

Morgan Henry Contracts Ltd has the following details in relation to a construction contract to build a motorway at the end of its financial year of 31 March 2013.

Contract M45	£000
Total contract price	26,000
Costs incurred to date	15,000
Costs to complete	4,000
Progress billings	12,000
Advance payments	3,000
%age complete 31 March 2013	60%
%age complete 31 March 2012	30%

The contract has been ongoing since June 2011 and Morgan Henry Contracts Ltd recognized revenue of £6.5 million and costs of £5 million in its financial statements to 31 March 2012. The company uses the stage of completion method to estimate revenues and expenses. Stage of completion is based on surveys of work performed.

Required

Prepare extracts of the statement of comprehensive income for Morgan Henry Contracts Ltd for the year to 31 March 2013 and the statement of financial position as at that date. Show, as far as possible, the disclosure requirements in accordance with IAS 11.

Suggested solution

Step 1: Calculate whether the contract will make an overall profit or loss

Contract M45	£000
Total contract price	26,000
Costs incurred to date	(15,000)
Costs to complete	(4,000)
Estimated profit	7,000

Step 2: Calculate turnover

Turnover: estimated total revenue × stage of completion = 26,000,000 × 60% = £15,600,000	
∴ cumulative turnover to be recognized	£15,600,000
Less: recognized year to 31 March 2012	£6,500,000
Revenue recognized year to 31 March 2013	£9,100,000

Step 3: Calculate cost of sales

Cost of sales = total estimated costs × stage of completion = 19,000,000 × 60% = £11,400,000	
∴ cumulative expenses recognized	£11,400,000
Less: recognized year to 31 March 2012	£5,000,000
Cost of sales recognized year to 31 March 2013	£6,400,000

Step 4 : Statement of financial position entries

	£000
Costs incurred	15,000
Profit recognized	4,200
Progress billings invoiced	(12,000)
Gross amounts due from customers	7,200

		31/3/12 £000	31/3/13 £000	Total £000
Profit recognized:	cumulative revenue	6,500	9,100	15,600
	cumulative expenses	5,000	6,400	11,400
	Profit	1,500	2,700	4,200

Morgan Henry Contracts
Statement of comprehensive income (extract)
Year to 31 March 2013

	£000
Turnover	9,100
Cost of sales	6,400
Gross profit	2,700

Statement of financial position (extract)
as at 31 March 2013

	£
Current assets	
Trade receivables	12,000
Gross amounts due from customers	7,200
Current liabilities	
Advance payments	3,000

Notes to the accounts

1. Turnover: turnover for the year on construction contracts amounted to £91,000,000. Turnover was calculated using the stage of completion and the total estimated revenue arising on contracts. Stage of completion was assessed based on surveys of work performed.

2.

Costs:	£000
Aggregate costs incurred	15,000
Aggregate profit less recognized losses	4,200

The effect of the disclosure requirements

The effect of the disclosure requirements in IAS 11 is to provide information both on the cumulative position of contracts – as in the aggregate costs incurred and aggregate profit recognized – but also on the turnover for the year under consideration.

It is worth pausing at this stage to consider what the statement of financial position amounts in relation to construction contracts actually represent.

Gross amount due to/from customers – by its very calculation – involves the incorporation, into the total, of unrealized profits (i.e. the profit recognized to date). This means that in such a statement of financial position figures will be incorporated that are not at lower of cost or net realizable value – but at some 'profit inclusive' value. In one sense, the accounting for construction contracts is akin to accounting for non-current assets, albeit in reverse. When accounting for non-current assets the net book value was found to be simply an accounting value representing the as yet unallocated cost of the non-current asset to profit or loss (i.e. the net book value is an intermediate stage in the allocation process).

Accounting for a long-term contract is very similar. Over the period of a contract, a given profit will be earned. By following the requirements of IAS 11, this profit can be allocated to accounting periods during which the contract is in progress. Until the contract is completed, therefore, the recognized profits are simply an intermediate stage in the overall profit measurement.

6.16 Comparison between GAAPs

In the UK, both inventories and long-term contracts are dealt with in one standard: SSAP 9. The principles followed in SSAP 9 are similar to those in IAS 2 and IAS 11, except for some differences in relation to contracts. SSAP 9 has more detailed presentation in the statement of financial position, although the net amounts in the statement of comprehensive income and statement of financial position are the same as IAS 11.

Under US GAAP, if an enterprise cannot determine contract revenue or costs, estimated costs to completion or the stage of completion, then the completed contract method is required. Under the completed contract method, net income is not recognized until the contract is complete. IAS 11 prohibits the use of the completed contract method.

6.17 IAS 11: a critical appraisal

As was demonstrated in our study of inventory valuations, the statement of financial position figure for inventory can be subjective. The valuations carried as construction contracts are subject to all the problems associated with inventory valuations – and more. It is easy to forget the principles that underpin accounting reporting – particularly when some of these principles conflict. A fundamental principle is that accounts are prepared following the historic cost convention; figures are recorded at their actual amounts and incorporated into the entity's financial reporting system at those historic amounts. In the case of construction contracts, this is what is being done in the recording of costs relating to specific contracts and recorded in the individual contract accounts. However, these contract accounts are not shown in the statement of comprehensive income but are instead held on the statement of financial position pending adjustments made in relation to recognizable revenue, expenses and profits. This is because of the nature of long-term construction contracts and the reporting problems that would exist if firms engaged in such contracts were unable to recognize profits until after a contract was completed; they would be placed in a situation in which reported profits might be subject to wide fluctuations from year to year. Reported profits would depend on the volume of contracts actually completed during a particular time period, which may bear no relation to the level of activity of the organization. Indeed, it is possible to envisage situations where a highly profitable firm is engaged in a small number of major contracts and yet appears to make heavy losses for a number of years followed by huge profits in the years in which the contracts terminate. In such circumstances the recognition of profit on construction contracts makes 'income smoothing' very desirable indeed. And therein lies the problem.

As has been demonstrated through our study of other areas in this book, as well as giving guidance to accountants in respect of the reporting of accounting transactions, standards also serve a regulatory function to try to prevent misleading users through the use of creative accounting. Unfortunately, income smoothing is just that – creative accounting. Moreover, if one considers just what is being recognized as revenue, it is clear that this in no way follows the historic cost recording principles. The amounts being recognized are an abstract based on the total contract revenue – revenue that no doubt has inflationary safeguards built in and that will be earned at some future date. Indeed, depending on the method chosen to determine the level of completion, the amount of contract costs recognized may bear very little resemblance to those costs actually incurred. Of course, it could be argued that all this information is available in the financial statements and the related notes, and that it is possible to extract from the accounts the detail required to make appropriate judgements on such activities. But this is not an easy topic. The accounting for construction contracts is complicated enough before one considers the inherent difficulties in obtaining the information to be accounted for in the first place. IAS 11 does not specify a single method that may be used to identify the stage of completion. The stage of completion of a contract can be determined in a variety of ways – including the proportion that contract costs incurred for work performed to date bear to the estimated total contract costs, surveys of work performed or completion of a physical proportion of the contract work. In some circumstances, the use of each of these methods to determine a level of completion may give vastly different results – and each would be acceptable, the IAS proviso being that whichever method is chosen, it should reliably measure the work performed.

It is clear therefore that the valuation of construction contracts is fraught with difficulty. From an auditor's perspective, it is unlikely that she or he will have the expertise to verify management's representations regarding stages of completion. The auditor's reliance on management will be great – and his auditor independence diminished. Fortunately, in many instances, the valuations will be made by independent, third-party valuers thus alleviating the auditor of this particular burden. From a user's perspective, however, an awareness of the principles underlying the reporting of construction contracts is essential to fully understand the figures within the financial statements. Moreover, since an element of subjectivity will once again be attached to the estimates made, however expertly calculated, the requirement to apply the chosen method of determining recognized profits in as consistent a manner as possible is essential if users of the financial statements are to place any credibility on them.

Proposed new standard

As was noted in the intermediate section of this chapter, IAS 11 and IAS 18 are currently under review in a project entitled Revenue Recognition. The exposure draft which was issued in 2010 would change the way in which revenue from construction contracts is recognized. The draft standard proposes that contract revenue would be recognized only if the customer controls the asset which is being constructed. In the case of an incomplete contract, revenue would only be recognized if the company had control of the partially completed asset. This would contrast markedly with the current 'stage of completion' method whereby revenue is recognized as work is performed, regardless of whether or not control has been passed to the customer.

> ## Section summary
>
> In Chapter 5 the difficulties of placing an accurate valuation on inventories was demonstrated. The valuation of long-term contracts is even more difficult. The standard's emphasis is on what can be recognized as revenue rather than on the statement of financial position figure, however, the two are inextricably linked. The standard allows attributable profit to date on a long-term contract to be taken to profit or loss when the earnings process is sufficiently far advanced and there is reasonable certainty of making a profit. This permitted treatment forms one exception to the rule of not recognizing profits until realized. This treatment also favours the accruals principle over prudence. Consequently, the analysis of a set of financial statements of a contracting business has to be approached in a very different way from a straight manufacturing business.

Chapter summary

IAS 11 *Construction Contracts*

- There is no reference to the length of a contract in its definition, but there is a requirement that the contract should be specifically negotiated.

- Contract revenue should include the amount agreed in the initial contract, plus revenue from variations in the original contract work, plus claims and incentive payments that are expected to be received and that can be measured reliably.

- Contract costs should comprise costs that relate directly to the specific contract, plus costs that are attributable to contract activity in general and can be allocated to the contract, and such other costs that can be specifically charged to the customer under the terms of the contract.

- When the outcome of a construction contract can be estimated reliably, revenues and costs should be estimated by reference to the stage of completion of the contract.
- To be able to make a reliable estimate, the enterprise must be able to make a reliable estimate of total contract revenue, the stage of completion and the costs to complete the contract.
- If the outcome cannot be measured reliably, no profit should be recognized; instead costs should be expensed and revenues should be recognized in line with recoverable costs.
- An expected loss on a construction contract should be recognized as an expense as soon as such a loss is probable.
- The stage of completion of a contract may be determined in a variety of ways:
  - the proportion that contract costs incurred for work performed to date bear to the estimated total contract costs,
  - surveys of work performed, or
  - completion of a physical proportion of the contract work.

 Key terms for review

Definitions can be found in the glossary at the end of the book.

Construction contract   Critical event   Revenue
Cost plus contract   Fixed price contract

? Review Questions

1. What is meant by revenue recognition?
2. What are the main issues in relation to revenue recognition?
3. Define what is meant by 'revenue' and explain how revenue should be measured in accordance with IAS 18.
4. What conditions must be satisfied before revenue relating to a sale of goods can be recognized?
5. What conditions must be satisfied before revenue relating to the rendering of services can be recognized?
6. Is recognition of revenue in accordance with IAS 18's objective?
7. Why does IAS 2 *Inventories* not apply to construction contracts?
8. By what methods can the stage of completion of a construction contract be determined?
9. What is the IAS 11 definition of a *construction contract*?
10. Explain how revenue and costs should be recognized in accordance with IAS 11 where the outcome of a construction contract can be estimated reliably.

 Exercises

Level I

1. Pillar Products plc entered into the following transactions in the year to 31 March 2013.

   (i) The company secured a consultancy contract for £2m with a customer. The terms of the contract state that payment will be made on delivery of the financial report. Work started on the contract on 1

November 2012 and completion is expected by 31 July 2013. At 31 March it was estimated that the contract was 60% complete.

(ii) Goods with an invoice value of £180,000 were delivered to a customer on 30 March 2013. The invoice relating to the sale was raised and recorded on 4 April 2013.

(iii) The company has a branch in France. A French company which deals in the same line of business as Pillar Products has a branch in the UK. In order to minimize transport costs Pillar Products agreed to sell goods with a value of £120,000 to the French company's UK branch. In return, the French company sold a similar batch of goods to Pillar Products French branch.

(iv) Pillar Products placed £2m on 6 months' deposit on 1 January 2013. All interest is payable at the end of the 6 months. Interest rates are 4% per annum.

Required

Explain how the above should be treated in the financial statements of Pillar Products plc for the year to 31 March 2013.

2. A specialist engineering company has the following transactions in the year to 31 December 2012.

(i) An order was received on 15 December 2012 for a machine tool costing £810,000. A 10% deposit was paid by the customer on placing the order – work will start on the order in February 2013.

(ii) Surplus goods from a previous order were sold to a customer for £550,000 on 1 October 2012. The customer was given 12 months' free credit. The company's average cost of borrowing is 8%.

(iii) In June 2012, the company delivered a cutting head to a Russian customer with a sales value of £1.2m. It was agreed that the Russian customer would give 40,000 barrels of oil worth £1.2m in exchange. This oil was used by a different division of the engineering company.

Required

Explain how these transactions should be dealt with in the financial statements of the company for the year to 31 December 2012.

3. Stone By Stone Ltd ('SBS') is a construction company involved in several building contracts. Details of two of the contracts in progress at the company's year end of 31 December 2012 are as follows.

Patterson Palace

This contract was originally negotiated in March 2010 at a price of £10.5m. In a bid to ensure speedy completion, an additional 5% incentive payment was included in the contract for completion by 31 March 2012.

During 2011, Lady Patterson amended the specification and both parties agreed that an increase of £0.5m should be made to the contract price. The incentive payment was also to apply to this variation.

At 31 December 2012, the contract is 95% complete and the engineers are confident it will be completed by mid-March 2013.

McLeod Mansion

This contract to construct a futuristic building was secured in January 2011 after a long period of tender and negotiation. SBS has estimated the total costs of the contract to be:

	£000
Materials	9,650
Labour	4,200
Subcontracted work	1,560
Professional fees	710

Equipment hire	250
Depreciation of plant and equipment	410
General administration	520
Development costs	260
Costs of contract tender	620
Production overheads	3,100

The development costs of £260,000 relate to the estimated costs of finalizing a new technique to be used to construct the building. As this technique is likely to be used on future contracts, SBS did not specify reimbursement of these in the terms of the contract.

It is company policy to provide 5% of total costs for rectification and guarantee work.

Of the £620,000 contract tender costs, £512,000 were incurred and written off to the statement of comprehensive income in the year to 31 December 2011.

Required

Calculate the total revenue for the Patterson Palace contract and the estimated total costs of the McLeod Mansion contract.

4. The following data relate to Contract RJC 19:

	£000
Total contract value	500
Value of work completed (certified)	400
Costs to date (all attributable to work completed)	500
Estimated costs to completion	80
Progress payments invoiced	540

Required

Prepare the relevant statement of comprehensive income and statement of financial position extracts in accordance with the requirements of IAS 11 *Construction Contracts*.

5. Metvon Ltd has a number of contracts in progress at its year end 31 December 2012. Details of two of these are given below:

	Contract 1	Contract 2
	£000	£000
Contract price	16,000	36,000
Progress billings invoiced	6,300	21,400
Progress billings received	4,850	20,000
Costs incurred to date	4,300	25,000
Estimated costs to complete	10,100	13,000
% completion	30%	65%

Both contracts were started in the current year.

The company uses the stage of completion method, and all costs and outstanding billings invoiced are regarded as recoverable.

Metvon can estimate reliably the outcome of contracts once they are 40% complete.

Required

Calculate the amounts to appear in the statement of comprehensive income of Metvon Ltd for the year to 31 December 2012, and the statement of financial position as at that date (disclosure notes are not required).

6. On 1 February 2010, Arena Construction Ltd obtained a contract to build a sports complex. The complex was to be built at a total cost of £4,500,000 and was scheduled for completion by 1 September 2012. One clause of the contract stated that Arena Construction Ltd was to deduct £10,000 from the £6,000,000 total contract price for each week that completion was delayed. Completion was delayed five weeks, which resulted in a £50,000 penalty. Below are data pertaining to the construction period:

	2010	2011	2012
	£	£	£
Costs incurred to date (cumulative)	1,500,000	3,220,000	4,600,000
Estimated costs to complete	3,000,000	1,380,000	–
Progress billings invoiced (cumulative)	1,000,000	2,500,000	5,950,000
Progress billings received (cumulative)	800,000	2,300,000	5,950,000

Arena Construction determines the stage of completion of a contract by reference to the proportion that contract costs incurred for work performed to date bear to estimated total contract costs.

The outcome of contracts can be estimated reliably only when a contract is at least 40% complete.

Required

Prepare extracts from the statements of comprehensive income and statements of financial position for each of the three years of the contract ending 31 December 2010, 31 December 2011 and 31 December 2012.

7. Buildwell Ltd commenced business on 1 April 2012 as building contractors. The following details relate to three contracts in progress at the company's year end of 31 March 2013:

Contract name	Station Road	Park Terrace	Castle Way
	£	£	£
Costs incurred to date	30,470	27,280	13,640
Value of work certified by			
Contractees' architects	38,250	22,015	14,300
Progress billings invoiced	33,000	17,600	11,000
Progress billings received	27,500	17,600	11,000
Estimate of:			
	£	£	£
Final cost including future costs of			
rectification and guarantee work	33,000	38,500	66,000
Final contract price	42,500	31,450	89,375

The company uses the stage of completion method to estimate revenues and expenses. Stage of completion is based upon surveys of works performed by the contractees' architects. Buildwell Ltd can estimate the outcome of a contract reliably only when it is at least 40% complete.

Required
Prepare extracts from the statement of comprehensive income and statement of financial position for the year ended 31 March 2013.

Level II

8. The following data relate to a profitable contract – contract F360M:

Contract F360M	£000
Costs incurred on contract	1,000
Appropriate proportion of total contract value reported as turnover for year	1,500
Costs incurred in reaching stage of completion recognized in turnover	900
Progress payments invoiced to customers	1,200

Required
Prepare journal entries to record the relevant information for the statement of comprehensive income and statement of financial position in accordance with IAS 11 *Construction Contracts* requirements, and show the relevant statement of comprehensive income and statement of financial position extracts.

9. Alternative Power Solutions Ltd ('APS') is a firm of building contractors specializing in the construction of offshore wind farms. At 31 December 2012 the company had three contracts in progress: North Shores, Western Beaches and Philorth Flats. North Shores was started during the year ended 31 December 2011, and Western Beaches and Philorth Flats were started during the year ended 31 December 2012.

Details of the contracts are as follows:

	North Shores 31/12/11 £000	North Shores 31/12/12 £000	Western Beaches 31/12/12 £000	Philorth Flats 31/12/12 £000
Contract value	250	250	320	420
Agreed variation	–	30	–	–
Progress billings (cumulative)				
Progress billings invoiced	40	240	260	340
Progress billings received	40	200	210	340
Costs to date (cumulative)				
Materials	20	100	84	69
Labour	5	20	54	71
Production overhead	10	80	82	80

Estimated additional costs to complete:

Materials	75	5	30	144
Labour	20	–	5	14
Production overhead	65	5	15	72
Percentage complete	20%	90%	80%	50%

Percentage complete is based upon surveyors' valuations. APS can estimate reliably the outcome of contracts once they are 30% complete.

Required

(a) Calculate, showing all workings, the amounts to be included in the financial statements for APS Ltd for the year ended 31 December 2012, in respect of each of the contracts for:

   (i) turnover

   (ii) cost of sales

   (iii) trade receivables, and

   (iv) gross amount due from customers or due to customers for contract work.

(b) Prepare the relevant statement of comprehensive income and statement of financial position extracts for the year ended 31 December 2012.

Appendix 6.1: Journals for construction contracts

The following journal entries are used to record the accounting entries in respect of construction contracts. During the year:

(1) Dr	Trade receivables	X	
	Cr Contract account		X
	Being progress billings invoiced.		

To record the progress billings invoiced to the customer.

(2) Dr	Bank	X	
	Cr Trade receivables		X
	Being amounts received from customers.		

To record the amounts received from the customer.

(3) Dr	Contract account	X	
	Cr Bank/trade creditors		X
	Being contract costs incurred in year.		

To record the costs incurred in the year.

At the year end, the relevant amounts are transferred from the contract account in the statement of financial position to the statement of comprehensive income on a work completed basis:

> (4) Dr   Contract account   X
>   Cr   Turnover   X
>   Being turnover recognized on contracts.

To record recognized turnover.

> (5)   Dr   Cost of sales   X
>   Cr   Contract account   X
>   Being cost of sales recognized on contracts.

To record recognized cost of sales.

Depending on the information provided, you may have to calculate some of the relevant amounts.

Appendix 6.2: Steps for construction contracts

Appendix 6.2 summarizes the steps to be followed in respect of construction contracts to ascertain the recognized turnover and cost of sales amounts, and to determine the statement of financial position entries.

Statement of comprehensive income

Step 1: calculate overall profit/loss on the contract.

Step 2: calculate turnover for each year of contract.

■ For profitable/reliable or loss-making contracts:

turnover = contract price × stage of completion (less previous recognized turnover)

■ For profitable/not reliable:

turnover = costs incurred (less previously recognized turnover)

Step 3: calculate cost of sales for each year of contract.

■ For profitable/reliable:

cost of sales = total estimated costs × stage of completion (less previously recognized cost of sales)

■ For profitable/not reliable:

cost of sales = costs incurred which are recoverable (less previously recognized cost of sales)

■ For loss making:

cost of sales = recognized turnover + full loss

That is, the full loss must be recognized immediately and the cost of sales is the balancing figure.

Stage of completion if not specified can be calculated as follows:

$$\text{Cost basis} = \frac{\text{costs to date}}{\text{total costs}}$$

$$\text{Survey of work to date} = \frac{\text{work certified to date}}{\text{contract value}}$$

Statement of financial position

Step 4: calculate the resultant statement of financial position amount.

Current assets	
Trade receivables	
Progress billings invoiced to date	X
Less: progress billings received to date	(X)
	X
Gross amounts due from customers*	
Costs incurred to date	X
Profit/(loss) recognized to date	X/(X)
Less: progress billings invoiced to date	(X)
	X
Creditors: amounts falling due within one year	
Gross amounts due to customers*	
Costs incurred to date	X
Profits/(loss) recognized to date	X/(X)
Loss: progress billings invoiced to date	(X)
	(X)
Advance payments received	X

* Note that these are calculated the same way. If the resultant amount is a positive figure, it should be disclosed as gross amounts due from customers within current assets. If it comes out as a negative, it should be disclosed as gross amounts due to customers within current liabilities.

References

IAS 18 *Revenue* IASB, 1993.
IAS 11 *Construction Contracts*. IASB, 1993.
Logica (2011) *Annual Report and Accounts*

Further reading

IAS2 *Inventories*. IASB, Period 2003.
IAS 16 *Property, Plant and Equipment*. IASB, amended 2012.
IAS 11 *Construction Contracts*.
Myers, J.H. (1959) The critical event and recognition of net profit. *Accounting Review*, 34, 28–32.
ASB (1999) *Statement of Principles for Financial Reporting*, ch. 5, paras 5.33–5.36.

When you have read this chapter, log on to the Online Learning Centre website at *www.mcgraw-hill.co.uk/textbooks/mckeith* to explore chapter-by-chapter test questions, further reading and more online study tools.

Chapter 7

Share Capital and Reserves

Learning Outcomes

After studying this chapter you should be able to:

- ✓ define share capital and reserves
- ✓ compare different classes of shares and explain key terms relating to share capital
- ✓ explain the concept of limited liability
- ✓ describe what is meant by capital maintenance, and how this is achieved in practice
- ✓ distinguish between distributable and non-distributable reserves
- ✓ describe and apply the rules in relation to the reduction of share capital for public and for private companies
- ✓ explain the uses to which non-distributable reserves may be put
- ✓ identify specific situations where a reduction in capital may be desirable
- ✓ prepare the appropriate entries to account for a reduction in capital
- ✓ describe and apply the requirements of IFRS 2 *Share-based Payment*
- ✓ gain an understanding of the complexities of the existing legislation in relation to limited companies, and the proposals for its simplification.

Introduction

Having looked in detail at the assets and other resources held by a business, it is perhaps now appropriate to consider what a business owes and what claims exist again those assets.

Section 1: Basic Principles

Share capital, reserves and liabilities all represent claims against the assets of a business. Liabilities – for example, trade payables or accruals – represent claims from those who trade or transact with the entity, whereas share capital and reserves represent the claims on the assets by the owners.

This chapter begins by defining share capital and explaining the accounting entries in respect of the issue of shares. There is then a brief explanation of limited liability in relation to companies limited by shares and an introduction to the doctrine of capital maintenance. Reserves are then defined and illustrated, and the accounting issues introduced. Liabilities are dealt with in the following chapter.

7.1 Share capital

In accounting, the term capital is used frequently, and consequently it is difficult to define it generally. However, it may mean the original fund with which a business was started and over time represents the claim by the business owner on the net assets of the business. This claim – also known as the ownership interest – will increase if the net assets increase and decrease if the net assets decrease. The ownership interest applies to the entire net assets (i.e. the total assets less the total liabilities).

In the case of a sole trader, this ownership interest would be represented by the capital account. In the case of a limited company, although the same broad principles apply, the situation is usually a little more complicated.

With a limited company, the ownership interest is split between the original investment and the subsequent changes in net assets made through profits and gains. The original investment is usually made in return for shares in the company, and the subsequent profits and gains are known as reserves. The ownership interest in a limited company will therefore consist of shares and reserves. These ownership or equity shares are known as ordinary shares. When a company is first formed, those who take steps to form it will decide how much needs to be raised by the potential shareholders in order to set up the company with the necessary assets to operate. Shares represent the basic units of ownership of a business and each share has a named value, which is called its nominal or par value.

This par value is at the discretion of the people who start up the company. In practice, £1 tends to be the maximum nominal value for shares, and 25 pence and 50 pence are common nominal values. Whatever amount is chosen, it will be written on the share certificate, which is the document given to each investor as evidence of being a shareholder.

It is important to note that the par value has little significance as it does not necessarily relate to the price that the share could be bought or sold for. It is simply the value that is attached to the divided units of total share capital. Indeed, for an existing company, any new shares issued after the company has started trading are likely to be issued at a price in excess of the nominal value.

Example

Suppose a company has share capital of £100,000. This could comprise:

- 100,000 shares of £1
- 200,000 shares of £0.50
- 400,000 shares of £0.25.

Authorized share capital

For a company formed under the Companies Act 1985, at the date of incorporation it would have been set up with a specified authorized share capital. This is the maximum amount of shares that may be issued by the company. The members of the company can, at a later date, increase the authorized share capital should the need arise. There is no upper limit on what a company may choose to set as its authorized share capital. The Companies Act 2006 has abolished the concept of authorized share capital for new companies but it continues to operate as a restriction for existing companies.

Issue of shares at the date of incorporation

When a company is first formed, shares will be issued to raise the appropriate funds required by the company to operate. It is likely that, at commencement, these shares will be issued at their par value. For example, 50,000 shares of £1 par value will raise £50,000. The accounting entry to record such an issue is:

Dr	Bank	£50,000	
	Cr Share capital		£50,000
Being issue of ordinary shares at par.			

This would give rise to a statement of financial position on incorporation as follows:

	£
Cash at bank	50,000
Net assets	50,000
Equity	
Share capital	
50,000 shares of £1 each	50,000

Note that the share capital represents the owners' interest in the net assets. That is, the claim that the owners – the shareholders – have is the amount of the net assets.

Let us assume that the company buys the necessary non-current assets and inventories and begins to trade. During the first year, the company makes a profit of £10,000. This, by definition, increases net assets by £10,000. At the end of this first year the statement of financial position would appear as follows:

	£
Net assets (assets less liabilities)	60,000
Equity	
Share capital	
50,000 shares of £1 each	50,000
Retained earnings	10,000
	60,000

The profit made by the company, retained earnings, is known as a revenue reserve – it has arisen from generating revenues. Note, however, that the ownership interest is now £60,000 and that this is made up of:

- share capital, and
- retained earnings.

The ownership interest in this company is called the shareholders' equity. That is, the residual interests in the assets of the company after deducting all its liabilities.

It is worth pausing here to consider the position regarding the shares. One year on, the net assets have a value of £60,000. Given that there are 50,000 shares in issue, this would suggest that each share would have a value of £1.20 (60,000/50,000 = £1.20). Note that the par value is not affected by this – it will remain at £1 per share. This difference between the par value and the net asset value gives rise to a specific accounting adjustment where shares are issued at a higher price than their par value and is most likely to happen after incorporation.

Issue of further shares after incorporation

As time goes by, a company will, it hopes, generate profits and increase net assets. This will have the effect of increasing the value of each share in issue. Indeed, the value of each share will, in an efficient market, be influenced not only by the underlying net assets in the company, but also the future expectations of the earnings of the company. This may mean that the market value attached to each share will be substantially higher than its par value.

If the company wishes to expand further, say by buying new non-current (fixed) assets, it may wish to raise finance by issuing new shares. Providing the company has sufficient authorized share capital, it can issue further shares to raise the required funds. Note, however, that while the par value remains the same, the market value may be somewhat different.

Example

A company has shares with a nominal value of £1 but finds that its shares are selling in the stock market for £5. The company decides to issue 20,000 new shares. These shares will be issued for their market value of £5 per share, thus raising £100,000.

Nominal value and premium

Company law requires that the company shows separately the nominal value of the shares and any amount extra over the nominal value. The nominal value is £1 and as the total amount collected is £5; this means that the extra amount is £4 per share. This extra amount is known as a premium. The increase of £100,000 in ownership interest will be recorded therefore as two separate items, namely the nominal value of £20,000 and the share premium of £80,000.

The accounting entry is:

Dr	Bank	£100,000	
	Cr	Share capital – ordinary	£20,000
	Cr	Share premium	£80,000
Being issue of ordinary shares.			

Subsequent share transfers: buying and selling

The issue of shares, whether it be at incorporation or some later date, will result in a cash inflow to the company. The shareholders', or members', details will be recorded in the Register of Members, which is maintained in public companies by the Company Secretary.

Subsequent share dealings between existing and new shareholders will not result in cash inflows to the company. Once the shares have been issued, and the funds received by the company in respect of the issue, there will be no further cash inflows to the company, irrespective of the price attached to the shares in the trading share market. The only involvement by the company will be to ensure that the details of the shareholders are correctly recorded in the Register of Members.

The role of shares

Shares are a form of company funding; a shareholder invests in a company and gets shares in return. A person who holds shares in a company does not own a share of the assets of that company. Instead, the shares carry certain rights from which the shareholder can benefit. The exact nature of those rights will depend upon the type, or 'class', of share.

Types of shares

The rights attached to shares depend upon the type of share held. Broadly speaking, there are two types of shares: ordinary shares and preference shares. Those shareholders holding ordinary shares will be entitled to a share of any dividend declared by the company and a share in the net assets of the company when it closes down or is wound up. In addition, ordinary shareholders will be able to vote on issues that affect the company (e.g. who should be the directors).

Preference shares, unlike ordinary shares, usually have a fixed dividend that is paid before dividends are paid to ordinary shareholders. Preference shares guarantee that, if a dividend is paid, the preference shareholders will be entitled to the first part of it up to a maximum value. The maximum is usually defined as a fixed percentage of the nominal value of the shares issued. For example, if a company has 100,000 preference shares of £1 each with a dividend rate of 9%, this means that the preference share-holders are entitled to receive the first £9,000 (i.e. 9% × £100,000) of any dividend that is paid by the company for a year. Any excess over £9,000 will be available to the ordinary shareholders.

In addition, preference shares normally carry a right to a preference in the order of payment in the event of the company going into liquidation. The rights of preference shareholders will be set out in the Articles of Association of the company. Some preference shareholders may have the right to share in a surplus of net assets on a winding up, but others may only be entitled to the amount of capital originally invested. Preference shares do not normally carry the rights to vote.

The accounting issue involved

From an accounting perspective, the rights attached to preference shares give rise to a particular account-ing issue, that issue being whether they should be classified as equity or debt. Preference shares may be redeemable (i.e. into cash) or non-redeemable; they may carry a right to dividends on a cumulative basis (i.e. if the directors do not pay dividends in a year, the preference shareholders will have a right to receive that year's dividend and any others that have not been paid before the ordinary shareholders can be paid any dividend). Some preference shares – known as participating preference shares – get a share of profits if the profit is over a certain figure. The fixed-return nature of preference shares tends to suggest they should be treated as a form of debt; however, from a legal viewpoint, preference shares are seen as more akin to equity. As will be seen in Chapter 8, Liabilities, a substance over form approach is taken in respect of some types of preference shares, which results in the legal form being disregarded in favour of the intended substance of the original issuing transaction.

BASIC

INTERMEDIATE

ADVANCED

Progress Point 7.1

Explain the following terms:

(a) nominal or par value
(b) share premium
(c) preference shares.

Solution

(a) The nominal or par value is the value put on a share when the company is initially formed.
(b) Share premium is the difference between the price at which a share is issued and the par value.
(c) Preference shares are a type of share that normally carry a right to preference over the ordinary shares in the payment of dividends, and to priority in terms of repayment in the event of liq-uidation. They may have cumulative rights with respect to dividends, be redeemable, or have rights to participate in profits under certain conditions.

7.2 Doctrine of capital maintenance

The doctrine of capital maintenance is a judge-made doctrine that concerns protecting the level of capital investment in a company by its shareholders.

A limited liability company is recognized as a separate legal entity that is distinct from its owners. The identifying feature of a company limited by shares is that the liability of the shareholders for the debts of the company is limited to the amount (if any) unpaid on the shares held by them. Because shareholders normally pay fully for their shares when they are issued, shareholders are rarely held liable for the company's debts.

The privilege of limited liability status requires some counter-measures to protect creditors' interests.

Limited liability

A limited company is, for legal purposes, treated as being a separate legal entity: it can sue and be sued; it can own property and can enter into contracts in its own name. This contrasts greatly with other types of business (e.g. sole traders or partnerships), where it is the owner or owners rather than the business that must sue, enter into contracts and so on, because these types of business have no separate legal identity.

In the event that a sole-trader business finds itself in a position where it is insolvent (i.e. where the liabilities exceed the business assets), the law gives creditors the right to demand payment from whatever other assets the sole trader may have, whether it be his personal bank accounts, investments or indeed his house. The sole trader could, in theory, lose everything and this is because the law makes no distinction between the sole trader as a business and the sole trader as a private individual.

With a limited company, because it is treated as being a separate legal entity, it is the company itself that has responsibility for its debts – not the owners of the company. It is this important distinction that distinguishes limited liability companies from other types of businesses. Moreover, once a shareholder has paid to the company that amount which has been agreed for the shares, that shareholder's obligation to the company – and indeed to the company's creditors – is satisfied. Consequently, shareholders' liabilities are limited to that amount which they have paid, or have agreed to pay, for their shares.

While this is clearly advantageous to shareholders and potential shareholders in that they know exactly what they may lose, it is not necessarily advantageous to the other possible stakeholders of the business. Limited liability is attractive to shareholders because they can, in effect, walk away from the company's debts. In practice, as well as equity finance, a company may also have loan finance and is likely to have other stakeholders, such as trade creditors. While it is probable that banks advancing loan funds to a company will have the debt secured on a specific asset – or group of assets, held by the company, it is unlikely that a supplier of goods will be able to obtain such a security. It is because of this inability to secure debts and the added limitation on the rights of creditors to claim against the private assets of the shareholders that there is a statutory requirement for a company to retain within the company specific amounts of net assets. This requirement is known as capital maintenance and involves placing restrictions on the amount of shareholders' equity that can be distributed to shareholders. As a general rule, a company's issued share capital is not repayable to shareholders and neither are any capital, non-distributable reserves. The doctrine of capital maintenance is considered in more detail later in this chapter.

Share capital and company accounts

The statement of financial position of a company shows, on the one hand, the resources held by the company, i.e. the current and non-current assets, and on the other the sources from which they were derived or who has a claim on them. The resources (i.e. the assets) will have debit balances, and the sources or claims on those assets will have credit balances. Liabilities, share capital and reserves are all credit balance items. Liabilities represent claims from those who trade and transact with the business on the resources the business holds; share capital and reserves represent claims by the owners on the net resources that the business holds.

Example

(i) Total sources/claims:

Total assets	500	Shareholders' equity	300
		Long-term debts	105
		Current liabilities	95
	500		500

(ii) Long-term sources/claims

Total assets less		Shareholders' equity	300
Current liabilities	405	Long-term debts	105
	405		405

(iii) Shareholders' sources/claims:

| Net assets | 300 | Shareholders' equity | 300 |

As the above example shows, the accounting equation (assets = liabilities + capital) is satisfied in each of the three cases, depending on the presentation adopted.

Example (i) shows the total assets and the total claims against those total assets.

Example (ii) shows the total assets less current liabilities and the long-term claims (including shareholders') against those total assets less current liabilities.

Example (iii) shows the net assets, i.e. the total assets less current and long-term liabilities and the shareholders' claims against those net assets. Note that the shareholders' claim is a residual one (i.e. it is the amount remaining after all liabilities have been deducted from total assets). In order to be able to correctly quantify shareholders' funds, it is necessary to correctly classify and quantify a company's liabilities. Moreover, a correct quantification and classification is essential if capital maintenance rules are to be adhered to.

Progress Point 7.2

Why is it important to distinguish between liabilities, share capital and reserves?

Solution

Liabilities are amounts owed by the business to third parties, whereas share capital and reserves are amounts owed by the business to the owners. The distinction is important, as when such items are included within the accounting equation, they have a direct effect on the net assets, and worth, of a business.

7.3 Reserves

With a limited company, the ownership interest (i.e. shareholders' equity) is split between the original investment, the share capital, and the subsequent changes in net assets made through profits and gains, the reserves.

Reserves created from trading profits are known as revenue reserves or retained earnings. Revenue reserves represent the retained trading profits of a business at the end of the financial year. It is important to understand what this balance represents. The profits earned by the company will have resulted in a corresponding increase in net assets. The amount retained is therefore being employed by the company among the various net assets. In this respect the term 'reserve' is perhaps misleading. It does not mean that a corresponding amount of money is being kept available to meet contingencies or future requirements. Retained profits form part of the equity of the owners, and therefore represent a claim on the assets of the business, and these assets are likely to include various items apart from cash.

Reserves are classified as either revenue reserves or capital reserves. Revenue reserves arise from trading profits. They also arise from gains made on the disposal of non-current assets.

Capital reserves are quite different from revenue reserves. A company may issue shares at a premium (i.e. where shares are issued at a price greater than their par value). The par value of the new shares is credited to the share capital account and the premium to a share premium account. The share premium account represents a part of the proceeds of the share issue. The only reason it is not included in the share capital account is that UK law requires that the excess of the issue price over the nominal value be shown separately. The premiums can be regarded as capital profits and, like retained profits, the amount adds to the total claims of the ordinary shareholders. The share premium account is an example of a capital reserve, and the main difference between a capital reserve and a revenue reserve is that a capital reserve cannot be used for a dividend distribution. Money is raised by a share issue specifically to provide additional resources and it would be inappropriate to pay back part of the proceeds to the same or other shareholders.

A revaluation reserve is another example of a capital reserve. A revaluation reserve is created when a non-current (fixed) asset is revalued upwards in the financial statements. When a revaluation takes place, the financial statements recognize the increase in value of the asset, and the uplift in value within the asset schedule is matched with a corresponding increase in the revaluation reserve. Such a recognition of increase in value is an unrealized gain. As the gain has not been realized it cannot be shown as revenue. It has not been represented by any cash receipt and depends upon the subjective view of the valuer. Moreover, although the recognition of the increase in value does increase shareholders' equity, the increase is not one that has been created through trading operations and cannot therefore be distributed. Again, it would be inappropriate to try to distribute some or all of such a reserve as this could mean that the asset giving rise to the revaluation itself would require to be sold in order to fund the distribution.

The accounting issue involved

Limited companies are required by law to distinguish between that part of their capital that may be distributed to the shareholders and that part that may not. The distributable part is that which has arisen from trading profits and from realized gains on the disposal of non-current assets less any taxes and previously distributed profits (i.e. revenue reserves).

The non-distributable part normally consists of that which has arisen from funds injected by shareholders in respect of share issues and that which has arisen from upward revaluations in company assets that remain in the company (i.e. share capital and capital reserves).

The reason for this distinction is the limited liability status that company shareholders enjoy. With a limited company, the business and the owners are legally separate and, in order to protect the company's creditors, the law insists that the shareholders cannot legally withdraw a specific part of the capital of the company. In other words, that part of the capital must be maintained. Section 2 of this chapter looks in detail at the concept of capital maintenance.

Progress Point 7.3

Why is it important to distinguish between capital and revenue reserves?

Solution

The concept of capital maintenance involves placing restrictions on the amount of shareholders' equity that can be distributed to shareholders. It is important to make the distinction because revenue reserves can be distributed to shareholders, whereas capital reserves cannot.

Section summary

Share capital, reserves and liabilities represent claims on the assets of a business.

The separate legal status of a limited liability company means that it is important to distinguish between those claims that arise from the owners (i.e. ownership interest), and those that arise from those who trade and transact with the business.

Share capital represents part of the original funding of a limited liability company. Each share that has been issued will have a par (or nominal) value, although this may be very different from the value at which the share could be traded in a stock market. Shares traded independently of a company do not result in any cash flows to the company.

Reserves are classified as revenue reserves or capital reserves. Revenue reserves may be distributed to shareholders, whereas capital reserves are non-distributable.

The concept of capital maintenance and creditor protection means that the distinction between liabilities, share capital and distributable and non-distributable reserves is essential.

Section 2: Intermediate Issues

In the introductory section to this chapter share capital was explained and defined, the issue of shares at incorporation and subsequent to incorporation was dealt with, and the two broad categories of shares – equity or preference – were introduced.

In addition, both revenue reserves and capital reserves were defined, and it was explained that only revenue reserves could be distributed to shareholders. Finally, creditor protection in relation to transacting with limited companies was introduced, along with the concept of capital maintenance.

This section now looks in more detail at share capital, capital maintenance and distributable profits.

7.4 Reduction of share capital

Once shares have been issued by a company, the share capital account is credited with the par (or nominal) value of the shares. This value forms part of the permanent capital of the company – capital that requires to be maintained in the interests of creditor protection.

There may, however, be genuine reasons why a company would wish to reduce its capital. In the UK, the Companies Act has provision for share capital to be reduced; however, as the intention is that this amount should not be reduced, for public companies such a reduction can only take place subject to the consent of the court. On 1 October 2008 the Companies Act 2006 introduced a new procedure for private companies to make share capital reductions. As an alternative to obtaining court approval, private companies have the option of reducing the amount of their share capital by a special resolution supported by a solvency statement made by the directors.

A reduction of capital is most commonly undertaken where:

■ the company's share capital exceeds the fair value of its underlying assets
■ the company has liquid assets surplus to its needs, or
■ the company redeems its shares.

The principle of capital maintenance requires that if any part of the permanent capital base is repaid to members, it must be:

■ replenished by a transfer out of profits, or
■ replaced by new capital.

However, subject to this rule, limited companies may reduce their share capital if:

■ there is authority for the reduction in the Articles or, if not authorized, there is no restriction of prohibition of a reduction in the Articles
■ a special resolution is passed by the shareholders
■ in respect of public companies, the court confirms the transaction.

In arriving at its decision, the court will consider whether the reduction of capital would prejudice the rights of creditors, and will usually require an undertaking from the company that it will not make any distributions until all creditors outstanding at the time of the transaction have been settled.

A typical capital reduction involves the transfer of an amount from share capital, share premium or capital redemption reserve either to a special reserve or to make good past losses. Capital reduction means that the share capital is subjected to a lessening of its nominal value, i.e. reducing a share nominal value from £1.00 to, say, £0.50.

The first two situations noted above will be considered in detail. The redemption of shares is covered later in this chapter.

Share capital exceeds fair value of underlying assets

This situation normally occurs when a company has accumulated trading losses that prevent it from making dividend payments under the distributable profits rules.

A typical statement of financial position might show the following:

Share capital 200,000 ordinary shares of £1	£200,000
Profit and loss account	(180,000)
	£20,000

The accounting issue involved is that a company that was loss making may well return to profitability but that, in the absence of any correction to the statement of financial position, the company would not be able to make future distributions based on the future profits until the accumulated losses had been eliminated. The Companies Act 2006 allows a company to reduce its capital where it has incurred losses and the share capital is no longer represented by available assets (i.e. the capital is reduced to reflect the actual level of asset backing).

The following example illustrates the mechanics of such a reduction.

Example

Assume that the capital and reserves of Fairfield plc were as follows at 31 December 2012:

Share capital 200,000 ordinary shares of £1	£200,000
Profit and loss account	(180,000)
	£20,000

The directors are confident that the company can return to profitability, and estimate that it will make profits in the year to 31 December 2013 of £4,000 and subsequent annual profits of £5,000.

The directors have presented their case for a reduction in share capital to the shareholders, and have obtained a special resolution and court approval to reduce the £1 ordinary shares to ordinary shares of 10p each. The reduction is dealt with through a 'capital reduction' account, which is debited with accumulated losses and credited with the amount written off the share capital. The accounting entries will be:

Dr	Capital reduction account	£180,000	
	Cr Profit and loss account		£180,000
Being transfer of accumulated losses.			

Dr	Share capital	£180,000	
	Cr Capital reduction account		£180,000
Being reduction of share capital.			

The statement of financial position of Fairfield plc immediately after the reduction will be:

Share capital 200,000 ordinary shares of 10p	£20,000
Profit and loss account	0
	£20,000

The advantages of this to the shareholders of Fairfield are immediately apparent. If the reduction of share capital had not taken place then the profits earned in 2013 and subsequent years would have to have been used to reduce the accumulated losses. This would mean that the company would be unable to pay a dividend for approximately 36 years if it continued at that level of profitability (i.e. until the accumulated profits had been eliminated and distributable reserves became available).

The advantages of this to the company are also immediately apparent – it would be extremely difficult to attract equity investment in the company if shareholders could not expect a dividend for over 30 years!

As for the creditors, then, as can be seen from the statements of financial position before and after the reduction, the net asset position remains the same (i.e. £20,000). The assurances given by the company to the courts so that existing creditors will be paid before any distributions are made should ensure that they are left no worse off.

Company has liquid assets surplus to its needs

In contrast to a company that has accumulated losses, it may be the case that a company has excess cash or other liquid reserves (i.e. it has assets that are no longer needed). This can happen following a contraction in the company's activities. It may be appropriate, therefore, for the company to reduce its capital by returning these excess funds to shareholders.

A typical statement of financial position might show the following:

	£
Excess cash	1,000,000
Other net assets	2,000,000
	3,000,000
Share capital 2,000,000 ordinary shares of £1	2,000,000
Retained earnings	1,000,000
	3,000,000

The accounting entries for the repayment are to credit cash and debit share capital. The directors have presented their case for a reduction to the shareholders to reduce the £1 ordinary shares to ordinary shares of £0.50 each. The accounting entries will be:

Dr	Share capital (2,000,000 × 50p)	£1,000,000	
	Cr Cash		£1,000,000
Being repayment of excess funds to shareholders.			

The statement of financial position immediately after the reduction will be:

Other net assets	£2,000,000
Share capital 2,000,000 ordinary shares of £0.50	£1,000,000
Retained earnings	£1,000,000
	£2,000,000

The benefits to the shareholders are again immediately apparent. They have been refunded one half of the par value of their shares – £1,000,000 in total.

From the company perspective, it has been able to effectively reduce its unwanted liquid resources.

The creditors, on the other hand, have been left exposed to a greater risk. The net assets prior to the reduction were £3,000,000 but reduced to £2,000,000 after the payment to the shareholders. This illustrates the need for creditor approval to be sought and obtained prior to such actions.

7.5 Capital maintenance and creditor protection

The concept of capital maintenance in relation to limited liability companies was explained in the introductory section to this chapter. The limitation of shareholders' liabilities to the amounts invested in their shares requires that additional protection is needed for creditors dealing with limited companies as opposed to dealing with unincorporated businesses. Such unincorporated businesses do not require specific capital maintenance rules as the business owners can themselves be held to account for their business's debts, with the only limits being the value of their personal assets.

The examples shown above are a good illustration of the two extremes faced by companies, their shareholders and their creditors. At the one extreme there was a loss-making company with accumulated losses and little in the way of net assets. At the other extreme there was a company with surplus liquid funds. In both instances, however, creditor protection rules required the permission of the courts before any capital reductions could be made which could potentially affect the claims on the net assets by the creditors. Note that the illustrations assumed that the companies were public companies. Private companies no longer need court approval.

The creditor perspective is now considered and we look in detail at the risks the creditor groups are exposed to, and the measures put in place to minimize those risks.

Risks faced by creditors

Broadly speaking, creditors are faced with two types of risk. First, there is the risk that a company will operate unsuccessfully and will not be in a position to settle its obligations; second, there is the risk that a company will be profitable and in a position to settle its obligations but will instead pay its shareholders rather than its creditors.

Creditor protection rules are not designed to protect against ordinary business risks (e.g. a company incurring trading losses that render it unable to meet its debts). The rules do, however, aim to protect the latter type of risk, and the Companies Act 2006 requires the amount available to meet creditors' claims to be calculated by reference to the company's annual financial statements. The question is how should the amounts available to meet creditors' claims be quantified?

There are two possible approaches to ensuring creditor protection by reference to a company's statement of financial position.

1. The assets could be considered in relation to the liabilities, and limits set to ensure that there are always assets with a realizable value sufficient to cover all outstanding liabilities. This is known as the direct approach.

2. The liability side of the statement of financial position could be considered in relation to reserves and these could be classified into distributable and non-distributable reserves, i.e. reserves that are and are not available to shareholders by way of dividend distributions. This is known as the indirect approach.

At first glance, the direct method would appear to have greater merit – it attempts to ensure that there are sufficient assets to cover the liabilities. On further consideration, however, the problems of asset valuation become very apparent. As was illustrated in Chapter 2, the book values of assets often bear little or no resemblance to their realizable values. Consequently, if the direct method were to be adopted, there could potentially be several different results as to the level of creditor cover, depending on whether historic cost, replacement cost or realizable values were adopted for asset valuation. As a result, the Companies Act opts for the indirect approach by specifying capital maintenance in terms of the shareholders' funds.

It is worth noting, however, that certain creditors effectively minimize their risk by adopting a direct approach and securing their debts on specific assets of the company. For example, it is common practice for a mortgage to be secured on the asset for which the loan was granted; indeed, banks often take out what is known as a 'floating charge' over all the assets in a company. This effectively secures one or more mortgages or loans over all the company's assets. Unfortunately, while this minimizes the risk to the banks, it nevertheless disadvantages the trade creditors, whose claims would be considered only once these priority rights have been settled.

We continue with our study of capital maintenance and creditor protection, and once more consider the importance of share capital. We have already seen that reduction of capital is an important issue – so too are a company's minimum capital requirements.

Minimum share capital

The minimum share capital requirement for a limited company depends on whether it is a public company or a private company. The main difference between these is that a public company can offer its shares for sale to the general public, whereas a private company is prohibited from doing so.

A public limited company – identified as such by having the words 'public limited company' or the abbreviation 'plc' after its name – requires to have a minimum share capital of £50,000. Indeed, a 'plc' is not permitted to commence trading unless it has issued this amount.

The minimum share capital requirement refers to the nominal (par) value of the share capital and not the market value of the shares in issue. The nominal value is used for identification but also, more importantly, for capital maintenance. It is questionable, however, whether this figure of £50,000 is adequate. Most 'plcs' tend to be very large indeed and, in relative terms, £50,000 is a small figure to be maintained.

There is effectively no minimum capital requirement for private companies. These can be set up with a very limited number of shares – a single £1 share is not uncommon and this clearly affords very little in the way of creditor protection. Furthermore, private companies form about 99% of the total of 1.5 million UK limited companies. Most private companies tend to be smaller businesses where the ownership is divided among relatively few shareholders, often family members. Given the number of such private companies, and the particularly low minimum capital requirement, it is questionable whether any creditor protection exists at all.

Creditor protection: distributable profits

A company can make distributions only out of revenue (distributable) reserves. A distribution is every transfer of a company's assets to its members, in cash or otherwise, except:

(a) bonus issue of shares

(b) redemption or purchase of own shares out of capital

(c) reduction in share capital through eliminating unpaid share capital, and

(d) a distribution of assets on a winding up.

By far the most common form of distribution is the payment of a dividend.

Profits available for distribution

These are distinguished between private and public companies, as follows.

Private companies

The definition of distributable profits under the Companies Act 2006 is:

> *Accumulated, realized profits, so far as not previously utilized by distribution or capitalization, less its accumulated, realized losses, as far as not previously written off in a reduction or re-organization of capital.*

This means that:

- unrealized profits cannot be distributed (i.e. on, say, a revaluation)

- there is no difference between realized revenue and realized capital profits (i.e. if a company sells a non-current asset at a profit then because the gain is realized it can still be distributed even though it is a capital gain)

- all accumulated net realized profits (i.e. realized profits less realized losses) in the statement of financial position must be considered (i.e. it is the statement of financial position retained earnings figure that is important and not the fact that a profit was made in a particular year); consequently, a company need not make a profit in the year that it pays a dividend as it can use reserves brought forward; on the other hand, a company may make a profit one year but not be able to pay a dividend as it has accumulated losses brought forward.

Public companies

The Companies Act specifies the reserves of a company which are undistributable.

The undistributable reserves of a public company are:

- its share capital

- its share premium

- its capital redemption reserve (covered in detail later in this chapter)

- the excess of accumulated unrealized profits over accumulated unrealized losses at the time of the intended distribution, and

- any reserves not allowed to be distributed under the Act or by the company's own Memorandum or Articles of Association.

This means that, when dealing with a public company, the distributable profits have to be reduced by any net unrealized loss. The following example illustrates the difference between a private and public company's distributable reserves.

Example

An analysis of the equity of a company's statement of financial position as at the end of its latest reporting period is as follows:

Equity	£000	£000
Share capital		3,000
Share premium		700
Capital redemption reserve		200
Permanent capital at beginning of year		3,900
Unrealized gain	200	
Unrealized losses	(300)	
		(100)
Permanent capital at end of year		3,800
Realized: current year's profits	600	
current year's losses	(100)	
	500	
Retained profits b/f	1,100	
		1,600
Net assets		5,400

Private company

The profits available for distribution were the above details to apply to a private company would be £1,600,000 (i.e. its accumulated net realized profit). No account need be taken of the accumulated net unrealized gain or losses.

Public company

The undistributable reserves of a public company are:

	£000
Share capital	3,000
Share premium	700
Capital redemption reserve	200
Excess of unrealized profits	
over unrealized losses	–
	3,900

The amount of distributable reserves were the above details to apply to a public company will be £5,400,000 – £3,900,000 (i.e. £1,500,000). That is, the distributable profits have to be reduced by any net unrealized loss, i.e. £1,600,000 – £100,000 = £1,500,000.

Progress Point 7.4

Greval Ltd had retained earnings of £100,000 at 31 December 2010. Its results for the next three years were as follows:

2011	£50,000 Loss
2012	£60,000 Loss
2013	£35,000 Profit

Assuming all amounts are distributable, what is the maximum dividend the company could pay in respect of each year?

Solution

The accumulated reserves require to be calculated.

	2011	2012	2013
	£	£	£
Balance b/f	100,000	50,000	(10,000)
Profit/(loss) for year	(50,000)	(60,000)	35,000
Balance c/f	50,000	(10,000)	25,000

The balance carried forward at each year-end date represents the maximum that can be paid out in each period. If, however, £50,000 is paid out in 2011, the cumulative losses at the start of 2013 would be £60,000 and no dividend would be payable in 2013. The balance carried forward on accumulated reserves at the end of 2013 if a £50,000 dividend had been paid in 2011 would be a £25,000 loss.

A company cannot lawfully make a distribution out of capital. Consequently, the directors, when proposing and making a dividend, must ensure that losses made since the last statement of financial position was drawn up do not make the distribution illegal.

In addition, directors have a fiduciary duty to protect the assets of the company and to ensure that the company can pay its debts when they fall due. Directors must therefore specifically consider whether the company will remain solvent following a proposed dividend.

Realized profits and losses

The Companies Act states that references to realized profit and realized loss are to such profits or losses as fall to be treated as realized in accordance with principles generally accepted, at the time the accounts are prepared.

A profit is realized when it arises from a transaction where the consideration received by a company is 'qualifying consideration'.

Qualifying consideration includes cash, an asset for which a liquid market exists (e.g. gilts), and amounts due to be settled in either of these where the debtor is capable of settling within a reasonable period of time, it is reasonably certain that the debtor will be capable of settling when called upon and there is an expectation that the receivable will be settled.

Therefore, a profit arising on a normal cash or credit sale will be a realized profit. Other realized profits arise from:

■ a foreign currency gain on a monetary asset or liability
■ a reversal of a loss previously regarded as realized (e.g. reversal of an impairment loss)

- a profit previously regarded as unrealized becoming realized due to sale for qualifying consideration (e.g. sale of a previously revalued asset)

- if a revalued asset is depreciated, an amount equal to the excess depreciation over the historical cost equivalent is treated as a realized profit.

Almost all losses are realized losses although a revaluation loss that cancels out a previous unrealized revaluation gain is not realized.

Example

Salton Ltd had the following balances at 31 December 2012.

	£000
Share capital	5,000
Share premium	4,000
Revaluation reserve	1,000
Retained earnings	7,000
	17,000

At 31 December 2012 there were no distributable profits other than the £7 million balance on retained earnings. During the year to 31 December 2013 the following occurred.

1. Salton Ltd made an after-tax profit of £900,000.

2. Dividends on ordinary shares of £200,000 and £80,000 were paid in July and October 2013 respectively.

3. The asset to which the £1 million revaluation reserve balance related was sold for a gain of £120,000. The gain is included in the profit after tax for the year.

4. Salton acquired a new business, Creatart Ltd, which was valued at £2 million. The consideration given was an investment that Salton had acquired for £1.4 million several years ago. The gain of £600,000 has been included in the profit after tax for the year.

Required

(a) Calculate the distributable profits of Salton Ltd at 31 December 2013.

(b) Prepare an extract of the equity section of the statement of financial position of Salton Ltd at 31 December 2013.

Solution

(a) Distributable profits:

	£000
At 31 December 2012	7,000
Add: profit for the year	900
Less: dividends	(280)
Add: realized revaluation gain	1,000
Less: unrealized gain	(600)
	8,020

Notes

1. The revaluation gain was unrealized until the asset was sold.
2. The gain on the investment is unrealized as it was not sold for qualifying consideration.

(b) Statement of financial position:

Workings:	Retained earnings £000	Revaluation reserve £000
At 31 December 2012	7,000	1,000
Add: profit for year	900	–
Less: dividends	(280)	
Sale of revalued asset	1,000	(1,000)
	8,620	–

Statement of financial position extract

31 December 2013

	£000
Share capital	5,000
Share premium	4,000
Revaluation reserve	–
Retained earnings	8,620
	17,620

This example illustrates a very important point. The realized profits of a company may be a different figure from the balance on retained earnings.

In this instance the difference is £600,000, that difference being the unrealized gain on the disposal of the investment that was sold for a non-qualifying consideration.

Non-distributable reserves: capital redemption reserve

In the introductory section to this chapter, two examples of non-distributable reserves were given, namely share premium and revaluation reserve. Both these are capital reserves and as they are not created by trading operations, they are not available for distribution to shareholders.

The capital redemption reserve is a further capital reserve. Before looking in detail at the capital redemption reserve, it will be beneficial to once more consider the reasoning behind the Companies Act capital maintenance requirements.

The general idea is that capital should not be returned to the shareholders except under certain circumstances. However, where a company has surplus assets and receives creditors and court approval, capital can be reduced and a return of capital made to shareholders. In addition, where a company has accumulated trading losses and its share capital exceeds the underlying net assets then again, subject to creditors' and court approval, share capital can be reduced.

The Companies Act restrictions are designed to prevent shareholders withdrawing their capital from the business, thus prejudicing the claims of creditors. There are, however, two further instances whereby a company can reduce its share capital and this is when it purchases or redeems its own shares.

7.6 Purchase and redemption of own shares

As far as the accounting entries are concerned, these are the same for both redemption and purchase of own shares. It will be helpful, however, to look at the distinction between the two.

'Redeeming' means the buying back of shares that were originally issued as being redeemable in that the company stated when they were issued that they would be, or could be, redeemed (i.e. bought back by the company). The terms of the redemption (the buying back) would be stated at the time the shares were issued.

In contrast, when shares are issued that are not stated to be 'redeemable' then, when they are bought back by the company, it is said to be the 'purchase' of its shares by the company.

The Companies Act permits a company, if it is authorized to do so by its Articles of Association, to:

(i) issue redeemable shares of any class (i.e. preference, ordinary), but subject to the proviso that the company can issue redeemable shares only if it also has in issue shares that are not redeemable; the reason for the restriction is that if a company issued only redeemable shares it could, in theory, if all the shares were redeemed, end up with no shareholders

(ii) purchase its own shares (i.e. shares that were not issued as being redeemable shares); again, there is a proviso that the company must, after the purchase, have other shares in issue at least some of which are not redeemable; this is to prevent the company redeeming its whole share capital and therefore ceasing to have members.

Advantages of purchase and redemption of shares

The advantages of a company being able to buy back its own shares rest primarily with private companies. For public companies, the main advantage is that those with surplus cash resources are able to return some of this surplus cash back to their shareholders by buying back some of their own shares.

For private companies the main advantage is that this facility helps to overcome the disadvantages of not having a ready market on which to trade the companies' shares, i.e. a stock exchange.

(i) It will help shareholders who have difficulty in selling their shares to another individual to be able to realize the value of their shareholding on, say, retirement or leaving the company.

(ii) It helps private companies raise finance as there is an exit route for those investors who previously purchased shares in the company. The fear of not being able to dispose of shares previously led to finance being relatively difficult for private companies to obtain from people other than the original main shareholders of the company.

(iii) Should a shareholder in a smaller family company die, the shares can be purchased and the proceeds used to assist with the settlement of any taxes on the shareholder's death.

(iv) Shareholders with grievances against the company can be bought out, thus eliminating future problems and contributing to the smooth running of the company.

(v) Should a family shareholder with a large number of shares die or retire, the facility to buy back some or all of the shares by the company may help the remaining shareholders keep control of the company (i.e. they will feel less pressured to sell the shares in the company to outsiders if they know that the company itself can be a source of funds to pay the exiting shareholder's estate).

(vi) Similar to public companies, the company could return surplus cash back to its shareholders.

(vii) Should a company, either private or public, whose shares are not listed on the stock exchange introduce a share scheme for employees, the employees would know that they could easily dispose of the shares instead of being stuck with them.

Companies Act requirements

The safeguards for the protection of 'capital' contained in the Companies Act are as follows:

■ no redemption can take place unless the shares are fully paid up; this is to protect those creditors who regard any uncalled capital as part of the capital base of the company

■ no redemption can take place that would result in there being no shareholders; this would in effect be a winding up or liquidation of the company and other rules would then apply.

Different rules apply to the redemption of shares by public companies and by private companies. Each will be considered in turn.

7.7 Redemption of shares by a public company

Although a public company is permitted to redeem or buy back shares, there is the overriding requirement that it maintain the same overall level of permanent capital for the protection of creditors. There are two ways in which this can be achieved, and these are illustrated below. Remember that the accounting entries will be same for redemption and buy back of shares – the only difference will be in the titles of the accounts used (i.e. in practice the accounts would state which shares were redeemable).

General rules and procedures

There is no restriction on the price that a company may pay on purchasing its shares (except for the following rules). If the shares are being purchased for more than nominal value the total payment is split into:

- the nominal value of shares purchased
- the premium on purchase (note that this is different to any share premium on issue).

The general rules applying to all companies are in Part 17, Chapter 10, of the Companies Act 2006.

The main provisions for protecting the permanent capital are as follows.

(i) The nominal value of the shares purchased must be replaced by either:
   (a) the proceeds of a fresh (new) issue of shares for the purpose (this includes the nominal value and any share premium raised in the new issue), or
   (b) a transfer from distributable profits to the capital redemption reserve (CRR); the CRR, like share capital and share premium, becomes part of 'permanent' capital; it can only be used to pay up a bonus issue, or
   (c) a combination of (a) and (b) if the proceeds in (a) are insufficient to replace the nominal value redeemed.

(ii) The premium (if any) paid on the purchase of shares must be charged wholly to distributable profits, unless the shares being purchased were originally issued at a premium *and* the purchase is being financed wholly or partly out of the proceeds of a new issue.

   In this case, some or all of the premium on purchase can be charged to the share premium account. The maximum that can be charged is the smaller of:

   (a) the premium on the issue of the original shares, and
   (b) the balance on the share premium account (after crediting any premium on the new issue).

   Any amount of the premium on purchase that cannot be charged (debited) to share premium should be debited to distributable profits.

If the company has an insufficient amount of distributable profits to write off any premium and transfer to the capital redemption reserve the scheme is illegal and should not be carried out. This may limit either the number of shares that can be purchased or the price that can be paid.

The following examples all assume that distributable profits equals the balance on retained earnings.

Shares purchased or redeemed must be cancelled and removed from issued share capital unless they are to be held as treasury shares. (Treasury shares are covered later in this chapter.) This does not alter the authorized share capital.

The following steps should be followed in any share purchase/redemptions.

Step 1: check legality

Check whether there are sufficient distributable profits to fund the purchase. If not, the proposal will be illegal.

Step 2: record the purchase/redemption
Split the purchase price being paid for the shares into nominal value of the shares being purchased and any premium element, and record:

Dr	Share capital (nominal value)
Dr	Premium on purchase (if any)
Cr	Bank
Being purchase of shares.	

Step 3: record any new issue
This is recorded as a normal new issue.

Dr	Bank
Cr	Share capital
Cr	Share premium (if any)
Being issue of shares.	

Step 4: eliminate the premium on purchase
Calculate if any of the premium on purchase can be charged to the share premium account, and record. Any amount that cannot be debited to share premium must be debited to retained earnings.

Dr	Share premium (if permissible)
Dr	Retained earnings (balance)
Cr	Premium on purchase
Being elimination of premium on purchase.	

Step 5: replace the nominal value of the shares purchased (if not met fully by the proceeds of a new issue)

Dr	Retained earnings reserve
Cr	Capital redemption reserve
Being transfer to Capital redemption reserve.	

Step 6: Prepare statement of financial position after purchase
That is, simply process the above transactions.

Redemption out of distributable profits
Where shares are redeemed (or, remember, bought back) by a company out of distributable profits, the Companies Act requires that an amount equal to the nominal value of the shares redeemed be transferred to a capital redemption reserve. Such a transfer is described as a capitalization, which means that profits have been capitalized and the permanent capital has been maintained. The following examples show the accounting adjustments required depending on whether the shares are redeemed at par or at a premium, and whether the shares being redeemed were originally issued at par or at a premium.

Example: redemption of shares at par out of distributable profits

The statement of financial position of the company prior to capitalization is as follows:

	£
Other net assets	7,500
Bank	2,500
	10,000
Ordinary share capital (£1 shares)	7,000
Retained earnings	3,000
	10,000

A total of 2,000 ordinary shares of £1 each are to be redeemed at par out of distributable profits. The journal entries to effect the transaction are as follows:

Dr	Ordinary share capital		£2,000	
	Cr	Bank		£2,000

Being ordinary shares purchased.

Dr	Retained earnings		£2,000	
	Cr	Capital redemption reserve		£2,000

Being transfer as required by Companies Act.

The statements of financial position before and after redemption are as follows:

	Balances before £	Purchases £	Transfer to CRR £	Balance after redemption £
Other net assets	7,500			7,500
Bank	2,500	(2,000)		500
	10,000			8,000
Ordinary share of £1	7,000	(2,000)		5,000
Capital redemption reserve	–		2,000	2,000
Retained earnings	3,000		(2,000)	1,000
	10,000			8,000

Note that the permanent capital (i.e. share capital) and (non-distributable) capital redemption reserve remain the same at £7,000.

BASIC

INTERMEDIATE

ADVANCED

Example: redemption of shares at a premium out of distributable profits

The statement of financial position of the company prior to capitalization is as follows:

	£
Other net assets	7,500
Bank	2,500
	10,000
Ordinary share capital (£1 shares)	7,000
Retained earnings	3,000
	10,000

A total of 1,500 ordinary shares of £1 are to be redeemed at a premium of £0.50 each (i.e. £1.50 per share) out of distributable profits, making a capital repayment of £2,250. The Companies Act requires that if shares are to be redeemed at a premium (and they had not originally been issued at a premium) then an amount equal to the premium must be transferred from distributable profits to the credit of the ordinary share redemption account. Again, this is to divert profits away from being distributable to part of the company's permanent capital.

The journal entries to effect the transaction are as follows:

Dr	Share capital	£1,500	
	Premium on purchase	£750	
	Cr Bank		£2,250
Being purchase of shares.			

Dr	Retained earnings	£750	
	Cr Premium on purchase		£750
Being elimination of premium on purchase.			

Dr	Retained earnings	£1,500	
	Cr Capital redemption reserve		£1,500
Being transfer as required by the Companies Act.			

The statement of financial position before and after redemption are as follows:

	Balance before redemption	Purchase	Write-off premium	Transfer to CRR	Balance after redemption
	£	£	£	£	£
Other net assets	7,500				7,500
Bank	2,500	(2,250)			250
	10,000				7,750
Ordinary share capital (£1 shares)	7,000	(1,500)			5,500
Capital redemption reserve				1,500	1,500
Retained earnings	3,000		(750)	(1,500)	750
Premium on redemption		(750)	750		–
	10,000				7,750

Note once again that the permanent capital, i.e. share capital, and capital redemption reserve remain the same before and after the capitalization at £7,000. The premium on redemption has been written off distributable profits.

Example: shares previously issued at a premium being redeemed at a premium out of distributable profits

This final example is used to illustrate a very important point. The Companies Act allows the write off to the share premium account of any premiums payable on the redemption or purchase of own shares provided the shares being redeemed were themselves issued at a premium but with an additional proviso that a new issue of shares is being made for the purpose. In this example the shares are being redeemed out of distributable profits and consequently the share premium account cannot be used.

The statement of financial position of the company prior to capitalization is as follows:

	£	
Other net assets	7,500	
Bank	4,500	
	12,000	
Ordinary shares of £1	7,000	
Share premium	1,750	(shares originally issued for £1.25)
Retained earnings	3,250	
	12,000	

A total of 1,500 ordinary shares of £1 are to be redeemed at a premium of £0.50 each (i.e. £1.50 per share) out of distributable profits, making a capital payment of £2,250.

The journal entries to effect the transaction are as follows:

Dr	Share capital	£1,500	
	Premium on purchase	£750	
	Cr Bank		£2,250
Being purchase of shares.			

| Dr | Retained earnings | £750 | |
| | Cr   Premium on purchase | | £750 |

Being elimination of premium on purchase.

| Dr | Retained earnings | £1,500 | |
| | Cr   Capital redemption reserve | | £1,500 |

Being transfer as required by the Companies Act.

The statements of financial position before and after redemption are as follows:

	Balance before redemption £	Purchase £	Write-off £	Transfer to CRR £	Balances after redemption £
Premium on redemption	–	750	(750)		–
Other net assets	7,500				7,500
Bank	4,500	(2,250)			2,250
	12,000				9,750
Ordinary share capital (£1 shares)	7,000	(1,500)			5,500
Share premium	1,750				1,750
Capital redemption reserve	–			1,500	1,500
Retained earnings	3,250		(750)	(1,500)	1,000
	12,000				9,750

BASIC

INTERMEDIATE

ADVANCED

Again, the permanent capital, i.e. share capital, and share premium and capital redemption reserve remains the same before and after capitalization at £8,750. Note, however, that the share premium account remains unaltered. Because the redemption was funded out of distributable profits and not a new issue of shares, the Companies Act prevented the share premium account being used to provide for the premium payable of £750 on the redemption of the shares – instead, this was written off the distributable reserves (i.e. retained earnings).

Progress Point 7.5

Rollrock plc is a successful manufacturer of decorative stones. The company is owned by the Johnston family, one of whose members wants to sell his 100,000 shares and retire. The other shareholders are keen to keep all the company's shares in the family, but none can afford to buy the retiring shareholder's shares. It has been decided, therefore, that the company will purchase the 100,000 £1 ordinary shares for £180,000.

Rollrock plc has the following statement of financial position at 30 September 2013.

	£000
Net assets	4,000
Equity	
Share capital – £1 shares fully paid	2,000
Share premium	500
Permanent capital	2,500
Retained earnings	1,500
	4,000

Required

(a) Prepare journal entries to record the purchase of shares.

(b) Prepare the statement of financial position of Rollrock plc after the share purchase.

Solution

(a) Journal entries:

Step 1: check legality

The purchase will cost £180,000; the company has distributable profits of £1,500,000. It is, therefore, a legal proposal.

Step 2: record the purchase

Dr	Share capital		£100,000	
Dr	Premium on purchase		£80,000	
	Cr	Bank		£180,000

Being purchase of shares at a premium.

Step 3: record any new issue

There is no new issue – the entire purchase is being funded out of distributable profits.

Step 4: eliminate the premium on purchase

Dr	Retained earnings		£80,000	
	Cr	Premium on purchase		£80,000

Being charge of premium to distributable profits.

Step 5: replace the nominal value of shares purchased

Dr	Retained earnings		£100,000	
	Cr	Capital redemption reserve		£100,000

Being transfer to capital redemption reserve in respect of nominal value of shares purchased.

The first journal reduces both bank and share capital by the appropriate amounts. The premium on purchase account is used to maintain the double entry. The balance on this account is cancelled with the next step.

The second journal is required by the Companies Act. As no new shares are being issued the premium on purchase has to be written off against distributable profits.

The third journal replaces the nominal value of the shares purchased with a transfer to the capital redemption reserve. None of this is funded by a new issue and the transfer is required by the Companies Act.

(b) Rollrock plc:

Statement of financial position at 30 September 2013	
	£000
Net assets	3,820
Equity	
Share capital – £1 shares fully paid	1,900
Share premium	500
Capital redemption reserve	100
Permanent capital	2,500
Retained earnings	1,320
	3,820

Both the company's total net assets and capital and reserves have been reduced by £180,000. The transfer to the CRR has, however, used part of the company's distributable profits to replace the permanent (share) capital reduced by the purchase.

Although the creditors' security has been affected by the outflow of cash and reduction in total equity, the important point is that the permanent capital has been maintained at £2,500,000. Note that the company could have paid a dividend of £180,000 and would have been in the same net asset position.

From a creditor perspective, it is never in their interests for the company to return equity to the shareholders, whether this is accomplished either by dividend or the repurchase of shares. There is, however, some protection in that distributable profits place an upper limit on such payments.

Redemption out of the proceeds of a new share issue

Instead of shares being redeemed out of distributable profits, in practice, shares are often redeemed out of the proceeds of a new issue – or indeed partly out of profits and partly out of the proceeds of a new issue.

Again, the following examples show the accounting adjustments required depending on whether the shares are redeemed at par or at a premium and whether those shares being redeemed were originally issued at par or at a premium.

Example: redemption of shares at par funded by new issue of shares at par

The statement of financial position of the company prior to the capitalization is as follows:

	£
Net assets	7,500
Bank	2,500
	10,000

Ordinary share capital (£1 shares)	7,000
Retained earnings	3,000
	10,000

A total of 2,000 ordinary shares of £1 are to be redeemed at par – a new issue of 2,000 ordinary £1 shares at par being made for the purpose.

The journal entries to effect the transaction are as follows:

Dr		Share capital	£2,000	
	Cr	Bank		£2,000
Being purchase of own shares.				

Dr		Bank	£2,000	
	Cr	Share capital		£2,000
Being proceeds of new issue of shares.				

The statements of financial position before and after redemption are as follows:

	Balances before redemption	New issue	Purchase	Balances after redemption
	£	£	£	£
Net assets	7,500			7,500
Bank	2,500	2,000	(2,000)	2,500
	10,000			10,000
Ordinary share capital	7,000	2,000	(2,000)	7,000
Retained earnings	3,000			3,000
	10,000			10,000

As can be seen, the permanent capital remains the same at £7,000.

Example: redemption of shares at par funded by new issue of shares at a premium

The statement of financial position of the company prior to the capitalization is as follows:

	£
Net assets	1,250
Bank	250
	1,500

Ordinary share capital (£1 shares)	1,200
Retained earnings	300
	1,500

A total of 100 ordinary shares of £1 are to be redeemed at par – a new issue of 80 ordinary £1 shares at a premium of £0.25 (i.e. £1.25) being made for the purpose.

The summarized journal entries to effect the transaction are as follows:

Dr		Share capital	£100	
	Cr	Bank		£100
Being payment on redemption.				

Dr		Bank	£100	
	Cr	Share capital		£80
		Share premium		£20
Being issue of shares at a premium.				

The statements of financial position before and after redemption are as follows:

	Balances before redemption	Dr	Cr	Balances after redemption
	£	£	£	£
Net assets	1,250			1,250
Bank	250	100	100	250
	1,500			1,500
Ordinary share capital	1,200	100	80	1,180
Share premium	–		20	20
Retained earnings	300			300
	1,500			1,500

Once again, the permanent capital, i.e. share capital and share premium remains the same before and after redemption at £1,200.

Example: shares previously issued at a premium being redeemed at a premium and funded by new issue of shares at a premium

As was noted above, where shares are redeemed at a premium, such a premium must be paid out of distributable profits except that where the shares being redeemed were themselves issued at a premium and a new issue of shares is being made for the purpose. In such instances, all or part of the premium now payable may be charged against the share premium account. The amount that may be charged against the share premium account is the lower of:

- the amount of the premium which the company received on the shares now being purchased, and
- the current balance on the share premium account, including any premium on the new issue of shares.

The statement of financial position of the company prior to the capitalization is as follows:

	£	
Net assets	1,250	
Bank	250	
	1,500	
Share capital (£1 shares)	1,000	
Share premium	200	(Shares originally issued at premium of £0.20 per share)
Retained earnings	300	
	1,500	

A total of 100 ordinary shares of £1 are to be redeemed at a premium of £0.80 (i.e. £180). The redemption price of £180 is to be funded by the issue of 90 ordinary shares of £1 at a premium of £1 per share.

Because the redemption is funded by a new issue, part of the premium payable on the redemption may be charged against the share premium account, i.e. the lower of:

- the original premium on the shares being purchased, i.e. $100 \times £0.20 = £20$, and
- the balance on the share premium account, including the premium on the new share issue, i.e. £290 (£200 + £90).

Therefore, £20 can be charged against the share premium account. The balance (£80 – £20) £60 must come from distributable profits.

The summarized journal entries to effect the transaction are as follows:

Dr		Share capital	£100	
Dr		Premium on purchase	£80	
	Cr	Bank		£180
Being payment on redemption.				

Dr		Bank	£180	
	Cr	Share capital		£90
		Share premium		£90
Being issue of shares at a premium.				

BASIC

INTERMEDIATE

ADVANCED

Dr	Share premium	£20	
Dr	Retained earnings	£60	
Cr	Premium on purchase		£80

Being share premium account used for redemption, and write-off of remaining premium.

The statements of financial position before and after the redemption are as follows:

	Balances before redemption	Dr	Cr	Balances after redemption
	£	£	£	£
Premium on purchase	–	80	80	–
Net assets	1,250			1,250
Bank	250	180	180	250
	1,500			1,500
Share capital (£1 shares)	1,000	100	90	990
Share premium	200	20	90	270
Retained earnings	300	60		240
	1,500			1,500

Note that the permanent capital, i.e. share capital, and share premium have in fact increased (i.e. £1,200 to £1,260). This is because of the Companies Act restriction on the amount of share premium payable which may be charged against the share premium account. Although capital maintenance is the main aim of the legislation, as this example shows, circumstances can arise that result in an increase in permanent capital. Circumstances may also arise that result in a decrease.

BASIC

INTERMEDIATE

ADVANCED

Progress Point 7.6

Using the statement of financial position information from Progress Point 7.5, suppose that the 100,000 £1 shares that Rollrock plc is buying back had originally been issued at a premium of £0.25 each and are being redeemed at £1.80 (i.e. at a premium of £0.80 each). The new issue is of 120,000 shares, issued at a premium of £0.50 per share.

Required

(a) Prepare journal entries to record the purchase of shares.

(b) Prepare the statement of financial position of Rollrock plc after the share purchase.

Solution

(a) Journal entries:

Step 1: check legality

There are sufficient distributable profits. The scheme is legal.

Step 2: record purchase
The premium on purchase is £80,000 (100,000 × 80p). The nominal value is £100,000.

Dr	Share capital	£100,000	
Dr	Premium on purchase	£80,000	
	Cr Bank		£180,000
Being purchase of own shares.			

Step 3: record new issue

Dr	Bank	£180,000	
	Cr Share capital		£120,000
	Cr Share premium		£60,000
Being recording of new issue of shares.			

Step 4: eliminate premium

Dr	Share premium	£25,000	
Dr	Retained earnings	£55,000	
	Cr Premium on purchase		£80,000
Being write-off of premium on purchase.			

The original share premium on the issue of the shares being bought back was £25,000 (100,000 × £0.25). The balance on the share premium account after the issue will be £500,000 + £60,000 = £560,000. Thus, the maximum premium that can be offset against the new issue will be £25,000 (i.e. the lower of the premium on the original issue of shares £25,000 and the balance on the share premium account £560,000).

Step 5: replace nominal value
The nominal value is fully replaced by the new issue. There is no need to transfer anything to the capital redemption reserve.

(b) Statement of financial position:

Rollrock plc	
Statement of financial position at 30 September 2013	
	£000
Net assets	4,000
Share capital – £1 shares fully paid	2,020
Share premium	535
Permanent capital	2,555
Retained earnings	1,445
	4,000

Note that, in this case, the permanent capital has increased as a result of the new issue.

At the beginning of this section it was noted that there were two ways in which a public company could redeem shares: out of distributable profits or out of the proceeds of a new issue. In practice, a redemption is likely to be made out of both (i.e. partly out of profits and partly out of the proceeds of a new issue). The final two examples in this section illustrate the accounting entries required when redemption is made partly out of profits and partly out of the proceeds of a new issue.

Example: redemption of shares at par – partly out of distributable profits, partly from issue of shares

The statement of financial position of a company prior to capitalization is as follows:

	£
Other net assets	7,500
Bank	2,500
	10,000
Ordinary share capital (£1 shares)	7,000
Retained earnings	3,000
	10,000

A total of 2,000 ordinary shares of £1 are to be redeemed at par – a new issue of 1,200 ordinary shares of £1 being made at par to raise £1,200 and the balance to be funded out of distributable profits.

The summarized journal entries to effect the transaction are as follows:

Dr	Ordinary share capital	£2,000	
	Cr ⸱ Bank		£2,000

Being payment on redemption.

Dr	Bank	£1,200	
	Cr Ordinary share capital		£1,200

Being issue of ordinary shares at par.

Dr	Retained earnings	£800	
	Cr Capital redemption reserve		£800

Being element of redemption not covered by new issue being transferred as per the Companies Act.

BASIC

INTERMEDIATE

ADVANCED

The statements of financial position before and after the redemption are as follows:

	Balances before redemption	Dr	Cr	Balances after redemption
	£	£	£	£
Net assets	7,500			7,500
Bank	2,500	1,200	2,000	1,700
	10,000			9,200
Share capital (£1 shares)	7,000	2,000	1,200	6,200
Capital redemption reserve	–		800	800
Retained earnings	3,000	800		2,200
	10,000			9,200

Note that the permanent capital, i.e. share capital, and capital redemption reserve remains the same before and after redemption at £7,000. The other accounting entries are what we would expect (i.e. the amount of the redemption not being funded by the new issue (£2,000 – £1,200 = £800) requires the transfer of an amount equal to the nominal value of the redeemed shares from distributable profits to the capital redemption reserve).

BASIC

INTERMEDIATE

ADVANCED

Example: shares previously issued at a premium being redeemed at a premium and being funded partly out of distributable profits and partly from a new issue of shares

The statement of financial position of a company prior to capitalization is as follows:

	£	
Net assets	1,250	
Bank	250	
	1,500	
Share capital (£1 shares)	1,000	
Share premium	200	(shares originally issued at a premium of £0.20 per share)
Retained earnings	300	
	1,500	

A total of 100 ordinary shares, which had originally been issued at a premium of £0.20 per share, are to be redeemed for £180. The redemption price of £180 is to be funded from the issue of 40 ordinary shares at a premium of £1 per share (i.e. £2 × 40 = £80) with the balance coming from distributable profits.

The premium payable on the purchase of the shares is £80 (£180 – £100) and because a new issue of shares is being made for the purpose, then part of the premium can be charged to the share premium account. The amount that may be charged is the lower of:

■ the original premium on the shares being purchased (i.e. 100 × £0.20 = £20), and

■ the balance on the share premium account, including the premium on the new share issue (i.e. £240 (£200 + £40)); therefore £20 can be charged against the share premium account and the balance (£80 – £20), £60, must be charged to distributable profits.

As part of the purchase price is being met from distributable profits, it is necessary to make a transfer between distributable profits and the capital redemption reserve. The Companies Act requires the amount to be transferred to be calculated by deducting the aggregate amount of the proceeds of the new issue from the nominal value of the shares purchased.

In this example the amount of the transfer is therefore:

	£
Nominal value of shares purchased (100 × £1)	100
Less: proceeds of new issue	80
Required transfer	20

The summarized journal entries required to effect the transaction are as follows:

Dr	Share capital	£100	
	Premium on purchase	£80	
	Cr Bank		£180

Being payment on redemption.

Dr	Bank	£80	
	Cr Share capital		£40
	Share premium		£40

Being issue of new shares at a premium.

Dr	Share premium	£20	
	Retained earnings	£60	
	Cr Premium on purchase		£80

Being share premium account used for redemption and write-off of remaining premium.

Dr	Retained earnings	£20	
	Cr Capital redemption reserve		£20

Being transfer required by the Companies Act.

BASIC

INTERMEDIATE

ADVANCED

The statements of financial position before and after the redemption are as follows:

	Balances before redemption	Dr	Cr	Balances after redemption
	£	£	£	£
Premium on purchase		80	80	–
Net assets	1,250			1,250
Bank	250	80	180	150
	1,500			1,400
Share capital (£1 shares)	1,000	100	40	940
Capital redemption reserve	–		20	20
Share premium	200	20	40	220
Retained earnings	300	60		220
		20		
	1,500			1,400

Note that the permanent capital, i.e. share capital and share premium and capital redemption reserve, has reduced from £1,200 to £1,180. The reason for this is that the proceeds of the new issue are treated as financing part of both the nominal value and the premium payable, but this is not recognized by the legislation in specifying the computation of the transfer to the capital redemption reserve. Let us reconsider the above workings. The proceeds of the new issue are £80, of which £20 is used to fund the premium on purchase. This therefore leaves £60 to replace the nominal value of the shares purchased. In order to maintain the permanent capital at £1,200, the transfer to capital redemption reserve would need to be £40. This would be calculated as follows:

		£
Nominal value of shares purchased		100
Less: net proceeds of new issue:		
total proceeds	80	
less: utilized to finance part of premium	20	
		60
Necessary transfer to capital redemption reserve		40

Why, then, has this reduction in permanent capital arisen? It is as a result of the wording of the Companies Act in relation to the transfer to the capital redemption reserve. As noted above, the Companies Act 2006 requires the amount to be calculated by deducting the aggregate amount of the proceeds of the new issue from the nominal value of the shares purchased (Section 733). Unfortunately, the Act does not take account of the amount of the proceeds used to finance the premium payable (in this case £20). Had the legislation referred to 'net' proceeds of the new issue then it would have had the desired effect in maintaining permanent capital by diverting sufficient reserves from distributable profits to the capital redemption reserve. That is:

	£
Nominal value of shares purchased	100
Less: net proceeds of new issue (80 – 20)	60
Required transfer	40

As it stands, therefore, the law seems to permit such a reduction in capital for both public and private companies. The law, it appears, has been poorly drafted.

Progress Point 7.7

Again, using the statement of financial position information from Progress Point 7.5, suppose that Rollrock plc purchased the 100,000 shares that had originally been issued at a premium of £0.25 each, for £1.80 per share. This time, however, Rollrock plc issues only 60,000 shares at a premium of £0.50, raising £90,000. The remainder of the purchase is funded out of profits.

Required

(a) Prepare journal entries to record the purchase of shares.

(b) Prepare the statement of financial position of Rollrock plc after the share purchase.

Solution

(a) Journal entries:

Step 1: check legality
Scheme is legal.

Step 2: record purchase

Dr	Share capital	£100,000	
Dr	Premium on purchase	£80,000	
	Cr Bank		£180,000
Being purchase of own shares.			

Step 3: record new issue

Dr	Bank	£90,000	
	Cr Share capital		£60,000
	Cr Share premium		£30,000
Being recording of new issue of shares.			

Step 4: eliminate premium

Dr	Share premium	£25,000	
Dr	Retained earnings	£55,000	
	Cr Premium on purchase		£80,000
Being write-off of premium on purchase of shares.			

That is, the lower of the premium on the original share issue and the balance on the share premium account is written off the share premium account.

BASIC

INTERMEDIATE

ADVANCED

Step 5: replace nominal value

Dr	Retained earnings	£10,000	
	Cr Capital redemption reserve		£10,000
Being transfer of distributable profits to the capital redemption reserve			

This transfer is required as the new issued raised only £90,000 of the £100,000 nominal value of shares purchased (i.e. there is a shortfall of £10,000).

(b) Statement of financial position:

Rollrock plc

Statement of financial position at 30 September 2013

	£000
Net assets	3,910
Capital and reserves	
Share capital – £1 shares fully paid	1,960
Share premium	505
Capital redemption reserve	10
Permanent capital	2,475
Retained earnings	1,435
	3,910

Note that there has been a reduction in the permanent share capital of £25,000 (2,500,000 – £2,475,000). This is because there is a certain amount of double counting in the application of the proceeds of the new issue to offset both the nominal value and the premium on the shares being repurchased. As noted earlier, this is probably an error in the way in which the rules have been drafted rather than an exception to the general principle that permanent capital should not be reduced.

In order to have maintained the permanent capital, the transfer to the capital redemption reserve should have been calculated as follows:

	£	£
Nominal value of shares purchased		100,000
Less: net proceeds of new issue: total proceeds	90,000	
less: utilized to finance part of premium (100,000 × 25p)	25,000	
		65,000
Necessary transfer to capital redemption reserve		35,000

7.8 Redemption of shares by a private company

Although the overriding aim of company law in relation to the redemption or buying back of shares is to maintain permanent capital, an unintended effect of the legislation is that there may be an increase or decrease in that permanent capital figure.

Private companies are, however, specifically permitted by the Companies Act to purchase their shares out of capital. This facility enables a private company to reduce its permanent capital without the formality and expense of undertaking a capital reduction scheme. This ability to purchase shares is of considerable benefit to, for example, a family-owned company where one shareholder wishes to realize his or her investment but the other shareholders are unwilling, or indeed unable, to purchase it.

Because a purchase of shares out of capital results in a fall in the resources potentially available to creditors, the legislation in the Companies Act 2006 provides a number of safeguards to protect their interests, as described below.

First of all, the payment out of capital must be permitted by the company's Articles of Association and authorized by a special resolution of the company. The directors also require to make a declaration of solvency to the effect that the company will still be able to pay its creditors after the redemption and during the year following redemption. As the protection of creditors rests on the validity of this declaration (i.e. the continuing solvency of the business), the law requires that the declaration be agreed and reported upon by the company's auditors. The auditors' report is to be addressed to the directors (not to the company or shareholders), which states that the auditor has enquired into the affairs of the company, the amount stated in the declaration as the permissible capital payment (explained below) is in his view properly determined, and that he is not aware of anything to indicate that the opinion expressed by the directors is unreasonable in all the circumstances. Furthermore, once the payment out of capital has been authorized, the company must publicize it in an official gazette or by individual notice to each creditor who may object to such a redemption through the courts. Finally, in the event that the declaration of solvency proves not to have been well founded and the company commences to wind up within a year of the payment out of capital and is unable to pay all its liabilities and the costs of winding up, then directors and past shareholders may be liable to contribute. The directors who have signed the declaration of solvency and/or the past shareholders whose shares were purchased may have to pay an amount not exceeding in total the permitted capital payment.

Note that a payment out of capital will arise only if the company cannot fund the purchase out of distributable profits and the proceeds of any fresh issue.

The mechanics of the share purchase itself also provide protection of creditors' interests. The first condition is that the company must use all its distributable profits before it may reduce its capital. Similarly, if a company issues shares to finance the purchase, either wholly or in part, then these proceeds must be used before any capital reduction may occur. In other words, the permanent capital will be the last element of the funding of the purchase. This is known as the 'permissible capital payment' and is the maximum amount by which the permanent capital may be reduced. The permissible capital payment is the amount by which the total amount paid on redemption of shares exceeds the aggregate of the distributable profits of a company and the proceeds of any new share issue specifically made for the purposes of redemption.

	£	£
Amount payable to purchase shares		X
Less: distributable profits	X	
proceeds of new share issue	X	
		X
Permissible capital payment		X

The accounting entries required to limit the reduction in permanent capital to the permissible capital payment are as follows:

- If the nominal value of shares redeemed exceeds the permissible capital payment, an amount equal to the excess must be transferred from distributable profits to the capital redemption reserve account.

- If the nominal value of shares redeemed is less than the permissible capital payment, an amount equal to this plus the proceeds of any new share issue may be used to reduce any undistributable reserves, e.g. revaluation reserve, capital redemption reserve, share premium account, or fully paid share capital. These should be used in order of least 'restriction' (e.g. revaluation reserve before share premium, share premium before share capital); as profit will have been eliminated by this there will be nothing to transfer to capital redemption reserve.

As noted above, the general effect is that, in limiting the reduction in permanent capital to the permissible amount, a private company first utilizes its distributable profit before reducing any undistributable reserves. As before, this is best illustrated by examples.

Example: nominal value of shares redeemed exceeds the permissible capital payment

The statement of financial position of a private company prior to redemption is as follows:

	£
Other net assets	240
Cash	260
	500
Share capital (£1 shares)	100
Share premium	240
Retained earnings	160
	500

The company agrees to buy 50 of its shares of £1 each from a retiring director and shareholder at a premium of £3 per share, i.e. $50 \times (£1 + £3) = £200$. No new shares are to be issued for the purpose.

Step 1

The first step is to calculate the permissible capital payment:

	£
Amount payable to redeem shares	200
Less: distributable profits	160
Permissible capital payment	40

Step 2

The next step is to determine how much of the distributable profits require to be diverted from the profit and loss account to the capital redemption reserve:

	£
Nominal value of shares redeemed	50
Less: permissible capital payment	40
Capital redemption reserve	10

The journal entries required to effect the transaction are as follows:

Dr	Ordinary share capital	£50
	Premium on redemption	£150
	Cr Cash	£200
Being cash paid at redemption.		

Dr	Retained earnings	£150
	Cr Premium on redemption	£150
Being premium funded from distributable reserves.		

Dr	Retained earnings	£10
	Cr Capital redemption reserve	£10
Being transfer to capital redemption reserve.		

The statements of financial position before and after redemption are as follows:

	Balances before redemption	Dr	Cr	Balances after redemption
	£	£	£	£
Other net assets	240			240
Cash	260		200	60
Premium on redemption		150	150	
	500			300
Share capital (£1 shares)	100	50		50
Capital redemption reserve	–		10	10
Share premium	240			240
Retained earnings	160	150		–
		10		
	500			300

Note that the permanent capital has reduced from £340 to £300 (i.e. by the amount of the permissible capital payment).

Looked at another way, the company paid £200 to redeem the shares. It had to use all of its distributable profits before it could reduce its capital. The company had distributable profits of £160 and therefore the difference (£200 – £160) had to come from permanent capital.

Example: nominal value of shares redeemed is less than the permissible capital payment

The statement of financial position of a private company prior to redemption is as follows:

	£
Other net assets	240
Cash	260
	500
Share capital (£1 shares)	100
Share premium	240
Retained earnings	160
	500

The company agrees to buy 50 of its shares of £1 each from a retiring director/shareholder at a premium of £5 per share (i.e. 50 × (£1 + £5) = £300). A total of 20 ordinary shares of £1 each are to be issued at a premium of £2 per share to help finance the redemption (i.e. 20 × (£1 + £2) = £60).

Step 1

The first step is to calculate the permissible capital payment:

	£	£
Amount payable to redeem shares		300
Less: distributable profits	160	
proceeds of new issue	60	
		220
Permissible capital payment		80

Step 2

The next step is to determine how much of the distributable profits requires to be diverted from retained earnings to the capital redemption reserve:

	£
Nominal value of shares redeemed	50
Less: permissible capital payment	80
Allowed reduction in permanent capital	(30)
Proceeds of new issue	(60)
Total allowed reduction in permanent capital	(90)

Remember that this example is illustrating the accounting procedures to be adopted where the nominal value of shares redeemed is less than the permissible capital payment. The permanent capital can therefore be reduced by the difference. However, the issue of the new shares has itself increased the permanent capital, and consequently the total reduction in undistributable reserves includes this new issue also.

The journal entries required to effect the transaction are as follows:

Dr	Share capital	£50	
	Premium on redemption	£250	
	Cr Cash		£300
Being cash paid at redemption.			

Dr	Cash	£60	
	Cr Share capital		£20
	Share premium		£40
Being cash received from new issue.			

Dr	Retained earnings	£160	
	Cr Premium on redemption		£160
Being part of premium funded from distributable profits.			

Dr	Share premium	£90	
	Cr Premium on redemption		£90
Being part of premium funded from permanent capital.			

The statements of financial position before and after the redemption are as follows:

	Balances before redemption	Journals Dr	Journals Cr	Balances after redemption
	£	£	£	£
Other net assets	240			240
Cash	260	60	30 0	20
Premium on redemption		250	16 0	–
			90	
	500			260
Share capital (£1 shares)	100	50	20	70
Share premium	240	90	40	190
Retained earnings	160	160		–
	500			260

Note that the permanent capital has reduced from £340 to £260, which in this case is the permissible capital payment. Consider what has happened. The company has bought back shares costing £300 and has partly financed this by issuing new shares for £60. There is therefore a shortfall to be funded of (£300 – £60) = £240. The company has distributable profits of £160 and these must be used first to finance the purchase. There is therefore a shortfall of £240 – £160 (i.e. £80), which requires to come from permanent capital. As can be seen from the movements on the accounts above, share capital has been reduced by £30 and share premium by £50.

Progress Point 7.8

Ferbrew Ltd has decided to buy 10,000 of its £1 ordinary shares from a retiring director at a price of £1.25 each (i.e. £12,500). The shares were originally issued at par. The purchase is to be partly financed by the issue of 2,000 new ordinary £1 shares at £1.30 each.

The statement of financial position of Ferbrew Ltd prior to the purchase is:

	£
Net assets	33,000
Equity	
Share capital (£1 shares)	25,000
Share premium	–
Permanent capital	25,000
Retained earnings	8,000
	33,000

Required

(a) Prepare journal entries to record the purchase of shares.

(b) Prepare the statement of financial position of Ferbrew Ltd after the share purchase.

Solution

(a) Journal entries:

Step 1: calculate permissible capital payment (PCP)

			£
	Amount payable to purchase shares		12,500
Less:	distributable profits	8,000	
	proceeds of new issue	2,600	
			10,600
	Permissible capital payment		1,900

Step 2: record purchase

Dr	Share capital	£10,000	
	Premium on purchase	£2,500	
	Cr	Bank	£12,500
Being purchase of shares.			

Step 3: record new issue

Dr	Bank	£2,600	
	Cr	Share capital	£2,000
	Cr	Share premium	£600
Being issue of new shares.			

Step 4: eliminate premium

Dr	Retained earnings	£2,500	
	Cr	Premium on purchase	£2,500
Being elimination of premium on purchase.			

Step 5: transfer to capital redemption reserve

The nominal value of shares redeemed (£10,000) exceeds the PCP (£1,900) and therefore a transfer must be made from distributable profits to the capital redemption reserve.

The remaining balance on retained earnings is:

	£
Retained earnings	8,000
Less: premium on shares purchased	2,500
Remaining balance	5,500

Because the premium on purchase is debited to retained earnings, only the remaining balance can be transferred to the capital redemption reserve.

Alternatively, the required transfer could have been calculated as follows:

	£
Nominal value of shares redeemed	10,000
Less: permissible capital payment	1,900
	8,100
Less: proceeds of new issue	2,600
Required transfer to CRR	5,500

BASIC

INTERMEDIATE

ADVANCED

| Dr | Retained earnings | £5,500 | |
| | Cr   Capital redemption reserve | | £5,500 |

Being transfer to capital redemption reserve.

(b) Statement of financial position:

Step 6

This gives a statement of financial position of:

	£
Net assets	23,100
Equity	
Share capital	17,000
Share premium	600
Capital redemption reserve	5,500
Permanent capital	23,100

The reduction in permanent capital is £1,900 (£25,000 – £23,100), which is the amount of the PCP.

Progress Point 7.9

Using the same statement of financial position and funding information from Progress Point 7.8, suppose the shares are purchased for £2.00 each (i.e. for £20,000).

Required

(a) Prepare journal entries to record the purchase of shares.

(b) Prepare the statement of financial position of Ferbrew Ltd after the share purchase.

Solution

(a) Journal entries:

Step 1: Calculate permissible capital payment (PCP)

	£	£
Amount payable to purchase shares		20,000
Less: distributable profits	8,000	
Proceeds of new issue	2,600	
		10,600
Permissible capital payment		9,400

Step 2: Record purchase

Dr	Share capital		£10,000	
	Premium on purchase		£10,000	
	Cr	Bank		£20,000
Being purchase of shares.				

Step 3: record new issue

Dr	Bank		£2,600	
	Cr	Share capital		£2,000
	Cr	Share premium		£600
Being issue of shares.				

Step 4: eliminate premium

The premium to be eliminated is £10,000. The balance on retained earnings is only £8,000. There is, therefore, insufficient in retained earnings to write off the premium. Other accounts must be used. These should be used in order of least restriction (e.g. revaluation reserve before share premium, share premium before share capital) – that is:

Dr	Retained earnings		£8,000	
Dr	Share premium		£600	
Dr	Share capital		£1,400	
	Cr	Premium on purchase		£10,000
Being elimination of premium on purchase.				

Step 5: transfer to capital redemption reserve

As retained earnings have been fully eliminated in writing off the premium there is nothing to transfer to the capital redemption reserve.

(b) Statement of financial position:

Step 6

This gives a statement of financial position of:

	£
Net assets	15,600
Share capital	15,600
Share premium	–
Capital redemption reserve	–
Retained earnings	–
Permanent capital	15,600

The reduction in permanent capital is £9,400 (£25,000 – £15,600), which is the amount of the PCP.

Note, however, how this has been achieved. The balance on the share capital account is only £15,600 despite there being 17,000 £1 shares in issue.

BASIC

INTERMEDIATE

ADVANCED

7.9 Treasury shares

Earlier in this section it was stated that shares redeemed or purchased must be cancelled.

In Europe and the USA, companies have been able to buy back shares and hold them for reissue. In the UK, regulations introduced in 2003 (now S724 of the Companies Act 2006) allow listed (full listing or AIM) companies to purchase their own shares and to hold them as **treasury shares** for sale at some future date. Under these regulations, purchased or redeemed shares do not need to be cancelled and they are not removed from issued share capital. Instead, these treasury shares are shown as a deduction from the existing shareholders' funds. To qualify, the company must have sufficient distributable profits to cover the purchase.

A maximum of 10% of any class of shares can be held as treasury shares at any one time. Treasury shares carry no rights to dividends or to vote. The company is recorded as holder of these shares in the register of members.

IAS 32 *Financial Instruments: Presentation*, paras 33 and 34, deals with this topic (see Chapter 8).

The amount of any treasury shares should be deducted from shareholders' funds. No gain or loss should be recognized in profit or loss on the purchase, sale, issue or cancellation of treasury shares. If treasury shares are cancelled, the usual rules for purchase of shares apply.

Accounting requirements

There are two common methods for accounting for treasury shares: the cost method and the par value method.

The most common method is the cost method, which provides that:

(i) **On purchase**

The treasury shares are debited at gross cost (i.e. purchase price not par value) to a treasury shares account, which is to be deducted from equity.

Journal:

```
Dr              Treasury shares
                Cr      Bank
Being purchase of treasury shares.
```

The treasury shares account records the consideration paid. Note that as the shares are not cancelled there is no debit to share capital.

(ii) **On resale**

The position on resale depends on whether the sales proceeds are greater than the purchase price.

(a) If the sales proceeds are higher than the purchase price, the treasury shares account is credited at cost and the excess is credited to share premium.

```
Dr      Bank
        Cr      Treasury shares
        Cr      Share premium
Being sale of treasury shares.
```

(b) If the sales proceeds are lower than the purchase price, the treasury shares account is credited with the original purchase price, and the deficit is debited to retained earnings.

```
Dr      Bank
Dr      Retained earnings
        Cr      Treasury shares
Being sale of treasury shares.
```

Note that, in both instances, no gain or loss is recognized in profit and loss – any gains or losses are recognized directly in equity.

Example

Exbere plc has 10 million 50p ordinary shares in issue. These were originally issued at a price of £1.50 each. On 1 January 2013, it purchased 1 million of these shares for £2.00 each. The shares are to be held as treasury shares.

The company resold the shares as follows:

- 15 April 2013 – 400,000 shares at £2.20 per share
- 25 October 2013 – 250,000 shares at £2.50 per share.

The company has a 31 December year end.

The journals to record the purchase and resale of the treasury shares during the year would be:

Purchase of treasury shares:

January 2013
| Dr | Treasury shares | £2,000,000 | |
| | Cr Bank | | £2,000,000 |

Being purchase of treasury shares.

April 2013
Dr	Bank	£880,000	
	Cr Treasury shares		£800,000
	Cr Share premium		£80,000

Being sale of treasury shares.

That is, the treasury shares account is credited with the original purchase price of the shares subsequently sold (i.e. 400,000 × £2.00), with the excess being credited to share premium.

October 2013
Dr	Bank	£625,000	
	Cr Treasury shares		£500,000
	Cr Share premium		£125,000

Being sale of treasury shares.

That is, again, the treasury shares account is credited with the original purchase price of the shares sold (250,000 × £2.00) with the excess being credited to share premium.

If a company holds shares as treasury shares and reissues some of these at below the initial purchase price it is prudent to write off the difference to retained earnings (not to profit or loss). Not to do so would be to anticipate the remaining shares being issued at an amount to cover the shortfall.

Example

A company purchases 2 million 50p ordinary shares for £2.50 each on 1 March 2013 and holds these as treasury shares. The shares are subsequently sold as follows:

- 1 August 2013 – 500,000 shares at £2.30
- 1 November 2013 – 1,500,000 shares at £2.80.

The company has a 31 December year end.

The journals to record the purchase and resale of the treasury shares during the year would be:
Purchase of treasury shares

March 2013			
Dr	Treasury shares	£5,000,000	
	Cr Bank		£5,000,000
Being purchase of treasury shares.			

Sale of treasury shares

August 2013			
Dr	Bank	£1,150,000	
	Retained earnings	£100,000	
	Cr Treasury shares		£1,250,000
Being sale of treasury shares.			

Note that the treasury shares account is credited with the original purchase price of the shares sold, i.e. (500,000 × £2.50), the deficit is charged to retained earnings.

November 2013			
Dr	Bank	£4,200,000	
	Cr Treasury shares		£3,750,000
	Share premium		£450,000
Being sale of treasury shares.			

Again, the treasury shares account is credited with the original purchase price of the shares sold (1,500,000 × £2.50), with the excess being credited to share premium.

Note that the £100,000 remains debited to retained earnings. It is not cancelled by part of the premium raised on the November sale.

The effect of the accounting treatment of treasury shares is as follows.

- If the disposal proceeds are equal to or less than the purchase price, the proceeds are treated as realized profit. This requires further explanation. Because the shares were originally purchased out of distributable profits, any proceeds received for their ultimate disposal – up to their purchase price – are credited back to realized profit. Note that this is not recognizing that a profit has been made when it clearly has not – it is just that it is returning to distributable profits some of the original purchase price that had been charged to distributable profits.

- If the disposal proceeds exceed the purchase price, an amount equal to the purchase price is treated as a realized profit and the excess is transferred to a share premium account. Again, there is a reversal of the amount that had originally been charged to distributable profits with the excess – the 'gain' – being credited to share premium.

Reasons for holding treasury shares

By holding treasury shares a company has greater flexibility to respond to investors' attitudes to gearing. Gearing is the measure of interest-bearing liabilities in relation to shareholders' equity. Consequently if a company holds treasury shares and investors perceive the level of gearing to be too high, the company can reissue the shares, thus increasing shareholders' equity and reducing the level of gearing.

In addition, by holding treasury shares a company has the capacity to satisfy loan conversions and employee share options without the need to issue new shares that would dilute the existing shareholdings.

Disclosure

The amount of treasury shares held should be disclosed as a deduction from shareholders' funds either on the face of the statement of financial position or in a note.

Example

Continuing with the information in the Exbere plc example, of the 1 million shares originally held as treasury shares, by the year end of 31 December 2013, 650,000 shares had been sold and £1.3 million (£800,000 + £500,000) credited to treasury shares. This left 350,000 shares at purchase price of £2.00 per share (i.e. £700,000 sitting as a debit in the treasury shares account).

Assume that at 31 December 2012 the company had the following balances:

	£
Ordinary share capital	5,000,000
Share premium	1,000,000
Retained earnings	3,500,000
	9,500,000

The retained profit for the year to 31 December 2013 was £400,000.

Assuming that the company discloses treasury shares on the face of the statement of financial position, the equity section of the statement of financial position at 31 December 2013 would be as follows:

Equity	
At 31 December 2013	
	£
Ordinary share capital	5,000,000
Share premium	1,205,000
Retained earnings	3,900,000
	10,105,000
Treasury shares	(700,000)
	9,405,000

Notes

Note that the share capital remains the same as the purchased shares have not been cancelled; the treasury shares held at the end of the reporting period are shown as a deduction from equity.

$$\text{Share premium} = \text{balance b/f} + \text{premiums on reissue.}$$

$$= £1,000,000 + £80,000 + £125,000$$

$$= £1,205,000$$

$$\text{Retained earnings} = \text{balance b/f} + \text{retained profit for the year.}$$

$$= £3,500,000 + £400,000$$

$$= \underline{£3,900,000}$$

7.10 Capital reserves put to use

The preceding examples have illustrated that capital reserves, once created, can be utilized. This is an important point to note. Our review of reserves thus far has effectively distinguished between distributable and non-distributable reserves, with capital reserves falling within the category of non-distributable. This does not mean that these reserves are not usable – it is just that they cannot be used to make distributions. The Companies Act specifies how capital reserves can be used and, in addition, a company's Articles of Association must also allow their use.

This is perhaps an appropriate point to look once more at capital reserves and how they may be used. As is often the case in accountancy, a full understanding of a particular topic often necessitates the introduction of a concept, and reference made to other concepts which, although essential to the understanding of the initial concept, have themselves not been explained. This has been the case with reserves, and in particular the capital redemption reserve, where the creation and subsequent use of the reserve have already been illustrated. Various capital reserves are now summarized, how they may be used is explained, and, as can be seen, this in itself leads to new issues requiring further illustration.

Capital redemption reserve

(a) As previously illustrated, the capital redemption reserve can be reduced in the case of a private company where the permissible capital payment is greater than the nominal value of shares purchased/ redeemed.

(b) It can be applied in paying up un-issued shares of a company as fully paid shares. These are known as bonus issues, capitalization issues or scrip issues. These are looked at in detail following this section.

Share premium account

(a) As with the capital redemption reserve, the share premium account can be used to issue bonus shares.

(b) Where an issue of shares resulted in a transfer to the share premium account, to write off expenses incurred on that issue.

(c) Where an issue of shares resulted in a transfer to the share premium account, to write off any commission paid on that issue.

Revaluation reserve

(a) The revaluation reserve can be reduced if, at any time, the asset whose increase in value gave rise to the revaluation falls in value.

(b) The revaluation reserve, as illustrated above, may also be reduced where the permissible capital payment exceeds the nominal value of the shares redeemed/purchased by a private company.

7.11 Bonus issues

Bonus issues – also referred to as capitalization issues or scrip issues – involve a transfer from one of the reserve accounts, distributable or non-distributable, to the share capital account to convert these reserves into shares. These shares can then be given to the existing shareholders in proportion to their holdings at the time of the issue. The shares will be treated as fully paid and usually do not include a premium element.

A bonus issue is often made when the market value of a share has grown to such an extent that it becomes difficult to trade on the stock market. It has the effect of lowering the value of each share without reducing the shareholders' collective or individual wealth. No new resources enter the company as a result of a bonus issue (i.e. there is no consideration received).

Example

The statement of financial position of a company is as follows:

	£
Net assets	128,000
Share capital (£1 shares)	50,000
Retained earnings	78,000
	128,000

The company decides to make a bonus issue of one new share to existing shareholders for every share owned by each shareholder. The journal entries required to effect the transaction are as follows:

Dr	Retained earnings	£50,000	
	Cr Share capital		£50,000

Being bonus issue – 50,000 shares.

The statement of financial position of the company immediately after this will be as follows:

	£
Net assets	128,000
Share capital (£1 shares) (50,000 + 50,000)	100,000
Retained earnings (78,000 – 50,000)	28,000
	128,000

As can be seen, the reserves have reduced by £50,000 and the share capital increased by £50,000. In other words, the reserves have been capitalized. Note that, in real terms, the shareholders are not any better off. Although they may own twice as many shares as they did previously, the total value of the company has remained the same at £128,000. The shares themselves will each be worth one half of the market price of an old share at the time of the issue.

If a company's articles of association give the power, a company can use any of its reserves to make a bonus issue (i.e. revaluation reserves, share premium account and capital redemption reserve).

Progress Point 7.10

The directors of Rosellie plc have decided to make a bonus issue from retained earnings of one new share for every three previously held. The company's statement of financial position at 31 December 2013, just before the issue, was as follows:

	£m
Non-current assets	14
Net current assets	4
Non-current liabilities	(5)
	13
Share capital (£1 ordinary)	9
Retained earnings	4
	13

Required

Prepare the journal entry required to record the bonus issue, and redraft the statement of financial position of Rosellie plc taking account of the bonus issue.

Solution

The bonus issue will be £9m/3 = £3m giving the following journal:

Dr	Retained earnings	£3m	
	Cr Share capital		£3m
Being the nominal value of shares created on bonus issue.			

The statement of financial position would become:

Rosellie plc
Statement of financial position at 31 December 2013

	£m
Non-current assets	14
Net current assets	4
Non-current liabiliies	(5)
	13
Share capital (£1 ordinary)	12
Retained earnings	1
	13

Note that net assets are unchanged as no new resources are raised in a bonus issue.

7.12 Share splits

There is another mechanism to reduce the market value per share, which does not involve the use of any reserve accounts. A company can split its shares into shares with a smaller par value. As with bonus issues, the effect is to reduce the market price per share but for each shareholder to hold the same total value.

Example

100,000 ordinary shares of £1 each could be subdivided into:

- 200,000 ordinary shares of £0.50, or
- 400,000 ordinary shares of £0.25 each.

7.13 Disclosure

The following disclosure is required by IAS 1.
   For each class of share capital:

- the number of shares authorized
- the number of shares issued and fully paid, and issued but not fully paid
- par value per share
- reconciliation of number of shares outstanding at the beginning and end of the period
- rights, preferences and restrictions attaching to each class of share
- shares of the entity held by the entity or by its subsidiaries and associates, and
- shares reserved for issue under options and contracts for the sale of shares, including the terms and amounts.

In addition, para. 97 of IAS 1 requires the amounts of transactions with shareholders and a reconciliation of the carrying amount for each class of share at the beginning and end of the period, separately disclosing each change.

Disclosure in practice

The reporting requirements in relation to share capital are dealt with in IAS 1. The relevant disclosures can be found within the accounting policies note and the notes to the statement of financial position.

Share capital

Ordinary shares are classified as equity. Incremental costs directly attributable to the issue of new shares or options are shown in equity as a deduction from the proceeds.

   Logica discloses in its policy note on share capital, the company's treatment of costs attributable to the issue of shares and that ordinary shares are classified as equity (see Figure 7.1).

   The share capital note from the Logica financial statements illustrates the disclosure requirements of IAS 1 in relation to share capital. A reconciliation of the number of shares at the beginning and end of the period is given, and the narrative element of the note gives details of the class of share in issue, the par value of those shares and the rights attaching to the shares.

Figure 7.1 Logica: share capital note

Allotted, called-up and fully paid	2011		2010	
	Number	£'m	Number	£'m
At 1 January	1,601,941,495	160.2	1,600,615,806	160.0
Allotted under share plans	10,032,071	1.0	1,325,689	0.2
At 31 December	1,611,973,566	161.2	1,601,941,495	160.2

The Company has one class of issued share capital, comprising ordinary shares of 10p each. Subject to the Company's Articles of Association and applicable law, the Company's ordinary shares confer on the holder: the right to receive notice of and vote at general meetings of the Company; the right to receive any surplus assets on a winding-up of the Company; and an entitlement to receive any dividend declared on ordinary shares.
Source: Logica (2011), p. 128

Other reserves

Figure 7.2 Logica other reserves note

	Treasury Shares	Translation reserve	Capital redemption reserve	Merger reserve	Other	Total
	£'m	£'m	£'m	£'m	£'m	£'m
At 1 January 2010	(35.1)	368.7	8.4	620.7	(1.5)	961.2
Exchange differences	–	12.2	–	–	(0.8)	11.4
At 1 January 2011	(35.1)	380.9	8.4	620.7	(2.3)	972.6
Cash flow hedges	–	–	–	–	(3.2)	(3.2)
Exchange differences	–	(53.5)	–	–	(0.5)	(54.0)
At 31 December 2011	(35.1)	327.4	8.4	620.7	(6.0)	915.4

Source: Logica (2011), p. 129

Treasury shares

Treasury shares

The Group holds shares in the Logica ESOP Trust for the benefit of Logica employees. The Trust purchases the Company's shares in the market for use in connection with the Group's employee share plans. As at the year end, the Treasury Shares reserve related solely to shares purchased and disposed of by the Trust, and would be deducted in determining the amount the Company had available for distribution at that date.

At 31 December 2011, the Trust owned 10,910,510 ordinary shares (2010: 11,807,522) with a nominal value of £1.1 million (2010: £1.2 million). The trustees of the Logica ESOP Trust have agreed to waive the right to future dividends on ordinary shares held by the Trust except for a nominal amount. At 31 December 2011 and 2010, the nominal amount payable to the Trust was 0.001 pence per share.

Translation reserve

The translation reserve represented the accumulated exchange differences arising from the following sources:

■ the impact of the translation of the statement of comprehensive income and net assets of subsidiaries with a functional currency other than pounds sterling;

- exchange differences recycled on disposal of foreign operations;
- exchange differences arising on the translation of net investments in a foreign operation where any subsidiary of the Group may have a receivable from or a payable to a foreign operation and settlement is neither planned nor likely; and
- exchange differences arising on hedging instruments that are designated hedges of a net investment in foreign operations, net of tax where applicable.

Capital redemption reserve

The capital redemption reserve is a non-distributable reserve and contained the nominal value of the shares re-purchased and cancelled.

Source: Logica (2011), p. 129

The capital redemption reserve note explains that the reserve comprises the nominal value of the repurchased shares. In addition to buying back and cancelling shares, Logica also holds treasury shares, as the extract above from the other reserves note discloses. As the note explains, these treasury shares are held for use in connection with employee share plans.

7.14 The position in practice

It is useful at this point to consider the position with share capital and reserves in practice.

The legislation governing share capital and reserves will be unique to the countries in which the accountant is based. The alteration of share capital as covered in this section has shown the importance of following the legislation prevalent in the reporting jurisdiction.

While an in-depth knowledge of the rules is not the aim of this book, an awareness of the possibilities to alter share capital very much is – particularly in relation to private companies. As noted earlier in this chapter, private companies form about 99% of the total of 1.5 million UK limited companies and it is therefore highly probably that, at some time, an issue in relation to the alteration of share capital will be encountered by the reader. Consequently, an awareness of the possible alterations that can be made to share capital is essential. Also essential is to be aware that before advising on any course of action in relation to such alterations, the Articles of Association must permit it, and the law prevailing in the reporting jurisdiction must be read in detail to establish exactly the correct procedures to be adopted.

Section summary

Share capital has been covered in detail, and in particular the rather complex topics of capital reduction, redemption and reconstruction.

The reasons why a company might wish to reduce its share capital and the legal process that must be undergone before such action can be taken was considered; after which we looked at the concept of capital maintenance and creditor protection, and how this affects companies' abilities to alter share capital and make distributions. Distributable profits were then defined, and non-distributable reserves introduced and explained in detail.

The purchase and redemption of shares by both public and private companies was illustrated, and it was explained that only private companies were permitted to purchase their shares out of capital. Finally, the chapter looked at how capital reserves could be put to use, and other forms of alteration of share capital, such as bonus issues and share splits.

The advanced section of this chapter goes on to consider some alternative uses of share capital, reviews recent changes to company law and what impact these changes have had on alternations to share capital.

Section 3: Advanced Aspects

7.15 Share-based payment

Introduction

The traditional view of share capital is as a means of funding a limited company and as a means of investment by investor shareholders. Shares are issued to raise funds for a company and the subsequent buying and selling of the shares on the stock market allows investors to invest when they believe a positive return is possible and to sell when they believe that a return has reached its maximum.

In recent years, however, the role of share capital has widened considerably and it is now frequently used as a means of rewarding employee performance and to remunerate directors, senior executives and other employees.

There are various reasons why share awards are becoming increasingly common. If company employees can benefit from their efforts then their interests can be aligned with those of the company's shareholders i.e. what will benefit the shareholders will also benefit the employees and consequently there is an incentive for the employees to ensure the long-term success of the company – that success reflecting in the value of the company's shares.

There can also be cash flow advantages to a company – if employees are rewarded in shares or perhaps, options to acquire shares, the company will not need to pay out cash to reward its employees. In a high-growth company this can be very beneficial when cash generated from operations is needed to fund continuing investment.

Finally, there can be tax benefits both for the company and for employees when share awards are given, thus making them more desirable than traditional forms of cash-based remuneration.

The accounting issue involved

The accounting issues with regard to share-based payments are how to measure the cost of the share awards conveyed and how to recognize these in the accounts. Indeed, if, as has been suggested above, share awards are used as a means of remunerating employees, then the measurement and recognition of their cost is essential if the statement of comprehensive income is to show an accurate profit figure. Moreover, if comparison is to be made between different companies with different remuneration packages, then to have no charge would be to underestimate the rewards given to employees and therefore overstate profit. Comparability is one of the enhancing qualitative characteristics of financial reporting information.

Consequently, the IASB have addressed these measurement and recognition issues in IFRS 2 *Share-based Payment* which is designed to cover all aspects of share-based payment awards whether these be share ownership schemes, share appreciation rights or other equity instruments. IFRS 2 is one of the more challenging accounting standards since it involves complex valuation issues and, as will be seen below, is sometimes counter-intuitive.

7.16 IFRS 2 *Share-based Payment*

Introduction

IFRS 2 prescribes the measurement and recognition principles for all share-based payment awards.

Definition

A share-based payment is a transaction in which the entity receives or acquires goods or services either as consideration for its equity instruments or by incurring liabilities for amounts based on the price of the entity's shares or other equity instruments of the entity.

Recognition principle

The general principle of IFRS 2 is that an entity recognizes an expense for goods and services (or an asset if the goods or services received meet the criteria for recognizing an asset), with the credit entry recognized either in equity or as a liability (depending on the classification of the share-based payment award).

Scope

IFRS 2 applies to all entities. There is no exemption for private or smaller entities; however, there are two exemptions to the general scope principle.

(a) the issuance of shares in a business combination should be accounted for under IFRS 3 *Business Combinations*

(b) contracts for the purchase of goods that are within the scope of IAS 32 and IFRS 9.

In order to fully understand the mechanics of share-based payments, it is essential to understand the following definitions:

(i) grant date – the date at which the entity and another party (including an employee) agree to a share-based payment arrangement

(ii) vesting conditions – the conditions that determine whether the entity receives the services that entitle the counterparty to receive cash, other assets or equity instruments of the entity under a share-based payment arrangement

(iii) vesting period – the period during which all the specified vesting conditions of a share-based payment arrangement are to be satisfied

(iv) vest – to become an entitlement i.e. when the counterparty's entitlement is no longer conditional on the satisfaction of any vesting conditions

(v) share option – a contract that gives the right, but not the obligation, to subscribe to the entity's shares at a fixed or determinable price for a specified period of time.

The IFRS sets out measurement principles and specific requirements for three types of share-based payment transactions.

(a) Equity-settled share-based payment transactions where the entity gives shares or share options in return for goods and services received.

(b) Cash-settled share-based payment transactions where the entity gives an amount of cash based on the value of the company's shares, in return for goods and services received. For example, employees may receive a bonus paid in cash based on the increase in the share price of the company over a particular period of time.

(c) Share-based payments transactions with cash alternatives where the company or the other party has a choice of whether the company settles in cash or shares (or options) in return for goods or services received. For example, a company or its employees may have a choice as to whether part of the remuneration package is given in cash or shares.

Recognition

An entity should:

(a) recognize the goods or services received or acquired in a share-based payment transaction when it obtains the goods or as the services are received (i.e. not when payments are made or shares are actually issued). If the goods and services do not qualify to be recognized as assets they should be recognized as expenses; and

(b) recognize a corresponding liability if payment is to be in cash, or an increase in equity for equity-settled transactions.

BASIC

INTERMEDIATE

ADVANCED

This can be illustrated diagrammatically as follows:

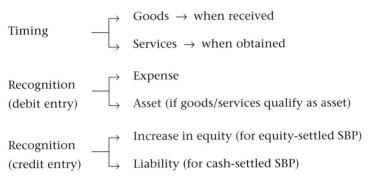

Timing
→ Goods → when received
→ Services → when obtained

Recognition
(debit entry)
→ Expense
→ Asset (if goods/services qualify as asset)

Recognition
(credit entry)
→ Increase in equity (for equity-settled SBP)
→ Liability (for cash-settled SBP)

The three arrangements noted above are now considered in more detail.

Equity-settled share-based transactions

The entity should measure the goods or services received and the corresponding increase in equity:

- directly, at the fair value of the goods and services received, unless that fair value cannot be estimated reliably;
- indirectly, by reference to the fair value of the equity instruments granted if the entity cannot estimate reliably the fair value of the goods and services received.

For transactions with employees, IFRS 2 notes that typically it is not possible to estimate reliably the fair value of services received for particular components of the employee's remuneration package and therefore the entity should measure the fair value of services received by reference to the fair value of the equity instruments granted. The fair value of those instruments should be measured at the grant date.

For transactions with others it is the date of receipt of the goods and services involved.

Example

A company issues shares on 1 June 2013 in order to pay for the purchase of inventory. The value of the inventory on 1 June 2013 is £3,000,000. The inventory was all sold on 31 December 2013. The shares were valued at £3,500,000 on 31 December 2013.

Required

How should this equity-settled share-based payment transaction be accounted for?

Solution

The company should measure the goods received and the corresponding increase in equity at the fair value of the goods received i.e. £3,000,000.

As the above example illustrates, the recognition date of goods in a share-based payment transaction is fairly obvious i.e. the goods should be recognized when received. However, it is often more difficult to determine when services are received. If shares are issued that vest immediately (i.e. the employees become unconditionally entitled to the shares) then it can be assumed that these are in consideration of past employee services and the expense should be recognized immediately on the grant date of the equity instrument.

If the equity instruments do not vest immediately the company should assume that the benefits received in return for the equity will be received over the vesting period. They should be accounted for as services received over the vesting period (normally debited to profit or loss) with a corresponding increase in equity.

If the vesting condition is merely the passing of time the company should assume that the benefits are received from the grant date to the vesting date.

Example

A company grants 2,000 share options to each of its three directors on 1 January 2013 subject to the directors being employed on 31 December 2015. The options vest on 31 December 2015. The fair value of each option on 1 January 2013 is £10 and it is anticipated that all of the options will vest on 31 December 2015. It is anticipated that all three directors will be employed on 31 December 2015.

Required

How should the share options be treated in the financial statements for the year ended 31 December 2013?

Answer

The company should presume that the services to be rendered by the directors as consideration for the share options will be received over the three-year vesting period. Consequently, in the year to 31 December 2013 the company should recognize an expense and a corresponding increase in equity calculated as follows:

$$2,000 \text{ options} \times 3 \text{ directors} \times £10 \times 1 \text{ year/3 years} = £20,000$$

For goods or services measured by reference to the fair value of the equity instruments granted, IFRS 2 specifies that vesting conditions, other than market conditions, should not be taken into account when estimating the fair value of the shares or share options at the measurement date. Instead, vesting conditions should be taken into account by adjusting the number of equity instruments included in the measurement of the transaction amount so that, ultimately, the amount recognized for goods and services received as consideration for the equity instruments granted is based on the number of equity instruments that eventually vest. Hence, on a cumulative basis, no amount is recognized for goods or services received if the equity instruments granted do not vest because of a failure to satisfy a vesting condition e.g. the counterparty fails to complete a specified service period. For example, if a company grants share options to employees that vest in the future if they are still employed the company would:

(i) calculate the fair value of the options at the grant date

(ii) charge this fair value to profit or loss over the vesting period

(iii) make adjustments at each accounting date to reflect the best estimate of the number of options that will eventually vest

(iv) increase equity by an amount equal to the profit or loss charge.

Example

A company grants 2,000 share options to each of its three directors on 1 January 2013 subject to the directors being employed on 31 December 2015. The options vest on 31 December 2015. The fair value of each option on 1 January 2013 is £10 and it is anticipated that all of the options will vest on 31 December 2015.

Required

How should the share options be treated in the financial statements in the years to 31 December 2013, 31 December 2014 and 31 December 2015 if, at the end of 31 December 2014, it is anticipated that there will only be two directors employed on 31 December 2015? At 31 December 2015, it is confirmed that there are two directors remaining.

Solution

Year to 31 December 2013

In this period the charge would be based on the original terms of the share option issue. The total value of the share option award at fair value at the grant date is:

$$2,000 \text{ options} \times 3 \text{ directors} \times £10 = £60,000$$

The charge to profit or loss for the period is therefore:

$$£60,000 \div 3 = £20,000$$

Year to 31 December 2014

In this year the number of directors still expected to be employed at the vesting date has reduced to two. The amended total expected share option award at the grant date would be:

$$2,000 \text{ options} \times 2 \text{ directors} \times £10 = £40,000$$

The charge to profit or loss is therefore:

£40,000 × 2/3	=	£26,667
Less: recognized to date	=	£20,000
Charge for year		£6,667

Year to 31 December 2015

In this year the actual number of options that vest is now known. The actual value of the option award at the grant date is:

$$2,000 \text{ options} \times 2 \text{ directors} \times £10 = £40,000$$

The charge to profit or loss is therefore:

£40,000 × 3/3	=	£40,000
Less: recognized to date	=	£26,667
Charge for year		£13,333

Note what is happening above. In the year to 31 December 2014, the year that it is anticipated that only two directors will be employed at the vesting date, the charge to profit or loss reflects the over-charge in the previous year i.e. had it been known at the outset that there would only be two directors being employed at the vesting date the fair value of the total award would have been as follows:

$$2,000 \text{ options} \times 2 \text{ directors} \times £10 = £40,000$$

and the annual charge would have been £40,000/3 = £13,333. However, in the year to 31 December 2013 a charge of £20,000 was made and so the overcharge (£20,000 − £13,333 = £6,667) is dealt with in the next available accounting period. By dealing with the adjustments as the facts become available, it ensures that the cumulative balance is the best estimate of the number of options that will eventually vest.

After vesting date

If the vesting conditions are based on the market price of the shares of the company, the company estimates the vesting period and does not change that estimate. If the employees decide not to exercise their options because the share price is lower than the exercise price, no adjustment is made to profit or loss. In such circumstances, a company would have recognized expenses through profit or loss for awards that ultimately had no value.

The rationale behind this rather counter-intuitive logic is this.

In arriving at the fair value of the equity instruments, the particular performance conditions will have been taken into account in estimating that fair value at the grant date. The charges to profit or loss reflect the number of options vested (whether or not these are exercised is not relevant to the calculation). Once the fair value of the option has been established at the grant date it cannot be adjusted for market price conditions. This means that options can be 'under water' (i.e. the share price less than the option price) and the company still recognizing a charge for these options.

The accounting entries

As was noted earlier in this section, the difficulties with IFRS 2 are as a result of the valuation issues that arise in determining the fair values attaching to the equity instruments awarded. The accounting entries are more straightforward.

The debit side of the entry – the charge – is to profit or loss and would be disclosed within the appropriate expense classification (e.g. distribution, administration etc.) as 'payroll costs' or perhaps 'share-based payment expenses'. If the goods or services acquired meet the appropriate recognition criteria for assets, then they should be disclosed as such.

In an equity-settled share-based payment transaction, the corresponding credit is to equity. Although IFRS 2 does not specify which item in equity is to be used, it is generally accepted that the entry should be to retained earnings. This results in the entries being disclosed in the statement of changes in equity (and not in the statement of comprehensive income). If shares are issued which vest immediately, the credit entry is treated in the same way as any other issue of shares.

Example

A company acquired a property on 31 March 2013 with an estimated market value at that date of £3.5 million. The consideration given was 1 million ordinary shares of 50p. On 31 March 2013, the ordinary shares of the company were trading at £3.55.

Required

How would this transaction be recorded in the books of the company?

Solution

IFRS 2 requires that the fair value of the goods received should be used as the basis of measuring the transaction unless no reliable estimate of fair value is available. There is no indication that the market value of £3.5 million is not reliable and therefore it should be used. The journal entry to record the transaction would be:

Dr	Property – at cost	£3,500,000
	Cr Share capital	£500,000
	Share premium	£3,000,000
Being purchase of property.		

The prescribed accounting treatment will ensure that the goods and services received are recognized over the period to vesting. Irrespective of what happens after the vesting date, no change is made to total equity. However, transfers within equity are permitted and may be appropriate. For example, if shares are issued on settlement the entry will be:

Dr	Equity
	Cr Share premium

Note that while there is nothing within the IFRS or indeed the Companies Act to prohibit the credit entry being recognized in retained earnings, nevertheless the credit entry is to be regarded as capital i.e an issue of shares. Consequently the amount of the credit is non-distributable even if it is not transferred to share premium.

The following progress point pools together all of the above issues and covers all aspects of a share-based payment award from its inception to its conclusion.

Progress Point 7.11

Gilmour Gates plc granted share options in respect of its ordinary £1 shares to its directors and staff on 1 January 2011. These can be exercised on 1 January 2014 or at any time within that calendar year at an exercise price of £100 per share. The 10 directors each received 500 options and the 60 staff received 200 options. Any new staff joining after January 2011 are not entitled to participate in this scheme. The fair value of each option at the grant date of 1 January 2011 was £30.

Required

How should the share options be treated in the financial statements and what would the accounting entries be in the years to 31 December 2011, 31 December 2012, 31 December 2013 and 31 December 2014 if:

- at the end of 2011, the directors estimate that all 10 directors will be eligible to exercise their rights but they expect that 30% of the staff will leave and forfeit their rights;
- in 2012, the directors new estimate is that all 10 directors will be eligible but only 15% of the staff are now expected to leave and forfeit their rights;
- in 2013, the exact details become available showing that 6 directors and 33 staff have become eligible to exercise their options
- in 2014 all eligible options are exercised by the directors and staff?

Solution

Year to 31 December 2011

At 31 December 2011, the directors must estimate how many of the directors and staff will still be employed at the vesting date and eligible to exercise their options. With the information available *at that time* the total cost of the options expected to vest is:

$$10 \text{ directors} \times £30 + 70\% \times 60 \text{ staff} \times 200 \text{ options} \times £30 = £402,000$$

The charge to profit or loss for the period given that the vesting period is 3 years is therefore £402,000 ÷ 3 years = £134,000.

The journal entries are:

Dr	Payroll costs	£134,000	
	Cr	Equity		£134,000
Being share-based payment expense.			

Year to 31 December 2012

The directors must reassess their estimate of how many of the directors and staff will still be employed at the vesting date and therefore eligible to exercise their options. The new information suggests that the revised total cost of the options expected to vest is:

$$10 \text{ directors} \times 500 \text{ options} \times £30 + 85\% \times 60 \text{ staff} \times 200 \text{ options} \times £30 = £456,000$$

As we are now two years into the three-year period we need to adjust the amounts involved so that the cumulative credit to equity is:

$$2 \text{ years}/3 \text{ years} \times £456,000 = £304,000$$

As we have already charged £134,000 in the year to 31 December 2011, we need to charge a further £170,000 i.e. £304,000 − £134,000 = £170,000.

The journal entries are:

Dr	Payroll costs		£170,000	
	Cr	Equity		£170,000
Being share-based payment expense.				

Year to 31 December 2013

By the end of 2013 the truth is known about how many directors and staff are eligible to exercise their options. The revised total cost of the options which actually vested is:

$$6 \text{ directors} \times 500 \text{ options} \times £30 + 33 \text{ staff} \times 200 \text{ options} \times £30 = £288,000$$

An adjustment needs to be made so that the cumulative credit to equity is £288,000. As £304,000 has already been charged, the adjustment is £288,000 − £304,000 = negative £16,000 i.e. there will be a negative payroll cost in this year.

The journal entries are:

Dr	Equity		£16,000	
	Cr	Payroll costs		£16,000
Being reduction in share-based payment expense.				

Year to 31 December 2014

All eligible options are exercised in this year i.e. 6 directors × 500 options + 33 staff × 200 options = 9,600 options. The exercise price is £100 and therefore the total cash generated will be £960,000.

The journal entries are:

Dr	Cash		£960,000	
	Cr	Share capital (£1 shares)		£9,600
	Cr	Share premium		£950,400
Being proceeds of exercise of options.				

As noted above, the issue of the shares on exercise is a capital transaction and, although not strictly required, it is useful to make a transfer to share premium of an amount equal to the cumulative increase in equity. i.e £134,000 + £170,000 − £16,000.

Dr	Equity		£288,000	
	Cr	Share premium		£288,000
Being transfer of reserve to share premium.				

Note that the charges to profit or loss and the cumulative amounts credited to equity are unaffected by the actual exercising of the share options. These charges would remain whether or not the options were actually exercised. The exercising of the options is treated in the same way as any other issue of shares i.e. it involves cash, share capital and, in this case, share premium.

Fair value of employee options

Our analysis thus far has been concerned with the accounting for equity-settled share-based payments and the fair values of the equity instruments which have been used in the examples have been provided to us. While detailed consideration of option valuation techniques is beyond the scope of this book, nevertheless, for completeness, it is worthwhile pausing at this stage to consider briefly how these fair values are arrived at.

IFRS 2 requires that fair values of equity instruments be measured based upon market prices if available, and taking account of the terms and conditions upon which these equity instruments were granted. If market prices are not available, a valuation technique to estimate what the price of those equity instruments would have been on the measurement date in an arm's length transaction between knowledgeable, willing parties should be used. The valuation technique should be consistent with generally accepted valuation methodologies for pricing financial instruments and should incorporate all factors and assumptions that knowledgeable, willing market participants would consider in setting the price.

If the particular option is traded on a market then the market price could be used to establish the fair value of an option at grant date. It is much more likely, however, that an option pricing model will have to be used. Examples of such option pricing models include:

> Black–Scholes: this option pricing model is used for options with a fixed exercise date that does not require adjustment for the inability of employees to exercise options during the vesting period; or

> binomial model: this model is used for options with a variable exercise date that will need adjustment for the inability of employees to exercise options during the vesting period.

IFRS 2 does not recommend any one pricing model but stipulates that whichever model is chosen, a number of factors affecting the fair value, such as exercise price, market price time to maturity and volatility of the share price, must be taken into account. In practice, the Black–Scholes model is probably most commonly used; however, many companies tend to vary the model to some extent to ensure it fits with the precise terms of their options.

Cash-settled share-based payments

For cash-settled share-based payment transactions, the entity should measure the goods or services acquired and the liabilities incurred at the fair value of the liability. With these transactions, the amount to be paid for the goods and services is *based* on the value of the company's shares but is *paid* in cash. The standard refers to these as share appreciation rights (SARs). With SARs the employees become entitled to a future cash payment, based on the increase in the entity's share price from a specified level over a specific period. Until the liability is settled, the entity should remeasure the fair value of the liability at the end of each reporting period and at the date of settlement, with any changes in fair value recognized in profit or loss for the period.

The entity should recognize the services received, and a liability to pay for these services, as the employees render service. For example, some SARs vest immediately and the employees are therefore not required to complete a specified period of service to become entitled to the cash payment. In the absence of evidence to the contrary the entity should presume that the services have been received and thus recognize immediately the services received and a liability to pay for them.

Example

Part of the contract of employment of the staff of a company is the right to receive payment in cash equivalent to 75% of the increase in value of a notional number of the company's shares during the year. On average, 250 employees receive 75% of the increase based upon 1,000 shares.

During the year to 31 December 2012 the share price increased from 450p per share to 520p.

Payment is made on 31 March 2013.

Required

Calculate the amount to appear in the financial statements for the year to 31 December 2012.

Solution:

Amount payable:

$$250 \text{ employees} \times 1,000 \text{ shares} \times 75\% \times (£5.20 - £4.50) = £131,250$$

And would be recorded as:

Dr	Payroll costs	£131,250	
	Cr Creditors		£131,250
Being payroll costs payable at year end.			

When the amount is finally settled on 31 March the payment would be recorded as follows:

Dr	Creditors	£131,250	
	Cr Bank		£131,250
Being payment of creditors.			

If the share appreciation rights do not vest until the employees have completed a specified period of service, the entity should recognize the services received, and a liability to pay for them, as the employees render service during that period i.e. the same approach as to equity-settled transactions applies.

The liability should be measured, initially and at the end of each reporting period until settled, at the fair value of the share appreciation rights, by applying an option pricing model, taking into account the terms and conditions on which the share appreciation rights were granted, and the extent to which the employees have rendered service to date.

Example

A company grants 500 share appreciation rights (SARs) to each of its 300 employees on condition that the employees remain with the company for the next two years. The SARs must be exercised at the start of year 3.

During year one, 10 staff leave and the company estimates that another 12 will leave in year two. During year two, 15 staff leave the company. At the end of year two the SARs of those remaining in the company vest.

The estimates of the fair values of the SARs for each year a liability exists are as follows:

Fair Value	
	£
Year 1	12.00
Year 2	14.30

Required

Calculate the amounts to appear in the statement of comprehensive income and statement of financial position of the company for years 1 and 2.

Year 1

An estimate is made of how many rights will vest based on the information available *at that time*.

$$(300 - 10 - 12) \text{ employees} \times 500 \text{ SARs} \times £12 = £1,668,000$$

The charge for the year is therefore:

$$£1,668,000 \times 1 \text{ year}/2 \text{ years} = £834,000$$

The statement of comprehensive income would be charged with staff costs and the corresponding liability disclosed in the statement of financial position as follows:

Dr	Staff costs	£834,000	
	Cr Creditors		£834,000
Being payroll costs due.			

Year 2

At year 2 the exact number of rights which will vest is known. The fair value of the SARs has increased based upon the information available and therefore the actual liability would be calculated as:

$$(300 - 10 - 15) \times 500 \text{ SARs} \times £14.30 = £1,966,250$$

An adjustment needs to be made so that the cumulative credit to creditors is £1,966,250. As £834,000 has already been credited, this leaves a further charge of £1,132,250. This would be recorded as:

Dr	Staff costs	£1,132,250	
	Cr Creditors		£1,132,250
Being payroll costs due.			

Year 3

When the SARs are exercised in year 3 the entries will be

Dr	Creditors	£1,966,250	
	Cr Bank		£1,966,250
Being payment of creditors.			

Share-based payment transactions with cash alternatives

These are share-based payment transactions in which the terms of the arrangement provide either the counterparty or the company with the choice of whether the transaction is settled in cash or equity instruments. Cash refers to cash and other assets. Transactions with employees are the most common examples of such transactions.

These should be accounted for as cash-settled share-based transactions if the company has incurred a liability to settle in cash or other assets, otherwise they should be accounted for as equity-settled share-based payments.

BASIC

INTERMEDIATE

ADVANCED

The company has an obligation if either:

(a) the counterparty has the choice, or

(b) the company has the choice but the settlement in equity option has no commercial substance or the company has a past practice or stated policy of settling in cash.

Where an obligation exists, the accounting treatment is the same as a cash-settled share-based payment transaction.

On the date of settlement, however, the counterparty might choose not to receive cash and instead opt for shares. Remember, the company is accounting for the transaction as best it can i.e. it cannot know for certain which course of action the counterparty will take until settlement. If this happens, the liability which has been built up should be transferred to equity as it represents the consideration received for the equity. For settlement in shares the journal entry would be:

Dr	Creditors	
	Cr	Share capital
	Cr	Share premium

Example

On 1 April 2012 a company grants its employees the choice of 500 ordinary shares of 50p each or the cash equivalent. The rights vest on the completion of two years' service and any employee who leaves within the two-year period forfeits the right to receive cash or shares. Settlement of any eligible awards is to be made on 1 April 2014.

During the two-year period to the vesting date of 31 March 2014 a liability of £639,400 is built up in relation to 278 eligible staff based upon a share price of £4.60 on 31 March 2014 i.e. 278 staff × 500 options × £4.60 = £639,400.

On the settlement date of 1 April 2014, 200 of the eligible staff opt for payment in cash and the remaining 78 opt for shares.

Required

What accounting entries are required to record the settlement on 1 April 2014?

Solution

Settlement is split between cash and shares. The cash payments reduce the liability by: 200 × 500 × £4.60 = £460,000. The balance £639,400 less £460,000 = £179,400 of the liability is effectively the proceeds from the issue of 39,000 (78 × 500) ordinary shares of 50p each.

The journal entries to record the settlement are:

Dr	Liability	£460,000	
	Cr Bank		£460,000
Being cash element of share-based payment liability.			

Dr	Liability	£179,400	
	Cr Share capital		£19,500	(39,000 × 50p)
	Cr Share premium		£159,900	(39,000 × £4.10)
Being transfer of shares to employees under share-based payment arrangement.				

Where no obligation exists the transaction should be accounted for as an equity-settled share-based payment transaction.

If, on the date of settlement, the company chooses to settle in cash then no new equity arises and the amount built up over the period has to be removed. The journal entry to record this would be:

Dr	Retained earnings	
	Cr	Bank

If the settlement is in shares there will be a transfer within equity – from retained earnings to share capital and share premium.

Example

A company has built up a reserve within retained earnings of £1,000,000 in relation to a share-based payment scheme where the company had the choice of settling in cash or shares. The company had intended to settle in shares at the outset and built up this reserve over the vesting period.

At the settlement date the company decided to settle one-quarter of the amount in cash and the remainder through the issue of £1 ordinary shares which had a market value of £5 at that date.

Required

What accounting entries are required on settlement?

Solution

The cash-based settlement of £250,000 (£1,000,000 ÷ 4) would be recorded as follows:

Dr	Retained earnings	£250,000	
	Cr	Bank	£250,000
Being cash settlement of share-based payment.			

The equity-settled element requires the issue of £750,000 ÷ 5 = 150,000 shares of £1 each (with a market value of £5).

Dr	Retained earnings	£750,000	
	Cr	Share capital		£150,000
	Cr	Share premium		£600,000
Being capitalization of retained earnings in issue of shares.			

Disclosure

IFRS 2 requires extensive disclosures to be made in the notes to the accounts that enable users of the financial statements to understand:

(a) the nature and extent of share-based payment arrangements that existed during the period

(b) how the fair value of the goods or services received, or the fair value of the equity instruments granted, during the period was determined; and

(c) the effect of share-based payment transactions on the entity's profit or loss for the period and on its financial position.

7.17 Changes to company law

As was seen in Section 2, the mechanics of reducing share capital and other capital reconstructions are both cumbersome and complex, involve applications to the Court and incur the associated court costs.

In 1999, the Company Law Review Steering Group (the Group) was appointed by the government to look into the possibilities of making changes to company law required for a competitive economy. A number of consultation documents were issued, one of which is on the formation of companies and the maintenance of their capital.

The Group made some important proposals for changes regarding the documents that companies should produce on their formation, and also regarding the question of their capital maintenance for the protection of their creditors.

The Companies Act 2006 incorporated many of the proposals.

7.18 Company formation

Prior to the Companies Act 2006 changes, when a company was formed there was a written document, the Memorandum and Articles of Association, which set out the powers of the company and was filed with the Registrar of Companies.

The Memorandum of Association describes and governs the relationship between the company and the outside world. The memorandum states the name of the company, the country in which the registered office is situated, the objectives of the company (i.e. activities the company may pursue), the authorized share capital, the nominal (par) value of the shares, a list of initial subscribers, and whether the liability of the members (i.e. shareholders) is limited.

The Articles of Association lay down the internal rules within which the directors run the company. The main items covered are:

(i) the issue of shares, the rights attaching to each class of share, the consent required for the alteration of the rights of any class of shareholders, and any restrictions on the transfer of shares

(ii) the procedure for board and general meetings, and for altering the authorized share capital

(iii) the election and retirement of directors, their duties and their powers, including borrowing powers

(iv) the declaration of dividends

(v) the procedure for winding up the company.

The Companies Act 2006 replaced the Memorandum and Articles of Association with two different documents and made it easier for companies to alter some of the contents of these. The Memorandum has been replaced with the 'Registration Form', which has broadly the same information but it is easier to change the contents; and the Articles with the 'Company Constitution', which again broadly resembles the previous document.

7.19 Capital maintenance

At present, any kind of shares issued by UK companies are required to have a nominal value. The Group proposed allowing companies to issue shares of no par value (NPV shares), i.e. shares without nominal values. This would affect the way a share is recorded and the way the permanent capital of a company is maintained. This proposal was not, however, adopted by the Companies Act 2006.

7.20 Shares of no par value

It can be seen that the idea of a fixed par value for a share can be very misleading, particularly to non-accountants. The value for which a share may be traded on the open market may vary considerably from the par value and this can be very confusing.

The requirement to have a nominal value is a legal requirement and is contained within the Companies Act. Similarly, it is the Companies Act that requires that, where shares are issued at a premium (i.e. at an amount higher than their par value), the share premium is kept separate.

The main argument for retaining nominal values of shares is that the share capital can be determined and therefore can be maintained. The nominal value is, however, an arbitrary value that was attached to each share when the company was first formed. The issue of shares at a premium on a later date will increase the permanent capital at that date. It is only by looking at the two together (i.e. share capital and share premium) that the permanent capital can be determined. The argument put forward, therefore, that by having a nominal value the capital can be determined and maintained, is flawed; it can only be determined by looking at both the share capital *and* the share premium. Moreover, the only reason that the issue of shares at a premium is split between share capital and share premium is because of a legal requirement. The permanent capital could still be determined and maintained if there were only one entry for the entire receipt.

A second argument put forward for having a nominal value attached to shares is that dividends paid by a company can be based on the nominal value of its shares. This argument, too, has flaws. If a par value is kept to, and the dividend based on this, then, over time, the dividend can look excessive, particularly in times of inflation.

Example

Lido bought 100 ordinary shares 40 years ago for £100. The dividend paid on the shares was 5% and this was sufficient, 40 years ago, to purchase a certain amount of goods. Forty years later, let us assume that the goods that are to be purchased now cost 20 times as much as they did (i.e. 40 years ago they cost £5 and now they cost £100). In order to keep Lido's dividends at the same rate of purchasing power, he would need a dividend of 100%. That is:

$$\frac{£100}{100 \text{ shares}} \times 100 = 100\%$$

Note that if the dividend was based on the current value it would probably be at a more realistic level – indeed, probably very close to the average return for the particular industry. It is just that the very misleading convention in accounting in the UK of calculating dividends in relation to the nominal amount of share capital gives this dramatic result.

The current report by the Group backs up study findings in 1952, which recommended the introduction of shares of no par value. Unfortunately, the then government failed to legislate for it. It is still not possible for the UK government to allow companies to issue NPV shares as the Directive requires public companies to have nominal values for their shares. The Group has expressed its wish for the Directive to be changed so that all companies are allowed to issue NPV shares. Until then, it is proposed that the new Statute should retain the requirements for shares to have a nominal or par value.

7.21 Share capital: authorized, minimum and share issue

Prior to the Companies Act 2006, companies had to have an authorized share capital, which limited the maximum number of shares they could issue. In practice, this limit was set much higher than was ever required and, because it could be raised with shareholders' agreement, it served no useful purpose. The 2006 Act abolished the concept of authorized share capital, for both public and private companies, for new companies from October 2008. Existing companies will, however, continue to be constrained by their authorized share capital, and will need to amend their Articles to abolish reference to authorized share capital if they want to allow the company to allot beyond that ceiling. The new rules instead require companies to deposit an initial statement of capital when incorporating, which will need to be updated when appropriate, such as when new shares are issued.

Currently, there is no requirement for private companies to have a minimum amount of share capital and no changes are proposed to this. There are no changes either to the minimum share capital of £50,000 required for public companies, although the Group does seek further consultation on this given that it is questionable whether this amount is adequate for creditor protection.

Shares will still be required to have a nominal value and, consequently, accounting for share issues will not change. Nominal values will continue to be credited to the share capital account, and any excess of net receipt over this value to the share premium account.

Simpler procedure for reducing share capital

The second section of this chapter explained that a company could reduce its share capital to:

- eliminate or reduce the part that has not been called up
- pay back that part which is in excess of its needs
- write off accumulated losses.

In all the above cases, prior to the passing of the Companies Act 2006, the court's consent was required to protect the interests of creditors.

Following implementation of the Companies Act 2006, private companies are now permitted to reduce their share capital by passing a special resolution but without the need for court approval.

Directors of all companies have to issue a formal solvency statement confirming that the company is solvent and will be able to pay its debts at all times within a year of the capital reduction. A director who makes a solvency statement without having reasonable grounds for the opinion expressed in it will be guilty of a criminal offence.

7.22 Repeal of restriction on assistance for acquisition of shares in private companies

The Companies Act 1985 prohibited private companies from giving financial assistance for the acquisition of their own shares unless certain conditions were satisfied. Under the Companies Act 2006 the prohibition has been wholly lifted for private companies but remains in place for public companies.

Implementation

The Companies Act 2006 was, after much publicity, passed by Parliament on 8 November 2006. It is a lengthy document, running to 1,300 sections. The aim of the Act is to consolidate most of the existing companies legislation and provide a focus on small businesses, using simplified language.

The government introduced these changes in an effort to make Britain an attractive place to set up and run a business, and to promote long-term investment. Time will tell whether the changes will have the desired effect.

Section summary

This advanced section has looked in detail at share-based payment transactions and in particular the requirements of IFRS 2. IFRS 2 requires that companies recognize a charge for share-based payments and that charge should be recognized at fair value. Thereafter companies should recognize the goods or services acquired in a share-based payment transaction over the period the goods or services are received.

Much of the legislation relating to share capital has been cumbersome and complex.

The Companies Act 2006 has been implemented to simplify many of the procedures that companies require to undertake in relation to company formations and subsequent alterations to share capital. The recognition by government that easing administrative burdens and providing flexibility to companies will help to promote long-term investment is welcomed; however, the protection of creditors' rights must also be maintained. Nevertheless, many of the issues covered in this chapter have illustrated the complexities caused by the historic legislation and also, in relation to minimum share capital, where the requirements are decidedly inadequate and out of date. The next few years offer a true indication of the success or otherwise of the changes.

Chapter summary

Companies Act: share capital and reserves

- Share capital is recorded at nominal value with any excess being recorded as share premium.
- A distribution can only be made from distributable reserves.
- The permanent capital of a company is made up of its share capital plus non-distributable reserves.
- In order to protect creditors, the permanent capital of a company must be maintained.
- If a company reduces its share capital by purchasing or redeeming its shares, the redemption must be from distributable profits or the proceeds of a new issue.
- The nominal value of the shares purchased must be replaced by either:
  - the proceeds of a new issue, or
  - a transfer from distributable profits to capital redemption reserve.
- Where shares are purchased at a premium the normal rule is that the premium is debited to distributable profits.
  - An exception is available where there is:
    - a new issue, and
    - the shares being redeemed were originally issued at a premium.
  - In such cases the premium on the repurchase can be debited to the share premium account up to the lower of:
    - the premium on the original issue, and
    - the balance on the share premium account (including the premium on the new issue).
- Private companies are allowed to reduce permanent capital by the amount of the permissible capital payment (PCP).
- The permissible capital payment is calculated as follows:

Amount payable to repurchase shares	X
Less: distributable profits	(X)
Less: proceeds of new issue	(X)
PCP	X

- The amount of any treasury shares should be deducted from shareholders' funds.
- No gain or loss should be recognized in profit or loss on the purchase, sale, issue or cancellation of treasury shares.

IFRS 2 *Share-based Payment*

- A share-based payment is a transaction in which the entity receives or acquires goods or services either as consideration for its equity instruments or by incurring liabilities for amounts based on the price of the entity's shares or other equity instruments of the entity.
- An equity-settled share-based payment transaction is a transaction in which the entity receives goods or services as consideration for equity instruments of the entity (including shares or share options):
  - If fair value of goods and services received is available, this should be used to measure the goods and services received and the corresponding increase in equity.
  - If no reliable fair value of goods or services received is available, the fair value of the shares given should be used.
  - The cost of the goods or services should be spread over the vesting period.
  - For transactions with employees, the entity is required to measure at the fair value of the equity instruments granted.
- A cash-settled share-based payment transaction is a transaction in which the entity acquires goods or services by incurring liabilities to the supplier of those goods or services for amounts that are based on the price (or value) of the entity's shares or other equity instruments of the entity:
  - Goods or services acquired and the corresponding liability incurred should be measured at the fair value of the liability.
  - The liability should be re-measured at each reporting date until settled with any changes in value reported in profit or loss for the period.
- A share-based payment transaction with cash alternatives is a transaction where either the entity or the counterparty has the choice whether the transaction is settled in cash or equity instruments:
  - These should be treated as a cash-settled share-based payment transaction if the company has an obligation to settle in cash, otherwise
  - These should be treated as an equity-settled share-based payment transaction.

✓ Key terms for review

Definitions can be found in the glossary at the end of the book.

Distributable reserves	Nominal value	Share-based payment transaction
Grant date	Non-distributable reserves	Treasury shares
Limited liability company	Permanent capital	Vesting period

? Review Questions

1. What are the advantages and disadvantages to a potential investor of investing in the following types of security:
   (a) ordinary shares
   (b) preference shares?
2. Explain the doctrine of capital maintenance.
3. Under what circumstances is a company permitted to reduce its capital?
4. Distinguish between profits available for distribution in private companies from those in public companies.

5. Outline the steps that should be followed in the event of a share purchase or share redemption by a public company.
6. What are the advantages to a private company of being permitted to buy back its own shares?
7. To what uses can a share premium account be put?
8. Explain what is meant by *share splits* and explain how they affect a company's share price.
9. Distinguish between the different types of share-based payment, namely equity-settled, cash-settled and equity with a cash alternative.
10. Describe the accounting entries required to record an equity-settled share-based payment transaction.
11. Describe the accounting entries required to record a cash-settled share-based payment transaction.

 ## Exercises

Level II

1. Rollside plc was incorporated on 15 March 2012 and issued 5,000,000 ordinary shares of 50p at par to raise capital to commence trading on 1 April 2012.

Authorized	£
5,000,000 ordinary shares at 50p each	2,500,000
Issued and fully paid	
500,000,000 ordinary shares of 50p each	2,050,000

During the year to 31 March 2013 the following occurred:

(i) In order to fund the construction of a new factory, 600,000 ordinary shares of 50p were each issued for £3.20 cash in August 2012.
(ii) At a special general meeting the authorized share capital was increased by 800,000 shares.

Required

(a) Prepare journal entries to record the initial issue of shares and the subsequent issue in August 2012.
(b) Prepare the disclosure note for share capital for inclusion in the 31 March 2013 financial statements, including comparatives.

2. Denside Ltd has the following summarized statement of financial position:

	£000
Cash	20
Other net assets	320
	340
Share capital (400,000 ordinary shares of 25p)	100
Share premium	40
Retained earnings	200
	340

The company is considering three possible changes to its capital structure:

(i) issue for cash 50,000 additional ordinary shares at £1 per share, fully paid, or

(ii) make a bonus issue from retained earnings of one ordinary share for every four previously held, or

(iii) make a 1-for-5 rights issue at £3 per share.

Required

(a) Prepare journal entries to record each of the above transactions.

(b) Show separately the impact of each change on the statement of financial position of the company.

3. Kenmac Ltd has decided to purchase shares with a nominal value of £110,000 (originally issued for £120,000) for £140,000. The purchase is to be funded out of distributable profits.

      The statement of financial position of Kenmac Ltd immediately prior to the purchase of the shares is as follows:

	£
Net assets	950,000
Share capital (£1 shares)	500,000
Share premium	250,000
Retained earnings	200,000
	950,000

Required

(a) Prepare journal entries to give effect to the above transaction.

(b) Prepare the statement of financial position of Kenmac Ltd immediately after the purchase.

4. Timor Ltd makes a fresh issue of ordinary shares to finance the purchase of its £1 ordinary shares, as follows:

Shares issued (£1 shares)	
Nominal value	£75,000
Issue price	£150,000
Shares purchased	
Nominal value of shares	£150,000
Originally issued at a premium of	£7,000
Premium on redemption	£30,000

The statement of financial position of Timor Ltd immediately before these transactions took place was as follows:

	£
Net assets	665,000
Share capital	450,000
Share premium (including the original	
premium on the shares to be redeemed)	35,000
Retained earnings	180,000
	£665,000

Required

(a) Prepare journal entries to record the above transactions.

(b) Prepare the statement of financial position of Timor Ltd after the repurchase of its shares.

(c) Comment on the permanent capital position of Timor Ltd after the repurchase of its shares.

5. A company granted share options to its 400 employees on 1 January 2010. Each employee will receive 600 share options if they remain in employment until 31 December 2012. At the grant date the share options were estimated to have a fair value of £2.50 each.

   During the year to 31 December 2010, 20 employees left the company and it is estimated that another 40 will leave by 31 December 2012.

   During 2011, 25 employees left and the company estimated that 25 would leave in 2012.

   During 2012, 18 staff left.

   All staff eligible exercised their options on 1 January 2013. The options permitted employees to buy £1 ordinary shares in the company for £2.40 each.

Required

(a) Calculate the amounts that will appear in the statement of comprehensive income and the statement of financial position for the years to 31 December 2010, 2011 and 2012.

(b) Prepare journal entries to record the exercise of the options on 1 January 2013.

6. A company operates an incentive scheme for employees. The scheme was introduced on 1 April 2010 when the company's 1,200 staff were offered 80% of the share price increase on an average 10,000 of notional shares over the period to 31 March 2013. The company's year end is 31 March and payment will be made on 1 May 2013. To be eligible, staff must have been employed by the company throughout the period.

Year end	Fair value of share appreciation rights	Number actually left in year	Extra expected to have left by 31 March 2013
31 March 2011	£1.20 per share	100	200
31 March 2012	£1.40 per share	110	120
31 March 2013	£1.55 per share	140	–

Required

Calculate the amounts that would appear in the statements of comprehensive income and statements of financial position for the years to 31 March 2011, 2012 and 2013.

Level III

7. The shareholders of Ustraco Ltd, a private company, wish to buy back 250,000 shares with a nominal value of £250,000 from a retiring director at a premium of £100,000. The company makes a fresh issue of 50,000 ordinary shares of £1 for £125,000.

   Before the transactions, the company's statement of financial position was as follows:

	£
Net assets	1,150,000
Share capital (£1 shares)	500,000
Share premium (Note 1)*	500,000
Retained earnings	150,000
	£1,150,000

Note 1: None of the share premium is attributable to the shares being redeemed.

Required

Calculate the permissible capital payment (PCP), the transfer to CRR (if any) and draft journal entries, and a statement of financial position that incorporates the above transactions.

8. Novaton plc purchased 5 million of its £1 ordinary shares for £6.40 each on 29 March 2012. The shares were held as treasury shares.

On 10 September 2012, Novaton sold 1.4 million of these shares at a price of £6.60 each.

The remaining treasury shares were sold at £6.33 on 13 October 2012.

Required

Prepare journal entries to record the above transactions.

9. The abbreviated statement of financial position of Netherfin plc, a listed company, at 31 March 2012, was as follows:

	£000
Net assets	25,000
Capital and reserves	
Share capital (25p ordinary)	2,000
Share premium	4,000
Revaluation reserve	2,500
Retained earnings	16,500
	25,000

The retained profit for the year to 31 March 2013 was £240,000. During the year to 31 March 2013 the following transactions took place:

22 June 2012	Netherfin plc purchased 4 million of its ordinary shares at £3.20 each to be held as treasury shares
17 September 2012	Sold 1 million of the treasury shares for £3.10 each
1 March 2013	Sold 1.5 million of the treasury shares for £3.40 each

Required

(a) Prepare journal entries to record the above transactions.

(b) Prepare the capital and reserves section of the statement of financial position as at 31 March 2013.

10. Cairnhall Ltd had the following balances at 31 March 2012.

	£000
Share capital (£1 shares)	10,000
Share premium	4,000
Capital redemption reserve	2,500
Revaluation reserve	1,500
Retained earnings	6,000
	24,000

The following information is available.

(i) The profit after tax of Cairnhall Ltd for the year to 31 March 2013 was £1,100,000.

(ii) Dividends of £400,000 and £300,000 were paid on 1 October 2012 and 18 March 2013, respectively.

(iii) Cairnhall Ltd revalues non-current assets but does not make transfer from revaluation reserve to retained earnings in respect of excess depreciation. At 31 March 2012, depreciation on revalued assets was £120,000 higher than the depreciation on the historical cost amount. In the year to 31 March 2013, depreciation on the revalued amount was £50,000, and depreciation would have been £30,000 based on historic cost.

(iv) A revaluation at 31 March 2013 gave rise to a revaluation loss of £350,000. This was debited to the revaluation reserve as it related to assets that had previously been revalued upwards.

(v) In March 2013, Cairnhall sold engineering equipment to a customer in China. In return, Cairnhall received electrical goods that it would use in its east European factories. As the value of the electrical goods exceeded the cost of the engineering equipment, £50,000 profit was included in Cairnhall's profits for the year.

(vi) On 30 June 2012, Cairnhall made a 1-for-10 bonus issue out of retained earnings.

(vii) At 31 March 2012 all the profits in retained earnings were distributable.

Required

(a) Calculate the distributable profits of Cairnhall Ltd as at 31 March 2013.

(b) Prepare an extract of the capital and reserves section of the statement of financial position of Cairnhall Ltd as at 31 March 2013.

References

Companies Act 1985.
Companies Act 2006.
IAS 1 *Presentation of Financial Statements*. IASB, revised 2004.
IAS 1 *Presentation of Financial Statements*. IASB, revised 2007.
IFRS 2 *Share-based payment*. IFRS, amended 2009.
Logica (2011) *Annual Report and Accounts*.

Further reading

IAS 32 *Financial Instruments Presentation*. IASB, amended 2012.
IFRS 3 *Business Combinations*. IFRS, amended 2010.
IFRS 9 *Financial Instruments*. IFRS, 2009.
Johnson T. (1997) *A Private Company's Purchase of Own Shares*. Butterworths.

Online **LearningCentre**

When you have read this chapter, log on to the Online Learning Centre website at *www.mcgraw-hill.co.uk/textbooks/mckeith* to explore chapter-by-chapter test questions, further reading and more online study tools.

Chapter 8

Liabilities

Learning Outcomes

After studying this chapter you should be able to:

- ✓ define liabilities
- ✓ define provisions
- ✓ explain and apply the rules for recognition of liabilities
- ✓ describe, apply and appraise the requirements of IAS 37 relating to provisions, contingent liabilities and contingent assets
- ✓ identify and account for events occurring after the end of the reporting period in accordance with IAS 10
- ✓ define, classify and categorize financial instruments.

Introduction

Liabilities represent claims against the assets of a business. This chapter considers the definition of liabilities and the importance of the correct classification of the various types of liabilities that may exist.

Section 1: Basic Principles

A liability is an amount owing at the end of the reporting period which a business is under an obligation to pay. There will usually be an invoice or other contractual document stating the liability. Monies owing for inventory, goods or other assets that have been received by the business at the end of the reporting period are liabilities. A bank overdraft (i.e. money owing to the bank because the account has usually, by prior arrangement, been overdrawn) is a liability; the outstanding amount of a loan to the business is a liability. These liabilities all arise because some benefit, whether in the form of goods, services or indeed money, has been received by the business, but has not yet been fully paid for. Furthermore, whoever supplied the benefit in the first instance has a claim on the assets of the business equal to the amount outstanding. A key characteristic of a liability is that it is an amount owing that can be determined with substantial accuracy.

Liabilities can be classified according to the period for which they are likely to be outstanding; current liabilities are those payable within a short period – usually within the next accounting period – likely to be one year; long-term liabilities are those payable in the future but not within the next accounting period (i.e. after one year).

8.1 The accounting issue involved

As noted above, a key characteristic of a liability is that it can be determined with substantial accuracy. Sometimes, however, the amount of an obligation may not be certain. When a known liability exists but cannot be determined with substantial accuracy, a provision may be made to account for the best estimate of the amount. A provision is an amount recognized in a set of financial statements for future expenditure that is certain or likely to be incurred but for which there is uncertainty about the amount that will be paid and/or when it will be paid. A provision is an amount written off by way of providing for depreciation, renewals or diminution in value of assets; or retained by way of providing for any known liability of which the amount cannot be determined with substantial accuracy (e.g. doubtful debts).

The difference between a provision and a liability often depends upon what is meant by substantial accuracy. The amount owing for electricity at the end of the reporting period would normally be known with precision – this would clearly be a liability; legal charges for a court case that has been heard but for which the lawyers have not yet submitted their bill, would be a provision.

Occasionally, it may be the case that an obligation may exist only if some future event happens, i.e. neither the existence nor the amount of the obligation is known with certainty at the end of the reporting period. Such obligations are known as contingent liabilities. The accounting treatment of such contingent liabilities will be covered in Section 2 of this chapter.

Progress Point 8.1

Explain the difference between a liability and a provision.

Solution
A liability is an amount owing, the timing and amount of which can be determined with substantial accuracy. A provision is a liability of uncertain timing or amount.

8.2 Definition of a liability

A liability is defined as: (Conceptual Framework, para. 4.4(b)):

> *a present obligation of the entity arising from past events, the settlement of which is expected to result in an outflow from the entity of resources embodying economic benefits.*

This definition is deliberately wide so that it can encompass all possible liabilities. As with the Conceptual Framework's definition of an asset, however, in order to understand this definition fully, each phrase must be considered separately.

(i) Present obligation

An essential characteristic of a liability is that the entity should have a present obligation. An obligation is a duty or responsibility to act or perform in a certain way. A legal obligation is evidence that a liability exists (e.g. under the law of contract there will be a binding obligation to make payment for goods and services).

The duty or responsibility may arise, however, from expectation of normal business practice (i.e. a constructive obligation). An example of a constructive obligation is to extend the benefits of a warranty for some period beyond the contractual warranty period, because this is an established practice (para. 4.15).

Note, however, that a present obligation is not the same as a future commitment. An entity may have a commitment to purchase an asset in the future at an agreed price. This does not, however, involve a net outflow of resources. The commitment itself does not give rise to a liability; it is only when the purchase has actually taken place and title has passed to the entity that the obligation to pay for it arises.

(ii) Past events

A liability does not arise from a decision to buy goods and services. While it could be argued that the decision is an event creating an obligation, the verification of such an event is extremely difficult, and likely to be subjective.

Accounting relies on objective measurement and, because most liabilities are related to a transaction, there tends to be documentary evidence that a transaction has taken place, e.g. taking delivery of a non-current asset, borrowing funds from a lender.

It may be the case that the existence of a liability is in doubt at the end of the reporting period. In such cases, subsequent events may help to confirm the position.

For example, when a company offers to repair goods under a warranty agreement, the liability exists from the time that the warranty is offered. Once a pattern of warranty repairs and costs is established, a company will be able to make an allowance for such warranty repairs. Until that pattern is established, however, the company will have to make an estimate of the liability – perhaps based on experience from other product lines. Where such an estimate is made, this is known as a provision. The Conceptual Framework requires that, where a provision involves a present obligation and satisfies the rest of the definition of a liability, it is a liability even if the amount has to be estimated.

(iii) Outflow of economic benefits

Cash is the usual economic benefit that is used in the settlement of obligations. There are other ways, however, in which a liability may be settled or discharged. For example, instead of a transfer of cash, there may be the transfer of a non-current asset or even the 'transfer' of a resource such as labour to settle an obligation. It is also possible to have a liability settled by replacement with another obligation – for example, a bank overdraft that is replaced by a bank term loan.

As was noted earlier, the definition of a liability has been made deliberately wide. By being so, it goes a long way to preventing liabilities from being 'hidden', perhaps by way of carefully worded agreements.

Table 8.1 gives examples of liabilities commonly found in statements of financial position, and illustrates the test aspects of the definition being satisfied.

It is conventional to classify liabilities into current liabilities and non-current (or long-term) liabilities. A current liability is a liability that satisfies any of the following criteria:

■ it is expected to be settled in the entity's normal operating cycle

■ it is held primarily for the purpose of being traded

■ it is due to be settled within one year of the end of the reporting period.

A non-current (long-term) liability is any liability that does not meet the definition of a current liability. In Table 8.1, items 1 to 3 would be classified as current liabilities, and items 4 and 5 would be classified as non-current liabilities because they will remain due by the business for longer than one year.

Table 8.1   Liabilities commonly found in statements of financial position

Liability	Obligation	Transfer of economic benefits	Past events
1. Bank overdraft	To repay the overdraft on demand	Cash	Overdrawing the bank account
2. Trade payables	To pay the suppliers for the goods or services received	Cash	Taking delivery of the goods or services and receiving the supplier's invoice
3. Taxation payable	To pay the cash to the tax authorities	Cash	The making of the profits giving rise to the tax payable
4. Bank loan (term loan)	To repay the loan by a due date – usually after one year	Cash	Receiving the borrowed funds
5. Debenture loan (long-term loans)	To repay the loan by a due date – usually after one year	Cash	Receiving the borrowed funds

Recognition of liabilities

Although an item may have passed the definition tests of a liability, this in itself does not qualify the item as a liability for inclusion in the statement of financial position. The item still requires to pass recognition tests. Recognition means reporting an item by means of words and amounts within the main financial statements in such a way that the item is included in the arithmetic totals.

A liability is recognized in the statement of financial position when:

■ it is probable that an outflow of resources embodying economic benefits will result from the settlement of a present obligation, and

■ the amount at which the settlement will take place can be measured reliably.

In order to satisfy the first criterion for recognition, an entity is likely to have strong evidence to prove the existence of a liability. For current liabilities, such as trade payables, there will be a payment made soon after the end of the reporting period and a past record of making such payments on time (e.g. within 30 days). In the case of non-current (long-term) liabilities such as a bank loan, there will be an agreement confirming the terms and dates of repayment.

The second criterion is usually satisfied by the existence of the document giving rise to the obligation in the first instance. For example, if goods or services have been supplied there will be an invoice from the supplier showing the amount due; in the case of a bank loan, there will be a bank statement showing the amount outstanding.

Non-recognition

It is worth pausing at this point to consider the types of item that pass the definition tests of liabilities but fail the recognition tests. In the main, these items fail because there is insufficient documentary evidence to allow confirmation of their existence or to quantify the measurable amount.

Examples of liabilities that pass the definition test but fail the recognition tests are:

■ a commitment to purchase non-current assets next year (but not a legally binding contract)

■ a remote, but potential, liability for a defective product, where no court action has yet commenced

■ a guarantee given to support the bank overdraft of another company, where there is very little likelihood of being called upon to meet the guarantee.

In the case of non-recognized liabilities, these are normally disclosed in a note to the accounts under the heading of contingent liabilities.

The above list of non-recognized liabilities all have some degree of uncertainty attached to them and, as a result, fail one or both of the recognition tests.

A commitment to purchase is not legally binding and there may not be an outflow of resources; the claim based on a product defect may go no further (i.e. there may not be court action and the amounts involved are uncertain); in the case of the guarantee, the facts as given would suggest that an outflow of resources is unlikely. These examples are designed to illustrate the accounting issue involved (i.e. recognition or disclosure – or indeed non-recognition and non-disclosure). In practice, the classification of items may not always be as clear cut and a great deal of subjectivity may be required.

Section summary

Liabilities represent claims on the assets of a business. Liabilities may be exact amounts in the case of trade payables as there is likely to be a legal document such as an invoice that will detail the amount outstanding. In the case of contingent liabilities they may also be extremely difficult to determine and to quantify.

Section 2: Intermediate Issues

In this section the reporting requirements of the standards dealing with liabilities and provisions, namely, IAS 37 *Provisions, Contingent Liabilities and Contingent Assets* and IAS 10 *Events After the Reporting Period*, are considered in detail.

8.3 IAS 37 *Provisions, Contingent Liabilities and Contingent Assets*

Objective

The objective of IAS 37 is to ensure that appropriate recognition criteria and measurement bases are applied to provisions, contingent liabilities and contingent assets, and that sufficient information is disclosed in the notes to the financial statements to enable users to understand their nature, timing and amount.

Traditional book-keeping methods tend to follow an objective, transaction-based system for recording financial data. Once accumulated, this data is then classified between revenue and capital following rules laid down within the accounting conventions, and then reported to users via the statement of comprehensive income and statement of financial position.

Unfortunately, even the most sophisticated accounting systems are transaction based and this means that judgements still have to be made – not only in the classification of items whose existence at the end of the reporting period is certain – but, in addition, of items whose existence at the end of the reporting period is uncertain. Furthermore, the outcomes of those uncertain events themselves often require to be considered.

Company financial statements are being used more and more by investors and lenders to determine the riskiness of their investments and, consequently, a greater level of information is being demanded than simply a summary of balances, many of them residual, at the end of the reporting period.

Given the importance of the statement of financial position in the decision-making process, it is essential that safeguards are in place to prevent presenting information in such a way as might mislead or misrepresent.

The key principle established by IAS 37 is that a provision should be recognized only when there is a liability (i.e. a present obligation arising from past events). Furthermore, the standard aims to ensure that only genuine obligations are dealt with in the financial statements, recognising that the accounting or not for such conditions can have a marked effect on both the statement of financial position and statement of comprehensive income of an entity. In particular it targets 'big bath' provisions, which companies had creatively used in the past to influence future profits. 'Big bath' accounting is covered in more detail later in this chapter (Section 8.9).

Scope

IAS 37 is to be applied to all entities when accounting for provisions, contingent liabilities and contingent assets, except those arising from:

- non-onerous executory contracts (see below)
- items covered by another IAS (e.g. IAS 11 *Construction Contracts*, IAS 12 *Income Taxes*, IAS 17 *Leases* and IAS 19 *Employee Benefits*).

Non-onerous executory contracts

A non-onerous executory contract is a contract where neither party has performed any of its obligations or both parties have performed obligations to an equal amount. Such contracts generally cover delivery of future services. For example:

- electricity, gas, rates
- purchase orders.

Key definitions

IAS 37 defines a provision as: 'a liability of uncertain timing or amount'.

Provisions are a sub-class of liabilities. The Conceptual Framework defines liabilities as: 'obligations of an entity arising from past events, the settlement of which is expected to result in an outflow of resources embodying economic benefits'.

It is clear, therefore, that intention without an obligation is insufficient to justify the creation of a provision.

Provisions could be made for a variety of items, including:

- reorganization costs
- warranties
- environmental costs
- major refits/refurbishments
- decommissioning costs
- legal cases against the company
- deferred tax
- losses on contracts.

It should be noted that certain 'provisions' are not covered by IAS 37. It is common practice for the word 'provision' to be applied to:

- provision for depreciation
- provision for bad debt
- provision for impairment.

In these cases, the word provision does not mean 'a liability of uncertain timing or amount'; instead it refers to adjusting the carrying amount of the asset.

Provisions and other liabilities

Uncertainty is a key feature of a provision. IAS 37 identifies four types of liabilities, as described below.

1 *Trade payables*: liabilities to pay for goods or services that have been received or supplied, and have been invoiced or formally agreed with the supplier (i.e. there is very little uncertainty).

2 *Accruals*: liabilities to pay for goods or services that have been received or supplied but have not been paid, invoiced or formally agreed with the supplier. Although it may be necessary to estimate the amount or timing of an accrual (e.g. telephone bill), the uncertainty is generally much less than

for provisions. Accruals are often reported as part of trade and other payables, while provisions are reported separately.

3 *Provisions*: liabilities because they are present obligations and it is probable that an outflow of resources embodying economic benefits will be required to settle the obligation.

4 *Contingent liabilities*: These are not recognized as liabilities because they are either:

   (a) possible obligations, as it is yet to be confirmed whether the entity has an obligation that could lead to the transfer of economic benefits, or

   (b) present obligations that do not meet the recognition criteria of IAS 37 because, either it is not probable that a transfer of economic resources will be required, or a sufficiently reliable estimate of the amount of the obligation cannot be made.

Relationship between provisions and contingent liabilities

It is worth pausing at this stage to consider the differences between a provision and a contingent liability.
   A *provision* requires:

- a present obligation from past events
- a probable outflow of economic benefits
- an evaluation of timing and amount.

A *contingent liability* occurs when one or more of the requirements for a provision are not met. That is:

- a possible obligation exists, and/or
- an outflow of economic benefits is not probable, and/or
- a reliable estimate of outflow cannot be made.

IAS 37 provides in an appendix a useful decision tree to determine whether a provision or contingent liability exists in a given set of circumstances (Figure 8.1).

Contingent asset

A contingent asset is:

- a possible asset that arises from past events, and
- whose existence will be confirmed only by the occurrence or non-occurrence of one or more uncertain future events not wholly within the control of the enterprise.

Recognition of a provision

As with assets and liabilities, a provision will require to pass recognition tests before it can be accrued in the financial statements.
   An enterprise must recognize a provision if, and only if:

- a present obligation (legal or constructive) has arisen as a result of a past event (the obligating event)
- payment is probable (more likely than not), and
- the amount can be estimated reliably.

An obligating event is an event that creates a legal or *constructive obligation* and, therefore, results in an enterprise having no realistic alternative but to settle the obligation. A *constructive obligation* arises if past practice creates valid expectation on the part of a third party – for example, a retail store that has a long-standing policy of allowing customers to return merchandise within, say, a 30-day period.
   A possible obligation (i.e. a contingent liability) is disclosed but not accrued. However, disclosure is not required if payment is remote.

Present obligation

In rare cases, for example in a lawsuit, it may not be clear whether an enterprise has a present obligation. In such cases, a past event is deemed to give rise to a present obligation if, taking account of all available

Figure 8.1 Decision tree

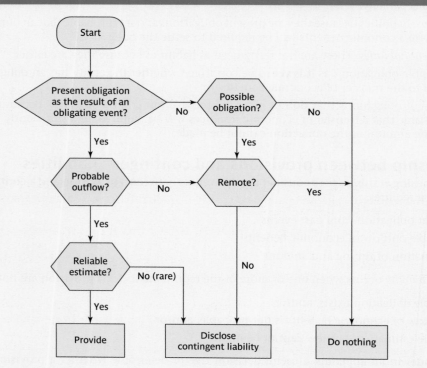

evidence, it is more likely than not that a present obligation exists at the end of the reporting period. A provision should be recognized for that present obligation if the other recognition criteria described above are met. If it is more likely than not that no present obligation exists, the enterprise should disclose a contingent liability, unless the possibility of an outflow of resources is remote.

A contingent asset is not recognized in the accounts but it is disclosed if the inflow of economic benefits is probable.

A contingent liability is not recognized in the financial statements but is disclosed as follows:

■ a brief description of the nature
■ an estimate of its financial effect
■ an indication of the uncertainties relating to the amount or timing of outflow
■ the possibility of any reimbursement.

Progress Point 8.2

Valentino Ltd has a number of retail clothes outlets. Explain how the following situations will be viewed under IAS 37 in the preparation of the accounts to 31 December 2012.

(a) Goods were delivered to the Knightsbridge branch in December 2012. No invoice has been received as yet, but there are no disputes surrounding the delivery.

(b) A competitor is claiming that Valentino Ltd infringed its copyright on a garment design, and has raised a court action. Valentino's lawyers believe it is probable that the competitor will not be successful in its court action.

(c) Although under no statutory obligation to do so, Valentino Ltd has a long-established policy of refunding customers for goods they return within one month of purchase, irrespective of whether they are faulty or not.

(d) The directors decided in October 2012 to close a branch of the company in Luton. The decision was minuted with closure due to take place following the summer season sales in August 2013. No official announcement has been made. Redundancy costs are estimated to be £750,000.

Solution

(a) Uninvoiced goods: there is no dispute with the delivery of the goods or the amount. It is simply that the invoice has yet to be received by Valentino Ltd. This should be treated as an accrual as there is little uncertainty as to the event.

(b) Competitor court action: Valentino's lawyers believe that it is probable that the competitor's court action will fail. There is therefore no present obligation and consequently no creditor, accrual or provision. However, Valentino's lawyers cannot be certain that the court action will fail and therefore there is a possible obligation that should be disclosed as a contingent liability.

(c) Refund policy: Valentino's established pattern of past practice gives rise to a constructive obligation. Although not a legal obligation, shoppers will have a valid expectation that Valentino will accept responsibility for refunding returned goods. Because of the uncertainty surrounding the amount and timing of refunds for the return of goods bought prior to 31 December 2012, a provision is required rather than an accrual or trade creditor.

(d) Closure of Luton branch: although the branch is scheduled for closure and the directors' intentions have been minuted prior to the year end, there is no liability as the company has neither a legal nor constructive obligation. No announcement has been made to affected parties and therefore no valid expectation has been created in those parties (e.g. employees, suppliers). Furthermore, the directors could, if they wished, reverse their decision. There has been no obligating event and therefore no provision, or any other form of liability, should be created.

Probable outflow of resources embodying economic benefits

The accounting treatment of events depends upon their probability. IAS 37 defines *probable* as meaning that the event is more likely than not to occur. When it is not probable, the company discloses a contingent liability unless the possibility is remote.

The accounting treatment is, therefore, dependent on how the preparer of the accounts defines the words probable, possible and remote – ultimately, a matter of personal degree.

The following examples will help to further illustrate the above. All information is at the enterprise's year end of 31 December 2012 unless otherwise stated.

Example 1

An airline enterprise is required by law to overhaul its aircraft every three years. The aircraft was purchased a year ago. At the end of the reporting period there is no obligation to overhaul the aircraft – indeed the enterprise could sell the aircraft to avoid the overhaul cost. This is neither a provision nor a contingent liability.

Example 2

An enterprise has guaranteed a loan taken out by one of its subsidiaries. The subsidiary has placed itself in liquidation and it appears that it has insufficient funds to repay the loan. The enterprise has an obligation to fulfil the guarantee and therefore it is probable that there will be an outflow of funds. A provision should be recognized in the accounts.

Example 3

The enterprise catered for a wedding reception in September 2012. Following the wedding, several people have died of food poisoning. The enterprise is disputing liability and its lawyers have advised that it is probable that it will not be found liable. There is no obligation and therefore no provision should be made. It is a contingent liability, which should be disclosed in the accounts unless the probability of any transfer of funds is remote.

Example 4

The enterprise has not received its electricity bill for the power supplied in the last quarter of the year. This is an accrual as there is very little uncertainty in respect of the timing of the amount due.

Progress Point 8.3

Andox Ltd, a supplier of medical equipment, is preparing its accounts for the year to 31 December 2012. The following information is available.

(a) Andox gives a one-year warranty on one of its products. Experience shows that these products are extremely reliable and none has ever been returned within the warranty period.

(b) Andox is defending a court case brought against it by a government department, claiming inadequate labelling on one of its products. The court upheld the department's complaint and, although not fining the company, instructed Andox Ltd to amend the labelling on all products produced from 1 December 2012. This led to the scrapping of stocks of labels, which cost £150,000.

Required

Explain whether a provision should be created for the above events.

Solution

(a) Warranty: although there is a present obligation arising from the issue of the warranty, it is not probable that an outflow of resources will take place. No provision should be recognized.

(b) Court ruling: there is a present obligation to comply with the court ruling. As there is no fine there is no outflow of resources. The loss of £150,000, although arising from the court case, is not an outflow of resources – it is a stock write-off. No provision should be created.

Damages	£
60% × £100,000	60,000
30% × £150,000	45,000
10% × £175,000	17,500
	122,500
Legal costs	50,000
Total provision required	172,500

Note that the full amount of the legal costs should be provided as the solicitors believe the company will lose the case and will have to meet the claimant's legal costs.

Risks and uncertainties

The risks and uncertainties surrounding the event in question should be taken into account in reaching the best estimate of a provision. This does not mean that an overly prudent view should be taken, but care should be exercised to ensure that liabilities are not understated.

Provisions are measured before the effect of any tax consequences. The tax effect will be shown in accordance with IAS 12 *Income Taxes* (see Chapter 9).

Progress Point 8.4

Fraselectric sells 10,000 washing machines each year, offering a one-year warranty. Past experience shows that 500 machines will require repair.

In addition, it sells two models of television: Standard and Deluxe. Sales for the year to 31 December 2012 were as follows:

	Sets	Sales price per set
		£
Standard	18,000	180
Deluxe	9,000	210

Engineers estimate that 5% of the Standard and 4% of the Deluxe sets sold will require repair within one year of sale. An additional 5% of the Deluxe sets will require to be repaired in the second year after sale. The Standard sets come with a one-year warranty, whereas the Deluxe sets have a two-year warranty. The average cost of repair is 20% of sales price. During 2012 the company spent £30,000 on warranty repairs of sets sold in the year.

Required

(i) Explain whether a provision should be recognized for washing machine repairs.

(ii) Calculate the provision for television warranties required at 31 December 2012 for sales made in that year.

Solution

(i) In the case of the washing machines, the chance of an individual machine requiring repair is 5% (i.e. 500/10,000). Nevertheless it is reasonable to expect that around 500 of the machines sold will require repair. This should be used as the basis for the provision.

(ii) The provision is calculated as follows:

Standard	$18{,}000 \times 5\% \times £180 \times 20\%$	=	32,400
Deluxe	$9{,}000 \times (4\% + 5\%) \times £210 \times 20\%$	=	34,020
			66,420
Less: paid in year			30,000
Provision required at year end			£36,420

Note that the amounts actually paid in the year in respect of warranty claims (£30,000) are deducted from the provision

Accounting for provisions

While the recognition and measurement of provisions can be complex, fortunately the actual accounting entries to create and utilize a provision are straightforward. A reorganization provision of £250,000 created in the 2012 accounts of a company is used to illustrate the entries.

Creation of a provision

Dr	Statement of comprehensive income	£250,000	
	Cr Provision for reorganization		£250,000

Being provision for reorganization.

Most provisions are created by charging the statement of comprehensive income with the expense while in the statement of financial position the item will appear under either non-current or current liabilities depending on when the provision is payable.

Note that it will not always be the case that the debit entry will be an expense. Sometimes a provision may form part of the cost of an asset. IAS 37 cites the example of the obligation for environmental clean-up when a new mine is opened or an offshore oil rig is installed (IAS 37, Example 3).

Utilization of a provision

As the expenditure in relation to a provision is incurred, it is debited directly to the provision that has been set up.

Continuing with the above example, assume that £120,000 was spent on reorganization in 2012.

The £120,000 should be charged to the provision as follows:

Dr	Provision for reorganization	£120,000	
	Cr Bank		£120,000

Being utilization of provision.

If the cost of the reorganization has been charged to the statement of comprehensive income, £120,000 should be released from the provision and credited to the statement of comprehensive income as follows:

Dr	Provision for reorganization	£120,000	
	Cr Statement of comprehensive income		£120,000

Being release from provision.

The effect being to cancel out the original charge to the statement of comprehensive income.

Review of a provision

The provision should be reviewed at the end of each reporting period to see whether it should be reduced or increased by crediting or debiting the statement of comprehensive income.

Continuing with the above example, assume that the reorganization was complete and that the remaining £130,000 was no longer required. The balance on the provision account should be transferred back to the statement of comprehensive income as follows:

Dr	Provision for reorganization	£130,000	
	Cr	Statement of comprehensive income	£130,000
Being writing back of provision.			

Discounting

IAS 37 (para. 45) requires that where the effect of the time value of money is material, the provision should be discounted to its present value. Because of the time value of money, provisions of equal monetary amount are more onerous the nearer they are to settlement.

Note that discounting is not optional. IAS 37 requires discounting if the effect is material.

The discount rate used should be a pre-tax rate that reflects current market assessments of the time value of money and the risks specific to the liability.

The unwinding of the discount is normally treated as an interest cost in the statement of comprehensive income.

Example

At 31 December 2012 a company involved in the manufacture of concrete products estimates that the cost of cleaning up a production site will be £10m in ten years' time. The risk adjusted discount rate is 5%.

Required

Calculate the provision in the statements of financial position at 31 December 2012, 2013 and 2014 and the entries in the statement of comprehensive income for 2013 and 2014.

Solution

	£
31 December 2012	
Statement of financial position ($£10,000,000/(1.05)^{10}$)	6,139,133
31 December 2013	
Statement of financial position ($£10,000,000/(1.05)^{9}$)	6,446,089
Statement of comprehensive income (6,446,089 – 6,139,133)	306,956
31 December 2014	
Statement of financial position ($£10,000,000/(1.05)^{8}$)	6,768,394
Statement of comprehensive income (6,768,394 – 6,446,089)	322,305

The statement of comprehensive income charge is a finance charge and represents the cost of not settling the obligation at the outset. A larger provision is required as the discount unwinds due to the cash outflow getting closer. The journal for 2013 would be:

Dr	Statement of comprehensive income (finance costs) £306,956		
	Cr	Provision	£306,956
Being increase in provision.			

Care should be taken where the estimate of the final obligation is changed for a provision that is discounted. Where this happens:

(i) calculate the unwinding of the discount up to the end of the reporting period and add to the opening provision; this is an interest expense

(ii) calculate the present value of the provision based on the new estimate

(iii) the difference between (i) and (ii) is a movement in the provision and is not a finance item. Normally it would be charged to the statement of comprehensive income as an increase in provision.

Application of the recognition and measurement rules: specific examples in IAS 37

Although a general standard, IAS 37 identifies three specific applications of recognition and measurement of provisions within the standard itself, as discussed below.

Future operating losses

Future operating losses do not meet the definition of a liability as there is no present obligation and therefore no liability. The loss will be recognized as it occurs. An expectation of future losses is an indication, however, of impairment and an entity should therefore test for this under IAS 36 *Impairment of Assets*.

Onerous contracts

An onerous contract is one in which the unavoidable costs of meeting the obligations under the contract exceed the economic benefits expected to be received under it. Onerous contracts will normally be for the long-term supply of goods of services. For example, an enterprise leases a factory under an operating lease. During the year it moves production to a new factory but the old factory lease cannot be cancelled and it cannot be relet. There is, therefore, a present obligation and a provision is required of the unavoidable lease payments in total.

If the contract can be cancelled without having to pay compensation, it is not onerous. IAS 37 requires that the present obligation under the onerous contract should be recognized and measured as a provision. The unavoidable costs reflect the net cost of exiting from the contract, i.e. the lower (i) of the cost of fulfilling the terms of the contract and (ii) any compensation or penalties arising from failure to fulfil it.

Note that the contract has to be loss making. A contract that is merely uneconomic in terms of earning a below-average expected rate of return is not classified as onerous.

Example

A company has an operating lease over a property which it entered into several years ago. The company no longer has a use for the property and has vacated it. The lease has a further three years to run at an annual cost of £10,000 per annum.

The company may be able to sub-lease the property but as a result of current market conditions, the annual rental from the sublease is likely to be only £8,000 per annum.

Alternatively, the landlord is prepared to terminate the lease and forgive the future rentals of £30,000 (£10,000 × 3) if the company makes a termination payment of £5,500.

Required

How should this be dealt with in the financial statements of the company?

Solution

Because the property has been vacated and the costs of meeting the continual rental payments are not expected to be recoverable by subleasing the property, a provision should be recognized.

The provision should be the lower of the cost of fulfilling the terms of the contract and any penalties arising from failure to fulfil it.

If the company were to fulfil the terms of the contract the net cost would be:

	£
Rentals paid (3 × £10,000)	30,000
Less: Sub-rentals received (3 × £8,000)	24,000
Net cost	6,000

If the company were to terminate the lease the cost would be £5,500.

Accordingly the company should recognize an onerous lease provision of £5,500, irrespective of whether it intends to terminate the lease or enter into a sub-lease.

Note that if the effects of discounting are material, the future rental payments and receipts should be disclosed to their present value. If the net present value of the future rental payments were less than £5,500, the provision would be for that lower amount.

Some long-term contracts for the supply of goods or services, when costs have risen or current market prices have fallen, may be onerous and, if so, a provision is recognized to the extent that future supplies must be made at a loss. No provision is recognized under a contract for the supply of goods which is profitable but at a reduced margin compared to other contracts, because there is no probable net transfer of economic benefits by the reporting entity.

Example

Esdaile Engineering Ltd, a manufacturer of specialist metal castings, prepares accounts annually to 31 December. At 31 December 2012, it had four contracts, W, X, Y and Z, which it believes to be onerous.

Contract W is for the future purchase of 1,000 tons of zinc, which were to be used in bronze manufacture. Esdaile Engineering Ltd sold off its bronze manufacturing business but was unable to assign this future contract. The contract price is £350 per tonne and at the year end the spot price is £280 per tonne. The terms of the contract specify that a cancellation fee of £100,000 is payable.

Contract X is for the purchase of 200 tonnes of titanium at a price of £1,500 per tonne. A change in processing technology means that Esdaile Engineering Ltd requires only 50 tonnes. The supplier is prepared to accept cancellation of the remainder of the contracted amount for a payment of £25,000. The year-end spot price is £1,300 per tonne.

Contract Y is for the purchase of 2,000 tonnes of special steel ingots at a cost of £600 per tonne. The company intends to use the ingots in manufacture where the processing costs will be £200 per tonne and the final product will be sold for £720 per tonne. Owing to the high quality of these ingots there is minimal wastage in the manufacturing process. The spot price on 31 December 2012 is £500 per tonne.

Contract Z is for the purchase of aluminium at a price of £25 per kg. The spot price of aluminium at 31 December 2012 is £21 per kg. The metal is to be used in the manufacture of blades for wind turbines. As a result of the fall in the price of aluminium, the selling price of these blades has fallen to £400. Costs of manufacture amount to £240 per blade. Each blade uses 5 kg of aluminium.

Required

How should the contracts be dealt with in the accounts of Esdaile Engineering Ltd for the year to 31 December 2012?

Solution

Contract W

Esdaile is unable to assign this contract to purchase zinc. Esdaile should, however, be able to sell zinc at the spot rate ruling on the date it requires to purchase it. As the spot rate is lower, the contract will be loss making and classified as onerous. The provision should be set at the lower of:

(i) the cost of fulfilling the terms of the contract:

$$1,000 \times (£350 - £280) = £70,000$$

and

(ii) the compensation payable arising from failure to fulfil it:

$$cancellation\ fee = £100,000$$

A provision for Contract W of £70,000 should be provided.

Contract X

The surplus quantity is 150 tonnes. Again, the contract is loss making and will be classified as onerous. The provision should be set at the lower of:

(i) the cost of fulfilling the terms of the contract and selling on the spot market:

$$150 \times (£1,500 - £1,300) = £30,000$$

and

(ii) the compensation payable arising from failure to fulfil the contract:

$$cancellation\ fee\ £25,000$$

Esdaile should opt to cancel the contract and provide the lower figure of £25,000.

Contract Y

A comparison requires to be made of the outcome were Esdaile Engineering Ltd to manufacture and sell the final product and the costs of selling the steel ingots on the spot market.

	£	£
Sales price		720
Production cost:		
Materials	600	
Processing	200	
		800
Loss per tonne		(80)

The costs of selling on the spot market would be:

	£
Contract price	600
Spot price	500
Loss per tonne	(100)

Esdaile Engineering Ltd should use the steel ingots rather than sell them as this results in a lower loss.
A provision should be made of 2,000 tonnes × £80 = £160,000.

Contract Z

Again, a comparison requires to be made of the outcome were Esdaile Engineering Ltd to manufacture and sell the blades and the costs of selling the aluminium on the spot market.

	£	£
Sales price		400
Production cost:		
Materials (5kg × £25)	125	
Manufacture	240	365
Profit		35

As a profit can be made on the use of the aluminium, the contract cannot be classified as onerous. No provision should be made.

Restructurings

IAS 37 provides specific guidance on how the general recognition criteria for provisions should be applied to restructurings.

IAS 37 (para. 10) defines restructurings as:

> *a programme that is planned and controlled by management and materially changes either:*
> *(a) the scope of a business undertaken by an enterprise; or*
> *(b) the manner in which that business is conducted.*

Examples given in paragraph 70 are:

- sale or termination of a line of business
- closure of business locations in a country or region, or the relocation of business activities from one country or region to another
- changes in management structure, for example, eliminating a layer of management
- fundamental reorganization of a company that has a material effect on the nature and focus of the entity's operations.

The kind of expenditure covered by such restructuring programmes includes redundancy costs, lease termination payments, the costs of breaking contracts and other direct costs of carrying out the reorganization. Such costs may not be capitalized as an asset.

The accounting issue involved

The accounting issue involved with restructurings concerns the general recognition criteria for provisions. That is, the point at which a present obligation arises as a result of a past event. IAS 37 (para. 72) gives guidance on restructuring provisions as follows.

A constructive obligation to restructure arises only when an entity

(a) has a detailed formal plan for the restructuring identifying at least
   (i) the business or part of a business concerned
   (ii) the principal locations affected

(iii) the location, function and approximate numbers of employees who will be compensated for terminating their services

(iv) the expenditures that will be undertaken

(v) when the plan will be implemented; and

(b) has raised a valid expectation in those affected that it will carry out the restructuring by starting to implement that plan or announcing its main features to those affected by it.

Those affected by a constructive obligation are likely to be customers, employees and suppliers. Note that both (a) and (b) are necessary to create a constructive obligation.

For an announcement to give rise to a constructive obligation its implementation needs to begin as soon as possible and to be completed in a timescale that makes significant changes to the plan unlikely.

If an entity starts to implement a restructuring plan or announces its main features only after the end of the reporting period but before the financial statements are authorized for issue, disclosure is required by IAS 10 *Events After the Reporting Period*. IAS 10 is considered later in this section. In summary, the effect of the conditions is to put the actual restructuring beyond any doubt.

In practice, the requirements relate to specific restructurings as follows.

Sale of operation

A restructuring provision should be accrued only once a binding sale agreement is in place. If the binding sale agreement comes after the end of the reporting period, disclosure only should be made and no accrual.

Closure or reorganization

A restructuring provision should be accrued only after a detailed formal plan is adopted and announced publicly. Note the need to publicly announce the plan – a board decision in itself is not enough.

Future operating losses

IAS 37 confirms that, even in a restructuring, provisions should not be recognized for future operating losses.

A provision for restructuring should include only direct expenditures caused by the restructuring and not costs associated with the ongoing activities of the enterprise. For example, the following costs, which relate to the future conduct of the business, are not included:

- retraining costs or relocation costs
- marketing costs
- investments in new systems and distribution networks.

Example

Lormac Logistics plc is a multinational transport company. Its board of directors has made the following decisions:

(a) Close its French operations by 30 September 2013: the decision was made on 4 December 2012. A detailed formal plan was approved on 28 December 2012 but there had been no formal communication with affected parties by 31 December 2012.

(b) Streamline operations by removing divisional managers: this decision was made on 11 December 2012 when a detailed plan was approved. Affected managers had been informed and discussions regarding severance payments had commenced by 31 December 2012.

Required

How should the above be dealt with in the accounts of Lormac Logistics for the year to 31 December 2012?

Solution

French operations

No constructive obligation exists as there was no announcement by the end of the reporting period. Although a formal plan exists and was approved by the end of the reporting period, the board of directors could still reverse its decision. No provision therefore should be made. If, however, the announcement was made before the accounts were authorized for issue, a disclosure note would be required if the closure is of such materiality it could influence the economic decisions of users of Lormac's financial statements.

Removal of managers

In this instance there is an approved plan, communication to affected parties has been made and implementation has begun. A constructive obligation exists and a provision should be made as it is probable that there will be an outflow of resources, i.e. severance payments. The provision should be based on the best estimate of the severance payments.

Other examples

In Appendix C to IAS 37 there are other examples of situations where provisions may be necessary. These include the following:

1. **Environmental provisions (e.g. contaminated land)**: Provisions for environmental liabilities should be recognized at the time and to the extent that the entity becomes obliged, legally or constructively, to rectify environmental damage or to perform restorative work on the environment. The *obligating event* is the environmental damage done and must have occurred at the end of the reporting period.

2. **Decommissioning provisions (e.g. offshore oilfield)**: A provision is required for obligations that exist at the end of the reporting period only. It should not be an allocation of total clean-up costs over the lifetime of an activity. If further damage is done by production, the costs of restoring the damage are costs of production, which should be recognized as a liability as production takes place. A provision is required for any decommissioning costs the company is obliged to incur as a result of planning permission, licensing agreements, etc.

Example

Valleyfield Ltd has been given permission to extract coal using an open-cast mine. It is expected that the coal will be extracted over 12 years and that the decommissioning costs at the end of that time will be £4 million. Of this, 20% relates to the removal of the fixed plant required to carry out the mining and the remainder is to rectify the damage caused by mining. The fixed plant has been constructed at a cost of £16 million. Extraction has not yet started. The licensing agreement was granted to Valleyfield Ltd on condition that the fixed plant be removed at the end of operations.

Required

How should the above be accounted for in the current year's accounts?

Solution

The construction of the fixed plant creates a legal obligation under the terms of the licence to remove the plant and is thus an obligating event. Provision should be made for the 20% of estimated costs related to the removal of the fixed plant (discounted to present value) and added to the cost of the fixed plant. No obligation exists to rectify the damage from extraction as this has not been started. No provision should be made for this.

3. **Refurbishment costs** The treatment of refurbishment costs is discussed in IAS 37, Appendix C, Examples 11, 11A and 11B. IAS 37 concludes that no provision should be made because there is no obligation that qualifies to be recognized as a liability.

When actual expenditure is incurred on refurbishment it should be written off to profit or loss or capitalized (if it meets the criteria for subsequent expenditure under IAS 16)

Use of provisions

Provisions should be used only for the purpose for which they were originally recognized. They should be reviewed at the end of each reporting period and adjusted to reflect the current best estimate. If it is no longer probable that an outflow of resources will be required to settle the obligation, the provision should be reversed. Note the effect of this requirement: it prevents the set-off of expenditures against a provision that was originally required for another purpose, which would conceal the impact of two different events.

8.4 Contingent liabilities

IAS 37 defines a contingent liability (para. 10) as:

> *(a) a possible obligation that arises from past events and whose existence will be confirmed only by the occurrence of one or more uncertain future events not wholly within the control of the entity, or*
> *(b) a present obligation that arises from past events but is not recognized because*
> *(i) it is not probable that an outflow of resources embodying economic benefits will be required to settle the obligation, or*
> *(ii) the amount of the obligation cannot be measured with sufficient reliability.*

Points (b)(i) and (ii) were covered earlier in the chapter and relate to actual obligations. Point (a) refers not to a present or actual obligation but to a possible obligation. This arises where it is more likely that no present obligation exists at the end of the reporting period but, because there is a possibility that a liability exists, it is described as a contingent liability and disclosed, with explanation, in the notes to the accounts. If the possibility of an outflow of resources is remote, no liability note is required.

For example, a competitor has raised a claim against the company for unauthorized use of a design. The company's solicitors advise that the claim is frivolous and the possibility of the claim being successful is remote. In this case, no disclosure is required.

Contingent liabilities are disclosed in the accounts (i.e. they are reported in the notes to the accounts). No amount is recognized (included in the arithmetic totals) for a contingent liability.

Given the uncertainty surrounding contingent liabilities, it may not be clear whether a present obligation arises from a past event. Changes in circumstances may make past events that were not obligations at the time they occurred, obligations now (e.g. changes to legislation with a retrospective effect create a legal obligation). Furthermore, contingent liabilities may develop in a way not initially expected. IAS 37 requires that contingent liabilities be assessed continually to determine whether an outflow of resources embodying economic benefits has become probable. If it becomes probable that an outflow of future economic benefits will be required for an item previously dealt with as a contingent liability, a provision should be recognized in the financial statements of the period in which the change in probability occurs.

Unless the possibility of any transfer in settlement is remote, an entity should disclose (para. 86) for each class of contingent liability:

(a) an estimate of its financial effect

(b) an indication of the uncertainties relating to the amount or timing of any outflow, and

(c) the possibility of any reimbursement.

8.5 Contingent assets

A contingent asset is defined (para. 10) as:

> *a possible asset that arises from past events and whose existence will be confirmed only by the occurrence or non-occurrence of one or more uncertain future events not wholly within the control of the enterprise.*

Contingent assets usually arise from unplanned or other unexpected events that give rise to the possibility of an inflow of economic benefits to the entity. IAS 37 (para. 32) gives the example of a claim that an entity is pursuing through legal processes, where the outcome is uncertain.

A contingent asset should not be recognized because it could result in the recognition of profit that may never be realized. When the realization of profit is virtually certain then the related asset is not a contingent asset and its recognition is appropriate. In other words, a contingent asset can never be recognized; an asset can only be recognized when it is no longer contingent and the future economic benefits are certain.

Where an inflow of economic benefits is probable, an entity should disclose a brief description of the nature of the contingent assets at the end of the reporting period and, where practicable, an estimate of their financial effect. The disclosure should not give a misleading indication of the likelihood of a profit arising.

Contingent assets should be assessed continually to ensure that developments are appropriately reflected in the financial statements. If it has become virtually certain that an inflow of economic benefits will arise, the asset and the related income are recognized in the financial statements of the period in which the change occurs.

8.6 Disclosure

The objective of IAS 37 with respect to disclosure is to ensure that sufficient information is disclosed in the notes to the financial statements to enable users to understand the nature, timing and amount of provisions, contingent liabilities and contingent assets.

For each class of provision, an entity shall disclose:

- the carrying amount at the beginning and the end of the period
- additional provisions recognized in the period, including increases to existing provisions
- amounts used (amounts charged against the provision)
- unused amounts reversed during the period.

For each class of provision, a brief description of:

- the nature of the obligation and the expected timing of any resulting outflows of economic benefits
- the uncertainties about the amount or timing of the outflows
- the amount of any expected reimbursement.

Disclosure in practice

IAS 37 requires both narrative and numerical disclosures.

Provisions

Logica outlines its policy on provisions in the accounting policies note where it identifies two specific items, namely restructurings and future committed property lease payments. In keeping with the requirements of the standard (para. 45), Logica measures provisions at their present value where the time value of money is material.

Provisions

Provisions are recognised when the Group has a present obligation (legal or constructive) as a result of a past event, it is probable that an outflow of resources embodying economic benefits will be required to settle the obligation and a reliable estimate can be made of the amount of the obligation. The expense relating to any provision is reflected in the consolidated statement of comprehensive income at a current pre-tax rate that reflects the risks specific to the liability. Where the provision is discounted, any increase in the provision due to the passage of time is recognised as a finance cost.

Source: Logica (2011), p. 99

Figure 8.2 Logica: provisions note

	Vacant properties £'m	Restructuring £'m	Other £'m	Total £'m
At 1 January 2011	31.9	16.4	18.2	66.5
Charged to the statement of comprehensive income	15.5	96.1	3.4	115.0
Utilised in the year	(8.2)	(28.8)	(3.5)	(40.5)
Unused amounts reversed	(2.7)	–	(1.1)	(3.8)
Unwinding of discount	1.3	–	–	1.3
Exchange differences	–	(0.1)	(0.7)	(0.8)
At 31 December 2011	37.8	83.6	16.3	137.7
Analysed as:				
Current liabilities				90.0
Non-current liabilities				47.7
				137.7

Vacant properties

At 31 December 2011, provisions for vacant properties represented residual lease commitments, together with associated outgoings, for the remaining period on certain property leases, after taking into account sub-tenant arrangements. The property costs provided for are mainly related to properties located in the UK, Netherlands, Sweden, and Australia. At 31 December 2011, non-current vacant property provisions amounted to £25.0 million (2010: £23.4 million) of which £10.2 million was payable between one and two years, £10.9 million between two and five years, and the balance thereafter. Of the amount charged to the statement of comprehensive income, £13.0 million related to the property rationalisation announced on 14 December 2011, and is included in property costs (Note 6).

Restructuring

At 31 December 2011, the restructuring provision mainly related to the restructuring of the businesses announced on 14 December 2011. The restructuring programme comprised property rationalisation, a reduction in headcount and other measures to reduce the cost base. £80.4 million of the amount charged to the statement of comprehensive income related to the 14 December 2011 accelerated restructuring (Note 6). Where appropriate, provisions arising from the property rationalisation are categorised as vacant property. At 31 December 2011, £73.2 million of the restructuring provision was payable within one year, with the remaining balance payable between one and two years.

Other

At 31 December 2011, the other provisions related to the value of legal claims. At 31 December 2011, £4.0 million of the other provision was payable within one year, with the remaining balance payable between two and five years.

Source: Logica (2011), p. 127

The provisions note from the Logica financial statements highlights the importance of both narrative and numerical disclosure. As required by IAS 37, for each class of provision, Logica has prepared a movements table showing the charges and credits being made during the year to 31 December 2011. Note the references to the unwinding of discounts, which indicate clearly that Logica does discount its provisions to present value. The narrative element of the disclosure note gives a brief description of each provision and includes, as IAS 37 requires, details of the timing, amount and uncertainties surrounding these provisions. Only by including both the narrative and numerical disclosures is the user in a position to determine the future cash flow effects of the various provisions.

Contingent liabilities

The size, structure and geographic spread of the Group and its activities naturally exposes it to potential scrutiny and possible legal claims including tax and other regulatory authorities in the normal course of operations. The results of tax audits and other similar enquiries are normally reflected in the accounts on an accruals basis where a recovery or liability can be predicted with reasonable certainty. Occasionally claims may be levied against the Group by such authorities, the outcomes of which cannot be predicted with reasonable certainty. While Logica strongly believes it complies with all relevant laws and regulations, and would vigorously defend itself against any such claims, if it was unsuccessful the enforcement of such claims could from time to time have a potentially material impact on the Group's results and financial position.

In 2009, the Group received a €59 million VAT claim from the French tax authorities. After €13 million tax relief received in 2011 this result in a net claim of €46 million. Interest continues to accrue on the claim amount.

The claim relates to the VAT treatment of goods exported from France during the years 2004 to 2006. The Group has carefully analysed these claims and obtained external experts' advice, as a result of which it considers that they are without merit and the Group is robustly contesting these claims through the appropriate channels. The initial ruling from the French courts is expected in the second quarter of 2012.

Any adverse judgement at the initial ruling may require Logica to make an interim settlement which it expects to do through a parent company or bank guarantee or in the form of a cash payment during the second quarter. In the event of such an adverse ruling, the Group intends to exercise its right to appeal. This would typically involve a protracted legal process.

Source: Logica (2011), p. 142

Contingent liabilities

Logica's disclosure of contingent liabilities highlights the current uncertainties facing the company.

8.7 International comparison

The equivalent UK standard is FRS 12 *Provisions, Contingent Liabilities and Contingent Assets*. It was developed jointly with the international standard and there are no substantial differences between the two. Indeed, the examples and decision trees used in both standards are identical.

US GAAP is similar again, but with the following minor differences.

- Measurement:
  - discount rate is pre-tax, reflecting current market assessment of time value of money (i.e. no account of risk is taken).
  - where a range of estimates of the outflow are available and all are equally likely, then the lowest is taken (not the midpoint as per IAS).
- Restructuring:
  - management approval and commitment is sufficient to recognize the restructuring; accordingly, under US GAAP, restructuring provisions are likely to occur at an earlier point than under IAS.

- Contingent asset:

  - under US GAAP insurance recoveries will be recognized when probable – IAS requires virtual certainty; accordingly, US GAAP will recognize the contingent asset at an earlier stage than IAS.

8.8 Problems in practice

As has been illustrated, the topic of provisions, contingent liabilities and contingent assets is controversial and involves a great deal of subjective judgement. The professional accountant, in attempting to adhere to the standard, may require to effectively interrogate management in an attempt to uncover any such potential items. It is worth bearing in mind that management may have strong reasons for including particular items (or not) as liabilities, as such liabilities can dramatically alter a set of financial statements. In practice, therefore, the most important quality that the reporting accountant must have is to be free from bias when evaluating such issues. The accountant's decision will necessarily be subjective. However, if that decision has been based on an objective application of the definition and recognition rules (without being overly pessimistic) then this should ensure that only useful information is reported or disclosed. If not, the alternative would be to take prudence to the extreme and to use the words of the standard, to report every possible eventuality whether 'probable, possible or remote'.

8.9 'Big bath' accounting

Earlier in this chapter, reference was made to 'big bath' accounting, and in particular that IAS 37 was primarily designed to target big bath provisions. Having now covered in detail the nature of provisions and contingent liabilities, it will be easier to explain and illustrate the term 'big bath' accounting.

Big bath accounting involves making provisions in order to smooth profits without any reasonable certainty that the provision will actually be required in subsequent periods.

Example

An enterprise with expected future profits of £2.5 million decides to recognize a provision for reorganization of future costs for future years of £2.0 million in the current year when its expected profits are £4.5 million.

The actual reorganization costs incurred are £0.5 million in the next year and £0.5 million in the year following. Thereafter, no further costs arise.

The effect of the proposed accounting treatment for the reorganization costs on the profits for the company for the current and future years is as follows:

	Year 1	Year 2	Year 3	Year 4
Profits	£4.5	£2.5	£2.5	£2.5
Provision (charged)/credited to profit or loss	(2.0)	0	1.0	0
Profits after provision	£2.5	£2.5	£3.5	£2.5
Provision b/f	0	2.0	1.5	0
Expense	0	(0.5)	(0.5)	0
Charge/(credit) to profit or loss	2.0	0	(1.0)	0
Provision c/f	£2.0	£1.5	£0	£0

As can be seen, the enterprise has charged the full amount of the provision in Year 1, when it has expected profits of £4.5 million. In Years 2 and 3, instead of charging the reorganization costs to profit or loss, the enterprise is able to charge these costs against the provision and so the profits in Years 2 and 3 are not reduced. Moreover, in Year 3, as the whole provision of £2.0 million was not required, the excess (£2.0 million provided – £1.0 million incurred) has been released back to profit or loss, increasing profits to £3.5 million. The enterprise has effectively taken a 'big bath' in Year 1, when the profits were substantial, and has protected future profits.

This potential for creative accounting highlights the need for a standard in this area. Indeed, without regulation, if the recognition of a provision were allowed to proceed on the intention to incur expenditure rather than an obligation to do so, then, this could result in even more creativity in accounting.

Sir David Tweedie, the former chairman of the IASB has said:

A main focus of [IAS 37] is 'big bath' provisions. Those who use them sometimes pray in aid of the concept of prudence. All too often however the provision is wildly excessive and conveniently finds its way back to [profit or loss] in a later period. The misleading practice needs to be stopped and [IAS 37] proposes that, in future, provisions should only be allowed when the company has an unavoidable obligation – an intention which may or may not be fulfilled will not be enough. Users of accounts can't be expected to be mind readers

Summary

The Appendix to IAS 37 summarizes the main requirements of the standard (see Tables 8.2 and 8.3).

Summary of provisions and contingent liabilities

Table 8.2   **Summary of IAS 37 (1)**

Obligation	Accounting effect	Disclosure
Present obligation that probably requires an outflow of resources	A provision is recognized	Amounts, nature, uncertainties, assumptions, reimbursements
Possible obligation or present obligation that may, but probably will not, require an outflow of resources	No provision recognized; contingent liability disclosed	Nature, estimate of financial effect, uncertainties, reimbursement
Possible obligation or present obligation where the outflow of resources is remote	No provision recognized; no contingent liability disclosed	No disclosure is required

Summary of contingent assets

Table 8.3   **Summary of IAS 37 (2)**

Economic benefits	Accounting effect	Disclosure
Inflow virtually certain	Asset rules apply, i.e. the asset is not contingent	N/A
Inflow probable but not virtually certain	No asset recognized; contingent asset disclosed	Nature, financial effect
Inflow not probable	No asset recognized; no contingent asset disclosed	Nil

The underlying requirements can be summarized more simply as follows:
IAS 37 effectively bans:

- big bath accounting
- creation of provisions where no obligation to a liability exists
- use of provisions to smooth profits

and requires greater disclosure in relation to provisions to aid the user's understanding and present a true and fair view.

8.10 IAS 10 *Events After the Reporting Period*

It is the uncertainty surrounding certain liabilities existing at the end of reporting period that gives rise to the accounting issues covered above. As time passes beyond the end of the reporting period, however, the certainty of some obligations may become clearer and, indeed, may even become confirmed. The process of preparing financial statements for publication can often take weeks – or even months – and the information that is available to the reporting accountant after the reporting period can be very useful in determining the appropriate accounting treatment for certain items.

Moreover, for the financial statements to be true and fair, any events occurring after the end of the reporting period and before the signing of the annual accounts must be considered if these events give significant and further information relevant to those financial statements. These events are described as events after the reporting period. The decision as to whether information is significant or not will be made, in the first instance, by the directors. If this information is not provided then the accounts will potentially be misleading.

Definitions

IAS 10 *Events After the Reporting Period* gives guidance on such matters. IAS 10 defines an event after the reporting period as an event that could be favourable or unfavourable, which occurs between the end of the reporting period and the date that the financial statements are authorised for issue.

An *adjusting event* is an event after the reporting period that provides further evidence of conditions that existed at the end of the reporting period, including an event that indicates that the going concern assumption in relation to the whole or part of the enterprise is not appropriate.

A *non-adjusting event* is an event after the end of the reporting period that is indicative of a condition that arose after the reporting period.

The key distinction, therefore, is whether the event after the reporting period (from the end of the reporting period to the date the accounts are authorized for issue) relates to a condition existing at the end of the reporting period.

Adjusting events after the reporting period

If information becomes available that gives further evidence of the conditions that existed at the end of the reporting period, the financial statements should be adjusted to include that information. There is no additional disclosure required.

The following examples are given in IAS 10 that require an entity to adjust the amounts recognised in its financial statements:

(a) The settlement after the reporting period of a court case that confirms that the entity had a present obligation at the end of the reporting period. The entity should adjust any previously recognized provision related to this court case or recognize a new provision. The entity does not merely disclose a contingent liability because the settlement provides additional evidence that would be considered in determining whether a contingent liability exists.

(b) The receipt of information after the reporting period indicating that an asset was impaired at the end of the reporting period, or that the amount of a previously recognized impairment loss for that asset needs to be adjusted, e.g.

(i) the bankruptcy of a customer that occurs after the reporting period usually confirms that a loss existed at the end of the reporting period on a trade receivable and that the entity needs to adjust the carrying amount of the trade receivable.

    (ii) the sale of inventories after the reporting period may give evidence about their net realisable value at the end of the reporting period.

(c) The subsequent determination of the cost of assets purchased, or the proceeds from assets sold, before the end of the reporting period.

(d) The subsequent determination of the amount of profit-sharing or bonus payments, if the entity had a present legal or constructive obligation at the end of the reporting period to make such payments as a result of events before that date.

(e) The discovery of fraud or errors that show that the financial statements are incorrect.

Non-adjusting events after the reporting period

The financial statements should not be adjusted for non-adjusting events (i.e. those events or conditions that arose after the reporting period). Non-adjusting events should, however, be disclosed if they are of such importance that non-disclosure would affect the ability of users to make proper evaluations and decisions. The required disclosure is:

- the nature of the event, and
- an estimate of its financial effect or a statement that a reasonable estimate of the effect cannot be made.

The following are examples of non-adjusting events after the reporting period that would generally result in disclosure:

(a) a major business combination after the reporting period or disposing of a major subsidiary;

(b) announcing a plan to discontinue an operation;

(c) major purchases of asses, other disposals of assets, or expropriation of major assets by government;

(d) the destruction of a major production plant by a fire after the reporting period;

(e) announcing or commencing the implementation of a major restructuring;

(f) major ordinary share transactions and potential ordinary share transactions after the reporting period;

(g) abnormally large changes after the reporting period in asset prices or foreign exchange rates;

(h) changes in tax rates or tax laws enacted or announced after the reporting period that have a significant effect on current and deferred tax assets and liabilities;

(i) entering into significant commitments or contingent liabilities, for example, by issuing significant guarantees; and

(j) commencing major litigation arising solely out of events that occurred after the reporting period.

Progress Point 8.5

Consider the following list of events after the reporting period and decide which should be classified as adjusting events and which are non-adjusting events in light of the above definitions:

(a) the receipt of a copy of the financial statements of an unlisted company, which provides evidence of an impairment in the value of a long-term investment at the end of the reporting period

(b) the receipt of proceeds of sales after the reporting period concerning the net realizable value of inventories held at the end of the reporting period

(c) issues of shares and debentures

(d) purchases and sales of non-current assets and investments

(e) the renegotiation of amounts owing by trade receivables, or the insolvency of a trade receivable

(f) losses of non-current assets or inventories as a result of a catastrophe such as fire or flood

(g) changes in rates of foreign exchange

(h) announcement of a major restructuring

(i) a valuation that provides evidence of an impairment in the value of a property

(j) the announcement of changes in the rates of tax

(k) the discovery of errors or frauds, which show that the financial statements to be issued were incorrect

(l) mergers and acquisitions.

Solution

Items (a), (b), (e), (i) and (k) would normally be adjusting events. The remainder are normally non-adjusting.

In deciding whether to disclose a non-adjusting event, a subjective decision will ultimately require to be made by the directors as to whether the information is significant or not.

Dividends

Paragraph 12 states, 'if an entity declares dividends to holders of equity instruments after the reporting period, the entity shall not recognise these dividends as a liability at the end of the reporting period'.

Consequently, if dividends are declared after the reporting period but before the financial statements are authorized for issue, they are treated as a non-adjusting event whose disclosure is required under the provisions of IAS 1 *Presentation of Financial Statements*. Under IAS 1 they will be disclosed in the notes to the accounts. Such dividends are not recognized as a liability at the end of the reporting period because they do not meet the criteria of a present obligation in IAS 37. Only dividends declared before the end of the reporting period are accrued as a liability, as only then do they meet the criteria of a present obligation.

Going concern

Paragraph 14 states, 'an entity shall not prepare its financial statements on a going concern basis if management determines after the reporting period either that it intends to liquidate the entity or to cease trading, or that it has no realistic alternative but to do so'.

If the going concern basis is no longer appropriate, the effect is so pervasive that the IASB sees this as a fundamental change in the basis of accounting rather than an adjustment to the financial statements in the manner of adjusting events.

The preparation of accounts when the company is not a going concern is beyond the scope of this textbook.

8.11 Disclosure in practice

Events after the reporting period

There were no events after the end of the reporting period to report in the 2011 accounts as the following extract shows.

Events after the Balance Sheet date

No important events have occurred since the year-end.

Source: Logica (2011), p. 57

In 2007 however, the following disclosure by Logica was a non-adjusting event after the reporting period. The fact that it was disclosed indicated that it was a material event and that non-disclosure could influence the economic decisions of users.

> On 15 February 2008, Energias de Portugal S.A. (EDP) notified the Group of its exercise of the EDP Put Option, under the terms of the shareholders agreement entered into between EDP and Logica on 20 April 2005. Accordingly, EDP gave notice that it will sell to Logica the remaining 40% interest in the equity shares of Edinfor – Sistemas Informáticos S.A. and the outstanding shareholder loans for the fixed price of €55.0 million. On 7 March 2008, the transaction completed resulting in Logica owning a 100% equity interest in Edinfor.
>
> *Source: Logica (2007), p. 145*

8.12 The position in practice

It is useful at this point to consider the position with liabilities and contingent liabilities in practice.

Liabilities ought to be relatively simple to determine. The Conceptual Framework definition, by including reference to a 'past event', goes a long way to guiding the accountant in determining both the existence and quantification of a liability (e.g. the purchase of goods giving rise to the existence of a liability and the invoice giving the amount). Contingent liabilities are more difficult both to ascertain and to determine. Business today has moved on greatly from the times when accounting standards were first being developed to give guidance on how to account for certain situations. An unavoidable consequence of this is that accountants have been expected to develop also, with the result that it is no longer sufficient to simply report on the obvious. In practice, accountants are expected to consider not only the figures that are included within the reporting system but also to consider those figures which have not been included in that system. Moreover, the accountant needs to consider situations with a broadened commercial awareness; in reviewing and discussing financial statements with management, the accountant needs to look beyond the figures and to the environment – social, economic and legal – in which the particular company operates in order to fully provide for any items whether requiring to be recognized, disclosed or not reported at all. Companies do not operate in a vacuum – and neither can the accountant.

BASIC

INTERMEDIATE

ADVANCED

> **Section summary**
>
> In this long intermediate section, liabilities have been looked at in detail and the Conceptual Framework definition used to help identify items that may require to be recognized, disclosed or simply ignored. IAS 37 has been covered in detail, and its objectives identified and appraised. IAS 10 identifies how to deal with events after the reporting period.

Section 3: Advanced Aspects

8.13 Financial instruments

Introduction

As business becomes more and more complex, so too does the accounting for the underlying transactions. In times when the primary focus of accounting was for traditional industries such as manufacturing, the main concern was accruing costs to be matched with revenues with a key point in the process being the point of revenue recognition i.e. the point at which an entity is considered to have an entitlement to cash or an obligation to settle claims by cash. At the end of the reporting period, any unsettled transactions would be recognized in the statement of financial position, classified as trade receivables, trade payables etc. In their simplest form, financial instruments are the contracts that give rise to unsettled transactions at the end of the reporting period. That is, the claims to cash (receivables) or the obligations to settle in cash (payables).

Such financial instruments are known as 'primary financial instruments'.

The development of sophisticated financial markets has resulted in companies being able to trade in a manner that 'traditional' accounting methods cannot adequately deal with. An entity can substantially alter its risk profile by using complex financing arrangements to take account of, for example, foreign currency movements if trading in a foreign jurisdiction; at a more speculative level the entity may use such financing arrangements to multiply the effects of changes in interest, foreign exchange or security prices thus multiplying the gains if prices move advantageously, or, alternatively, multiplying the losses if they move adversely. Such transactions, where part of the financial risk of a primary instrument is transferred, are known as derivative financial instruments.

The market for financial instruments has expanded tremendously over the past 20 years. Many companies have moved from using only straightforward financial instruments (such as cash, trade debtors and creditors, long-term debt and investments in bonds and shares) to the adoption of sophisticated risk management strategies using derivatives and complex combinations of financial instruments. It is now possible to manage virtually any financial risk or speculate on key rates and prices in the increasingly global economy. However, while the types and availability of financial instruments have advanced considerably, traditional accounting recognition, measurement and disclosure principles have struggled to keep pace. Four standards have been issued by the IASB in response, to deal with these issues:

1. IAS 32 *Financial Instruments: Presentation*
2. IAS 39 *Financial Instruments: Recognition and Measurement*
3. IFRS 7 *Financial Instruments: Disclosures*
4. IFRS 9 *Financial Instruments.*

These standards define the term financial instrument, identify several types of financial instrument and prescribe the accounting treatment of each type.

This area of accounting can be extremely complex and a detailed coverage of financial instruments is beyond the scope of this book. The aim of this section therefore is simply to provide a basic introduction to the accounting issues involved. It is important to bear in mind, however, that while these standards are detailed, they become complex only when dealing with more complex situations. They make no significant difference to accounting for more basic items such as cash, trade receivables, trade payables and straightforward borrowings.

Definitions

IAS 32 provides, in paragraph 11, key definitions which apply throughout all of the standards in relation to financial instruments.

- A financial instrument is any contract that gives rise to a financial asset of one entity and a financial liability or equity instrument of another entity.
- A financial asset is any asset that is:
  (a) cash
  (b) an equity instrument of another entity (e.g. an investment in the shares of another company)
  (c) a contractual right
    (i) to receive cash or another financial asset from another entity (e.g. a customer, loan made to a supplier), or
    (ii) to exchange financial instruments with another entity under conditions that are potentially favourable to the entity (e.g. in the money option).

Physical assets such as property, plant and equipment or inventory are not financial assets as they do not give a right to receive cash or another financial asset. It is important to note, however, that it would be expected that they would ultimately generate cash. Similarly, intangible assets such as brands and patents are not financial assets. Finally, prepayments are not financial assets as they will not be settled for cash or another financial instrument. Their settlement is by the delivery of goods and services.

- A financial liability is any liability that is:
  - (a) a contractual obligation to deliver cash or another financial asset to another entity
  - (b) a contractual obligation to exchange financial instruments with another entity under conditions that are potentially unfavourable.

Examples include:

- trade payables and accruals – settlement will normally involve a transfer of cash
- forward contract to acquire $1m dollars at £1 = $1.50 when current exchange rate is £1 = $1.60; that is, there is an unfavourable exchange resulting in a contract to pay $1m/1.50 = £666,667 when it could be acquired for $1m/1.60 = £625,000
- bank loan.

Tax liabilities and deferred income are not financial liabilities as they do not derive from contractual obligations. Tax is a statutory obligation, not a contractual obligation. Deferred income is not a financial liability as there is no obligation relating to deferred income. It exists because of the revenue recognition policy of the company.

- An equity instrument is any contract that evidences a residual interest in the assets of an entity after deducting all of its liabilities. This definition includes shares (ordinary and some preference), and warrants and options to acquire shares.

In addition, IFRS 9 provides the following definition:

- A derivative is a financial instrument that changes in value with an underlying economic item (e.g. interest rate, exchange rate or share price), requires no or relatively little investment, and is settled at a future date. Common types of derivatives include forward exchange contracts, interest rate swaps and options.

BASIC

INTERMEDIATE

ADVANCED

Example

On 31 December 2012 a company acquires an option to purchase 20,000 shares in ABC plc at 50p per share. The option is exercisable on 31 March 2013. The cost of the option is £750. The share price of ABC plc on 31 December 2012 is 48p.

Required

Explain whether the option meets the definition of a derivative.

Solution

The tests to see whether the option meets the definition of a derivative are as follows.

- (a) *Change in value*: the value of the option will change in response to changes in the share price of ABC plc. If the share price increases between 31 December and 31 March the value of the option will increase, and vice versa.
- (b) *Initial investment*: the cost of the option (£750) is relatively little compared to what would have to be paid for the shares themselves (£9,600, i.e. 20,000 × 48p).
- (c) *Settled at a future date*: if the option is exercised it will be in March 2013 (i.e. in the future).

All the above tests are satisfied and the option therefore meets the definition of a derivative.

Progress Point 8.6

Explain whether the following transactions give rise to a financial instrument as defined by IAS 32:

(a) a company sells goods to a customer on credit

(b) a company has a corporation tax bill outstanding of £250,000

(c) a company makes an issue of ordinary shares

(d) a company prepays rates of £50,000

(e) a company buys goods from a supplier on credit.

Solution

(a) The sale of goods on credit results in a contractual obligation on the part of the customer to pay for the goods. The contract is a financial instrument because:

   (i) the company now has a trade receivable (a financial asset)

   (ii) the customer now has a trade payable (a financial liability).

(b) The payment of taxation is a statutory obligation, not a contractual one. Because the payment of taxation does not derive from a contractual obligation it is not a financial liability.

(c) The issue of ordinary shares creates a contract between the company and its shareholders, which entitles them to a residual interest in the assets of the company after deducting all of its liabilities. The contract is a financial instrument because:

   (i) the shareholders now own the shares (a financial asset)

   (ii) the company has additional share capital (an equity instrument).

(d) The prepayment is not a financial asset as it will not be settled for cash or another financial instrument. The prepayment will be settled by the delivery of services. This contract is not a financial instrument.

(e) The purchase of goods on credit creates a contractual obligation on the part of the company to pay for the goods. This contract is a financial instrument because:

   (i) the supplier now has a trade receivable (a financial asset)

   (ii) the company now has a trade payable (a financial liability).

The accounting issue involved

The accounting issue involved is that an industry evolved in the development of 'new financial instruments' that were designed to exploit loopholes in tax regulations and/or the Companies Act definitions, so that companies could pay less tax or have stronger-looking statements of financial position. Some of these instruments have features of equity and liabilities. The intention behind IAS 32 and IFRS 9 is to clarify the accounting treatment of these items. If the requirements of IAS 32 did not exist, an entity might be able to incur a financial liability but then present this liability as equity, and consequently improve the gearing ratio but at the same time reduce the reliability of the reported information.

8.14 IAS 32 *Financial Instruments: Presentation*

Objective

The objective of IAS 32 is to establish principles for presenting financial instruments as liabilities or equity and for offsetting financial assets and financial liabilities. It applies to the classification of financial instruments, from the perspective of the issuer, into financial assets, financial liabilities and equity instruments;

the classification of related interest, dividends, losses and gains; and the circumstances in which financial assets and financial liabilities should be offset.

Classification of financial instruments

The fundamental principle of IAS 32 is that a financial instrument should be classified as either a financial liability or an equity instrument according to the substance of the contract, not its legal form. Consequently, even though the legal form of a financial instrument might be a share issue, the instrument could still be regarded as giving rise to a financial liability if the underlying substance of the transaction indicates that this is the case.

A key distinction between a financial liability and an equity instrument is whether a contractual obligation exists. A financial instrument should be classified as an equity instrument if, and only if, the instrument includes no contractual obligation to deliver cash or another financial asset to another entity.

Example

A company has the following items in issue at 31 December 2012

- 5 million £1 4.5% bonds 2015
- 12 million ordinary shares of 25p.

Required

Explain how these should be classified in the statement of financial position of the company at 31 December 2012.

Solution

Bonds

The bonds represent a financial liability as they contain contractual obligations. The first is in respect of the annual interest payable on them of £225,000 (£5,000,000 × 4.5%) and the second is the obligation to repay the bonds in 2015. Either obligation is sufficient to identify the bonds as debt.

Ordinary shares

The ordinary shares are an equity instrument. Although the ordinary shareholders will expect to receive dividends, and indeed, once any dividends have been properly declared the company has a legal obligation to pay these to the shareholders, the key point is that the company is under no obligation to declare a dividend in the first place. No obligation means no liability. Similarly, the shareholders do not have a right to receive back the money they paid for the shares.

Redeemable preference shares

In judging whether an obligation exists, IAS 32 requires a substance over form approach to distinguish between liabilities and equity. This leads to most preference shares and some ordinary shares being classified as liabilities.

Preference shares or ordinary shares that either the company is obliged to redeem at a certain date or redeem at the option of the holders are liabilities because there is an obligation to transfer financial assets to the holder.

In the event that preference shares are not redeemable, an assessment of the substance of the contractual arrangements needs to be made. Where distributions are at the discretion of the issuer, the shares are equity. Most preference shares, however, carry an obligation to pay a stated dividend (e.g. 5%). This obligation is contingent only on the company having sufficient reserves legally to pay the dividend. The standard clarifies this point by stating that the decision to classify as a liability or equity item is not affected by the amount of the company's reserves or its history of making distributions. Such preference shares will, therefore, be classified as liabilities.

It is worth covering at this stage how the dividends from such preference shares should be dealt with. IAS 32 adopts a consistent approach and requires that interest and dividends relating to financial liabilities should be recognized as an expense in profit or loss. Consequently, any dividends paid to the holders of redeemable preference shares must be treated as an expense and presented in the statement of comprehensive income. Furthermore, any accrued dividends unpaid at the end of an accounting period should be treated in the same way as accrued interest. This should be compared with dividends on equity instruments, which are required to be presented in the statement of changes in equity. Moreover dividends proposed at the year end on equity instruments will not be recognized but will instead be disclosed in the notes.

Although this treatment might at first appear counter-intuitive, it is in fact the reverse. It is the logical consequence of the IAS 32 principle that the accounting treatment of a financial instrument should follow its substance rather than its legal form.

Compound financial instruments

Some financial instruments, known as compound financial instruments, have both a liability component and an equity component from the issuer's perspective. Where an instrument has both an equity and liability element, IAS 32 requires that the two should be accounted for and presented separately.

The most common is convertible debt (i.e. loan stock), which is convertible to ordinary shares at the option of the lender. Legally this is one instrument but in substance combines a financial liability (the contractual obligation to transfer cash on repayment and normally to pay interest up until that point) and an equity instrument (a call option granting the holder the right, for a specified period, to convert to ordinary shares). The two elements should be classified separately – one within liabilities and the other as part of reserves in equity (a separate reserve should be used to record this part). The option to convert is termed an 'embedded derivative' in IAS 39.

IAS 32 does not address measurement issues but suggests (para. 31) a method for separating the total amount of a convertible instrument into the liability and equity elements.

(a) The carrying amount of the liability element should first be calculated by measuring the fair value of a similar liability that does not have conversion rights.

(b) The fair value of the equity element is then determined by deducting the fair value of the liability element from the fair value of the whole instrument. IAS 39 states that the fair value of the whole instrument is normally equal to the amount of the consideration that was received when the instrument was issued.

IAS 32 defines fair value as 'the amount for which an asset could be exchanged, or a liability settled, between knowledgeable willing parties in an arm's length transaction'.

Example

A company issued the following instrument at par on 31 March 2012:

2 million 50p 3% convertible bonds 2018

The value of 2 million 50p 3% bonds 2018 without the conversion rights is estimated to be £960,000.

Required

State the amounts that should appear for the above items in the accounts of the company as at 31 March 2012.

Solution

Bonds	£
Total amount raised at issue (2 million × 50p)	1,000,000
Allocated to liability (fair value of bond without rights)	960,000
Allocated to equity (difference)	40,000

Note that the classification of the liability component is made at issuance and is not revised for subsequent changes in market interest rates, share prices or other event that changes the likelihood that the conversion option will be exercised (para. 28).

8.15 IAS 39 *Financial Instruments: Recognition and Measurement*

The objective of IAS 39 is to establish principles for recognizing and measuring financial assets, financial liabilities and some contracts to buy or sell non-financial items. The recognition principles determine when a financial asset or liability should be shown on an entity's balance sheet, while the measurement principles determine the amount at which a financial asset or liability should be shown.

It should be noted that the IASB is to replace IAS 39 over a period of time. The first instalment, dealing with classification and measurement of financial assets, was issued as IFRS 9 *Financial Instruments* in November 2009. The requirements for classification and measurement of financial liabilities and derecognition of financial assets and liabilities were added to IFRS 9 in October 2010. As a consequence, parts of IAS 39 are being superseded and it was originally planned that these parts would become obsolete and IFRS 9 effective for annual periods beginning on or after 1 January 2013. However, on 16 December 2011, the IASB amended the mandatory effective date of IFRS 9 to annual periods beginning on or after 1 January 2015, although earlier application is still permitted. The IASB intends to expand IFRS 9 to add new requirements for impairment of financial assets measured at amortized cost, and hedge accounting. When these projects are complete, IFRS 9 will be a complete replacement for IAS 39.

Consequently, at time of writing (April 2012) IAS 39 remains in force and therefore this chapter concentrates on the requirements of IAS 39. However, any significant changes introduced by IFRS 9 are explained where relevant.

Recognition and derecognition

IAS 39 and IFRS 9 state that an entity should recognize a financial asset or a financial liability in its statement of financial position when, and only when, it becomes a party to the contractual provisions of the instrument.

This means that derivatives (e.g. forward contracts) will be included in the statement of financial position from the date of the commitment, rather than on the date on which settlement takes place. In many cases, however, these will have no initial monetary value as there is no cost attached to them at the outset. They may have a value in the future as the underlying variable changes or due to the time value of money.

The rules within IAS 39 and IFRS 9 in relation to derecognition are very detailed.

The main requirements are as follows:

(a) a financial asset is derecognized when the entity's contractual rights to receive cash flows from the asset expire

(b) a financial liability is derecognized when the entity's contractual obligations expire, are discharged or cancelled.

Initial measurement of financial assets and liabilities

Both IAS 39 and IFRS 9 require that all financial assets and liabilities should be measured initially at fair value (with the exception of financial assets not at fair value through profit or loss) plus transaction costs directly attributable to the acquisition or issue of the financial asset or financial liability. Fair value is the amount paid for the asset or received for the liability.

Transaction costs include fees and commissions paid to advisers, agents, brokers and so on, as well as transfer taxes (e.g. stamp duty). They do not include internal administrative or holding costs.

Transaction costs are an addition to the cost of a financial asset and a reduction in a net liability.

Example

A company had the following transactions in the year to 31 March 2012:

(i) entered into a forward contract to acquire $20m in 3 months' time at £1: $1.65; there were no costs or fees arising

(ii) acquired 300,000 shares in Ulpas plc for £5 per share; commission and stamp duty totalled £15,000

(iii) issued 5 million £13.5% bonds 2020 at a discount of 25%; the bonds will be redeemed at 110p in 2020; arrangement fees of £45,000 were paid.

Required

Prepare journal entries to record the initial measurement of the above items.

Solution

(i) Forward contract: although the company is party to a contract there is no cost to record on initial measurement. No journal entry is required.

(ii) Acquisition of shares: the cost of the shares (300,000 × £5 = 1,500,000), together with the commission and stamp duty (£15,000), would be recorded.

Dr	Investment	£1,515,000	
	Cr Bank		£1,515,000
Being cost of acquisition of shares.			

(iii) Issue of bonds: the issue of bonds is at a discount and raises 5 million × £1 × 75% = £3,750,000. The costs of the issue are £45,000.

Dr	Bank	£3,750,000	
	Cr Non-current liability bonds		£3,750,000
Being issue of bonds at discount.			

Dr	Non-current liabilities – bonds	£45,000	
	Cr Bank		£45,000
Being cost of issuing bonds.			

The bonds would be initially recorded at £3,705,000 (£3,750,000 less £45,000).

Subsequent measurement of financial assets

Many financial instruments will change in value after initial recognition. IAS 39 identifies and defines four categories of financial asset and prescribes how each category should be measured after its initial recognition.

(i) Financial assets at fair value through profit or loss

These are usually financial assets that have been acquired for the purpose of generating a profit from short-term fluctuations. However, on initial recognition, an entity may designate any financial asset as being 'at fair value through profit or loss' if this would result in more relevant information.

After initial recognition, financial assets that fall into this category should be measured at their fair value, with any gains or losses arising from fluctuations in fair value being recognized in profit or loss for the period in which they arise.

Fair value should not include any deduction for transaction costs that might arise on the disposal of the asset. Market value is the best indicator of fair value but, in the absence of a reliable market value, a valuation technique (e.g. dividend valuation model) should give a reliable figure. Where available, bid prices should be used.

(ii) Held-to-maturity investments

These are financial assets with fixed or determinable payments and fixed maturity that the entity has the positive intent and ability to hold to maturity. After initial recognition, held-to-maturity investments should be measured at their amortized cost using the effective interest method (see below).

(iii) Loans and receivables

These are financial assets with fixed or determinable payments that are not quoted in an active market. This category will mainly comprise trade receivables and other debtors and loans made by a company.

After initial recognition, loans and receivables should be measured at their amortized cost using the effective interest method. This method involves discounting the amounts expected to be received when the loan or receivable is settled. The standard does not required amortized cost to be applied to short-term receivables unless the effect of discounting would be material. In respect of short-term receivables, usually it would not be.

(iv) Available-for-sale financial assets

These are any other financial assets that do not fall into the above categories. Common examples are investments in shares and debt of other companies. Shares in private companies, whose fair value cannot be measured reliably, are included in this category.

After initial recognition, available-for-sale financial assets should generally be valued at their fair value with gains or losses arising from fluctuations in fair value being recognized in other comprehensive income. In cases where it is impossible to measure the fair value of unquoted shares reliably (e.g. private companies), these should be valued at cost.

Example

A company purchased 100,000 ordinary shares of 25p in A plc, a listed company, for £3.60 per share on 24 February 2012. Broker's commission on the purchase was £3,000.

At 31 December 2012, the year end of the company, the shares of A plc were quoted at a bid/offer price of £3.95/£3.98. Selling costs are estimated at 0.5% of the sales proceeds.

The shares are in the available-for-sale category.

Required

State the amounts at which the shares would be recorded on 24 February and 31 December 2012.

Solution

The shares would initially be recorded at their purchase price and acquisition costs. That is:

$$100,000 \times £3.60 + 3,000 = £363,000$$

As the investment is in the available-for-sale category it should be included at fair value at the end of the reporting period. At 31 December, the investment in A plc would be included at £395,000 (100,000 × £3.95, i.e. the bid price). No deduction would be made for selling costs. The gain in value of £32,000 would be recognized in other comprehensive income.

IFRS 9 position

Under IFRS 9 the available-for-sale and held-to-maturity categories are eliminated in an attempt to simplify the process of accounting for such financial instruments. Although the standard retains a mixed measurement model with some assets measured at amortized cost and others at fair value, the distinction between the two models is based on the business model of each entity and a requirement to assess whether the cash flows of the instrument are only principal and interest.

The business model approach is fundamental to the standard and is an attempt to align the accounting for financial assets with the way the entity deploys the assets in the business while also looking at the characteristics of the business. A debt instrument that meets both the 'business model test' and 'contractual cash flow characteristics test' is normally measured at amortized cost.

■ *Business model test*: the objective of the entity's business model is to hold the financial asset to collect the contractual cash flows (rather than to sell the instrument prior to its contractual maturity to realise its fair value changes).

■ *Cash flow characteristics test:* the contractual terms of the financial asset give rise on specific dates to cash flows that are solely payments of principal and interest on the principal outstanding.

A debt instrument, such as a loan receivable, that is held within a business model whose objective is to collect the contractual cash flows and has contractual cash flows that are solely payments of principal and interest must be measured at amortized cost. All other debt instruments must be measured at fair value through profit or loss (FVTPL).

An investment such as a convertible loan note would not qualify for measurement at amortized cost because of the inclusion of the conversion option as this is not deemed to represent payments of principal and interest.

IFRS 9 allows an entity to classify financial assets that meet the amortized cost criteria as FVTPL where it eliminates or significantly reduces an accounting mismatch.

Any changes in the fair value of financial assets that are measured at fair value are usually recognized in profit or loss. However, an entity may elect that gains and losses arising in relation to an investment in an equity instrument may be recognized in other comprehensive income as long as the instrument is not held for trading. Any dividend income from the investment would be recognized in profit or loss.

Subsequent measurement: financial assets at amortized cost

As noted above, certain financial assets such as loans and receivables should be measured subsequent to initial recognition at their amortized cost using the effective interest method.

The amount under amortized cost is as follows:

	The amount on initial recognition (or balance b/f from a previous period)
plus	Amortization (i.e. the finance income for the period)
minus	Repayments
minus	Any reduction for impairment or uncollectibility (e.g. bad debt provision)
=	Balance carried forward at end of period

The effective interest method uses the internal rate of return to calculate the amortization each year. The effective interest rate is the rate that exactly discounts estimated future cash receipts through the expected life of the financial asset to the net carrying amount of the financial asset.

Example

AB plc makes a loan of £600,000 to YZ plc on 1 February 2013. Interest of 3% per annum is due annually in arrears. YZ plc must repay £738,000 on 31 January 2018. This gives an effective interest rate of approximately 7% per annum. The loan is classified as loans and receivables.

Required

State the amounts at which the loan to YZ plc would be disclosed in AB plc's accounts for the years ended 31 January 2014, 2015, 2016, 2017 and 2018.

Solution

The amortized cost of the loan at the end of each year is calculated as follows:

Year to 31 Jan	Opening carrying value £	Finance income (7%) £	Received in year (3%) £	Closing carrying value £
2014	600,000	42,000	(18,000)	624,000
2015	624,000	43,680	(18,000)	649,680
2016	649,680	45,478	(18,000)	677,158
2017	677,158	47,401	(18,000)	706,559
2018	706,559	49,459	(18,000)	738,018
Rounding		(18)		(18)
				738,000

Notes

(i)   The loan carries 3% interest but yields a higher return as an additional £138,000 (£738,000 – £600,000) will be received in 2018. The effective interest method spreads this premium over the life of the loan.

(ii) The finance income would be recorded in profit or loss each year.

(iii) The annual repayments made by YZ plc are £18,000 (£600,000 × 3%).

Impairment and uncollectibility of financial assets

Although IAS 36 (covered in Chapter 3) deals with impairment of assets, it excludes financial assets from its scope. IAS 39 has its own rules for impairment, covered in paragraphs 58–70.

IAS 39 requires an entity to assess at the end of each reporting period whether there is any objective evidence of impairment. If any such evidence exists (e.g. borrower enters liquidation), the entity is required to do a detailed impairment calculation to determine whether an impairment loss should be recognized. The amount of this loss should be measured as the difference between:

■ the carrying amount of the asset, and
■ the present value of the estimated cash flows discounted at the financial asset's original effective interest rate.

The carrying amount of the asset should be reduced by the amount of the impairment loss with the loss itself being written off as an expense.

If, in a subsequent period, the amount of the impairment loss relating to a financial asset carried at amortized cost or a debt instrument carried as available-for-sale decreases due to an event occurring after the impairment was originally recognized, the previously recognized impairment loss is reversed through profit or loss. Impairments relating to investments in available-for-sale equity instruments are not reversed.

One of the most common examples of an impairment loss is when a trade receivable becomes wholly or partly non-collectible – the loss is either written off as a bad debt or a provision made for doubtful receivables. Such a short-term receivable will likely be measured at its invoice amount rather than amortized cost and so the amount of any impairment loss will simply be the difference between the current carrying amount of the receivable and the undiscounted amounts expected to be received from it.

Progress Point 8.7

Castle Contracts plc has the following financial assets at 31 December 2012.

> Trade receivables of £2,257,000
> 250,000 ordinary shares of 25p in Airthfield Ltd

Additional information

(i) Credit sales are due for settlement within 30 days of the invoice date. At 31 December 2012 a bad debt provision of 1.5% of trade receivables was required.

(ii) The shares in Airthfield Ltd cost £140,000. Airthfield is unlisted and the directors of Castle Contracts plc are unable to determine a reliable fair value at 31 December 2012.

The shares are designated as available for sale.

Required

State the amounts at which the above financial assets should be included in the financial statements of Castle Contracts plc at 31 December 2012.

Solution

(i) Trade receivables: there is an obvious indicator of impairment (i.e. the bad debt provision). There is no need to discount the balance as this would not be material given the credit terms.

	£
Carrying value = 2,257,000 − (2,257,000 × 1.5 = 33,855) =	<u>2,223,145</u>

(ii) Investment in Airthfield Ltd: this should be valued at cost as there is no reliable fair value, i.e.

£ <u>140,000</u>

Subsequent measurement of financial liabilities

After initial recognition, all liabilities should be measured at amortized cost using the effective interest method. There are exceptions to this rule, two of which are considered below.

Financial liabilities at fair value through profit and loss

These consist mainly of financial liabilities that are held for trading. In a similar manner to financial assets, however, an entity may designate any financial liability as being 'at fair value through profit and loss' if doing so would result in more relevant information.

After initial recognition, these should be measured at fair value, with gains or losses arising from fluctuations in fair value being recognized in profit or loss for the period in which they arise.

Trade payables

Short-term payables (e.g. trade payables) may be measured at the original invoice amount if the effect of discounting is not material.

Example

Metston plc issued 5 million 50p 7% bonds on 1 January 2012. The bonds are issued at a 10% discount (so only £2,250,000 is received) from the lenders, and costs of issue amount to £120,000. Interest is to be paid annually at the end of each year and the bonds are to be repaid at a premium of 20% on 31 December 2016. The effective rate of interest has been calculated at approximately 14.3%.

Required

(i) State the amount at which the bonds should be measured on 1 January 2012.

(ii) Calculate the amortization of the cost of the bond over the five years to 31 December 2016.

Solution

(i) The bonds should initially be measured at their fair value which is equal to the amount of the consideration received when the liability was incurred less directly attributable transaction costs. This is calculated as follows:

	£
Face value of bonds 5,000,000 × 50p	2,500,000
Less: 10% discount	(250,000)
Less: costs of issue	(120,000)
	£2,130,000

That is, the consideration received less costs directly attributable to the issue

(ii) The bonds should be measured at amortized cost using the effective interest method. The amortized cost can be calculated by multiplying the amount outstanding for the period by the effective interest rate. Any payments of principal or interest should be deducted in calculating the carrying value. Workings are as follows:

Year to 31 Dec	Opening carrying value	Finance cost (14.3%)	Payments in year	Closing carrying value
	£	£	£	£
2012	2,130,000	304,590	(175,000)	2,259,590
2013	2,259,590	323,121	(175,000)	2,407,711
2014	2,407,711	344,303	(175,000)	2,577,014
2015	2,577,014	368,513	(175,000)	2,770,527
2016	2,770,527	404,473*	(3,175,000)	–
		£1,745,000		

Balancing amount

Notes

1. The finance cost is a constant percentage of the carrying value (14.3%).

2. The annual payments are those determined by the bond rate (i.e. 7% × 5m × 50p = £175,000).

3. The liability progressively increases to the amount that will be repaid at the end of 2016 (i.e. the interest charge for the year of £175,000, the face value of the bonds, £2,500,000, and the premium of £500,000 (£2,500,000 × 20%)).

4. The total finance costs amounted to:

	£
Issue costs	120,000
Discount	250,000
Interest (5 yrs × £175,000)	875,000
Premium	500,000
	1,745,000

Note how these have been spread over the life of the bond by the use of the effective interest rate. This rate takes account of all the costs to the company and is therefore higher than the rate at which the annual interest rate payments are calculated (7%).

IFRS 9 position

Most of the requirements in IAS 39 for classification and measurement of financial liabilities have been carried forward unchanged to IFRS 9.

IFRS 9 requires gains and losses on financial liabilities at fair value through profit or loss to be split into the amount of the change in fair value that is attributable to changes in the credit risk of the liability (covered later in this chapter), which should be presented in other comprehensive income, and the remaining amount of the change in the fair value of the liability which should be presented in profit or loss.

Status of IFRS 9

It should be remembered that mandatory application of IFRS 9 has been pushed back to amend the effective date to annual periods beginning on or after 1 January 2015. Early adoption was permitted starting in 2009; however, because an early adopter continues to apply IAS 39 for other requirements for financial instruments that are not covered by IFRS 9, such a decision would be a major step for any entity. It would seem desirable to wait until the whole of the new standard has been finalized to minimize the costs of compliance.

The aim of the revision of IAS 39 is to remove inconsistencies between US GAAP and IFRS in accounting for financial instruments and on 27 January 2012, the IASB and the Financial Accounting Standards Board (FASB) announced that they have agreed to work together to seek to reduce differences in their respective classification and measurement models for financial instruments. This will enable easy comparisons to be made between entities applying IFRSs and those using US GAAP.

8.16 IFRS 7 *Financial Instruments: Disclosures*

Objective

The objective of IFRS 7 is to require entities to provide disclosures in their financial statements that enable users to evaluate:

(a) the significance of financial instruments for the financial position and the financial performance of the entity concerned; and

(b) the nature and extent of risks to which the entity is exposed from financial instruments, and how the entity manages those risks.

Significance of financial instruments for financial position and performance

The main disclosures to evaluate the significance of financial instruments for an entity's financial position and performance are as follows.

Statement of financial position (paras 8 – 19)
Categories of financial assets and financial liabilities
The carrying amount of each of the following categories of financial assets and liabilities should be shown either in the statement of financial position or in the notes:

 (i) financial assets measured at fair value through profit and loss

 (ii) held to maturity investments

(iii) loans and receivables

(iv) available-for-sale financial assets

 (v) financial liabilities at fair value through profit and loss

(vi) financial liabilities measured at amortized cost.

If an entity has adopted IFRS 9, categories (ii), (iii) and (iv) will not apply. Instead, the entity should disclose the carrying amounts of financial assets measured at amortized cost and financial assets measured at fair value through other comprehensive income.

Allowance account for credit losses
When financial assets are impaired by credit losses and the entity records the impairment in a separate allowance account rather then directly reducing the carrying amount of the asset, it shall disclose a reconciliation of changes in that account during the period for each class of financial assets.

Statement of comprehensive income
Items of income, expense, gains or losses
The following should be disclosed either in the statement of comprehensive income or in the notes:

 (i) net gains and losses on
   – financial assets or liabilities at fair value through profit or loss
   – available-for-sale assets showing the amount recognized in equity and the amount removed from equity (on disposal)
   – loans and receivables, and
   – financial liabilities measured at amortized cost

 (ii) total interest income and total interest expense for financial assets and liabilities measured at amortized cost

(iii) the amount of any impairment loss for each class of financial asset.

Other disclosures
These might include:

- accounting policies (i.e. the measurement bases and other accounting policies used in relation to financial statements)
- fair value of each class of financial assets and liabilities should be disclosed in a way that facilitates comparison with carrying amounts.

Nature and extent of risks arising from financial instruments
IFRS 7 identifies three main types of risk typically associated with financial instruments and defines these in Appendix A to the standard.

(a) **Credit risk.** The risk that one party to a financial instrument will cause a financial loss for the other party by failing to discharge an obligation.

(b) **Liquidity risk.** The risk that an entity will encounter difficulty in meeting obligations associated with financial liabilities that are settled by delivering cash or another financial asset.

(c) **Market risk.** The risk that the fair value or future cash flows of a financial instrument will fluctuate because of changes in market prices. Market risk comprises three types of risk:

  (i) *currency risk* – the risk that the fair value or future cash flows of a financial instrument will fluctuate because of changes in foreign exchange rates

  (ii) *interest rate risk* – the risk that the fair value or future cash flows of a financial instrument will fluctuate because of changes in market interest rates

  (iii) *other price risk* – the risk that the fair value or future cash flows of a financial instrument will fluctuate because of factors specific to the individual financial instrument or its issuer, or factors affecting all similar financial instruments traded in the market.

IFRS 7 requires entities to disclose information that enables the users of the financial statements to evaluate the nature and extent of the risks arising from financial instruments. Qualitative and quantitative disclosures of exposures to the following risks are required.

Qualitative disclosures

For each type of risk arising from financial instruments an entity should disclose:

(a) the exposures to risk and how they arise;

(b) its objectives, policies and processes for managing the risk and the methods used to measure the risk; and

(c) any changes in (a) or (b) from the previous period

Quantitative disclosures

Specific detailed disclosures are also required in relation to credit risk, liquidity risk and market risk as follows:

(a) **Credit risk.** For each class of financial instrument the entity should disclose:

  (i) the amount that best represents its maximum exposure to credit risk at the end of the reporting period

  (ii) a description of collateral held as security

  (iii) an age analysis of financial assets that are overdue but not impaired

  (iv) an analysis of financial assets that are impaired.

(b) **Liquidity risk.** The entity should disclose a maturity analysis for financial liabilities and a description of how inherent liquidity risk is managed.

(c) **Market risk.** The entity should disclose a sensitivity analysis for each type of market risk to which the entity is exposed showing how profit or loss and equity would have been affected by changes in the relevant risk variable that were reasonably possible at that date e.g. exchange rates or market interest rates.

Section summary

Accounting standards are generally about measurement, presentation and disclosure. All three issues are usually covered within a single standard.

The fact that there is a separate accounting standard for each issue is a measure of the complexity of accounting for financial instruments. As business transactions have become increasingly complex, the need for standards regulating such transactions is paramount if financial statements are to be relied upon.

Chapter summary

IAS 37 *Provisions, Contingent Liabilities and Contingent Assets*

- A provision is defined as a liability of uncertain timing or amount.
- A liability requires there to be an obligation at the end of the reporting period.
- A provision should be recognized if:
  - a present obligation has arisen as a result of a past event
  - a payment is probable (i.e. more likely than not)
  - the amount can be estimated reliably.
- A contingent liability is a possible obligation that arises from past events and whose existence will be confirmed only by the occurrence or non-occurrence of one or more uncertain future events not wholly within the control of the entity.
- Contingent liabilities should not be recognized as liabilities but disclosed, unless the possibility of an outflow of resources is remote.
- A contingent asset is a possible asset that arises from past events, and whose existence will be confirmed only by the occurrence or non-occurrence of one or more uncertain future events not wholly within the control of the enterprise.
- Contingent assets should not be recognized but should be disclosed where an inflow of benefits is probable:
  - when the realization of income is virtually certain, then the related asset is not a contingent asset and its recognition (as an asset) is appropriate.
- A provision should be recognized at the best estimate of the expenditure required to settle the present obligation at the end of the reporting period.
- The risks and uncertainties that surround many events and circumstances should be taken into account in reaching the best estimate of a provision.
- Where the effect of the time value of money is material, the amount of a provision should be the present value of the expenditures expected to be required to settle the obligation.
- Provisions should be reviewed at the end of each reporting period and adjusted to reflect the current best estimate. If it is no longer probable that an outflow of resources will be required to settle the obligation, the provision shall be reversed.
- Provisions should be used only for the purpose for which they were originally recognized.
- Provisions should not be recognized for future operating losses.
- If an entity has a contract that is onerous, the present obligation under the contract should be recognized and measured as a provision.
- A constructive obligation to restructure arises only when an entity has a detailed formal plan for the restructuring and has raised a valid expectation in those affected that it will carry out the restructuring.

IAS 10 *Events After the Reporting Period*

- Events after the reporting period are those events that occur between the end of the reporting period and the date when the financial statements are authorized for issue.
- Adjusting events after the reporting period provide additional evidence of conditions that existed at the end of the reporting period and require figures to be adjusted accordingly.
- Non-adjusting events after the end of the reporting period are material events that occur in the period between the end of the reporting period and the date when the financial statements are authorized for issue, and are sufficiently important to be brought to the attention of users by way of a note.
- Proposed dividends should not be recognised as a liability at the end of the reporting period.

IAS 32 *Financial Instruments: Presentation*

- A financial instrument is a contract that gives rise to a financial asset for one entity and a financial liability (or equity instrument) for another.
- Financial instruments should be classified as either a financial liability or an equity instrument according to the substance of the contract, not its legal form.
- An equity instrument is a financial instrument that includes no contractual obligation to deliver cash (or any other financial asset) to another entity.
- Redeemable preference shares are generally classed as financial liabilities. Dividends from preference shares classified as financial liabilities should be treated as an expense.
- A compound financial instrument should be separated into its two components by evaluating the liability component first and then deducting this from the fair value of the whole instrument to give the equity component.
- The entity must make the decision as to classification at the time the instrument is initially recognized.
- The classification is not subsequently changed based on changed circumstances.

IAS 39 *Financial Instruments: Recognition and Measurement*

- A financial asset or a financial liability should be recognized when (and only when) the entity becomes a party to the contractual provisions of the instrument.
- Financial assets and financial liabilities should be measured initially at their fair value plus transaction costs.
- Financial assets should be held at fair value except that the following should be held at amortized cost using the effective interest method:
  - (a) loans and receivables
  - (b) held-to-maturity investments.
- Financial assets whose fair value cannot be measured reliably should be held at cost.
- Gains and losses should be recognized in profit or loss except those arising from available-for-sale financial assets, which should be recognized in other comprehensive income.
- Financial liabilities should be measured at amortized cost using the effective interest method, except that fair value should be used for those held for trading.
- Gains and losses should be recognized in profit or loss.
- A financial asset is derecognized when the entity's contractual rights to receive cash flows from the asset expire.
- A financial liability is derecognized when the entity's contractual obligations expire, are discharged or cancelled.

IFRS 9 *Financial Instruments*

- IFRS 9 will eventually replace IAS 39 in its entirety.
- On 12 November 2009, IFRS 9 was issued as the first step towards replacing IAS 39. It introduced new requirements for classifying and measuring financial assets, effective from 1 January 2013.
- All financial assets are measured at fair value other than those measured at amortized cost. A financial asset is measured at amortized cost if it gives rise to cash flows that are solely payments of principal and interest and the asset is held solely to collect these cash flows.
- On 28 October 2010, IFRS 9 was reissued incorporating new requirements on accounting for financial liabilities, and carrying over from IAS 39 the requirements for derecognition of financial assets and financial liabilities.

- Subsequent to initial recognition, financial liabilities at fair value through profit or loss are measured at fair value. Most other financial liabilities are measured at amortized cost using the effective interest method.
- On 16 December 2011, the IASB amended the effective date of IFRS 9 to annual periods beginning on or after 1 January 2015.
- IFRS 9 will be expanded to add new requirements for impairment of financial assets measured at amortized cost, and hedge accounting. When these projects are completed, IFRS 9 will be a complete replacement for IAS 39.

IFRS 7 *Financial Instruments: Disclosures*

- An entity must group its financial instruments into classes of similar instruments.
- The two main categories of disclosures required are:
  - (i) information about the significance of financial instruments
  - (ii) information about the nature and extent of risks arising from financial instruments.

✓ Key terms for review

Definitions can be found in the glossary at the end of the book.

Compound financial instruments	Financial asset	Non-current (long-term) liability
Contingent liability	Financial instrument	Provision
Credit risk	Financial liability	Recognition of a liability
Current liability	Liability	Restructurings
Derivative	Liquidity risk	
Equity instrument	Market risk	

? Review questions

1. What is the definition of a liability according to the IASB Framework?
2. When should a liability be recognized in the statement of financial position?
3. According to IAS 37, what is the definition of a *contingent asset*?
4. Explain how the amount of a provision should be measured.
5. What are the accounting entries required to:
   (a) create a provision?
   (b) utilize a provision?
6. Explain the term *'big bath'* accounting.
7. Explain, according to IAS 10, what is meant by an *event after the reporting period*.
8. Define the term *financial instrument*.
9. At what point should a company recognize a financial asset or liability in its statement of financial position?
10. What is meant by the term *amortized cost*?
11. Explain what is meant by the terms:
    (a) credit risk
    (b) liquidity risk
    (c) market risk.

Exercises

Level I

1. Briefly explain the differences between creditors, accruals, provisions and contingent liabilities.

Level II

2. Cragg Cycles Ltd is an outdoor pursuits company operating a number of retail outlets. The finance director is unsure how the following should be dealt with under IAS 37 in the preparation of the financial statements for the year to 31 December 2012.

   (i) At a board of directors meeting on 30 November 2012, it was decided to close one of the company's three outlets in Inverness. Redundancies and other costs will arise. The staff and customers have been advised of the closure by 31 December 2012 and the company has informed the landlord that the lease of the property will not be renewed at the end of its current term (March 2013).

   (ii) Cragg Cycles Ltd has a subsidiary company, Hangliders 4 U Ltd. Cragg Cycles Ltd has guaranteed the borrowings of its subsidiary, which is currently very profitable and in a sound financial state.

   (iii) In October 2012, a member of staff was injured while demonstrating a mountain bicycle. The Health & Safety Executive has alleged that the company was at fault. Cragg Cycles Ltd's solicitors believe the company will lose any case brought against it.

   ### Required
   Advise the finance director on the status of the above situations in relation to the accounts of Cragg Cycles Ltd for the year to 31 December 2012.

3. Andlaw Ltd has produced the following figures at its year end of 31 December:

	2010	2011	2012
	£	£	£
Operating profit after charging	200,000	180,000	170,000
reorganization costs paid	–	20,000	30,000

   The reorganization was approved by the directors in 2009.

   ### Required

   (a) Assuming a provision for reorganization costs of £50,000 was created in the year to 31 December 2010, show the effect on the profits of the three years and compare this with the situation where no provision is created.

   (b) Comment on your findings.

4. As the financial director of Bellrock plc, you have the following to consider in the accounts for the year to 31 December 2012.

   (i) A customer has made a claim against Bellrock for defective goods. The claim is nearing settlement and Bellrock's legal advisers think it is probable that a sum of £300,000 will be paid by Bellrock in settlement, in addition to all legal costs.

   (ii) Bellrock sells goods with a warranty. If minor defects arose in all products sold, repair costs of £2 million would arise. If major defects arose in all products sold, repair costs of £8 million would arise. Bellrock's experience is that 20% of sales lead to claims for minor defects and 5% lead to claims for major defects.

(iii) In September 2012 Bellrock relocated to new office premises. The lease on the old premises runs to 31 December 2014 at a rent of £180,000 per year. Bellrock has been unable to find a tenant to sub-let the old office premises.

(iv) A law passed in October 2012 requires the fitting of new smoke filters at a cost of £150,000 by March 2013. This work has not yet been carried out.

(v) Bellrock has a provision of £200,000 brought forward at 1 January 2012 against a legal claim. During the year to 31 December 2012, Bellrock won this court action and therefore the provision is no longer needed. However, environmental penalties of some £200,000 have been threatened by the Health & Safety Executive and it is probable that this cost will have to be paid. The directors have therefore proposed that the provision be carried forward.

Required

Explain, quantifying your answer where possible, how the above should be accounted for in accordance with IAS 37.

5. Watfield Engineering Ltd sells and services forestry equipment. Provisions have to made in the accounts of Watfield Engineering Ltd for the year to 30 September 2012.

(i) As part of the servicing schedule of forestry vehicles, Watfield is required to replace the engine oil. A special tank is used to collect the old oil, which is emptied on a regular basis and recycled. A leak developed in the tank, causing environmental damage to a nearby river. The company has spent £50,000 on clear-up costs at the year end but further work requires to be done. Advisers estimate that there is a 50% likelihood that the additional work will cost £75,000, a 30% chance it will cost £90,000 and a 20% chance it will cost £110,000.

(ii) Watfield Engineering Ltd sells log splitters. The following details are available:

Model	Warranty period	Number of units sold in year
Basic	1 year	400
Standard	1 year	310
Super	2 years	250

The company estimates that 15%, 12% and 20% of Basic, Standard and Super, respectively, will require repair within the warranty period. Estimated repair costs are £150, £200 and £220 for Basic, Standard and Super, respectively. During the year the company spent £15,500 on repairing log splitters sold in the year.

(iii) At 30 September 2011, the accounts contained a provision of £195,000 relating to potential damages arising from a court case being brought against the company. The company reached an out-of-court settlement in December 2011, with Watfield making a full and final payment of £148,000.

Required

(a) Explain, using appropriate figures, the effect of the above on the financial statements of Watfield Engineering Ltd for the year to 30 September 2012.

(b) Prepare the provisions disclosure note for inclusion in the 30 September 2012 accounts.

6. Davpet Ltd built an oil rig in 2010. A decommissioning provision was created at 30 June 2010 based on:

Estimated decommissioning costs	£5.5 m
Discount rate	6%
Estimated decommissioning date	30 June 2022

Owing to changes in legislation in June 2012, it is now estimated that decommissioning costs will be £7.0m in 2022. It is company policy to capitalize the decommissioning costs.

Required

(a) Calculate the provision required in the accounts of Davpet Ltd at 30 June 2012 and prepare journal entries to show all movements on the provision for the year to 30 June 2012.

(b) Prepare the provisions disclosure note for inclusion in the 30 June 2012 accounts.

7. Brax plc has the following transactions in the year to 31 December 2012.

(i) Purchased plant and machinery for £75,000 in October 2012. The estimated useful life of the plant and machinery is five years. The invoice from the supplier was still outstanding at 31 December 2012.

(ii) Issued 2 million ordinary shares of £0.50 at £3.20 each in May 2012.

(iii) Accrued £15,000 of electricity costs as at 31 December 2012.

(iv) Borrowed £300,000 from a bank as a five-year term loan.

(v) Received a government grant of £20,000 in relation to the plant and machinery mentioned in (i) above.

Required

Identify any financial assets, financial liabilities and equity instruments arising from each of the above transactions.

8. Emack plc acquired 570,000 ordinary shares of £1 each in Amber Ltd in January 2011 for £1,700,000. Broker's commission and stamp duty amounted to £33,000. Emack holds the shares as an available for sale asset.
The fair value of the shares was as follows:

- 31 December 2011 – £3.10 per share
- 31 December 2012 – £3.23 per share.

The shares were sold in March 2013 for £3.15 per share.

Required

State how the above would be dealt with in the accounts of Emack plc for the years to 31 December 2011, 2012 and 2013.

9. Edsant plc has the following financial instruments at 1 January 2012.

- Financial asset interest-free loan to a supplier of £450,000. The loan was originally made on 1 January 2010 and is due to be repaid in 2014 with an internal rate of return of 2.5%. The loan is included under loans and receivables.

- Financial liability 5,000,000 £14% bonds 2020 were issued on 1 January 2009. These bonds were issued at par with issue costs of £100,000. The effective interest rate is 4.5% per annum. Interest on the bonds is payable annually in arrears. The bonds were not designated as financial liabilities at fair value through profit or loss.

Required

Calculate the amounts to appear in the statement of comprehensive income of Edsant plc for the year to 31 December 2012 in relation to the above items.

Level III

10. Brownbev Ltd is a brewer of specialist beers. During the audit of the accounts to 31 March 2013 the following items have been brought to your attention as audit manager. The financial accountant has asked you to provide him with some notes so that he can discuss them with the finance director. The company's annual general meeting is held in July each year and the accounts are normally approved in June.

(i) At 31 March 2013 a provision of £100,000 was made for the cost of a court case against the company. During April 2013 an out-of-court settlement of £125,000 was agreed. Legal fees, which had not been provided for, of £10,000 were also incurred.

(ii) On 15 March 2013 a contract was signed for the purchase of new brewing equipment costing £750,000 to be delivered and paid for on 30 June 2013. The equipment will be brought into use immediately on delivery.

(iii) During March 2013 Brownbev Ltd began legal proceedings against a competitor company whose website was using a domain name registered by Brownbev. On 28 March 2013, Brownbev's solicitors filed a claim for £100,000 in damages. The solicitors have advised that the case is likely to take several months to settle and the outcome is uncertain at this stage. Legal fees, for which no provision has as yet been made, are expected to be £20,000.

(iv) On 25 April 2013, the board of directors proposed a final dividend of £1 per ordinary share be paid for the year ended 31 March 2013, subject to approval at the shareholders' AGM.

(v) At the AGM, the board of directors will announce the amalgamation of two of its microbreweries in Scotland on 30 September 2013. This will result in initial redundancy costs of £200,000, but annual savings of £450,000.

Required

Prepare notes for the financial accountant, setting out and explaining how the above matters should be accounted for and disclosed in the financial statements of Brownbev Ltd for the year ended 31 March 2013.

References

IAS 10 *Events after the Reporting Period*. IASB, 2007.
IAS 32 *Financial Instruments: Presentation*. IASB, revised 2003.
IAS 37 *Provisions, Contingent Liabilities and Contingent Assets*. IASB, 1998.
IAS 39 *Financial Instruments: Recognition and Measurement*. IASB, amended 2009.
IFRS 7 *Financial Instruments: Disclosures*. IFRS, amended 2010.
IFRS 9 *Financial Instruments*. IFRS, 2009.
Logica (2007) *Annual Report and Accounts*
Logica (2011) *Annual Report and Accounts*

Further reading

Weetman, P. (1998) *Assets and Liabilities: Their definition and recognition*. Certified Accountants Publications Limited, London.
IAS 12 *Income Taxes*. IASB, amended 2010.
IAS 36 *Impairment of Assets*. ISAB, amended 2009.

When you have read this chapter, log on to the Online Learning Centre website at *www.mcgraw-hill.co.uk/textbooks/mckeith* to explore chapter-by-chapter test questions, further reading and more online study tools.

Chapter 9

Taxation

Learning Outcomes

After studying this chapter you should be able to:

- ✓ prepare the accounting entries required to account for corporate income taxes
- ✓ explain why differences arise between accounting profits and taxable profits
- ✓ explain deferred tax
- ✓ explain and appraise the arguments for and against providing for deferred tax
- ✓ identify several methods of accounting for deferred tax
- ✓ apply the requirements of IAS 12 *Income Taxes*
- ✓ critically appraise whether IAS 12 is effective in providing useful information to user groups.

Introduction

Taxation and the payment of tax evokes a great deal of interest and emotion. Taxation, unlike other expenses that are incurred *in earning* profits, and indeed are matched with the revenues they generate, is charged *as a result of* earning profits. In practice, paying taxation is seldom welcomed and more often resented by all concerned.

This chapter deals with accounting for taxation, together with the reporting of the tax liability for a company. The chapter will not deal directly with the calculation of the tax liability itself; however, some knowledge and understanding about taxation is inevitably required.

In practice, depending on the size of the particular organization, a company may have its own tax department responsible for the calculation of the annual tax charge. Alternatively, the company may employ a firm of taxation specialists to calculate its annual liability for taxation.

Once the tax charge has been established, the details will be passed over to the reporting accountant for inclusion within the financial statements. Consequently, although taxation rates and rules may change, and so affect the calculation of the tax liability, the accounting treatment of the calculated liability will remain broadly the same.

Section 1: Basic Principles

9.1 Corporate income taxes

The tax charged on a company's profits – corporate income tax – is governed by the law prevailing in any given country. In the United Kingdom, this tax is known as corporation tax and is calculated under rules and rates set by the UK Parliament each year in the Finance Act. The date of payment of the corporation tax is dependent upon whether a company is classified as small or large. A company is large for tax purposes when its taxable profits exceed £1.5m.

The corporation tax of small companies is due in one payment and is to be paid nine months and one day after the end of its accounting period. For example, a small company with a year ending on 31 March 2012 will be required to pay its corporation tax on 1 January 2013. In this instance, corporation tax payable would be classified as a current liability.

A large company must pay corporation tax in instalments. These instalments are based on the company's own estimates of its corporation tax liability for the accounting year. Payments are made in four equal instalments due on the fourteenth day of the seventh, tenth, thirteenth and sixteenth month after the *start* of the accounting year.

For example, a large company with an accounting year *ended* on 31 December 2012 would require to pay its corporation tax in four equal instalments based on the *start* of the accounting year. In this case the start of the accounting year is 1 January 2012, and so corporation tax would be payable as follows:

- Instalment 1 – 14 July 2012
- Instalment 2 – 14 October 2012
- Instalment 3 – 14 January 2013
- Instalment 4 – 14 April 2013

At 31 December 2012, the company would disclose the 14 January and 14 April 2013 amounts as current liabilities. It is important to note that this system imposes upon companies the problem of estimating taxable profits as the year proceeds, in order to calculate the instalments payable.

Example

A small company for tax purposes has a corporation tax liability of £20,000 in respect of its profits for the year of £100,000. The corporation tax rate is 20%.

Statement of comprehensive income extract	
	£
Profit on ordinary activities before tax	100,000
Tax on profit on ordinary activities (Note 1)	20,000
Profit on ordinary activities after tax	80,000

This would be disclosed in the financial statements as follows:

Notes to the accounts extract	
	£
Note 1: Taxation	
UK corporation tax on the profits for the year at 20%	20,000

Statement of financial position extract

	£
Current liabilities	
Other creditors including taxation and Social Security	20,000

The journal entry required to record a company's corporate income tax liability is as follows:

Dr	Corporation tax charge (statement of comprehensive income)	£20,000	
	Cr Corporation tax payable (statement of financial position)		£20,000

Being corporation tax charge.

Progress Point 9.1

Castle Coaches Ltd has an estimated corporation tax charge of £3.2 million for the year to 31 December 2012. It paid £800,000 (the instalments being calculated based on the estimated profits, i.e. £3.2 million/4 = £800,000) of the tax on 14 July and 14 October 2012. The profit before tax was £9,400,000.

Required

(a) Prepare journal entries to record the corporation tax transactions arising in the year to 31 December 2012.

(b) Prepare extracts from the statement of comprehensive income of Castle Coaches Ltd for the year to 31 December 2012 and the statement of financial position at that date.

Solution

(a) Journal entries
The transactions in 2012 would be recorded as:

Dr	Tax expense (Statement of comprehensive income)	£1,600,000	
	Cr Bank		£1,600,000

Being first and second instalments paid.

Dr	Tax expense (Statement of comprehensive income)	£1,600,000	
	Cr Corporation tax payable		£1,600,000

Being corporation tax outstanding at year end (i.e. third and fourth instalments).

Statement of comprehensive income extract

	£
Profit on ordinary activities before tax	9,400,000
Tax on profit on ordinary activities	3,200,000
Profit on ordinary activities after tax	6,200,000

> **Statement of financial position extract**
>
> Creditors: amounts falling due within one year
>
> Corporation tax   1,600,000

NB: The third and fourth instalments would be paid on 14 January 2013 and 14 April 2013. These will be recorded as:

> Dr   Corporation tax creditor
>   Cr   Bank
> Being corporation tax paid.

9.2 The accounting issue involved

The complicating factor when accounting for taxation is that while accounting profits form the starting point for the computation of taxable profits and the resulting taxation charge, accounting profits and taxable profits are seldom the same. Consequently, the actual taxation paid by a company can often bear no resemblance to the expected payment based upon a user's knowledge of the prevailing tax rate and the accounting profits earned by a company.

For example, a company reporting accounting profits of £1,000,000, when the prevailing tax rate is 30%, might be expected to show a corporation tax charge of £300,000 (i.e. £1,000,000 × 30%), but may actually show a quite different tax figure.

This is because the tax rules for allowing expenses to be charged against profit differ from the accounting rules. This means that, from an accounting point of view, all expenses, including provisions and adjustments for accruals and prepayments, will be included in the calculation of the accounting profit. However, this accounting profit may not be acceptable to the authorities as the basis for the taxation charge.

9.3 Differences between accounting profits and taxable profits

In arriving at accounting profits, accountants will deduct those expenses that have been incurred in earning those profits. Unfortunately, the tax authorities specifically disallow certain items of expenditure and allow others, which accounting profits do not. This gives rise to two types of differences.

1. Permanent differences: these are items that, while allowable deductions in arriving at accounting profits, will *never* be allowed as a deduction for tax purposes.
2. Timing differences: these are items that are legitimate deductions in arriving at both accounting and taxable profits, but in different time periods.

Permanent differences

Permanent differences arise in respect of expenditure that is deductible in arriving at accounting profits but is specifically prohibited from being a deduction in arriving at taxable profits.

Examples of such expenses are:

- entertaining, and
- company formation fees.

In the case of entertaining expenses, the tax authorities do not allow this as a taxable deduction because it is open to abuse. For example, suppose Businessman A took out B for lunch and claimed the cost of the meal as a business expense for tax purposes. This is effectively giving A tax relief on normal living expenditure, the rationale being that everyone has to eat! Company formation fees are deemed to be of a capital nature and are therefore not deductible against revenues. With the knowledge of what constitutes a permanent difference, the tax charge as determined for the tax authorities can be reconciled with the accounting profit as the following example illustrates.

Example

	£	£
Gross profit		100,000
Expenses		
Rent	10,000	
Rates	8,000	
Entertainment	2,000	
		20,000
Net accounting profit		80,000
Taxation (see note)		24,600
Profit after tax		55,400

BASIC

INTERMEDIATE

ADVANCED

Note: The taxation charge is calculated as follows, assuming a corporation tax rate of 30%:

	£
Net accounting profit as reported	80,000
Add disallowable expenditure:	
Entertainment	2,000
Taxable profit	82,000
Corporation tax at 30%	24,600

In this instance, with the knowledge that entertainment is not permitted as a deduction in arriving at taxable profits, a user would be able to reconcile the tax charge to the accounting profits.

Timing differences

Timing differences arise in respect of items that are legitimate credits or deductions in arriving at both accounting and taxable profits, but in different time periods. They are said to 'originate' in the first of these periods and 'reverse' in one or more subsequent periods.

The most common example of a timing difference is the difference between the accounting reliefs given in respect of the depreciation charges of a non-current asset and the statutory tax reliefs granted in respect of the purchases of such assets.

Depreciation can be a very subjective calculation since it depends upon several factors, such as the life of the asset and residual value. A different depreciation charge may be calculated in respect of the same asset. It is for this reason, and indeed to avoid manipulating taxable profits, that depreciation is not an allowable expense for tax purposes. Instead, tax allowances, known as capital allowances, are given as deductions in arriving at taxable profits.

Capital allowances are in effect 'statutory depreciation charges', which are given at predetermined rates set by governments. Such rates do not take account of factors, such as useful economic life, pattern of benefit or expected residual value. Moreover, capital allowances are often given at enhanced rates to encourage investment in plant and equipment, which often means that the timing of the accounting and taxation reliefs may differ.

Over the lifetime of any particular asset, a company will receive the same amount of reliefs for accounting purposes (through the statement of comprehensive income in a combination of depreciation and profit or loss on disposal) as it will for tax purposes (in a combination of capital allowances and balancing adjustments on disposal). It is because of the way the capital allowances are given that the timing of the reliefs may differ. Indeed, if the differences in any particular year are significant, this can have a considerable bearing on the tax payable by a company, and on the relationship between the accounting profit and the tax payable.

Progress Point 9.2

Explain what is meant by timing differences.

Solution

Timing differences represent items of income or expenditure which are taxable or deductible, but are so in periods different from those in which they are dealt with in the accounts. They therefore arise when items of income and expenditure enter into the measurement of profit for both accounting and taxation purposes, but in different accounting periods. Timing differences originate in one period and are capable of reversal in one or more periods.

Example

A company buys a van for £3,000, which is to be depreciated over four years at £750 per annum. At the end of Year 4, the company disposes of the van for £200.

The statutory tax reliefs given on the van are as follows:

Year 1:	40% first year allowance (FYA)
Year 2 onwards:	25% writing down allowance (WDA) on written-down value (WDV)

The accounting deductions given will be as follows:

	Year 1	Year 2	Year 3	Year 4	Relief
	£	£	£	£	£
Depreciation	750	750	750	750	3,000
Gain on disposal	–	–	–	(200)	(200)
	750	750	750	550	2,800

Note that over the four years the expenses recorded equal the net cost of the van to the company, i.e. cost less residual proceeds received (3,000 – 200 = £2,800).

The taxation reliefs given will be as follows:

	Cost	fya/wda	wdv
Year 1	3,000	1,200 (40% cost)	1,800
Year 2		450 (25% wda)	1,350
Year 3		338 (25% wda)	1,012

In year 4, the year of disposal, there is no writing-down allowance; instead, the sales proceeds are set against the written-down value at the beginning of that year (i.e. £1,012 – 200 = £812) to give the balancing allowance.

Note again that the taxation reliefs (1,200 + 450 + 338 + 812) granted equal the net cost of the van to the company (2,800).

Assume that the company, over the four years of owning the asset, has the following results.

If the taxation charge was based on the accounting profits then the expected tax charges would be as follows:

	Year 1	Year 2	Year 3	Year 4	Total
Profit before depreciation	10,000	11,000	9,500	12,000	
Depreciation (as calculated)	750	750	750	550	
Accounting profits	9,250	10,250	8,750	11,450	
Expected tax charge (30%)	2,775	3,075	2,625	3,435	11,910

The taxable profits, however, would be calculated as follows:

	Year 1	Year 2	Year 3	Year 4	Total
Profit before depreciation	10,000	11,000	9,500	12,000	
Capital allowances	1,200	450	338	812	
Taxable profits	2,775	10,550	9,162	11,188	
Actual tax charge (30%)	2,640	3,165	2,749	3,356	11,910

Comparison

	Year 1	Year 2	Year 3	Year 4	Total
Expected tax charge	2,775	3,075	2,625	3,435	11,910
Actual tax charge	2,640	3,165	2,749	3,356	11,910
Difference	135	(90)	(124)	79	–

Alternatively this difference may be calculated as:

Comparison of reliefs

	Year 1	Year 2	Year 3	Year 4	Total
Accounting reliefs	750	750	750	550	2,800
Taxation reliefs	1,200	450	338	812	2,800
	450	(300)	(412)	262	
Taxation impact (30%)	135	(90)	(124)	(79)	

As can be seen, in each of the years, there is a difference between the expected tax charge found by multiplying the accounting profit by the appropriate corporation tax rate, and the actual tax charge. The difference is a result of the timing of the capital allowances (reliefs available as deductions against taxable profits) being different from the depreciation (deductions against accounting profits). However, as the example illustrates, the total tax charge for the period as a whole remains the same at £11,190. It is simply that the timing of the tax charges differs. Note that the actual tax charges would still be *payable* on their due dates regardless of the accounting charges.

The difference between the depreciation charge in any year and the tax allowance for that year is referred to as the 'timing difference'. In the above example, the tax allowances have the effect of reducing the actual tax charge to below the expected tax charge in Years 1 and 4, and increasing the actual tax charge above the expected tax charge in Years 2 and 3. The difference in Year 1 is known as the 'originating difference', caused by the capital allowances given being *higher* than the depreciation disallowed (i.e. accelerated capital allowances). The differences in Years 2 to 4 are known as 'reversing differences', caused by the capital allowances given being *lower* than the depreciation disallowed.

9.4 Deferred tax account

BASIC

INTERMEDIATE

ADVANCED

It is possible to account for this distortion in the tax charge by creating a special account called a deferred tax account. A deferred tax account recognizes the tax effects of timing differences in the current period and is used to make appropriate adjustments to the tax charge in future periods.

Continuing with our earlier illustration, the additional tax charge required in Year 1 to equalize the expected tax charge with the actual tax charge would be £135 (i.e. £2,775 – £2,640). This is the amount that requires to be transferred *into* the deferred tax account and is calculated as follows:

$$\text{Tax rate} \times (\text{tax allowances given} - \text{depreciation disallowed})$$
$$\text{i.e. } 30\% \times (1,200 - 750) = £135.$$

Year 1

In Year 1, the effect of this adjustment on the tax charge in the statement of comprehensive income would be as follows:

Statement of comprehensive income (Year 1)		
	£	£
Profits		9,250
Taxation: Actual	2,640	
Deferred	135	
Total tax charge		2,775
Profit after tax		6,475

By making the deferred tax adjustment, the taxation charge and after-tax profit figure become the same as if the accounting profit had been multiplied by the tax rate and had itself been used in the tax calculation (i.e. £9,250 × 30% = £2,775).

Note, however, that the deferred tax adjustment does not affect the amount or timing of the tax payable to the tax authorities – it is merely an accounting adjustment that effectively equalises the tax charge to the expected tax charge that would have resulted had there been no timing differences. The actual tax due will be payable on its due date.

The journal entry required to record this transfer is as follows:

		£	£
Dr	Tax expense	135	
	Cr Provision for deferred tax		135
Being originating difference.			

The provision for deferred tax is shown separately in the statement of financial position under the heading 'Provision for liabilities'.

Statement of financial position extract	
Current liabilities	£
Corporation tax payable	2,640
Provision for liabilities	
Deferred tax	135

What does the provision for deferred tax represent?

The provision for deferred tax represents the additional tax that would have become due had the timing differences not arisen. The taxable profits are lower than the accounting profits because the capital allowances are higher than the depreciation charge. The provision for deferred tax equalizes the total tax charge with the expected tax charge. Given that, over the lifetime of the asset, these timing differences will reverse, the amount in the provision for deferred tax account will be used to make the total tax charge equal to the expected tax charge in subsequent accounting periods. This procedure follows the accruals principle and matches the tax charge with the accounting profits earned in a particular accounting period.

Year 2

Carrying on with the example, the position in Year 2 is as follows:

$$\text{Transfer to/(from) deferred tax} = \text{tax rate} \times (\text{tax allowances given} - \text{depreciation disallowed})$$
$$= 30\% \times (450 - 750)$$
$$= \underline{(90)}$$

In Year 2, the timing difference is the opposite from that in Year 1. Rather than a transfer into the provision for deferred tax account being required, a transfer out of the provision account is required. This is because, in Year 2, the capital allowances given are *less* than the depreciation charge disallowed, which means the actual tax charge is *higher* than the expected tax charge. This transfer is made into profit or loss. Such a transfer is known as a 'reversal'.

The journal adjustment required to record this transfer is as follows:

		£	£
Dr	Provision for deferred tax	90	
	Cr Taxation expense		90
Being transfer from deferred taxation.			

The statement of comprehensive income and statement of financial position extracts would be as follows:

Statement of comprehensive income: Year 2		
	£	£
Profits		10,250
Taxation: actual	3,165	
deferred	(90)	
Total tax charge		3,075
Profit after tax		7,175

Again, the transfer from deferred tax results in the tax charge shown in the statement of comprehensive income as being the same as that which would have occurred had depreciation been allowed as a deduction for tax purposes and no timing differences had therefore arisen. (i.e. £10,250 × 30% = £3,075).

Statement of financial position: Year 2	
Current liabilities	£
Corporation tax payable	3,165
Provision for liabilities	
Deferred tax (135 – 90)	45

Year 3

Adopting the same procedure for Year 3 gives the following:

Transfer to/(from) deferred tax = tax rate × (tax allowances given – depreciation disallowed)

$$= 30\% \times (338 - 750)$$

Transfer (from) deferred tax = (124)

The journal entry required to record this transfer is as follows:

		£	£
Dr	Provision for deferred tax	124	
	Cr Taxation expense		124
Being transfer from deferred taxation.			

The statement of comprehensive income extract for year 3 will be as follows:

Statement of comprehensive income: Year 3		
	£	£
Profits		8,750
Taxation: Actual	2,749	
deferred	(124)	
Total tax charge		2,625
Profit after tax		6,125

Once more, the effect of the transfer results in the tax charge being the same as that which would have occurred had depreciation been allowed as a deduction for tax purposes and no timing differences had therefore arisen (i.e. £8,750 × 30% – £2,625).

The statement of financial position for Year 3 is slightly more complex. At the end of Year 2 the balance on the deferred tax provision was £45 credit. As a result of the transfer made to profit or loss of £124, this means that a deferred tax asset of £79 (£124 – £45) needs to be created.

Statement of financial position extract: Year 3	
	£
Deferred tax asset	79
Current liabilities	£
Corporation tax payable	2,749
Provision for liabilities	
Deferred tax	–

Year 4

Finally, in Year 4, the van that was originally purchased, and that has given rise to the timing differences, is sold. The deferred tax adjustment is as follows:

$$\text{Transfer to/(from) deferred tax} = \text{tax rate} \times (\text{tax allowances given} - \text{depreciation disallowed})$$
$$= 30\% \times (812 - 550)$$
$$\text{Transfer to deferred tax} = 79$$

In Year 4, the tax allowance is greater than the depreciation charge and consequently a transfer to deferred tax is required. The actual tax charge is lower than expected as a result of the tax allowances being greater than the depreciation deduction.

The journal entry required is as follows:

		£	£
Dr	Taxation expense	79	
	Cr Provision for deferred tax		79
Being transfer to deferred taxation.			

The statement of comprehensive income extract will be as follows:

Statement of comprehensive income: Year 4		
	£	£
Profits		11,450
Taxation: actual	3,356	
deferred	79	
Total tax charge		3,435
Profit after tax		8,015

As would be expected, the effect of the transfer results in the tax charge being equal to the expected tax charge (i.e. £11,450 × 30% = £3,435).

The statement of financial position extracts will be as follows:

Statement of financial position extract: Year 4	
	£
Deferred tax asset (79 – 79)	–
Current liabilities	
Corporation tax payable	3,356
Provision for liabilities	
Deferred tax	–

By the end of Year 4, the timing differences have equalized and no further deferred tax adjustments are required.

Overview

As a result of the timing differences between the tax allowances given and the depreciation charged on the van, the actual tax charge for each of the years did not bear any relationship to the accounting profits earned. By utilizing the deferred tax account, and making appropriate transfers to and from that account, the total tax charge and after-tax profit figures became the same as if the accounting profits had themselves been used in the tax calculations (and no timing differences had therefore arisen).

The accounting issue involved

The earlier example has demonstrated the effects of timing differences. As a consequence of taxation reliefs being granted in different time periods from depreciation being claimed, and the resulting difference between taxable profits and accounting profits, the actual tax paid by a company often bears no relationship to the accounting profit earned.

Why it matters

The example was based on the assumption that first year tax allowances of 40% were granted. In practice, initial tax allowances can be as much as 100%. In such cases, all the tax relief in respect of an asset purchase is claimed in Year 1, while the depreciation charges may be allocated over two, three or more years. This can result in the actual tax charge in the year of purchase being unexpectedly low and the subsequent years' tax charges being higher than expected. The deferred tax adjustment effectively allocates the tax relief over the lifetime of the asset and in a manner reflecting the consumption of that asset.

Given the effect the deferred tax charge can have on the reported results of an entity, as would be expected, there are strong arguments for as well as against providing for deferred tax.

Advantages of providing for deferred tax

A key accounting indicator used by investors is that of earnings per share (EPS); this is calculated using after-tax profits.

Taxation is a function of the profit for the period together with the company's tax circumstances. These circumstances may result in higher or lower taxable profits. As a result, the total tax charge will, if comparison between other companies/years is to be possible, require to be adjusted to remove the distortions caused by timing differences.

Consequently, unless an adjustment is made within the total tax charge, the actual tax charge will not accurately reflect the total tax cost of a company's current profits. In the year in which an asset is purchased, and where significant initial allowances have been granted, a low tax charge will be recorded; if this tax charge is expressed as a percentage of profits it will give a low tax rate. This low rate will not be sustainable, however, as the tax charge in future years increases. Therefore, without making an adjustment to account for the timing differences, the future tax cost of the accelerated capital allowances claim is ignored, and the profit after tax figure will not reflect the true performance of the company.

A further benefit of providing for deferred tax is that it reduces shareholder pressure for dividends. By smoothing after-tax reported profits, less pressure will be put on directors to pay dividends than would be the case were a company to show a low tax charge and hence higher after-tax profits. Moreover, the paradox of such a situation is that in arriving at the capital allowances claim, the company may well have invested heavily in capital expenditure and would not have cash resources left. In other words, it is as a result of spending its cash resources that the company has managed to reduce its tax liability.

It would also appear to be desirable to show the true liability for tax based on accounting profits as opposed to taxable profits, by showing a combination of actual tax charge and the deferred tax element that remains as a provision.

To provide for deferred tax in full would therefore appear to adhere to both the prudence and accruals concepts. This is known as full provisioning for deferred tax.

Disadvantages of providing for deferred tax

There is no requirement for a company's tax charge to bear a relationship to its reported income. As was noted in the introduction to this chapter, taxation is an expense that is unique. It is not incurred in earning profits, but rather is incurred as a result of earning profits and consequently the accruals concept would appear not to be applicable to such a rogue expense.

Moreover, the tax payable by a company is that tax which has been calculated in respect of its taxable profits. The deferred tax adjustment does not affect the tax payable and, consequently, providing the actual tax liability is disclosed then the prudence concept is effectively satisfied.

Providing for deferred tax may also mask any perceived tax benefits given by the government. The government may try to encourage investment in capital equipment by offering incentives such as initial allowances, but if the reduced actual tax charge is effectively masked by the overall tax charge (i.e. current tax and deferred tax), then any perceived tax benefits will not be readily evident from the financial statements.

At the individual company level, the benefits of good tax planning (i.e. investment strategies) are not reflected in the financial statements.

A real-life example will illustrate the problem.

Example

A few years ago, the writer met with a client just before the company's year end. The company had traded very successfully during the year and was to invest heavily in new equipment in order to take advantage of the initial allowances available at that time and which would substantially reduce the company's tax liability. The company duly invested in the equipment and the financial statements were compiled shortly after the year end. The company's actual tax charge had been significantly reduced; however, the provision for deferred tax returned the total tax charge back to the expected tax charge based on the accounting profit. At a meeting held to discuss the draft accounts, the CEO was extremely unhappy. He questioned the advice that had been given to him in respect of the investment in the equipment since the tax charge did not appear to reflect the tax savings that had been discussed at the time.

It took a great deal of time and effort to convince the CEO that the investment strategy had worked and the company's tax liability had been reduced. The provision for deferred tax had most certainly been unhelpful in this instance.

The flow-through approach

As an alternative to providing for deferred tax, the flow-through approach ignores the effects of timing differences and accounts only for that tax payable in respect of the period in question. The tax charge is therefore the amount payable based on the profits of that year, with no attempt to reallocate it between periods by reference to timing differences.

Section summary

Although accounting profits form the basis for the computation of taxable profits, accounting profits and taxable profits are seldom the same. This is because the tax rules for deductibility of expenses differ from accounting rules, and means that the profit or loss as stated in the statement of comprehensive income may not be that which the tax authorities will accept as the basis for the taxation charge.

These differences can be permanent differences or timing differences. Permanent differences are as a result of items of income or expenditure which are included in arriving at accounting profits but which are not taken account of in arriving at taxable profits. There is no need to adjust the accounts for permanent differences. Timing differences are as a result of items of income or expenditure which are taxable or deductible, but in different periods from those in which they are dealt with in the accounts.

It is possible to account for the distortions caused by timing differences by creating a deferred tax account and providing in full for the future tax consequence of current tax savings. This approach is known as full deferred tax accounting. The flow-through approach, on the other hand, ignores the effects of timing differences and accounts only for that tax payable in respect of the period in question.

Section 2: Intermediate Issues

9.5 Deferred tax

Section 1 explained how the deferred tax adjustment could be used to remove distortions in calculated tax figures caused by accelerated capital allowances. Some of the advantages of providing for deferred tax were outlined; however, there were also advantages in adopting the 'flow through' approach, which ignores the effects of timing differences and instead accounts only for the tax payable in respect of the period in question.

The examples presented were concerned with the deferred tax position in relation to individual assets only. This section now considers the position in relation to a collection of assets held by a company, and looks at the deferred tax implications.

The accounting issue involved

At the individual asset level, it is possible to estimate, over the lifetime of the asset, the originating and reversing differences, and account for the deferred tax adjustments accordingly. The position with regard to all the assets that a company may acquire is somewhat more complex. Most businesses will tend to replace assets regularly and, over time, inflationary pressures will tend to push up the prices of the replacement assets. In addition, companies are not static and will tend to grow over time.

If the taxation rules in place are such that initial allowances in the year of acquisition are greater than the depreciation being charged then there is the possibility that each year there will be an originating difference and therefore no reversing differences. Moreover, where such circumstances prevail, providing in full for deferred tax will result in the balance on the deferred tax account becoming larger and larger each year with no net reversing differences to reduce that balance.

Following a full provision approach may well cause difficulties when interpreting financial statements. As was noted in Section 1, deferred tax is disclosed separately on the statement of financial position under the heading 'Provision for liabilities'. Consequently, such a classification results in the net assets figure being reduced by a 'liability' that will never crystallize. Moreover, by its inclusion in the statement of financial position, an item that will not be payable in the foreseeable future would appear to be inconsistent with the going concern concept – that is, if the going concern concept applies then investment will continue and therefore originating differences will continue to be created. Only cessation of the company or contraction of its business and reduced investment would result in there being reversals to the provision.

514

Partial provision: a partial solution

In order to avoid the problems caused by providing in full for deferred tax, and the disadvantages caused by following the 'flow through' approach, a partial provision approach could be adopted. As its name suggests, a partial provision falls between no provision for deferred tax at all and full provision. The level of provision provided is that part of the deferred tax liability that is likely to become payable in the future, or to 'crystallize in the foreseeable future'.

This partial provision approach estimates how much of the provision is likely to crystallize into a liability. This crystallization is assumed to happen when the depreciation charge in succeeding years exceeds the capital allowances (i.e. when there are reversing as opposed to originating differences).

Example

Neat plc is calculating the necessary provision for deferred tax using partial provision of the end of Year 5. It has forecast the following information, taking account of expected expenditure, capital allowances and depreciation for the next four years. Corporation tax is expected to remain at 30% throughout the period.

	Year 6	Year 7	Year 8	Year 9
	£000	£000	£000	£000
Capital allowances	1,600	1,750	1,100	2,400
Depreciation	1,400	1,600	1,670	1,000
Net originating differences	(200)	(150)	–	(1,400)
Net reversing differences	–	–	570	–

In this illustration, the depreciation charge exceeds the capital allowances claim in Year 8. It will be in this year, therefore, that the taxable profits will exceed the accounting profits by £570,000. Given that the tax rate in Year 8 is expected to be 30%, the amount of tax involved is 30% of £570,000, which is £171,000.

Consequently, the provision required for deferred tax at the end of Year 8 needs to be £171,000.

The statement of comprehensive income charges and statement of financial position extracts would be as follows:

Statement of comprehensive income extracts

	Year 5	Year 6	Year 7	Year 8
	£	£	£	£
Deferred tax	171,000	–	–	(171,000)

Statement of financial position extracts

	Year 5	Year 6	Year 7	Year 8
	£	£	£	£
Provision for liabilities				
Deferred tax	171,000	171,000	171,000	0

However, it could be argued that to make all the required provision in Year 5 is being excessively prudent. Indeed, this approach is known as the 'most prudent partial provision'.

Based on Neat plc's forecasts, the provision could be built up as follows, taking a cumulative view of the position in future years. Instead of providing for all of the deferred tax balance in Year 5, only an amount that results in the required provision being accumulated by the beginning of Year 8 need be provided for. Given this approach, the net reversing difference in Year 8 is preceded by net originating differences in

Year 7 and Year 6. Therefore, it would be possible to make additional provisions in those two years in order to determine the amount of the provision required in Year 5:

		£000
i.e. Net reversing differences in Year 8		570
Less: future net originating differences		
Year 6	200	
Year 7	150	
		350
		220

Minimum provision necessary at Year 5		£
£220,000 × 30%	=	66,000

Using this minimum partial provision approach results in the following statement of comprehensive income and statement of financial position extracts being reported.

Statement of comprehensive income extracts				
	Year 5	Year 6	Year 7	Year 8
	£	£	£	£
Deferred tax	66,000	60,000	45,000	(171,000)

Statement of financial position extracts				
	Year 5	Year 6	Year 7	Year 8
Provision for liabilities	£	£	£	£
Deferred tax	66,000	126,000	171,000	–

In Year 5, the provision is set to £66,000 and if the forecasts on expenditure, tax and depreciation are met, net originating differences in Year 6 of £60,000 (£200,000 × 30%) and Year 7 of £45,000 (£150,000 × 30%) will result in there being an accumulated provision of £171,000 by the beginning of the year in which the reversal takes place.

In Year 8 there is a net originating difference and no further details available, therefore no further calculations using partial provisioning can be made.

Comparison of methods

Statement of comprehensive income extracts				
	Year 5	Year 6	Year 7	Year 8
	£	£	£	£
Most prudent partial provision				
Deferred tax	171,000	–	–	(171,000)
Minimum partial provision				
Deferred tax	66,000	60,000	45,000	(171,000)

BASIC

INTERMEDIATE

ADVANCED

Statement of financial position extracts				
	Year 5	Year 6	Year 7	Year 8
	£	£	£	£
Most prudent partial provision				
Provision for deferred tax	171,000	171,000	171,000	–
Minimum partial provision				
Provision for deferred tax	66,000	60,000	45,000	(171,000)

As can be seen from the comparison, there are marked variations between the two.

Partial arts

So which one is correct?

Both are!

Unfortunately, both methods are perfectly acceptable. Adopting a partial provision approach to providing for deferred tax necessarily involves making estimates, taking judgements and making assumptions about future investment plans, future tax rates as well as the inherent subjectivity in determining depreciation charges and estimating useful lives, patterns of benefit and residual values. Full provisioning, on the other hand, is made on the basis of the knowledge of what has happened in the past. Regrettably, given the level of potential variation, partial provisioning could also allow for manipulation of deferred tax and, consequently, reported after-tax profits.

Changes in tax rates

The analysis thus far has assumed that tax rates over time have remained the same. Further complications, and choices, arise when the rate of tax changes. There are effectively two rates that could be adopted:

1. the rate ruling at the time the original timing difference occurred; this approach is known as the deferral method

2. the current rate of tax ruling at the date the statement of financial position is prepared; this is known as the liability method.

Deferral method

Under the deferral method, the tax effects of the timing differences that have arisen in each year are calculated. The tax effect is then debited or credited to profit or loss as part of the annual tax charge and the corresponding adjustment made to the deferred tax provision in the statement of financial position. The balances on the deferred tax account are regarded as deferred credits or deferred charges rather than as amounts payable or recoverable, and are not revised on changes in the rate of tax. The deferral method places an emphasis on the statement of comprehensive income charge. In principle, all reversing timing differences in respect of an asset are reversed at the same rate of tax that applied to the originating timing difference on that asset. This approach, known as the 'strict deferral method', inevitably involves extensive recording of dates and rates – particularly when more than one asset is concerned. In practice, as a consequence of the extremely onerous record-keeping requirements, a 'net change method' is used instead, whereby the net amount of all originating and reversing timing differences is calculated. If this produces a net originating difference then the current tax rate will be applied. If, however, there is a net reversing difference then either:

- a first in, first out (FIFO) basis is used, whereby the rate applying to the earlier timing differences making up the deferred tax account is used, or

- an average basis is applied, the rate being arrived at by comparing the balance on the deferred tax account at the beginning of the period with the total of related timing differences.

Liability method

Under the liability method, the tax effects of timing differences are regarded as liabilities for taxes payable in the future. Whenever there is a change in the rate of tax, the balance on the deferred tax account is adjusted to that current rate of tax on accumulated timing differences. The corresponding statement of comprehensive income charge will normally be shown as part of the taxation charge. The liability method places an emphasis on the liability disclosed in the statement of financial position on the basis that the most recent rate of tax is the best available estimate of the tax payable if timing differences reverse. This approach allows calculations to be made in total and therefore it is not necessary to keep such detailed records as would be required for the deferral method.

Example

An asset attracts capital allowances as follows: £200,000 in 2012 and £150,000 in 2013. Depreciation on the asset, calculated using the straight line method is £100,000 per annum. The tax rate is 30% in 2012 and 25% in 2013.

	2012	2013
	£	£
Depreciation charge	100,000	100,000
Tax allowance	200,000	150,000
Timing difference	100,000	50,000

Deferral method

	2012	2013
	£	£
Deferred tax charge	30,000	12,500
Deferred tax balance	30,000	42,500 (100,000 × 30% + 50,000 × 25%)

Liability method

	2012	2013	
	£	£	
Deferred tax charge	30,000	7,500	(25% × 50,000) + (100,000 × (25% − 30%))
Deferred tax balance	30,000	37,500	(25% × 150,000)

BASIC

INTERMEDIATE

ADVANCED

Deferral versus liability method

Advantages of the deferral method:

(a) The deferral method is more in accordance with the accruals (matching) concept in that the tax benefit derived from an originating difference is carried forward to the years of reversal.

(b) It avoids undue fluctuations in the deferred tax charge arising from changes in the tax rate.

Advantages of the liability method:

(a) The figure for deferred tax in the statement of financial position represents the best current estimate of the future liability.

(b) The calculation of the provision is more straightforward.

The remainder of this section considers what other variations between accounting practice and taxation law give rise to timing differences and how these, and other taxes should be accounted for under IAS 12 *Income Taxes*.

9.6 IAS 12 *Income Taxes*

Objective and Scope

The objective of IAS 12 is to prescribe the accounting treatment for income taxes. Income taxes include all domestic and foreign taxes which are based on taxable profits. IAS 12 applies to current tax as well as deferred tax.

Current tax

Current tax is defined in IAS 12 as the amount of income taxes payable (recoverable) in respect of the taxable profit (tax loss) for a period.

Recognition and measurement

The main requirements of IAS 12 with regard to current tax are as follows:

(a) Current tax for the current and prior periods should be recognized as a liability to the extent that it has not been settled, and as an asset to the extent that the amounts already paid exceed the amount due.

(b) The benefit of a tax loss that can be carried back to recover current tax of a prior period should be recognized as an asset.

(c) Current tax assets and liabilities should be measured at the amount expected to be paid to (recovered from) taxation authorities, using the rates that have been enacted or substantially enacted by the end of the reporting period.

(d) Current tax should be recognized as income (in the case of tax recoverable) or an expense and included in profit or loss for the period, except to the extent that the tax arises from a transaction or event which is recognized, in the same or a different period, outside profit or loss, either in other comprehensive income or directly in equity, in which case it should be recognized in other comprehensive income or directly in equity.

(e) Any adjustments necessary so as to reflect over- or under-provisions of current tax in previous periods should be included in the tax expense for the current period and, if material, disclosed separately in the notes.

Example

A company estimates that its current tax liability for the year to 30 June 2013 is £530,000. This figure has been based upon new tax rates which were announced in March 2012 and which are fully expected to be enacted by July 2013. If the new tax rates are not enacted then the tax due would be £550,000. Being a large company for taxation purposes, it has made payments on account during the year to 30 June 2013 of £275,000 towards its current tax liability for the year. In the previous year, the current tax liability was underestimated by £30,000.

Required

Calculate the current tax expense which should be reported in the statement of comprehensive income for the year to 30 June 2013 and the amount of the current tax liability which should be shown in the statement of financial position at that date.

Solution

As the new tax rates are fully expected to be enacted by the end of the reporting period, the current tax for the year is £530,000. However, as there was an underprovision in the previous year of £30,000, this should also be included in the tax expense for the year.

The charge would therefore appear in the statement of comprehensive income as £560,000 made up as follows:

	£
Current tax	530,000
Underprovision in previous year	30,000
Total current tax	560,000

The payments on account of £275,000 reduce the current tax liability shown in the statement of financial position to £255,000 (£530,000 – £275,000).

Deferred tax

IAS 12 applies to deferred tax as well as current tax. In its objectives the standard states that the principal issue in accounting for income taxes is how to account for the current and future tax consequences of the future recovery (settlement) of the carrying amount of assets (liabilities) that are recognized in an entity's statement of financial position. It continues by stating that it is inherent in the recognition of an asset or a liability that the reporting entity expects to recover or settle the carrying amount of that asset or liability. If it is probable that recovery or settlement of that carrying amount will make future tax payments larger (smaller) than they would be if such recovery or settlement were to have no tax consequences, the standard requires an entity to recognize a deferred tax liability (deferred tax asset). The approach is based on the balance sheet (as called in the standard) and focuses on temporary differences.

Temporary differences vs timing differences

Temporary differences are differences between the carrying amount of an asset or liability in the statement of financial position and its tax base. The tax base of an asset or liability is the amount attributed to that asset or liability for tax purposes.

The essential difference between the 'timing difference' approach and the 'temporary difference' approach is that timing differences are differences between taxable profit and accounting profit and therefore the emphasis is on the statement of comprehensive income, whereas the temporary difference approach effectively provides for the tax that would be payable if the statement of financial position were liquidated at book value. What this means is that all timing differences are temporary differences but not all temporary differences are necessarily timing differences. An example of this would be the revaluation of an asset in the financial statements. While a revaluation would give rise to a change in the carrying amount of an asset in the financial statements, this accounting adjustment would have no effect whatsoever on that asset's value for tax purposes. That tax value would remain at its original value and would be unaffected by the adopted treatment in the financial statements.

IAS 12 therefore extends the principles outlined earlier in relation to timing differences and requires that deferred tax be accounted for on the future tax consequences of all items that are included in the financial statements and are dealt with for accounting purposes differently than for tax purposes. If we consider the asset revaluation example noted above, what this means is that as well as the revaluation of the asset being recognized in the accounts, the potential tax which would arise were that asset to be sold at its new revalued amount would also be recognized. In other words, the matching principle is being extended further to include taxation adjustments that are implied by the valuations of the assets and liabilities included within the financial statements. Items whose accounting treatments and taxation treatments differ – income or expenses – by their very nature must be unsettled at the end of the reporting period (otherwise they would be permanent differences), and will therefore appear as assets or liabilities in the statement of financial position. IAS 12 requires that where those assets and liabilities are recognized, then the taxation effects of their inclusion as assets and liabilities must also be recognized.

Recognition and measurement of deferred tax liabilities and deferred tax assets

IAS 12 requires that a deferred tax liability must be recognized for all taxable temporary differences and a deferred tax asset must be recognized for all deductible temporary differences to the extent that it is probable that taxable profits will be available in the future against which these deductible temporary differences can be utilized.

In terms of measurement, deferred tax assets and liabilities must be measured at the tax rates that are expected to apply to the period when the asset is realized or the liability is settled, based on tax rates (and tax laws) that have been enacted or substantively enacted by the end of the reporting period.

The tax base concept

The tax base of an asset or liability is the amount attributed to that asset or liability for tax purposes.

One way of understanding this concept is to consider what amount would appear in the statement of financial position if it was drawn up based on tax rules as opposed to accounting principles.

It follows that, in order to calculate the deferred tax expense (or benefit) and the related deferred tax liability (asset), a company will require to determine the tax values of its assets and liabilities and then compare them with their carrying amounts in the published accounts.

Assets

The tax base of an asset is the amount that will be deductible for tax purposes against any taxable economic benefits that will flow to an entity when it recovers the carrying amount of the asset. If those economic benefits will not be taxable, the tax base of the asset is equal to its carrying amount.

It is assumed that assets in a statement of financial position will generate future income or benefits at least equal to their carrying amounts (otherwise the carrying amounts will be overstated). These benefits might be:

(a) selling the asset e.g. inventories

(b) using the asset e.g. property, plant and equipment

(c) realizing the asset e.g. trade receivables

The issue involved

The issue involved is that the benefits obtained may or may not be taxable. If it is probable that the recovery of the asset will make future tax payments larger (smaller) in future, a deferred tax liability (deferred tax asset) should be recognized. If we consider the examples above, this will help explain this rather complicated concept.

(a) When a company sells inventory, that inventory is a deductible expense in the financial statements but also is deductible when calculating the tax due. In this case, the tax system and the accounting system are in harmony and there is no deferred tax problem. The tax base of the inventory will be the same as the carrying value in the accounts. This means that there is no temporary difference and therefore no deferred tax implications.

(b) As we have seen, the tax allowances given on property, plant and equipment can be quite different from the depreciation charges calculated by a company on that property, plant and equipment. Suppose we have a machine which cost £30,000 and is written down to £25,000. For tax purposes, its written-down value is £18,000. The remaining cost of the machine will be deductible in future periods either as depreciation or through a deduction on disposal. For tax purposes, however, only £18,000 is available to offset against the revenues generated from that asset. In this case while the carrying value of the asset is £25,000, the tax base of the asset is only £18,000. The tax base and the carrying value are different and consequently this gives rise to a deferred tax issue.

(c) Where a company has trade receivables and where the related revenue has already been included in accounting and taxable profit, the ultimate receipt of the monies from the customers will not be taxable i.e. the tax was chargeable on the revenue which gave rise to the trade receivables. In this case, the tax base of the trade receivables will be the same as the carrying value in the accounts. This means that there is no temporary difference and therefore no deferred tax implications.

Liabilities

The tax base of a liability is its carrying amount, less any amount that will be deductible for tax purposes in respect of that liability in future periods.

It is assumed that liabilities will be settled (benefits transferred) at amounts at least equal to their carrying amounts. If it is probable that the settlement of a liability will make future tax payments smaller (larger), a deferred tax asset (liability) should be recognized.

The issue involved

The settlement of a liability has no effect on accounting profit – it is simply a movement on the statement of financial position – and usually has no effect on taxable profit either, and consequently liabilities tend not to cause any deferred tax problems. However, under certain circumstances, the settlement of a liability may trigger a deduction for tax purposes and this will give rise to a deferred tax adjustment. This is why the definition above defines the tax base of a liability in terms of the amount of the deduction that will be allowable for tax purposes when the liability is settled. The following examples help to illustrate this point.

(a) Current liabilities include accrued expenses with a carrying amount of £1,000. The related expense has already been deducted when calculating both accounting and taxable profit. In this case, when the accrued expenses are paid, the payment will not be deductible for tax purposes i.e. it had already been included in arriving at taxable profits when it was accrued. Consequently, the tax base of the accrued expenses will be the same as their carrying amount i.e. £1,000. This means that there is no temporary difference and therefore no deferred tax implications.

(b) Current liabilities include accrued expenses with a carrying amount of £500. The related expense has been include in arriving at accounting profit but will not be deducted for tax purposes until it is paid. In this case, when the accrued expenses are paid the payment will be deductible for tax purposes. Consequently the tax base of the accrued expenses is nil. This means that there is a temporary difference and therefore deferred tax implications.

(c) A loan payable has a carrying amount of £10,000. The repayment of the loan will have no tax consequences. In this case, when the loan is repaid there will be no deduction for tax purposes i.e. it is simply a movement within the statement of financial position. Consequently the tax base of the loan will be the same as its carrying amount i.e. £10,000. This means that there is no temporary difference and therefore no deferred tax implications.

Taxable and deductible temporary differences

Temporary differences can be either taxable temporary differences or deductible temporary differences:

(a) Taxable temporary differences are temporary differences that will result in taxable amounts in determining taxable profit of future periods when the carrying amount of the asset or liability is recovered or settled. Taxable temporary differences give rise to deferred tax liabilities.

(b) Deductible temporary differences are temporary differences that will result in amounts that are deductible in determining taxable profit of future periods when the carrying amount of the asset or liability is recovered or settled. Deductible temporary differences give rise to deferred tax assets.

IAS 12 requires that for each type of temporary difference, the amount of the deferred tax asset or liability recognized in the statement of financial position, and the amount of the deferred tax expense or income recognized in the period, be disclosed separately.

Example – Taxable temporary difference

Tartan plc accrued income from Sodik Inc (a foreign company) of £150,000 as at 31 December 2012. The amount was received during 2013. This income is taxed on a receipts basis and, consequently, Tartan plc is not subject to corporation tax until the income is received in 2013 at which point it will be taxable at 30%.

However, the company has a potential tax liability at 2012 in respect of the accrued income. Indeed, by accruing the income as receivable, Tartan plc is confident of its ultimate receipt. Tartan plc therefore has a liability for the related tax, which will fall due on receipt. This tax is accounted for not as current tax, but as deferred tax.

The journal entry to record this will be:

	£	£
Dr Taxation charge	45,000	
Cr Deferred tax liability		45,000
Being deferred tax on income receivable.		

The effect of this adjustment is that the tax expense in 2012 is set to that level that is implied by including the accrued income within the 31 December 2012 accounts. The extract from Tartan's statement of comprehensive income in respect of this income will show:

Statement of comprehensive income extract 31 December 2012

	£
Income	150,000
Taxation	
Current tax	0
Deferred tax	45,000

In 2013, when the actual tax is paid on the amounts received, the tax expense is reduced by the deferred tax previously accounted for. The distorting effects of the temporary differences are therefore removed and the tax expense reflects that level of charge which is implied by the level of profit. In 2013, the journal entry to reduce the tax expense will be

	£	£
Dr Deferred tax liability	45,000	
Cr Taxation charge		45,000
Being transfer from deferred tax.		

The extract from Tartan's statement of comprehensive income in respect of this income will show:

Statement of comprehensive income extract 31 December 2013

	£
Income	0
Taxation	
Current tax	45,000
Deferred tax	(45,000)

That is, Tartan will account for the actual tax but this will be reduced by the transfer from deferred tax which was accounted for in the previous year when the income was recognized.

Example – deductible temporary difference

A company has a pension liability of £100,000 recognized in its statement of financial position at the year end. Under UK tax rules, pension contributions are deducted for tax purposes when they are paid.

This company will require to make the appropriate pension contributions to clear the liability in future years by increasing its contributions. This will result in future years' tax liabilities being reduced as the contributions are paid and the taxable profits reduced. This future tax relief will be shown in the accounts now as a deferred tax asset (i.e. £100,000 × 30% = £30,000).

The journal entry to record this will be:

		£	£
Dr	Deferred tax liability	30,000	
	Cr Deferred tax charge		30,000
Being deferred tax asset on pension liability.			

As before, the effect of this adjustment is that the tax expense is set to that level that is implied by having the accrued pension liability within the accounts i.e. the actual tax charge is higher than would be expected given the accounting profit but this is accordingly reduced by the transfer to the deferred tax asset account. In future years when the pension contributions are paid, the deferred tax asset account will be credited and the taxation expense debited with the increased charge.

Progress Point 9.3

Norwood plc accrued income from a foreign company of £100,000 at 31 December 2012 – the income being received in February 2013. This income is taxable on receipt. Given a corporation tax rate of 30%, calculate and record any deferred tax asset or liability arising.

Solution

The income would not be subject to corporation tax until the year to 31 December 2013 (i.e. the year of receipt). Its tax effect would not therefore be recognized in the corporation tax charge for the year to 31 December 2012. However, assuming that the asset (i.e. the accrued income) will generate income at least equal to its carrying amount, the asset will make future tax payments higher (i.e. in the year to 31 December 2013). A deferred tax liability at 31 December 2012 should therefore be created of £100,000 × 30%, as follows:

Dr	Deferred tax expense	£30,000	
	Cr Deferred tax liability		£30,000
Being deferred tax on income receivable.			

This liability will be reversed in the year to 31 December 2013, when the income is received and subject to corporation tax.

The UK position

As was noted in the introduction to this chapter, tax rates and rules can differ year on year and between jurisdictions. In order to further illustrate the issues, some temporary differences which arise under the

UK system of taxation are examined. The following are examples of temporary differences under current UK tax legislation.

Tangible non-current assets held at cost and on which capital allowances are available

The temporary difference equals:

		£
Carrying amount	NBV (net book value)	X
Tax base	Tax WDV (written down value)	X
Temporary difference		X

If NBV > Tax WDV = deferred tax liability.
If NBV < Tax WDV = deferred tax asset.

Tangible non-current assets held at value

The same principles apply as those for assets held at cost, except net book value is based on revalued figures.

Note that where there is a revaluation, deferred tax is provided even if there is no intention to sell the asset. If such assets were sold at the revalued amount then a profit would arise that could be subject to tax. Although no actual tax is payable in respect of the upward revaluation, IAS 12 requires that the implicitly deferred tax be accounted for. The deferred tax on the revaluation gain is recognized in other comprehensive income rather than in profit or loss – the reason being that as the revaluation itself is recognized in other comprehensive income, the related tax effects are also recognized in other comprehensive income.

The journal entry to record this will be:

> Dr   Income tax (other comprehensive income)
>   Cr   Deferred tax liability
> Being deferred tax on revalued assets.

Accrued income

There are no deferred tax consequences unless the income is taxed when received (i.e. on a cash basis).
If income is taxed on a cash basis, the temporary difference equals:

Carrying amount (accrued income)	X
Tax base	0
Taxable temporary difference	X

Note that while, for accounting purposes, the accrued income has been included in arriving at accounting profits, for tax purposes the income will be taxed when received; in other words, in the financial statements for the following year. As far as the tax authorities are concerned, the tax base will be nil. In the following year, the position will be reversed and the tax base will take on the value of the amount received while the carrying value in the statement of financial position will be nil (i.e. it has now been received).

Example

Ferdz provided for deferred tax of £60,000 in respect of accrued income receivable of £200,000 in the year to 31 December 2012. This income was received in February 2013 and is subject to tax on receipt. In the financial statements to 31 December 2013, the credit would be released to the tax expense in the statement of comprehensive income.

i.e. Carrying value (2013)	0	
Tax base	200,000	
Temporary difference	(200,000)	
Deferred tax @ 30%	£60,000	Dr

The journal entry will be:

	£	£
Dr Deferred tax liability	60,000	
Cr Deferred tax income		60,000
Being reversal of deferred tax liability.		

The effect of this is that the tax expense in 2012 is set to that level that is implied by including the accrued income within those financial statements. And in 2013, when the actual tax is paid on the amounts received, the tax expense is reduced by the deferred tax previously accounted for. The distorting effects of the temporary differences are therefore removed and the tax expense reflects that level of charge which is implied by the level of profit.

Pension asset

In respect of defined benefit plans (i.e. plans that specify the amounts payable to pensioners on retirement), a pension asset may be recognized in the statement of financial position. A pension asset represents a recognized surplus of invested funds, which means that the company may pay reduced contributions in the future or may even receive a refund of contributions paid. Consequently, by recognizing the pension asset now, the future tax consequences of this recognition, i.e. lower future pension payments and therefore higher taxable profits and higher tax, also have to be recognized. This will result in a deferred tax liability calculated as follows:

Carrying amount: pension asset	X
Less: tax base	0
Taxable temporary difference	X

In this instance the tax base is nil as the tax authorities will not recognize the surplus until the refund or reduced contribution takes place. (Remember that tax relief for pension premiums is granted when the premium is paid.)

Provisions

Certain provisions are not allowable deductions for tax purposes. While specific bad debt provisions are acceptable deductions, general bad debt provisions are not allowable until the debt is specifically provided for or written off. General bad debt provisions can therefore give rise to temporary differences.

The deductible temporary difference is calculated as follows:

	£
Carrying amount: general bad debt provision	X
Tax base	0
Deductible temporary difference	X

This gives rise to a deferred tax asset as the tax relief in respect of the provision will be receivable in the future when the bad debts are either specifically provided for or written off. The journal entry will be:

Dr Deferred tax asset
    Cr Deferred tax income
Being deferred tax asset on provisions.

Example

Included in arriving at the accounting profit of £900,000 of Emerson for the year to 31 December 2012 is a general bad debt provision of £50,000. The extract tax expense entries are as follows:

	£	£
Profit before tax		900,000
Current tax	285,000	
Deferred tax	(15,000)	
Total tax expense		270,000
Profit after tax		630,000

Note that the general bad debt provision is not deductible for tax purposes and the current tax charge is calculated as follows (£900,000 + £50,000 = £950,000 × 30% = £285,000). The deferred tax credit is calculated as follows (£50,000 × 30% = £15,000), with the corresponding debit being shown as a deferred tax asset.

Suppose that in the year to 31 December 2013, the customer's debts, which gave rise to the general provision of £50,000, are now written off. Assuming Emerson had accounting profits of £800,000, the extract tax expense entries would be as follows:

	£	£
Profit before tax		800,000
Current tax	225,000	
Deferred tax	15,000	
Total tax expense		240,000
Profit after tax		560,000

Note that the bad debts written off would now be deductible for tax purposes and the current tax charge would be calculated as follows (£800,000 − £50,000 = £750,000 × 30% = £225,000). The deferred tax asset created at 31 December 2012 would now be reversed in the year to 31 December 2013.

As can be seen, for each of the years concerned, the total tax expense becomes that charge which is expected or implied by the level of profits and the prevailing tax rate. In the year to 2012, the tax expense is reduced – a lower tax charge is expected given the level of profits but the non-deductibility of the general bad debt provision results in a higher current tax charge. In the year to 2013, the tax expense is increased – a higher tax charge is expected given the level of profits, however the actual bad debts written off now become tax deductible expenses and result in there being a lower current tax charge than the profits would imply.

Pension liability

A pension liability for a defined benefit plan relates to a recognized deficit. This means that the fund has insufficient investments to meet its future pension obligations and will require additional contributions in the future in order to rectify the situation. As pension contributions are deductible when they are paid, the recognition of the pension deficit now gives corresponding rise to a deferred tax asset (i.e. the future tax relief that will result from the future contributions paid).

The deductible temporary difference is calculated as follows:

Carrying amount: pension liability	X
Tax base: nil	0
Deductible temporary difference	X

Progress Point 9.4

Majestic plc has the following items in its statement of financial position at 31 March 2013:

	£
Tangible non-current assets	
Buildings	2,200,000
Plant and machinery	1,300,000
Current assets	
Inventories	280,000
Trade receivables	505,000
Prepayments and accrued income	85,000
Bank	110,000
Pension asset	200,000

Additional information

1. The buildings have a tax written-down value of £1,590,000. They were revalued from their net book value of £1,800,000 to £2,200,000 on 31 March 2013.
2. Plant and machinery has a tax written-down value of £410,000.
3. Trade receivables are stated net of bad debts of £8,000, a specific provision of £5,000 and a general provision of £4,500.
4. Prepayments and accrued income include accrued foreign interest receivable of £40,000. This interest will be taxed on receipt.

5. At 31 March 2012, Majestic plc had a deferred tax liability of £95,000, which related solely to accelerated capital allowances.

Required

Calculate, assuming a corporation tax rate of 30%, the required deferred tax balance at 31 March 2013. Prepare the appropriate journal entry at 31 March 2013 to record deferred tax for the year and show the amount of deferred tax assets and liabilities recognized in the statement of financial position in respect of each type of temporary difference identified.

Solution

Step 1

The first stage in the calculation is to determine the temporary differences:

	Carrying amount	Tax base	Taxable/(deductible) temporary differences
	£	£	£
Non-current assets			
Buildings	2,200,000	1,590,000	610,000
Plant and machinery	1,300,000	410,000	890,000
Current assets			
Inventories	280,000	280,000	–
Trade receivables	505,000	509,500	(4,500)
Prepayments	45,000	45,000	–
Accrued income	40,000	–	40,000
Bank	110,000	110,000	–
Pension asset	200,000	–	200,000
			1,735,500

Note that inventories, prepayments and bank have a tax base equal to the carrying amount. Trade receivables have been adjusted for the non-deductible general provision; accrued income has a tax base of nil as it will not be taxed until received; the pension asset represents a surplus of funds, indicating that future pension contributions will be lower – its tax base is therefore nil.

Step 2

Calculate the deferred tax liability at 31 March 2013 as follows:

Temporary differences × tax rate	
1,735,500 × 30% =	£520,650
Deferred tax liability at 31 March 2012	£95,000
∴ Increase required	£425,650

Step 3

Prepare journal.

NB: the amount of tax relating to the revaluation should be charged to other comprehensive income.

That is:

$$(2,200,000 - 1,800,000) \times 30\% = £120,000$$

Journal:

		£	£
Dr	Deferred tax expense (other comprehensive income)	120,000	
Dr	Deferred tax expense (profit or loss)	305,650	
Cr	Deferred tax liability		425,650
Being increase in deferred tax liability for the year.			

Step 4

The detail of the temporary differences of deferred tax is as follows:

	Accelerated capital allowances	Revaluation	Overseas dividends	Pension asset	Total liabilities	Assets: bad debt provn
	£	£	£	£	£	£
At 31/3/12	(95,000)				(95,000)	
(Charged) to profit or loss	(235,000)[1]		(12,000)[2]	(60,000)[3]	(307,000)	
Credited to profit or loss						1,350[4]
Charged to other comprehensive income		(120,000)			(120,000)	
	(330,000)	(120,000)	(12,000)	(60,000)	(522,000)	1,350
				Net	£520,650	

Notes

1 Buildings: (1,800,000 – 1,590,000) = 210,000
   Plant and machinery (1,300,000 – 410,000) = 890,000
   1,100,000 × 30% = 330,000
   Balance at 31 March 2012 95,000
   Increase in deferred tax 235,000

2 Overseas interest:
   40,000 × 30% = £12,000

3 Pension asset:
   £200,000 × 30% £60,000

4 Bad debt provision:
   £4,500 × 30% = £1,350

Deferred tax assets: tax losses

So far in this chapter, our discussion of deferred tax assets has centred on when, as a result of temporary differences, the tax benefits of a transaction are deferred to a future period rather than being recognized in the current period.

There are, however, specific business situations that may also give rise to the creation of deferred tax assets. Such situations arise when the company in question has made a tax loss.

Tax losses may be used to reduce future taxable profits and therefore reduce future tax payable.

IAS 12 requires that a deferred tax asset in respect of the carry forward of unused tax losses should only be to the extent that it is possible that future taxable profits will be available against which the unused tax losses can be used. This means that deferred tax assets may be recognized on a partial basis.

Example

A company has calculated deferred tax assets of £1,000,000 at 31 March 2013, resulting from trading losses incurred in the year. Taxable profits for the year to 31 March 2014 are estimated at £200,000; however due to market uncertainties, no profits can be anticipated in the following year to 31 March 2015.

Given a tax rate of 30%, the amount of deferred tax asset that should be recognized is £60,000 (i.e. 30% × £200,000). The deferred tax asset would be set to the level of the future tax liability, which would be implied from the next year's profit of £200,000.

Suppose, however, that in the year to 2015, and for the foreseeable future, the company is expected to make significant profits. In this event, the restriction on the amount of deferred tax asset to be created would be lifted and the company would account for the tax effects of the full deferred tax assets of £1,000,000.

As the above example illustrates, the calculation may be very subjective and can only ever be an estimate – an estimate based on a forecast of future profitability. IAS 12 requires an enterprise to assess, at the end of each reporting period, unrecognized deferred tax assets. Consequently, where tax losses exist that previously were unrecognized as deferred tax assets, they may subsequently be recognized to the extent that it has become probable that future taxable profit will allow the deferred tax asset to be recovered.

For example, an improvement in trading conditions may make it more probable that the enterprise will make sufficient taxable profit in the future for the deferred tax asset.

Other factors to consider include:

- whether the enterprise has sufficient taxable temporary differences that will result in taxable amounts against which the losses/credits can be used
- whether it is probable that the enterprise will have taxable profits before the losses/credits expire
- whether the unused tax losses result from identifiable causes that are unlikely to recur
- whether tax planning opportunities are available that will create taxable profits against which the losses/credits can be used.

Progress Point 9.5

At 31 March 2013, Obsidian plc had calculated the following amounts in respect of deferred tax:

	2013	2012
	£000	£000
Accelerated capital allowances	(964)	(993)
Revaluations	(430)	(360)
	(1,394)	(1,353)

In addition, following an unexpected change in the market in the year to 31 March 2012, Obsidian had recognized unrelieved trading losses of £1,500,000, which were expected to be able to be used against future taxable profits and temporary difference reversals. During the year to 31 March 2013, Obsidian made a trading profit (before loss relief) of £600,000, and £600,000 of the available trading losses will be utilized to eliminate the taxable profits.

At 31 March 2013, it is estimated that only £700,000 of the remaining trading losses are useable in the foreseeable future as part of the trade has been discontinued. Deferred tax has been calculated at 30%.

Required

Prepare the statement of financial position note for deferred tax for the year to 31 March 2013.

Solution

The first step in preparing the statement of financial position note is to ascertain the balances at 31 March 2012 (i.e. the opening balance for the year to 31 March 2013). In terms of the deferred tax liability balances, these are as outlined in the example (i.e. £993,000 in respect of accelerated capital allowances and £360,000 in respect of revaluations).

The deferred tax asset at 31 March 2012 is calculated as follows: Obsidian has unrelieved trading losses of £1,500,000 and *at that time* it believed that these would be able to be used against future profits. The deferred tax asset recognized is therefore £1,500,000 × 30% (i.e. £450,000).

At 31 March 2013, the closing deferred tax liability balances have been given in the example and consequently the differences need only be accounted for in the disclosure note.

The deferred tax asset to be recognized *at 31 March 2013* is calculated as follows: Obsidian has estimated that only £700,000 of the unrelieved losses will be able to be used against future profits. The deferred tax asset recognized at this time will be £700,000 × 30% = £210,000. Again, the change will be disclosed in the note.

Deferred tax liability and asset:				
	Liability Accelerated capital allowances	Revaluations	Total	Asset Unrelieved trading losses
	£000	£000	£000	£000
At 31 March 2012 (charged)/ credited to profit or loss	(993)	(360)	(1,353)	450
Charged to other comprehensive income		(70)	(70)	
At 31 March 2013	(964)	(430)	(1,394)	210

Note that the charge to profit or loss in respect of unrelieved trading losses of £240,000 is made up of:

(a) the charge resulting from the use of the trading losses in the year of £600,000	£
i.e. £600,000 × 30%	= 180,000
(b) the charge resulting from the write-off of the losses which are now deemed to be unrelievable of £200,000	
i.e. (£1,500,000 − 600,000 − 700,000) × 30%	= 60,000
	240,000

9.7 Presentation

The tax expense (or income) related to profit or loss from ordinary activities should be presented as part of profit or loss in the statement of comprehensive income.

For transactions and other events recognized outside profit or loss i.e. either in other comprehensive income or directly in equity, any related tax effects are also recognized outside profit or loss either in other comprehensive income or directly in equity, respectively.

Offset of current tax assets and liabilities

An entity should offset current tax assets and current tax liabilities if, and only if, the entity:

(a) has a legally enforceable right to set off the recognized amounts; and

(b) intends either to settle on a net basis, or to realize the asset and settle the liability simultaneously.

The standard explains that an entity normally has a legally enforceable right to set off current tax assets against current tax liabilities when they relate to taxes levied by the same tax authority, and that authority permits the entity to make or receive a single net payment.

Offset of deferred tax assets and liabilities

An entity should offset deferred tax assets and deferred tax liabilities if, and only if:

(a) the entity has a legally enforceable right to set off current tax assets against current tax liabilities; and

(b) the deferred tax assets and the deferred tax liabilities relate to income taxes levied by the same tax authority on either:

 (i) the same taxable entity; or

 (ii) different taxable entities which intend either to settle current tax liabilities and assets on a net basis, or to realize the assets and settle the liabilities simultaneously, in each future period in which significant amounts of deferred tax liabilities or assets are expected to be settled or recovered.

What this means in practice is that generally, deferred tax assets and liabilities arising in the same legal entity can be offset. However, when, for example, the taxable entity has capital losses carried forward that can only be used to reduce capital gains, those losses can only be offset against deferred tax liabilities to the extent that recognized deferred tax liabilities arise from unrealized capital gains.

9.8 Disclosure

The disclosure requirements in IAS 12 are extensive and the standard must be read in detail.

Statement of comprehensive income

The major components of tax expense (income) should be disclosed separately, including:

- current tax expense (income)
- any adjustments recognized in the period for current tax of prior periods;
- the amount of deferred tax expense (income) relating to the origination and reversal of temporary differences;
- the amount of the benefit arising from a previously unrecognized tax loss, tax credit or temporary difference of a prior period that is used to reduce current tax expense;
- the amount of the benefit from a previously unrecognized tax loss, tax credit or temporary difference of a prior period that is used to reduce deferred tax expense;

■ an explanation of the relationship between the tax expense (income) and accounting profit in either or both of the following forms:

- a numerical reconciliation between tax expense (income) and the product of accounting profit multiplied by the applicable tax rate(s), disclosing also the basis on which the applicable tax rate(s) is (are) computed; or

- a numerical reconciliation between the average effective tax rate (being the tax expense (income) divided by the accounting profit) and the applicable tax rate, disclosing also the basis on which the applicable tax rate is computed.

The purpose of this is so that users can see whether the tax charge in a particular year is unusual and to understand significant factors that could affect accounts in the future. An example of the first of these methods is as follows.

Example

A company has an accounting profit before tax of £5,000,000. Of these profits, £4,000,000 are taxable at the UK rate of 30% and £1,000,000 are earned overseas and taxed at a local rate of 42%. Included in the £4,000,000 UK-based profits are disallowable expenses of £120,000 and non-chargeable income of £25,000.

The actual tax charge is £1,648,500.

Required

Prepare a tax reconciliation.

Solution

	£
Accounting profit	5,000,000
Tax at the UK rate of 30%	1,500,000
Tax effect of disallowable items (£120,000 × 30%)	36,000
Tax effect of non-chargeable items (£25,000 × 30%)	(7,500)
Effect of higher tax rates on overseas income (£1,000,000 × (42% − 30%))	120,000
Actual tax charge	1,648,500

Statement of financial position

The following should also be disclosed separately:

■ For each type of temporary difference, and each type of unused tax losses and unused tax credits:

- the amount of the deferred tax assets and liabilities recognized in the statement of financial position for each period presented;

- the amount of the deferred tax income or expense recognized in profit or loss if this is not apparent from the changes in the amounts recognized in the statement of financial position.

■ The amount (and expiry date, if any) of deductible temporary differences, unused tax losses, and unused tax credits for which no deferred tax asset is recognized in the statement of financial position.

■ When an entity presents current and non-current assets, and current and non-current liabilities, as separate classifications in its statement of financial position, it should not classify deferred tax assets (liabilities) as current assets (liabilities).

Other disclosure requirements

Other disclosure requirements include:

- The aggregate current and deferred tax relating to items that are charged or credited directly to equity.
- The amount of income tax relating to each component of other comprehensive income i.e. revaluation surplus, foreign exchange reserve.
- Deferred tax should be distinguished from current tax.
- When changes in tax rates or tax laws are enacted or announced after the reporting period, any significant impact on the entity's current and deferred tax assets and liabilities.

Disclosure in practice

As noted above, the disclosure requirements in respect of IAS 12 *Income Taxes* are extensive, and disclosures can be found within the accounting policies, statement of comprehensive income, statement of financial position, and the notes to the accounts.

Taxation

Logica's policy note on taxation details the rates at which tax is recognized, and its policies on providing for deferred tax assets and liabilities. Note that Logica does not discount deferred tax liabilities.

Taxation

Current tax is recognised based on the amounts expected to be paid or recovered under the tax rates and laws that have been enacted or substantively enacted at the end of the reporting period.

Deferred tax is provided in full on temporary differences that arise between the carrying amounts of assets and liabilities for financial reporting purposes and their corresponding tax bases. Deferred tax is recorded on all temporary differences except in respect of investments in subsidiaries and joint ventures where the timing of the reversal of the temporary difference is controlled by the Group and it is probable that it will not reverse in the foreseeable future.

Deferred tax assets are recognised to the extent that it is probable that future taxable profits will be available against which the asset can be offset.

Deferred tax is measured on an undiscounted basis using the tax rates and laws that have been enacted or substantively enacted at the end of the reporting period.

Current and deferred taxes are recognised in the statement of comprehensive income, except when the tax relates to items charged or credited directly to equity, in which case the tax is also dealt with directly in equity.

Source: Logica (2011), p. 99

Figure 9.1 Logica: income statement extract		
Profit before tax	32.7	192.9
Taxation	(5.5)	(40.8)
Net profit for the year	27.2	152.1
Source: Logica (2011), p. 92		

The effective tax rate on operations for the year, before the share of post-tax profits from associates, exceptional items and amortisation of intangible assets initially recognised on acquisition, was 23% (2010: 23%), of which a charge of £15.7 million (2010: £14.5 million) related to the UK.

The effective tax rate on exceptional items was 0% (2010: 23.5%) and the effective tax rate on amortisation of intangible assets initially recognised on acquisition was 28.8% (2010: 28.9%).

Figure 9.2 Logica: taxation note

	2011 £'m	2010 £'m
Current tax:		
UK corporation tax	10.3	15.7
Overseas tax	35.7	34.5
	46.0	50.2
Deferred tax:		
UK corporation tax	5.4	(1.2)
Overseas tax	(45.9)	(8.2)
	(40.5)	(9.4)
	5.5	40.8

Source: Logica (2011), p. 108

The tax charge from operations is lower than the standard rate of corporation tax in the UK applied to profit before tax. The differences are explained below.

Figure 9.3 Logica: analysis of taxation charge

	2011 £'m	2010 £'m
Profit before tax	32.7	192.9
Less: share of post-tax profits from associates	(1.0)	(0.6)
Profit before tax excluding share of post-tax profits from associates	31.7	192.3
Tax at the UK corporation tax rate of 26.5% (2010: 28.0%)	8.4	53.8
Adjustments in respect of previous years	8.7	(12.3)
Adjustment in respect of foreign tax rates	16.9	11.8
Tax loss utillzation	(21.5)	(7.1)
Income not subject to tax	(9.4)	(16.5)
Deferred tax assets not recognised	2.4	11.1
Tax charge	5.5	40.8

The current tax related to exceptional items for the year ended 31 December 2011 was £nil (2010: tax credit £0.4 million).

In addition to the changes in rates of Corporation tax disclosed above, a number of further changes to the UK Corporation tax system were announced in the March 2011 UK Budget Statement. Further reductions to the main rate are proposed to reduce the rate by 1% per annum to 23% by 1 April 2014. These further changes had not been substantively enacted at the balance sheet date and, therefore, are not included in these financial statements.

Source: Logica (2011), p. 109

The tax charge for the year to 31 December 2011 as recognized in Logica's statement of comprehensive income is £5.5 million. The accompanying note to the statement of comprehensive income charge shows how this tax charge is made up and there is also a reconciliation of the tax charge to the accounting profit.

BASIC

INTERMEDIATE

ADVANCED

Figure 9.4 Logica: deferred tax disclosure note

	Property, plant and equipment £'m	Intangible assets £'m	Retirement benefits £'m	Tax losses £'m	Other £'m	Total £'m
At 1 January 2010	7.2	(50.0)	9.4	28.0	4.9	(0.5)
(Charge)/credit to profit or loss for the year	1.3	16.2	(0.8)	(8.9)	1.6	9.4
Credit to equity	–	–	0.6	–	–	0.6
Acquisition of subsidiaries	–	–	–	–	(0.1)	(0.1)
Exchange differences	0.2	(1.4)	0.2	0.7	0.1	(0.2)
At 1 January 2011	8.7	(35.2)	9.4	19.8	6.5	9.2
(Charge)/credit to profit or loss for the year	(1.7)	12.1	(1.4)	26.5	5.0	40.5
Charge to equity	–	–	(7.3)	–	–	(7.3)
Acquisition of subsidiaries	–	(3.4)	–	–	(0.7)	(4.1)
Exchange differences	(0.2)	0.8	(0.2)	(0.4)	(0.3)	(0.3)
At 31 December 2011	6.8	(25.7)	0.5	45.9	10.5	38.0

Deferred tax assets and liabilities are offset where there is a legally enforceable right of offset and the Group intends to settle the balances on a net basis. An analysis of the deferred tax balances for financial reporting purposes is shown in the table below:

Figure 9.5 Logica: analysis of deferred tax balances

	2011 £'m	2010 £'m
Deferred tax assets	84.0	70.3
Deferred tax liabilities	(46.0)	(61.1)
	38.0	9.2

Source: Logica (2011), p. 128

The deferred tax provisions note discloses the amount of deferred tax assets and liabilities recognized in the statement of financial position for each type of temporary difference and in respect of unused tax losses. Note that Logica has netted off its deferred tax assets and liabilities. This is because it intends to settle the balances on a net basis.

9.9 Discounting

In some countries (e.g. the Netherlands, the UK) companies are allowed under national accounting rules to discount their deferred tax balances.

A major conceptual issue is whether the objective of discounting deferred tax is to reflect the fair value of deferred tax (for which discounting can be seen as a surrogate) or to reflect the time value of money. If the objective is to reflect the time value of money then problems can arise in determining the future cash flows to be discounted, and the discount rate to be used.

With regard to future cash flows, some argue that it is unrealistic to discount the deferred tax inherent in timing differences at the end of the reporting period since it may well be that these timing differences have no effect on tax cash flows in the year that they reverse. For example, future investment and the related capital allowances may postpone the deferred tax liability.

Another view is that discounting may give rise to double counting since the purchase price of an asset already reflects the net present value of future income earned from the asset. If depreciation is already discounted, then it is not appropriate to discount further the deferred tax arising from it.

IAS 12 does not permit the discounting of deferred tax balances, with one exception. It allows discounting of deferred tax where it relates to a pre-tax amount that is itself discounted – that is, the application of a tax rate to an already discounted item will automatically result in a deferred tax charge that is discounted.

Section summary

Three approaches to accounting for the tax effects of timing differences arising from accelerated capital allowances have been put forward:

1. the flow through approach
2. the full deferral approach
3. the partial deferral approach.

Two further methods have been put forward to calculate a deferred tax balance namely the liability method and the deferral method. The requirements of IAS 12 have been looked at in detail together with the concepts of the tax base and temporary differences.

Section 3: Advanced Aspects

9.10 Deferred tax: a critical appraisal

Many of the ideas introduced so far in this chapter have, by the very complexity of their nature, been relatively advanced. This section and the remainder of the chapter take an overview of the concepts and arguments put forward earlier and make a critical appraisal of the IAS 12 approach and the deferred tax issue in general.

The temporary difference approach – the conceptual arguments

Timing differences were explained and illustrated in the introductory section to this chapter. The timing difference approach provides for the reversal of cumulative differences between the statement of comprehensive income and the tax computation. Under this approach deferred tax is calculated not as a liability, but is more in the nature of deferred income or expenditure and utilized to correct the distorting effects timing differences can create in terms of the annual tax charge. On the other hand, the temporary difference approach effectively provides for the tax that would be payable if the statement of financial position were to be liquidated at book value. The reason for this temporary difference approach and the shift of emphasis from the statement of comprehensive income to the statement of financial position was as a result of the IASB's Conceptual Framework requirement that all items in the statement of financial position, other than shareholder's equity, must be either assets or liabilities as defined in the Conceptual Framework.

The IASB believes that the temporary difference approach gives rise to assets and liabilities as defined in its Conceptual Framework for the following reasons. It is inherent in the recognition of an asset or liability that a reporting entity expects to recover or settle the carrying amount of that asset or liability. If it is probable that recovery or settlement of that carrying amount will make future tax payments larger (smaller) than they would be if such recovery or settlement were to have no tax consequences, then to ignore these tax consequences would be to contradict the accounting assumption inherent in the statement of financial position that the reported amounts of assets and liabilities will be recovered or settled. In other words, if the tax effects are ignored, then the amounts actually recovered or settled could be different from their carrying amounts.

It must be questioned, however, whether this is a valid argument to put forward. As noted above, the temporary difference approach provides for the tax that would be payable if the statement of financial position were to be liquidated at book value. The Conceptual Framework states that financial statements are normally prepared on a going concern basis and that the reporting entity will continue for the foreseeable future. Consequently, to provide for the tax consequence of a transaction which would *only* happen were the entity to be liquidated would appear to contradict this fundamental assumption underlying the preparation of the financial statements. Moreover, to include deferred tax as a liability would appear to be contradicting the Conceptual Framework's own definition of a liability (i.e. a present obligation arising from a past event). The only liability that actually exists is the one due to the tax authorities i.e. current tax.

A further issue arises with regard to recovery of an asset. While the temporary difference approach recognizes as a liability the tax cost of the recovery of an asset, it nevertheless omits to address the many other expenses that are often incurred in order to recover the carrying value of an asset. Expenses such as rent, rates, salaries, etc. may also be incurred in the recovery process. If an asset such as inventory is considered, and if the rationale of the temporary difference approach is carried to its logical conclusion, then these costs should be recognized as liabilities as well. Such costs are just as certain to arise as the tax but they are clearly not liabilities at the end of the reporting period. However, if these are not recognized as they do not meet the recognition criteria of liabilities as defined in the Conceptual Framework, then, under the temporary difference approach, neither is deferred tax.

It could be argued that the only reason the temporary difference approach has been adopted is simply because deferred tax accounting has been generally accepted accounting practice for a number of years. That is, had it not already been accepted practice, it is extremely unlikely that it would ever have been regarded as being a requirement to fulfil the Conceptual Framework's recognition criteria of an asset or a liability.

Tax bases

Practical issues can also arise when calculating the tax base of assets or liabilities. The tax base is defined as the amount attributed to that item for tax purposes. While in some cases, for example, the tax written down value of an asset, the amount is quite obvious, in other cases it is often far less so. A good example of this is a bank loan – neither the receipt nor settlement of which has any tax consequences. Such an item is therefore a 'nothing' for tax purposes and this would suggest that its tax base should be nil.

However, that would mean that a deferred tax asset would be provided for on the carrying amount of the loan and that would clearly not be correct i.e. carrying amount – tax base = temporary difference. The temporary difference must be nil and in order to achieve that, its tax base must be the same as its carrying amount. IAS 12 addresses this issue by providing that in the case of:

(a) an asset the recovery of which does not give rise to taxable income; and

(b) a liability the settlement of which is not deductible for tax purposes, the tax base is to be taken as being the carrying amount. That is, there is no temporary difference and therefore no deferred tax.

It could be argued therefore that the tax base definition in IAS 12 has simply been expanded so that it achieves the correct result. If an item is not relevant for tax purposes then its tax base would be more obviously nil than its carrying amount. IAS 12 clearly recognizes that this problem exists and states that 'where the tax base of an asset or liability is not immediately apparent, it is helpful to consider the fundamental principle upon which this Standard is based: that an entity should, with certain limited exceptions, recognize a deferred tax liability (asset) whenever recovery or settlement of the carrying amount of an asset or liability would make future tax payments larger (smaller) than they would be if such recovery or settlement were to have no tax consequences'. Although not formally stating this, it could be interpreted as saying that the tax base of an item is whatever it needs to be in order to end up with the correct deferred tax amount!

All this centres upon the fact that the temporary difference approach focuses on assets and liabilities while in reality tax is charged on gains and losses. By adopting a balance sheet approach rather than an income statement approach, the relevant 'legs' of the double entry are being ignored. It is income and expenses that give rise to profits and tax and therefore it is the income statement 'legs' of the double entry that are relevant. The origination and settlement of a loan have no impact on the income statement and therefore would not give rise to any temporary differences – regardless of the wording of the standard. As has been illustrated above, a balance sheet approach can very easily lead to confusion.

Deferred tax in general

As we have noted above, deferred tax is not a liability. It is not, as is stated in the Conceptual Framework, a 'present obligation' of an enterprise, and consequently it could be argued that deferred tax should not appear at all in the financial statements. Moreover, it could be argued that only the actual amount of tax payable by an enterprise should be incorporated within the financial statements. This would avoid any confusion over what the taxation charge represents and the potential to mislead users with tax charges that bear little resemblance to actual tax payable i.e. the tax disclosed would be that tax that was actually payable – not the tax that would have been payable had the adjustments required by taxation law not occurred. Furthermore, taxation rules are quite separate and distinct from accounting standards requirements. Tax is calculated on taxable income, not accounting income, and it could be argued that there is no requirement for the tax charge to bear any relationship to reported income.

Additional information could be made available in the notes to the accounts, which would explain the difference between the actual tax payable and the expected tax charge based on the operating results.

We have seen, however, the distorting effects that temporary differences can have on an enterprise's taxation charges. In times of enhanced taxation allowances, which may be to encourage investment in non-current assets, an actual tax charge can be significantly lower than an implied tax charge based on the level of profit. This in turn, if no deferred tax adjustments are made, will give rise to an increased after-tax profit, which in turn may result in pressure from shareholders for the enterprise to pay dividends. Paradoxically, given that the investment in the assets giving rise to the tax allowances may have used up the enterprise's cash reserves, such shareholder pressure comes at a time when the enterprise may have little or no cash reserves left. The ability, therefore, to smooth out the distortions can be seen as desirable.

But is income smoothing desirable?

Is this ability by preparers of financial statements to dramatically alter an overall taxation charge by the use of a deferred tax charge desirable? Financial statements should be free from bias and objective – however, as we have seen, the very nature of the deferred tax calculation and the inherent subjectivity within opens to question the effectiveness of the deferred tax charge in meeting this reporting requirement.

However, one of the most fundamental of accounting concepts is that financial statements are prepared on the accruals basis of accounting. The use of deferred tax adjustments effectively takes accrual accounting to the maximum possible degree by accounting for the taxation implications of all temporary differences. For example, if a statement of financial position includes an asset at a revalued amount then it seems perfectly plausible to argue that the implicit taxation arising on this future economic benefit should be provided for at the same time.

BASIC

INTERMEDIATE

ADVANCED

Should deferred tax be provided for?

There are strong arguments for and against this question, but perhaps the question can best be answered by once more taking a critical look at the user of the financial statements.

The business owner, the supplier, the creditor, the unsophisticated investor – for these groups deferred tax is likely to cause as much confusion and mislead as much as its intention is to remove confusion and provide more useful information. We are not, therefore, any further forward in obtaining an answer to our question.

Consider, however, the board of directors of a capital-intensive listed company who will be judged by shareholders on their efforts in increasing stock prices and profits. Full provisioning for deferred tax may, as we have illustrated, result in the creation of ever-increasing liability balances that reduce reserves and, consequently, stock prices. Moreover, their investment strategies – and related successes – may be masked by the deferred tax charges when they may well have planned for investment at tax-opportune moments. In such circumstances, we may conclude that management may well be opposed to deferred tax accounting.

Consider, however, the sophisticated investor who bases investment decisions on the basis of future cash flows. The inclusion of the deferred tax adjustments allowing the timing of tax payments to be incorporated within the investors' analysis is doubtless invaluable. We have, therefore, a strong argument for deferred tax accounting.

Arguments for and against deferred tax accounting can be found when considering any user group. Is it possible, therefore, to rely on the Conceptual Framework to provide an answer?

The answer is probably yes – but perhaps not in the obvious definitions of assets and liabilities, future economic benefits or present obligations. One of the other most fundamental of accounting concepts is that of consistency of accounting treatment: consistency between similar transactions between one year and the next, and between one company and another. It seems reasonable to suggest therefore that, regardless of the arguments for and against deferred tax accounting, provided that companies treat similar transactions in a similar manner – which adherence to the IASs should ensure – and adequate disclosure of the nature of the taxation balances is made, then all users of the financial statements will be able to extract the information they require and disregard that which they do not.

> ### Section summary
> This advanced section has looked critically at the deferred tax provision and in particular the underlying approach adopted by IAS 12. It has also questioned whether accounting for deferred tax is useful to decision makers.

Chapter summary

IAS 12 *Income Taxes*

- Current tax is the amount of tax payable or recoverable in respect of the taxable profit or loss for an accounting period.
- Current tax for the current and prior periods should be recognized as a liability to the extent that it has not been settled, and as an asset to the extent that the amounts already paid exceed the amount due.
- The benefit of a tax loss that can be carried back to recover current tax of a prior period should be recognized as an asset.

- Current tax assets and liabilities should be measured at the amount expected to be paid to (recovered from) taxation authorities, using the rates/laws that have been enacted by the end of the reporting period.
- A temporary difference arises if an item of income or expense is recognized in the financial statements in one accounting period but is dealt with for tax purposes in a different period.
- IAS 12 identifies temporary differences by comparing the tax base of each asset and liability at the end of the reporting period with its carrying amount. The tax base of an item is the amount attributed to that item for tax purposes.
- A temporary difference arises if the tax base of an asset or liability is different from its carrying amount.
- Deferred tax liabilities should be recognized for all taxable temporary differences and measured at the tax rates that are expected to apply to the period when the liability is settled (liability method).
- Deferred tax assets should be recognized for deductible temporary differences, unused tax losses and unused tax credits to the extent that it is probable that taxable profit will be available against which the deductible temporary differences can be utilized, and measured at the tax rates that are expected to apply to the period when the asset is realized.
- Current and deferred tax should be recognized as income or expense, and included in net profit or loss for the period.

✓ Key terms for review

Definitions can be found in the glossary at the end of the book.

Accounting profit	Current tax	Taxable profit
Accounting profits and taxable profits	Deductible temporary differences	Taxable temporary differences
	Tax base	Temporary differences

? Review questions

1. Why does the charge to taxation in a company's accounts not equal the profit multiplied by the current rate of corporation tax?
2. Distinguish between permanent differences and temporary differences.
3. Explain and distinguish between the flow-through, full deferral and partial deferral approaches to providing for deferred tax.
4. Explain and distinguish between the liability method and deferral method of providing for deferred tax.
5. Distinguish between current tax and deferred tax.
6. Define the term current tax, and explain how it should be accounted for under IAS 12.
7. Distinguish between timing differences and temporary differences.
8. Define the term temporary differences, and explain the difference between taxable temporary differences and deductible temporary differences.
9. What is the tax base of an asset or a liability?
10. Is income smoothing a sufficient reason to provide for deferred tax?

Exercises

Level I

1. VSDA Ltd had pre-tax profits for the last three years as follows:

	£
Year to 31 March 2011	125,000
Year to 31 March 2012	130,000
Year to 31 March 2013	135,000

In the year to 31 March 2011, there was a difference between accounting and taxable profits that gave rise to a taxable temporary difference of £50,000. £10,000 of this was reversed in the year to 31 March 2012 and the remaining £40,000 was reversed in the year to 31 March 2013. The company was subject to corporation tax at 20% throughout the three year period.

Required

Show the relevant statement of comprehensive income extracts for each year incorporating the appropriate deferred tax transfers and the statement of financial position extracts at each year end.

2. Ostman Ltd purchased a machine on 1 April 2008 for £25,000. The company prepares its accounts to 31 March each year and its policy is to depreciate machinery at the rate of 15% per annum on the straight line basis. Tax allowances have been granted on the purchase of the machine at a rate of 25% per annum on the reducing balance basis.

   The rate of corporation tax applicable to the company has been as follows:

Year ended 31 March	2009	26%
Year ended 31 March	2010	25%
Year ended 31 March	2011	25%
Year ended 31 March	2012	24%
Year ended 31 March	2013	24%

Required

(a) Calculate the deferred tax provision using the deferral method.
(b) Calculate the deferred tax provision using the liability method.

3. A company has the following assets and liabilities in its statement of financial position at 31 March 2013.

   (i) A machine which cost £80,000 has a carrying value of £20,000. For tax purposes, it has a tax written-down value of £30,000.
   (ii) A receivable is shown at £35,000. The corresponding credit entry of income has been included in accounting profit in the year to 31 March 2013. £25,000 of this income has been taxed in the year to 31 March 2013 but the remaining £10,000 will not be taxed until it is received.
   (iii) A loan payable of £70,000. The repayment of the loan will have no tax consequences.
   (iv) An amount payable is shown at £5,000. Although the related expense has been deducted in arriving at accounting profit, it will not be deductible for tax purposes until it is paid.

Required

Compare the tax base of each of these assets and liabilities and identify any taxable or deductible temporary differences.

Level II

4. Company A has a piece of machinery bought for £100,000 on 1 January 2012. It adopts the straight line method of providing for depreciation and estimates that the asset has a useful life of 10 years with no residual value.

   Company B also bought an asset for £100,000 on 1 January 2012. It also adopts the straight line method of providing for depreciation, and estimates that the asset it purchased has a useful life of three years and no residual value.

   Tax allowances of 25% are available on both assets and the rate of corporation tax is 30%. Neither company has deferred tax balances at 31 December 2011.

   ### Required

   (a) For each company:
      (i) calculate the deferred tax asset/liability at 31 December 2012 and prepare the necessary journal entry, and
      (ii) repeat (i) at 31 December 2013 and 2014. Assume that Company B does not sell the asset until 2015.

   (b) For Company A, calculate the year in which the temporary difference reverses (i.e. begins to decline).

5. Dambysil plc is a profitable company that manufactures greenhouse accessories. On 31 December 2012, the net book value of non-current assets in the published accounts was £5,000,000. The tax written-down value of these assets was £4,250,000. Previously no deferred taxation has been provided.

   Dambysil plc has produced a budget indicating the likely expenditure over the next few years and, from this, the following information regarding depreciation and tax allowances (capital allowances) has been derived.

Year ended 31 December	WDA £000	Depreciation £000
2013	125	25
2014	25	50
2015	25	75
2016	175	50

From 2016 onwards, it is expected that tax allowances will be well in excess of depreciation.

Required

(a) Assuming that the corporation tax rate is 30%, calculate the deferred tax charge (or credit) for each of the four years to 31 December 2016, and the deferred tax asset or liability for inclusion in the statement of financial position at each year end, and show the relevant statement of comprehensive income and statement of financial position extracts, under each of the following:
   (i) on a full provision basis
   (ii) on a partial provision basis.

(b) IAS 12 *Income Taxes* recommends full deferral when providing for deferred tax. Critically appraise this approach and explain what other methods could be used.

Level III

6. Herbox plc prepares accounts to 31 December each year. The following information has been provided by the directors of Herbox as at 31 December 2012.

   (i) At 31 December 2012, the net book value of plant and machinery was £50m. The tax written-down value at that date was £38m.

   (ii) The directors revalued land from £25m to £35m on 31 December 2012.

   (iii) The figure of trade receivables in Herbox plc's statement of financial position at that date consisted of:

	£
Gross receivables	18
Less: bad debts	(2)
Less: specific provision	(1)
Less: general provision	(3)
Net receivables	12

   (iv) Herbox had £1m accrued overseas dividend income at 31 December 2012. This dividend is taxable on receipt.

   (v) Herbox had no deferred tax asset or liability at 31 December 2011.

   (vi) Assume a corporation tax rate of 30%.

   Required

   Calculate the required deferred tax balance at 31 December 2012.

7. Rivendell plc is a manufacturer of loft ladders. At 31 March 2012 Rivendell had a deferred tax provision of £2.25m, made up as follows:

	£
Accelerated capital allowances	1.95m
Accrued interest receivable	0.30m
	2.25m

At 31 March 2013, the statement of financial position showed plant and machinery costing £120m with a net book value of £70m. Capital (tax) allowances so far given on these assets amount to £58m.

In 2003 Rivendell had purchased some land costing £6m, with a view to building a new display showroom. Planning permission had been difficult to obtain; however, following a change in local authority policy, this has now been granted. At 31 March 2013 the land was valued at £7.8m and as the directors intend to use this land as security for loan purposes, they have decided to incorporate the revalued amount in the financial statements.

Rivendell received £1,000,000 in interest during the year to 31 March 2013 from funds held in a foreign bank account. This interest had been accrued in the financial statements to 31 March 2012. Corporation tax is payable on receipt of this interest.

The company incurred taxable losses in the year to 31 March 2013 of £4.8m. Rivendell has been consistently profitable for the last ten years and the loss arose from the closure of an old product range. The new range was introduced late in the year and the company is now trading profitably. Indeed, budgets indicate that the company will be profitable for the foreseeable future.

Assume a tax rate of 30%.

Required

(a) Calculate the required deferred tax provision as at 31 March 2013.

(b) Prepare the relevant statement of comprehensive income and statement of financial position extracts for deferred tax as required by IAS 12 for the year ended 31 March 2013.

(c) Prepare the deferred tax disclosure note.

8. Arkling plc had recognized the following deferred tax balances at 31 March 2012.

Type of temporary difference	Temporary difference	Deferred tax asset/(liability)
	£m	£m
Accelerated capital allowances	(10)	(3)
Revaluations	(10)	(3)
Tax losses	35	10.5
Other	(15)	(4.5)

At 31 March 2012, Arkling had additional tax losses of £8,500,000, which had not been recognized. At that time, it was not certain that there would be future taxable profits against which these losses could be utilized. Consequently, Arkling recognized only the amount of losses sufficient to cover the deferred tax liabilities in respect of the taxable temporary difference relating to accelerated capital allowances, revaluations and the other taxable temporary differences existing at that date.

Additional information

(i) At 31 March 2012, the net book value of assets qualifying for capital allowances was £90m and the tax written-down value was £80m. During the year to 31 March 2013, Arkling acquired new assets qualifying for capital allowances, costing £15m. The depreciation charge for the year to 31 March 2013 was £20m and the capital allowances claimed amounted to £24m. All the assets qualifying for capital allowances are plant and equipment.

(ii) The company acquired a new office block in June 2012 costing £9.5m. There were no capital allowances available on this building.

(iii) Following a general downturn in the property market, properties that had previously been revalued upwards in the year to 31 March 2012 were revalued downwards as at 31 March 2013. A downward revaluation of £5m occurred.

(iv) The other temporary differences existing at 31 March 2012 reversed during the current year.

(v) During the year to 31 March 2013, Arkling had accounting profits before tax of £29m. The taxable profits came to £41.5m, arrived at after adjusting for depreciation, capital allowances, other temporary differences and disallowable expenditure. The tax losses brought forward have been set off against the taxable profits to fully eliminate the tax payable. Disallowable expenditure in the tax computation amounted to £1.5m.

Required

(a) Calculate the required deferred tax balance as at 31 March 2013, and the amounts to be taken to the statement of comprehensive income.

(b) Prepare an extract of the statement of comprehensive income of Arkling for the year to 31 March 2013.

(c) Prepare the deferred tax liability disclosure note as at 31 March 2013.

(d) Prepare a tax reconciliation for the year to 31 March 2013.

References

IAS 12 *Income Taxes*. IASB, 2000.
Logica (2011) *Annual Report and Accounts*.

Further reading

FRS 19 *Current Tax*. ASB, 1999.
FRS 16 *Deferred Tax*. ASB, 2002.
IFRS: www.ifrs.org
Macdonald, G. (2002) The Taxation of Business Income: Aligning taxable income with accounting income. Tax Law Committee Discussion Paper No. 2, Institute for Fiscal Studies, London.
Stylianou, J. (1997) Deferred tax – partial arts. *Accountancy Age*, April.

When you have read this chapter, log on to the Online Learning Centre website at *www.mcgraw-hill.co.uk/textbooks/mckeith* to explore chapter-by-chapter test questions, further reading and more online study tools.

Chapter 10

Statement of Cash Flows

Learning Outcomes

After studying this chapter you should be able to:

- ✓ explain the difference between cash and profit
- ✓ explain the additional information that the statement of cash flows can provide
- ✓ distinguish between operating activities, investing activities and financing activities
- ✓ explain the difference between the direct method and indirect method of determining cash flows from operating activities
- ✓ define the terms cash and cash equivalents
- ✓ identify non-cash transactions
- ✓ outline and explain the requirements of IAS 7 *Statement of Cash Flows*
- ✓ prepare a statement of cash flows in accordance with IAS 7 *Statement of Cash Flows*.

Introduction

It is widely recognized that the ability to generate cash is essential for a company's survival. Indeed, it is often said that cash is the 'lifeblood' of a business. A business that cannot pay its suppliers or employees will not survive. The ability to earn profits, however, does not necessarily result in a healthy cash balance.

This chapter first of all considers the differences between cash and profit (profit vs cash flow) and explores the reasons why these differences arise. A simple example is used to illustrate these differences. A statement of cash flows is then constructed, providing step-by-step guidance on how to prepare the statement from a statement of comprehensive income and statement of financial position. The next section outlines the requirements of IAS 7 *Statement of Cash Flows*, and discusses in detail the specific requirements of this standard. The final section considers the history of the development of statements of cash flows and illustrates some of the more complicated issues which can arise in practice.

Section 1: Basic Principles

Accountants frequently meet with clients to review their financial statements. When the level of profit made is being considered, the discussion almost always results in the comment from the clients to the effect that it is a pity that the bank balance does not appear to reflect the level of the profit achieved. It can be quite puzzling for clients to understand why, after a year of good profits, their bank overdraft is bigger at the end of the year than it was at the start. Or indeed why the bank balance has increased more than profit.

10.1 Cash vs profit

The ability to generate cash is crucial to the survival of a business. Indeed, many profitable businesses fail because they cannot generate enough cash to meet short-term commitments. Other things being equal, in the longer term profits do have the effect of increasing the bank balance. However, in the short term, the making of a profit will not necessarily result in an increased cash balance.

Consider the following scenario.

A fruit seller has a market stall and £100 cash. He buys some apples for £100 and during the day sells them all for £130.

His trading account for the day would be as follows:

Sales	£130
Purchases	£100
Profit	£30

Suppose all the transactions were for cash. How much *cash* is left at the end of the day?

Sales (all for cash)	£130
Purchases (all for cash)	£100
Profit	£30

Because all the transactions were for cash, the profit earned will be reflected in the cash position at the end of the day.

Cash at start of day	£100
Less cash purchases	£100
	0
Add cash from sales	£130
Cash at end of day	£130
Cash at start of day	£100
Cash at end of day	£130
Increase in cash	£30

So in this instance profit and increase in cash are equal.

Consider the situation where all purchases are for cash, and some of the sales are for cash and some on credit. Suppose cash sales are £100 and credit sales are £30. As before, profit will still be £30.

Sales (cash)	£100
Sales (credit)	£30
	£130
Purchases (all for cash)	£100
Profit	£30

However, this time, cash at the end of the day will be £100.

Cash at start of day	£100
Less cash used for purchases	£100
	0
Add cash from sales	£100
Cash at end	£100
Cash at start	£100
Cash at end	£100
Increase in cash	£0

Profit and increase in cash are not equal.

It can be seen that the reason for this is that some sales were made on credit during the day. These credit sales had no effect on cash but were included in arriving at the profit figure. It is possible to reconcile the profit figure with the change in cash as follows:

Profit per accounts	£30
Less: credit sales	(30)
Change in cash	0

In other words, the sales that are on credit do not increase cash, instead they increase trade receivables. Therefore, the following reconciliation can also be made:

Profit per accounts	£30
Less: increase in trade receivables	(30)
Change in cash	0

Consider the situation where the purchases are for cash, but all the sales are on credit. Again, as before, profit is still £30.

Sales (all on credit)	£130
Purchases (all for cash)	£100
Profit	£30

However, this time, cash at the end of the day will be zero since no cash will have been received from sales.

Cash at start of day	£100
Less cash purchases	£100
	0
Add cash from sales	0 (all sales are on credit)
Cash at end of day	£0
Cash at start	£100
Cash at end	£0
Decrease in cash	£100

Given that all the cash was spent on apples and no cash was collected from selling them, cash at the end of the day will be zero. However, a profit of £30 has been made. Again, in this instance, profit and increase in cash are not equal.

Once more, reconciliation can be made of the profit with the change in cash. In this scenario, all the sales were on credit, therefore cash is not affected. Instead there is an increase in trade receivables of the full amount of the credit sales. Therefore:

Profit per accounts	£30
Less: increase in trade receivables	(130)
Change in cash (decrease)	(100)

The market trader would be in difficulty if he is not able to buy more apples on credit to sell the next day because he has no cash left.

This simple example leads to two important issues:

1. the important distinction between cash and profit
2. the usefulness of the information provided by the statement of comprehensive income and the statement of financial position in helping the business identify whether or not it will be able to generate sufficient cash to finance its operations.

Statement of financial position

The statement of financial position discloses the cash/bank balances, the near cash assets, such as debtors, and the short-term liabilities, such as creditors. However, the statement of financial position provides an overview at a specific point in time, so it is a static picture. The statement of financial position does not show how the business has financed its activities during the period under review.

Progress Point 10.1

Why does the making of a profit not necessarily result in an increase in cash?

Solution

The reason a profit does not necessarily result in an increase in cash is due to the fact that profit is determined by comparing income with expenditure and not receipts with payments. Where a business has sold goods on credit this will be recorded as income; however, it will not result in an inflow of cash until that cash is received from the customer.

Statement of comprehensive income

The statement of comprehensive income shows revenues and expenses rather than cash receipts and payments. The profit shown in the statement of comprehensive income is the difference between the revenues and expenses for the period. This may have little or no relationship to the cash generated for the period.

This anomaly identified above can be illustrated as follows.

Example

Current assets and current liabilities of a business at the start of a period are as follows:

Inventories	£200
Trade receivables	£30
Cash	£50
Trade payables	£20

During the year the following transactions took place.

1. 100 items bought on credit costing £2 each
2. 180 items sold on credit for £4 each
3. Cash paid to suppliers £180
4. Cash received from customers £700.

The information given above can be put together in the following summary statement

Summary statement

	Opening position			Closing position
Inventories	£200	+ £200 (1)	− £360 (2)	£40
Receivables	£30	+ £720 (2)	− £700 (4)	£50
Cash	£50	− £180 (3)	+ £700 (4)	£570
Payables	£20	+ £200 (1)	− £180 (3)	£40
Net current assets	£260			£620

Net current assets is the total of current assets (inventories, receivables and cash) less the current liabilities (payables). Net current assets are more commonly referred to as working capital. In this case net current assets have increased by £360 (£620 – £260) over the period.

The transactions may be explained as follows.

1. Items bought on credit for £200 (100 × £2). This will have the effect of increasing inventory and increasing trade payables by £200.
2. Items sold on credit for £720 (180 × £4). This will have the effect of increasing trade receivables by £720 and decreasing inventory by £360, that is at cost (180 × £2).
3. Cash paid to suppliers. This will decrease trade payables and decrease cash by £180.
4. Cash received from customers. This will increase cash by £700 and decrease trade receivables by £700.

Profit versus cash

Using the above summary statement, a statement of comprehensive income can now be prepared:

Statement of comprehensive income for the period ended X		
Sales		£720
Less cost of sales		
Inventory at start	£200	
Add purchases	200	
	400	
Less inventory at end	40	£360
Profit		£360

This is the same as the increase in net current assets (working capital) over the same period.

What has happened to cash? Cash at the start is £50 and cash at the end is £570, so cash has gone up by £520 but profit has gone up by only £360. What is the explanation for the difference?

In general terms the reason for the difference is one of timing. For example, some of the cash has still to be received from the customers and is in trade receivables. However, credit sales will already have been taken account of as part of total sales and so will already have been taken into account in the calculation of profit.

The specific reasons for the difference between cash and profit can be identified and measured separately. The statement of cash flows combines these individual changes and measures the overall change.

Consider each possible change in isolation.

Inventory

If inventory increases over the period, the implication is that the business is buying more stock, so the likely impact of this would be to decrease cash. If inventory decreases over the period, the opposite would be true. It could be implied that the company is selling inventory and so cash would increase. In this instance, inventory has decreased, implying that it has been sold, so increasing cash.

Trade receivables

If trade receivables increase over the period it is as though the customers are not paying. The increase in trade receivables causes the sales figure shown in the statement of comprehensive income to be higher than the amount actually received from the customers. Cash is not coming in as quickly. This situation will have a negative impact on cash and so will notionally decrease cash. However, if trade receivables are falling over the period it is as though the customers are paying more quickly. This will have a positive impact on cash and so will notionally increase cash. In the illustration given, trade receivables have increased. This suggests that while sales have been made, the amount of cash generated from these sales has been less than the sales. In the example, trade receivables have increased, so notionally decreasing cash.

Trade payables

If trade payables are increasing over the period it is as though the business is not paying its suppliers and so is retaining cash in the business. This will have a positive impact on cash and will increase cash. Conversely, if trade payables are decreasing over the period, it is as though the company is paying the suppliers more quickly. This will have a negative impact on cash and will lead to a cash decrease. In the example, trade payables have increased. Purchases have been recognized in the statement of comprehensive income as an expense, thus reducing profit. However, since these purchases were on credit the impact of this is to increase trade payables and so notionally increase cash.

In order to identify the effects the increases or decreases in these items between the beginning and end of the accounting period have, the profit figure should be adjusted as follows:

	Increases	Decreases
Inventories	Subtract	Add
Trade receivables and prepaid expenses	Subtract	Add
Trade payables and accrual expenses	Add	Subtract

The effect of these adjustments is to change the basis of accounting from the accruals basis to the cash basis. Using the example, the various changes can now be combined as follows:

Statement of cash flows	
Profit for the period	£360
Changes having a positive impact on cash	
Decrease in inventories	£160
Increase in trade payables	£20
	£540
Changes having a negative impact on cash	
Increase in trade receivables	£20
Increase in cash	£520
Opening cash	£50
Closing cash	£570
Increase in cash	£520

This example also shows how valuable information about the profit of a business can be extracted. From the computation above, the cash generated from the trading activities of the business can be seen. The business has made a profit, which will increase working capital (net current assets). The composition of the current assets and current liabilities will determine whether sufficient cash has been generated to allow a business to survive. The statement of cash flows allows the *quality* of the profit to be tested.

The statement of cash flows combines these individual changes and shows the overall impact of them on the cash position. While profit and cash rarely equal each other, the fact that a company makes a profit will tend to have a positive impact on net assets and therefore on cash. Profit will contribute to the change in cash over the period.

Progress Point 10.2

Explain whether each of the following statements is true or false.
(a) Accounting profit is the difference between cash received and cash paid.
(b) A decrease in trade receivables increases the cash position.
(c) An increase in trade payables decreases the cash position.
(d) An increase in inventories increases the cash position.

BASIC

INTERMEDIATE

ADVANCED

> ## Suggested solution
>
> (a) False: accounting profit is the difference between revenues earned and expenses incurred whether or not they have been received or paid.
>
> (b) True: if trade receivables have decreased, this means that money has been received from customers.
>
> (c) False: if trade payables have increased, this means that suppliers are not being paid, so cash is being retained in the business.
>
> (d) False: if inventories are increasing this means that the business is buying more inventory and so this is likely to decrease the cash position.

Continuing with the example, suppose the company has depreciating assets and the depreciation charge for the period is £100.

The profit will be reduced by £100, from £360 to £260. What is the impact on cash?

There is no impact on cash. This is because depreciation represents a charge for using non-current assets and is matched against the revenues generated from using such assets. However, the business does not actually pay depreciation in cash, so there is no effect on cash.

Depreciation reduces the profit but has no effect on cash. In order to reconcile profit with the change in cash, any factors that distort one, but not the other must be eliminated. Given that depreciation reduces profit and not cash then depreciation must be added back on to profit.

Building on the earlier example:

Statement of cash flows	
Profit for the period (after depreciation)	£260
Add back depreciation	£100
	£360
Changes having a positive impact on cash	
Decrease in inventories	£160
Increase in trade payables	£20
	£540
Changes having a negative impact on Cash	
Increase in trade receivables	£20
Increase in cash	£520
Opening cash	£50
Closing cash	£570
Increase in cash	£520

Other items that have an impact on profit but not on cash

Loss on sale of non-current asset

This arises when cash received from the sale of an asset is less than the net book value of the asset. This loss on sale will be deducted from the profit figure in the statement of comprehensive income and so has the effect of decreasing profit. However, it has no impact on cash. As with depreciation, this loss on sale will have to be added back on to profit. Note however that the proceeds from the sale of the asset will cause an increase in the cash balance.

Gain on sale of non-current asset

This arises when cash received from the sale of an asset is greater than the net book value of the asset. This gain on sale is added to the profit in the statement of comprehensive income, and so has the effect of increasing profit. However, it has no impact on cash. This time, it will have to be deducted from profit. As above, the proceeds from the sale of the asset will cause an increase in the cash balance.

In both the above cases, it is the actual cash received from disposing of the assets that will have an impact on cash.

Progress Point 10.3

(a) Explain the effect of each of the following on the statement of financial position, statement of comprehensive income and statement of cash flows.

(i) Depreciation of £10,000 is charged.

(ii) Credit sales of £8,000 are made.

(iii) Inventories costing £13,000 are purchased on credit.

(iv) A non-current asset with a net book value of £5,000 is sold for £3,000.

(v) Land is revalued from its original cost of £130,000 to £200,000.

(b) The information relating to current assets and current liabilities of a business is as follows. At start of year.

Inventories (100 items at £3 each)	£300
Trade receivables	£50
Cash	£75
Trade payables	£35

During the year, the following transactions took place:

1. 80 items bought on credit, each costing £3
2. 150 items sold on credit for £5 each
3. Cash paid to suppliers £175
4. Cash received from customers £600

Calculate the change in the cash balance and net current assets, and reconcile these using a statement of cash flows.

Solution

(a)

(i) Statement of financial position: the depreciation charge will reduce the net book value of non-current assets by £10,000.

Statement of comprehensive income: profit is reduced by £10,000 depreciation.

Statement of cash flows: no effect as no cash flow has occurred.

(ii) Statement of financial position: there will be an increase in trade receivables of £8,000.

Statement of comprehensive income: there will be an increase in sales revenue of £8,000.

Statement of cash flows: no effect as no cash flow has occurred.

(iii) Statement of financial position: there will be an increase in trade payables of £13,000.

Statement of comprehensive income: there will be an increase in purchases of £13,000.

Statement of cash flows: no effect as no cash flow has occurred.

(iv) Statement of financial position: the non-current assets are reduced by £5,000 and the cash is increased by £3,000.

Statement of comprehensive income: profit is reduced by the £2,000 loss on the sale of the non-current asset.

Statement of cash flows: there will be a cash inflow of £3,000 from the sale of the non-current asset.

(v) Statement of financial position: the carrying value of the land is increased by £70,000 and the same amount is credited to a revaluation reserve.

Statement of comprehensive income: the gain is shown in other comprehensive income.

Statement of cash flows: no effect as no cash flow has occurred.

(b)

Net current assets	At start		At end
Inventories	£300	+ 240 − 450	£90
Trade receivables	£50	+ 750 − 600	£200
Cash	£75	+ 600 − 175	£500
Trade payables	(£35)	+ 240 − 175	(£100)
	£390		£690

∴ Change in cash balance = £75 − £500: increase £425

Change in net assets = £390 − £690: increase £300

Statement of cash flows

	£
Profit for the period (increase in net assets)	300
Add: decrease in inventories	210
increase in trade payables	65
	575
Less: increase in trade receivables	150
increase in cash	£425

Section summary

As the above examples have illustrated, by analysing the changes in a company's statement of financial position and the items in its statement of comprehensive income it is possible to identify the reasons for a given change in that company's bank balance. This is extremely useful and beneficial. Just because a business is profitable does not necessarily mean that it has adequate funds in its bank. As has been explained, the use of the accruals basis for the reporting of profits is one reason for this apparent anomaly. There are several other reasons why a business might report a healthy profit and yet suffer severe cash problems:

(a) The purchase of non-current assets causes an immediate reduction in cash; however, this does not show in the statement of comprehensive income. Instead, the depreciation charge will reflect the company's usage of that asset but over an extended time period.

(b) A company may build up a stock of inventories in anticipation of attracting new customers. Again, these inventories may have to be paid for quickly while the revenues from their sale may take many months. The purchase of these inventories will have no effect on reported profits until they are sold.

(c) If a company has a bank loan, it will only be the loan interest that is shown in the statement of comprehensive income. The repayment of the capital element of the loan will have no effect on profit but it will deplete the cash balance.

It is for reasons such as these that the size of a company's profit is not a reliable indicator of its cash situation. Note, incidentally, that a healthy bank balance is not in itself a reliable indicator of the success of a company either. Companies may obtain cash by:

(a) selling non-current assets
(b) obtaining loan finance
(c) issuing share capital or debentures.

In order to be able to fully evaluate a company's performance, an analysis of the flows of cash in and out of a business is essential. Moreover, if these inflows and outflows are classified its categories which summarize the various activities of a company then this will further assist in the assessment of the liquidity, solvency and financial adaptability of that company. All these different receipts and payments can be brought together in the form of a statement that summarizes the sources of the cash and the uses of the cash. Such a summary is known as a statement of cash flows. The next section looks in detail at how this statement should be prepared in accordance with IAS7 Statement of Cash Flows.

Section 2: Intermediate Issues

10.2 IAS 7 Statement of Cash Flows

Objective and scope

IAS 7 recognizes that information about the cash flows of an entity is useful in providing users of financial statements with a basis to assess the ability of the entity to generate cash and the needs of the entity to utilize those cash flows.

The objective of the standard is to require the provision of information about the historical changes in cash and cash equivalents of an entity by means of a statement of cash flows which classifies cash flows during the period from operating, investing and financing activities.

IAS 7 requires that all entities which comply with international standards should produce such a statement as an integral part of its financial statements. Although the title of IAS 7 is Statement of Cash Flows, entities are not required to use that title for the statement itself. For example some entities use the title 'cash flow statement'.

Benefits of cash flow information

A number of benefits of a statement of cash flows are outlined in the standard, as follows.

- It gives the business the ability to influence cash flows in light of changing circumstances.
- It enables the operating performance of different businesses to be compared.
- Historical cash flow information is often used as an indicator of the amount, timing and uncertainty of future cash flows.

- It is useful for checking the accuracy of past assessments of future cash flows.
- It is useful for examining the relationship between profitability and net cash flow, and the impact of changing prices.

Definitions

IAS 7 defines the following terms which are used in the standard.

- *Cash* comprises cash in hand and demand deposits.
- *Cash equivalents* are short-term highly liquid investments that are readily convertible to known amounts of cash and which are subject to an insignificant risk of changes in value.
- *Cash flows* are inflows and outflows of cash and cash equivalents.
- *Operating activities* are the principal revenue-producing activities of the entity and other activities that are not investing or financing activities.
- *Investing activities* are the acquisition and disposal of long-term assets and other investments not included in cash equivalents.
- *Financing activities* are activities that result in changes in the size and composition of the contributed equity and borrowings of the entity.

Cash and cash equivalents

IAS 7 takes the view that cash equivalents are virtually indistinguishable from cash itself and should therefore be treated as cash rather than as investments.

The decision on how to classify such items can be difficult, however, and involves a degree of subjectivity. For example, many businesses put surplus funds on deposit, perhaps for a number of months, and the decision as to how to classify such items can be difficult. Cash equivalents are held for the purpose of meeting short-term cash commitments rather than for investment or other purposes. For an investment to qualify as a cash equivalent it must be readily convertible to a known amount of cash and be subject to an insignificant risk of changes in value.

Normally, only an investment with a short maturity of, say, three months or less would qualify under the definition. Equity investments are excluded unless they are cash equivalents in substance – for example, redeemable preference shares acquired within a short period of their maturity and with a specified redemption date.

Bank borrowings can be equally problematic. A bank overdraft, repayable on demand, could be viewed as part of cash and cash equivalents where it forms an integral part of a business's cash management policy. A mortgage over ten years, say, would almost certainly be a financing activity.

The decision of how to classify such items can be subjective: one business may classify an investment as a cash equivalent, while another may treat the same investment as an investing item. In general terms, however, an investment normally qualifies as a cash equivalent only where it is readily convertible to a known amount of cash, is not subject to a significant risk of changes in value, and where it has a short maturity (three months or less) from date of acquisition.

Note that cash flows under IAS 7 exclude movements between cash in hand and highly liquid investments because these are components of a business's cash management rather than part of the operating, investing and financing activities.

Example: Cash and cash equivalents

Explain how the following items would be classified in accordance with IAS 7.

(i) A company places £1m on a seven-day call deposit.

(ii) A company has an account with its bank under which the company has to give 90 days' notice to the bank before it can withdraw money.

(iii) A company buys a two-year bond in the market when the bond has only two months remaining before its redemption date. The purchase is made for investment purposes.

Solution

(i) Cash is defined as cash on hand and demand deposits. Because seven days' notice of withdrawal is required, this would not be classified as cash; the deposit could however, be reported as a cash equivalent.

(ii) The company has to give 90 days' notice to the bank before it can withdraw the cash. The account does not meet the definition of cash because it is not a demand deposit. However, as only 90 days' notice is required, it may meet the definition of a cash equivalent.

(iii) The bond does not qualify as a cash equivalent because, even though it meets the definition in IAS 7 para 6, it is held for investment purposes and not for the purpose of meeting short-term cash commitments.

Presentation of a statement of cash flows

IAS 7 requires that the statement of cash flows should report cash flows classified by operating, investing and financing activities.

This classification is to allow users to assess how these types of activity impact on the financial position of the business. The various components of the classifications will be those most appropriate to the business. The standard notes that a single transaction may fall into different classifications. For example, where the repayment of a loan includes both interest and capital, the interest payment may be included in operating activities, whereas the capital repayment is a financing cash flow.

Operating activities

Operating activities are defined as the 'principal revenue-producing activities of the business and other activities that are not investing or financing activities'. So, by definition, all cash flows that are neither investing nor financing will be deemed to be part of operating activities. The standard states that operating cash flow information is valuable since:

■ it provides an important indication of the extent to which a business has generated enough cash flows from its operating activities to pay dividends, to make investments, to repay debts and to increase its scale of operating activity without borrowing

■ it may assist in forecasting future cash flows.

Examples of cash flows from operating activities given in the standard include:

■ cash receipts from sale of goods or performing a service

■ cash receipts from fees, royalties, commissions and other revenue

■ cash payments to suppliers for goods and services

■ cash payment to employees

■ cash payments or refunds of taxes (unless they can be specifically identified with financing and investing activities).

Investing activities

IAS 7 defines investing activities as 'the acquisition and disposal of long-term assets and other investments not included in cash equivalents'. According to the standard, this classification allows users of the financial statements to understand the extent to which expenditures have been made for resources intended to provide future income and cash flows. Cash flows from investing activities include:

■ payments made to acquire, and receipts from the sale of long-term assets, including those payments and receipts relating to capitalized development costs and self-constructed assets

■ payments made to acquire and receipts from the sale of equity or debt instruments of other businesses and interests in jointly controlled entities

- advances and loans made to and repaid by other parties
- cash payments for and receipts from futures, forward, option and swap contracts (except when these contracts are held for trading purposes).

Financing activities

IAS 7 defines financing activities as 'those activities that result in changes in the size and composition of the contributed equity and borrowings of the entity'. Examples of cash flows arising from financing activities include:

- share issues
- redemption of shares
- issue and repayment of debentures and other long-term borrowing
- payments made under a lease.

Allocation of items to operating, investing and financing activities

There may be situations where it is not clear how cash flows should be classified. IAS 7 provides additional guidance on the classification of interest, dividends and taxation.

Interest and dividends

IAS 7 notes that there is no consensus on the classification of these cash flows, and suggests that interest paid can be classified either as operating or financing activities. Interest and dividends received can be included in either operating or investing cash flows. The standard allows dividends paid to be classified as a financing cash flow, since such dividends are a cost of obtaining financial resources, or as an operating cash flow.

The standard requires the total amount of interest paid to be disclosed whether it has been recognized as an expense or has been capitalized as part of the cost of an asset (as allowed under IAS 23).

Taxation

Cash flows arising from taxes on income should be disclosed separately within operating cash flows unless they can be specifically identified with investing or financing activities. In general terms, tax paid is usually classified as an operating cash flow since it is often impractical to match such cash flows with specific investing and financing activities.

Progress Point 10.4

Explain the effect of each of the items below on the statement of financial position, statement of comprehensive income, and statement of cash flows, indicating whether they are operating, investing or financing activities

(a) During the year the company purchased a new piece of machinery costing £15,000.
(b) A loan of £12,000 was taken out to help finance the purchase of the machine.
(c) The company paid back a long-term loan to the bank of £80,000.
(d) The company made an issue of 100,000 8% £1 preference shares at a price of £1.20 per share.
(e) The company received bank interest of £1,000.

Solution

(a) Statement of financial position: the non-current assets are increased by £15,000 and the cash is reduced by £15,000.

Statement of comprehensive income: no effect.

Statement of cash flows: the statement of cash flows will show cash outflows from investing activities of £15,000.

(b) Statement of financial position: cash is increased by £12,000 and liabilities (loans) will increase by £12,000.

Statement of comprehensive income: no effect.

Statement of cash flows: the statement of cash flows will show cash inflows from financing activities of £12,000.

(c) Statement of financial position: long-term liabilities are reduced by £80,000 and the bank balance is reduced by a similar amount.

Statement of comprehensive income: no effect as we are merely using an asset to discharge a liability.

Statement of cash flows: the financing section of the statement of cash flows will show a cash outflow of £80,000.

(d) Statement of financial position: increase issued preference share capital by £100,000 and increase the share premium account by £20,000.

Statement of comprehensive income: no effect.

Statement of cash flows: cash flows from financing activities will show an inflow of £120,000 (i.e. 100,000 shares at £1.20 each).

(e) Statement of financial position: cash will increase by £1,000.

Statement of comprehensive income: included in arriving at profit from operating activities.

Statement of cash flows: included in arriving at net cash inflow from operating activities.

10.3 Preparation of statement of cash flows

Comprehensive example

The following information comprises the statement of comprehensive income of XYZ for the year ended 31 March Year 4, together with statements of financial position of the business as at 31 March Year 4 and Year 3 and the statement of changes in equity between Year 3 and Year 4.

Statement of comprehensive income

Year ended 31 March Year 4	£	£
Sales		100
Cost of sales		30
Gross profit		70
Expenses		
Depreciation	5	
Loss on disposal	2	
Wages and salaries	13	20
Operating profit		50
Taxation		10
Profit for the year		40

Statement of financial position

As at 31 March	Year 4		Year 3	
	£	£	£	£
Non-current assets (cost)		98		80
Less depreciation		33		30
		65		50
Current assets				
Inventories	10		15	
Trade receivables	34		21	
Cash	12		3	
	56		39	
Current liabilities				
Trade payables	6		9	
Taxation	10		8	
Dividends payable	5		7	
	21		24	
Total net current assets		35		15
Net assets		100		65
Equity				
Share capital		45		45
Retained earnings		55		20
		100		65

BASIC

INTERMEDIATE

ADVANCED

Statement of changes in equity

	Share Capital	Retained Earnings	Total Equity
	£	£	£
Balance at 31 March Year 3	45	20	65
Total comprehensive income		40	40
Final dividend declared		(5)	(5)
Balance at 31 March Year 4	45	55	100

- The following additional information is also given.
  Assets, which originally cost £12 and had a net book value at time of sale of £10, were sold for £8.

- From the information given above, a statement of cash flows will now be prepared.

The cash flows will be calculated for each of the headings *of Operating activities, Investing activities* and *Financing activities.*

Working notes

In order to prepare the statement of cash flows it is necessary to group the items into the above headings. To do this, some additional information needs to be extracted from the information given.

Step 1: analyse the changes in non-current assets

In order to find out the how much depreciation has been charged and how much has been spent on non-current assets, it helps to construct a schedule of non-current assets, a little 'magic square', as follows:

	Cost	Depreciation	Net book value
	£	£	£
Position at start (Year 3)	80	30	50
Assets sold	12	2	10
	68	28	40
Position at end	98	33	65
Increase in assets	30	5	25

Explanation of the statement

The increase in assets of £30 represents the amount of non-current assets bought during the year.

An increase in depreciation of £5 represents the depreciation for the year.

Assets that cost £12 with a net book value of £10 at the time of sale were sold for £8. This means that there was a loss on the sale of these assets of £2 (£10 – £8). There was also a cash inflow of £8 associated with the sale of these assets.

Step 2: find out how much tax has been paid

From the statement of financial position and statement of comprehensive income the following information can be determined:

Tax owing in Year 3	8 (from statement of financial position)
Amount of tax for end year 4	10 (from statement of comprehensive income)
	18
Tax owing in Year 4	10 (from statement of financial position)
Therefore tax paid during the year	8

Step 3: identify the changes in current assets and current liabilities other than cash

Decrease in inventory	£5 (£15 – £10)
Increase in trade receivables	£13 (£21 – £34)
Decrease in trade payables	£3 (£9 – £6)

Step 4: combine the information to determine the cash flow from operating activities

Cash flow from operating activities

		£
Profit before tax		50
Add:	Depreciation	5
	loss on disposal	2
		57
Add:	decrease in inventory	5
Less:	increase in trade receivables	(13)
	decrease in trade payables	(3)
		46
Less:	taxation paid	8
Net cash flows from operating activities		38

Step 5: identify the cash flows from investing activities

	£
Purchase of non-current assets	(30)
Proceeds from sale of non-current assets	8
Net cash used in investing activities	(22)

Step 6: identify the cash flow from financing activities

In this example, the company had declared final dividends before the year end of £5. We need to calculate what amount of dividends the company actually paid in cash.

Dividend owing at the start	£7 (statement of financial position Year 3)
Dividend proposed	£5 (statement of changes in equity)
	£12
Dividend owing at the end	£5 (statement of financial position Year 4)
Therefore dividend paid	£7

Step 7: combine all the above information to produce the complete statement of cash flows

Statement of cash flows

Cash flow from operating activities (step 4)	£38
Cash flow from investing activities (step 5)	(£22)
Cash flow from financing activities (step 6)	(£7)
Net cash inflow	£9

This net cash inflow can be verified by comparing the change in the cash over the period:

Cash at start	£3 (statement of financial position Year 3)
Cash at end	£12 (statement of financial position Year 4)
Increase in cash	£9

10.4 Reporting cash flows from operating activities: direct or indirect

The method shown above of calculating cash flows from operating activities is known as the indirect, or net, method. It involves starting with the operating profit and adjusting it for non-cash charges and credits so that one figure of operating cash flow is shown.

Another method exists, however, known as the direct or gross method, which involves showing the individual operating cash receipts from customers, and cash payments to suppliers and employees.

In order to use the direct method of calculating operating cash flows using our earlier example, cash receipts from customers and cash payments made to suppliers and other cash payments made will have to be calculated.

Calculation of direct cash flows

Cash receipts from customers	
Trade receivables at start of period	£21 (statement of financial position Year 3)
Sales for period	£100 (statement of comprehensive income account)
	£121
Trade receivables at end of period	£34 (statement of financial position Year 4)
Therefore cash received	£87

Cash paid to suppliers
This needs to be done in two stages.

Stage 1
First of all, the purchases for the year need to be calculated. From the statement of comprehensive income the cost of sales figure of £30 is given. From the statement of financial position the opening and closing inventories can be identified. This information can be used to calculate the purchases:

Opening inventory	£15 (statement of financial position Year 3)
Add purchases	£x (missing number)
Less closing inventory	£10 (statement of financial position Year 4)
Cost of sales	£30 (statement of comprehensive income)

The missing number, purchases, is deduced to be £25.

$$(£15 + £x - £10) = £30 \therefore x = £25.$$

Stage 2

Trade payables at start of period	£9 (statement of financial position Year 3)
Purchases	£25 (stage 1)
	£34
Trade payables at end of period	£6
Therefore cash paid	£28

Other cash paid

This will be the amount shown in the statement of comprehensive income for wages and salaries of £13.

Cash flow from operating activities (direct method)	
Cash receipts from customers	£87
Cash paid to suppliers	(£28)
Cash paid to employees	(£13)
Cash generated from operations	£46
Taxation paid	£8
	£38

The operating cash flow figure is the same regardless of the method used. This example allowed the calculation to be made using either method. In practice, companies operate accounting systems that are geared towards accrual accounting and, consequently, the detailed information required to enable the calculation to be made using the direct method may not always be available.

Progress Point 10.5

(a) The direct method of reporting cash flows from operating activities is the easiest to understand but most companies use the indirect method. Why do you think this might be so?

(b) The cash flows below were extracted from the accounts of Gemmill Ltd, a landscaping business.

	£
Loan repaid	25,000
Purchase of office equipment	15,000
Sale of property	25,000
Interest paid	350
Dividend received	1,150
Payments to suppliers	175,000
Payments to employees	55,000
Expenses paid	10,000
Receipts from customers	250,000

Prepare a statement of cash flows using the direct method to report cash flows from operating activities for the year ended 31 December 2012.

Solution

(a) Under the direct method of reporting cash flows from operating activities, cash inflows and outflows are directly reported, starting with the major categories of gross receipts and payments. This means that cash flows such as receipts from customers and payments to suppliers are stated separately within the operating activities. By contrast, the indirect method starts from operating profit, and adjusts for movements in working capital and for non-cash items such as depreciation. Because the direct method deals with the natural cycle of cash flows (i.e. receipts and payments), it is easier to understand. Again, by contrast, it is less easy to grasp the adjustments to operating profit required by the indirect method. The reason most companies use the indirect method is primarily because the statement of cash flows is prepared from the existing statement of comprehensive income and statement of financial position. It is therefore a matter of putting through a set of overall adjustments. In addition, the direct method potentially requires a lot of work to analyse the constituent cash flows from the cash book. This will involve additional expense, which companies may not wish to incur. Finally, for reasons of confidentiality, companies may not wish to reveal comprehensive details of their cash flows from customers or to suppliers.

(b) Gemmill Ltd

Statement of cash flows (direct method) Year ended 31 December 2012		
Cash flow from operating activities	£	£
Receipts from customers	250,000	
Payments to suppliers	(175,000)	
Payment to employees	(55,000)	
Expenses paid	(10,000)	
Net cash inflow from operating activities		10,000
Cash flow from financing activities		
Loan repaid	(25,000)	
Interest paid (i)	(350)	
Net cash flow from financing activities		(25,350)
Cash flow from investing activities		
Dividend received (ii)	1,150	
Purchase of office equipment	(15,000)	
Sale of property	25,000	
		11,150
Decrease in cash		(4,200)

Notes:

(i) interest paid may be classified as either an operating or financing activity

(ii) dividends received may be classified as either operating or investing activities.

Progress Point 10.6

The following information relates to Runstone Ltd.

Statement of comprehensive income for year ended 31 December Year 4		
	£000	£000
Sales		500
Cost of sales		350
Gross profit		150
Expenses	121	
Depreciation	10	
		131
Net profit		19

Statement of financial position as at 31 December		
	Year 4	Year 3
	£000	£000
Non-current assets	130	130
Less depreciation to date	20	10
	110	120
Inventory	32	25
Trade receivables	60	40
Bank	–	5
	92	70
Trade payables	36	48
Bank overdraft	5	–
	41	48
	161	142
Equity		
Issued share capital	100	100
Retained profit	61	42
	161	142

Prepare a statement of cash flows using the indirect (net) method of reporting cash flows from operating activities that explains the changes in the bank account of Runstone Ltd between Year 3 and Year 4.

Solution

	(£000)
Profit for the year	19
Add: depreciation	10
	29
Increase in inventories	(7)
Increase in trade receivables	(20)
Decrease in trade payables	(12)
Decrease in cash	(10)
Cash in Year 3	£5
Bank overdraft in Year 4	£5

Cash has moved from £5 in Year 3 to an overdraft in Year 4, a decrease of £10 over the period.

Although Runstone made a profit of £19,000, a £10,000 depreciation charge had been deducted in arriving at that profit figure. The depreciation charge does not involve a flow of cash and must be added back to the profit figure in order to compensate for the fact that there is no cash impact. Inventory increased by £7 over the period, implying that some cash was used to buy this inventory. Trade receivables increased by £20,000, which meant that although sales had been made, no cash was generated from £20,000 of these sales. In other words, no cash income. Trade payables decreased over the period, implying that some of the cash has been used to pay them and so depleting the cash balance further. The net effect of all of the above has been to turn a positive bank figure of £5 – into an overdraft of £5 – a reduction of £10.

Examination issues

Students, and indeed many qualified accountants (!), often dread having to prepare a statement of cash flows. However, adopting a consistent, methodical approach to preparing the statement should ensure that those concerns are left unfounded.

A typical examination question on statements of cash flows will involve a statement of comprehensive income and statements of financial position at the beginning and the end of the reporting period and a number of additional notes.

The secret to preparing a statement of cash flows that corresponds to the changes in cash as disclosed in the statement of financial position is to ensure that you deal with every item, on a line by line basis, in the statement of comprehensive income and the statement of financial position. A good approach is to 'tick off' each item as you consider it and this ensures that you have considered all the data and avoids having to consider or re-read data you have already dealt with. It is also helpful to draft a pro-forma statement with the appropriate headings ready to be completed as you work your way down the statement of financial position and statement of comprehensive income.

If you are required to report cash flows from operating activities using the indirect method, the problem is often deciding which profit figure to use as your starting point. The illustrative example in IAS 7 starts with 'profit before taxation' and so this is the preferred starting point.

The figure is then adjusted for non-cash transactions (e.g. depreciation) and changes during the period in working capital such as inventories and operating receivables and payables. This latter point is very important. What you are trying to do is match like with like i.e. the operating items in the statement of comprehensive income with their corresponding operating receivables and payables in the statement of financial position. If, for example, there are any amounts payable in respect of the acquisition of non-current assets (i.e. investing cash flows), these must be excluded from the movement in trade payables to be included in the reconciliation. Similarly, if there are amounts due in respect of accrued interest then these too should be adjusted for.

Having calculated the net cash flow from operating activities the next stage is to consider the investing and financing activities. Typically you will have opening and closing balances from the statement of financial position and a number of movements in the year – except the one you are after i.e. the cash flow. The purchase of fixed assets is often one of the more complicated figures to calculate.

Remember that you can calculate the net cash inflow or outflow by reference to the opening and closing statements of financial position. You know, therefore, the figure you are trying to reconcile to. If it does not balance, look to see if there are any figures that are 'unticked'. Next, look to see if the difference corresponds to any of the figures in the statements of financial position or comprehensive income. Another useful 'tool' is to divide the amount by which the statement is out by two, to see if this highlights anything. For example, you may had added a figure when you should have subtracted it, or vice versa. If the balancing figure divides by nine it is possible you may have made a transposition error.

Whatever approach you choose to adopt, its success will be improved by practice. With this in mind, try working through the next Progress Point which illustrates many of the points discussed in the chapter.

Progress Point 10.7

An extract from the statement of comprehensive income of Telbat Ltd for the year to 31 December 2012 is shown below, together with the company's statement of financial position at that date together with comparatives for the previous year.

Statement of comprehensive income (extract) for the year to 31 December 2012	
	£000
Operating profit	532
Interest	(180)
Profit before taxation	352
Taxation	(183)
Profit for the year	169

Statement of financial position at 31 December 2012		
	2012	2011
	£000	£000
Non-current assets		
Plant & equipment	1,813	1,524
Current assets		
Inventory	106	102
Trade receivables	164	189
Cash & cash equivalents	197	191
Total assets	2,280	2,006
Equity and liabilities		
Ordinary share capital	800	800
Retained earnings	228	124
	1,028	924
Non-current liabilities		
Debentures	1,000	800
Current liabilities		
Trade payables	124	168
Interest payable	45	40
Current taxation	83	74
Total liabilities	252	282
Total equity and liabilities	2,280	2,00

Notes:

(i) Operating profit is arrived at after charging depreciation for the year of £167,000.

(ii) During the year a machine which had originally cost £120,000 and had a net book value of £24,000 was sold at a loss of £14,000. This loss is included in arriving at the operating profit figure.

(iii) The company acquired two pieces of machinery during the year. At the year end, the entire cost of one of the machines, £40,000 was unpaid and included within the trade payables figure.

(iv) Dividends of £65,000 were paid during the year.

Required

Prepare the statement of cash flows for the year to 31 December 2012 in accordance with the requirements of IAS 7 using the indirect method to calculate the cash flows from operating activities.

Solution

The items in the statement of financial position will be considered line by line.

(i) Plant & equipment

There have been both purchases and sales of plant and equipment and so we need to ascertain the relevant amounts. In addition, we are told that the cost of one of the machines, £40,000 has not been paid for and is included in trade payables.

	£000
Net book value at 31 December 2011	1,524
Less: Disposal at net book value	(24)
Depreciation	(167)
	1,333
Net book value at 31 December 2012	1,813
Purchases of plant & equipment	480

However, £40,000 remains payable for the second machine, therefore the actual cash flows in respect of purchases of plant and equipment are £480,000 – £40,000 = £440,000.

(ii) Sale of plant & equipment

Net book value of assets sold	24
Loss on sale	14
Sales proceeds	10

(iii) The changes in the current assets are dealt with in the statement of cash flows.

(iv) There have been no changes to share capital; however, there must have been an issue of debentures during the year of £1,000,000 – £800,000 = £200,000.

(v) The changes in the current liabilities are dealt with in the statement of cash flows after adjusting the trade payables for the amount relating to the purchase of the plant and equipment. Remember that we are only dealing with those changes in current assets and current liabilities that relate to operating revenues and expenses. The relevant trade payables figure at 31 December 2012 is therefore £124,000 – £40,000 = £84,000.

BASIC

INTERMEDIATE

ADVANCED

BASIC

INTERMEDIATE

ADVANCED

(vi)   IAS 7 requires separate disclosures of interest and taxation paid in the year so we need to calculate these amounts as follows:

	£000
Interest: Opening balance	40
Add: charge for year	180
	220
Less: Closing balance	45
Interest paid	175
Taxation: Opening balance	74
Add: Charge for year	183
	257
Less: Closing balance	83
Taxation paid	174

(vii)   We are now in a position to draft the statement of cash flows using the profit before taxation
figure as the starting point in the calculation of cash flows from operating activities.

(viii)   Remember that we know the figure we are trying to reconcile to i.e. the change in the cash
and cash equivalents balance over the year.

	£000
At 31 December 2011	191
At 31 December 2012	197
Increase	6

Statement of cash flows for the year to 31 December 2012

Cash flows from operating activities

	£000	£000
Profit before taxation	352	
Adjustments for:		
Depreciation	167	
Loss on sale	14	
Interest expense	180	
Profit before working capital changes	713	
Increase in inventories	(4)	

Decrease in trade receiveables	25	
Decrease in trade payables (168 – 84)	(84)	
Cash generated from operations	650	
Interest paid	(175)	
Taxation paid	(174)	
Net cash from operating activities		301
Cash flows from investing activities		
Purchase of plant and equipment	(440)	
Disposal of plant and equipment	10	
Net cash flow from investing activities		(430)
Cash flows from financing activities		
Issue of debentures	200	
Dividends paid	(65)	
Net cash flow from financing activities		135
Net increase in cash and cash equivalents		6
Cash and cash equivalents at 1 January 2012		191
Cash and cash equivalents at 31 December 2012		197

10.5 Disclosure requirements

IAS 7 requires entities to disclose the components of cash and cash equivalents and to present a reconciliation of the amounts in its statement of cash flows with the equivalent items reported in the statement of financial position.

In addition, where investing and financing transactions are undertaken that do not require the use of cash or cash equivalents, these should be disclosed elsewhere in the financial statements in a way that provides all the relevant information about these investing and financing activities.

10.6 Disclosure in practice

The disclosure requirements of IAS 7 *Statement of Cash Flows* are contained with the statement itself together with notes to the financial statements.

Logica's statement of cash flows (Figure 10.1) reports, as required by IAS 7, cash flows for the year ended 31 December 2011, classified by operating, investing and financing activities.

Figure 10.1 Logica: consolidated cash flow statement

Consolidated statement of cash flows
for the year ended 31 December 2011

	2011 £'m	2010 £'m
Cash flows from operating activities		
Net cash inflow from trading operations	226.4	270.1
Cash outflow related to restructuring and integration activities	(18.4)	(36.8)
Cash outflow related to business acquired/disposed of	(2.7)	(4.8)
Cash generated from operations	205.3	228.5
Finance costs paid	(21.5)	(20.1)
Income tax paid	(36.4)	(50.9)
Net cash inflow from operating activities	147.4	157.5
Cash flows from investing activities		
Finance income received	6.8	3.8
Dividends received from associates	1.0	0.4
Proceeds on disposal of property, plant and equipment	0.3	0.2
Purchases of property, plant and equipment	(49.7)	(45.8)
Expenditure on other intangible assets	(29.2)	(28.8)
Repurchase of non-controlling interests	(0.1)	–
Acquisition of subsidiaries and other businesses, net of cash acquired	(16.7)	(8.9)
Proceeds on disposal of subsidiaries and other businesses, net of cash disposed	–	3.2
Net cash outflow from investing activities	(87.6)	(75.9)
Cash flows from financing activities		
Proceeds from issue of shares allotted under share plans	3.6	0.4
Refund of expenses related to shares issued in prior years	–	5.6
Proceeds from bank borrowings	30.0	230.9
Repayments of bank borrowings	(179.8)	(399.8)
Proceeds from private placement debt notes, net of issuance cost	187.8	88.9
Repayments of finance leases	(2.4)	(3.4)
Repayments of other borrowings	(1.3)	(0.7)
Net proceeds from forward contracts	(0.4)	(17.7)
Dividends paid to the Company's shareholders	(70.2)	(66.8)
Net cash outflow from financing activities	(32.7)	(162.6)
Net increase/(decrease) in cash, cash equivalents and bank overdrafts	27.1	(81.0)
Cash, cash equivalents and bank overdrafts at the beginning of the year	30.6	110.1
Net increase/(decrease) in cash, cash equivalents and bank overdrafts	27.1	(81.0)
Effect of foreign exchange rates	(1.1)	1.5
Cash, cash equivalents and bank overdrafts at the end of the year	56.6	30.6

Source: Logica (2011), p. 153

BASIC

INTERMEDIATE

ADVANCED

Figure 10.2 Logica: reconciliation of operating profit to cash generated from continuing operations

	2011	2010
	£'m	£'m
At 1 January	0.1	0.1
Repurchase of non-controlling interests	(0.1)	–
At 31 December	–	0.1

Reconciliation of operating profit to cash generated from operations

	2011	2010
	£'m	£'m
Operating profit from operations	54.5	210.6
Adjustments for:		
Share-based payment expense	7.0	12.1
Depreciation of property, plant and equipment	46.6	42.7
Loss on disposal of non-current assets	0.8	2.5
Net movement in provision for impairment of trade receivables	(0.3)	–
Loss on sale of subsidiaries and disposed of/held-for-sale businesses	–	1.7
Unrealised foreign exchange differences	(2.8)	–
Government grant income	(2.6)	–
Amortisation of intangible assets	72.8	74.9
Non-cash element of expense for defined benefit plans	(17.6)	(7.1)
	103.9	126.8
Net movements in provisions	70.7	(52.7)
Movements in working capital:		
Financial assets	–	(0.1)
Inventories	0.2	0.1
Trade and other receivables	(27.7)	(116.1)
Trade and other payables	3.7	59.9
	(23.8)	(56.2)
Cash generated from operations	205.3	228.5
Add back: Cash outflow related to restructuring and integration activities	18.4	36.8
Add back: Cash outflow related to business acquired/disposed of	2.7	4.8
Net cash inflow from trading operations	226.4	270.1

Source: Logica (2011), p. 130

BASIC

INTERMEDIATE

ADVANCED

Cash generated from continuing operations is detailed further in this note to the statement. The adjustments made include many of those that have been dealt with in this chapter. The complexities of Logica's operating activities mean that additional adjustments are required in respect of defined benefit plans, share-based payments and defined benefit plans.

The Group defines net debt as borrowings, including related derivatives, less cash:

Figure 10.3 Logica: reconciliation of movements in net debt

	At 1 January 2011	Cash flows	Other non-cash movements	Acquisitions	Exchange differences	At 31 December 2011
	£'m	£'m	£'m	£'m	£'m	£'m
Cash and cash equivalents	56.4	51.0	–	(16.7)	(1.1)	89.6
Bank overdrafts	(25.8)	(7.2)	–	–	–	(33.0)
	30.6	43.8	–	(16.7)	(1.1)	56.6
Finance leases	(4.2)	2.4	(0.6)	(0.8)	0.1	(3.1)
Bank loans	(216.3)	149.8	(1.7)	(3.6)	(0.2)	(72.0)
Private placement debt notes	(88.7)	(187.8)	(17.7)	–	(3.1)	(297.3)
Other borrowings	(1.6)	1.3	(0.1)	(5.5)	0.1	(5.8)
Derivatives in respect of net debt (Note 26)	–	–	12.2	–	14.4	26.6
Net debt	(280.2)	9.5	(7.9)	(26.6)	10.2	(295.0)

Figure 10.4 Logica: cash and cash equivalents

Cash, cash equivalents and bank overdrafts at the end of the reporting period comprised:

	2011	2010
	£'m	£'m
Cash at bank and in hand	78.9	56.4
Short-term deposits	10.7	–
	89.6	56.4
Bank overdrafts	(33.0)	(25.8)
Cash, cash equivalents and bank overdrafts	56.6	30.6

The Group's credit risk on cash, cash equivalents and bank overdrafts is limited because the counterparties are well-established banks with high credit ratings. Included in cash at bank and in hand were overdrafts that were part of cash pooling arrangements for which a legal right of off-set existed against positive cash balances that were of an equal or greater amount at the end of the reporting period. The Directors estimate that the carrying value of cash and cash equivalents approximated their fair value.

The Group's policy for cash investments requires that cash and deposits only be placed with counterparties that have a minimum A1/P1 short term rating and A- equivalent long term credit rating. The reference to ratings must include at least one from either Standard & Poor's or Moody's. Cash and deposits are limited to £25.0 million per bank where the bank has a minimum AA-rating and £10.0 million per bank where the bank is rated A or A-. No credit limits were exceeded during the reporting period and management does not expect any losses from non-performance by any of these counterparties.

Source: Logica (2011), p. 119f.

BASIC

INTERMEDIATE

ADVANCED

The reconciliation of movements in net debt discloses the classifications of finances and borrowings adopted by Logica. Note that Logica takes a prudent view with its cash investments; no more than £25 million is deposited with any one bank.

Section summary

IAS 7 requires that the statement of cash flows should report cash flows classified by operating, investing and financial activities. In arriving at cash flows from operating activities, IAS 7 allows an entity to choose between the direct method and the indirect method. In addition there are choices about the presentation of dividends and interest. Finally, the definition of cash and cash equivalents can cause problems where different entities classify cash equivalents differently, leading to a lack of comparability. Notwithstanding, the production of cash flow information provides valuable information to users.

Section 3: Advanced Aspects

This section extends and expands the previous two sections. It begins by considering some of the more problematic situations found in practice and then considers the historical development of statements of cash flows in terms of the publication of SFAC No. 1 *Objective of Financial Statements by Business Enterprises*. Finally a critical appraisal is made of the standard and its objectives.

Non-cash transactions

In the examples so far, the only illustrations of non-cash transactions have been depreciation, losses on disposal or gains on disposal of assets.

IAS 7 states that investing and financing transactions that do not require the use of cash or cash equivalents should be excluded from a statement of cash flows, and should be disclosed elsewhere in the financial statements in a way that provides all the relevant information about these investing and financing cash flows.

Examples of investing and financing transactions that do not result in cash flows and consequently are excluded from the statement of cash flows include:

(a) the acquisition of an asset by way of a finance lease (but the payments for lease rentals would be cash flows);

(b) the acquisition or disposal of assets (other than cash) in return for equity securities;

(c) exchanges of non-monetary assets such as property, plant and equipment, and inventories;

(d) the issue of bonus shares to holders of the entity's equity;

(e) the conversion of debt securities into equity securities.

In this example, from an initial examination of the movement in the share capital in the statement of financial position it would appear that there has been a share issue. The notes to the accounts, however, will explain the reason for the change in share capital. The conversion from debentures into share capital has been made, so no flows of cash have taken place.

As noted earlier, where transactions of a non-cash nature occur, the standard requires that they be disclosed elsewhere in the financial statements in a way that provides all of the relevant information about those investing and financing activities. This disclosure will normally be in narrative form in the notes.

Example: Finance Lease Contract

The notes to the accounts of Roughwall show the following non-current asset note:

	Freehold property	Plant and machinery	Total
	£	£	£
Cost at 1 January 2012	750,000	200,000	950,000
Additions	–	150,000	150,000
Disposals	–	–	–
Cost at 31 December 2012	750,000	350,000	1,110,000

Assume that included in the additions to non-current assets figure of £150,000 is an amount of £100,000 in respect of assets held under finance leases. Such a transaction, although reflected in the statement of financial position by recognizing an asset and a corresponding liability, should not be reflected in the statement of cash flows because the reporting entity neither pays nor receives cash. It would not be appropriate to show a cash outflow in respect of an asset purchase and the drawdown of a loan.

BASIC

INTERMEDIATE

ADVANCED

Example: non-cash transaction where debt is converted to equity

Statement of financial position extract		
	Year 4	Year 3
	£000	£000
Debentures	100	200
Share capital	200	100

Notes to the accounts

During the year £100,000 10% debentures were converted to £100,000 ordinary shares.

10.7 Development of statement of cash flows

In November 1987 the requirement to produce a statement of cash flow was required in the USA when SFAS 95 was issued by the FASB. This requirement by the USA started a trend in financial reporting that extended worldwide. It had been long recognized by the FASB, since the publication of SFAC No. 1 *Objectives of Financial Reporting by Business Enterprises* in 1978, that investors, potential investors, creditors and other users of financial information needed information to assess the amounts, timing and uncertainty of prospective net inflows to the related enterprise.

SFAC No. 5 *Recognition and Measurement in Financial Statements of Business Enterprises*, published in December 1984, stated that a 'full set of financial statements for a period should show:... cash flows during the period'.

In July 1977 the IASC originally approved IAS 7 *Statement of Changes in Financial Position*, which required the presentation of a statement of sources and use of funds. IAS 7 was revised in 1992 and renamed *Cash Flow Statements*; it required businesses to prepare a cash flow statement. An amended version of IAS 7 is now mandatory for financial periods beginning on or after 1 January 2005. In September 2007, IAS 7 was retitled *Statement of Cash Flows* as a consequential amendment resulting from revisions to IAS 1.

10.8 IAS 7: a critical appraisal

The objective as stated by IAS 7 is 'to require the provision of information about the historical changes in cash and cash equivalents of an entity by means of a cash flow statement which classified cash flows during the period from operating, investing and financing activities' (IAS 7). The aim of the standard is to give users of financial statements a basis on which to evaluate the ability of a business to generate cash and cash equivalents.

IAS 7 goes on to state that a statement of cash flows, when used in conjunction with the rest of the financial statements, provides information that enables users to evaluate the changes in net assets of an entity, its financial structure (including its liquidity and solvency) and its ability to affect the amounts and timings of cash flows in order to adapt to changing circumstances and opportunities. In addition, it contends that cash flow information is useful in assessing the ability of the entity to generate cash and cash equivalents and enables users to develop models to assess and compare the present value of the future cash flows of different entities.

However, although these benefits are outlined in the standard it is questionable if all those benefits referred to can really be derived from the statement of cash flows. After all, the statement of cash flows shows only the changes in the cash of a business on a historic basis.

The statement of cash flows is useful in that it highlights the differences and the similarities between the various elements of profitability and net cash flow. Also, cash flow information is less easily manipulated or influenced by the effect of different accounting treatments. It has to be said that, even in conjunction with the other information obtainable for the financial statements, it would be difficult for a user of accounting information to assess the extent to which an organization could adapt to changing financial circumstances, the timing and certainty of future cash flows and indeed the impact of changing prices.

A statement of cash flows does, however, highlight the significant components of cash generation. The format of the statement separating cash flows into operating, investing and financing cash flows enables users to determine where cash has been generated from and where it has been spent. This can assist in making predictions about future sources of cash and the areas in which it will be spent. Cash is undoubtedly more easily understood by users and less easy to manipulate than profit. Indeed, if a company is only maintaining a positive cash balance by selling off its assets then this would be brought out in the statement of cash flows. In addition, statements of financial position may be strengthened by the revaluation of non-current assets; again such masking of potential problems is exposed by the disclosures in the statement of cash flows.

It could be argued that the adequacy of IAS 7 in providing information to suit the user's needs depends on the user. Some users may find the headings confusing and the computation of cash flows from operating activities impossible to follow. In addition, comparison between companies may prove problematic where different classifications of items are prevalent e.g. interest and dividends.

IAS 7 currently allows an entity to choose between the direct and indirect methods of reporting cash flows from operating activities. Those in favour of the indirect method argue that this highlights the difference between the profit for the year and net cash flows from operating activities and therefore gives an indication of the quality of a company's reported earnings. The direct method provides more obvious information about the sources and uses of cash and therefore helps in the estimation of future cash flows. Research has shown that the direct method is a better predictor of company failure providing information that is not unavailable using the indirect method.

By allowing a choice, it is highly unlikely that companies would choose to use the direct method if it was likely to indicate that the company was at risk of failure.

It could be argued that the IAS 7 approach in allowing a choice is flawed and indeed the IASB are currently working on a revised version of IAS 7 which is likely to remove the choice and require all companies to use the direct method. If such a requirement is made then the extraction of the information by companies to prepare the statement is likely to be extremely costly; many companies operate accounting systems that are geared towards accrual accounting and not receipts and payments accounting. Finally, for reasons of confidentiality, companies may not wish to reveal comprehensive details of their cash flows from customers or to suppliers.

Section summary

Both preparers and users of financial statements can generally understand IAS 7. The objective of the standard is to require information about the changes in cash and cash equivalents to be disclosed. The application is relatively straightforward in that it requires cash flows to be classified under one of three headings. Businesses have some discretion over the treatment of interest and dividend cash flows provided these are separately disclosed and are treated consistently from period to period. The current version of IAS 7 allows companies to choose between the direct or indirect methods of reporting cash flows from operating activities.

Chapter summary

IAS 7 *Statement of Cash Flows*

- Requires the presentation of information about the changes in cash and cash equivalents by means of a statement of cash flows.
- Cash comprises cash on hand and demand deposits.
- Cash equivalents are short-term highly liquid investments that are readily convertible to known amounts of cash.
- Statement classifies cash flows according to operating, investing and financing activities.
- Operating activities are the principal revenue-producing activities of the entity.
- Investing activities are the acquisition and disposal of long-term assets and other investments not included in cash equivalents.
- Financing activities are activities that alter the equity capital and borrowing structure of the enterprise.
- Cash flows from operating activities may be reported using either:
  - (a) the direct method, whereby major classes of gross cash receipts and gross cash payments are disclosed, or
  - (b) the indirect method, whereby profit or loss is adjusted for non-cash charges and credits, changes in working capital and items of income or expense associated with investing or financing cash flows.
- Investing and financing activities that do not require the use of cash or cash equivalents should be excluded from a statement of cash flows.
- Cash and cash equivalents are disclosed and reconciled with the amounts in the cash flow statement.

✓ Key terms for review

Definitions can be found in the glossary at the end of the book.

Cash equivalents	Financing activities	Operating activities
Cash flows	Investing activities	Profit vs cash flow

? Review questions

1. Why is it that a profitable business can find itself short of cash?
2. Is it possible for a business to make losses year after year but still increase its bank balance?
3. What is the main aim of a statement of cash flows?
4. How does an increase in the depreciation charge affect the operating profit and the net cash flow from operating activities?
5. Distinguish between the *direct method* and *indirect method* of calculating the net cash flow from operating activities.
6. List the main adjustments that are required if the indirect method of calculating the net cash flow from operating activities is used.
7. Explain what is meant by *cash and cash equivalents*.
8. Explain each of the following terms, which are defined in IAS 7:
   (a) operating activities
   (b) investing activities
   (c) financing activities.
9. How are non-cash investing and financing transactions dealt with in accordance with IAS 7?
10. Which entities have to prepare a statement of cash flows?

✎ Exercises

Level I

1. A company has the following statement of comprehensive income for the year ended 31 December 2012 and statement of financial position extracts at that date.

Statement of comprehensive income for the year to 31 December 2012	
	£
Turnover	1,200,000
Cost of sales	(840,000)
Gross profit	360,000
Distribution and administration expenses	(120,000)
Profit before tax	240,000

Statement of financial position extracts at 31 December 2012		
	2012	2011
	£	£
Current assets		
Inventories	160,000	140,000
Trade receivables	288,000	235,000
Current liabilities		
Trade payables	168,000	138,000

You are given the following information.

(i) Expenses includes depreciation of £36,000.

(ii) During the year the company disposed of an item of plant for £24,000, which had a net book value of £18,000. The profit had been netted off expenses.

Required

(a) Show how the net cash flow from operating activities would be presented in the statement of cash flows under the direct method.

(b) Using the same information, show the net cash flow from operating activities using the indirect method.

2. The following are extracts from the financial statements of Sparrow Ltd for the year ended 31 December 2012.

Statement of comprehensive income

	£000
Profit before tax	2,408
Tax	620
Profit for the year	1,788

Statement of financial position

	2012	2011
	£000	£000
Non-current assets		
Property, plant & equipment	7,265	5,760
Current assets		
Inventories	3,604	3,720
Trade receivables	5,001	4,896
Bank	–	544
	8,605	9,160
Current liabilities		
Trade payables	1,854	2,072
Bank overdraft	116	–
Taxation	620	856
Dividend payable	600	500
	3,190	3,428
Total assets less current liabilities	12,680	11,492
Equity		
Share capital	10,000	10,000
Retained earnings	2,680	1,492
	12,680	11,492

Additional information:

(i) In arriving at profit before tax, depreciation for the year of £3,905,000 had been charged.

(ii) Dividends of £600,000 had been declared on 15 December 2012.

Required

Prepare a statement of cash flows for the year ended 31 December 2012 as required by IAS 7 using the indirect method to calculate cash flows from operating activities.

Level II

3. The following are extracts from the statement of comprehensive income and the statements of financial position of Croft Ltd ('Croft').

Statement of comprehensive income
year to 30 April 2013

	£
Turnover	4,200,000
Cost of sales	(2,870,000)
Gross profit	1,330,000
Distribution costs	(280,000)
Administrative expenses	(473,000)
Operating profit	577,000
Interest	(23,000)
Profit before tax	554,000

Statement of financial position as at 30 April

	2013	2012
	£	£
Current assets		
Inventory	318,000	292,000
Trade receivables	416,000	389,000
Cash and cash equivalents	71,000	25,000
Current liabilities		
Trade payables	373,000	320,000
Accruals	61,000	85,000

Notes

(1) Operating profit includes a gain of £5,000 on the disposal of a non-current asset and £12,000 amortization of a government grant. These were deducted in arriving at net administrative expenses.

(2) Accruals at 30 April 2013 includes £16,000 accrued interest (for 2012 the amount was £14,000).

(3) Cost of sales includes depreciation of £215,000.

Required

(a) Prepare the cash generated from operating activities under the indirect method.

(b) Using the following additional information, produce the cash generated from operating activities under the direct method.

    (i) Cost of sales, distribution costs and administrative expenses include wage and salary costs, all of which were paid by the year end.

    (ii) Administrative expenses includes £17,000 bad debt written off in the year.

4. Margot Ltd had the following non-current asset balances at 1 January 2012:

	Land	Machinery
	£	£
NBV	1,000,000	2,800,000

During the year to 31 December 2012 the following occurred:

  (i) land was revalued upwards by £600,000

 (ii) depreciation of £1,016,000 at 20% straight line was charged on machinery

(iii) a piece of machinery, bought in 2009 for £410,000 was sold for £120,000

(iv) machinery with a fair value of £70,000 was obtained under a new finance lease during the year.

At 31 December 2012 the company had the following non-current asset balances:

	Land	Machinery
	£	£
NBV	1,850,000	3,110,000

It is the policy of the company to charge a full year's depreciation in the year of purchase and none in the year of disposal.

Required

Calculate purchases of non-current assets for the year to 31 December 2012.

5. Sharma plc's draft statement of comprehensive income for the year ended 31 December 2012 and statements of financial position at 31 December 2012 and 31 December 2011 were as follows:

Sharma plc
Statement of comprehensive income for the year ended 31 December 2012

	£000
Sales	360
Distribution and administrative expenses	186

Operating profit	174
Interest payable	14
Profit before tax	160
Taxation	62
Profit for year	98

Statement of financial position as at 31 December 2012

	2012		2011	
	£000	£000	£000	£000
Non-current assets:				
Property, plant and equipment at cost		798		780
Depreciation		159		112
		639		668
Current assets:				
Inventory	12		10	
Trade receivables	33		25	
Bank deposit account	24		28	
	69		63	
Current liabilities:				
Bank overdraft	10		8	
Trade payables	6		3	
Taxation	51		43	
	67		54	
Net current assets		2		9
		641		677
Long-term loans		100		250
		541		427
Share capital (£1 shares)		180		170
Share premium		18		12
Retained earnings		343		245
		541		427

In addition, the following information is available.

(i) Included within distribution and administration expenses were:
   - Depreciation   £59,000
   - Loss on disposal   £9,000
(ii) During the year, the company paid £45,000 for a new piece of machinery.

Required

Prepare a statement of cash flows for Sharma plc for the year ended 31 December 2012 as required by IAS 7, using the indirect method to calculate cash flows from operating activities.

6. The following information has been extracted from the draft financial statements of T plc:

T plc
Statement of comprehensive income
for the year ended 30 September 2013

	£000
Sales	15,000
Cost of sales	(9,000)
	6,000
Other operating expenses	(2,400)
	3,600
Interest	(24)
Profit before taxation	3,576
Taxation	(1,040)
Profit for the year	2,536

T plc
Statement of changes in equity (retained earnings only)
for the year to 30 September 2013

	£000
Balance at 30 September 2012	4,400
Profit for the year	2,536
Dividends	(1,100)
Balance at 30 September 2013	5,836

T plc
Statement of financial position at 30 September

	2013		2012	
	£000	£000	£000	£000
Non-current assets:	18,160		14,500	
Current assets:				
Inventory	1,600		1,100	
Trade receivables	1,500		800	
Bank	150		1,200	
	3,250		3,100	
Current liabilities:				
Trade payables	(700)		(800)	

Dividends payable	(700)	(600)
Taxation	(1,040)	(685)
	(2,440)	(2,085)
Net current assets	810	1,015
	18,970	15,515
Long-term loans	(1,700)	(2,900)
	17,270	12,615
Deferred tax	(600)	(400)
Equity	16,670	12,215
Ordinary share capital (£1 share)	2,500	2,000
Share premium	8,334	5,815
Retained earnings	5,836	4,400
	16,670	12,215

Non-current assets schedule

	Land and buildings £000	Plant and machinery £000	Total £000
Cost			
30 September 2012	8,400	10,800	19,200
Additions	2,800	5,200	8,000
Disposals	–	(2,600)	(2,600)
30 September 2013	11,200	13,400	24,600
Depreciation			
30 September 2012	1,300	3,400	4,700
Disposals	–	(900)	(900)
Charge for year	240	2,400	2,640
30 September 2013	1,540	4,900	6,440
Net book value			
30 September 2013	9,660	8,500	18,160
30 September 2012	7,100	7,400	14,500

The plant and machinery that was disposed of during the year was sold for £730,000.

Required

(a) Prepare T plc's complete statement of changes in equity for the year ended 30 September 2013.
(b) Prepare T plc's statement of cash flows using the indirect method to arrive at cash flows from operating activities for the year ended 30 September 2013.

Level III

7. The following information relates to Ronile plc for the year ended 31 December 2012.

Statement of financial position as at 31 December 2012

	2012 £000	2011 £000
Non-current assets		
Property – at cost	90	60
Plant & equipment	125	48
	215	108
Current assets		
Inventory	170	140
Trade receivables	120	100
Cash at bank	2	1
	292	241
Total assets	507	349
Equity		
Ordinary share capital (£1 share)	250	200
Share premium account	25	–
Retained earnings	108	70
	383	270
Liabilities		
Trade payables	64	40
Interest payable	2	1
Corporation tax	26	16
Dividends payable	20	16
Bank overdraft	12	6
	124	79
	507	349

Statement of comprehensive income for the year ended 31 December 2012

	£000	£000
Revenue		300
Cost of sales		180
Gross profit		120
Distribution	15	
Administration	19	
		34
Operating profit		86
Interest payable		2
Profit before tax		84
Taxation		26
Profit for the year		58

Additional information:

(i) A final dividend of £20,000 for the year to 31 December 2012 was declared on 1 December 2012.

(ii) Cost of sales includes depreciation on plant and equipment of £28,000.

Required

(a) Prepare Ronile plc's statement of changes in equity for the year to 31 December 2012.

(b) Prepare a statement of cash flows for Ronile plc for the year to 31 December 2012 in accordance with IAS 7.

8. You have been provided with the following information relating to Belgar plc for the year to 31 March 2013.

Statement of comprehensive income for the year to 31 March 2013

	£000
Turnover	4,850
Cost of sales	600
Gross profit	4,250
Distribution and administration expenses	2,875
Operating profit	1,375
Interest	300
Profit before tax	1,075
Taxation	670
Profit for the period	405

Statements of financial position at 31 March 2013

	2013		2012	
	£000	£000	£000	£000
Non-current assets:				
Land and buildings at cost		3,500		1,800
Plant and machinery at cost	6,100		5,800	
Less: depreciation	3,900		3,850	
	2,200		1,950	
		5,700		3,750
Current assets				
Inventory and work in progress	3,435		3,150	
Trade receivables	2,200		1,900	
Bank	160		500	
	5,795		5,550	
Current liabilities				
Bank overdraft	(1,750)		(1,500)	
Trade payables	(1,450)		(1,550)	
Taxation	(820)		(1,150)	
	(4,020)		(4,200)	
Net current assets	1,775		1,350	
	7,475		5,100	
Debentures – 8% £1	2,000		–	
	5,475		5,100	
Share capital – fully paid	1,200		1,000	
Ordinary £1 shares	550		600	
Share premium	3,725		3,500	
Retained profits	5,475		5,100	

Additional information:

(i) The ordinary dividend paid during the year and charged against the profit after tax was £180,000.

(ii) Interest of £300,000 was made up of:
   - Debenture interest £160,000 (£80,000 accrual included in creditors)
   - Overdraft interest £140,000 (all paid in year)

(iii) During the year, plant and equipment that had cost £1,200,000, and on which depreciation of £590,000 had been provided, was sold for £565,000.

(iv) There had been a rights issue of ordinary shares at the rate of 1 for 10 at a price of £1.50 per share payable in full on 1 April 2012.

(v) Subsequently, a bonus issue of 1 for 11 shares had been made utilizing the share premium account.

(vi) The 8% debentures had been issued at par on 1 April 2012, payable in full.

Required

Prepare the statement of cash flows for the year to 31 March 2013 for Belgar plc in accordance with IAS 7, using the indirect method to calculate the cash flows from operating activities.

References

IAS 1 *Presentation of Financial Statements*. IAS, amended 2012.
IAS 7 *Statement of Cash Flows*. IASB, amended 2009.
IAS 23 *Borrowing Costs*. IASB, amended 2008.
Logica (2011) *Annual Report and Accounts*

Further reading

Holmes, G., Sugden, A., and Gee, P. (2008) *Interpreting Company Reports and Accounts* (10th edn). FT/ Prentice Hall.
IFRS: www.ifrs.org.
SFAS 95 *Statement of Cash flows*. FASB, November 1987.

Online LearningCentre

When you have read this chapter, log on to the Online Learning Centre website at *www.mcgraw-hill.co.uk/textbooks/mckeith* to explore chapter-by-chapter test questions, further reading and more online study tools.

Chapter 11

Business Combinations

Learning Outcomes

After studying this chapter you should be able to:

- ✓ record an investment in another company
- ✓ explain what is meant by a set of consolidated financial statements
- ✓ calculate and adjust for goodwill, non-controlling interests and pre-acquisition reserves
- ✓ prepare a consolidated statement of financial position and statement of comprehensive income
- ✓ adjust the financial statements to take account of inter-company transactions
- ✓ explain the equity method of accounting and apply this method to account for an investment in an associate
- ✓ outline the main accounting requirements of IFRS 3, IFRS 10, IFRS 11 and IAS 28
- ✓ outline the main disclosure requirements of IFRS 12.

Introduction

Companies, as well as individuals, can be investors. Such companies may buy and sell shares issued by other companies. The way a company accounts for such investments depends, in part, on why an investment was acquired and the power an investment gives to the investor company. Investments in other companies need to be accounted for. This chapter will introduce the different methods of investing in other companies, and illustrate the methods of accounting for such investments. It will then go on to deal with basic group structures and discuss the accounting regulations governing the preparation of group accounts. The final section will examine the theoretical rationale underlying the alternative methods of preparing group accounts.

There are different ways in which one company can combine with another company. For example, the various assets and liabilities of two or more businesses may be acquired by a newly formed business and the original businesses cease to exist. This is called an *amalgamation*. An alternative way of combining is by *absorption*. This is where various assets (and sometimes liabilities) of a business are acquired by another business and are part of the acquiring company's own assets (and liabilities). A third way is where one company acquires shares in another company, with each continuing to exist independently. It is this third method that will be the subject of this chapter.

Section 1: Basic Principles

A company can make an investment by acquiring shares in another company. These investments can be at different levels – for example, 1%, 10%, 100%. The level of investment gives different degrees of 'power' to the acquiring company.

11.1 Initial recording of an investment

An investment arises when one company, the investor, buys shares in another company or undertaking, the investee. The investor is acquiring a new asset and will have to pay for this 'asset'. The payment is often referred to as the *consideration*.

Example 1

Alpha Ltd buys 25,000 £1 ordinary shares of Beta Ltd at £4 each. Alpha pays cash. In the accounts of Alpha there will be a 'new' asset, the investment in Beta, and, in order to acquire this asset, Alpha will have used up cash. So, this transaction will be recorded as follows:

Dr	Investment in Beta	£100,000	
	Cr Bank		£100,000
Being investment in Beta.			

Note that although the par value of the shares is £1, the price paid for each share is £4.

It would also be possible for one company to pay for the shares in another company by issuing new ordinary shares of its own.

Example 2

Alpha buys 25,000 £1 ordinary shares of Beta at £4 each. To finance the purchase, Alpha issues 20,000 of its 25p ordinary shares. The market value of each Alpha share is £5.

The 'cost' of the investment in Beta is what Alpha had to give to acquire the shares. Alpha has to give shares worth £100,000 (25,000 × £4) to acquire its shares in Beta. These shares are worth £5 each – that is, £100,000 (20,000 × £5) in total. To record this transaction, Alpha will have a 'new' asset, the investment in Beta, but this time will have issued shares to pay for it. The issue of shares will result in the share capital being increased. The share capital account can only be increased by the par value of the shares. The difference between the market value of the shares, £5.00, and the par value, 25p, is classed as a share premium (£5.00 – £0.25) of £4.75.

So, the transaction will be recorded as follows:

Dr	Investment in Beta	£100,000	
	Cr Share capital (20,000 × £0.25)		£5,000
	Share premium (20,000 × £4.75)		£95,000
Being investment in Beta.			

The shares in Beta will be bought from existing shareholders, perhaps through the stock exchange. It is important to realize that the statement of financial position of Beta (the investee company) will not be affected. This is because the transaction is between the investor company (Alpha) and the shareholders of Beta. All Beta has to do is to record the change in its register of members.

11.2 The investors' accounts

Once an investment has been made, the investor must decide how to classify this in its statement of financial position. If the investment is to be held for a short period of time it should be classified as a current asset investment. If, on the other hand, it is to be held for a long period of time, it will be classified as a non-current asset.

In the statement of financial position, the investment will be initially recorded at cost. The investment can remain at this amount or can be revalued to fair value every year (see Chapter 2).

The investor company (Alpha in the example above) will be entitled to receive a dividend from Beta. This will constitute investment income in the statement of comprehensive income in Alpha. Only dividends that are realized from the investor's point of view should be included. While it is prudent to include only those dividends actually received, any dividend that has been declared by the investee company, but has not actually been received, will normally be shown as a dividend receivable.

Example

Alpha Ltd owns 100% of the ordinary shares of Beta Ltd. On 15 October Year 8, Beta pays a dividend of £60,000. On 31 December Year 8, Beta declares a dividend of £100,000. Assuming that the dividend declared on 31 December will be paid, and that there is no intention on the part of Alpha to sell the shares in Beta, the accounting entries for the year to 31 December Year 8 will be as follows:

Dr	Bank	£60,000	
	Cr Investment income		£60,000
Being dividend received.			

Dr	Receivables (dividends receivable)	£100,000	
	Cr Investment income		£100,000
Being accrued dividends receivable.			

11.3 Investments that give control or influence

It may be that the purchase of shares in one company by another gives the investing company some degree of control or influence over the other company. The relationship between the two companies will depend on this degree of control. The degree of control may be linked to the percentage shareholding. There are four categories of investment that can be determined. These can be identified as follows.

1. Where Company A acquires a small stake in Company B – for example, 0.1%: this will constitute a simple investment and will be recorded in the statement of financial position of Company A as an asset. Examples 1 and 2 (page 592) relate to this situation.

2. Where Company A has a substantial stake in Company B such that it is able to exercise total control over the operating and financial policies of Company B. In other words, where Company A can exert a 'dominant influence' over Company B. Such control normally exists when Company A has more than 50% of Company B. If 'dominant influence' exists, then Company B is by definition a subsidiary company.

3. Where Company A has a stake in Company B, but this stake is not large enough to give Company A total control, but does allow Company A to participate in the operating and financial policy decisions, but not to control these: this gives Company A a 'significant influence' and usually arises from a holding of between 20% and 50% of the shares. If such a degree of influence was held by Company A, then Company B would be by definition an associate company.

4. Where Company A has a stake in Company B and shares control jointly with others (venturers), through some contractual arrangement. All the venturers will have to agree on key operating and financial policies with no single venturer in a position to exercise total control. In this case a joint venture would exist.

Definitions

The following definitions are necessary for a full understanding of this topic:

(i) Consolidated financial statements – the financial statements of a group in which the assets, liabilities, equity, income, expenses and cash flows of the parent and its subsidiaries are presented as those of a single economic entity.

(ii) Group – a parent and its subsidiaries.

(iii) Non-controlling interest – equity in a subsidiary not attributable, directly or indirectly, to a parent.

(iv) Parent – an entity that controls one or more entities.

(v) Control of an investee – an investor controls an investee when the investor is exposed, or has rights, to variable returns from its involvement with the investee and has the ability to affect those returns through its power over the investee.

(vi) Subsidiary – an entity that is controlled by another entity.

Progress Point 11.1

X Ltd buys a stake in Y Ltd, comprising 100,000 ordinary shares of £1 each. In order to finance this purchase, X Ltd issues 40,000 ordinary shares of £1 each. The current market price of the shares in X Ltd is £5 and in Y Ltd is £2.

(a) How would X Ltd record its investment in Y Ltd?

(b) If Y Ltd paid an interim dividend of £10,000 and declared a final dividend of £50,000, show how this would be recorded in the accounts of X Ltd.

(c) Under what circumstances would Y Ltd be:

   (i) an associate

  (ii) a subsidiary

 (iii) a joint venture?

Solution

(a) Cost of investment in Y Ltd = (100,000 × £2) = £200,000.

Shares issued by X Ltd = 40,000.

Value of the 'consideration' = 40,000 × £5 = £200,000.

To record this share issue, share capital would be increased at par (40,000 × £1) and the excess (£5 − £1) would be put into the share premium account (40,000 × £4).

So the transaction would be recorded in the books of X Ltd as follows:

Dr	Investment in Y Ltd	£200,000	
	Cr Share capital		£40,000
	Share premium		£160,000
Being cost of investment in Y Ltd.			

(b)

Dr	Bank account (dividend received)	£10,000	
	Cr Investment income		£10,000
Being dividend received.			

Dr	Receivables (dividend receivable)	£50,000	
	Cr Investment income		£50,000
Being dividends receivable accrued.			

(c)

  (i) Y Ltd would be an associate if X Ltd had a participating interest, and was able to exert a significant influence over its operating and financial policies. Such an influence would be deemed to exist if X Ltd held a stake of between 20% and 50%.

 (ii) Y Ltd would be a subsidiary if X Ltd was able to exert a dominant influence and so have total control over its operating and financial policies. Total control would tend to exist if X Ltd had a stake of more than 50%.

(iii) Y Ltd would constitute a joint venture if it was jointly controlled by X Ltd and other venturers, such that no one venturer was in a position to control Y Ltd unilaterally.

11.4 The accounting issue involved

The accounting issue involved is this. If, by virtue of an entity's shareholding in another entity, the first entity is effectively able to control the net assets of the second entity, then it is as if the first entity has purchased the net assets of the second entity and can control them as if the assets belonged to it. Consequently, when looked at in combination, a more meaningful representation of the relationship

BASIC

INTERMEDIATE

ADVANCED

would be given by combining the assets and liabilities of the two entities rather than by simply disclosing that the first entity had purchased shares in the second entity. Moreover, if the two entities trade with one another then, as far as the combined companies are concerned, it would be more meaningful to cancel out any transactions that had taken place between them and show instead the trading activities of the combined unit. That is, only the transactions outside the combined unit would be disclosed. This is the purpose of consolidated financial statements – to give a more meaningful depiction of a company's results when that company has a controlling interest in one or more other companies.

11.5 Subsidiary companies

As was noted above, a subsidiary company is one in which another company (called the parent or holding company) has total control over the operating and financial policies. When one company acquires a substantial stake in another company then this has to be accounted for. If the relationship that exists between those companies is that of parent and subsidiary, then a special technique of accounting is used. This accounting technique is called acquisition accounting, sometimes called the purchase method.

Acquisition of a subsidiary

Company H plc is interested in acquiring Company S plc. The statement of financial position of S plc is as follows:

Statement of financial position of S plc as at 31 December Year 1	
	£m
Non-current assets	150
Current assets:	
Cash	100
Creditors due within one year	
Trade payables	(50)
	200
Capital and reserves	
Ordinary shares of £1	150
Retained earnings	50
	200

From this statement of financial position it can be seen that the net assets of S plc are worth £200. The statement of financial position of H plc is as follows:

Statement of financial position of H plc as at 31 December Year 1	
	£m
Non-current assets	600
Current assets:	
Cash	440
Current liabilities	
Trade payables	(40)
	1,000
Capital and reserves	
Ordinary shares of £1	800
Retained earnings	200
	1,000

On 31 December Year 1, H plc decides to buy all of the shares in S plc and is prepared to pay £300m. Assuming that the purchase was for cash, how would the statement of financial position of H plc change? H plc will now have a new asset, Investment in Company S, and will have used up cash in acquiring this 'asset'. The statement of financial position of H plc after the acquisition of the shares in S plc will now be as follows:

Statement of financial position of H plc (after acquisition of S plc) as at 31 December Year 1	£m
Non-current assets	600
Investment in S	300
Current assets:	
Cash	140
Current liabilities	
Trade payables	(40)
	1,000
Capital and reserves	
Ordinary shares of £1	800
Retained earnings	200
	1,000

Note that after the acquisition by H plc, the statement of financial position of S plc will not change. All that has happened is that the ownership of the shares has passed to H plc. At this stage it is important to appreciate that H plc and S plc are still separate companies, and will continue trading as such. They will maintain their own accounting records. However, H plc will have to account for its interest in S plc by preparing group financial statements.

Using the statements of financial position of H plc and S plc, the group statement of financial position can now be prepared.

Example

Summary statements of financial position as at 31 December Year 1		
	H plc	S plc
	£m	£m
Non-current assets	600	150
Investment in S	300	
Current assets: cash	140	100
Trade payables	(40)	(50)
	1,000	200
Share capital	800	150
Retained earnings	200	50
	1,000	200

Some initial points to note:

1. The group is a single entity and a single entity cannot have an investment in itself, nor can it issue share to itself.

2. The assets *controlled* by H plc should be reflected in the group accounts.

3. Any profits earned as a result of H plc's control should be shown in the group accounts. These are the profits earned after acquisition – that is, *post-acquisition*.

Some preliminary points

Showing an *Investment in S* in the group statement of financial position does not make sense, since this would imply the group has an investment in itself. This cannot be, since the group is a single entity. This investment in S must be eliminated from the group statement of financial position.

The Investment in S represents the price paid by H plc to acquire the net assets of S plc through its purchase of the share capital of S plc.

Since H plc controls all the non-current assets of S plc, in order to give a true and fair view, the total assets of both companies will be shown in the group statement of financial position.

Stage 1

Compare the price paid to acquire S plc (i.e. the Investment in S), with the 'value' of S plc at the date it was acquired (i.e. the date of acquisition).

H plc paid £300m for S plc. At the time of the purchase the 'value' of S plc was £200m. So H plc was prepared to pay an additional £100m for something that is not shown in the statement of financial position. This 'something' could be the reputation of S plc, its experienced staff, its market position, established customers and so on. This additional amount paid to acquire control of S plc is called goodwill.

Goodwill is measured as the excess of the cost of the investment over the 'value' of the proportion of net assets acquired. The net assets acquired can be measured either as non-current assets plus net current assets, or as share capital and reserves. Usually in the preparation of group accounts it is easier to use the share capital and reserves measure, so this measure will be used in the examples that follow.

The calculation of goodwill will be:

'Value' of S plc at the date of acquisition	
	£m
Share capital	150
Retained earnings	50
	200
Proportion acquired (100%)	200
Price paid	300
Therefore goodwill	100

Stage 2

Calculate the total retained earnings of the group. The retained earnings of the group will comprise the profits of H plc plus H's share of the profit of S plc which have been earned since acquisition. This is because at the date of acquisition, H plc acquired the net assets of S plc, which are represented by the share capital and reserves. So the goodwill figure of £100m has already taken account of any profits which existed at the date of acquisition. Such profits are referred to as pre-acquisition profits.

The calculation of the profits of the group will be:

	£m	
Profit of H plc	200	
H's share of the profit of S earned since date of acquisition	0	(all the profit of S is pre-acquisition)
	200	

The group statement of financial position can now be prepared.

Statement of financial position of H group as at 31 December Year 1

	£m	
Non-current assets	750	(total of H and S, since H controls these)
Goodwill	100	
Current assets: cash	240	(total of H and S)
Trade payables	(90)	(total of H and S)
	1,000	
Share capital	800	(only share capital of H)
Retained earnings	200	(profit of H and any post-acquisition profit of S)
	1,000	

Goodwill is dealt with in full in Chapter 3. However, it is useful to note as a reminder that goodwill can be either positive, as in this example, or negative. Positive goodwill arises when the price paid is greater than the value of the net assets acquired. In other words, the acquiring company pays a premium.

When the price paid is less than the value of the net assets acquired, then negative goodwill arises. This is not very common.

Note that positive goodwill should remain in the statement of financial position at cost but should be tested annually for impairment while negative goodwill should be treated as income and included in the acquirer's profit or loss (see Chapter 3).

When the holding is less than 100%

Up to now the assumption made is that H plc owns 100% of S plc. Suppose that H plc had acquired only 75% of S plc. Who owns the other 25%? This other 25% may be held by many different shareholders. Collectively, this other ownership is called the non-controlling (minority) interest (NCI). If there is a non-controlling interest of 25% this has to be accounted for. The fact that H plc owns 75% of S plc means that H plc still has control over S plc.

Applying the same principles as indicated above, the group statement of financial position can now be prepared.

Stage 1: goodwill calculation

Goodwill is calculated in the same way as before. However, this time the proportion of the assets acquired is less than 100%. The calculation is as follows:

	'Value' of S at date of acquisition	
	£m	
Share capital	150	
Retained earnings	50	
	200	
Proportion acquired	150	(75% of £200)
Price paid	300	
Goodwill	150	

Stage 2: calculate the total retained profit of the group

This is done as follows:

	£m	
Profit of H plc	200	
H's share of the profit of S earned since date of acquisition (75% × £0)	0	(all the profit of S is pre-acquisition)
	200	

Given that H plc has less than 100% of S plc, the non-controlling interest must be accounted for.

Stage 3: calculate the non-controlling (non-controlling interest)

As indicated above, the non-controlling interest is 25%. If the net assets of S plc are 'valued' at £200m, then the non-controlling interest in these will be £50m (25% of £200m).

The statement of financial position of the H group can now be prepared.

	Statement of financial position of H group as at 31 December Year 1	
	£m	(total of H and S, since H controls these)
Non-current assets	750	
Goodwill	150	
Current assets: cash	240	(total of H and S)
Trade payables	(90)	(total of H and S)
	1,050	
Share capital	800	(only share capital of H)
Retained earnings	200	(profit of H and any post-acquisition profit of S)
Non-controlling interest	50	(the part of net assets not controlled by H)
	1,050	

Progress Point 11.2

The statement of financial position of A plc and S plc are given as follows:

Statement of financial position as at 30 June Year 2		A plc		S plc
		£200		£140
Tangible non-current assets		£200		£140
Investment in S		175		–
		375		140
Current assets:				
Inventory	60		40	
Trade receivables	30		15	
	90		55	
Current liabilities				
Trade payables	(70)	20	(35)	20
		395		160
Capital and reserves				
Ordinary share capital of £1		150		100
Retained earnings		245		60
		395		160

(a) Prepare the consolidated statement of financial position of the A group, assuming A plc has acquired 100% of S plc on 30 June Year 2.

(b) Prepare the consolidated statement of financial position of the A group, assuming A plc has acquired 80% of S plc on 30 June Year 2.

Solution

(a) Where control is 100% the calculation of goodwill is as follows:

'Value' of S at date of acquisition	
Share capital	100
Retained earnings	60
	160
Proportion acquired (100%)	160
Price paid	175
Goodwill	15

Retained earnings of group		
Profit of A	£245	
Add A's share of post-acquisition profit of S	£0	(all profit is pre-acquisition)
	£245	

> ### Consolidated statement of financial position of A group as at 30 June Year 2
>
> | | | |
> |---|---:|---:|
> | Tangible non-current assets (£200 + £140) | | £340 |
> | Goodwill | | 15 |
> | Current assets | | |
> | Inventory (£60 + £40) | 100 | |
> | Trade receivables (£30 + £15) | 45 | |
> | | 145 | |
> | Trade payables (£70 + £35) | (105) | 40 |
> | | | £395 |
> | | | |
> | Capital and reserves | | |
> | Ordinary share capital | | £150 |
> | Retained earnings | | 245 |
> | | | £395 |

(b) Where control is 80%, calculation of goodwill is as follows.

> ### 'Value' of S at date of acquisition
>
> | | |
> |---|---:|
> | Share capital | £100 |
> | Retained earnings | 60 |
> | | 160 |
> | Proportion acquired (80%) | 128 |
> | Price paid | 175 |
> | Goodwill | 47 |

Non-controlling interest

If the majority acquire 80% then the minority proportion is 20%. So non-controlling interest is 20% of £160 = £32.

Group retained earnings will be the same as in (a).

> ### Consolidated statement of financial position of A group as at 30 June Year 2
>
> | | | |
> |---|---:|---:|
> | Tangible non-current assets (£200 + £140) | | £340 |
> | Goodwill | | 47 |
> | Current assets | | |
> | Inventory (£60 + £40) | 100 | |
> | Trade receivables (£30 + £15) | 45 | |
> | | 145 | |
> | Trade payables (£70 + £35) | (105) | 40 |
> | | | £427 |
> | | | |
> | Capital and reserves | | |
> | Ordinary share capital | | £150 |
> | Retained earnings | | 245 |
> | Non-controlling interest | | 32 |
> | | | £427 |

Consolidation in periods after acquisition

So far consolidation at the date of acquisition has been considered. This section will consider the preparation of consolidated statements of financial position when the subsidiary was acquired some time ago.

An important date in the preparation of the group financial statements is the date at which acquisition takes place.

To illustrate this point, assume that company S was formed in Year 0. In Year 3 it was acquired by Company H. Profits reported by Company S are as follows:

- Year 3: £10,000 (date of acquisition)
- Year 5: £25,000

The total accumulated profit in Year 5 can be allocated as shown in Figure 11.1.

From Figure 11.1, it can be seen that the total retained earnings of Company S at Year 5 (i.e. at the date of consolidation) is £25,000. However, at the date Company S was acquired (i.e. date of acquisition) the accumulated profit was £10,000. This means that, since acquisition, retained earnings have increased from £10,000 to £25,000, an increase of £15,000. The date of acquisition divides the life of the company into two: the period before acquisition, or *pre-acquisition*, and the period after acquisition, or *post-acquisition*. This means that any profits earned since the date of acquisition (i.e. the post-acquisition profit) will amount to £15,000 (£25,000 – £10,000).

Why is the distinction important?

The distinction is important because profits earned before the date of acquisition are accounted for differently to those earned after the date of acquisition. Pre-acquisition profits are used in the calculation of the goodwill figure – in other words, capitalized – while post-acquisition profits become part of the group profit (Figure 11.2).

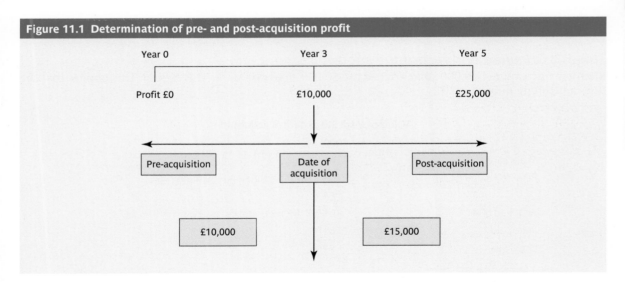

Figure 11.1 Determination of pre- and post-acquisition profit

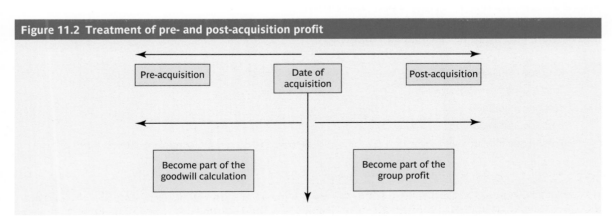

Figure 11.2 Treatment of pre- and post-acquisition profit

Note that **non-controlling interest** will not be affected. Non-controlling interest is entitled to a share in both pre and post-acquisition profits.

Example: Matthew Ltd and Mark Ltd

On 31 March Year 3 Matthew Ltd acquired 40,000 of the £1 ordinary shares in Mark Ltd. On this date, the retained profit of Mark Ltd was £27,000. The statements of financial position of the two companies a year later are as follows:

	Matthew Ltd	Mark Ltd
	£000	£000
Investment in Mark Ltd	83	
Net assets	659	153
	742	153
Share capital £1 ordinary shares	150	50
Retained earnings	592	103
	742	153

Prepare the consolidated statement of financial position at 31 March Year 4.

This can be done through the stages indicated above.

Stage 1: calculate and record the goodwill

Matthew has acquired 40,000 shares out of the 50,000 shares of Mark. This is 80%. This implies that the non-controlling interest is 20%.

'Value' of Mark Ltd at date of acquisition		
	£000	
Share capital	50	
Retained earnings	27	(this is the pre-acquisition profit)
	77	
Acquired 80%	61.6	(non-controlling interest = 20% = £15.4)
Price paid	83.0	
Goodwill	21.4	

Stage 2: calculate the group retained earnings

This is the retained earnings of Matthew Ltd plus Matthew's share of the post-acquisition retained earnings of Mark Ltd. It can be calculated as follows:

Retained earnings of Matthew		£592.0
Total retained earnings of Mark	£103.0	
Less pre-acquisition	£27.0	
Post-acquisition portion	£76.0	
Portion due to Matthew =	80% = £60.8	(non-controlling interest = £15.2)
	£652.8	

Stage 3: calculate and record the non-controlling interest

The non-controlling interest are entitled to a share in both the pre- and post-acquisition profits.

'Value' of Mark Ltd at date of consolidation

	£000	
Share capital	50	
Retained earnings	103	(this is both pre- and post-acquisition)
	153	
NCI = 20% =	30.6	(£15.4 + £15.2)

The group statement of financial position can now be prepared:

Matthew Group
Statement of financial position as at 31 March Year 4

Net assets (£659 + £153)	£812.0
Goodwill (Stage 1)	21.4
	£833.4
Capital and reserves	
Share capital	£150.0
Retained earnings (Stage 2)	652.8
NCI (Stage 3)	30.6
	£833.4

BASIC

INTERMEDIATE

ADVANCED

Consolidated statement of comprehensive income

The consolidated statement of comprehensive income shows the profit generated by all the resources disclosed in the consolidated statement of financial position. In other words, the resources of the net assets of the parent company, and its subsidiaries.

The consolidated statement of comprehensive income follows two basic principles.

1. All the items shown in the statement of comprehensive income, down to profit after tax, will add together the income and expenses of both the parent and the subsidiary.

2. If the subsidiary is only partly owned, there will be a non-controlling interest in the profit for the year of the subsidiary (after taxation). The profit attributable to the non-controlling interest will be deducted from the group profit.

Example

P acquired 80% of the ordinary share capital of S. The statements of comprehensive income for the year ended 30 November 2012 were as follows:

	P	S
	£000	£000
Sales revenue	8,500	2,200
Cost of sales and expenses	7,650	1,980
Profit before tax	850	220
Taxation	400	100
Profit after tax	450	120

The subsidiary is partly owned (80%) so there will be a non-controlling interest in the profit for the year (after tax) of the subsidiary. This is calculated as follows:

$$20\% \text{ of } £120,000 = £24,000$$

As indicated above, all the items in the statement of comprehensive income of both the parent and subsidiary are added together, down to the profit after tax. In this example, the consolidated statement of comprehensive income would be as follows:

Consolidated statement of comprehensive income	
	£000
Sales revenue (£8,500 + £2,200)	10,700
Cost of sales and expenses (£7,650 + £1,980)	9,630
Group profit before tax	1,070
Taxation (£400 + £100)	500
Net profit for the period	570
Amount attributable to:	
Equity holder of the parent (£570 − £24 NCI)	546
NCI (20% of £120)	24
	570

Section summary

The owners of a company are its shareholders. The purchase of ordinary shares usually gives a shareholder three main rights – rights which are proportionate to the number of shares held by them i.e.

 (i) voting rights

(ii) a right to an interest in the net assets of the company

(iii) a right to an interest in the profits earned by the company.

Because of the voting rights attached to the shares, any shareholders who own more than 50% of the voting shares of the company can control the election of directors and consequently, can control the policies of the company through the directors.

Where that shareholder is another company and the first company is able to control the net assets of the second company, a more meaningful representation is given by combining the assets and liabilities of the two companies and reporting these in a consolidated set of accounts.

Section 2: Intermediate Issues

This section will develop the basic principles identified in Section 1. It will consider additional adjustments necessary to calculate the goodwill figure. In addition, it will consider the treatment of inter-company transactions and how these impact on the group financial statements.

11.6 Fair value adjustments

When one company is acquired by another company, any price paid will reflect the underlying values of the net assets of the company being acquired. It is likely therefore that, at the date of acquisition, the assets of the company being acquired will be revalued. This will mean adjusting the values of each individual asset and liability on the balance sheet and bringing them up to date. In other words, the net assets of the company being acquired will be restated to current values at the date of acquisition. Although there is no specific requirement to do so, it is likely that the acquiring company will also take the opportunity to bring its statement of financial position up to date too.

Example

P plc bought 3,200 ordinary shares in S plc several years ago. At the time P plc bought the holding in S plc, the balance in retained earnings of S plc was £1,200. The statements of financial position of P plc and S plc at 31 December Year 6 (i.e. now) are as follows:

	Statements of financial position as at 31 December Year 6	
	P plc	S plc
Non-current assets	£1,900	£4,000
Investment in S plc	8,500	
Current assets	800	2,500
Current liabilities	(700)	(500)
	10,500	6,000
Share capital (£1 shares)	9,000	4,000
Retained earnings	1,500	2,000
	10,500	6,000

At the date of acquisition the non-current assets of S plc were revalued to £6,000. None of the other net assets required any adjustment.

The statement of financial position of S plc does not reflect this adjustment. In order to take account of the revaluation, the non-current assets of S plc will need to be increased to £6,000 and a revaluation reserve of £2,000 will need to be created.

Statement of financial position of S plc after the fair value adjustment:	
	S plc
Non-current assets	£6,000
Current assets	2,500
Current liabilities	(500)
	8,000

Share capital (£1 shares)	£4,000
Retained earnings	£2,000
Revaluation reserve	£2,000
	£8,000

Note that, since the adjustment to fair value occurred at the date of acquisition, it will be treated as pre-acquisition and so will become part of the goodwill figure.

The group statement of financial position can now be prepared using the stages discussed above.

Stage 1: goodwill calculation

This time the fair value of the assets is taken and compared with the cost of the investment, as follows:

Fair value of S at date of acquisition		
Share capital	£4,000	
Retained earnings	1,200	
Revaluation reserve	2,000	
	7,200	
80% acquired	5,760	(3,200 shares out of 4,000)
Price paid	8,500	
Goodwill	2,740	

Stage 2: calculate the total retained earnings of the group

This is done as follows:

Profit of P plc		£1,500
P's share of the profit		
of S earned since date of		
acquisition:		
Total profit of S plc	£2,000	
Less pre-acquisition	£1,200	
Post-acquisition	£ 800	
Whereof	80%	£640
		£2,140

Stage 3: calculate the non-controlling interest

Non-controlling interest will be entitled to 20% of the 'fair value' of the company at date of consolidation = 20% of £8,000 = £1,600. Note that this does include the non-current assets at fair value.

The statement of financial position of the P group can now be prepared:

BASIC

INTERMEDIATE

ADVANCED

Statement of financial position of P group
as at 31 December Year 6

Non-current assets	£7,900	(£1,900 + £4,000 + £2,000)
Goodwill	£2,740	
Current assets	£3,300	
Current liabilities	(£1,200)	
	£12,740	
Share capital	£9,000	
Retained earnings	£2,140	
Non-controlling interest	£1,600	
	£12,740	

BASIC

INTERMEDIATE

ADVANCED

11.7 Acquisition for consideration other than cash

Often when a company acquires another company, instead of paying cash, the acquiring company will issue shares to substitute for the shares it acquires. When there is a non-cash acquisition the investment in the subsidiary will be recorded at fair value. In this case the fair value of the investment in a subsidiary will be based on the number of shares issued and the current market price of each share.

Example

Statements of financial position of:	H plc	S plc
Net assets	£1,600	£1,200
Share capital (£1 shares)	£1,000	£800
Retained earnings	£600	£400
	£1,600	£1,200

H plc is to acquire 100% of S plc. The terms of the acquisition are that H plc will issue shares on a 1 for 2 basis to acquire S plc. The fair value of the net assets of S plc at date of acquisition is £1,500. The market value of each share in H plc at date of acquisition is £5.

The figures for the group financial statements can be determined as before.

Stage 1: calculate the goodwill

In this case the fair value of the net assets of S plc will be measured and compared with the fair value of the shares given by H plc – that is, the 'consideration'. In order to acquire its stake in S plc, H plc gives up shares currently worth £5 each. In other words:

Number of shares in S plc = 800 (par value £1)
H plc gives 1 of its shares for every 2 in S plc, so H plc will issue 400 shares.
Fair value of those shares = £5 × 400 = £2,000
This is called the 'fair value of the consideration'.

In order to calculate goodwill, the fair value of the consideration needs to be measured against the fair value of the net assets.

Fair value of net assets:	
Share capital	£800
Retained earnings	£400
Revaluation reserve	£300
	£1,500
Fair value of consideration	£2,000
Therefore: goodwill =	£500

The issue of shares by H plc will be recorded in the accounts of H plc as normal. The share capital will be increased by the amount of shares issued, at par. Any excess will be transferred to the share premium account. In this case the issue of 400 shares at a market price of £5 per share will be recorded as follows:

Dr	Investment in S plc	£2,000	
	Cr Share capital		£400
	Cr Share premium		£1,600
Being investment in S.			

Stage 2: calculate the group profit

In this example the group profit will only be the profit of H plc since all of the profit of S plc is pre-acquisition.

Stage 3: calculate the non-controlling interest

In this case there is no non-controlling interest since it was a 100% acquisition.

So the group statement of financial position is as follows:

Statement of financial position of H Group		
Net assets	£3,100	(£1,600 + £1,200 + £300)
Goodwill	£500	
	£3,600	
Share capital	£1,400	(£1,000 + £400)
Share premium	£1,600	
Retained earnings	£600	
	£3,600	

11.8 Inter-company trading

Where there is a transfer of goods from one company to another at *cost*

Example
P has a subsidiary S. P transfers (sells) goods to S at cost: £10,000. Normally, each company will keep a record of its transactions with the other company using current accounts. So P will keep a record of its transaction with S in 'Current Account S' and S will keep a record of its transactions with P in 'Current Account P'. Because they are inter-company, these accounts will represent the amounts owing to, and from, each of the companies. The balances in them should be equal and opposite, and will be eliminated on consolidation.

Where there is a transfer of goods from one company to another at *profit*
In this situation one company will sell goods to the other company at selling price.

Example holding company sells to subsidiary
H has a 60% interest in S. H buys an item of inventory for £100 and sells it to S for £125. S subsequently sells this item for £140.

As far as the individual companies are concerned, each will make a profit. H's profit is calculated as follows:

Cost of item of inventory	£100
Sold to S for	£125
Profit made by H	£25

S's profit will be calculated as follows:

Cost of item of inventory from H	£125
Sold for	£140
Profit	£15

As far as the group is concerned, the profit will be:

Profit of H	£25
Profit of S	£15
Group profit	£40

This is the profit that would be expected since the cost of the item is £100 and was ultimately sold for £140, giving a profit of £40.

Since this item is subsequently sold, all of the group profit would be realized. However, what happens if, at the end of the year, the item is not sold by S but remains in the inventory of S? As far as the *group* is concerned, the profit made by H has not been realized, since it is still in the inventory of S. Both the group profit and group inventory figures will be overstated and will require to be adjusted as follows:

- reduce the group profit by the amount of the unrealized profit
- reduce the group inventory by the amount of the unrealized profit.

If instead of the sale being from H to S, it was the other way round – from S to H – how would the situation change?

The principle is exactly the same. The amount of unrealized profit must be eliminated, but this time there will be a non-controlling interest to be accounted for. The unrealized profit element, using the above example, is £40. The non-controlling interest in this is 40%, which is £16. The adjustment required is as follows:

- reduce group profit by majority share (60%) – £24
- reduce non-controlling interest – £16
- reduce group inventory – £40.

Progress Point 11.3

H acquired 90% of S on 1 January 2012. S sold some goods to H at a selling price of £18,000, and a mark-up of 25% on cost. Two-thirds of these goods remained in inventory at the year end. How would this be accounted for in the group financial statements?

Solution

The first thing to notice is that the sale is from the subsidiary company to the holding company (i.e. from S to H), so there will be a non-controlling interest to account for. S sells to H at a mark-up of 25% on cost, so cost plus 25% of cost equals selling price. Therefore:

$$
\begin{aligned}
\text{Let cost} &= C \\
C + 25\% \text{ of } C &= £18,000 \\
C + 0.25C &= £18,000 \\
1.25C &= £18,000 \\
C &= £14,400 \ (£18,000/1.25) \\
\text{Profit} = £18,000 - £14,400 &= £3,600
\end{aligned}
$$

Given that two-thirds of the inventory remains unsold implies that two-thirds of the profit will be unrealized.

$$\text{Amount of unrealized profit} = \text{two-thirds of } £3,600 = £2,400$$

So, in the group financial statements:

- reduce group profit by majority share (90%) £2,160 Dr
- reduce non-controlling interest (10%) £240 Dr
- reduce inventory £2,400 Cr.

11.9 Transfer of non-current assets

The transfer of non-current assets between group companies causes similar problems to those concerned with internal inventory transfers. The objective is to make adjustments on consolidation, which will show the assets at cost to the group – in other words, as if the transfer had not taken place.

Where a non-current asset transfer occurs within a group at an amount greater than the net book value of the asset in the books of the transferor, any profit made on the transfer must be eliminated since this profit is unrealized.

However, the transaction has an additional effect as far as the group is concerned since the asset will have been subject to depreciation in the books of both companies. The depreciation charged by each company may be different, which means that the same asset will be subject to both a different amount and different pattern of depreciation as a result of the transfer.

Example

T Ltd owns 75% of the ordinary shares of H Ltd. In April 2012, H Ltd sold a piece of machinery to T Ltd for £450,000. H Ltd had bought this machinery in 2008 for £700,000. The policy of both companies is to depreciate machinery over a total useful life of ten years using the straight line method. When assets are transferred it is group policy to depreciate over the remaining useful life of the assets. A full year's depreciation is charged in the year of acquisition, and none in the year of disposal.

When the asset was owned by H Ltd the pattern of depreciation would have been as follows:

1/1/08	Cost of asset		£700,000
31/12/08	Depreciation	£70,000	
31/12/09	Depreciation	£70,000	
31/12/10	Depreciation	£70,000	
31/12/11	Depreciation	£70,000	£280,000
	Net book value		£420,000
	Sold for		£450,000
	Profit on sale		£30,000

When the asset is transferred to T Ltd, the cost is £450,000 and the asset will be depreciated over the remaining six years at a depreciation charge of £75,000 p.a. So, at 31 December 2012, the asset will be shown in the books of T Ltd as follows:

Cost of asset	£450,000
Depreciation	£75,000
Net book value at 31 December 2012	£375,000

As far as the *group* is concerned, the profit of £30,000 is unrealized and must be eliminated. Also, the depreciation by T is based on the transfer price, and not on the cost to the group. In order to restore the carrying amount of non-current assets to that which would have existed had the inter-company transfer not taken place, four adjustments may have to be made.

1. The asset must be adjusted back to the original cost to the group.
2. The profit on sale must be removed since, from a group point of view, it is unrealized.

3. The depreciation charge for the year must be adjusted to what it would have been, based on the cost to the group.

4. Aggregate depreciation needs to reflect the amount it would be had all the depreciation calculations been based on the original cost of the asset.

The profit made by H Ltd is unrealized and must be eliminated from the group accounts. This is done as follows:

- Reduce the group profit by (75% of £30,000)   £22,500 Dr
- Reduce non-controlling interest by (25% of £30,000) £7,500 Dr
- Reduce the non-current assets by   £30,000 Cr

The depreciation charged by T Ltd will be higher than it ought to be since it will be based on the 'new' cost of the asset to T Ltd. Had the asset not been transferred it would have been depreciated by £70,000. When it was transferred the depreciation increased to £75,000. Therefore there is an excess depreciation of £5,000 that must be adjusted.

The adjustment is made to both the income statement (profit will be understated), and to the provision for depreciation (which will be overstated). So:

- reduce the provision for depreciation   £5,000 Dr
- increase group profit (75% of £5,000)   £3,750 Cr
- increase non-controlling interest (25% of £5,000) £1,250 Cr

These adjustments will have the effect of restoring the asset to the position it would have been in had the transfer not taken place.

Progress Point 11.4

Alpha Ltd owns 80% of the ordinary shares of Beta Ltd. On 1 January Year 3 Beta sold a machine to Alpha for £7,000. Its original cost in Year 0 was £8,000 and it was depreciated by Beta at 10% straight line. The policy of both companies is to depreciate machinery over a total useful life of ten years using the straight line method. When assets are transferred it is group policy to depreciate over the remaining useful life of the assets. A full year's depreciation is charged in the year of acquisition, and none in the year of disposal.

The non-current assets schedules of Alpha and Beta at 31 December Year 6 show the following:

	Alpha	Beta
Non-current assets at cost	£38,000	£27,000
Depreciation	£14,000	£10,000
Net book value	£24,000	£17,000

Show how this asset transfer would be shown in the group accounts at 31 December Year 6.

Solution

In this example the transfer is from Beta (subsidiary) to Alpha (parent). As far as the asset is concerned, the pattern of depreciation will be as follows:

In the books of Beta			
Year 0	Cost of asset		£8,000
31/12 Year 0	Depreciation	£800	
31/12 Year 1	Depreciation	£800	
31/12 Year 2	Depreciation	£800	£2,400
Net book value when sold			£5,600
Sold to Alpha for			£7,000
Profit on sale			£1,400

When the asset is sold to Alpha the cost to Alpha will be £7,000. The asset has a life of ten years, and has already been depreciated for three years, so there are seven years left of the asset's life. The depreciation in the books of Alpha will be spread over the remaining life of seven years, and will be charged at the rate of 1/7 (i.e. £1,000 p.a.).

In the books of Alpha			
Cost of asset from Beta			£7,000
31/12 Year 3	Depreciation	£1,000	
31/12 Year 4	Depreciation	£1,000	
31/12 Year 5	Depreciation	£1,000	
31/12 Year 6	Depreciation	£1,000	£4,000
Net book value at 31 December Year 6			£3,000

BASIC

INTERMEDIATE

ADVANCED

1. Unrealised profit of £1,400 needs to be eliminated

Reduce the profit by (80% of £1,400)	£1,120 Dr
Reduce non-controlling interest (20% of £1,400)	£280 Dr
Reduce non-current assets	£1,400 Cr

2. Adjust for excess depreciation

If the asset had not been transferred to Alpha, then Beta would have continued to charge depreciation at £800 per annum. However, Alpha charged depreciation at £1,000 per annum. So:

Depreciation that ought to be charged (£800 × 4)	£3,200
Depreciation actually charged (£1,000 × 4)	£4,000
Excess depreciation charges	£800

The adjustment will be made as follows:

Reduce provision for depreciation	£800 Dr	
Increase group profit (80% of £800)		£640 Cr
Increase non-controlling interest (20% of £800)		£160 Cr

Cost of assets to the group
    As far as the group is concerned, it is as though the transfer had not taken place.

Beta	Cost	Depreciation	Net book value
Balance at start	£27,000	£10,000	£17,000
Add back asset	£8,000	£5,600	£2,400
	£35,000	£15,600	£19,400
Alpha			
Balance at start	£38,000	£14,000	£24,000
Remove asset	£7,000	£4,000	£3,000
	£31,000	£10,000	£21,000
Group			
Alpha	£31,000	£10,000	£21,000
Beta	£35,000	£15,600	£19,400
	£66,000	£25,600	£40,400

11.10 Transfer at a loss

Where the asset is transferred at a loss, the same principles apply, except that transfer below net book value may imply impairment, in which case the asset should be carried at the reduced amount and the loss retained. This would be a 'realized' loss and so no consolidation adjustment would be required.

11.11 Debentures

Holding bonds, debentures, loan stock in a subsidiary does not give ownership rights and normally does not give any control, as such items are liabilities and not capital. Therefore the parent does not require to hold any of the subsidiary's debt. However, the parent may hold some or all of the subsidiay's debt, as there is nothing to stop this happening.

Where debt of a group company is held by another member of the group, then such a holding is deemed to be inter-company and must be eliminated on consolidation.

Any balance outstanding after elimination will represent the holding outside the group and must be shown in the consolidated statement of financial position. Remember that external debt holders are long-term creditors and not shareholders. In the consolidated statement of financial position they should be shown as long-term creditors and not included in the non-controlling interest.

11.12 Preference shares

It may be that the parent company acquires some preference shares in a subsidiary. Normally, preference shares are not required for control since they do not carry any voting rights. However, the purchase of preference shares in an existing subsidiary requires that the goodwill on acquisition be calculated. This calculation is the same as that required for the acquisition of ordinary shares. The net assets acquired are equivalent only to the nominal value of the shares acquired because preference shareholders do not have ownership rights over the reserves of a company.

Example

XY Ltd is a subsidiary of AB Ltd. AB Ltd purchased 75% of the preference share capital of XY Ltd for £375,000. The preference share capital of XY Ltd comprises 400,000 shares of £1 each.
Goodwill is calculated as before:

Nominal value of preference shares	£400,000
Proportion acquired = 75% =	£300,000
Price paid	£375,000
Goodwill	£75,000

This goodwill on acquisition of preference shares is not separately identified in the statement of financial position. It is combined with goodwill arising on acquisition of ordinary shares. Any balance of preference shares not held by the group is included in the consolidated statement of financial position as part of non-controlling interest. In this case the non-controlling interest element would be £100,000 (25% of £400,000).

11.13 Consolidated statement of comprehensive income: development of issues

Impairment of goodwill

Once any impairment has been identified during the year, the charge for the year will be shown in the consolidated statement of comprehensive income. This will usually be done through the operating expenses.

Dividends

A payment of a dividend from a subsidiary to a parent company will need to be eliminated. This is in essence an intra-group transaction. Only dividends paid by the parent company to its own shareholders will appear in the consolidated financial statements. Any dividend income shown in the consolidated statement of comprehensive income must only be from investments other than in a subsidiary.

The principles outlined relating to the cancellation of internal dividends on ordinary shares also apply to preference dividends on consolidation. However, since preference shareholders are entitled to their dividends before ordinary shareholders, preference dividends must be deducted before calculating the non-controlling interest in profits available to ordinary shareholders.

Example

H plc holds 60% of the ordinary shares of S plc and 80% of the preference shares. The following information relates to the year ending 31 December Year 1.
Profit after taxation of S plc is £15,000.

Dividends:	H plc	S plc
	£	£
Ordinary	5,000	2,000
Preference	2,000	4,000

In order to calculate the non-controlling interest in the profit for the year of S plc, the preference dividend must be taken into account. The non-controlling interest would be calculated as follows:

Profit for the year of S plc after tax	£15,000	
Less preference dividend	£4,000	NCI = 20%
Available for ordinary shareholders	£11,000	NCI = 40%
Total non-controlling interest:		
20% of £4,000	£800	
40% of £11,000	£4,400	
	£5,200	

Progress point 11.5

The statements of comprehensive income of P Ltd and S Ltd for the year ended 31 August Year 4 are shown below. P acquired 75% of the ordinary shares capital of S several years ago.

Statements of comprehensive income		
	P Ltd	S Ltd
	£	£
Sales revenue	2,400	800
Cost of sales and expenses	(2,160)	(720)
Trading profit	240	80
Dividend from S	2	–
Profit before tax	242	80
Taxation	(115)	(40)
Profit after tax	127	40

Prepare the consolidated statement of comprehensive income for the year ended 31 August Year 4.

Solution
Working 1: non-controlling interest
Non-controlling interest will be 25% of profit of S for the year, after tax:
= 25% of £40 = £10

P consolidated statement of comprehensive income for year ended 31 August Year 4	
Sales revenue (£2,400 + £800)	£3,200
Cost of sales and expenses (£2,160 + £720)	£2,880
Group profit before tax	£320
Taxation (£115 + £40)	£155
Profit for the year	£165
Attributable to:	
Group	£155
Non-controlling interest	£10

Sales, purchases and inventories

The general principle that applies to the above items is that any intra-group trading must be eliminated from the consolidated statement of comprehensive income. In the case of sales and purchases, the sales from one company in the group will be the purchases of another company within the group. So for the consolidated statement of comprehensive income:

Consolidated sales revenue
Revenue of the parent company
Add revenue of the subsidiary company
Less any intra-group sales

Consolidated cost of sales
Cost of sales of the parent company
Add cost of sales of the subsidiary
Less intra-group sales

If there are any intra-group goods sold that are still in the closing inventory, their value must be adjusted to the lower of cost and net realizable value to the group, as is the case with the consolidated statement of financial position. In other words, any unrealized profit must be removed. This is usually done in practice by increasing the cost of sales figure.

Example

The statements of comprehensive income of P Ltd and its subsidiary L Ltd for the year ended 31 December Year 5 are given as follows:

	P Ltd	L Ltd
	£000	£000
Sales revenue	3,200	2,560
Cost of sales	2,200	1,480
Gross profit	1,000	1,080
Distribution costs	160	120
Admin costs	400	80
	440	880
Dividend income	160	0
	600	880
Taxation	400	480
Net profit for the year after tax	200	400

Additional information

1. P Ltd acquired 80% of the ordinary shares of L Ltd on 31 December Year 1, when the share capital was £800,000 and the balance on L's retained earnings was £600,000.

2. A goodwill impairment of £38,000 was necessary. Impairments are to be included within administrative expenses.

3. P Ltd sold goods to L Ltd, at a selling price of £600,000. Not all of these goods had been sold externally by the year end. The profit element included in the closing inventory of L was £30,000.

In order to prepare the consolidated statement of comprehensive income the sales revenue and cost of sales need to be adjusted to take account of intra-company trading. The unrealized profit will also have to be eliminated from the closing inventory. As was stated above, this is usually achieved by increasing the cost of sales. The goodwill impaired will be accounted for by increasing the administration expenses by the amount impaired. Finally, the non-controlling interest in the profit for the year of L will be disclosed.

The consolidated statement of comprehensive income would be as follows:

	£000
Sales revenue (£3,200 + £2560 − £600)	5,160
Cost of sales (£2,200 + £1,480 − £600 + £30)	3,110
Gross profit	2,050
Distribution costs	280
Admin costs (£400 + £80 + £38 (goodwill))	518
Profit before taxation	1,252
Taxation (£400 + £480)	880
Profit after tax	372
Amount attributable to:	
Equity shareholders of P	292
Non-controlling interest	80

Note: the non-controlling interest is calculated as 20% of the profit for the year after tax of L. This equals: 20% of £400 = £80.

11.14 Interest

If loans are outstanding between group companies, intra-group loan interest will be paid and received. Both the loan and the loan interest must be excluded from the consolidated financial statements.

11.15 Acquisition of a subsidiary during its accounting period

Up to now the acquisition of a subsidiary has happened at the end of the accounting period. In practice it is unlikely that the date of acquisition will coincide precisely with the end of the accounting period. It is more likely that the date of acquisition will occur during the accounting period.

When a parent company acquires ordinary shares in a subsidiary during the accounting period it will not be necessary to prepare consolidated financial statements immediately. These statements will be prepared at the normal year end of the company. However, the principles of consolidation are unchanged in that it is necessary to calculate goodwill based on conditions existing at the date of acquisition. Where the subsidiary has been acquired during the accounting period, some of the reserves at the date the statement of financial position is prepared will be attributable to post-acquisition, and some to pre-acquisition.

The objectives of the adjustments in this situation are:

- to ensure that all reserves at the date of acquisition are capitalized as part of the calculation of goodwill so that the purchase price is compared with the net assets at the date of acquisition
- to ensure that the consolidated statement of comprehensive income includes the results of the new subsidiary only from the date of acquisition.

If a separate set of accounts is not prepared for the subsidiary at the date of acquisition, the balance on reserves at that date will have to be estimated. Time apportionment of the profit of the subsidiary for the relevant accounting period is acceptable.

In addition, it should be noted that to ensure that the consolidated statement of comprehensive income only includes the results of the new subsidiary, it will be necessary to apportion the items in the statement of comprehensive income on a time basis also.

However, if the circumstances suggest that apportionment on a time basis would be unacceptable, then a basis that reflects the circumstances should be used – for example, if there is some kind of seasonality in the business cycle of the company. The objective is to calculate as accurately as possible the net assets of the company at the date of acquisition.

Example

Bright Ltd purchased 80% of Spark Ltd on 30 June 2012 for £600,000. The accounts for Spark Ltd for the year ended 31 December 2012 were as follows:

Statement of comprehensive income for period ended 31 December 2012	
Sales revenue	£400,000
Cost of sales and expenses	£235,000
Profit before taxation	£165,000
Taxation	£60,000
Profit after tax	£105,000

Statement of financial position as at 31 December 2012	
Net assets	£790,000
Share capital	£50,000
Retained earnings	£740,000
	£790,000

The following information is available.

1. The trade of Spark Ltd is seasonal, and the timing of the profit is such that 75% of the profit arises in the last six months of the year.
2. Goodwill is not impaired.

The goodwill on acquisition will be calculated as follows.
Fair value of net assets acquired at date of acquisition:

Share capital	£50,000
Retained earnings at 31 December 2011	
= £740,000 – £105,000	£635,000
Retained earnings from 1 Jan 2012 to	
30 June 2012 are split 25%/75%. So	
pre-acquisition part = 25% of £105,000	£26,250
	£711,250
Whereof 80%	£569,000
Price paid	£600,000
Goodwill	£31,000

As far as non-controlling interest is concerned, this would normally be calculated at the end of the reporting period. However, if the subsidiary is acquired during the year, there would not be a non-controlling interest at the start of the year because there would be no subsidiary. In this situation, the non-controlling interest is calculated at the date of acquisition.

In the example given, the non-controlling interest at date of acquisition is 20% of £711,250 = £142,250. However, the non-controlling interest will also be entitled to a share in the profits earned since acquisition. These are the profits earned from 1 July 2012 to 31 December 2012 = 75% of £105,000 = £78,750. Non-controlling interest will be 20% of this, which is £15,750 (20% of £78,750). Total non-controlling interest shown in the group statement of financial position would be £158,000 (£142,250 + £15,750).

In the group statement of comprehensive income, 75% of the sales revenue and costs of the subsidiary will be added to those of the parent, so that only the results of the new subsidiary from date of acquisition will be included. So, using the figures from the above example, the amounts to be included in the consolidated statement of comprehensive income from Spark Ltd will be as follows:

Sales revenue (75% of £400,000)	£300,000
Cost of sales and expenses (75% of £235,000)	(176,250)
Profit before taxation	123,750
Taxation	(45,000)
Profit after tax	78,750

Progress point 11.6

Kay Ltd acquired 60% of Gregor Ltd on 30 June 2012.

The financial statements of the two companies for the year ended 30 September 2012 are as follows:

Statement of comprehensive income

	Kay Ltd	Gregor Ltd
	£	£
Sales revenue	900,000	750,000
Cost of sales	(650,000)	(450,000)
Gross profit	250,000	300,000
Operating expenses	(100,000)	(80,000)
Interest expense	(60,000)	(20,000)
Profit before tax	90,000	200,000
Taxation	(30,000)	(65,000)
Profit after tax	60,000	135,000

Statement of financial position

	£	£
Tangible non-current assets	784,000	485,000
Investment in Gregor	460,750	
Current assets	215,250	210,000
Current liabilities	(100,000)	(25,000)
	1,360,000	670,000
Share capital £1 ordinary shares	400,000	150,000
Share premium	350,000	50,000
Retained earnings	610,000	470,000
	1,360,000	670,000

Additional information:

1. There has been no impairment of goodwill.
2. Profits of Gregor accrue evenly throughout the year.

Required

Prepare the consolidated statement of comprehensive income for the year ended 30 September 2012 together with a consolidated statement of financial position as at that date.

Solution

Kay acquired Gregor on 30 June. Group financial statements have to be prepared on 30 September, so the revenues and costs will have to be apportioned 9/12 (pre-acquisition) and 3/12 (post-acquisition). In addition, the revenues and costs of Gregor shown in the statement of comprehensive income will have to be apportioned from date of acquisition to date of consolidation. The adjusted statement of comprehensive income of Gregor will therefore be as follows:

Adjusted statement of comprehensive income of Gregor Ltd	
Sales (3/12 of £750,000)	£187,500
Cost of sales (3/12 of £450,000)	(£112,500)
Gross profit	£75,000
Operating expenses (3/12 of £80,000)	(£20,000)
Interest (3/12 of £20,000)	(£5,000)
Profit before tax	£50,000
Taxation (3/12 of £65,000)	(£16,250)
Profit after tax	£33,750

The information required for the consolidated statement of financial position can be prepared in accordance with the stages outlined previously.

Stage 1: calculate and record goodwill

Fair value of Gregor at date of acquisition		
Share capital		£150,000
Share premium		£50,000
Retained earnings		
This can be split into two time periods:		
(i) at 1/10/11 (£470,000 – £135,000)	£335,000	
(ii) from 1/10/11 to 30/06/12 (£135,000 × 9/12)	101,250	436,250
		£636,250
Portion acquired = 60%		£381,750
Price paid		460,750
Goodwill		£79,000

Stage 2: calculate total retained earnings of the group

Retained profit of Kay		£610,000
Add Kay's share of the post-acquisition profit of Gregor		
In this example only 3/12th of £135,000 is post-acquisition.		
So post-acquisition profit	£33,750	
Share of this attributable to Kay = 60%		20,250
Total group retained earnings		£630,250

Stage 3: calculate total non-controlling interest

Remember there is no need to divide reserves into pre- and post-acquisition as far as the non-controlling interest are concerned. The non-controlling interest are entitled to a share in both pre- and post-acquisition profits.

Fair value of Gregor at date of consolidation	
Share capital	£150,000
Share premium	50,000
Retained earnings	470,000
	£670,000
NCI share = 40%	£268,000

The non-controlling interest can be shown to comprise two components, as follows.

1. Non-controlling interest at date of acquisition:

Share capital	£150,000	
Share premium	£50,000	
Profit	£436,250	(from Stage 1 above)
	£636,250	
Non-controlling interest share = 40%		£254,500

2. Non-controlling interest in the profit for the year of Gregor since acquisition.

= 3/12 of £135,000 × 40%	£13,500
Total non-controlling interest	£268,000

The group financial statements can now be prepared.

Group statement of comprehensive income	
Sales revenue (£900,000 + £187,500)	£1,087,500
Cost of sales (£650,000 + £112,500)	(762,500)
Gross profit	325,000
Operating expenses (£100,000 + £20,000)	(120,000)
Interest (£60,000 + £5,000)	(65,000)
Profit before tax	£140,000
Taxation (£30,000 + £16,250)	£46,250
Profit after taxation	£93,750
Attributable to:	
Group shareholders	£80,250
Non-controlling interest	£13,500

Group statement of financial position	
Tangible non-current assets (£784,000 + £485,000)	£1,269,000
Goodwill	79,000
Current assets (£215,250 + £210,000)	425,250
Current liabilities (£100,000 + £25,000)	(125,000)
	£1,648,250
Share capital	£400,000
Share premium	350,000
Retained earnings	630,250
Non-controlling interest	268,000
	£1,648,250

BASIC

INTERMEDIATE

ADVANCED

11.16 Accounting for associates and joint ventures

The definitions of associates and joint ventures have already been given in the first section. This part will now deal with the accounting issues relating to associates and joint ventures. The accounting for both associates and joint ventures are identical.

Associates

As an investor has significant influence over an associate it has a measure of responsibility for the performance of the associate, and for the return on its investment. Significant influence is the power to participate in the financial and operating policy decisions of the investee company by the investor, but does not give the investor control over those policies.

Significant influence would not be evidenced merely by retaining the investment at cost and recording the dividends received. Neither is consolidation, either full or partial, appropriate, since the investor company does not control the net assets of an associate.

In terms of accounting for an associate an investor accounts for its stewardship by including its share of the profits and net assets of an associate in its consolidated financial statements using a method of accounting called equity accounting.

Equity accounting is a method of accounting that brings an associate investment into the parent company's financial statements initially at cost. The carrying amount of the investment is then adjusted in each period for the group share of the profit of the associate less any impairment losses. The investment in the associate is calculated at:

- cost of investment
- add group share of post-acquisition retained profit
- less any impairment losses

or

- share of the net assets of the associate
- add premium on acquisition (goodwill)
- less any impairment losses.

The equity method of accounting requires that the consolidated statement of comprehensive income does not include any dividend income from the associate, but instead includes the group's share of the associate company's profit for the year.

The following example illustrates these two basic points.

Example

H plc acquired 25% of A plc when the share capital of A was £40 and its retained earnings were £12.

Statements of financial position as at 31 December 2012		
	H plc	A plc
	£	£
Assets	105	72
Investment in A	20	0
Current liabilities	(25)	(12)
	100	60
Share capital	60	40
Retained earnings	40	20
	100	60

Statements of comprehensive income for the year ending 31 December 2012

	H plc	A plc
	£	£
Trading profit	20	8
Dividend received	1	0
Profit for the year	21	8

Under the equity method of accounting the investment in the associate will be calculated as follows:

Cost of investment	£20	
Add share of post-acquisition profit	2	(25% of £20 – £12)
	£22	

Alternatively, the investment in the associate can be calculated by adding the goodwill figure to the share of net assets acquired.

Calculation of goodwill:

Fair value of A at date of acquisition	
Share capital	£40
Retained earnings	£12
	£52
Share acquired = 25%	£13
Cost	£20
Goodwill	£7

So, investment in associate:

Share of net assets (25% of £60)	£15
Add goodwill	£7
	£22

H Group Statement of comprehensive income

Profit (H only)	£20
Share of profit of A (25% of £8)	£2
	£22

H Group statement of financial position

Assets (only assets of H)	£105
Investment in associate	£22
Current liabilities	(25)
	£102
Share capital	£60
Retained earnings (£40 + 25% of £8)	£42
	£102

Progress Point 11.7

The following question brings together some aspects of accounting for subsidiary companies and incorporating the results of an associate.

The following are the statements of financial position of D, L and P as at 31 December 2012.

	D £000	L £000	P £000
Non-current assets	1,120	980	840
Investments:			
672,000 shares in L	744		
168,000 shares in P	224		
	2,088		
Current assets:			
Inventory	280	640	190
Receivables	190	310	100
Cash	35	58	46
	505	1,008	336
	2,593	1,988	1,176
Equity and liabilities			
Capital and reserves			
Ordinary shares of £1	1,120	840	560
Retained earnings	1,232	602	448
	2,352	1,442	1,008
Current liabilities			
Payables	150	480	136
Taxation	91	66	32
	241	546	168
	2,593	1,988	1,176

The following information is also relevant.

1. D acquired its shares in L on 1 January, 2012 when the retained profit of L was £56,000.
2. D acquired its shares in P on 1 January, 2012 when the retained profit of P was £140,000.
3. An impairment test at the year end shows that goodwill for L has been impaired by £3,360 and the investment in P by £2,800.

Required
Prepare the consolidated statement of financial position at 31 December 2012.

Solution
The solution to this question can be prepared using the stages as already outlined in previous examples.

D in L
D holds 672,000 shares out of 840,000 shares in L. This is a holding of 80%, therefore L would be a subsidiary of D.

Stage 1: calculate the goodwill

Fair value of L at date of acquisition:	
Share capital	£840,000
Retained earnings	56,000
	896,000
Whereof 80%	£716,800
Price paid	£744,000
Goodwill	£27,200

Stage 2: calculate the group retained earnings
This will comprise the profit of D, plus D's share of the post-acquisition profits of both L and P.

Profit of D		£1,232,000
Profit of L	£602,000	
Less pre-acquisition	56,000	
Post-acquisition	546,000	
	80%	436,800
Profit of P	£448,000	
Less pre-acquisition	140,000	
Post-acquisition	308,000	
	30%	92,400
		£1,761,200

BASIC

INTERMEDIATE

ADVANCED

Stage 3: non-controlling interest

Fair value of L at date of consolidation:

Share capital	£840,000
Retained profit	602,000
	£1,440,000
Whereof 20%	£288,400

There is no non-controlling interest in an associate.

Associate company (D in P)

D owns 168,000 shares out of 560,000 shares in P, this is 30%. P is deemed to be an associate.
The value of the investment in the associate needs to be calculated as was explained above.
It can be calculated in one of two ways:

Share of net assets of P (30% of £1,008,000)	£302,400
Add goodwill	14,000
	£316,400

Value of P at date of acquisition	
Share capital	£560,000
Retained earnings	140,000
	£700,000
Whereof 30%	£210,000
Price paid	£224,000
Goodwill	£14,000

or

At cost	£224,000
Add share of post-acquisition profit	£92,400
	£316,400

Stage 4: impairment of goodwill

The impairment in the year to 31 December 2012 is:
For the subsidiary L:

Dr Retained earnings	£3,360	
Cr Goodwill		£3,360
Being impairment of goodwill in L Ltd.		

And for the Associate P:

Dr Retained earnings	£2,800	
Cr Investment in associate		£2,800
Being impairment of goodwill in P Ltd.		

D Group statement of financial position

Tangible assets (£1,120,000 + £980,000)		£2,100,000
Investment in associate (316,400 − 2,800)		313,600
Goodwill (27,200 − 3,360)		23,840
Current assets:		
Inventory (280,000 + £640,000)	£920,000	
Receivables (£190,000 + £310,000)	£500,000	
Cash (£35,000 + £58,000)	93,000	1,513,000
		£3,950,440
Capital and reserves		
Ordinary shares		£1,120,000
Retained earnings (1,761,200 − 3,360 − 2,800)		£1,755,040
Non-controlling interest		288,400
Current liabilities:		
Payables	£630,000	
Taxation	£157,000	£787,000
		£3,950,440

BASIC

INTERMEDIATE

ADVANCED

11.17 Associate companies: development of issues

Fair values and the associate

If the fair value of the net assets of the associate at date of acquisition is materially different from their book values, then the net assets of the associate should be adjusted in the same way as for a subsidiary.

Balances with the associate

The associate company is considered to be outside the group, so any balances between group companies and the associate will remain in the consolidated statement of financial position.

Unrealized profit in inventory

This is treated in the same way as was illustrated for subsidiaries in that it has to be eliminated, as follows.

(i) If parent company sells to associate:

in this case the profit element is included in the accounts of the parent company, so

remove from group retained earnings (Dr)
remove from investment in associate (Cr)

(ii) If associate sells to parent:
in this case the profit element is included in the accounts of the associate, so

remove from group retained earnings (Dr)
remove from group inventory (Cr).

In addition, since the associate is considered to be outside the group any sales or purchases between group companies and the associate are not normally eliminated. These will remain part of the consolidated figures in the statement of comprehensive income.

Progress Point 11.8

The statements of comprehensive income of the B group for the period ending 31 December 2012 are given below.

	B	K	S
	£000	£000	£000
Sales revenue	385	100	60
Cost of sales	(185)	(60)	(20)
Gross profit	200	40	40
Operating expenses	(50)	(15)	(10)
Profit before tax	150	25	30
Taxation	(50)	(12)	(10)
Profit after tax	100	13	20

The following information is also given.

1. B acquired a 30% stake in S a number of years ago.
2. B acquired a 90% stake in K a number of years ago.
3. During the year, S sold goods to B for £28,000. None of these goods was in the inventory at the end of the year.
4. Goodwill and the investment in the associate were impaired for the first time during the year as follows:

   - S £2,000
   - K £3,000.

Impairment of the goodwill of the subsidiary should be charged to operating expenses.

Required
Prepare the consolidated statement of comprehensive income for B group incorporating the results of the associated company.

Solution

Consolidated statement of comprehensive income (incorporating the results of the associate)	
	£000
Sales revenue (£385 + £100)	£485
Cost of sales (£185 + £60)	(245)
Gross profit	240
Operating expenses (£50 + £15 + £3 impairment)	68
Profit before tax	172
Share of profit of associate (30% of £20 – impairment £2)	4
	176
Less taxation	£62
	£114
Attributable to	
Equity holders of the parent	£112.7
Non-controlling interests (10% of £13,000)	£1.3

Note that although S had sold goods to B during the year for £28,000, at the year end none of these goods were in inventory. This implies that the goods had been sold by B and therefore, as far as the group is concerned, any profits had been realized.

11.18 The relevant IFRSs

The topic of consolidation is often found to be extremely difficult and for that reason the mechanics of the consolidation process, rather than the requirements of the IFRS have been the priority of this chapter so far. It is perhaps appropriate at this stage to briefly consider the reporting aspects and the relevant IFRSs dealing with consolidated financial statements.

As part of the ongoing project with the US FASB aimed at reducing differences between international standards and US GAAP, the standards formerly dealing with the various aspects of group accounting and business combinations have all recently been revised and in some cases replaced.

In May 2011, the IASB issued a suite of standards dealing with consolidated financial statements to update and replace the standards which were currently in place. These new standards, which are considered in detail in the advanced aspects section of this chapter, are required to be applied for annual periods beginning on or after 1 January 2013, although early application is permitted. If an entity wishes to adopt one of these standards early then it must adopt all of the standards at the same time and disclose that fact.

One of these standards is IFRS 12 *Disclosure of Interests in Other Entities*. Of particular significance are the IASB's reasons for issuing this standard. The standards which were in existence prior to 2011, namely IAS 27 *Consolidated and Separate Financial Statements*, IAS 28 *Investments in Associates* and IAS 31 *Interests in Joint Ventures* all contained requirements regarding disclosures. In revising and replacing these standards, the IASB also identified an opportunity to integrate and make consistent the disclosure requirements for subsidiaries, joint arrangements and associates and present these requirements in a single IFRS. The Board concluded that such a combined disclosure standard would make it easier to understand and apply the disclosure requirements for subsidiaries, joint ventures, and associates. Consequently the 2011 standards do not contain any disclosure requirements and instead refer to IFRS 12. We now look in detail at the content of this standard.

11.19 Disclosure requirements

IFRS 12 *Disclosure of interests in other entities*
Objective
The objective of IFRS 12 is to require an entity to disclose information that enables users of its financial statements to evaluate:

(a) the nature of, and risks associated with, its interests in other entities; and

(b) the effects of those interests on its financial position, financial performance and cash flows

Scope
The IFRS applies to entities that have an interest in a subsidiary, a joint arrangement, an associate or an unconsolidated structured entity.

Disclosure objectives
IFRS 12 establishes disclosure objectives according to which an entity discloses information that enables users of its financial statements:

(a) to understand:

    (i) the significant judgements and assumptions made in determining the nature of its interest in another entity or arrangement (i.e. control, joint control or significant influence), and in determining the type of joint arrangement in which it has an interest; and

    (ii) the interest that non-controlling interests have in the group's activities and cash flows; and

(b) to evaluate:

    (i) the nature and extent of significant restrictions on its ability to access or use assets, and settle liabilities, of the group;

    (ii) the nature of, and changes in, the risks associated with its interests in consolidated structured activities;

    (iii) the nature and extent of its interest in unconsolidated structured entities, and the nature of, and changes in, the risks associated with those interests;

    (iv) the nature, extent and financial effects of its interests in joint arrangements and associates, and the nature of the risks associated with those interests;

    (v) the consequences of changes in a parent's ownership interest in a subsidiary that do not result in a loss of control; and

    (vi) the consequences of losing control of a subsidiary during the reporting period.

Although IFRS 12 specifies minimum disclosures, if these are not sufficient to meet the disclosure objectives, an entity should disclose whatever additional information is necessary to meet that objective.

11.20 Disclosure in practice

In terms of the information given in the financial statements, if the company has subsidiaries, then group accounts will be prepared. These group accounts will include a consolidated statement of comprehensive income, statement of financial position and statement of cash flows for the group. Each of these statements will be prepared in accordance with the principles outlined in this chapter.

Figure 11.3 Logica: example of consolidated statement of comprehensive income

Consolidated statement of comprehensive income
for the year ended 31 December 2011

	2011 £'m	2010 £'m
Revenue	3,921.3	3,696.8
Net operating costs	(3,866.8)	(3,486.2)
Operating profit	**54.5**	210.6
Analysed as:		
Operating profit before exceptional items	**59.3**	212.3
Exceptional items	(4.8)	(1.7)
Operating profit	**54.5**	210.6
Finance costs	**(36.1)**	(27.2)
Finance income	**13.3**	8.9
Share of post-tax profits from associates	1.0	0.6
Profit before tax	**32.7**	192.9
Taxation	**(5.5)**	(40.8)
Net profit for the year	**27.2**	152.1
Other comprehensive income/(expense)		
Actuarial gains/(losses) on retirement benefit schemes	**26.7**	(3.1)
Tax on items taken directly to equity	**(7.3)**	0.6
Cash flow hedges	**(3.2)**	–
Interest rate swaps fair value difference	**0.1**	(0.1)
Exchange differences on translation of foreign operations	(54.0)	11.4
Other comprehensive income/(expense) for the year, net of tax	(37.7)	8.8
Total comprehensive income/(expense) for the year	(10.5)	160.9
Profit attributable to:		
Owners of the parent	27.2	152.1
	27.2	152.1
Total comprehensive income/(expense) attributable to:		
Owners of the parent	(10.5)	160.9
	(10.5)	160.9

Source: Logica (2011), p. 92

An example of the consolidated statement of comprehensive income and statement of financial position can be seen in the financial report of Logica (see Figure 11.3).

Note that the profit for the year is allocated to the equity holder of the parent and to the non-controlling interests.

Additional information on the basis of consolidation is given in the accounting policy section of Logica. Note that this gives information on how Logica accounted for its interest in its associates and joint ventures, using the equity method as described in this chapter. The business combinations are accounted for using the 'purchase method', that is acquisition accounting. Notice too that intercompany transactions are eliminated on consolidation.

Figure 11.4 Logica: example of consolidated statement of financial position

Consolidated statement of financial position
31 December 2011

	2011 £'m	2010 £'m
Non-current assets		
Goodwill	1,883.4	1,906.5
Other intangible assets	174.0	200.7
Property, plant and equipment	139.7	138.5
Investments in associates	2.6	2.7
Financial assets	41.5	12.5
Retirement benefit assets	52.4	38.7
Deferred tax assets	84.0	70.3
	2,377.6	2,369.9
Current assets		
Inventories	0.8	1.0
Trade and other receivables	1,262.0	1,252.3
Current tax assets	24.8	11.4
Cash and cash equivalents	89.6	56.4
	1,377.2	1,321.1
Current liabilities		
Other borrowings	(35.1)	(204.3)
Trade and other payables	(1,061.9)	(1,062.4)
Current tax liabilities	(89.3)	(66.6)
Provisions	(90.0)	(29.4)
	(1,276.3)	(1,362.7)
Net current assets/(liabilities)	100.9	(41.6)
Total assets less current liabilities	2,478.5	2,328.3
Non-current liabilities		
Borrowings	(376.1)	(132.3)
Retirement benefit obligations	(69.7)	(95.2)
Deferred tax liabilities	(46.0)	(61.1)
Provisions	(47.7)	(37.1)
Other non-current liabilities	(5.8)	(1.4)
	(545.3)	(327.1)
Net assets	1,933.2	2,001.2
Equity		
Share capital	161.2	160.2
Share premium account	1,110.6	1,107.4
Other reserves	661.4	733.5
Total shareholders' equity	1,933.2	2,001.1
Non-controlling interests	–	0.1
Total equity	1,933.2	2,001.2

Source: Logica (2011), p. 93

Consolidation
Subsidiaries

Subsidiaries are all entities (including special purpose entities) over which the Group has the power to govern the financial and operating policies generally accompanying a shareholding of more than one half of the voting rights. The existence and effect of potential voting rights that are currently exercisable or convertible are considered when assessing whether the Group controls another entity. The Group also assesses existence of control where it does not have more than 50% of the voting power but is able to govern the financial and operating policies by virtue of de facto control. De facto control may arise in circumstances where the size of the Group's voting rights relative to the size and dispersion of holdings of other shareholders give the Group the power to govern the financial and operating policies.

Subsidiaries are fully consolidated from the date on which control is transferred to the Group. They are de-consolidated from the date that control ceases.

The Group applies the acquisition method of accounting to account for business combinations. The consideration transferred for the acquisition of a subsidiary is the fair values of the assets transferred, the liabilities incurred and the equity borrowings issued by the Group. The consideration transferred includes the fair value of any asset or liability resulting from a contingent consideration arrangement. Identifiable assets acquired and liabilities and contingent liabilities assumed in a business combination are measured initially at their fair values at the acquisition date. The Group recognises any non-controlling interest in the acquiree on an acquisition-by-acquisition basis, either at fair value or at the non-controlling interest's proportionate share of the recognised amounts of the acquiree's identifiable net assets.

Acquisition-related costs are expensed as incurred.

If the business combination is achieved in stages, the acquisition date fair value of the acquirer's previously held equity interest in the acquiree is remeasured to fair value at the acquisition date through profit or loss.

Any contingent consideration to be transferred by the Group is recognized at fair value at the acquisition date. Subsequent changes to the fair value of the contingent consideration that is deemed to be an asset or liability is recognised in accordance with IAS 39 either in profit or loss or as a change to other comprehensive income. Contingent consideration that is classified as equity is not remeasured, and its subsequent settlement is accounted for within equity. Goodwill is initially measured as the excess of the aggregate of the consideration transferred and the fair value of non-controlling interest over the net identifiable assets acquired and liabilities assumed. If this consideration is lower than the fair value of the net assets of the subsidiary acquired, the difference is recognised in profit or loss.

Inter-company transactions, balances, income and expenses on transactions between Group companies are eliminated. Profits and losses resulting from inter- company transactions that are recognized in assets are also eliminated. Accounting policies of subsidiaries have been changed where necessary to ensure consistency with the policies adopted by the Group.

Changes in ownership interests in subsidiaries without change of control

Transactions with non-controlling interests that do not result in loss of control are accounted for as equity transactions – that is, as transactions with the owners in their capacity as owners. The difference between fair value of any consideration paid and the relevant share acquired of the carrying value of net assets of the subsidiary is recorded in equity. Gains or losses on disposals to non-controlling interests are also recorded in equity.

Disposal of subsidiaries

When the Group ceases to have control any retained interest in the entity is re-measured to its fair value at the date when control is lost, with the change in carrying amount recognised in profit or loss. The fair value is the initial carrying amount for the purposes of subsequently accounting for the retained interest as an associate, joint venture or financial asset. In addition, any amounts previously recognised in other comprehensive income in respect of that entity are accounted for as if the Group had directly disposed of the related assets or liabilities. This may mean that amounts previously recognized in other comprehensive income are reclassified to profit or loss.

Associates

Associates are all entities over which the Group has significant influence but not control, generally accompanying a shareholding of between 20% and 50% of the voting rights. Investments in associates are accounted for using the equity method of accounting. Under the equity method, the investment is initially recognised at cost, and the carrying amount is increased or decreased to recognise the investor's share of the profit or loss of the investee after the date of acquisition. The Group's investment in associates includes goodwill identified on acquisition. If the ownership interest in an associate is reduced but significant influence is retained, only a proportionate share of the amounts previously recognised in other comprehensive income is reclassified to profit or loss where appropriate.

The Group's share of post-acquisition profits or losses is recognised in the income statement, and its share of post-acquisition movements in other comprehensive income is recognised in other comprehensive income with a corresponding adjustment to the carrying amount of the investment. When the Group's share of losses in an associate equals or exceeds its interest in the associate, including any other unsecured receivables, the Group does not recognise further losses, unless it has incurred legal or constructive obligations or made payments on behalf of the associate. Profits and losses resulting from upstream and downstream transactions between the Group and its associates are recognised in the Group's financial statements only to the extent of unrelated investor's interests in the associates. Unrealised losses are eliminated unless the transaction provides evidence of an impairment of the asset transferred. Accounting policies of associates have been changed where necessary to ensure consistency with the policies adopted by the Group. Dilution gains and losses arising in investments in associates are recognised in the income statement.

Source: Logica (2011), p. 96f.

Information specific to any investment in associate companies is disclosed separately. The information given by Logica in Figure 11.5 is fairly detailed. It is likely that this is an overseas associate since there is an exchange difference shown. Note that the share of the post-tax profit of the associate is given.

In the notes to the accounts of Logica, full details are given of the non-controlling interests (see Figure 11.6).

Figure 11.5: Logica: investment in associates

Investments in associates	2011 £'m
At 1 January 2011	2.7
Share of post-tax profits of associates	1.0
Dividends received	(1.0)
Exchange differences	(0.1)
At 31 December 2011	**2.6**

Summarised information in respect of associates at 31 December 2011 is provided below on a 100% interest basis.

	2011 £'m	2010 £'m
Assets	21.1	22.8
Liabilities	(15.2)	(15.5)
Revenue	30.2	33.5
Net profit	1.7	4.2

Source: Logica (2011), p. 116

Figure 11.6 Logica: non-controlling interests		
	2011 £'m	2010 £'m
At 1 January	0.1	0.1
Repurchase of non-controlling interests	(0.1)	–
At 31 December	–	0.1
Source: Logica (2011), p. 130		

Section summary

Subsidiary

This is defined in IAS 27. The method of accounting used is acquisition accounting. The accounts of the subsidiary are combined with those of the parent to produce the consolidated financial statements. Any goodwill arising is shown in the statement of financial position and is tested for impairment. All aspects of intra-company trading are eliminated so that the figures remaining are at 'cost to the group'.

Associate

Defined in IAS 28(2011) and accounted for using the equity method. This method estimates the value of the investment in the associate and is calculated by adding the cost of the investment to the parent company's share of any post-acquisition profit.

Joint venture

This is defined in IAS 28(2011). The required treatment of a joint venture is by using the equity method.

All these techniques of accounting for business acquisitions have been dealt with elsewhere in this chapter.

Section 3: Advanced Aspects

The previous two sections have concentrated heavily on the preparation of consolidated financial statements. Various technical aspects were explored in greater detail, and the examples and progress points given have focused mainly on the construction of consolidated financial statements incorporating these adjustments. This section now goes on to examine the rationale for group accounts, and explores the underlying conceptual thinking behind group accounts. It also identifies aspects of the regulatory framework, in particular international accounting standards, as they apply to the preparation of group accounts.

11.21 Background to the preparation of consolidated accounts

In 1983 the Seventh Council Directive of the European Communities was issued. This directive specifies that a member state should require any parent undertaking that is subject to its national laws to prepare consolidated accounts. Furthermore a consolidated annual report needs to be prepared if such an undertaking has control of another undertaking, either by ownership of shares, voting rights or through a dominant influence.

Concepts underlying group accounts

A parent company is a company that has one or more subsidiary companies. The shareholders of a parent company are not entitled to receive any information from the subsidiary companies because they are not shareholders of these companies. However, in order to give the holding company shareholders information on the financial position of a group of companies, consolidated financial statements are prepared.

Consolidated financial statements are designed to give effect to the economic substance of intragroup relationships rather than the strict legal form of such relationships. The traditional approach to preparing group accounts focuses on providing information for the equity investors for the parent company. Any interests that the minority shareholder has is seen as of secondary importance. This approach is sometimes referred to as the parent company concept. Under this concept there is an assumption that the parent company has the power to exercise control over the subsidiary company.

Consolidation is the process whereby the individual accounts of the parent company and each of the subsidiaries are combined as though it were a single company. This combination requires that each item in the individual company accounts is aggregated on a line-by-line basis, eliminating in the process any double counting.

Control

Control is important in determining how a particular investment is to be classified. Under the Seventh Directive, two concepts of control are identified: legal concept and entity (economic) concept.

Legal concept

Formerly, legal definitions of control were based on an ownership holding of more than 50% of equity (rather than voting) shares. In addition to this, control of the composition of the board of directors would have given a parent–subsidiary relationship. This legal concept of control is evident in the Seventh Directive's definition of subsidiary undertaking. However, the Seventh Directive's definition of control is much broader and takes into account the economic concept of control.

Entity (economic) concept

This concept focuses on the existence of the group as an economic unit, rather than looking at it only through the eyes of the dominant shareholder group. The main focus of this concept is on the resources controlled by the company, and it views the identity of owners with claims on such resources as being less important. No distinction is made between the treatment given to different classes of shareholders, whether majority or minority, and all transactions between the shareholders are regarded as internal to the group.

Proprietary (parent entity) concept

This concept emphasizes ownership through a controlling shareholding interest. Consolidated financial statements are therefore prepared for the shareholders of the holding company. This means that the minority shareholders are treated as 'outsiders' and the interests of this group of shareholders are reflected in the consolidated financial statements as a kind of liability. An alternative is to omit the minority altogether and consolidate the parent company's proportion of the assets and liabilities of the subsidiary. This approach is the proportionate consolidation method, as described in previous section. The proprietary concept is sometimes known as the 'parent entity' concept and there is a variant of it known as the 'parent entity extension' concept.

The parent company approach to consolidation was used extensively in the UK, where it was known as acquisition accounting. This is the method of accounting that has been demonstrated in the earlier sections of this chapter.

Recent changes to international accounting standards seem to be moving the accounting for groups away from the parent company approach and towards the entity approach. In terms of the accounting regulation, which will be discussed in more detail later, it is the parent company concept that is required by international accounting standards (IFRS 3). However, some changes to the new international standard on *Presentation of Financial Statements* (IAS 1), as illustrated in Chapter 1, have introduced a slight move-ment towards the entity concept. This is because IAS 1 now requires that the consolidated statement of comprehensive income be analysed to show only the parent share of the profit for the year, and the non-controlling interest in that profit. Previously, the non-controlling interest was deducted on the face of the statement of comprehensive income.

IAS 1 also requires that non-controlling interest be shown on the consolidated statement of financial position as part of equity. Before, the parent company approach showed this minority outside of equity.

Regulatory framework

The content of consolidated financial statements is dealt with in IFRS 10. The methods of accounting for business combinations and how to deal with goodwill arising on consolidation are dealt with by IFRS 3, which we will look at now.

11.22 IFRS 3 *Business Combinations*

IFRS 3 (Revised) *Business Combinations* was published in January 2008 and has created significant changes in accounting for business combinations. Some of the more significant changes are in relation to the purchase consideration, which now includes the fair value of all the interests that the acquirer may have held previously in the acquired business. This includes any interest in an associate or joint venture, or any other equity interest.

If an acquiree has held a previous stake in a business, this is seen as being 'given up' to acquire the entity, and a gain or loss is recorded on its disposal. If the acquirer already held an interest in the acquired entity before acquisition, the standard requires that this existing stake is re-measured to fair value at the date of acquisition. If the value of the stake has increased, there will be a gain recognized in the statement of comprehensive income of the acquirer at the date of the business combination. (Note that it is possible for a loss to occur if the existing interest has a book value in excess of the proportion of fair value obtained and no impairment had previously been recorded. This loss situation is not expected to occur very often.)

Goodwill and non-controlling interests

The revised standard gives entities the option, on an individual transaction basis, to measure non-con-trolling interest at either:

(a) the fair value of their proportion of identifiable assets, or

(b) full fair value.

If option (a) is chosen, then this will result in a goodwill calculation that is basically the same as the origi-nal IFRS. If option (b) is chosen, the goodwill will be recorded on the non-controlling interest as well as on the acquired controlling interest. Goodwill continues to be a residual, but it will be a different residual under IFRS 3 (Revised) if the full fair value method is used. This is partly because all of the consideration (including any previously held interest in the acquired business) is measured at fair value, but also because goodwill can be measured in two different ways, as described below.

Partial goodwill method

This is the difference between the consideration paid and the purchaser's share of the identifiable net assets acquired. This is classed as a partial goodwill method because the non-controlling interest (minor-ity) is recognized at its share of identifiable net assets and does not include any goodwill.

Full goodwill method

This approach results in the recognition of the whole goodwill of the acquired business and not just the acquir-er's share of goodwill. Under this method goodwill is measured as the difference between the aggregate of:

■ the consideration transferred (generally measured at fair value at the date of acquisition)

■ the amount of any non-controlling (minority) interest

■ the fair value at date of acquisition of any previously held equity interest in the acquiree (if any)

■ the identifiable net assets at date of acquisition.

Non-controlling interests can be measured in one of two ways:

1. at fair value (this results in the full goodwill approach)
2. at the non-controlling interest's proportionate share of the acquiree's net assets.

The following examples will illustrate the point.

Example 1

On 1 September Year 10, A plc acquires 60% of B plc for £10,000. Prior to the acquisition it has been determined that:

■ the fair value of the non-controlling interest in B plc is £6,000

■ the fair value of the identifiable net assets of B plc is £9,000.

Show the calculation of goodwill under IFRS 3 (Revised).

IFRS3 (Revised)

Under this method, non-controlling interest can be measured either:

(a) at fair value, or

(b) at proportionate share.

	Fair value	Proportionate share	
Fair value of identifiable net assets	£9,000	£9,000	
Non-controlling interest	6,000	3,600	(40% of £9,000)
	3,000	5,400	
Fair value of consideration	£10,000	£10,000	
Goodwill	£7,000	£4,600	

Example 2

On 1 September Year 10, A plc acquires 50% of B plc for £10,000. Prior to this, A plc held 10% of the equity of B plc, which had a fair value of £1,000 immediately prior to the acquisition of the additional 50% of B plc. A plc has determined the following:

■ the fair value of the non-controlling interest in B plc is £6,000

■ the fair value of the identifiable net assets of B plc is £9,000.

Show the calculation of goodwill under IFRS 3 (Revised).

IFRS3 (Revised)

Under this method, non-controlling interest can be measured either:

(a) at fair value, or

(b) at proportionate share (as before).

	Fair value	Proportionate share	
Fair value of identifiable net assets	£9,000	£9,000	
Non-controlling interest	6,000	3,600	(40% of £9,000)
	3,000	5,400	
Previously held equity at fair value*	1,500	1,500	
	1,500	3,900	
Fair value of consideration for 50%	£10,000	£10,000	
Goodwill	£8,500	£6,100	

* The fair value of the 40% non-controlling interest is now £6,000. So a holding of 10% would have a fair value now of £1,500. This is an increase of £500 (£1,500 – £1,000) over the previous fair value and will be recorded as a profit.

Fair value aspects

The revised IFRS 3 has introduced some changes to both assets and liabilities recognized in the acquisition statement of financial position. The existing requirement to recognize all the identifiable assets and liabilities is retained. With the exception of certain items, such as pension obligations and deferred taxation, most assets are recognized at fair value. Additional clarification has been given by the IASB, which might result in more intangible assets being recognized. Acquirers are required to recognize brands, licences and customer relationships, and other intangible assets. Other ongoing projects on standards linked to business combinations may affect their recognition or measurement. Such projects are on provisions (IAS 37) and on deferred tax (IAS 12).

Disclosure requirements of IFRS 3

IFRS 3 requires disclosures such that users of financial statements can evaluate the nature and financial effect of business combinations. Disclosure is required as follows:

- names of combining entities
- date of acquisition
- proportion of company acquired
- cost of the combination, together with components of the cost
- any operations disposed of due to the combination
- details of fair values and carrying values of assets, liabilities and contingent liabilities acquired
- any negative goodwill
- amount of post-acquisition profit included in the statement of comprehensive income of the acquirer.
- where non-controlling interest is measured at fair value, the valuation methods used will need to be disclosed
- in a step acquisition, the fair value of any previously held equity interest will require to be disclosed, and any gain or loss resulting from re-measurement will need to be recognized in the statement of comprehensive income.

11.23 IFRS 10 *Consolidated Financial Statements*

In May 2011, the IASB issued IFRS 10 *Consolidated Financial Statements*. IFRS 10 is part of a suite of standards issued together, which must all be adopted at the same time. The other Standards are IFRS 11 *Joint Arrangements*, IFRS 12 *Disclosure of Interest in Other Entities*, IAS 27 *Separate Financial Statements* and IAS 28 *Investments in Associates and Joint Ventures*.

IFRS 10 replaced IAS 27 (Revised) *Consolidated and Separate Financial Statements* for annual periods beginning on or after 1 January 2013 with earlier application permitted.

Objective

The objective of the standard is to establish principles for the presentation and preparation of consolidated financial statements when an entity controls one or more other entities.

To meet the objective, IFRS 10

(a) requires an entity (the parent) that controls one or more other entities (subsidiaries) to present consolidated financial statements;

(b) defines the principle of control, and establishes control as the basis for consolidation;

(c) sets out how to apply the principle of control to indentify whether an investor controls an investee and therefore must consolidate the investee; and

(d) sets out the accounting requirements for the preparation of consolidated financial statements

This standard requires a parent company to prepare consolidated financial statements except when:

- the parent is a wholly owned or partly owned subsidiary of another company
- the company's shares are not publicly traded
- the ultimate or any intermediate parent produces consolidated financial statements available for public use that comply with IFRS.

Control

An investor controls an investee when it is exposed, or has rights, to variable returns from its involvement with the investee and has the ability to affect those returns through its power over the investee.

Consolidation procedures

IFRS 10 requires an entity to use uniform accounting policies for reporting like transactions and other events in similar circumstances. Intragroup balances and transactions must be eliminated. Non-controlling interests in subsidiaries must be presented in the consolidated statement of financial position within equity, separately from the equity of the owners of the parent.

Disclosure

The disclosure requirements for interests in subsidiaries are specified in IFRS 12 *Disclosure of Interests in Other Entities*.

11.24 IAS 28 (2011) *Investments in Associates and Joint Ventures*

Introduction

In May 2011, the IASB issued IAS 28 which:

(a) prescribes the accounting for investments in associates; and

(b) sets out the requirements for the application of the equity method when accounting for investments in associates and joint ventures.

An associate is defined in IAS 28 as an entity over which the investor has significant influence. Significant influence is deemed to apply where the investor holds, directly or indirectly, 20% or more of the voting power of the investee unless it be can clearly demonstrated that this is not the case. Significant influence is usually in evidence where there is:

- some representation on the board of directors
- some participation in the policy-making process
- interchange of managerial personnel.

A joint venture is a joint arrangement whereby the parties that have joint control of the arrangement have rights to the net assets of the arrangement. A joint venturer should recognize its interest in a joint venture as an investment and should account for that investment using the equity method in accordance with IAS 28 unless the entity is exempted from applying the equity method as specified in the standard.

The equity method

Under the equity method, on initial recognition the investment in an associate or a joint venture is recognized at cost, and the carrying amount is increased or decreased to recognize the investor's share of the profit or loss of the investee after the date of acquisition. The investor's share of the investee's profit or loss is recognized in the investor's profit or loss.

Disclosure

The disclosure requirements for entities with joint control of, or significant influence over, an investee are specified in IFRS 12 *Disclosure of Interests in Other Entities*.

11.25 IFRS 11 *Joint Arrangements*

Objective

The objective of IFRS 11 is to establish principles for financial reporting by entities that have an interest in joint arrangements (i.e. arrangements that are controlled jointly). The IFRS defines joint control and requires a party to a joint arrangement:

- to determine the type of joint arrangement in which it is involved by assessing its rights and obligations arising from the arrangement; and
- to account for those rights and obligations in accordance with that type of joint arrangement

Scope

The IFRS is to be applied by all entities that are a party to a joint arrangement. A joint arrangement is an arrangement of which two or more parties have joint control. Joint control is defined in the standard as the contractually agreed sharing control of an arrangement, which exists only when decisions about the relevant activities (i.e. activities that significantly affect the returns of the arrangement) require the unanimous consent of the parties sharing control.

Entities within the scope of the IFRS 11 are required to analyse each joint arrangement and classify it as either a:

(i) joint operation; or

(ii) joint venture

Joint operation

A joint operation is a joint arrangement whereby the parties that have control of the arrangement (i.e. joint operators) have rights to the assets, and obligations for the liabilities, relating to the investment.

It involves the use of the assets and other resources of the joint operators rather than the establishment of a corporation, partnership or other entity. Each operator uses its own property, plant and equipment and inventories. It also incurs its own expenses and liabilities, and raises its own finance. The agreement usually provides a means by which the revenue from the sale of the joint product and any expenses incurrent in common are shared among the joint operators.

An example of this is where joint operators combine their operations, resources and expertise to manufacture jointly a particular product (e.g. a ship).

The IFRS requires a joint operator to recognize and measure the assets and liabilities (and recognize the related revenues and expenses) in relation to its interest in the arrangement in accordance with relevant IFRSs applicable to the particular assets, liabilities, revenues and expenses.

Joint venture

A joint venture is a joint arrangement whereby the parties that have joint control of the arrangement (i.e. joint venturers) have rights to the net assets of the arrangement. The IFRS requires a joint venturer to recognize an investment and to account for that investment using the equity method in accordance with IAS 28 *Investments in Associates and Joint Ventures*, unless the entity is exempted from applying the equity method as specified in that standard.

Determining whether a joint arrangement is a joint operation or a joint venture

An entity determines the type of joint arrangement in which it is involved by considering its rights and obligations. An entity assesses its rights and obligations by considering:

(i) the structure of the arrangement i.e. if a joint arrangement is not structured through a separate vehicle, it should be classified as a joint operation

(ii) the legal form of the arrangement i.e. if the legal form of the separate vehicle gives the parties rights to the assets, and obligations for the liabilities, relating to the arrangement, it should be classified as a joint operation

(iii) the contractual terms agreed to by the parties to the arrangement i.e. if the terms of the contractual arrangement specify that the parties have rights to the assets, and obligations for the liabilities, relating to the arrangement, it should be classified as a joint operation

(iv) other facts and circumstances to assess whether the parties do in fact have rights to the assets and obligations for the liabilities of the arrangement, in which case the arrangement is classified as a joint operation.

Disclosure

The disclosure requirements for parties with joint control of a joint arrangement are specified in IFRS 12 *Disclosure of Interests in Other Entities*.

Section summary

This section has looked at methods of accounting for an entity's investment in another entity depending on the level of investment made. We have seen that acquisition accounting is used for the consolidation of a subsidiary, while equity accounting is used for associated companies and joint ventures.

Notwithstanding the technical complexities of the mechanics of the consolidation process, the determination of the required method of accounting is also made complex as a result of the basis for consolidation being dependant upon the principle of control.

A detailed examination of the consolidation process is beyond the scope of this text and there are many more aspects still to be considered. However, as this chapter comes to a close it is perhaps worth considering whether the requirements of the standards provide a true and fair view to investors or whether the underlying concepts are so complex that the fundamental characteristic of faithful presentation, and the enhancing characteristic of understandability, can be applied to consolidated financial statements.

Chapter summary

IFRS 3 (Revised) *Business Combinations*

- The acquisition method is used for all business combinations as follows:
  - identify the acquirer
  - determine the acquisition date
  - recognize and measure the identifiable assets acquired, the liabilities assumed and any non-controlling interest (NCI) in the acquiree
  - recognize and measure goodwill or a gain from a bargain purchase.
- Assets and liabilities are measured at their acquisition date fair value.
- At acquisition, the non-controlling interest in the acquiree is measured at fair value (of the NCI) *or* at the NCI's proportionate share of the acquiree's identifiable net assets. The choice is applicable on a transaction-by-transaction basis.
- Recognizes goodwill at date of acquisition, measured as the excess of (a) over (b), where (a) is the total of consideration transferred plus amount of any NCI plus the fair value of the acquirer's previously held equity interest in the acquiree at date of acquisition (where the business combination is achieved in stages), and (b) is the total fair value of identifiable net assets acquired.
- Where business combinations are achieved in stages (piecemeal acquisition) an acquirer must remeasure its previously held equity interest at fair value at date of acquisition. Any resulting gain (or loss) should be recognized in profit or loss.

IFRS 10 *Consolidated Financial Statements*

- Requires a parent entity to present consolidated financial statements.
- Defines and establishes control as the basis for consolidation.
- Consolidated financial statements are prepared by combining like items of assets, liabilities, equity, income, expenses and cash flows of the parent with those of its subsidiaries.
- All intra-group items are cancelled out.
- A reporting entity includes the income and expenses of a subsidiary in the consolidated financial statements from the date it gains control.
- Any unrealized profit on assets transferred between group companies is eliminated in full on consolidation.
- A parent presents the extent to which the net assets of the group are attributable to a non-controlling interest within equity, separately from the equity of the owners of the parent.

IAS 28 (2011) *Investments in Associates and Joint Ventures*

- An associate is an entity over which the investor has significant influence.
- Significant influence is presumed to exist where the investor holds 20% or more of the voting power of the entity.
- A joint venture is an arrangement whereby the parties have rights to the net assets of the arrangement.
- Associates and joint ventures should be accounted for using the equity method.
- The equity method involves recognizing the investment initially at cost and adjusting it thereafter for the post-acquisition change in the investor's share of the investee's net assets.

IFRS 11 *Joint Arrangements*

- A joint arrangement is an arrangement of which two or more parties have joint control.
- A joint arrangement is either a joint operation or a joint venture.

- A joint operation is a joint arrangement whereby the parties that have joint control of the arrangement have rights to the assets, and obligations for the liabilities, relating to the arrangement. Those parties are called joint operators.
- A joint operator recognizes in relation to its interest in a joint operation:
  - its assets, including its share of any assets held jointly;
  - its liabilities, including its share of any liabilities incurred jointly;
  - its revenue from the sale of its share of the output of the joint operation;
  - its share of the revenue from the sale of the output by the joint operation; and
  - its expenses, including its share of any expenses incurred jointly.
- A joint operator accounts for the assets, liabilities, revenue and expenses relating to its involvement in a joint operation in accordance with the relevant IFRSs.

IFRS 12 *Disclosure of Interests in Other Entities*

- Requires the disclosure of information that enables users of financial statements to evaluate:
  - the nature of, and risks associated with, an entity's interest in other entities
  - the effects of those interests on an entity's financial position, financial performance and cash flows.
- Disclosure is required of the significant judgements and assumptions an entity has made in determining:
  - that it has control of another entity
  - that it has joint control of an arrangement or significant influence over another entity
  - the type of joint arrangement (i.e. joint operation or joint venture) when the arrangement has been structured through a separate vehicle.
- Disclosure is required of information that enables users of an entity's consolidated financial statements to:
  - understand the composition of the group
  - understand the interest that any non-controlling interests have in the group's activities and cash flows
  - evaluate the nature and extent of significant restrictions on the entity's ability to access or use assets, and settle liabilities, of the group
  - evaluate the nature of, and changes in, the risks associated with the entity's interests in consolidated structured entities
  - evaluate the consequences of changes in an equity's ownership interest in a subsidiary that do not result in a loss of control
  - evaluate the consequences of losing control of a subsidiary during the reporting period.
- Disclosure is required of information that enables users of an entity's financial statements to:
  - understand the nature, extent and financial effects of its interests in joint arrangements and associates, including the nature and effects of its contractual relationship with the other investors with joint control of, or significant influence over, joint arrangements and associates
  - the nature of, and changes in, the risks associated with its interests in joint ventures and associates.
- Disclosure is required of information that enables users of an entity's financial statements to:
  - understand the nature and extent of its interests in unconsolidated structured entities
  - evaluate the nature of, and changes in, the risks associated with its interests in unconsolidated structured entities.

✓ Key terms for review

Definitions can be found in the glossary at the end of the book.

Acquisition accounting

Associate company

Consolidated financial statements

Date of acquisition

Date of consolidation

Equity accounting

Goodwill

Group

Joint arrangement

Joint operation

Joint venture

Non-controlling (minority) interest

Parent

Pre-acquisition profits and reserves

Subsidiary company

? Review questions

1. What is the philosophy underlying the *proprietary* approach?
2. What is the philosophy underlying the *entity* approach?
3. Explain how negative goodwill may arise and how it should be accounted for.
4. Explain why it is only the net assets of the subsidiary that are adjusted to fair value at the date of acquisition for the purpose of consolidated accounts, and not those of the parent.
5. Explain why the non-controlling interest is calculated at the end of the reporting period, while goodwill is calculated at the date of acquisition.
6. Explain why pre-acquisition profits of a subsidiary are treated differently from post-acquisition profits.
7. Why is it important to remove unrealized profits arising from transactions between companies in a group?
8. Explain what is meant by the term 'joint arrangement' and what types of joint arrangement exist.
9. Explain what is meant by the term 'significant influence'.
10. Explain how associated companies are accounted for in a consolidation, and how this differs from the treatment of a subsidiary.

✎ Exercises

Level I

1. The following are the summarized statements of financial position of H Ltd and S Ltd which were drawn up immediately after H Ltd acquired control of S Ltd.

	H Ltd £	S Ltd £
Investment in S Ltd 60,000 shares	70,000	–
Property, plant & equipment	18,000	34,000
Net current assets	12,000	26,000
	100,000	60,000
Share capital – £1 shares	100,000	60,000
	100,000	60,000

Required

Prepare the consolidated statement of financial position for the H Group.

2. The following are the summarized statements of financial position of Aston Ltd, Bentley Ltd and Caterham Ltd at 31 December 2012.

	Aston Ltd	Bentley Ltd	Catarham Ltd
	£	£	£
Investment in Bentley Ltd at cost	60,000	–	–
Investment in Caterham Ltd at cost	150,000	–	–
Sundry assets	290,000	200,000	350,000
Sundry liabilities	(160,600)	(109,000)	(113,700)
	339,400	91,000	236,300
Share capital (£1 shares)	200,000	100,000	150,000
Retained earnings	139,400	(9,000)	85,300
	339,400	91,000	236,300

(handwritten note next to Caterham retained earnings: 86 300)

Additional information

(i) Aston acquired 80,000 shares in Bentley Ltd when the balance on Bentley's retained earnings showed a deficit of £10,800.

(ii) Aston acquired 90,000 shares in Caterham Ltd when the balance on Caterham's retained earnings were £92,300.

(iii) No dividends were paid or proposed by any of the companies in the relevant years.

Required

Prepare the consolidated financial position for the group at 31 December 2012.

Level II

3. The statements of financial position sheets of Parent plc and Daughter plc as at 31 December 2012 were as follows:

	Parent	Daughter
	£	£
Net assets	45,000	10,800
Share capital (£1 shares)	40,500	9,000
Retained earnings	4,500	1,800
	45,000	10,800

On 31 December 2012, Parent plc acquired all the ordinary shares in Daughter plc. The purchase consideration was satisfied by the issue of one new ordinary share in Parent plc for every three held in Daughter plc. The fair value of a £1 ordinary share in Parent plc was £2. The fair value of the net assets in Daughter plc was £15,000.

Required

Prepare the consolidated statement of financial position at 31 December 2012

4. Red plc acquired 80,000 shares in Blue plc on 31 December 2009. At that date, the retained profit of Blue plc was £200,000 and the revaluation reserve was £50,000. The summarized statements of financial position of the two companies at 31 December 2012 are as follows:

	Red plc	Blue plc
	£	£
Investment in Blue	315,000	
Non-current assets	400,000	250,000
Net current assets	135,000	200,000
	850,000	450,000
Share capital (£1 shares)	250,000	100,000
Revaluation reserve	100,000	50,000
Retained profit	500,000	300,000
	850,000	450,000

Required

(a) Prepare the consolidated statement of financial position for the Red Group as at 31 December 2012.

(b) If Red plc has acquired 20,000 shares in Blue plc, instead of 80,000, and had appointed a member to the board of directors of Blue plc, how would this affect the consolidated statement of financial position under (a) above? Show the new statement of financial position.

5. On 31 March 2013 Jardine plc declared unconditional its offer for the entire share capital of Walker plc. The agreed consideration was in the form of five new ordinary shares of 50p each issued by Jardine plc for every four held in Walker plc. The fair value of the shares issued by Jardine plc was £1.30 per share.

The statements of financial position of the two companies at 31 March 2013, prior to the implementation of the business combination, were as follows:

	Jardine	Walker
	£000	£000
Tangible non-current assets	4,500	1,200
Net current assets	1,700	1,300
	6,200	2,500
Creditors	2,000	900
	4,200	1,600
Share capital (par value 50p each)	2,000	800
Share premium	400	–
Retained earnings	1,800	800
	4,200	1,600

ı the course of negotiations it was established that the fair value of the tangible fixed assets of Walker plc as £700,000 greater than the existing book value.

Required

Show the statement of financial position after the business combination.

6. T plc acquired 75% of the ordinary share capital of S plc when shareholders' funds of S plc were:

	£000
Ordinary share capital £1 shares	400
Reserves	800
	1,200

T plc acquired 25% of the ordinary share capital of A plc when shareholders' funds of A plc were:

	£000
Ordinary share capital £1 shares	200
Reserves	360
	560

The statements of financial position of the three companies at 31 December 2012 were:

	T plc £000	S plc £000	A plc £000
Non-current assets	2,200	1,400	700
Investment in S	1,600		
Investment in A	168		
Net current assets	1,200	1,000	500
	5,168	2,400	1,200
Share capital	1,000	400	200
Retained earnings	2,168	1,200	600
14% debentures	2,000	800	400
	5,168	2,400	1,200

Required

Prepare the consolidated statement of financial position for the T group as at 31 December 2012, assuring T plc appoints a member to the board of A plc.

7. The following information concerns Landlord Ltd and its subsidiary undertaking Tennant.
Trial balance as at 31 December 2012

	Landlord £	Tennant £
Land and buildings at cost	35,000	
Machinery at cost	80,000	30,000
Accumulated depreciation on machinery	(35,000)	(17,000)
Investment in Tennant (9,000 shares) at cost	16,000	
Amount due by Tennant	8,000	

Inventories	27,000	9,000
Accounts receivable	20,000	6,000
	£151,000	£28,000
Ordinary shares of £1 each	120,000	12,000
General reserve		4,000
Retained earnings	21,000	8,000
Accounts payable	10,000	4,000
	£151,000	£28,000

Additional notes

(i) Landlord bought 9,000 shares in Tennant at a time when the general reserve of Tennant was £2,000 and retained profits were £4,000.

(ii) Six years earlier, Tennant bought a machine for £20,000 and immediately transferred it to Landlord for £40,000. This machine had an estimated life of ten years and has been depreciated at 10% per annum in the books of Landlord.

(iii) The amount due by Tennant at 31 December 2012 represents goods in transit that were received and recorded by Tennant in January 2013. These goods were priced so as to give Landlord a gross profit of 25%.

Required

Prepare the consolidated statement of financial position as at 31 December 2012 for Landlord and its subsidiary, Tennant.

8. The following are the summarized accounts of A, D and G for the year ended 31 December 2012.

Statements of comprehensive income	A	D	G
Sales revenue	£573,600	£314,000	£150,000
Operating costs	(300,000)	(200,000)	(90,000)
Operating profit	273,600	114,000	60,000
Interest payable	(20,000)	(14,000)	(8,000)
Dividend income from D	14,400		
Dividend income from G	4,000		
Other dividend income	10,000	–	–
Profit before tax	282,000	100,000	52,000
Tax	(72,000)	(30,000)	(16,000)
Profit for the year	£210,000	£70,000	£36,000

Statements of financial position	A	D	G
Investment in D (60%)	60,000		
Investment in G (25%)	50,000		
Other assets	300,000	120,000	100,000
	410,000	120,000	100,000
Ordinary shares	20,000	30,000	10,000
Retained earnings	330,000	66,000	70,000
Current liabilities	60,000	24,000	20,000
	410,000	120,000	100,000

Additional information

(i) The shares in D and G were acquired on 1 January 2012.

(ii) Goodwill in the subsidiary has suffered an impairment of 20% of its value, and the associate has suffered an impairment of £7,000.

(iii) A has accounted for the dividends from both the subsidiary and associate.

Required

Prepare the consolidated statement of comprehensive income for the year ended 31 December 2012, together with a statement of financial position as at that date.

9. Hook plc is a well-established firm in the fishing industry. The summary statement of financial position of Hook plc on 1 January 2012 is as follows:

Summary statement of financial position	
	£000
Assets:	
Cash	40
Other assets	180
	220
Share capital	100
Reserves	60
Liabilities	60
	220

On 1 January 2012, Hook plc enters into a joint venture with Line plc. They establish a new firm, Sinker, and each invests cash of £10,000 in it. Sinker raises a long-term loan to finance the purchase of non-current assets. When the investment is made in Sinker the summary statement of financial position is as follows:

Summary statement of financial position of Sinker		
		£000
Assets:		
Cash		10
Other assets		90
		100
Share capital:		
Hook	10	
Line	10	20
Long-term debt		80
		100

For the period ended 31 December 2012, Sinker reports revenues of £70,000 and a profit of £10,000. pays a dividend of £8,000. In the same period Hook plc reports revenues of £150,000 and a profit from own activities of £20,000. It pays a dividend of £12,000. Year end liabilities are still £60,000. There are inter-company transactions between Hook plc and Sinker, except for the dividend.

Required

(a) Explain the circumstances under which Hook plc would account for its investment in Sinker, under:
  (i) the equity method of consolidation
  (ii) proportionate consolidation.

(b) For each of the methods listed in (a) above, prepare statements of comprehensive income for the year ended 31 December 2012, together with statements of financial position as at that date.

References

IAS 27 *Consolidated and Separate Financial Statements*. IASB, revised 2008.
IAS 31 *Interests in Joint Ventures*. IASB, revised 2003.
IFRS 3 *Business Combinations*. IASB, revised 2008.
IFRS 10 *Consolidated Financial Statements*.
IFRS 11 *Joint Arrangements*.
IAS 28 *(2011) Investments in Associates and Joint Ventures*.
IFRS 12 *Disclosure of Interest in Other Entities*.
Logica (2011) *Annual Report and Accounts*.

Further reading

Deloitte: Business Combinations and Changes in Ownership Interests. Deloitte, 2008.
KPMG: *Business Combinations. IFRS 3*, revised January 2008.
RSM International: *The New Approach to Business Combination Introduced by the Revised IFRS 3 and the Revised IAS 27*.

Online LearningCentre

When you have read this chapter, log on to the Online Learning Centre website at *www.mcgraw-hill.co.uk/textbooks/mckeith* to explore chapter-by-chapter test questions, further reading and more online study tools.

Chapter 12

Foreign Currency Translation

Learning Outcomes

After studying this chapter you should be able to:

- ✓ record transactions denominated in a foreign currency
- ✓ calculate any exchange gain or loss arising in the accounts of the individual company
- ✓ describe the regulations governing foreign currency transactions for individual companies
- ✓ translate the accounts of overseas subsidiaries
- ✓ describe the disclosure requirements of IAS 21 *The effects of changes in foreign exchange rates* in terms of foreign currency translation.

Introduction

This chapter will look at the issues that arise when one company has dealings with another company located overseas. This other company could simply be a customer or supplier of goods or services, or it could be an overseas subsidiary. There will be an impact on the accounts given that the rate of exchange between domestic and foreign currencies is not stable. The reporting requirements of IAS 21, which looks at the accounting aspects of overseas dealings, will be examined. In the first instance, this chapter will deal with situations where companies have individual dealings with another company in terms of individual transactions. The intermediate section will consider the situation when a company located in one country has a subsidiary company located in another country. In order to prepare the group financial statements, the accounts of the overseas company must be converted, or translated, into the holding company's currency. Finally, the advanced section looks in detail at the reporting requirements of IAS 21 *The Effects of Changes in Foreign Exchange Rates*.

Section 1: Basic Principles

Businesses are becoming increasingly international. It is not unusual for firms to import or export goods and services to firms in other countries. These transactions may involve the purchase of, for example, raw materials from a foreign supplier. In order to pay for such materials, the purchaser will have to acquire some foreign currency. A similar situation would arise if a company sold to an overseas buyer and received payment in a foreign currency.

Most exchange rates are not fixed but vary from day to day. This fluctuation can pose problems for a company dealing with overseas suppliers or customers. When a foreign currency transaction is completed within an accounting period, currency conversion will be required. This currency conversion can be regarded as comprising two separate aspects: the purchase or sale of an asset, and the receipt or payment of cash for these assets.

12.1 Conversion and translation of currency

Conversion is the exchange of one currency for another, while translation is the expression of another currency in terms of the currency of the reporting entity.

Functional currency

In terms of foreign currency translation requirements, the functional currency concept is central. IAS 21 defines the functional currency as 'the currency of the primary economic environment in which the entity operates'. In general terms, the primary economic environment in which an entity operates is normally the one in which it mainly generates and spends cash. Although the functional currency is not necessarily the 'local' currency of the country in which the entity operates, in most cases it will be. The currency in which the financial statements are presented is called the presentation currency.

Foreign currency transactions

In order to record foreign currency transactions in its own accounts, a company has to convert (i.e. translate) these transactions into the currency in which the financial statements are presented.

Monetary and non-monetary items

The distinction between monetary items and non-monetary items is important, since the rate used in the translation of these items differs.

The general approach taken is as follows.

1. When a company enters into a transaction with an overseas company, the exchange rate to be used is the one in operation at the date the transaction took place. This rate is referred to as the '*spot*' rate.

2. Items in the statement of financial position that can be classified as monetary assets, or monetary liabilities – for example, cash, accounts payable, accounts receivable, loans – should be translated at the rate ruling at the end of the reporting period. This rate is referred to as the '*closing*' rate.

3. Items that are classified as non-monetary items – for example, property, plant and equipment, inventory – are generally measured in terms of historic cost and will be translated at the rate ruling at the date these items were acquired. This rate is referred to as the '*historic*' rate. However, it should be noted that, if the carrying amount of an asset is determined by comparing two or more amounts – for example, lower of cost or net realizable value in the case of inventory, then:

   (i) cost (or carrying amount) will be translated at the spot rate

   (ii) net realizable value will be translated at the closing rate.

   Sales and purchases of goods will be translated at the rate ruling when the sale or purchase was made.

4. If any non-monetary item is carried at fair value, then the exchange rate used should be that at the date the fair value was determined.

BASIC

INTERMEDIATE

ADVANCED

Gain and losses arising on exchange rate movements

Gains and losses will arise when there is a movement in the exchange rate between the date of transaction, the date of preparation of the financial statements and the date of settlement.

For example, a UK company buys an item of inventory from an overseas company in the USA. The item costs $100 and at the date of purchase the exchange rate is £1 = $1.5. If payment is made immediately, then no problem arises. The amount to be paid will be $100/1.5 = £66.67. However, if payment is not made until one month later and the exchange rate at this time was £1 = $1.6, then the amount owing to the US company would be £62.50 ($100/1.6). This means that a payment of £62.50 is required to be made, instead of £66.67. The difference of £4.17 is the 'gain' the company has made because of the exchange rate movement. This exchange difference needs to be accounted for, and the regulations governing the treatment of exchange gains and losses are contained in IAS 21.

12.2 Accounting treatment of exchange gains and losses

As indicated above, exchange gains and losses arise when there is a delay between entering into a transaction and receiving payment, and during this period of 'delay' the exchange rate moves.

These problems are illustrated further in the following examples.

BASIC

INTERMEDIATE

ADVANCED

Example 1

A UK company buys goods for resale from a US company at a cost of $450,000. When the transaction was entered into, the exchange rate ruling was £1 = $1.5. This initial purchase will be recorded at £300,000 ($450,000/1.5) and the amount to be paid to the US company will be the same.

Dr	Purchases	£300,000	
	Cr Accounts payable (US company)		£300,000
Being goods purchased			

When the accounts payable are settled, then the rate at date of settlement will be used. So, using the above example, if the US supplier was paid when the rate was £1 = $1.2, then the amount paid would be £375,000 ($450,000/1.2).

Dr	Accounts payable	£375,000	
	Cr Bank		£375,000
Being payment made to settle debt.			

This is more than the initial liability of £300,000. The fact that the payment was made when the rate moved from 1.5 to 1.2 meant that the company had to pay more to settle the account. This difference of £75,000 (£375,000 – £300,000) is a loss on exchange as more was paid to the US supplier than originally recorded. In accordance with IAS 21, this loss on exchange should be recognized in profit or loss for the year:

Dr	Loss on exchange	£75,000	
	Cr Accounts payable		£75,000
Being loss on exchange.			

The above entries can be combined as follows:

Dr	Loss on exchange	£75,000	
Dr	Accounts payable	£300,000	
	Cr Bank		£375,000

The purchases remain at the historic amount.

If the supplier is paid when the rate is £1 = $1.8 then a different situation emerges. The amount to be paid this time would be £250,000 ($450,000/1.8). This is less than the initial payment recorded, so in this situation a gain on exchange arises. The gain amounts to £50,000 (£300,000 – £250,000) and arises because less was paid to the US supplier than originally recorded. In accordance with IAS 21, this gain is also recognized in profit or loss for the year. The accounting entries for this would be:

Dr	Accounts payable	£300,000	
	Cr Bank		£250,000
	Cr Gain on exchange		£50,000
Being gain on exchange.			

As indicated above, in the general approach to foreign currency translation, any non-monetary items, such as non-current assets, inventory and equity investments, should be recorded at the rate ruling at the date of the transaction. These items are not re-translated at any time in the future unless there is a fair value adjustment. However, if there are monetary assets and liabilities in existence at the end of the reporting period, then these should be re-translated at the rate of exchange ruling at that date. This is referred to as the 'closing rate'. By using the closing rate, this means that those monetary items are shown in the statement of financial position at an up-to-date rate. In other words, as though they were payable (or recoverable) at the end of the reporting period.

If there are any exchange gains or losses arising on transactions and outstanding monetary items, then these gains or losses should be recognized in profit or loss for the year.

Progress Point 12.1

A company acquired non-depreciable land in Sweden for SKr 70m cash on 1 January 2009. On 31 December 2012 the land was estimated to have a value of SKr 90m and the directors have decided to incorporate this value into the financial statements as at that date.

Exchange rates are:

	SKr : £1
1 January 2009	14
31 December 2012	15

Required
Prepare the relevant journal entries to account for the land in 2009 and 2012.

BASIC

INTERMEDIATE

ADVANCED

Solution

2009

The purchase of the land (a non-monetary item) will be translated at the exchange rate ruling on the date of the transaction i.e. SKr 70m ÷ 14 = £5m

Dr	Land	£5,000,000	
	Cr Bank		£5,000,000
Being acquisition of property.			

2012

The land is to be carried at its revalued amount. The exchange rate to be used is that prevailing at the date the fair value was determined i.e. SKr 90m ÷ 15 = £6m.

The journal entry to record the uplift in value would be:

Dr	Land	£1,000,000	
	Cr Revaluation reserve		£1,000,000
Being revaluation of land.			

Example 2

A UK company buys a non-current asset on credit from a US company on 1 November 2012. The asset cost $3 million and the rate of exchange at the date of purchase was £1 = $1.5. Assume the company's financial year is from 1 January to 31 December.

This transaction will be recorded at the rate ruling when the transaction was undertaken. The non-current asset will be recorded at £2 million ($3 million/1.5) and the corresponding account payable will be recorded at the same amount.

Dr	Non-current asset	£2,000,000	
	Cr Accounts payable		£2,000,000
Being purchase of non-current asset.			

At the end of the reporting period, when the statement of financial position is to be prepared, the accounts payable, a monetary item, will be shown at the rate ruling at the end of the reporting period – that is, the closing rate. The non-current asset, on the other hand, will not be re-translated. It is a non-monetary item and so will remain recorded at the rate of the original transaction – in other words, the historic rate.

If the rate of exchange at the end of the reporting period was £1 = £1.6, then in the statement of financial position, the accounts payable would be £1.875 million (£3 million/1.6). The difference between the original accounts payable of £2 million and the £1.875 million represents an exchange gain of £125,000. At the date of purchase the amount owed was £2 million and at the end of the reporting period the amount owed is £1.875 million – a 'saving' of £125,000. This would be recorded in the accounts as follows:

Dr	Accounts payable	£125,000	
	Cr Exchange gain		£125,000
Being exchange gain.			

Note that the gain is taken to profit or loss, in accordance with IAS 21.

To take this scenario to its logical conclusion, if the account payable was paid on 15 January 2013, when the exchange rate was £1 = $1.55, then at 15 January, the account payable would now be £1.935m ($3 million/1.55) and it is this amount that will require to be paid. The account payable at the end of the reporting period was shown as £1.875 million and at the date of payment is £1.935 million, resulting in an exchange loss of £60,000 (£1.935 – £1.875). The transaction will be recorded as follows:

Dr	Accounts payable	£1,875,000	
Dr	Exchange loss	60,000	
	Cr Bank		£1,935,000

As before, the loss will be included in profit or loss for the year ended 2013 as it arises from exchange movements from 1 to 15 January 2013.

Progress Point 12.2

ABC is a UK company that sells goods in the USA. An invoice is raised on 15 December 2012 for $100,000 in respect of the goods sold. On 10 January 2013, the invoice was paid. The financial year of ABC runs from 1 January to 31 December. The relevant exchange rates are as follows:

15 December 2012	£1 = $1.75
31 December 2012	£1 = $1.80
10 January 2013	£1 = $1.78

Required
Show how any exchange movements will be recorded in the financial statement of ABC.

Solution

(a) To record the initial transaction: at date of transaction the amount owing from the US company will be £57,143 ($100,000/1.75).

Dr	Accounts receivable	£57,143	
	Cr Sales		£57,143

(b) When the accounts are prepared at 31 December, the accounts receivable, a monetary item, will be re-translated at the rate ruling at that date. The amount will be £55,556 ($100,000/1.80). This will mean that there is a loss on exchange of £1,587 (£57,143 – £55,556). It is a loss because less will be received from the debtor than was originally anticipated.

Dr	Loss on exchange	£1,587	
	Cr Accounts receivable		£1,587

BASIC

INTERMEDIATE

ADVANCED

(c) At the date of settlement the actual amount received will be £56,179 ($100,000/1.78). There will now be a gain on exchange of £623 (£56,179 – £55,556). It is a gain this time because more will be received (£56,179) than was anticipated (£55,556).

Dr	Bank	£56,179	
	Cr Gain on exchange		£623
	Cr Accounts receivable		£55,556

Hedging

One of the ways in which companies minimize the risk of exchange rate movements is to take out hedges against individual transactions. For example, a UK company wants to buy a piece of machinery from a US company for $10,000. If the exchange rate at the date the transaction was undertaken was £1 = $2 then the UK company would be required to pay £5,000 ($10,000/2).

However, if the machine was not to be delivered for six months, then by the time the payment is required to be made the exchange rate may have moved to, say, £1 = $1.8. This would mean that the UK company would be liable now to pay £5,556 (rounded) [$10,000/1.8], which is more than would have been paid initially (had the exchange rate remained fixed).

In order to avoid this risk, the company can enter into a deal to buy dollars in advance, and so fix the rate. This is known as buying forward. In other words, if the UK company bought dollars forward at the time it entered into the transaction with the US company, then the exchange rate would have been fixed at the outset at £1 = $2. This technique is known as hedging. When such a transaction takes place, the asset would be recorded in the UK company's books at the exchange rate built in to the forward contract, not at the rate in existence when the asset is delivered.

If there is no hedge, then the individual transactions are translated at the rate ruling when the transaction took place.

> ## Section summary
>
> A foreign currency transaction is one that is denominated or requires settlement in a foreign currency. Such transactions are recorded initially at the exchange rate on the date of the transaction. Unsettled foreign currency transactions at the end of the reporting period may give rise to foreign currency items in an entity's statement of financial position. Monetary foreign currency items are translated using the exchange rate at the end of the reporting period. Non-monetary foreign currency items are translated using the exchange rate on the date of the transaction. If any non-monetary items are carried at fair value then the exchange rate used should be that at the date the fair value was determined.

Section 2: Intermediate Issues

A company may conduct foreign operations through an overseas subsidiary company. This overseas subsidiary will maintain its own accounting records in the currency of the foreign country; this will be in the local currency. In order for the results of the foreign operation to be included in the overall results of the parent company, the financial statements of the foreign operation need to be translated into the currency used by the parent company. How this translation process is done depends on the nature of the relationship between the subsidiary company and the parent company.

This section outlines the different relationships between the subsidiary and the parent company, and illustrates the different methods used for translating and presenting the results of overseas operations.

12.3 Monetary and non-monetary items

In the introductory section there was a brief explanation of how exchange gains or losses arise. This now needs to be formalized and related to what will be described later as monetary items. Monetary items refer to monetary assets and liabilities such as cash, accounts receivable and payable, loans and over-drafts. These items are important because if a company holds them over a period during which the rate of exchange changes, a gain or loss will arise.

To illustrate this, consider the following example. A company has overseas accounts receivable in the USA of $100,000 at a time when the exchange rate is £1 = $2. The company could reasonably expect to receive £50,000. However, if by the time the monies are to be received the exchange rate becomes £1 = $1.8, the amount receivable will now be £55,555. The company will receive £5,555 more than expected. This represents a gain from holding accounts receivable. Of course, the situation would be reversed if the rate became £1 = $2.2. This time the amount to be received would be £45,454, which is lower by £4,545, resulting in a loss.

The same general principle can be applied to all monetary assets.

In terms of monetary liabilities the situation would be similar. If the same company had outstanding accounts payable of $80,000 at a time when the exchange rate is £1 = $2 then the company would reasonably expect to pay £40,000. If, however, by the time payment was made the rate had become £1 = $1.8 then the amount to be paid would become £44,444. This is not good news since the company will have to pay £4,444 more than expected and so will result in a loss from holding a monetary liability. If, however, the rate became £1 = $2.2 then the amount required to settle the liability would become £36,363. This is less than was originally owed and so results in a gain to the company from holding a monetary liability.

The same general principle can be applied to all monetary liabilities.

The distinction between monetary and non-monetary assets and liabilities becomes important later when dealing with what is known as the temporal method of translation. In this method it is necessary to identify the gain or loss from holding net monetary items. This is described in more detail later in this section.

Functional and presentation currencies

At this stage it is necessary to further develop an understanding of functional and presentation currencies. There are two areas in which these currencies are applied:

1. in translating the results of foreign operations to be included in the consolidated financial statements of the entity, and

2. in translating the financial statements of foreign operations into a presentation currency.

In essence there are two different types of translation process. To help understand this it is necessary to distinguish between three different 'types' of currency.

1. Local currency: this is the currency in which the foreign operation measures and records its transactions.

2. Functional currency: this has already been defined above, as the currency of the primary economic environment in which the entity operates. It is the currency that affects the economic wealth of the entity.

3. Presentation currency: this is the currency in which the financial statements are presented.

Example

Home Ltd is a UK company that has an overseas subsidiary, Overseas Ltd, which operates in France. The operations in France are to sell goods manufactured in Singapore. In this scenario, Overseas Ltd would probably maintain its accounts in euros (the local currency) while the functional currency could be the Singapore $ (reflecting the major economic operations in Singapore). However, for presentation of the financial statements of Home Ltd, the presentation currency could be the £ sterling.

As the accounts are maintained in euros, they may have first of all to be translated into the functional currency, the Singapore $, and then translated into £ sterling for presentation purposes.

It is these two translation processes that are referred to in IAS 21.

Choice of functional currency

As the foreign subsidiary operates in another country, it is important that any financial effects on the parent entity of a change in the exchange rate are apparent from the process of translation. Given that the parent entity has an investment in a foreign operation, it is exposed to a change in the exchange rate because it has assets in that other country. Any choice of translation method must deal with the extent to which the parent company is exposed to exchange rate movements. The impact of any exchange rate movements will have an effect depending on the economic relationship between the parent and the subsidiary.

Consider the following examples, which illustrate the case of a UK company that wishes to sell its product in the USA.

Example 1

On 1 January 2013 the UK company acquires premises in the USA to be used as a distribution depot. The building cost $1.2 million. The UK company also put £60,000 into a business bank account in the USA. This £60,000 is equivalent to $90,000 (£60,000 × 1.5). At the end of January 2013 total sales on credit in the USA amounted to $450,000 and these goods had cost £275,000 to manufacture. The rate of exchange during January was £1 = $1.5. The accounts receivable were collected in February 2013 when the rate of exchange was £1 = £1.6.

The UK company has no subsidiary but has acquired an overseas asset, put money into an overseas bank and has sold goods. These can be looked at as a series of transactions (as was shown in the introductory section) and would be recorded by the UK company in £ sterling in its own records as follows.

(a) Acquiring the building:

Dr	Building ($1,200,000/1.5)	£800,000
	Cr Cash	£800,000
Being purchase of buildings.		

(b) Paying cash into the bank account:

Dr	Bank (US bank)	£60,000
	Cr Cash	£60,000
Being cash paid into bank account.		

(c) Selling goods on credit:

Dr	Accounts receivable ($450,000/1.5)	£300,000
	Cr Sales	£300,000
Being goods sold on credit.		

(d) Cost of goods sold:

Dr	Cost of sales	£275,000
	Cr Inventory	£275,000
Being cost of sales.		

Assume that the cash is received from the customers in February 2013 and that the exchange rate has moved to £1 = $1.6. The amount received would be $450,000/1.6 = £281,250. The amount originally receivable was £300,000 so there is a loss on exchange of £18,750 (£300,000 – £281,250). It is a loss on exchange because less was actually received than was expected (see introductory section).

This loss on exchange would be taken to profit or loss. The transactions would be recorded as follows:

(e)

Dr	Loss on exchange	£18,750	
Dr	Cash	£281,250	
	Cr Accounts receivable		£300,000
Being exchange loss.			

In addition to this there would be an exchange difference arising from the fact that the US company has $90,000 in the bank account. The bank account is a monetary asset and, as such, any movement in the exchange rate will affect the 'value' of such an asset.

The $90,000 in the bank account was put in when the rate was £1 = £1.5, so this was equivalent to £60,000. However, when the rate moved to £1 = $1.6, the equivalent amount was now £56,250 ($90,000/1.6). The monetary asset has therefore lost 'value' to the extent of £4,850 (£60,000 – £56,250). This loss in 'value' has arisen because of an exchange rate movement and will be recorded as a loss on exchange. The bank account will have to be reduced and a loss on exchange recorded.

(f)

Dr	Loss on exchange	£4,750	
	Cr Bank		£4,750
Being loss from holding monetary asset.			

Example 2

Instead of dealing with customers in the USA, the UK company formed an overseas subsidiary company, Overseas Ltd, to deal with the US operations. This situation is similar to the one above in that all the goods are transferred from the UK parent company to the US subsidiary at cost. The goods are sold in the USA by the subsidiary and the profits are sent back to the UK parent.

The underlying transactions are the same as for Example 1. The fact that a subsidiary has been formed does not change the underlying economic effects of the transactions. The translation of the US subsidiary must show the position as if the parent had undertaken the transactions itself. This is the purpose behind the choice of the functional currency approach.

The basic underlying transactions would be as follows.

(a) On receipt of inventory at cost:

Dr	Inventory	$412,500	
	Cr Accounts payable		$412,500

(b) On sale of inventory on credit:

Dr	Accounts receivable	$450,000	
	Cr Sales		$450,000

(c) Cost of goods sold:

Dr	Cost of sales	$412,500	
	Cr Inventory		$412,500

The opening statement of financial position of the US subsidiary would be as follows:

Building	$1,200,000
Inventory (transferred at cost) (£275,000 × 1.5)	412,500
Accounts payable (amount owing for inventory)	(412,500)
Bank account	90,000
	$1,290,000
Capital	$1,290,000

Assume:

(i)   all the inventory is sold on credit at the end of January 2013

(ii) the financial statements of the subsidiary have to be prepared at the end of February 2013 when the exchange rate is £1 = $1.6.

At the end of February the financial statements of the US company would be as follows:

Statement of comprehensive income (local currency)

Sales	$450,000
Cost of sales	412,500
Profit	37,500

Statement of financial position (local currency)

Building	$1,200,000
Accounts receivable	450,000
Bank	90,000
Accounts payable	(412,500)
Net assets	$1,327,500
Capital	$1,290,000
Profit for period	37,500
	$1,327,000

Although the financial statements are shown in the *local currency*, the *functional currency* is the £ sterling since this is the currency of the primary economic environment affecting the overseas subsidiary. The inventories are manufactured in the UK, the parent is financing the subsidiary and the cash flows that influence the parent to continue to trade in the US come from the UK.

In this scenario, the subsidiary is simply an extension of the parent company and is used for transforming foreign currency transactions into cash flows. In this situation, the financial statements of the subsidiary must now be translated into the functional currency, the £ sterling, and must show:

- the assets of the subsidiary at cost to the parent – in other words, what the parent would have paid in its own currency to acquire the asset
- the revenues and expenses of the subsidiary at what it would have cost the parent at the date the transactions occurred
- any gain or loss from holding monetary items (monetary assets and monetary liabilities); any gains or losses on holding monetary items should be shown in profit or loss since they affect the parent directly.

The financial statements of the subsidiary would be translated into the functional currency as follows:

Statement of comprehensive income

		Rate	
Sales	$450,000	1.5	£300,000
Cost of sales	412,500	1.5	275,000
Profit	37,500		25,000
Loss on holding net monetary assets (see Note 1)			5,312
			£19,688

Statement of financial position

Building	$1,200,000	1.5	£800,000
Accounts receivable	450,000	1.6	281,250
Bank	90,000	1.6	56,250
Accounts payable	(412,500)	1.6	(257,812)
	$1,327,500		£879,688
Capital	$1,290,000	1.5	860,000
Profit for period	37,500		19,688
	$1,327,500		£879,688

Note 1: net monetary items

As explained above, monetary items comprise items such as cash, accounts payable and, accounts receivable. In the above scenario the monetary items are as follows:

Cash	$90,000	monetary asset
Accounts receivable	$450,000	monetary asset
Accounts payable	$412,500	monetary liability

So overall the company has net monetary assets of $127,500 ($90,000 + $450,000 – $412,000). These net monetary assets are in existence at the end of January when the exchange rate is £1 = $1.5. When the financial statements are prepared at the end of February, the exchange rate is now £1 = $1.6.

So, net monetary assets:

- At end of January   £85,000 ($127,500/1.5)
- At balance sheet date   £79,688 ($127,500/1.6)

The 'value' of these assets has fallen by £5,312, which represents the loss from holding net monetary items and is shown in arriving at profit or loss in the statement of comprehensive income.

Example 3

Assume in this scenario that the UK company sets up a subsidiary company in the USA with $1,290,000 as in Example 2, the money being used to buy a building and set up a bank account. However, this time, the US subsidiary is established to manufacture products in the USA for sale in the USA. Also, US workers are used in the manufacturing process and any profits made by the company are used to expand the business in the USA. The parent company receives remittances from the subsidiary in the form of dividends.

This is a completely different scenario from that presented in Example 2. The subsidiary is not just an extension of the parent. The cash flows for the subsidiary are dependent this time on the economic environment of the USA not the UK. If there is a change in exchange rate between the £ and the $, then there will not be an immediate effect on the operations of the US subsidiary. In this case the functional currency will be the US$ not the UK£. However, given that the US company is a subsidiary of the UK company, the accounts of the US subsidiary will have to be translated into the *presentation* currency.

In analysing the success or otherwise of the overseas subsidiary, the interrelationships between sales, profits, assets and equity should be the same whether expressed in $s or £s. The translation process should adjust all such items by the same exchange rate to retain these interrelationships. In this case the closing rate would be used.

Where the functional currency of a subsidiary is different to the presentation currency of the group, then the financial statements should be translated into the presentation currency as follows:

- statement of financial position – items should be translated at the rate of exchange at the end of the reporting period, the closing rate
- statement of comprehensive income – items should ideally be translated at the rate of exchange ruling at the date of each transaction, but for practical purposes an average rate is usually used
- any exchange differences arising are recognized in other comprehensive income
- the cumulative amount of the exchange differences is presented in a separate component of equity until disposal of the foreign operation. In this case it is being referred to as 'translation reserve'.

Since translation differences do not have much effect on the present and future cash flows from foreign operations, they are not recognized in profit or loss.
Using the information from Example 2:

Statement of comprehensive income

		Rate	
Sales	$450,000	1.5	£300,000
Cost of sales	412,500	1.5	275,000
Profit	37,500		25,000
Other comprehensive income			
Exchange loss			(55,312)
Total comprehensive income	$37,500		£(30,312)

Statement of financial position

		Rate	
Building	$1,200,000	1.6	£750,000
Accounts receivable	450,000	1.6	281,250

Bank	90,000	1.6	56,250
Accounts payable	(412,500)	1.6	(257,812)
	$1,327,500		£829,688
Capital	$1,290,000	1.5	860,000
Retained earnings	37,500		25,000
Translation reserve	0		(55,312)
	$1,327,500		£829,688

How can the exchange difference (the amount in other comprehensive income) be explained? It can be verified as follows.

The statements of financial position of both years can be linked as follows;

$$\text{Opening net assets} + \text{Profit} = \text{Closing net assets}$$
$$\$1,290,000 + \$37,500 = \$1,327,500$$

The opening net assets 'come in' when the rate is £1 = £1.5, and 'go out' as part of closing net assets when the rate is £1 = £1.6. The same is true of the profit. Profit is calculated when the transactions take place. At this time the rate is £1 = $1.5. However, the profit of $37,500 is part of the closing net asset figure of $1,327,500 and the closing net assets have been translated at the rate of £1 = $1.6. So the exchange difference may be explained as follows.

Explanation of exchange difference

Opening net assets			
At opening rate	$1,290,000/1.5	=	£860,000
At closing rate	$1,290,000/1.6	=	£806,250
Exchange loss (assets have decreased)			£53,750

Profit for the year			
At rate	£37,500/1.5	=	£25,000
At closing rate	£37,500/1.6	=	£23,437
Exchange loss (profit has gone down)			£1,562
Total loss to other comprehensive income		=	£55,312

Examples 2 and 3 give rise to two different methods of translation. In Example 2 the overseas subsidiary was seen as an extension of the parent company and as such the functional currency was that of the parent company. In this scenario the accounts of the subsidiary were translated into that currency. If an overseas subsidiary is an 'extension' of the parent company then the currency of the parent company is the functional currency. The method illustrated in Example 2 is referred to as the temporal method of foreign exchange translation.

In Example 3 the overseas subsidiary is independent of the parent. The functional currency will most likely be the 'local' currency: the US$. Once in the functional currency, the accounts of the subsidiary have to then be translated from functional currency to presentation currency. The method illustrated in Example 3 is referred to as the closing rate method, or the net investment method of foreign exchange translation.

The methods of foreign currency translation illustrated above are dealt with formally in IAS 21 *The Effects of Changes in Foreign Exchange Rates*.

BASIC

INTERMEDIATE

ADVANCED

Progress Point 12.3

A plc acquired 100% of an American subsidiary X Inc on 31 December 2011. The summarized statements of financial position of X Inc are as follows:

	2012	2011
	$	$
Net assets	14,000	9,000
Share capital	4,000	4,000
Retained earnings	10,000	5,000
	14,000	9,000

Exchange rates were as follows:

31 December 2011	£1 = $2.00
Average for year to 31 December 2012	£1 = $1.94
31 December 2012	£1 = $1.90

Required

(i) Assuming the net investment method is used to translate the financial statements, what translation differences arise in the year to 31 December 2012?

(ii) Identify and explain the reasons for the translation difference.

Solution

(i) Statement of financial position

	$	Rate	£
Net assets	14,000	1.90	7,368
Share capital	4,000	2.00	2,000
Retained earnings b/f	5,000	2.00	2,500
Profit for the year	5,000	1.94	2,577
Translation difference			291
	14,000		7,368

(ii) Analysis of translation difference

Opening net assets	$9,000 ÷ 2.00 =	4,500
	$9,000 ÷ 1.90 =	4,737
	Gain on exchange	237

Profit for the year	$5,000 ÷ 1.94 =	2,577
	$5,000 ÷ 1.90 =	2,631
	Gain on exchange	54
	Total gain on exchange	291

The translation difference arises because of the increase in net assets (the profit) being translated at the rate of $1.90 : £1 for the purposes of the net asset calculation in the statement of financial position, and at the average rate of £1.94 in the statement of comprehensive income.

12.4 IAS 21 *The Effects of Changes in Foreign Exchange Rates*

Objective and scope

An entity may enter into foreign currency transactions in two principal ways:

- it may enter directly into transactions denominated in a foreign currency; and
- it may have foreign operations.

In addition, an entity may present its financial statements in a foreign currency.

IAS 21 prescribes how to account for transactions in a foreign currency and how to translate foreign operations for inclusion in the financial statements of an entity, whether by consolidation or the equity method. The standard also addresses how to translate financial statements into a presentation currency.

Definitions

A *foreign operation* is an entity that is a subsidiary, associate, joint venture or branch of a reporting entity, the activities of which are based or conducted in a country or currency other than those of the reporting entity.

It should be noted from this definition that it is possible for a branch of a reporting entity to have a different functional currency from that of the entity itself.

The *functional currency* of an entity is the currency of the primary economic environment in which the entity operates.

Monetary items are units of currency held and assets and liabilities to be received or paid in a fixed or determinable number of units of currency.

Net investment in a foreign operation is the amount of the reporting entity's interest in the net assets of that operation.

Presentation currency is the currency in which the financial statements are presented.

Functional currency

As stated above, an entity's functional currency is the currency of the primary economic environment in which the entity operates. In preparing financial statements, each entity is required to determine its functional currency in accordance with IAS 21 paragraphs 9–14 (covered in the advanced aspects section of this chapter). This requirement applies whether the entity is a stand-alone entity, an entity with foreign operations (such as a parent) or a foreign operation (such as a subsidiary or branch).

It is important to note that an entity's functional currency is a matter of fact and not one of choice. In practice, judgement is required in assessing which currency is the functional currency.

Reporting foreign currency transactions in the functional currency: the temporal method

The process of translating one currency into another is detailed in paragraphs 21 and 23 of IAS 21. Paragraph 21 deals with items reflected in the statement of comprehensive income that concern transactions occurring in the current period. IAS 21 does not use the term 'temporal method' to describe these translation procedures. According to the standard, accounting for non-autonomous foreign operations is considered to be equivalent to the accounting for foreign currency transactions. According to the standard, a foreign currency transaction shall be recorded on initial recognition in the functional currency. This is done by applying the spot rate of exchange between the functional currency and the foreign currency at the date of the transaction.

Strictly speaking, then, in translating revenues and expenses in the statement of comprehensive income each item of revenue and expense should be translated at the spot rate of exchange between the functional currency and the foreign currency on the date that the transaction occurred. In the real world, given the very large number of transactions that a company would have, IAS 21 provides for an averaging system to be used. A rate that approximates the actual rate at the date of the transaction can be used. An average rate for the month might be used for all transactions occurring within this period.

Basic principles of translation

Statement of financial position items

- Assets and liabilities: assets and liabilities need to be first of all classified as either monetary or non-monetary. Monetary assets and monetary liabilities are translated at the rate existing at the end of the reporting period, the closing rate. Non-monetary assets are recorded at the rate ruling when the asset was acquired, the historic rate. If a non-monetary asset has been revalued then the rate ruling at the date of revaluation would be used. Non-monetary liabilities are translated at the date of valuation.
- Share capital: if this is capital created by an investment or that exists at the date of acquisition then this is translated at the rate ruling when the investment was made (or at date of acquisition).
- Retained earnings and other reserves: if these reserves are on hand at the date of acquisition, then they are translated at the rate existing at acquisition. If the reserves result from internal transfers then the rate to be used is the one that existed at the date the amounts transferred were originally recognized in equity.

Statement of comprehensive income items

- Income and expenses: in general these are translated at the rates in existence when the transactions were entered into. For items that relate to non-monetary items, such as depreciation, the rates to be used are those used to translate the related non-monetary item.
- Dividends paid: translated at the rate ruling at the date of payment.
- Dividends declared: translated at the rate ruling at the date the dividend was declared.
- Transfers to and from reserves: if internal transfers are made, then the rates applicable are those existing when the amounts transferred were originally recognized in equity.

Given that non-monetary items are translated at the historic rate, no exchange difference will arise on these items. Any exchange difference that does arise will be from holding monetary items. In addition, items such as sales, purchases and expenses give rise to monetary items such as cash, and accounts receivable and payable. Exchange differences can be explained therefore by looking at movements in the monetary items over the period.

In accordance with IAS 21, any exchange differences arising are to be recognized in profit or loss in the period in which they arise.

Example

H plc has a wholly owned overseas subsidiary S Ltd, which it acquired on 1 January 2012. The summary financial statements of S as at 1 January 2012 and at 31 December 2012 are as follows:

	Statement of financial position as at			
	1 Jan 2012		31 Dec 2012	
	AUS$	AUS$	AUS$	AUS$
Tangible non-current assets		450		330
Current assets:				
Inventory	240		360	
Accounts receivable	120		240	
	360		600	
Accounts payable	210		240	
		150		360
		600		690
Share capital		600		600
Retained profit		0		90
		600		690

Statement of comprehensive income
for the year ending 31 December 2012

	AUS$	AUS$
Sales revenue		1,500
Cost of sales		
Opening inventory	240	
Purchases	1,200	
	1,440	
Closing inventory	360	1,080
Gross profit		420
Depreciation	120	
Taxation	150	
		270
Total comprehensive income		150

Statement of changes in equity
for the year to 31 December 2012

	Share capital AUS$	Retained earnings AUS$	Total equity AUS$
Balance at 1 January 2012	600	0	600
Total comprehensive income		150	150
Dividends		(60)	(60)
Balance at 31 December 2012	600	90	690

Assuming that the functional currency of S Ltd is that of the UK, translate the financial statements of S Ltd into the functional currency using the temporal method. Identify and explain any exchange difference arising. The movements in the exchange rate are as follows:

1 January 2012	£1 = AUS$3
Average rate for opening inventory	£1 = AUS$3
Average for the year	£1 = AUS$2.5
Average rate for closing inventory	£1 = AUS$2
31 December 2012	£1 = AUS$2

Explanation

The temporal method described above uses a mixture of rates:

- non-monetary items are translated at historic rate
- monetary items are translated at closing rate
- income and expenses shown in the statement of comprehensive income are translated at the date the transaction occurred.

Depreciation will be translated at the rate that applied when the asset to which the depreciation related was acquired. In this case it is the opening rate.

Statement of comprehensive income
for the year ending 31 December 2012

	AUS$	AUS$	Rate	£	£
Sales revenue		1,500	2.5		600
Cost of sales					
Opening inventory	240		3	80	
Purchases	1,200		2.5	480	
	1,440			560	
Closing inventory	360	1,080	2	180	380
Gross profit		420			220
Depreciation	120		3	40	
Taxation	150		2	75	
		270			115
Profit for the year		150			105*

At this stage the statement of comprehensive income is incomplete. The exchange difference is missing. The exchange difference can be identified from the translated statement of financial position.

Statement of financial position
as at 31 December 2012

	AUS$	AUS$	Rate	£	£
Tangible non-current assets		330	3		110
Current assets:					
Inventory	360		2	180	
Accounts receivable	240		2	120	
	600			300	
Accounts payable	(240)		2	(120)	
		360			180
		690			290
Share capital		600	3		200
Retained profit		90			90*
		690			290

* At this stage, in order to make the statement of financial position balance, the retained profit needs to be £90.

However, the profit shown in the statement of comprehensive income is £105. The dividend paid for the year of AUS$60 will be translated at the rate of £1 = AUS$2 i.e. £30 will be deducted from this amount in the statement of changes in equity but this will then leave the profit shown at £75 (£105 – £30 = £75). The profit in the statement of changes in equity is lower than it ought to be. The difference, £15, is the amount that needs to be added to the profit of £75 to bring it up to £90. The £15 is the gain on exchange that needs to be shown in profit or loss in the statement of comprehensive income.

The complete statement of comprehensive income and the movement in retained earnings over the year can now be shown as follows:

Statement of comprehensive income
for the year ending 31 December 2012

	AUS$	AUS$	Rate	£	£
Sales revenue		1,500	2.5		600
Cost of sales					
Opening inventory	240		3	80	
Purchases	1,200		2.5	480	
	1,440			560	
Closing inventory	360	1,080	2	180	380
Gross profit		420			220
Depreciation	120		3	40	
Exchange gain				(15)	
Taxation	150	270	2	75	100
Profit for the year		150			120

Statement of changes in equity
for the year ended 31 December 2012

	Share capital £	Retained earnings £	Total equity £
Balance at 1 January 2012	200	0	200
Total comprehensive income	–	120	120
Dividends	–	(30)	(30)
Balance at 31 December 2012	200	90	290

This is one way of determining the exchange difference. However, the exchange difference can also be calculated separately. As was described above, any exchange difference can arise only from the monetary items, since the non-monetary items are translated at the historic rate (i.e. the rate in existence when these items were acquired), so no exchange difference arises. Monetary items, on the other hand, are translated at the closing rate.

Calculation of the exchange difference
From the opening statement of financial position the opening net monetary position can be established:

Accounts receivable	120
Accounts payable	210
Net monetary liabilities	(90)

During the year sales were made and inventory was purchased. This would have an impact on the opening monetary position. Sales would have a positive impact (increase accounts receivable) and purchases would have a negative impact (increase accounts payable) on the monetary position.

Also, when payments are made for tax and dividends, this too would have a negative impact since it would reduce cash (a monetary asset). A statement can be prepared as follows:

Statement of net monetary position:	AUS$	AUS$
Opening net monetary liabilities		(90)
Sales during year	1,500	
Purchases during year	(1,200)	300
		210
Payments at year end		
Tax	150	
Dividends	60	210
		0
Closing monetary position		
Accounts receivable		240
Accounts payable		240
		0

Keep in mind that the assumption made for sales and purchases is that since they occurred during the year, an *average* rate has been used in this example to translate these items. This impact can be seen in Figure 12.1.

From Figure 12.1, it can be seen that the company holds net monetary liabilities until transactions are undertaken. Remember it is assumed that these transactions are averaged over the year, so the mid-year point is taken.

Once sales and purchases have been made, the net monetary position changes from (90) to 210 and remains at that point until the final payments are made for tax and dividends. Using this figure, the exchange difference can be calculated as follows:

Opening net monetary liabilities	
(90/3)	£30
(90/2.5)	£36
Exchange loss	(£6)

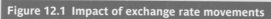

Figure 12.1 Impact of exchange rate movements

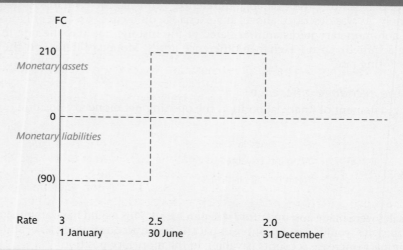

This is a loss on exchange since when the rate moves from 3 to 2.5, liabilities increase from £30 to £36, so the company has to pay more than anticipated.

When the sales and purchases are made, the net monetary liabilities changes to net monetary assets.

Net monetary assets	
(210/2.5)	£84
(210/2.0)	£105
Exchange gain	£21

This is an exchange gain since more will be received than was expected.

Overall there is an exchange gain of £15 (£21 – £6) from holding net monetary items. It is this gain of £15 that appears in profit or loss.

Translation into the presentation currency: the net investment (closing rate) method

Once the financial statements of a subsidiary are prepared in the relevant functional currency these statements have now to be translated into the presentation currency. The principles of translation are given in IAS 21, paragraph 39.

A presentation currency is defined as the currency in which the financial statements are presented. Unlike an entity's functional currency (which is a matter of fact) the presentation currency can be any currency of choice. This choice is available both in the entity's 'main' financial statements and, if prepared, any separate financial statements.

An entity normally presents its financial statements in the same currency as its functional currency; however, an entity may choose to present its financial statements in a different currency. Presenting the financial statements in a currency other than the functional currency does not change the way in which the underlying items is measured. It merely expresses the underlying amounts, which are measured in the functional currency, in a different currency.

Basic principles of translation
Statement of financial position items

- Assets and liabilities: all assets and liabilities (whether monetary or non-monetary) are translated at the exchange rate ruling at the end of the reporting period; this is the closing rate.
- Share capital: if this capital is created by an investment, or exists at the date of acquisition this is translated at the rate that existed at the date of acquisition; this is the historic rate.
- Retained earnings and other reserves: if these reserves are on hand at acquisition date then they are translated at the rate current at this acquisition date. If reserves are post-acquisition and created by an internal transfer within equity, they are then translated at the rate existing at the date the reserve from which the transfer was made was originally recognized in the accounts. If the reserves are post-acquisition, and not created as a result of an internal transfer – for example, an asset revaluation surplus – then the rate to be used is that which is in existence when the reserve is created.

Statement of comprehensive income items

- Income and expenses: these should be translated at the rates current at the date at which the transactions took place. For such items as sales and purchases of inventory, which will occur on a regular basis throughout the period, average rates may be used. In relation to items such as depreciation, which are in essence allocations for a period, an average exchange rate may be used.
- Dividends paid: these are translated at the rates current when the dividends are paid.
- Dividends declared: these are translated at the rate ruling when the dividend is declared.
- Transfers to and from reserves: if these transfers are internal then the rate used is the one ruling when the amounts transferred were originally recognized in equity.

Exchange differences

- all resulting exchange differences should be recognized in other comprehensive income.

Using the previous example, the financial statements can now be translated into the presentation currency. The example is repeated here for convenience.

Example

H plc has a wholly owned overseas subsidiary S Ltd, which it acquired on 1 January 2012. The summary financial statements of S as at 1 January 2012 and at 31 December 2012 are as follows. These statements are presented in the functional currency.

Statement of financial position as at				
	1 Jan 2012		31 Dec 2012	
	AUS$	AUS$	AUS$	AUS$
Tangible non-current assets		450		330
Current assets:				
Inventory	240		360	
Accounts receivable	120		240	
	360		600	
Accounts payable	210		240	
		150		360
		600		690
Share capital		600		600
Retained profit		0		90
		600		690

Statement of comprehensive income for the year ending 31 December 2012		
	AUS$	AUS$
Sales revenue		1,500
Cost of sales		
Opening inventory	240	
Purchases	1,200	
	1,440	
Closing inventory	360	1,080
Gross profit		420
Depreciation	120	
Taxation	150	
Profit for the year		270
		150

Statement of changes in equity
for the year to 31 December 2012

	Share capital AUS$	Retained earnings AUS$	Total equity AUS$
Balance at 1 January 2012	600	0	600
Total comprehensive income	–	150	150
Dividends	–	(60)	(60)
Balance at 31 December 2012	600	90	690

Assuming that the *presentation* currency of S Ltd is that of the UK, translate the financial statement of S Ltd into the *presentation* currency using the *closing rate method*. Identify and explain any exchange difference arising.

The movements in the exchange rate are as follows:

1 January 2012	£1 = AUS$3
Average rate for opening inventory	£1 = AUS$3
Average for the year	£1 = AUS$2.5
Average rate for closing inventory	£1 = AUS$2
31 December 2012	£1 = AUS$2

This time the income and expenses within the statement of comprehensive income will be translated using rates in existence when the transactions were undertaken. In general this is usually the average rate for the period. In this example the average rate is used except for opening and closing inventory, and taxation and dividends, since it is known when those items were paid/acquired.

Statement of comprehensive income
for the year ending 31 December 2012

	AUS$	AUS$	Rate	£	£
Sales revenue		1,500	2.5		600
Cost of sales					
Opening inventory	240		3.0	80	
Purchases	1,200		2.5	480	
	1,440			560	
Closing inventory	360	1,080	2.0	180	380
Gross profit		420			220
Depreciation	120		2.5	48	
Taxation	150		2.0	75	
		270			123
		150			97

The dividend paid of AUS$60 would be shown in the statement of changes in equity and would be translated as follows resulting in a closing balance on retained earnings of £67. Note that the translated total comprehensive income figure of £97 is arrived at using three different exchange rates. It is not translated using only the average rate for the year.

Provisional statement of changes in equity (extract) for the year to 31 December 2012			
	Retained earnings AUS$	Rate	£
Balance at 1 January 2012	0		0
Profit for the year	150		97
Dividends	(60)	2.0	(30)
Balance at 31 December 2012	90		67

The statement of financial position will be translated using the closing rate, except for the share capital. Retained profit is the profit for the year, so in this instance the profit shown in the statement of changes in equity will be carried forward into the statement of financial position.

Statement of financial position					
	AUS$	AUS$	Rate	£	£
Tangible non-current assets		330	2		165
Current assets:					
Inventory	360		2	180	
Accounts receivable	240		2	120	
	600			300	
Accounts payable	(240)		2	(120)	
		360			180
		690			345
Share capital		600	3		200
Retained profit		90			67
		690			267
Difference (translation reserve)					78
					345

The translated statement of financial position does not initially balance; the difference of £78 (£345 – £267) is the amount of the exchange difference. In this case it is an exchange gain of £78 and should be recognized in other comprehensive income and presented in a separate component of equity under the heading translation reserve.

The statement of comprehensive income in £ sterling would be:

Statement of comprehensive income for the year to 31 December 2012		
	£	£
Sales revenue		600
Cost of sales		
Opening inventory	80	
Purchases	480	
	560	
Closing inventory	180	
		380
Gross profit		220

Depreciation	48
Taxation	75
	123
Profit for the year	97
Other comprehensive income	
Exchange gain	78
Total comprehensive income	175

And the final statement of changes in equity would show:

	Share capital £	Retained earnings £	Translation reserve £	Total equity £
Balance at 1 January 2012	200	0	0	200
Total comprehensive income	–	97	78	175
Dividends	–	(30)	–	(30)
Balance at 31 December 2012	200	67	78	345

Note that the exchange gain is presented in a separate component of equity – in this case translation reserve.

This is one way of determining the exchange difference, by simply using the balancing figure in the statement of financial position. However, the exchange difference can also be calculated separately. This example is slightly more complicated than that shown in the example on page 680, but the basic principle explained there still applies. Remember, the opening and closing statements of financial position are linked by the profit for the year.

$$\text{Opening net assets} + \text{Profit} = \text{Closing net assets}$$
$$\text{AUS\$600} + \text{AUS\$90} = \text{AUS\$690}$$

Note that the figure for closing net assets contains both the opening net assets plus the profit. Under the closing rate method, the opening net assets would 'come in' at a rate of 3 and 'go out' at a rate of 2.

An exchange difference will arise as follows:

Opening net assets	
$600/3 (opening rate)	£200
$600/2 (closing rate)	£300
Gain on exchange	£100

This is an exchange gain because assets have increased in 'value', i.e. are shown at a higher amount.

The profit for the year is slightly more complicated this time, because of the different rates used to translate the opening and closing inventory, and also the payment of the dividend and taxation at the year end. All other items of revenue and expenditure are taken at the average rate for the year. In general terms an increase in revenue will result in an exchange gain, while an increase in a cost will result in an exchange loss.

The exchange difference relating to the profit for the year can be deconstructed as follows.

Sales revenue	
£1,500/2.5	£600
£1,500/2	£750
Exchange gain	£150

Opening inventory	
$240/3	£80
$240/2	£120
Exchange loss	£40

Purchases	
$1,200/2.5	£480
$1,200/2	£600
Exchange loss	£120

Closing inventory

No exchange difference arises as it is translated at the closing rate in both the statement of comprehensive income and in the closing statement of financial position.

Depreciation	
$120/2.5	£48
$120/2	£60
Exchange loss	£12

Taxation and dividends

Again no exchange difference arises as they are translated at the closing rate both in the statement of comprehensive income and in the closing statement of financial position.

Overall exchange difference in the profit	
Exchange gain on sales	£150
Exchange loss on opening inventory	(£40)
Exchange loss on purchases	(£120)
Exchange loss on depreciation	(£12)
Net exchange loss in profit	(£22)

Total exchange gain	
Opening net assets	£100
Profit	(£22)
Exchange gain	£78

Progress Point 12.4

(a) Explain what is meant by an entity's functional currency.

(b) If an entity presents its financial statements in a currency other than its functional currency, explain how the entity's financial statements are translated into the chosen presentation currency.

Solution

(a) An entity's functional currency is the currency of the primary economic environment in which the entity operates.

(b) The financial statements are translated into the presentation currency as follows:

- assets and liabilities are translated at the closing rate at the end of the period
- income and expenses are translated at the exchange rates which applied on the dates of the transactions concerned.
- resulting exchange differences are recognized in other comprehensive income

Progress Point 12.5

Alba plc has a subsidiary, NS Ltd, a company incorporated in the USA. The following information relates to the subsidiary for 2013.

Statement of financial position as at 31 December 2012 and 2013		
	2012	2013
	$000	$000
Tangible non-current assets	32,200	32,000
Monetary assets	5,300	7,600
Monetary liabilities	(6,500)	(5,000)
	31,000	34,600
Share capital	28,000	28,000
Retained profit	3,000	6,600
	31,000	34,600

Statement of comprehensive income for period ended 31 December 2013	
	$000
Sales revenue	10,080
Cost of sales	(3,960)
Gross profit	6,120

BASIC

INTERMEDIATE

ADVANCED

Depreciation	(200)
Other operating expenses	(240)
Operating profit	5,680
Taxation	(2,080)
Profit for the year	3,600

Sterling exchange rates were:

31 December 2012	£1 = $2.00
Average rate for 2013	£1 = $1.8
31 December 2013	£1 = $1.6

Required

(a) Translate the statement of financial position and statement of comprehensive income into:

   (i) the functional currency of Alba plc using the temporal method

   (ii) the presentation currency of Alba plc using the net investment method.

(b) For each of (i) and (ii) above, calculate the exchange difference, and explain how the exchange difference is to be treated in the financial statements.

(c) Prepare a statement showing how the exchange difference is calculated.

Solution

(i) Translation into functional currency (temporal method)

   (a)

Statement of financial position			
	$000	Rate	£000
Tangible non-current assets	32,000	2.0	16,000
Monetary assets	7,600	1.6	4,750
Monetary liabilities	(5,000)	1.6	(3,125)
	34,600		17,625
Share capital	28,000	2.0	14,000
Retained profit			
2012	3,000	2.0	1,500
2013	3,600	Balancing figure	2,125
	34,600		17,625

Statement of comprehensive income			
	$000		£000
Sales revenue	10,080	1.8	5,600
Cost of sales	(3,960)	1.8	2,200
Gross profit	6,120		3,400

Depreciation	(200)	2.0	(100)
Other operating expenses	(240)	1.8	(133)
Operating profit	5,680		3,167
Taxation	(2,080)	1.6	1,300
	3,600	1.8	1,867
Exchange gain			258
Profit for the year	3,600		2,125

(b) The exchange gain is £258 and can be determined from the statement of financial position figure for retained profit for the year. The figure required to 'balance' the statement of financial position is £2,125, while the translated figure in the statement of comprehensive income is £1,867. This results in a difference of £258, which is the amount of the exchange gain. In the temporal method this exchange gain is recognized as income when calculating profit or loss for the period.

(c) As has been seen before, any exchange difference under this method results in an exchange difference from holding monetary items. Since other assets and liabilities are translated at the historic rate, then there is no exchange difference arising from these items.

Statement of net monetary position

Opening monetary position:		
Monetary assets		$5,300
Monetary liabilities		$6,500
Net monetary liabilities	(1)	($1,200)
Sales		$10,080
Cost of sales		($3,960)
Expenses		($240)
	(2)	$5,880
Net monetary assets	(1)–(2)	$4,680
Taxation		(2,080)
Closing net monetary assets		$2,600

This can be verified from the closing statement of financial position:

Net monetary assets	$7,600
Net monetary liabilities	$5,000
	$2,600

Determination of gain or loss from holding net monetary items.

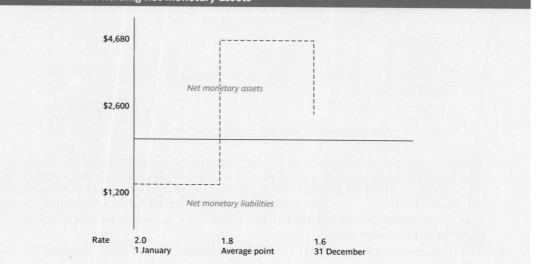

Figure 12.2 Gain from holding net monetary assets

The gain from holding net monetary assets can be shown diagrammatically, as in Figure 12.2

Opening net monetary liabilities	
$1,200/2	£600
$1,200/1.8	£667
Loss from holding NML	(£67)
Monetary assets	
$4,680/1.8	£2,600
$4,680/1.6	£2,925
Gain from holding NMA	£325
Total gain (£325 – £67)	£258

This gain is shown in the statement of comprehensive income as part of profit for the year.

(ii) Translation into presentation currency (net investment method)

(a)

Statement of financial position			
	$000	Rate	£000
Tangible non-current assets	32,000	1.6	20,000
Current assets	7,600	1.6	4,750
Current liabilities	(5,000)	1.6	(3,125)
	34,600		21,625
Share capital	28,000	2.0	14,000
Retained profit			
2012	3,000	2.0	1,500
2013	3,600	1.8	2,000
	34,600		17,500
Translation reserve (balancing figure)			4,125
			21,625

Statement of comprehensive income			
Sales revenue	10,080	1.8	5,600
Cost of sales	(3,960)	1.8	2,200
Gross profit	6,120		3,400
Depreciation	(200)	1.8	(111)
Other operating expenses	(240)	1.8	(133)
Operating profit	5,680		3,156
Taxation	(2,080)	1.8	(1,156)
Profit for the year	3,600	1.8	2,000
Other comprehensive income			
Exchange gain	–		4,125
Total comprehensive income	3,600		6,125

(b)

Opening net assets	+	Profit	=	Closing net assets
$31,000	+	$3,600	=	$34,600
This would be translated				
$31,000/2.0	+	$3,600/1.8	=	$34,600/1.6
£15,500	+	£2,000	=	£21,625

The closing net assets should be £17,500 (i.e. £15,500 + £2,000) and not £21,625. Over the period the net assets have increased in 'value' by £4,125 (£21,625 – £17,500). The difference represents a gain on exchange, and will be recognized in other comprehensive income.

(c)

Explanation of exchange difference			
Opening net assets			
At opening rate	$31,000/2	=	£15,500
At closing rate	$31,000/1.6	=	£19,375
Exchange gain			£3,875
Profit for year			
At average rate	$3,600/1.8	=	£2,000
At closing rate	$3,600/1.6	=	£2,250
Exchange gain			£250
Total gain to other comprehensive income			£4,125	(£3,875 + 250)

Disclosure

The following should be disclosed:

(a) the amount of exchange differences recognized in profit or loss except for those arising on financial instruments measured at fair value through profit or loss in accordance with IFRS 9; and

(b) net exchange differences recognized in other comprehensive income and accumulated in a separate component of equity, and a reconciliation of the amount of such exchange differences at the beginning and end of the period.

IAS 21 is silent regarding where in profit or loss foreign currency exchange gains and losses should be presented. The presentation should follow the nature of the transactions to which the foreign currency gains and losses are linked e.g. recognizing foreign currency gains and losses relating to operational activities (on trade receivables, trade payables etc.) within income from operations, and recognizing foreign currency exchange gains and losses related to debt, in finance costs. When relevant to an understanding of the entity's financial performance, presentation as a separate line item will be appropriate.

Disclosures are also required

- If there has been a change in the functional currency of either the reporting entity or a significant foreign operation; and
- If the presentation currency is not same as the functional currency. The functional currency should be disclosed, together with the reason for using a different presentation currency.

12.5 Disclosure in practice

The main source of information concerning the disclosure of information regarding foreign currency is contained in the policy notes and in the notes to the group financial statements. As far as Logica is concerned, information is given on both the choice of functional currency and of the presentation currency. The functional currency is the pound sterling, presumably reflecting the primary economic environment in which the company operates.

The note concerning the functional currency is given in the accounting policy section, as follows:

Foreign currencies

The functional currency of the Company is pounds sterling. Transactions denominated in foreign currencies are translated into the functional currency of the Company at the rates prevailing at the dates of the individual transactions. Foreign currency monetary assets and liabilities are translated at the rates prevailing at the balance sheet date. Exchange gains and losses arising are charged or credited to the profit and loss account within net operating costs.

Source: Logica (2011), p. 145

This clearly follows the requirements of IAS 21, translating the monetary items at the closing rate and putting any exchange gains or losses into profit or loss in the statement of comprehensive income.

In terms of the presentation currency, again the pound sterling, the notes to the group financial statements, accounting policy section, show the following:

Foreign currencies

The presentation currency of the Group is pounds sterling. The Group also presents primary statements in euro, see pages 151 to 153.

Items included in the separate financial statements of Group entities are measured in the functional currency of each entity. Transactions denominated in foreign currencies are translated into the functional currency of the entity at the rates prevailing at the dates of the individual transactions. Foreign currency monetary assets and liabilities are translated at the rates prevailing at the end of the reporting period. Exchange gains and losses arising are charged or credited to net operating costs or finance costs/income in the statement of comprehensive income, as appropriate, except when deferred in equity as qualifying cash flow hedges and qualifying net investment hedges.

The statement of comprehensive income and statement of financial position of foreign entities are translated into pounds sterling on consolidation at the average rates for the period and the rates prevailing at the end of the reporting period respectively. Exchange gains and losses arising on the translation of the Group's net investment in foreign entities, and of financial instruments designated as hedges of such investments, are recognised as a separate component of shareholders' equity. On disposal of a foreign entity, the cumulative translation differences are recycled to the statement of comprehensive income and recognised as part of the gain or loss on disposal.

Goodwill and fair value adjustments arising on the acquisition of a foreign entity are treated as assets and liabilities of the foreign entity and translated at the rates prevailing at the end of the reporting period.

The most important foreign currencies for the Group are the euro and the Swedish krona. The relevant exchange rates to pounds sterling are shown in the table below.

Source: Logica (2011), p. 99

In this section further reference is made to the policy regarding functional currency. Note this time that, in terms of translation into the presentation currency, the net investment method is followed, in that income and expenses are translated using average rates for the period, while the rate ruling at the end of the reporting period is used for statement of financial position items. The exchange difference this time is shown in other comprehensive income.

Some additional information on the exchange differences is given in the statement of comprehensive income, as shown in Figure 12.3.

Figure 12.3 Logica: exchange differences

Other comprehensive income/(expense)		
Actuarial gains/(losses) on defined benefit schemes	30.7	(3.6)
Tax on items taken directly to equity	(8.4)	0.7
Cash flow hedges	(3.7)	–
Interest rate swaps fair value difference	0.1	(0.1)
Exchange differences on translation of foreign operations	(62.1)	13.3
Other comprehensive income/(expense) for the period, net of tax	(43.4)	10.3
Total comprehensive income/(expense) for the period	(12.0)	188.3
Profit attributable to:		
Owners of the parent	31.4	178.0
	31.4	178.0

Source: Logica (2011), p. 151

The company also gives an indication of the most important currencies for the group: the euro and the Swedish krona. This is given as part of the accounting policy section, as shown in Figure 12.4.

The most important foreign currencies for the Group are the euro and the Swedish krona. The relevant exchange rates to pounds sterling were:

Figure 12.4 Logica: foreign currencies used

	2011		2010	
	Average	Closing	Average	Closing
£1 = €	1.15	1.20	1.17	1.17
£1 = SEK	10.41	10.65	11.12	10.53

Source: Logica (2011), p. 100

Section summary

IAS 21 requires the translation of transactions and operations in a way that reflects the economic circumstances of the transaction. For companies entering into individual foreign transactions there are no significant problems. For companies with foreign operations, however, this approach has led to two methods of translation.

A foreign operation which has the same functional currency as its parent is treated as an integral part of the parent's operations and is therefore translated in the same way as individual company transactions.

A foreign operation with a functional currency different to that of the parent's (or a company with different functional and presentation currencies) follows different rules.

Section 3: Advanced Aspects

This section will outline in a little more detail some of the issues raised in the previous sections. In particular, it will look at the specific requirements of IAS 21 *The Effects of Changes in Foreign Exchange Rates*. It will outline the specific requirement for the identification of the functional currency, and the rationale for the differences in treatment of some items under the temporal and closing rate methods of translation. Some of these requirements have already been illustrated in Section 2 of this chapter. Hedging transactions will be examined further.

12.6 Functional currency: further aspects

In the intermediate section of this chapter, the functional currency was defined as that currency of the primary economic environment in which the entity operates. This tends to oversimplify the issue. In reality it might not be so simple to determine the functional currency of an entity. IAS 21 elaborates on this definition in paragraphs 9 to 14 of the standard.

In general terms the functional currency is normally the one in which the entity generates and spends cash (para. 9). So it is important to consider:

- the currency in which the sales prices are denominated or the currency that influences sales prices
- the currency of the country that influences the sales prices through specific regulations or through various competitive forces
- the currency in which manufacturing costs are determined, either in terms of how such costs are settled or in terms of how such costs are influenced.

According to paragraph 10, there are two factors to consider:

1. the currency in which funds from financing activities are generated
2. the currency in which receipts from operating activities are retained.

It is also important to consider the following questions (under para. 11).

- Are the activities of the foreign operation carried out as an extension of the reporting entity?
- Are the number of transactions with the reporting entity a high or low proportion of the activities of the foreign operation?
- Do the cash flows of the foreign operation directly affect the cash flows of the reporting entity?
- Are the cash flows from the foreign operation readily available for remittance to it?
- Are the cash flows from the foreign operation sufficient to service existing or expected debt obligations (without funds being made available from the reporting entity)?

Finally, paragraph 12 indicates that management should use judgement to determine which currency most faithfully reflects the economic effects of the underlying transactions and events.

Foreign currency translation: a critical appraisal

Owing to the complexities surrounding this topic, this chapter has deliberately followed the requirements of IAS 21 in its approach, rather than question the rationale behind the logic or, indeed, suggest alternative approaches. Having reached this advanced section it is perhaps appropriate to look more closely at this logic and whether any alternatives exist to deal with the translation methods for financial statements of foreign operations.

When translating any particular item there are two basic possibilities:

(i) the item could be translated using the exchange rate ruling when the item was created (historic rate)
(ii) the item could be translated using the exchange rate ruling when the item is being reported (current or closing rate).

Before IAS 21 was developed, there were four distinct methods which could be used in the translation process:

(a) Closing rate method – all assets and liabilities are translated at the current rate of exchange i.e. the exchange rate ruling at the end of the reporting period.
(b) Temporal method – assets and liabilities carried at current values are translated at the current rate of exchange e.g. cash, receivables, payables, investments at market value etc. Assets and liabilities carried at historic values are translated at the rate of exchange ruling at the dates the items were established e.g. property, prepayments, investments at cost etc.
(c) Current/non-current method – all current assets and current liabilities are translated at the current rate of exchange. Non-current assets and liabilities are translated at historic rates i.e. the exchange rate in effect at the time the asset was acquired or the liability incurred.
(d) Monetary/non-monetary method – monetary assets and liabilities are translated at the current rate of exchange. Non-monetary assets and liabilities are translated at the historic rate.

Each had its own supporters who provided strong arguments for and against the use of each particular method.

The closing rate method was the first to evolve and emerged when exchange rates were relatively stable. However, when exchange rates fluctuated there were problems with the translation of non-monetary items. When an item being carried at historic cost was translated using closing (current) rates, it was argued that the result was multiplying unrelated numbers i.e historical cost × closing rate.

The monetary/non-monetary method emerged as a consequence of the deficiencies of the closing rate method. This resolved the problems with the translation of non-monetary items noted above with the closing rate method so that all such items were translated at the historic rate. Monetary items continued to be translated using the historic rate. However, this method did not find favour with US companies, particularly when consolidated accounts were drawn up in a relatively weak currency. Results were being produced which neither made economic nor commercial sense.

There was relatively little difference between the monetary/non-monetary method and the temporal method which used translation rates determined by the valuation basis used for the asset and liability classes i.e. items valued at historic cost were translated at the historical rate; items valued at current value were translated at the closing rate. The most frequent cause of a difference between the two methods is where inventories are shown at net realizable value.

The use of the current/non-current method resulted in long-term liabilities being translated using historical rates of exchange. This resulted in inconsistency of treatment between current liabilities which were translated using the closing rate – giving the most up-to-date relevant information relating to amounts outstanding, and long-term liabilities which, when translated, gave an equivalent of the historic amount of the loan and, therefore, out-of-date information.

After several years of debate it was agreed that an approach to translation which is related to the cash flow consequences of exchange movements should determine the appropriate method to be used. Exchange differences which give rise to cash flows i.e. those resulting from business transactions should be reported as part of profit or loss for the period; other exchange differences which do not give rise to cash flows because they result from retranslations of the parent company's long-term investment in the foreign subsidiary are reported as other comprehensive income and as a movement in equity. This gave rise to the permitted methods for translation as being the temporal method and the closing rate method.

Translation methods: further discussion
Temporal method (translation into the functional currency)

As described above, the temporal method views the subsidiary as an extension of the parent and treats the transactions as though they were carried out by the parent. It is: to be used where the trade of the foreign enterprise is more dependent on the economic environment of the parent company's currency than of its own reporting currency. This method requires translation into the functional currency by applying the spot rate of exchange at the date of the transactions. This has been illustrated in the intermediate section of this chapter. However, what is the situation at the next and subsequent balance sheet dates?

This is particularly important in the case of borrowings in foreign currencies. These loans may be over a number of years and will by necessity have to appear in several statements of financial position before final repayment. The accounting question that arises is: at what amount should the loan liability be stated in each of the statements of financial position between the receipt of the loan and the final repayment? Depending on how the exchange rate moves, it may be that a company has to repay more than it borrowed. If this is the case, then the difference will need to be recognized as a loss at some point. The question is how, and when should the loss be recognized?

From a shareholder's perspective, the most useful information would be how much has to finally be paid to settle the loan and what is the amount of the total loss over the period. The question is, therefore, should the exchange loss be recognized only at this time? Suppose it was an exchange gain, what then? IAS 21 takes the view that such items should be translated at the rate existing at the end of the reporting period. This is the closing rate. Any difference arising because of a movement in the exchange rate is to be taken to profit or loss. What is the rationale for this treatment? The view is that the closing rate gives the best approximation of the future repayment and is the best information available.

According to IAS 21 the treatment of items depends on the nature of the item (i.e. whether monetary or non-monetary). This means that all exchange differences arising on such items, whether gains or losses, are to be recognized in profit or loss. Of course, any such gains will be unrealized until the monetary item is settled (e.g. when a loan is repaid). This is one of the few cases when an unrealized gain is taken to profit or loss. That said, it is open to question whether or not a difference on translation is truly a gain or a loss. Given that exchange rates may fluctuate both up and down, is there any reason to suppose that any translation difference is purely temporary? For example, the rate of exchange may be, for example, £1 = $2 at the end of the reporting period, but the very next week may have changed to £1 = $1.8. How valid is it to recognize a gain or loss at the end of the reporting period if the position has already changed when the statements are in the process of being prepared? Again, if the gain or loss is temporary, should it be recognized in profit or loss at all?

Notwithstanding, the use of the temporal method ensures that the principles of historical cost accounting are maintained. Moreover, the activities of the foreign enterprise that are being treated as an extension of the parent company is in line with the conceptual basis of consolidation. Finally, it recognizes that the risk of translation differences being realized depends on the nature of the item being accounted for.

Closing rate method: translation into the presentation currency

This method is to be used when the foreign subsidiary carries out its activities on a day to day basis as a separate, autonomous, semi-independent unit. The parent company is not involved in the day-to-day transactions of the subsidiary and instead regards its investment as being in the net worth of the subsidiary rather than in the subsidiary's individual assets.

As such, this method of translation recognizes the subsidiary as an independent entity. The method of translation uses the closing rate to translate the items in the statement of financial position. As regards the mechanics of translation, if the subsidiary is 'independent' then the assets and liabilities of such an entity will interact with each other rather than with those of the parent. Assume the assets of the subsidiary were acquired by means of a long-term loan. If these assets were translated at the rate ruling when they were acquired, and long-term loans at the rate ruling at the end of the reporting period, then different rates would be being used to translate items that are interdependent. In this case the rationale for the closing rate method seems to make sense, in that it preserves this interrelationship.

However, there is one major conceptual flaw in this approach. By consolidating the subsidiary using the current (closing) exchange rate, the assets of the subsidiary will be 'imported' into the group accounts at current values. This represents some form of hidden revaluation. According to the purchasing power parity theory, exchange rates move in response to inflation and the use of current rates for non-current assets means that an inflation adjustment is being automatically built in to the group accounts. In terms of pure historical cost accounting, it is not acceptable to revalue some assets and not others. Revaluation should be applied systematically and not on the haphazard basis of currency inflation. Surely in this instance the correct rate ought to be the historic rate!

As with the temporal method, the closing rate method does have many benefits. Because the foreign subsidiary's accounts are translated using effectively one rate, the accounting ratios of the subsidiary are not distorted on consolidation, the method is simple to operate and understand, and the most up-to-date information on exchange rates is used.

Nevertheless, translation exposure can be dramatically different for the two methods depending on the underlying assets and liabilities of the subsidiary company being translated, as the following illustration shows.

Comparison of temporal method and closing rate method
Temporal method
The following example will be used to illustrate the main differences.

Example
A UK company invests $6m in a US subsidiary on 1 January 2012. The subsidiary borrows $4 from a local bank and buys assets for $10m. At 31 December 2012 the US subsidiary made a profit of $1m.

During the year to 31 December 2012, the exchange rates moved as follows:

At 1 January 2012	£1 = £1.8
Average for the year	£1 = £1.5
At 31 December 2012	£1 = £1.4

The statement of financial position of the subsidiary in 'local' currency at the start and end of the period will be as follows:

	At start		At end
	$000		$000
Assets	10,000		10,000
		Monetary assets	2,500
		Monetary liabilities	(1,500)
			11,000
Long-term loan	(4,000)		(4,000)
	6,000		7,000
Share capital	6,000		6,000
Retained profit	0		1,000
	6,000		7,000

As far as the subsidiary is concerned, this is quite a good set of results. Net assets have increased by 17% from $6,000 to $7,000. Now consider the situation when the results of the subsidiary are translated using the temporal method:

	At start £000		At end £000	Rate
Assets	5,555		5,555	1.8
		Monetary assets	1,786	1.4
		Monetary liabilities	(1,071)	1.4
			6,270	
Long-term loan	(2,222)		(2,857)	1.4
	3,333		3,413	
Share capital	3,333		3,333	
Retained profit	0		667	1.5
	3,333	Exchange loss	(587)	
			3,413	

When translated, the results do not look nearly so good. Net assets have only grown by a modest 2.4% in comparison with the 17% shown in the local currency accounts. Why has this situation arisen? The reason is that the long-term loan has been translated at the current (closing) rate of 1.4 while the assets to which the loan relates have been translated at the historic rate of 1.8. This is because the assets and liabilities are viewed from the parent company viewpoint. Prudence requires that the growth in the liability be shown at current value if the liability is recognized, whereas the assets should be shown at historic cost. Should the liability also be shown on the same basis as the asset to which it relates, thus ignoring prudence, or should the asset be revalued?

This example of a local loan to finance the purchase of a local asset is common practice in international business. If the parent company had not borrowed but had invested $10m directly, then it would have experienced greater exposure to exchange rate movements. What has happened in this situation is that the company has acquired assets of $10m with a currency risk of $6m. The loan is balanced by the asset, since any rate change will affect the loan (liability) and the asset in opposite ways, so cancelling each other out. This has been referred to in the previous section as a currency hedge. The problem with the temporal method in this regard is that it fails to recognize the economic existence of the hedge in so much as the rate change is reflected in the accounts only in so far as it affects the liability and not where it affects the asset.

Closing rate (net investment) method

Example

	At start £000		At end £000	Rate
Assets	5,555		7,142	1.4
		Monetary assets	1,786	1.4
		Monetary liabilities	(1,071)	1.4
			7,857	
Long-term loan	(2,222)		(2,857)	1.4
	3,333		5,000	

Share capital	3,333			3,333	
Retained profit	0			667	1.5
	3,333	Exchange gain		1,000	
				5,000	

The use of the closing rate method ties the rate change to both assets and liabilities, and so reflects the current exchange value for both.

Comparison of translated statements of financial position at the end of the period:

	Temporal		Closing rate	
	£000			£000
Assets	5,555			7,142
Monetary assets	1,786			1,786
Monetary liabilities	(1,071)			(1,071)
	6,270			7,857
Long-term loan	(2,857)			(2,857)
	3,413			5,000
Share capital	3,333			3,333
Retained profit	667			667
Exchange loss	(587)	Exchange gain		1,000
	3,413			5,000

The numbers chosen in the example showed a picture of a situation in which sterling was weakening against the dollar. Under the temporal method, the impact was to show an increased liability.

Note that if the exchange rate had moved in the other direction, then the impact would have been the complete opposite. The asset would have remained at its 'old' sterling value, while the liability would have decreased. The exchange difference would have been positive. Under the net investment method, if this had been the case, both the asset and liability would have declined and so would have given a negative exchange difference.

Impact of exchange differences on performance

Using the example above to measure return on equity gives the following measures:

Return on equity (%)	
In local currency ($)	16.67
Temporal method	2.4
Closing rate method	50.0

Three different measures of performance are shown, depending on the method of translation chosen. From an interpretation point of view this can present problems for the analyst. The effect of translation differences can be highlighted in two ways.

1. The differences will be reflected in the analysis of non-current assets. When the closing rate method is used it will change the value of the assets. This change ought to be disclosed in the note to the non-current assets.

2. It is also important to look at the translation difference recognized in other comprehensive income. Is it material?

In the accounting policy notes companies need to disclose the method used to translate foreign subsidiaries. The amounts written off must also be disclosed, showing details of what has been taken directly to equity. This will appear in the statement of changes in equity.

Hedging a net investment

A description of the mechanics of hedging was given in the introductory section. There is, however, a major loophole in IAS 21, concerned with currency hedges. It is likely that a multinational company will have investments in many countries. These investments will be denominated in many different currencies and will potentially be exposed to exchange rate movements. Multinational companies will try to minimize this exposure by borrowing in foreign currencies. If, for example, a UK company wants to invest in a subsidiary in the USA, it will try to borrow the money in the USA to finance the deal. The cash flow from the investment in the overseas subsidiary may be used to pay interest on the borrowing, and may ultimately be used to repay the debt. Any movement in the exchange rate will have no impact since both the loan and the investment will 'cancel' each other out.

Companies will hedge their investments and will borrow in those currencies that will reflect their future expected cash flows. As was indicated above, such borrowings will have to be translated into the functional currency using the closing rate, while the underlying investment will be translated at the historic rate. If this were the case, then the borrowing and the investment would not 'balance' out.

However, IAS 39 *Financial Instruments: Recognition and measurement* allows any translation gains and losses on loans that are hedges to be taken directly to equity, without going through the statement of comprehensive income. Multinational companies, however, tend not to hedge individual investments, but rather take out a 'basket' of currency loans to hedge a 'basket' of investments. It is not possible therefore to link individual assets to individual loans. At the end of the reporting period it is up to the company to disclose which items are trading debts and so will be taken to profit or loss, and which are hedges. This system is clearly open to abuse.

Foreign operations in a high inflationary economy

This is a special situation and is subject to special rules under IAS 21. If the foreign operation is an autonomous unit and is based in an economy experiencing a very high rate of inflation, the closing rate method may distort the financial results of the foreign company. In particular, the tangible non-current assets may be severely understated. There are two ways of dealing with this problem:

1. adjust the financial statements in the local currency to take account of the impact of inflation before they are translated;
2. assume that the overseas operation is an integral part of the parent company, and use the temporal method to translate the accounts.

While both approaches are in use, the first must be used where a company has an autonomous subsidiary in a country experiencing hyperinflation.

Section summary

Group financial statements of multinational companies may contain information that is aggregated and contain a combination of financial statements denominated in many difference currencies. Where there are fluctuating exchange rates this gives rise to accounting problems in terms of the exchange rate to be used, and in the treatment of any gain or loss that arises on translation.

The translation of foreign currency for presentation in the financial statements has been a difficult area of accounting for many years and several different views have been put forward as the preferred approach – each with its own advantages and disadvantages.

In terms of the accounting regulation, IAS 21 sets the functional currency of a foreign subsidiary, which is integrated with the operations of the parent, and for which the temporal method is more appropriate, to that of the parent. Is it is therefore translated in the same way as individual company transactions. IAS 21 refers only to the closing rate method as the method to be used when translating financial statements of overseas subsidiaries into the presentation currency of the parent. Any difference on exchange arising is then treated as other comprehensive income.

Chapter summary

IAS 21 *The Effects of Changes in Foreign Exchange Rates*

- Where there are transactions denominated in foreign currencies, such transactions denominated in the 'local' currency need to be translated into the functional currency.
  - Business transactions are translated at the rate ruling at the date of the transaction.
  - Monetary items are translated at the rate ruling at the end of the reporting period.
  - Any exchange differences, whether a gain or a loss, are recognized in profit or loss.
- For consolidation purposes there are two methods that have been put forward for translation purposes depending on the relationship between the parent and the subsidiary.
- If the subsidiary is seen to be an extension of the parent then the translation of the subsidiary is done as though the transactions were those of the parent itself. The method applied in this case has been referred to as the temporal method. Under this method a mixture of different rates will be applied.
  - Non-current assets are translated at the rate ruling when the asset was acquired.
  - Monetary items are translated at the rate ruling at the end of the reporting period.
  - Revenues and expenses are translated at the average rate for the period.
  - Any exchange differences are recognized in profit or loss.
- If the subsidiary is seen to be an independent entity, then the method of translation applied is referred to as the closing rate (net investment) method. Under this method:
  - assets and liabilities are translated at the rate ruling at the end of the reporting period, the closing rate
  - revenues and expenses are translated (usually) at the average rate for the period
  - any exchange differences arising are recognized in other comprehensive income.
- While the closing rate method preserves the relationship between assets and liabilities within the statement of financial position of the company, there may be a problem with assets that have been 'revalued' in terms of the foreign currency exchange rate movement. Such 'revalued' assets will then be incorporated into a historical cost statement of financial position, so the information given may be misleading.

✓ Key terms for review

Definitions can be found in the glossary at the end of the book.

Closing rate method	Local currency	Temporal method
Exchange difference	Monetary items	Transaction
Functional currency	Non-monetary items	Translation
Hedge	Presentation currency	Translation reserve

? Review questions

1. Explain the difference between foreign currency translation and foreign currency conversion.
2. What justification is there to recognize unrealized gains arising from the translation of an unsettled foreign currency transaction at the end of a reporting period?

3. Distinguish between a company's *functional* currency and its *presentational* currency.

4. What factors should a company take into account when determining which is its functional currency?

5. Identify the circumstances under which IAS 21 permits the use of the closing rate method and the temporal method for translation of financial statements.

6. What does the net investment (closing rate) method assume is most relevant at the consolidated financial statements stage of translation?

7. Explain the differences in treatment and the effect of translating financial statements using the temporal and closing rate method.

8. Should the different relationships between a parent operation and its controlled foreign operation affect the treatment of exchange profits or losses in the consolidated financial statements?

9. IAS 21 requires the use of the net investment method when translating the financial statements of foreign operations with a functional currency different to that of the parent's. What other methods have been put forward over the years to translate the financial statements of foreign operations?

10. Explain what is meant by 'hedge accounting', and give an example of when a company may use a hedge transaction.

 Exercises

Level I

1. DLJ Ltd had the following transactions in the year to 31 March 2013.

   (i) On 11 January 2013, goods were purchased from an American supplier for $900,000. The goods were recorded at the spot rate of £1 = $1.60. DLJ Ltd had not settled the liability by 31 March 2013 when the exchange rate was £1= $1.64.

   (ii) Trade receivables are translated into Sterling automatically by the sales ledger using the spot rate ruling on the date of the transaction. At 31 March 2013, the balance on the sales ledger in respect of amounts due from American customers showed a Sterling amount owing of £283,230. The dollar amount of the American customers was $456,000.

   (iii) DLJ Ltd borrowed $4m 1 April 2012. This was correctly recorded using the spot rate at that date of £1 = $1.58. No adjustments have been made to the loan balance since that date.

   (iv) DLJ Ltd includes foreign gains and losses in administrative expenses.

Required

Prepare journal entries to record any necessary adjustment relating to the above information.

2. Nyleve Ltd is preparing its financial statements for the year to 31 December 2012. In June 2011, Nyleve Ltd purchased some land in Switzerland for CHFr 1,300,000. In line with Nyleve's accounting policies on non-current assets, the land was revalued by an independent valuer on 31 December 2012 and is to be incorporated into the financial statements at the revalued amount. The land was valued at CHFr 1,650,000.

Exchange rates were as follows:

	CHFr : £1
June 2011	3.2
December 2011	3.4
December 2012	3.1

Required

Calculate and explain the accounting treatment for the land purchase and subsequent revaluation.

3. X Inc is a wholly owned US subsidiary of A plc and was acquired on 31 December 2011. The statements of financial position of X Inc are as follows:

	Dec 11	Dec 12
	$	$
Net assets	10,000	14,000
Share capital	4,000	4,000
Retained earnings	6,000	10,000
	10,000	14,000
Statement of comprehensive income		
Revenues		10,000
Expenses		6,000
Profit for the year		4,000

Exchange rates were as follows:

At 31 December 2011	£1 = $2.00
Average for year	£1 = $1.94
At 31 December 2012	£1 = $1.90

Required

Translate the statement of financial position of X at 31 December 2012 into the presentation currency of the pound, for inclusion in the group accounts of A plc.

Level II

4. This extends the previous example. The statement of financial position of X Inc one year on is added so that the statements for three years are as follows:

Statement of financial position			
	Dec 11	Dec 12	Dec 13
	$	$	$
Net assets	10,000	14,000	19,000
Share capital	4,000	4,000	4,000
Retained earnings	6,000	10,000	15,000
	10,000	14,000	19,000

Statement of comprehensive income (extract) for the year ended 31 December 2013

Net profit for the year	$5,000

Exchange rates were as follows:

At 31 December 2011	£1 = $2.00
Average for 2012	£1 = $1.94
At 31 December 2012	£1 = $1.90
Average for 2013	£1 = $1.80
At 31 December 2013	£1 = $1.75

Required

Translate the statement of financial position of X Inc at 31 December 2013 into the presentation currency of the pound, for inclusion in the group accounts of A plc.

5. ABC plc is a trading company that has its head office in London and operates in the UK, Japan and eastern Europe. One of its investments is a wholly owned subsidiary company, XYZ Ltd, which is registered and operates in the Czech Republic. This subsidiary was acquired on the 1 April 2012 at which time the share capital and reserves amounted to 2.4 million Czech crowns. During the year to 31 March 2013, XYZ Ltd made a profit of 600,000 crowns.

Exchange rate movements during the year to March 2013 were as follows:

1 April 2012	£1 = 41.8 crowns
Average for year	£1 = 48.0 crowns
31 March 2013	£1 = 48.5 crowns.

Required

(a) Prepare a summary statement of financial position of XYZ Ltd translated into the presentation currency (sterling) for inclusion in the group financial statements.

(b) Calculate the difference arising on exchange and explain how this difference has arisen.

(c) Explain how the accounting treatment of XYZ Ltd would have differed if its operations were a direct extension of the parent company rather than a separate independent operation.

6. Sterling Engineering acquired Pathfoot Products Ltd, a Latvian-based manufacturing company, on 31 March 2012. The statements of financial position of the new company are given below. No new assets have been acquired by Pathfoot Products Ltd since the date of acquisition.

	31 March 2012		31 March 2013	
	Lats (m)	Lats (m)	Lats (m)	Lats (m)
Non-current assets		24.5		20.3
Current assets				
Inventory	34.5		39.5	

Accounts receivable	24.2		15.8	
Cash	3.5	62.2	16.5	71.8
		86.7		92.1
Accounts payable		45.2		22.6
		41.5		69.5
Long-term loan		16.5		51.5
		25.0		18.0
Share capital		15.6		15.6
Reserves		7.0		7.0
Retained profit (loss)		2.4		(4.6)
		25.0		18.0

Statement of comprehensive income for the year ended 31 March 2013

		Lats (m)
Sales		8.0
Cost of sales		
Opening inventory	34.5	
Purchases	10.0	
	44.5	
Closing inventory	39.5	5.0
		3.0
Other costs (including depreciation)	(10.0)	
Loss for the year		(7.0)

Exchange rate movements:

31 March 2012	£1 = 6.5 lats
Average for year	£1 = 7.8 lats
31 March 2013	£1 = 10.4 lats

Required

Translate the statement of financial position of Pathfoot Products Ltd at 31 March 2013, together with the statement of comprehensive income, into:

(a) functional currency

(b) presentation currency.

in accordance with IAS 21.

7. The following are the summary accounts of Overseas Ltd, in foreign currency (limas).

Statement of financial position as at 31 December 2012

	Limas
Ordinary share capital	630,000
Retained earnings	80,000
	710,000
Plant and machinery at cost	700,000
Less depreciation	70,000
	630,000
Inventory at cost	210,000
Net monetary current assets	40,000
	880,000
Less long-term loan	170,000
	710,000

Statement of comprehensive income for the year ended 31 December 2012

			Limas
Cash sales		900,000	
Less:	cost of sales:		
	Purchases	960,000	
	Closing inventory	(210,000)	
		750,000	
	Depreciation	70,000	
			820,000
Operating profit before tax			80,000

During the year the relevant exchange rates were:

	Limas to the £1
1 January 2012	14
Average for the year	12
Average at the acquisition of closing inventory	11
31 December 2012	10

Your UK company, Sterling Ltd, had acquired Overseas Ltd on 1 January 2012 by subscribing £45,000 of share capital when the exchange rate was 14 limas to the £1. The long-term loan had been raised on the same date. On that day, Overseas Ltd had purchased the plant and equipment for 700,000 limas. It is being depreciated by the straight line method over ten years.

Required

(a) Translate the statement of financial position and statement of comprehensive income of Overseas Ltd into the functional currency.

(b) Translate the statement of financial position and statement of comprehensive income of Overseas Ltd into the presentation currency.

(c) For each of the requirements (a) and (b) above, provide a detailed explanation of any exchange difference that arises.

Level III

8. Home Ltd is incorporated in the UK and rents mobile homes to holidaymakers in this country and Carea. The company has a head office in the UK and a branch in Carea where the local currency is 'mics'. The following balances are extracted from the books of the head office and its 'self-accounting' branch at 31 December 2012.

	Head office £	Branch (Mics)
Debit balances		
Non-current assets – cost	450,000	900,000
Receivables	17,600	36,000
Operating costs	103,700	225,000
Amount due from branch	42,600	–
	613,900	1,161,000
Credit balances		
Share capital	200,000	–
Retained earnings 1 June 2012	110,800	–
Sales	186,300	480,000
Payables	9,700	25,000
Amount due to head office	–	420,000
Accumulated depreciation	107,100	236,000
	613,900	1,161,000

Exchange rates were as follows:

	Mics to the £
1 January 2012	6
Average for year	5
31 January 2012	4

The non-current assets of the branch were acquired when there were 8 mics to the £.
There are no cash or goods in transit between head office and branch at the year end.

Required

Prepare the final accounts of Home Ltd for 2012. The accounts should be expressed in £ Sterling and for this purpose, the conversion of the branch should be translated into the functional currency (i.e. the temporal method).

References

IAS 21 *The Effects of Changes in Foreign Exchange Rates*. IASB, revised 1993.
IFRS 9 *Financial Instruments*. IFRS, 2009.
IAS 39 *Financial Instruments: Recognition and Measurement*. IASB, amended 2009.
Logica (2011) *Annual Report and Accounts*.

Further reading

Revsine, L. (1987) The rationale underlying the functional currency choice. In R. Bloom and P.Y. Elgers (eds) *Accounting Theory and Policy*. Harcourt Brace Jovanovich.

When you have read this chapter, log on to the Online Learning Centre website at *www.mcgraw-hill.co.uk/textbooks/mckeith* to explore chapter-by-chapter test questions, further reading and more online study tools.

Chapter 13

Interpretation of Financial Statements

Learning Outcomes

After studying this chapter you should be able to:

- ✓ explain what is meant by horizontal analysis
- ✓ explain what is meant by vertical analysis
- ✓ calculate specific accounting ratios
- ✓ use ratio analysis to evaluate the performance of a company
- ✓ explain the limitations of ratio analysis
- ✓ identify and explain indicators of financial distress.

Introduction

Interpretation of financial statements is probably one of the most interesting aspects of financial reporting, but will present many challenges. In order to judge the extent to which a company has performed over a number of years requires a good understanding of how the accounting numbers have been compiled and also what can cause an accounting number to change.

Having gained an understanding of the individual figures making up a set of financial statements, it is now appropriate to consider these individual figures in the overall context of a set of financial statements. A constant theme throughout this text is that decision making is the main use to which financial statements are put. Indeed, the Conceptual Framework states that the objective of preparing financial statements is to provide users with information which will help them to make decisions about providing resources to an entity. In order to make decisions based on financial statement information there must be standards, budgets, expectations or benchmarks against which the reported financial information is compared and assessed. The study of such relationships, interpretation of financial statements, is the subject of this chapter.

In particular, this chapter describes the techniques of analysis available, including horizontal, vertical and ratio analysis, to evaluate a company's performance. It will evaluate these techniques and develop an understanding of how the accounting numbers interact with each other to give an indication of the financial health of a company.

Section 1: Basic Principles

Interpretation of financial statements is useful in providing information for decision making. For example:

- How much would a bank be prepared to lend to the company?
- Would an investor be prepared to buy shares in the company?
- Should a supplier be willing to supply goods to the company?

These kinds of questions can be answered, to an extent, by using accounting information. However, it is important to realize at the outset that the technique of interpretation can be used in conjunction with any additional information available. That is, information not necessarily disclosed in the financial statements – for example, general economic conditions, inflation, state of the industry.

The application of financial statement analysis provides only part of the information used by decision makers. In order to produce a good analysis, what is needed is an enquiring frame of mind. What exactly do the accounting numbers tell? In order to build up a methodology for analysis, it is useful to start with a general overview of the company.

13.1 The interpretation process

There are various 'tools' available to the user in the interpretation process. Techniques such as horizontal analysis, vertical analysis and ratio analysis can all be used to extract data from a set of financial statements. The best 'tool' is, however, to have an inquisitive and enquiring frame of mind.

In practice, before applying any specialist techniques to analyse a firm's financial statements it is necessary to specify the objectives of the analysis and indentify the financial statements user for whom the analysis is being prepared. Thereafter, the interpretation process should begin with a general overview of the financial statements to be analysed. This will allow the figures to be put into context – for example, have sales increased/decreased? Has the overdraft gone up/reduced? What is particularly important at this stage is to remember that a company does not operate in a vacuum; the reported figures must be put in context of the wider economy and, in particular, the economic conditions that persist in the industry of which the company is a part.

General overview

Information disclosed in financial reports may relate to an individual company or to a group of companies. This information will show, for example:

- different kinds of assets and how they are financed
- relationship between items (e.g. debt/shareholders' funds, current assets/current liabilities)
- level of sales and profits
- earnings per share, dividends.

From the information given in the financial statements of a company it is possible to get an overview of how successful the company has been over the period under review. The main financial statements need to be examined but it is important to note that any analysis must be set in context. It is important to:

- compare like with like in terms of companies in the same industry – it is not much use comparing a company in the retail sector with one in the manufacturing sector; any analysis would be flawed
- it is also a good idea to compare with industry norms, to ensure that the comparison is like with like.

In terms of the information provided, two broad techniques of analysis are available: horizontal analysis and vertical analysis.

Horizontal analysis

The is where trends can be examined over a number of accounting periods. Horizontal analysis is useful where comparisons are for periods greater than two years. Companies do publish historical summaries covering five years, and in some cases, ten years.

Consider the following example.

Example

	Year 1	Year 2	Year 3	Year 4	Year 5
Sales (£m)	630	819	1,046	1,298	1,562
Profit	45	48	56	73	94
Net assets	500	600	700	850	900
Dividends	2	4	5	6	8

These figures do not give an immediate indication of how well, for example, the company's sales performance is. In order to get a better picture of movements in numbers, indexing may be used.

The way indexing works is that a base year is chosen, and this is set at 100. All the other figures are then adjusted to correspond with this figure. So if Year 1 is chosen as the base year, the £630 sales figure is set equal to 100. The corresponding numbers are adjusted as follows.

If £630 = 100, then the Year 2 sales of £819 will be equal to:

$$£819 \times 100 / £630 = 130$$

Each sales figure is then related to the base year of Year 1.
Year 3 sales will be equal to:

$$£1046 \times 100 / 630 = 166$$

So a table can be compiled as follows:
Year 1 = 100

	Year 1	Year 2	Year 3	Year 4	Year 5
Sales	100	130	166	206	248

In terms of how the information is presented it is much easier to see the growth in sales. However, care should be taken when looking at growth rates. In the above example, although sales are growing, the rate of growth year on year may not be growing. Continuing with the above example:

	Year 1	Year 2	Year 3	Year 4	Year 5
Sales	100	130	166	206	248
Increase over previous year		30	36	40	42
% increase over previous year		30%	28%	24%	20%

This shows that, although there is a growth in sales over the five-year period, the rate of growth is slowing down, from 30% in Year 1 to only 20% in the final period.

In addition to this, there are some problems with historical summaries.

- There is nothing to compare them with, so they suffer from a lack of comparability
- The information given is not audited so there is no independent verification of the numbers contained in the historical summary.
- If the company changes an accounting policy – for example, on revaluation – there is no indication as to how this accounting policy change affects the accounting numbers.
- If the company acquires a new subsidiary during the year, it may be difficult to detect this since acquisitions are not always reported.
- The figures give will not be adjusted to take account of inflation, although this can be done as a separate exercise using some inflation index, such as the Retail Price Index.
- The information contained in a historical summary is not mandatory, so directors can choose its contents. Information given in historical summaries is not standard across companies.

Vertical analysis

While horizontal analysis tends to work year on year, comparing each item with the previous year to get the percentage change, or as was indicated above to see the trend in a particular item, it is also possible to work vertically: vertical analysis. This is done by equating the total to 100 and then producing what are known as 'common size' statements. This can be done for both statements of financial position and statements of comprehensive income. The following example illustrates a common size statement for a statement of financial position. The individual statement of financial position figures are shown as a percentage of the total net assets of the company.

Example

Statement of financial position as at ...	£000	% of total net assets
Non-current assets		
Land	32,300	127
Machinery	3,100	12
Vehicles	9,500	38
	44,900	177
Current assets		
Inventory	8,600	34
Receivables	2,600	10
Cash	600	2
	11,800	46
Current liabilities		
Payables	17,700	70
Net current liabilities	(5,900)	(24)
Total assets less current liabilities	39,000	153
Long-term loan	(13,700)	(53)
Net assets	25,300	100
Share capital	20,000	79
Retained earnings	5,300	21
	25,300	100

This method has some advantages in that inter-company comparison is made easier since the items in the financial statements are reduced to a common scale. This shows more clearly any changes in the financial structure of the company. Vertical analysis can be used over several years to show how the sales and profitability pattern, or the financial structure of a company, is changing.

Comparisons between companies (cross-sectional analysis)

As noted above, common-sized financial statements can be used to compare multiple companies at the same point in time. It is particularly useful when comparing companies of different sizes. It is often useful to 'benchmark' a company against the best performing company in its industry as a whole. A company can also be compared to the industry average by obtaining or calculating industry average data. This gives a quick overview of where the firm stands in the industry with respect to key items in the financial statements.

Progress Point 13.1

The summarized common-size statements of financial position for five companies are given below. In addition, the industries in which the five companies operate are as detailed below.

Required

Which company is represented by which common-size statement of financial position and explain the reasons for your choice.

Industry:

A. General engineering
B. Whisky distillers and blenders
C. Software development
D. House builders
E. Pharmaceutical.

Common-size statements of financial position					
	1	2	3	4	5
Land and property	11	12	31	5	40
Plant and equipment	9	3	28	25	47
Intangible assets	–	–	–	70	76
Inventory and work-in-progress	75	111	43	5	37
Trade receivables	18	36	36	25	60
Cash	1	1	5	5	60
	114	163	143	135	320
Trade payables	9	45	34	10	112
Bank overdraft	5	18	9	25	14
Long-term liabilities	–	–	–	–	(94)
Net assets	100	100	100	100	100

Solution

In order to answer this question it is necessary to first of all identify attributes of companies which would be particular to the specific industries.

A. **General engineering = Statement of financial position number 3**

A general engineering company would have high investment in plant and equipment and would also likely have a factory representing a significant amount for land and property. There would also be relatively significant inventories and trade receivables with a corresponding level of trade payables.

B. **Whisky distillers and blenders = Statement of financial position number 1**

There would be high inventories and work-in-progress as a result of the lengthy maturation process. There would likely be a reasonable investment in land and property but more particularly plant and equipment in items such as distilling equipment, storage tanks, etc.

C. **Software development = Statement of financial position number 4**

There would be a significant investment in intangible assets representing software and a considerable investment in property, plant and equipment representing office premises and computer equipment. Trade debtors are likely to form a significant part of the statement of financial position as credit will be given to purchasers of software. There will likely be a bank overdraft to finance monthly running costs such as payroll etc. Trade payables will be relatively small consisting of office supplies, utilities etc.

D. **House builder = Statement of financial position 2**

There would be high work-in-progress as a result of the long-term process of house-building. There would also be significant trade payables representing purchases of materials etc.

E. **Pharmaceutical = Statement of financial position number 5**

The pharmaceutical company is likely to have significant intangible assets representing patents on drugs etc and capitalized development expenditure. There are also likely to be significant amounts of plant and equipment as well as research facilities housing that equipment. There will be significant inventories of drugs and trade receivables are likely to be high representing the amounts due from their sale. Long-term borrowings financing the property elements of the statement of financial position would be expected.

BASIC

INTERMEDIATE

ADVANCED

Section summary

Before undertaking the analysis of any company's financial statements, it is necessary to specify the objectives of the analysis. Horizontal or trend analysis allows comparison of one company's results over a number of years whereas vertical analysis allows comparison of different sized companies by expressing their accounting information in common-size statements.

Section 2: Intermediate Issues

Once a general overview of the company is undertaken using trend analysis, it is possible to do a more detailed analysis using accounting ratios. These ratios will direct the focus of the user to highlight areas of good and bad performance, and identify any significant change. Once change has been identified this is only the first step: it is very important to know the reason why the change has taken place.

13.2 Ratio analysis

Ratios describe the relationship between different accounting numbers in the financial statements. At the outset it is important to note that some ratios are more useful than others, so care must be taken in interpreting these, otherwise the results may be misleading. It is also important to set the ratios in context. A ratio by itself will be meaningless. Ratios need to be compared with:

- the same ratios in the preceding period
- budgeted ratios for the same period
- ratios for other companies in the same sector.

In order that comparison is possible it is important to compare 'like with like'. The precise implications of a given ratio are only possible if it is accompanied by a clear definition of its constituent parts. Before the reliability of a ratio can be assessed, the reliability of the underlying business operations must be ascertained.

The definitions of ratios themselves may vary. There is no universal definition of an accounting ratio. No accounting standards have ever been published on the subject of ratios. Other textbooks may give different definitions of the same ratios. What is important is to ensure that when calculating ratios a consistent approach is used.

Purpose of ratio analysis

The annual financial statements of an organization can provide a lot of financial information that is difficult to interpret. Looking at the statement of comprehensive income, this may show an increase in profit before tax. However, this does not mean that the company is making efficient use of all its resources. In general, ratio analysis has the following uses:

- it helps to review the performance of an organization over time
- it makes it possible to compare the performance of an organization with that of its competitors
- it makes it possible to compare the performance of an organization with the industry average
- it enables any problems within a company to be highlighted and corrective action can then be taken.

Ratio analysis is a useful tool for any of the stakeholders in an organization. For example, a supplier may want to ensure that any new customer will be able to pay for goods and services. The liquidity of the business will be important in this context. The efficiency of an organization in generating profits will be of interest to potential shareholders. Lenders will be interested in the risk of the organization, to ensure that the business is not overexposed to long-term debt and can afford to meet any interest payments when they become due. Management of the business will be interested in those ratios that highlight the efficiency of the business.

Progress Point 13.2

Steelies plc is a medium-sized engineering company whose shares are listed on the Stock Exchange.

The company recently applied to its bankers for a 7-year loan of £1,000,000 to finance a modernization and expansion programme.

Mr Love, a recently retired civil servant, is considering investing £50,000 of his lump sum pension in the company's ordinary shares in order to provide both an income during his retirement and a legacy to his grandchildren after his death.

Both the bank and Mr Love have acquired copies of the company's most recent annual report and accounts.

Required

Identify, separately for each of the two parties, those aspects of the company's performance and financial position which would be of particular interest and relevance to their respective circumstances.

Solution

The bank will be interested in two main aspects:

(i) the ability to repay the loan as and when it falls due
(ii) the ability to pay interest on the due dates.

In addition, the bank will be looking to see if the loan can be secured over any of the company's assets.

Mr Love will be interested in the expected return on his investment. This means that recent performance of the company and its future plans will be important to him. The possible capital growth of his investment will also be of interest to him.

Limitations of accounting data

Before looking in detail at the various ratios commonly used to analyse financial statements, it is perhaps appropriate to look at their limitations, which arise mainly from the limitations that are inherent in the accounting data being used.

Our studies thus far in this book have shown that there is scope for differences in accounting treatment for the same transaction, which can lead to tremendous variation in reported figures. For example, the use of the straight line method of providing for depreciation can give a significantly different charge from that obtained by using the reducing balance method. In addition, account must be taken of the distortions that may arise when comparing accounts based on historic cost principles and where one company has chosen to revalue its assets. The figures contained in financial statements themselves can contain assumptions and estimates that can be very subjective.

In practice it is not always possible to obtain all the required accounting information in order to calculate a desired ratio. As has been seen, the content and presentation of limited company financial statements are summarized and prescribed, and it may not be possible to extract the required information to prepare the ratio.

Moreover, the use of year-end figures extracted from financial statements may not be representative of the year as a whole; many companies choose a quiet time of year for their year end, and consequently inventory, trade receivable and trade payable levels may be uncharacteristically low. Any seasonal factors may be missed entirely.

Problems can also arise due to the time lag in preparation and publication of the accounts following the end of a company's reporting period. Unless information is available in a timely fashion it may be too late to take corrective or preventative actions.

Finally, traditional accounting statements deal only with those items that are measurable in money terms and therefore cannot disclose important facts that are not monetary (e.g. a loyal workforce).

Limitations of ratio analysis

It is important to note that the ratios in themselves are of little informational benefit; it is only when they are compared against other years or other firms, or perhaps against budgeted figures or other profit centres within a firm, that they provide the information necessary to interpret what has happened and to predict what will happen. Problems often arise with inter-temporal analysis in establishing a normal base year with which to compare other years, or in selecting an industry norm if inter-firm comparisons are being attempted.

It is important that like-for-like comparisons are made. In the case of inter-temporal analysis this should be readily achievable but care will still need to be taken to ensure that no changes in accounting policy have taken place that could distort the results. In addition, changes in technology make time comparisons difficult where prices and asset efficiency have changed – what was once an acceptable ratio may not be now.

International comparisons can be even more problematic as there is the added problem of the different accounting policies that may exist in different countries.

In the case of inter-firm comparisons within the same industry, provided that each company uses exactly the same basis in calculating ratios, this provides a controlled and objective means of evaluation. This is because every company is subject to identical economic and market conditions in the review period and this therefore allows a much truer comparison than a single company's fluctuating results over several years.

The precise implication of a given ratio is possible only if it is accompanied by a clear definition of its constituent parts. Unfortunately, the use of accounting information in published accounts is generally summarized and there may not be sufficiently detailed information available to calculate the ratios required. In addition, the definitions of ratios themselves may vary from source to source as they are not universally defined.

Finally, it must be remembered that ratios only identify symptoms and not causes of problems and, as such, must be used in conjunction with other available information.

BASIC

INTERMEDIATE

ADVANCED

13.3 The use of ratios in practice

Having collected the data, the information provided by the ratios can be used to interpret what has happened and to predict what will happen.

As noted earlier, ratios in themselves provide little informational benefit. They need to be compared against other years' ratios, other companies' ratios, budgeted ratios or against other profit centres within the same firm.

This comparison of ratios will direct attention to key areas requiring analysis, and identify areas of good and bad performance. The ratios may highlight areas of significant change, and provide an indication of the profitability and cash position of a company.

By highlighting areas of good and bad performance, ratios can assist management in identifying where their strengths and weaknesses are and where further effort should be directed. Ratios help in identifying the success or otherwise of particular choices of action as comparison can be made of the pre- and post-action results. Although there can be differences in accounting treatment of particular items between different companies, such variations should not exist when making inter-temporal comparison and therefore a comparison of like for like can be made. The use of historic costs can also be overcome in certain circumstances and current values used to replace outdated asset values.

While ratios in themselves are of little benefit, ratio analysis as a technique should not be used in isolation either. It is essential that the findings are incorporated into an overall analysis. It is necessary to establish *why* there has been a change and not simply identify that there *has* been a change. Any interpretation or analysis must be taken in context with all the other available information about the company and its environment. Companies do not operate in a vacuum and are instead part of the industries in which they operate, the economy and, indeed, the world economy. As such, the sources of information available with which to assist in any analysis are numerous.

Accounting ratios

The accounting ratios most often used can be grouped as follows:

- profitability
- liquidity
- management (or activity)
- risk.

In order to illustrate the calculation and interpretation of the ratios, the following example will be used.

Example

Choclatier Ltd is a company that makes luxury confectionery. The following is a summarized extract from the financial statements of the company.

Statements of comprehensive income for the year ended 30 June			
	Notes	2013 £000	2012 £000
Turnover		6,200	5,800
Cost of sales		(4,800)	(4,600)
Gross profit		1,400	1,200
Operating expenses		(668)	(650)
Operating profit		732	550
Net interest payable	1	(45)	(30)
Profit before tax		687	520
Tax		(180)	(91)
Profit for the year		507	429

Statement of changes in equity (retained earnings only) for the year to 30 June

	2013 £000	2012 £000
Balance at 30 June 2012 (2011)	861	452
Profit for the year	507	429
Dividends paid	(40)	(20)
Balance at 30 June 2013 (2012)	1,328	861

Statements of financial position as at 30 June

	Notes	2013 £000	2012 £000
Non-current assets			
Intangible assets		200	200
Property, plant & equipment		1,400	1,100
		1,600	1,300
Current assets			
Inventory		400	350
Accounts receivable	2	1,825	1,721
Cash		3	120
Current liabilities	3	(1640)	(1,790)
Net current assets		588	401
Total assets less current liabilities		2,188	1,701
Non-current liabilities			
12% debentures		(250)	(250)
Provision for liabilities and charges	4	(40)	(20)
Total net assets		1,898	1,431
Equity and reserves			
Share capital		450	450
Share premium		120	120
Retained earnings		1,328	861
		1,898	1,431

Notes to the accounts

Note 1: interest

Payable on overdrafts and other loans	17	10
Payable on debentures	30	30
Receivable on short-term deposits	(2)	(10)
	45	30

BASIC

INTERMEDIATE

ADVANCED

Note 2: accounts receivable

Amounts falling due within one year		
Trade receivables	1,590	1,537
Prepayments	190	90
	1,780	1,627
Amounts falling due after one year		
Trade receivables	25	80
Prepayments	20	14
	45	94
Total receivables	1,825	1,721

Note 3: payables

Trade payables	1,200	1,090
Accruals	141	560
Taxation	210	75
Other taxes	89	65
	1,640	1,790

Note 4: provisions for liabilities and charges

Deferred tax	40	20

When analysing the financial performance of an organization it is rarely possible to produce a good analysis without making use of the notes to the accounts in addition to the statement of comprehensive income and the statement of financial position. Ratios will give a better analysis if the numbers used in them are meaningful.

Profitability ratios

The most commonly calculated ratios that consider the profitability and trading activities of an organization are:

- return on capital employed (ROCE)
- return on equity (ROE)
- net profit margin
- asset turnover
- gross margin.

Return on capital employed (ROCE)

Return on capital employed (ROCE) measures the return made by the organization from using its capital resources. This is sometimes referred to as the primary ratio and gives an indication of how efficient the organization is at generating profits from its capital. It is calculated by:

$$\frac{\text{Profit before interest and taxation (PBIT)}}{\text{Capital employed}} \times 100 \%$$

Capital employed refers to the funds provided by shareholders and long-term lenders. It will include provision for liabilities and charges as these are essentially long-term debt, and also non-controlling interests. It can be measured from both sides of the statement of financial position, viz:

Total assets less current liabilities

or

Share capital + reserves + creditors (due more than 1 year) + non-controlling interests + provisions for liabilities and charges.

For Choclatier Ltd, in the above example, the ROCE will be calculated as follows:

2013	2012
$\frac{£732}{£2,188} \times 100$	$\frac{£550}{£1,701} \times 100$
33%	32%

These figures indicate that an investment in this organization gives a higher return than that available from, say, a deposit account. So from that point of view these ratios are good. However, one major problem with ROCE is that it is particularly sensitive to the valuation of the non-current assets of the organization. A company that does not revalue assets on a regular basis will show a high ROCE. If the assets were to be shown at market value (assuming it is higher than original cost) then the ROCE will fall. It is important when making comparisons therefore to adjust for any differences in valuation policies.

A question which often arises is whether the bank overdraft of a company is being used to partly finance its long-term activities. If so, then it ought to be included as part of capital employed.

As well as looking at the movement from previous years and comparing it with other organizations, the analyst may compare the calculated ROCE with commercial bank deposit rates. If the ROCE is higher than these rates, then the company is making a better return from trading than it would have had it (theoretically) invested its capital in deposit accounts.

Overall, ROCE will be improved by reducing costs and increasing sales, which will improve the PBIT part of the ratio.

In terms of how useful the measure is, it should be noted that:

- if the return is low, then it may be wiped out if there is a downturn in the fortunes of the company or in the economy
- in terms of the cost of borrowing, if ROCE is lower then any increase in borrowing will reduce earnings per share (EPS)
- it can be a useful guide in assessing possible acquisitions; if potential ROCE is not good, then it would not be a good idea to go ahead with the acquisition
- any persistent low ROCE for any part of a business may suggest it should be disposed of (provided it is not an integral part of the business).

It is useful to note the effect on the ratio of acquiring a new subsidiary. In accordance with acquisition accounting, the total assets of subsidiary will be included but only profits since date of acquisition (post-acquisition) will be included. In a year in which an acquisition is made, ROCE may fall.

Return on equity (ROE)

Return on equity (ROE) is similar to ROCE but considers the profit made by the company in relation to the capital contributed by shareholders. Note that the long-term debt and the costs associated with this are excluded. The ratio is calculated as follows:

$$\frac{\text{Profit after interest but before tax}}{\text{Shareholders' funds}} \times 100$$

For Choclatier, the ratio is as follows:

2013	2012
$\dfrac{£687}{£1,898} \times 100$	$\dfrac{£520}{£1,431} \times 100$
36%	36%

Shareholders in this instance should be satisfied with what appears to be a healthy return on their invested capital. However, it would be necessary to compare with similar ratios from competitors and the industry average to determine whether or not this ROE is as healthy as it appears.

Net profit margin

Net profit margin simply considers PBIT as a percentage of sales and is calculated as follows:

$$\frac{\text{PBIT(profit before interest and tax)}}{\text{Sales}} \times 100$$

Generally, low margins show poor performance, but care needs to be taken in interpreting this, since low margins:

- may be set by management to increase market share
- may be caused by expansion costs (new product launching).

On the other hand, high margins show good performance, but may mean that the company will attract competition.

Note that the trading profit margins are important since both management and investment analysts tend to base their forecasts of future profitability on projected turnover multiplied by estimated future margins.

For Choclatier, net profit margin is as follows:

2013	2012
$\dfrac{£732}{£6,200} \times 100$	$\dfrac{£550}{£5,800} \times 100$
$= \underline{11.8\%}$	$\underline{10\%}$

Asset turnover

Before interpreting the net profit margin ratio is it important also to calculate the asset turnover ratio. Asset turnover is calculated as:

$$\frac{\text{Turnover}}{\text{Capital employed}}$$

The answer this time is not a percentage, but the number of times turnover exceeds capital employed. This ratio provides useful information about the efficiency of the company at generating sales from its capital. However, it is important to examine the underlying causes of any change in this ratio. For example, any increase in asset turnover may be due to various factors, such as:

- *An increase in sales*: if so, then this is acceptable since the company will be generating a higher turnover so using the asset base efficiently.
- *A reduction in capital employed* will increase asset turnover, but this would not be acceptable since this would imply a failure by the company to maintain its asset base, so there may be problems arising in the future.
- *A drop in inventory level*: again this would not be a good indicator of financial health.

In addition to this it is important to watch out for signs of overtrading. Overtrading occurs when a business expands too rapidly on an insufficient capital base. More on this later.

The current ratio of Choclatier is calculated as follows:

	2013	2012
CA : CL	£2,183 : £1,640	£2,097 : £1,790
=	1.33 : 1	1.17 : 1

Receivables due after one year have been excluded.

The figures show that the current ratio of Choclatier appears to be reasonable. The ratio has increased from 1.17 to 1.33, but this hides the fact that the company has considerably less cash in 2013 than in 2012, as is apparent from the statement of financial position.

Quick assets ratio

Not all current assets are readily converted into cash to meet debts (e.g. stock and work in progress may take time to convert into cash). The quick assets ratio, sometimes called the 'acid test' or 'liquidity ratio', recognizes this, eliminates inventory and applies the 'acid test' to see what would happen if the company had to settle all its creditors straight away. If the current ratio is less than 1 : 1 it would not be able to do so.

The quick assets ratio is calculated as follows:

current assets less inventory : current liabilities

Some companies which normally sell for cash (e.g. supermarkets), may operate with a quick ratio of less than 1 : 1. In fact some supermarket chains have a liquidity ratio of around 0.15 : 1. It is also worth noting that neither the current ratio nor the liquidity ratio takes, into account any overdraft limit the company may have. The fact that the organization can have access to liquid funds (not apparent from the statement of financial position) can significantly change the overall view of the liquidity of the organization.

However, there are problems indicated if the ratio is poorer when compared to other companies or if there is a declining trend in the ratio. A low and declining ratio often indicates a rising overdraft, so it is important to consider the bank's position.

As far as Choclatier is concerned, the liquid ratio is:

	2013	2012
CA – Inventory : CL	£1,783 : £1,640	£1,747 : £1,790
=	1.09 : 1	0.98 : 1

As with the current ratio, there is nothing to suggest that there are any problems with liquidity.

If there are liquidity problems it would be important for the analyst to examine the statement of cash flows. This statement would let the analyst see if there are any potential problems with the movement of cash.

While the statement of cash flows might highlight a deteriorating cash situation, it still does not tell the analyst how near the company is to its overdraft limit. Nor does it give any indication of whether any of the borrowing agreements have been broken or whether the bank is happy with the situation. There is some further discussion of the statement of cash flows in the advanced section of this chapter.

Activity ratios

Activity ratios are designed to provide some information about the efficiency with which management controls the business. The ratios that are considered most helpful are:

- inventory turnover
- trade receivables collection period
- trade payables payment period.

Inventory turnover

The inventory turnover ratio calculates how quickly the company is turning over its inventory during the year. This can give an indication of slow-moving inventories, or how efficient the inventory control policy of the company is. The ratio is calculated as follows:

$$\frac{\text{Cost of sales}}{\text{Average inventory}}$$

It is better to use the average inventory figure for this ratio, but the year-end figure would be acceptable. Again different industries will show different numbers for inventory turnover. For example, a company in heavy engineering may have a inventory turnover of 1, whereas a company in the retail industry may have a inventory turnover of 10.

Again it is the trend in the number that is important. A decrease in the ratio may highlight a slowdown in trading or a build-up in the levels of inventory, which would indicate that too much money may be tied up in inventory.

As an alternative to the rate of inventory turnover, it is possible to calculate the number of days inventory is held for i.e. the inventory holding period. This is done as follows:

$$\text{Inventory holding period in days} = \frac{\text{Average inventory}}{\text{Cost of sales}} \times 365$$

Adding together the number of trade receivable days and inventory holding period days gives an indication of how long it takes the company to convert inventory into cash. A continual increase in this number could indicate liquidity problems.

Inventory turnover of Choclatier:

2013	2012
£4,800	£4,600
£400	£350
= 12 times	13 times

Inventory turnover has fallen from 13 to 12, which may be as a result of a slowdown in demand for the product. It is important to monitor the trend in this because, if the ratio continues to fall, this would be an indication of serious problems for the company.

Trade receivables collection period

The trade receivables collection period ratio measures how effective the business is in collecting its debts. The ratio is a measure of how many days' credit customers are taking to pay. It is calculated as follows:

$$\text{Trade receivables collection period (in days)} = \frac{\text{Accounts receivable}}{\text{Credit sales}} \times 365$$

In calculating this ratio, problems can arise in what should be included – for example:

- Should the average or year-end receivables be used?
- Should credit sales or total sales be used?
- Should total receivables be used, or only those due within one year?

As before, it is the trend that is important here. If the ratio is seen to be continually increasing over time, this could be an indication of a problem with credit control and with bad debts. On the other hand, a falling collection period is generally a good sign, but could reflect a shortage of cash and may be as a result of trade receivables being pressured to pay or extra discounts being given for prompt payment.

Other factors to consider when interpreting this ratio are as follows:

■ What is the composition of trade receivables? Is there an undue proportion of debt due from one major customer? If so, what would happen if this customer had problems paying?
■ What would be the impact on trade receivables if one or two of the customers failed to pay?
■ What is the age pattern of trade receivables? How long have some of the debts been outstanding?
■ Is there adequate provision for bad and doubtful receivables?

Trade receivables collection period for Choclatier:

2013	2012
$\dfrac{£1,615}{£6,200} \times 365$	$\dfrac{£1,617}{£5,800} \times 365$
$= 95\,\text{days}$	$102\,\text{days}$

This ratio includes long-term receivables.

If the long-term receivables were excluded, the collection period still appears to be rather high (although this needs to be compared to the industry as a whole). The 2013 figure is better than the previous year's, but there is still an indication of poor credit control. It may also mean that there are significant bad debts, but this is not apparent from the financial information.

It is sometimes helpful to see how much cash could be released if the collection period was reduced. So if the company reduced the collection period from 95 days to, say, 70 days, how much cash would be released? The trade receivable collection period figure is reduced by 25 days. The value of one day's sales is calculated by dividing the year-end receivables of £1,615 by 95. So the value of 25 days' sales is:

$$\frac{£1,615}{95} \times 25 = £425$$

So Choclatier could release approximately £425,000 if it reduced the collection period from 95 days to 70 days.

Trade payables payment period

The trade payables payment period (or payment period taken) ratio calculates how many days credit the business is taking from suppliers. This ratio is calculated as follows:

$$\frac{\text{Trade payables}}{\text{Credit purchases}} \times 365$$

The figure for credit purchases is often difficult to obtain and the cost of sales figure is often used as a substitute.

As has been stated before, it is the trend in the ratio that is important. A steady increase in the ratio may highlight the fact that the company is making better use of interest-free credit, or it could be that the business has no cash to pay its suppliers. It just might mean that the business is taking longer to pay its suppliers, which may damage its credit standing.

Trade payables payment period of Choclatier:

2013	2012
$\dfrac{£1,200}{£4,800} \times 365$	$\dfrac{£1,090}{£4,600} \times 365$
$= 91\,\text{days}$	$86\,\text{days}$

Given that the cost of sales has been used for this calculation, the ratio is only approximate. Note that the company is taking longer to collect debts than it is to pay debts. This means the company is a net provider of funds: not good working capital management. It would also help to quantify any changes in cash terms (as was the case with the receivables).

Risk ratios

In general, shareholders and lenders will be interested in those ratios that provide a measure of risk. If a company if financed partly by borrowing, it will be exposed to a degree of risk. The higher the borrowing the higher will be the exposure to risk. This is because interest must be paid whether or not a company has made profits. The ratios considered most useful in this connection are:

- gearing ratio, and
- interest cover.

Gearing ratio

Gearing is concerned with the capital structure of the company and has been defined in a number of ways. The intention of gearing is to show what proportion of the assets of the company has been financed by lenders rather than shareholders.

There are different ways of calculating the gearing ratio, but they all measure the proportion of capital employed that is borrowed. The problem is in defining what is meant by 'capital employed' and what is meant by 'borrowing'. There are two generally accepted ways of measuring gearing:

1. **Debt/equity:**

   Debt   Interest-bearing loans + preference share capital (include short-term borrowing where interest is payable, e.g. bank overdraft)

   Equity   Ordinary shareholders' funds (i.e. share capital + reserves + non-controlling interests)

2. **Debt/capital employed:**

   Debt is same as in (1) above

   Capital employed   Shareholders' funds + non-controlling interests + provisions + all long- and short-term borrowing + preference shares (if redeemable)

In both of the above definitions, preference shareholders have essentially been classified as debt rather than equity. Strictly speaking, preference shareholders are not really debt. However, the holders of preference shares do have a prior claim on the profits and net assets of the company over the ordinary shareholder. Preference shares are therefore included in order to show the risks the ordinary shareholders are exposed to.

Which is the better measure? 'It depends' would be the obvious answer. The debt/equity ratio is a more sensitive measure of gearing. That said, high gearing is risky, while low gearing may provide scope to increase borrowing. The higher the level of gearing, the greater the risk that there will not be enough profits available for dividend payments to shareholders. In addition, the more highly geared a company is, the more sensitive it is to changes in interest rates. If interest rates increase, then highly geared companies will have a higher interest charge to pay, and so profits may suffer. However, the converse is also true. If interest rates fall, then profits of a highly geared company will improve and so shareholders will gain.

Also, in periods of profit fluctuation, a highly geared company will experience a much greater impact with regard to this. Consider the following example.

Example: gearing effect

The capital structure of two companies, A and B, is given as:

	Company A	Company B
	£	£
Share capital	600	200
Reserves	300	300
	900	500
Long-term borrowing (10%)	100	500
	1,000	1,000

Gearing ratios:

(a) Debt/equity

$$\frac{£100}{£900} \times 100 \qquad \frac{£500}{£500} \times 100$$

$$\underline{11\%} \qquad \underline{100\%}$$

(b) Debt/capital employed

$$\frac{£100}{£1,000} \times \qquad \frac{£500}{£1,000} \times 100$$

$$\underline{10\%} \qquad \underline{50\%}$$

Company A would be a low-geared company, while company B is a high-geared company. A further analysis of Company A shows the following statements of comprehensive income for two years:

	Year 1	Year 2
Profit (before interest)	£100	£80
Interest	£10	£10
	£90	£70
Less taxation (assume 30%)	£27	£21
	£63	£49

This shows that, when profits fall from £100 to £80 (20%), the profit after taxation is only marginally affected: falls from £63 to £49 (22%). However, the situation as far as company B is concerned is more dramatic.

Company B:

	Year 1	Year 2
Profit (before interest)	£100	£80
Interest	£50	£50
	£50	£30
Less taxation (assume 30%)	£15	£9
	£35	£21

This time, when profit drops by 20%, profit after taxation falls by 40% (£35 to £21).

The converse of this is also true. If profits increase from £80 to £100 a similar effect is seen. For company A, the increase in profit is 25% (£80 to £100), while the increase in profit after taxation is 28%. For company B, the effect is more dramatic. Profits go up to 25% as before, but profit after taxation rises by 66% (£21 to £35).

There is no one particular level of gearing that is deemed to be 'risky', and high gearing is not necessarily bad. As long as the company is generating sufficient and increasing profits, and will be able to meet interest costs, then a highly geared company will survive. The danger for highly geared companies arises when profits start to decline, as is seen in the example above.

For Choclatier:

	2013	2012
Debt/equity	$\dfrac{£250}{£1,898} \times 100$	$\dfrac{£250}{£1,431} \times 100$
	13.1%	17.5%
Debt/capital employed	$\dfrac{£250}{£2,188} \times 100$	$\dfrac{£250}{£1,707} \times 100$
	11.4%	14.6%

These figures show a relatively low level of borrowing, so clearly Choclatier is not exposed to a high level of risk. If the company wished to borrow more for expansion, it looks as though this would be easy to do.

Interest cover

This ratio shows how many times the company can pay its interest charges. In other words, how much the profits of the company can fall before the interest payments are threatened. This ratio is of particular interest to the providers of loans. A high figure for interest cover indicates that lenders are in are in a secure position and that the company's profits could fall substantially before there was any concern as to whether interest payments would not be met. **Interest cover** is calculated as follows:

$$\frac{\text{Profit before interest and tax}}{\text{Interest}} = \text{number of times}$$

The ideal level of cover depends on the current economic climate of a country. If economic conditions are tight, then interest cover should be higher than when the economy is stable or in a state of growth.

For Choclatier:

		2013	2012
Interest cover	=	$\dfrac{£732}{£47}$	$\dfrac{£550}{£40}$
		15.6 times	13.8 times

These figures show that Choclatier is exposed to very little risk. The interest cover is good, showing that it can easily afford the interest charges.

Complete analysis of Choclatier

The ratios calculated above for Choclatier can now be summarized (Table 13.1):

When the above ratios are reviewed together it allows the analyst to build up a picture of the main strengths and weaknesses of a company. It is important to realize that the ratios interlink and any conclusion reached should take all the relevant ratios into account.

However, before reaching any conclusions it is import to remember that these ratios have been calculated for only two years, therefore it is not possible to determine whether the movement indicated is part of an overall trend or whether it is a one-off movement. Further details to support the conclusions may be available from other sources of information. There are no industry averages given.

Overall summary of Choclatier

The company appears to be in a fairly healthy state. Shareholders are getting a good return on their investment when compared with commercial borrowing rates. Is this a fair reflection? Perhaps not, since the non-current assets of the company may still be stated at historic cost. This will have had a positive impact on ROCE and ROE. Further investigation is required on this point.

BASIC

INTERMEDIATE

ADVANCED

Table 13.1 **Summary of ratios for Choclatiers**

Ratio	2013	2012
ROCE	33%	32%
ROE	36%	36%
Net profit margin	12%	10%
Asset turnover	2.83 times	3.41 times
Gross margin	23%	21%
Current ratio	1.33 : 1	1.17 : 1
Quick assets ratio	1.09 : 1	0.98 : 1
Trade receivables collection period (days)	95 days	102 days
Trade payables payment period (days)	91 days	86 days
Inventory turnover	12 times	13 times
Debt/equity	13%	17%
Debt/capital employed	11%	15%
Interest cover	15.6 times	13.8 times

Profitability is strong and looks to be improving. The company has only a small amount of long-term debt, so interest payments are not a problem. However, the increase in profitability has led to a relative fall in asset turnover, indicating that the company is less efficient at generating sales. In addition to this, inventory turnover has fallen. This fall may be due to price increases. The ratios show that the movement in the numbers is small, but indicate that this needs to be monitored in the future.

Working capital is one area causing concern. The trade receivables collection period appears to be high and, given the length of the trade payables payment period, the company is a net provider of funds, albeit only just. In general, this is not good working capital management and this area requires further scrutiny since the proper management of working capital is fundamental to any organization. Profits are good, however, and the company would be able to cope with any bad debts that may arise.

In conclusion, profits, liquidity and gearing appear to be good, but the company needs to reassess its management of working capital.

Progress Point 13.3

Scamp Ltd had traded profitably for a number of years in the electronic component industry. Recently the bank overdraft has been steadily rising and Scamp is becoming concerned. The bank has contacted the company and has requested that the overdraft be reduced in the short term. The following summarized income statements and balance sheets have been give for the past three years.

Statements of comprehensive income for the year ending 31 March			
	2011	2012	2013
	£000	£000	£000
Sales	3,825	4,100	4,550

Cost of sales	2,563	2,788	3,185
Gross profit	1,262	1,312	1,365
Admin expenses	450	495	545
Distribution expenses	150	160	178
Interest payable	80	105	140
	680	760	863
Profit before taxation	582	552	502
Taxation	232	222	200
Profit for the year	350	330	302

Statement of changes in equity (retained earnings only)
for the year ended 31 March

	2011	2012	2013
	£000	£000	£000
Balance at 31 March	310	610	890
Profit for the year	350	330	302
Dividends paid	(50)	(50)	(60)
Balance at 31 March	610	890	1,132

Statements of financial position
as at 31 March

	2011	2012	2013
	£000	£000	£000
Land and buildings	300	293	286
Plant and machinery	600	690	750
	900	983	1,036
Current assets			
Inventory	700	850	1,100
Trade receivables	740	920	1,105
Cash	20	30	35
	1,460	1,800	2,240
Current liabilities			
Trade payables	400	415	425
Bank overdraft	720	828	1,019
Other creditors (including taxation)	220	230	250
	1,340	1,473	1,694
Net current assets	120	327	546
Deferred taxation	(110)	(120)	(150)
	910	1,190	1,432
Equity and reserves			
Share capital	300	300	300
Retained earnings	610	890	1,132
	910	1,190	1,432

The following additional information is also available.

1. The current market value of the property is £800,000.
2. The bank overdraft is secured over the assets of the company.
3. To increase capacity a new machine will be required. This machine will cost £200,000.

Required

(a) Using appropriate accounting ratios, explain why the liquidity position has deteriorated.
(b) Outline what corrective action, if any, the company can take.
(c) What alternative sources of finance should be considered?

Solution

Ratio/trend	2011	2012	2013
Sales growth (2011 = 100)	100	107	119
Profit growth (2011 = 100)	100	93	81
ROCE	$\dfrac{(£582 + £80)}{£1,020} \times 100$	$\dfrac{(£552 + £105)}{£1,190} \times 100$	$\dfrac{(£502 + £140)}{£1,432} \times 100$
	65%	50%	41%
Gross profit/sales	$\dfrac{£1,262}{£3,825} \times 100$	$\dfrac{£1,312}{£4,100} \times 100$	$\dfrac{£1,365}{£4,550} \times 100$
	33%	32%	30%
Profit margin	$\dfrac{£300}{£3,825} \times 100$	$\dfrac{£280}{£4,100} \times 100$	$\dfrac{£242}{£4,550} \times 100$
	8%	7%	5%
Inventory turnover	$\dfrac{£2,563}{£700}$	$\dfrac{£2,788}{£850}$	$\dfrac{£3,185}{£1,100}$
	3.7 times	3.3 times	2.9 times
Receivables collection period	$\dfrac{£740}{£3,825} \times 365$	$\dfrac{£920}{£4,100} \times 365$	$\dfrac{£1,105}{£4,550} \times 365$
	71 days	81 days	89 days
Payable days	$\dfrac{£400}{£2,563} \times 365$	$\dfrac{£415}{£2,788} \times 365$	$\dfrac{£425}{£3,185} \times 365$
	57 days	54 days	48 days
Working capital	£1,460 : £1,340	£1,800 : £1,473	£2,240 : £1,694
	1.09 : 1	1.22 : 1	1.32 : 1
Quick asset ratio	£760 : £1,340	£950 · £1,473	£1,140 · £1,694
	0.57 : 1	0.64 : 1	0.67 : 1
Debt/equity	$\dfrac{£720}{£920} \times 100$	$\dfrac{£828}{£1,190} \times 100$	$\dfrac{£1,091}{£1,432} \times 100$
	78%	70%	71%

Summary of current situation (based on the information given in the table above)

Over the three-year period, sales have increased by 19%. Profitability has fallen over the same period. ROCE has dropped from 65% to 41%. Gross profit margin has fallen by 3%, from 33% to 30%, over the three-year period, while administration and distribution costs are running at around 16% of sales. Net profit margin has declined, also perhaps indicating that operating costs need to be more actively controlled.

Profit before taxation and the retained profit have been steadily declining over the period. Efficiency of operations, as measured by activity ratios, has also been deteriorating. This reinforces the reduction in profitability.

Inventory turnover has fallen from 3.7 times to 2.9 times, meaning that inventory held at the end of March 2013 represented over four months' cost of sales. Given that the weekly cost of sales averages around £61,000, a reduction in stock turnover of 4 would release cash of around £300,000.

Control of trade receivables has also deteriorated from 71 days, sales outstanding to 89 days. This level is fairly high and therefore unacceptable. With sales at just under £90,000 a week, stricter control of receivables, reducing them to the 2011 level, would release £220,000, and a reduction to 70 days would release £230,000 for use elsewhere in the business.

Trade payables are currently being paid earlier: in 48 days rather than 57 days. This may be due in part to suppliers suspecting that the company has cash flow problems and therefore pushing to get paid. An alternative explanation could simply be lack of control in the company because the bank has not been limiting its funding.

The current liquidity position as indicated by the current and quick ratios is static but showing a gradual improvement. It does, however, reflect increasing inventories and receivables being financed by an increasing overdraft.

The gearing of the company has decreased over the period and currently stands at a ratio of debt/equity of 71%. If the revaluation of the premises were to be incorporated in the books, then the gearing would be lowered to 52%.

Corrective action

Over the next few months it would be helpful if the company could:

- start an aggressive marketing policy to sell surplus inventory
- improve inventory control procedures and increase inventory turnover to four times a year (i.e. maintain three months' inventory levels)
- improve control of trade receivables and bring the average amount outstanding to 70 days over time, and in the longer term aim for a lower level
- enter into a discussion with the bank with a view to reducing the overdraft.

Other ratios

The ratios used up to now provide an overall picture of how the company is performing, and will be of use to a wide variety of interested parties. However, it may be that some groups – for example, shareholders and potential shareholders – will be more interested in other aspects of the business and will be concerned about their investment. The following additional investment ratios will be of use to a shareholder or potential shareholder.

Shareholder ratios

A potential shareholder in a company will be interested in both the security of any investment and in the return such an investment gives. In addition to the ratios previously mentioned, particularly those looking at profitability and risk, a potential shareholder will be interested in:

- earnings per share
- price/earnings ratio

- earnings yield
- dividend cover
- dividend yield.

Earnings per share (EPS)

This ratio shows how much of the profit left over is available to the ordinary shareholder. Earnings per share (EPS) is a measure of a company's profitability and of the company's ability to pay dividends. It is calculated as:

$$\frac{\text{Profit after tax and preference dividends}}{\text{Number of ordinary shares in issue}}$$

The calculation of earnings per share can be more complicated if, for example, the company issues some new shares during the year, or when other financial instruments such as debentures can be converted into ordinary shares.

This is a very important ratio, frequently used as an indicator of performance, and its importance is recognized by the fact that companies are required to present their EPS figure in the statement of comprehensive income.

Price/earnings ratio (PER)

The price/earnings ratio (PER) is a measure of how the stock market rates the company. This ratio is calculated as:

$$\frac{\text{Market price per ordinary share}}{\text{Basic earnings per share}}$$

The ratio indicates how many times' the earnings an investor is prepared to pay to buy a share. The price/earnings ratio that can be expected generally depends on four things:

1. overall level of the stock market
2. the industry in which the company operates
3. the company's record
4. how the market views the company's prospects.

In general terms, the higher the PER, the more valuable the earnings of the company. At first, this might seem to be counter-intuitive as one might expect that a share with a low P/E ratio would be regarded as an attractive investment i.e. the share price would be nearer the earnings per share and would therefore appear to reflect 'value'. However, because EPS is a measure of past performance and the market price of a share reflects the stock market's expectations of a company's future performance, a high P/E ratio is seen as an indication that the market expects the company to perform well in the future.

Earnings yield

The earnings yield ratio is simply the inverse of the PER and shows earnings per unit of the company's share price. This is calculated as follows:

$$\text{Earnings yield} = \frac{1}{\text{PER}} = \frac{\text{Earnings per share}}{\text{Share prices}}$$

Dividend cover

The dividend cover is a measure of how many times the dividends actually paid are covered by the profits that were available for distribution to shareholders.

$$\text{Dividend cover} = \frac{\text{Profit after tax and preference dividend}}{\text{Dividends paid}}$$

Dividend cover is an important indicator for a potential investor. It indicates what size of dividend an investor might expect to receive given a specific level of company profits. Alternatively, it indicates how far earnings would have to fall before the dividend paid by the company would be reduced.

A high dividend cover indicates that, relative to the potential for paying dividends, a company is retaining a substantial part of its profits. This may not be popular with the ordinary shareholders but would indicate that the company has sufficient funds with which to pay the dividends from. A low dividend cover could signal that a company may have difficulty in maintaining an acceptable level of dividend.

Dividend yield

The dividend yield measures the annual return received by way of a dividend as a percentage of the current share price. It must be remembered that this is not a measure of the total return of the shareholder because it does not take account of the growth in the value of shares. Also, it is based on the current share price, which may not be the same as the price paid by the shareholder to acquire the share. The ratio is calculated as follows:

$$\text{Dividend yield} = \frac{\text{Dividend per share}}{\text{Share price}} \times 100$$

The ratios given are some of the main ratios that are useful in the interpretation of the financial statements of a company. This list is neither definitive nor exhaustive. Other ratios may be used – for example, sales per employee or sales per square metre. What is important is that ratios are not calculated just for the sake of calculating them, so make sure there is a purpose behind the calculation of any ratio you use.

Progress Point 13.4

A company has issued share capital of £100,000 comprising 100,000 ordinary shares of £1 each. The company has a profit after tax of £15,000 and pays a dividend of 10% of its ordinary share capital. The market price of the company's shares is £1.50.

Required
Calculate the

(a) earnings per share
(b) dividend yield
(c) the price/earnings ratio.

Solution

(a) Earnings per share $= \dfrac{\text{profit attributable to ordinary shareholders}}{\text{number of ordinary shares in issue}}$

$\qquad\qquad\qquad\quad = \dfrac{\pounds15,000}{100,00}$

$\qquad\qquad\qquad\quad = \underline{\pounds0.15}$

(b) Dividend yield $= \dfrac{\text{dividend per share}}{\text{share price}} \times$

$\qquad\qquad\qquad = \dfrac{\pounds1 \times 10\%}{1.50}$

$\qquad\qquad\qquad = \underline{6.67\%}$

(c) Price/earnings ratio $= \dfrac{\text{market price per ordinary share}}{\text{earnings per share}}$

$\qquad\qquad\qquad\quad = \dfrac{\pounds1.50\%}{\pounds0.15}$

$\qquad\qquad\qquad\quad = \underline{\underline{10}}$

BASIC

INTERMEDIATE

ADVANCED

Limitations of ratio analysis

Having spent the bulk of the chapter explaining and defining ratios, it is important to remember that ratio analysis needs to be used with care. It does not provide all the answers. What ratio analysis does is to highlight areas within an organization that require further investigation. Ratios do have limitations and these need to be taken into consideration when using ratio analysis.

- Ratios use statement of financial position information only applicable at the end of the reporting period. Any seasonal factors may be missed altogether.

- The figures contained in financial statements themselves can contain certain assumptions and estimates, which can be very subjective.

- Sometimes organizations manipulate the year-end financial statements to improve the appearance of the ratios.

- Accounting policies may differ between organizations, which can make comparisons difficult – for example, the treatment of development costs.

- Accounting standards, when introduced for the first time, can make comparisons with previous periods difficult. The ratios may have to be recalculated.

- Care needs to be exercised in order to take all other relevant factors into account when interpreting the ratios. If the organization, for example, has been the subject of a recent takeover then any cost reduction might be as a result of the takeover rather than an improvement in efficiency.

In addition to all this there are other sources of information contained within a company's financial statements that should always be taken into account. The sources of information available with which to assist in any analysis are numerous.

BASIC

INTERMEDIATE

ADVANCED

Progress Point 13.5

Company X and Company Y are similar-sized companies selling toys. Both companies have sales of £100,000 and both companies show a gross profit of 50%. In carrying out an analysis of the companies' inventory turnover ratios, you discover the following results:

Company X = 1.25 times   Company Y = 5 times

Required

(a) What is the average inventory held by each company?

(b) If they are similar companies, what could cause such a significant difference?

(c) What does this tell us about the use of ratios?

Solution

(a) $\text{Average inventory} = \dfrac{\text{Cost of sales}}{\text{rate of inventory turnover}}$ $\dfrac{50,000 \text{ X}}{1.25} = £40,000$ $\dfrac{50,000 \text{ Y}}{5} = £10,000$

(b) The calculations in (a) show that company X has average inventory of £40,000 while company Y has average inventory of only £10,000. This difference can be explained by the choice of year end adopted by each company. The companies both sell toys and consequently if Company X had a year end of say 31 October, it would likely have a high level of inventories in anticipation of the Christmas rush. If Company Y, on the other hand, had a year end of 31 January it would likely be carrying very low inventories after the Christmas sales.

(c) This tells us that ratios can be very misleading!

Internal sources of information

If the analysis is of a public limited company, there will be an annual report. This should be referred to, to provide information about the company's products, performance and capital investment strategy. A change in sales, for example, may be explained in the chairman's statement while the directors' report may give reasons for other significant changes that have been identified. The accounting policies notes may explain the reason for a change in results, while the notes to the financial statements can be used to provide greater detail on the summarized statement of comprehensive income and statement of financial position figures.

External sources of information

Benchmark information may be available from trade journals and published accounts of companies in the same industry sector. In addition, relevant information can be found in the finance sections of many newspapers and government statistics are also available. For more tailored information, it is possible to contact specialist agencies that sell industry-specific facts. There are numerous sources of inter-firm information but there are two main distinctions: there are those that gather their data from external published accounts and those that collect the data directly from surveyed companies on a strictly confidential basis.

Organizations that prepare inter-firm comparisons from external published accounts face all the limitations noted earlier associated with company accounts. There are, however, certain advantages of using such agencies: the scope of the comparison can be extremely wide and can include an analysis of any firm that produces published accounts. The quality of ratio analysis is improved because the survey organizations attempt to standardize the basis of every ratio in the survey, and the information can be accessed easily and at relatively low cost.

Data collected directly from member companies of the private inter-firm comparison scheme are usually available only to participating companies. The advantage of these schemes is that the data collected consist of a comprehensive analysis of every firm in the scheme and are more reliable due to there not being any statutory restrictions in place governing the content and presentation of the financial statement information. The disadvantages are that there are onerous requirements concerning the quality of information that companies contribute to private schemes, all information must comply with strict uniformity requirements, and it is relatively costly.

The information obtained from these internal and external sources would be used in conjunction with ratio analysis to explain further changes or results that the ratios themselves had identified.

13.4 Disclosure in practice

Logica gives the following five-year financial summary.

Five-year summary (unaudited)

The five-year financial summary below includes selected information on a calendar year basis, which has been extracted from audited financial statements.

Figure 13.1 Logica: five-year summary

	2007 £'m	2008 £'m	2009 £'m	2010 £'m	2011 £'m
Revenue	3,073.2	3,588.0	3,701.6	3,696.8	**3,921.3**
Adjusted operating profit[1]	207.6	267.4	272.3	271.9	**113.8**
Operating profit before goodwill amortisation/ impairment and exceptional items	132.9	178.7	183.8	212.3	**59.3**

Figure 13.1 (Continued)

Goodwill amortisation/impairment and exceptional items	(23.2)	(92.3)	(117.5)	(1.7)	**(4.8)**
Share of post-tax profits from associates	1.2	0.7	0.5	0.6	**1.0**
Net finance costs payable	(26.8)	(43.3)	(24.2)	(18.3)	**(22.8)**
Profit on ordinary activities before tax	84.1	43.8	42.6	192.9	**32.7**
Tax on profit on ordinary activities	(5.4)	(4.9)	(2.5)	(40.8)	**(5.5)**
Profit on ordinary activities after tax	78.7	38.9	40.1	152.1	**27.2**
Result from discontinued operation[2]	89.4	–	–	–	**–**
Non-controlling interests	1.8	(0.2)	–	–	**–**
Profit for the year attributable to ordinary shareholders	169.9	38.7	40.1	152.1	**27.2**
Closing number of employees from continuing operations	38,740	39,937	38,780	39,284	**41,784**
Turnover growth from continuing operations	27%	17%	3%	(0.1)%	**6.1%**
Adjusted operating margin from continuing operations[3]	6.8%	7.5%	7.4%	7.4%	**2.9%**
Adjusted basic earnings per share from continuing operations[4]	10.2p	12.3p	12.5p	12.3p	**4.5p**
Dividends per share[5]	5.80p	3.00p	3.30p	4.20p	**4.40p**

[1] Adjusted operating profit represented operating profit from continuing operations before amortisation of intangible assets initially recognised on acquisition and exceptional items. As disclosed in Note 3 to the consolidated financial statements restructuring programmes are no longer treated as exceptional items. The adjusted operating profit for prior years disclosed above has not been restated to reflect this change. Restructuring charges were £nil in 2007, £84.3 million in 2008, £95.1 million in 2009 and £nil in 2010. Adjusted operating profit under IFRSs is defined in Note 8 to the consolidated financial statements.

[2] For the year ended 31 December 2007, the result from discontinued operation represented the Telecoms Products operation, which was disposed on 18 June 2007.

[3] The adjusted operating margin is from continuing operations before exceptional items and amortisation of those intangible assets initially recognised at fair value in a business combination.

[4] Adjusted basic earnings per share under IFRSs is defined in Note 15 to consolidated financial statements.

[5] Dividends per share are presented according to the financial year to which they relate rather than the basis of recognition for accounting purposes.

Source: Logica (2011), p. 154

The main pieces of information in the five-year summary are clearly the revenue and profit items. Note that basic earnings per share is given as is the dividend per share. Also, the number of employees over the five-year period this has increased from nearly 39,000 to 42,000, clearly an indication of growth from the point of view of the company, and one that it would wish to highlight.

Section summary

Ratio analysis is a technique for the analysis and interpretation of company financial statements. It involves the compilation of accounting ratios to explain relationships within a firm over a number of years or to make comparisons with ratios produced for other businesses. The use of ratio analysis is limited to a certain extent by the limitations inherent in accounting data and the availability of benchmark figures against which ratios can be compared. Ratios are commonly grouped into profitability, liquidity, activity, risk and shareholder ratios. There are numerous sources of information available to users of financial statements to obtain information in a form suitable for specific needs.

Section 3: Advanced Aspects

In Chapter 10, statements of cash flows were shown to provide additional information showing cash inflows and outflows. In addition, such statements can be incorporated within ratio analysis to provide additional insights into the company's financial position.

13.5 Statement of cash flows: some further aspects

The statement of cash flows can also be used to derive accounting ratios. As before, the analysis should begin with a general overview and once the figures have been put in context, then ratios may be calculated to focus the user's attention on areas requiring further analysis. Such questions may be in relation to, for example, identifying future cash requirements.

A general concern may relate to when any existing borrowing will require to be repaid. On a more detailed level, the analysis may consider, for example, working capital requirements and the desire of a company to expand. This may involve the use of ratios to assist in analysing the cash requirements, and whether these can be met internally or from external sources.

A ratio that is calculated from the statement of cash flows is the cash flow ratio. It is calculated as follows:

$$\frac{\text{Total cash inflows}}{\text{Total cash outflows}}$$

A ratio greater than 1 indicates a net inflow of cash, while a ratio of less than 1 indicates a net outflow of cash.

Working capital requirements

In general, when a business expands, working capital will rise in line with the increase in turnover. In order to see the relationship between working capital and sales, it makes sense to use the working capital ratio, which is calculated as follows:

$$\frac{\text{Inventory} + \text{trade receivables} - \text{trade payables} \times 100}{\text{Sales}}$$

The answer is usually expressed as a percentage.

A company with a low working capital ratio will find it easier to expand than one with a high working capital ratio. In general terms, any business that can sell its goods before it has to pay for them will not need any additional working capital for expansion. Conversely, companies that have to carry large amounts of inventory will need additional working capital if they want to expand.

In addition, expenditure on non-current assets will be difficult to determine with any degree of accuracy unless the company discloses the information.

Increasing cash: possible solutions

What can a company do if the cash flow looks certain to be less than that required to meet these commitments? The following are some suggestions.

- Use its overdraft, but there would be problems if the overdraft was at its limit. As indicated above, there is no way of knowing this.
- Borrow more on a longer-term basis. Again the borrowing limits would need to be adhered to.
- If the company has investments it could sell these; or it may be able to sell some of the business activities. Care needs to be taken with this not to damage the business.
- Sell and lease back some of the properties of the business.
- Reduce capital expenditure.

- Tighten credit and inventory controls.
- Cut dividend payments.
- Sell more shares i.e. new issues.

If a company has a cash shortfall and does not take action, then it will inevitably go into an overtrading situation, which will cause a cash crisis, unless as a last resort, the company reduces its level of trading.

An important number derived from the statement of cash flows is what is known as free cash flow (FCF). This is the cash that is left over to spend once all the fixed commitments have been made. Fixed commitments include those items that must be paid, such as taxation and interest, and, to an extent, dividends. Although there is no legal requirement to pay a dividend, any company that cuts its dividend or does not pay a dividend without a very good reason is asking for trouble!

Working capital and overtrading

Working capital is defined as current assets less current liabilities. It is that part of the financing of a firm used to generate profits. Working capital is the life-blood of any business. The faster the working capital cycle can be made to operate, the faster profits will accumulate.

Problems can arise, however, where a business has too little working capital. Working capital may become depleted for several reasons, the most common of these being excessive dividends or drawings, or the purchase of non-current assets.

An expanding business may need to buy new equipment or premises to meet increased demand for its products or services. Unless a business has adequate reserves, it may have little working capital left if it has financed the purchase of non-current assets using working capital. Such an investment will remove some of the current assets into non-current assets and so have an impact on working capital.

As a result of this, the company may have to rely on extended trade credit in order to purchase goods for resale. If creditors demand payment, the only way to settle the debts may be to sell some of its non-current assets. The next step is likely to be bankruptcy as a business will not be able to function without its full complement of non-current assets. A business that tries to manage with inadequate working capital is said to be *overtrading*.

How, then, does the company expand?

Clearly, not every business will end up bankrupt if it tries to expand. If the fall in working capital caused by the purchase of non-current assets is quickly replaced by extra profits from increased trade then no problems ought to arise. Where a business grows steadily, this should not be problematic either. The danger comes when the expansion is too rapid and the working capital is inadequate to meet this rapid expansion.

The following example will help illustrate this point.

Example

Oakwood has the following statement of financial position at 31 December:

Non-current assets		£70,000
Current assets		
Inventory	£20,000	
Trade receivables	£40,000	
Bank	£20,000	
	£80,000	
Trade payables	£30,000	
Net current assets		£50,000
		£120,000

Issued share capital	£100,000
Retained earnings	£20,000
	£120,000

The working capital is £50,000 and the company makes profits of £15,000 per annum.

A competitor company has announced that it is to leave the market, which will enable Oakwood to double its profits – however, this will involve the purchase of a new storage facility costing £160,000. Oakwood requires an overdraft facility from the bank of £140,000 to supplement the cash it already has.

Non-current assets		£230,000
Current assets		
Inventory	£20,000	
Trade receivables	£40,000	
Bank	0	
	£60,000	
Trade payables	£30,000	
Bank overdraft	£140,000	
	£170,000	
Net current liabilities		£(110,000)
		£120,000
Issued share capital		£100,000
Retained earnings		£20,000
		£120,000

The statement of financial position would now be as follows:

The working capital is now minus £110,000. Current liabilities exceed current assets.

Oakwood now faces three potential problems.

1. Unless the bank overdraft can be increased further, the company will have to rely on extended trade credit to purchase additional inventories.
2. The working capital, which has been depleted, will be replaced only gradually as profits are earned and this is likely to take at least four years (i.e. $4 \times £30,000$ profits).
3. If inventory is not turned over quickly and cash generated to pay suppliers, then the company could be forced into liquidation.

This is of course an extreme example. It is unlikely that a bank would allow a company to use an overdraft to facilitate such an expansion. However, rapid expansion on a smaller scale is quite common, and unfortunately, so are the related problems when it is not financed correctly.

Expansion on such a scale is better financed by the use of long-term loans, the term length matched as far as possible with the length of time the company is likely to benefit from the use of the asset. Alternatively, the company could issue new shares.

BASIC

INTERMEDIATE

ADVANCED

Financed in this way, the working capital remains intact. Remember that working capital consists of current assets less current liabilities. Non-current assets, long-term loans and share capital do not form part of working capital. They are long-term assets and long-term sources of finance.

Indicators of financial distress

Broadly speaking, 'financial distress' describes the situation where a company is unable to meet its liabilities as they fall due.

A number of methods have been devised to give some indication of when a company is likely to become insolvent. Ratio analysis is one such method.

Ratio analysis

As has been seen earlier in this chapter, ratio analysis is often used to determine the financial health of a company. However, it can also be used to indicate any potential financial distress. If profitability and liquidity ratios are falling and management ratios show a reduction in efficiency, while at the same time the gearing ratios are increasing, then this may show early signs of trouble ahead. The company may not have long to survive. Ratio analysis, then, is a good first step in gauging the health of a company.

It is unlikely that the directors of a company will admit that the company is in trouble. Forecast information provided by directors will be of limited use in that they will be designed to show an improving position. The financial statements themselves will provide more robust information. By making good use of accounting ratios, financial statements will show the trends in profitability and in liquidity. However, when calculating ratios it is important to keep the following points in mind.

■ Have there been any significant changes in management recently? If the company has not been successful in the recent past, then it is unlikely that improvement will happen unless there is a change in management.

■ Has anything happened to the auditors? Have they been changed recently? If so, this may indicate a disagreement over some issue of reporting.

■ Is staff morale good? Employees will be concerned about their jobs if they sense that there a problems within the business.

■ As far as borrowing is concerned, does the management of the company match borrowings to assets acquired?

■ The creation of intangible assets or of a revaluation reserve may indicate that management is desperate to improve the appearance of the financial position of the business.

■ Is directors' remuneration realistic in terms of the company's performance?

Multivariate ratio analysis

The ratio analysis considered thus far in this chapter is of a 'univariate' type. That is, each ratio is considered separately and then all ratios, once calculated, are assessed together and a judgement made on the state of the company. In contrast, the technique known as 'multivariate' analysis combines several key ratios to produce a single index number. This number can then be compared to previous years, other companies and industrial averages. Multivariate analysis has been widely used in predicting corporate failure.

Z-score

One example of multivariate analysis is the 'Z-score' devised by Professor Edward Altman. This was developed back in 1968 as a way of overcoming some of the basic difficulties in using accounting ratios to predict the financial health of a company. The Z-score is calculated by adding together a number of ratios, with each ratio being weighted according to its usefulness as a predictor of financial failure. The weightings were arrived at as the result of research into the relative importance of each ratio to a company's survival.

The Z-score is calculated as follows:

$$Z = 1.2 \text{ (working capital/total assets)}$$

$$+ 1.4 \text{ (retained earnings/total assets)}$$

+ 3.3 (profit before interest and tax/total assets)

+ 0.6 (market capitalisation/book value of debts)

+ 1.0 (sales/total assets)

A score of 3.0 and above is considered to be a sign of a healthy company, whereas a score of less than 1.8 may mean that a company is heading for bankruptcy. The Z-score is used in practice by banks and other institutions for assessing the risk of their customers. There are some limitations of this model that need to be recognized:

■ There is no scientific proof of the model.
■ The information used in the model is historic.
■ Different companies may classify similar items in a different way.
■ There is no specified time-frame within which the company being assessed is deemed to be 'safe'.

A-score

A third method of predicting corporate failure is completely different from the above ratio-based methods. As such, it avoids the problems inherent in these methods.

A-scores concentrate on non-financial signs of failure and are based on the premise that financial difficulties are the direct result of management defects and errors which have existed in the company for many years.

The A-score uses a list of questions that have a specific score associated with them. A company could score up to 100 points, depending on the answers to the questions. A score of more than 25 is deemed to be bad, and may indicate that a company is heading for failure. The A-score questions are divided into three sections, concerned with defects, mistakes and symptoms. Defects deal with issues relating to reaction to change, management and accounting; mistakes deal with gearing and trading levels, while symptoms deal with the results of ratio analysis.

In order to calculate a company A-score, different scores are allocated to each defect, mistake and symptom according to their importance. The scores are then added and compared with the benchmark values. If companies achieve:

(i) an overall score of over 25; or
(ii) a defect score of over 10; or
(iii) a mistakes score of over 15,

then the company is demonstrating typical signs leading up to failure. Typically, companies not at risk will score well below 18, and companies which are at risk will score well over 25.

The scoring system attaches a weight to individual components within defects, mistakes and symptoms. By way of illustration, the weights applied within defects are as follows:

Defects in accountancy:	Weight
There are no budgets for budgetary control	3
There are no current cash flow plans	3
There is no costing system or product costs	3
There is a poor response to change	15

The use of the A-score is clearly highly subjective and it is difficult to rationalize either the weightings or the additive nature of the scoring system. Nevertheless, as has been a key benefit of ratio analysis, it is the identification of a defect or mistake that is important as this can in itself give direction to further investigation.

It is important to note that the use of the Z- and A-scores is not commonplace. The results of ratio analysis are more likely to guide accountants, together with general observations about the company – for example, the company not being able to pay its debts, not replacing equipment, staff leaving. The A-score is more like a 'scorecard' approach: in certain industries these are used to analyse company performance.

Section summary

There are various 'tools' and techniques available with which to analyse a company's financial statements. Horizontal analysis can be used to compare a company's performance over a period of time, while vertical analysis and the use of common-size statements can be used to compare companies of different sizes.

Ratio analysis helps to direct attention to areas of the business that need further investigation. Ratios can be compared against preceding period's ratios, budgeted ratios, ratios of other companies in the same industry and industry averages.

Unfortunately, the calculation of ratios is often hampered by the lack of uniformity and comparability of published financial statements.

Multivariate analysis attempts to combine ratios together into a single index number which is then used to judge a company's financial health.

Finally, we looked at the calculation of the A-score which concentrates on non-financial signs of corporate failure.

Chapter summary

Ratio analysis

- Ratio analysis is a very important tool that can be used by the stakeholders of a company to analyse the profitability, liquidity, management and risk of a company by using the information contained in its annual statements.

- It is possible to get a broad indication of the health of a company by doing a trend analysis and by using common-size statements. Using accounting ratios is also a good technique of analysis and there are a number of ratios that can be computed. These are described fully in the chapter.

- When computing ratios it is important to be consistent, to calculate those ratios that are relevant in the analysis, and to be aware of the limitations inherent in ratio analysis. In terms of specific ratios, bear in mind the following information.

ROCE

- Beware of revaluation of non-current assets, which has an adverse effect on ROCE. A revaluation will increase the denominator of the ratio, so the ratio itself will decrease. Note the use of the bank overdraft as a long-term source of finance and take care to include this in capital employed. It is important to analyse the movements in this ratio in terms of net profit margin and asset turnover.

Current ratio

- If the ratio is increasing then this may suggest poor working capital management, while if the ratio is deteriorating this may suggest liquidity problems.

- Trade receivable and payable days: these can be compared to establish whether the company is a net provider or recipient of funds.

Overall interpretation

- There is no ideal ratio. A better comparison is with the industry average and with the trend in ratios over time. It is not helpful to analyse each ratio in isolation, it is better to consider the ratios collectively to give a more complete picture.
- Ratios are generally useful as a guide in attempting to identify financial distress. They can be used in conjunction with the Z-score and the A-score, together with general observations about the company, in order to get a proper understanding of the future financial health of the company.

✓ Key terms for review

Definitions can be found in the glossary at the end of the book.

A-score	Gross margin	Ratio analysis
Asset turnover	Horizontal analysis	Return on capital employed (ROCE)
Current ratio	Interest cover	Return on equity (ROE)
Dividend cover	Inventory holding period	Trade receivables collection period
Dividend yield	Inventory turnover	Trade payables payment period
Earnings per share (EPS)	Net profit margin	Vertical analysis
Earnings yield	Price/earnings ratio (PER)	Z-score
Gearing ratio	Quick asset ratio	

? Review questions

1. Explain what is meant by the term *horizontal analysis*.
2. Explain what is meant by the term *vertical analysis*.
3. Explain whether the advantages of ratio analysis outweigh the disadvantages.
4. Explain the uses and limitations of ratio analysis when used to interpret the published financial statements of a company.
5. Identify and explain the ratios that provide information on performance for investors.
6. Explain why liquidity is important to a company.
7. Identify and explain the ratios that provide information on liquidity.
8. Identify and explain the ratios that provide information on profitability.
9. What methods have been devised to give indications of financial distress?
10. What sources of information outside the business are available to assist in the interpretation process?

✎ Exercises

Level I

1. The following are the summarized accounts of two companies for the year ended 31 October 2012.

Statement of financial position as at 31 October 2012

	£000	£000	£000	£000
Non-current assets		383		204
Current assets				
Inventory	156		36	
Trade receivables	120		72	
Bank	252		116	
	528		224	
Current liabilities				
Trade payables	191		137	
		337		87
		720		291
Non-current liability				
11% Loan (repayable 2018)		(220)		–
		500		291
Equity				
Ordinary Shares		300		140
Retained earnings		200		151
		500		291

Statement of comprehensive income

	Walker Ltd		Grant Ltd	
	£000	£000	£000	£000
Sales		1,080		1,080
Cost of Sales:				
Opening inventory	144		24	
Purchases	822		930	
	966		954	
Closing inventory		810		918
Gross profit		270		162
Expenses	155		72	
Interest	25		–	
Net profit		90		90

Required

(a) Compute the following for each company:

   Gross profit percentage

   Return on net assets

   Inventory turnover (times)

   Current ratio

   Acid test (liquid ratio)

   Trade receivables collection period (months)

   Trade payables payment period (months).

(b) Assuming that both companies sell similar products, discuss the relative performance of each.

2. The following are summarized financial statements of the two retailing concerns, Mason Ltd and Quinn Ltd, both of which deal in the same kind of goods in the same town. It is the policy of one concern to cut is prices and operate on a reduced gross profit margin in order to increase sales. The other concern, however, pays more attention to customer service and impressive shop layout.

Statements of comprehensive income

	Mason Ltd		Quinn Ltd	
	£	£	£	£
Sales		100,000		100,000
Opening inventory	16,000		4,000	
Purchases	78,000		75,000	
	94,000		79,000	
Closing inventory	24,000	70,000	6,000	73,000
Gross profit		30,000		27,000
Overhead expenses		23,700		21,240
Net profit		6,300		5,760

Statements of financial position

	Mason Ltd		Quinn Ltd	
Non-current assets		65,000		40,000
Current assets	24,000		6,000	
Trade receivables	8,500		2,125	
Bank	2,500		9,875	
	35,000		18,000	
Current liabilities	10,000		10,000	
Net current assets		25,000		8,000
Net assets		90,000		48,000
Issued share capital		40,000		40,000
Retained earnings		50,000		8,000
		90,000		48,000

Required

(a) Set out and complete a table in the following form:

	Mason Ltd	Quinn Ltd
Current ratio		
Liquid ratio		
Rate of inventory turnover		
Gross profit percentage		
Net profit percentage		
Return on capital employed		

(b) State the conclusions to be drawn from the above ratios taking account of what is already known about the two businesses.

Level II

3. Carousel Ltd has been trading for three years. The financial statements for the three years to 31 December 2012 are as follows:

Statements of comprehensive income for the years ended			
	31 Dec 2010	31 Dec 2011	31 Dec 2012
	£000	£000	£000
Turnover	300	320	480
Cost of sales	180	192	312
Gross profit	120	128	168
Overheads			
Wages	40	44	52
Rent, rates & insurance	16	16	16
Distribution costs	8	11	16
Miscellaneous expenses	12	12	12
Depreciation	8	8	12
	84	91	108
Operating profit	36	37	60

Statements of changes in equity (retained earnings only)			
	31 Dec 2010	31 Dec 2011	31 Dec 2012
Balance b/f	–	0	4
Profit for the year	36	37	60
Dividends paid	(36)	(33)	(48)
Balance c/f	0	4	16

Statements of financial position as at			
	31 Dec 2010	31 Dec 2011	31 Dec 2012
	£000	£000	£000
Non-current assets	88	92	80
Inventory	20	28	76

Trade receivables	24	26	56
Bank	4	–	–
	136	146	212
Trade payables	16	20	60
Bank overdraft	–	2	16
	16	22	76
Net Assets	120	124	136
Share capital (£1 shares)	120	120	120
Retained earnings	–	4	16
	120	124	136

Additional information

During the first two years, half of the sales were for cash and the other half on credit. In the third year however, credit sales amounted for two thirds of the total sales.

Required

(a) Compute the following for each of the three years

Gross profit percentage

Return on net assets

Rate of inventory turnover

Current ratio

Acid test (liquid ratio)

Trade receivables collection period (months)

Trade payables payment period using Cost of Sales (months)

(b) With reference to the ratios calculated in part (a) above, write a report analysing the financial position of the company over the three-year period.

4. Fastbru plc is a listed company. The principal business of the company is the manufacture and distribution of soft drinks. The company has been in operation for ten years but the major shareholders have become particularly concerned about the performance of the company over the last two years. At a recent meeting the board of directors of Fastbru adopted a short-term plan for recovery. The key elements of this plan were:

(i) to restructure the finances of the company by issuing more shares and reducing bank borrowing

(ii) to change the operating practices of the distribution network, which has relied on local depots holding inventories for distribution by local carriers to retailers.

The financial statements of the company for the three years ended 31 December 2010–2012 are given below:

Statement of comprehensive income for the year ended 31 December

	2010 £000	2011 £000	2012 £000
Turnover	5,210	5,295	5,380
Cost of sales	3,768	3,836	3,904
Gross profit	1,442	1,459	1,476
Distribution and administration costs	1,117	1,176	1,208
Operating profit	325	283	268
Interest paid	55	67	100
Profit before tax	270	216	168
Taxation	85	65	44
Profit for the year	185	159	124

Statement of changes in equity (retained earnings only) for the year to 31 December

	2010 £000	2011 £000	2012 £000
Balance at 1 January	770	835	874
Profit for the year	185	159	124
Dividends paid	(120)	(120)	(120)
Balance at 31 December	835	874	878

Statements of financial position as at 31 December

	2010 £000	2011 £000	2012 £000
Tangible non-current assets:			
Land and buildings	1,093	1,053	1,013
Plant, machinery, and motor vans	898	1,242	1,420
	1,991	2,295	2,433
Current assets:			
Inventories	355	525	789
Trade receivables	204	231	323
Cash	52	25	17
	611	781	1,129
Current liabilities			
Bank overdraft	–	115	458
Trade payables	182	249	375
Other payables	41	48	65
	223	412	898

Net current assets	388	369	231
Total assets less current liabilities	2,379	2,664	2,664
Non-current liabilities			
Long-term loan (secured)	544	540	536
	1,835	2,124	2,128
Equity and reserves:			
Issued ordinary share capital			
(£1 each)	1,000	1,250	1,250
Retained earnings	835	874	878
	1,835	2,124	2,128

The following are average industry ratios for the sector in which Fastbru plc operates. These ratios have been consistent over the year period 2010–2012.

Return on capital employed	13%
Gross margin	25%
Sales to net assets	300%
Gearing	40%
Inventory turnover (based on year-end figures)	12 times
Interest cover	3 times

Required

(a) Calculate from the financial statements of Fastbru plc, for each of the three years given, the same ratios as given for the industry sector.

(b) Compare the ratios calculated in (a) above with the industry average and comment on this comparison.

(c) Based on your answers to (a) and (b) above, discuss the merits of the key elements of the recovery plan to be adopted by the directors.

5. CFC International, Inc., a US-based company headquartered in Chicago, is a worldwide holography and speciality-coated film company. It designs, manufactures and markets chemically complex, multi-layer, transferable coatings and sophisticated holographic technologies. Its coatings provide superior performance for a wide variety of consumer and industrial products (both for product authentication and eye-catching packaging), under a wide range of operating solutions. The company does this by coating rolls of plastic film and selling them to its customers, who transfer the coatings to their products for protective or informative purposes. CFC International makes its coatings by mixing pigments, solvents and resins into formulations, which come in many colours, patterns and surface finishes designed to resist chemical and physical abuse.

CFC International manufactures its own coatings, which provide the company with the flexibility to customize and meet its customers' specific needs. For a relatively small cost compared to the cost of the finished products, CFC's technology adds to the functionality and increases the customer value of a variety of everyday products (e.g. toothpaste packaging and credit cards).

Below are provided:

■ the consolidated statements of comprehensive income for the financial years ended 31 December 1997–1999 (source: Annual Report, 1999)

■ the common-size statements of comprehensive income for the same period.

Statement of comprehensive income

In US$	1999	1998	1997
Net sales	66,147,299	51,047,399	42,319,147
Cost of goods sold	44,714,285	31,914,511	26,063,431
Gross profit	21,433,014	19,132,888	16,255,716
Marketing and selling expenses	7,048,868	5,544,129	4,813,880
General and administrative expenses	7,689,424	4,871,277	4,032,066
Research and development expenses	2,021,555	1,585,458	1,343,678
	16,759,847	12,000,864	10,189,624
Operating income	4,673,167	7,132,024	6,066,092
Other expenses/(income):			
interest	1,029,755	569,573	412,920
miscellaneous	475,881	311,823	(65,183)
	1,505,636	881,396	347,737
Income before income taxes and minority interest	3,167,531	6,250,628	5,718,355
Provision for income taxes	922,219	2,259,607	2,207,021
	2,245,312	3,991,021	3,511,334
Minority interest	0	− 343,029	− 290,131
Net income	2,245,312	3,647,992	3,221,203

Common-size statement of comprehensive income

	1999	1998	1997
Net sales	100.0%	100.0%	100.0%
Cost of goods sold	67.6%	62.5%	61.6%
Gross profit	32.4%	37.5%	38.4%
Marketing and selling expenses	10.7%	10.9%	11.4%
General and administrative expenses	11.6%	9.5%	9.5%
Research and development expenses	3.1%	3.1%	3.2%
	25.3%	23.5%	24.1%
Operating income	7.1%	14.0%	14.3%
Other expenses (income):			
interest	1.6%	1.1%	1.0%
miscellaneous	0.7%	0.6%	− 0.2%
	2.3%	1.7%	0.8%
Income before income taxes and minority interest	4.8%	12.2%	13.5%
Provision for income taxes	1.4%	4.4%	5.2%
	3.4%	7.8%	8.3%
Minority interest	0.0%	− 0.7%	− 0.7%
Net income	3.4%	7.1%	7.6%

Analyse and comment on these different statements. What can you infer happened during these three years? What are the significant evolutions an analyst or investor might be interested in?

6. Summary financial statements for a company in the automobile industry are given below for the years ended 31 December 2014 and 2013.

Statements of comprehensive income for the year ended		
	31 Dec 2014	31 Dec 2013
	£000	£000
Revenue	26,590,603	24,505,864
Cost of sales	23,428,829	21,989,159
Gross profit	3,161,774	2,516,705
Distribution costs	1,876,600	1,754,315
Administrative expenses	240,062	241,914
Operating profit	1,045,112	520,486
Other income	515,244	819,054
Interest payable	250,355	196,190
Profit before tax	1,310,001	1,143,350
Tax	485,868	272,229
Profit after tax	824,133	871,121
Earnings per share:		
Basic	19.17	20.21

Statements of financial position as at	31 Dec 2014	31 Dec 2013
	£000	£000
Non-current assets	8,596,613	8,970,805
Current assets:		
Inventory	2,041,837	1,831,613
Trade receivables	1,497,703	1,393,050
Investments	870,957	949,726
Cash in bank	3,104,976	1,759,211
	7,515,473	5,933,600
Current liabilities:		
Loans and finance leases	3,143,189	2,435,314
Trade payables	2,149,818	2,074,061
Accruals	348,047	127,923
	5,805,949	4,785,537
Net current assets	1,709,524	1,148,063
Non-current liabilities	4,201,887	4,291,056
Net assets	6,104,250	5,827,812
Called-up share capital	110,080	110,080
Other reserves	251,730	56,730
Retained earnings	5,742,440	5,656,945
Non-controlling interests	–	4,057
	6,104,250	5,827,812

Required

Prepare a report on the financial performance of the company for the year ended 31 December 2014, using the 2013 information for comparative purposes. In analysing the company's performance, you should use ratio analysis to measure its profitability, liquidity and gearing.

7. ABCD Ltd is a company engaged in building construction and renovation for private-sector customers. The company has a healthy order book but, despite this, is experiencing considerable cash flow problems. In view of this the company has approached its bankers and had requested an extension of overdraft facilities. This request has been refused until the company can explain the reasons for the cash flow problems and establish a recovery plan.

Extracts from the management accounting information provide the following summarized information.

Statements of financial position

	2010 £000	2011 £000	2012 £000
Non-current assets	84	96	128
Current assets:			
Inventory	28	24	30
Work in progress	620	740	640
Payments on account	(500)	(530)	(300)
Trade receivables	250	190	260
	398	424	630
Current liabilities			
Trade payables	298	274	396
Bank overdraft	140	60	158
	438	334	554
Net current assets (liabilities)	(40)	90	76
Total net assets	44	186	204

Statements of comprehensive income

	2010 £000	2011 £000	2012 £000
Sales:			
New houses	1,150	796	604
Commercial developments	400	856	1,146
	1,550	1,652	1,750
Cost of sales:			
Materials	656	690	740
Labour	486	540	716
Overheads	154	166	190
	1,296	1,396	1,646
Gross profit	254	256	104
Administration overheads	90	98	88
	164	158	16
Interest payable	21	10	23
Profit (loss) before tax	143	148	(7)

The following information has been provided by the directors.

(i) Non-current assets are made up of:
- old building, which has been converted to offices and stores
- a house that is currently rented to a tenant
- plant
- machinery
- motor vehicles.

The property was recently valued at £40,000 more than its book value, but this has not been incorporated into the accounts.

(ii) Some land suitable for a private housing development is owned by the company.

(iii) The overdraft limit is £130,000, which was agreed in 2009.

Required

Identify and discuss the possible reasons for the cash flow problems of the company. List the points that should be included in the action plan for recovery.

8. Gold Ltd is a metal manufacturing company. The managing director is concerned that sales cannot continue at their current level without increased borrowing. The management accounts for the period 2010 to 2012 are as follows:

Gold Ltd
Statements of comprehensive income for the year ending 31 March

	2010 £	2011 £	2012 £
Net sales	3,315,000	3,442,500	3,570,000
Cost of goods sold	(2,652,000)	(2,754,000)	(2,856,000)
Gross profit	663,000	688,500	714,000
Administration and selling expenses	(255,000)	(280,500)	(306,000)
Depreciation	(102,000)	(127,500)	(153,000)
Miscellaneous expenses	(51,000)	(107,100)	(153,000)
Net profit before tax	255,000	173,400	102,000
Taxation	(76,500)	(52,020)	(30,600)
Net profit after tax	178,500	121,380	71,400

Statement of financial position as at 31 March

	2010 £	2011 £	2012 £
Non-current assets:			
Land and buildings	61,200	163,200	153,000
Machinery	188,700	147,900	127,500
Other non-current assets	35,700	10,200	7,600
	285,600	321,300	288,100

Current assets:			
Inventory	382,500	637,500	1,032,800
Trade receivables	306,000	346,800	484,500
Cash	76,500	35,700	25,500
	765,000	1,020,000	1,542,800
Total assets	1,050,600	1,341,300	1,830,900
Equity and reserves			
Ordinary shares	459,000	459,000	459,000
Retained earnings	351,900	438,600	489,600
	810,900	897,600	948,600
Long-term loan	56,100	51,000	45,900
Current liabilities			
Accruals	61,200	71,400	96,900
Trade payables	122,400	193,800	382,500
Bank overdraft	0	127,500	357,000
	1,050,600	1,341,300	1,830,900

The following are the industry ratios for the metal manufacturing industry. These ratios are based on year-end statement of financial position figures.

Metal manufacturing industry ratios:	
Quick ratio	1.0 : 1
Current ratio	27 : 1
Inventory turnover	7 times
Trade receivables collection period	32 days
Asset turnover	13 times
Return on total assets	19%
Return on capital employed	36%
Debt/equity ratio	50%
Profit margin	7%

Required
Write a report to the managing director analysing the financial position of Gold in light of the industrial average ratios. Your report should include an analysis of the firm's strengths and weaknesses.

References
Altman, E. (1968) Financial ratios, discriminant analysis and the prediction of corporate bankruptcy. *Journal of Finance*, 23, 4, 589–609.

Logica (2011) *Annual Report and Accounts*.

Further reading

Company REFS – Really Essential Financial Statistics: Tables Volume, devised by Jim Slater, Hemmington Scott.

Dun & Bradstreet: *Key Business Ratios: The Guide to British Business Performance*. Dun & Bradstreet Ltd.

Extel (1992) *Handbook of Market Leaders*. Extel Financial Ltd.

Holmes, G., Sugden, A. and Gee, P. (2008) *Interpreting Company Reports and Accounts*. FT/PrenticeHall,

HS Financial Publishing: *The Company Guide*. HS Financial Publishing.

Stead, M. (1995) *How to Use Company Accounts for Successful Investment Decisions*. FT Pitman.

Taffler, R. (1982) Forecasting company failure in the UK using discriminant analysis and financial ratio data. *Journal of the Royal Statistical Society*, Series A, 145, 3, 342–58.

Glossary

A

Accounting policies The detailed methods of valuation and measurement that an entity chooses in preparing its financial statements.

Accounting profit Accounting profit is profit or loss for a period before deducting tax expense.

Accounting profits and taxable profits Accounting profits and taxable profits are seldom the same because the tax rules for allowing expenses to be charged against profit differ from the accounting rules.

Acquisition accounting This is sometimes called the purchase method and is the method required to account for an interest in a subsidiary company.

Amortization Amortization is the systematic allocation of the depreciable amount of an intangible asset over its useful life.

A-score The A-score uses a list of questions that have a specific score associated with them. A company could score up to 100 points, depending on the responses to the questions. The result of such a score is used to predict the likelihood of a company failing.

Asset An asset is a resource controlled by the enterprise as a result of past events, and from which future economic benefits are expected to flow to the enterprise.

Asset turnover A ratio that provides useful information about the efficiency of the company at generating sales from its capital.

Associate company This is where one company has a substantial stake in another company such that it gives some degree of influence, but not total control, over the operating and financial policies. This is a 'significant' degree of influence.

Audit The examination by an independent external examiner of an entity's financial statements.

B

Borrowing costs Borrowing costs are interest or other costs incurred by an entity in connection with the borrowing of funds.

Brand The registered trade mark of a particular product.

C

Carrying amount Carrying amount is the amount at which an asset is recognized after deducting any accumulated depreciation and accumulated impairment losses.

Cash Cash comprises cash on hand and demand deposits.

Cash equivalents Cash equivalents are short-term highly liquid investments that are readily convertible to known amounts of cash and subject to an insignificant risk of changes in value.

Cash flows Cash flows are inflows and outflows of cash and cash equivalents.

Cash generating unit A cash generating unit is the smallest identifiable group of assets that generates cash inflows that are largely independent of the cash inflows from other assets or groups of assets.

Closing rate method This is sometimes referred to as the net investment method. It is the method that is dealt with explicitly in IAS 21 for translating into the presentation currency, and is used as the method of translation when the subsidiary company is an independent entity. All statement of financial position items are translated at the rate of exchange ruling at that time (i.e. the closing rate); all statement of comprehensive income items are (mainly) translated at the average rate. Any exchange differences are shown as a movement on reserves.

Compound financial instruments A compound financial instrument is a financial instrument containing both a liability component and an equity component.

Conceptual framework A set of agreed fundamental principles that underpin financial accounting.

Consolidated financial statements The financial statements of a group presented as those of a single economic entity. Often referred to as group accounts.

Construction contract A construction contract is a contract specifically negotiated for the construction of an asset, or a combination of assets that are closely interrelated or interdependent in terms of their design, technology and function, or their ultimate purpose or use.

Contingent liability A contingent liability is an obligation that is not recognized in the statement of financial position because it depends upon some future event happening.

Cost The cost of a non-current asset is the cost of making it ready for use.

Cost of goods sold The materials, labour and other costs directly related to the goods sold.

Cost plus contract A cost plus contract is a construction contract in which the contractor is reimbursed for allowable or otherwise defined costs, plus a percentage of these costs or a fixed fee.

Costs of disposal Costs of disposal are incremental costs directly attributable to the disposal of an asset or cash generating unit, excluding finance costs and income tax expense.

Credit risk The risk that one party to a financial instrument will cause a financial loss for the other party by failing to discharge an obligation.

Critical event The point in the business cycle at which revenue may be recognized.

Current asset An asset that is reasonably expected to be realized in cash, or sold, or otherwise consumed during the normal operating cycle of the business, or within one accounting year if longer.

Current entry value A market buying price to replace an asset.

Current exit value The price at which an asset could be sold.

Current liability A current liability is a liability that satisfies any of the following criteria: (a) it is expected to be settled in the entity's normal operating cycle; (b) it is held primarily for the purpose of being traded; (c) it is due to be settled within 12 months after the end of the reporting period.

Current purchasing power (CPP) A method of adjusting historical cost accounting financial statements to take account of general price level changes.

Current ratio A ratio that focuses on the working capital of a business. It assesses the ability of the company to meet its short-term debt.

Current tax Current tax is the amount of income taxes payable (recoverable) in respect of the taxable profit (tax loss) for a period.

D

Date of acquisition This is the date at which a parent company acquires its stake in the subsidiary company.

Date of consolidation This is the date at which the financial statements are being prepared.

Deductible temporary differences Deductible temporary differences are temporary differences that will result in amounts that are deductible in determining taxable profit (tax loss) of future periods when the carrying amount of the asset or liability is recovered or settled.

Depreciable amount Depreciable amount is the cost of an asset, or other amount substituted for cost, less its residual value.

Depreciation Depreciation is the systematic allocation of the depreciable amount of an asset over its useful life.

Deprival value The amount by which a business would be worse off if it were deprived of a particular asset. Also referred to as its 'value to the business' or 'value to the owner'.

Derivative A derivative is a financial instrument that changes in value with an underlying item, requires no or relatively little investment, and is settled at a future date.

Development Development is the application of research findings or other knowledge to a plan or design for the production of new or substantially improved materials, devices, products, processes, systems or services before the start of commercial production or use.

Distributable reserves Distributable reserves are reserves that can be distributed to shareholders by way of dividends and other distributions (e.g. revenue reserves).

Dividend This is the return paid to shareholders as a reward for holding shares in a company. Dividends are payable only when the directors of the company declare them. There are usually two dividends declared during the year: one part way through the year (i.e. an interim dividend) and one at the end of the financial year (a final dividend).

Dividend cover The dividend cover is a measure of how many times the dividends actually paid are covered by the profits that were available for distribution to shareholders.

Dividend yield The dividend yield measures the annual return received by way of a dividend as a percentage of the current share price.

E

Earnings per share (EPS) A ratio that shows how much of the profit remaining is available to the ordinary shareholder. Earnings per share is a measure of a company's profitability and of the company's ability to pay dividends.

Earnings yield This ratio is simply the inverse of the *price/earnings ratio*, and shows earnings per unit of the company's share price.

Economic value The value of the expected earnings from using the item in question discounted at an appropriate rate to give a present-day value.

Equity accounting This method of accounting is required to account for an interest in an associate or joint venture.

Equity instrument An equity instrument is any contract that evidences a residual interest in the assets of an entity after deducting all of its liabilities. Ordinary shares are the most common example of an equity instrument.

Exchange difference This refers to any gain or loss arising from a movement in the exchange rate.

F

Fair value Fair value is the amount for which an asset could be exchanged between knowledgeable, willing parties in an arm's-length transaction.

Fair value less costs to sell Fair value less costs to sell is the amount obtainable from the sale of an asset or cash generating unit in an arm's-length transaction between knowledgeable, willing parties, less the costs of disposal.

Finance lease A finance lease is a lease that transfers substantially all the risks and rewards incidental to ownership of an asset to the lessee. The underlying substance of the transaction is a financing arrangement.

Finance lease (initial recognition) Lessees shall recognize, at the commencement of the lease term, finance leases as assets and liabilities in their statements of financial position at amounts equal to the fair value of the leased property or, if, lower, the present value of the minimum lease payments.

Financial asset A financial asset is any asset that is: (a) cash; (b) an equity instrument of another entity; (c) a contractual right to receive cash or another financial asset from another entity.

Financial instrument Any contract that gives rise to a financial asset for one party and a financial liability or equity instrument for another.

Financial liability A financial liability is any liability that is a contractual obligation to deliver cash or another financial asset to another entity.

Financing activities Financing activities are activities that result in changes in the size and composition of the contributed equity and borrowings of the entity.

Fixed price contract A fixed price contract is a construction contract in which the contractor agrees to a fixed contract price, or a fixed rate per unit of output, which in some cases is subject to cost escalation clauses.

Functional currency The currency of the primary economic environment in which a company operates.

G

Gearing ratio Gearing is concerned with the capital structure of the company. This ratio shows what proportion of the assets of the company have been financed by borrowing.

Goodwill Sometimes referred to as 'cost of control' or 'premium on acquisition', goodwill is calculated as the excess of the cost of an investment in a subsidiary over the 'value' of the proportion of net assets acquired.

Grant date The date at which the entity and another party agree to a share-based payment arrangement.

Grants related to assets Grants related to assets are government grants whose primary condition is that an entity qualifying for them should purchase, construct or otherwise acquire long-term assets.

Gross investment (in the lease) Gross investment in the lease is the aggregate of the minimum lease payments receivable by the lessor under a finance lease and any unguaranteed residual value accruing to the lessor.

Gross margin A ratio that measures the ability of a business to sell goods for more than they cost to make.

Group A parent and all its subsidiaries.

H

Hedge A finance technique to minimize the risk of exchange rate movements by entering into an agreement to buy currency ahead of time and so fix the exchange rate.

Hicks' definition of income Income is that amount which an individual can consume and still be as well off at the end of the period as he or she was at the start of the period.

Holding gains Gains that arise as a result of holding assets.

Horizontal analysis Used to examine trends over a number of accounting periods. Horizontal analysis is useful where comparisons are for periods greater than two years.

I

Impairment loss An impairment loss is the amount by which the carrying amount of an asset exceeds its recoverable amount.

Income ex-ante Income ex-ante measures relate to measures made from a point in time at the start of the period. They are essentially forward looking.

Income ex-post Income ex-post measures relate to measures made from a point in time at the end of the period. They are essentially backward looking.

Initial recognition of finance lease See *Finance lease (initial recognition)*.

Intangible asset An intangible asset is an identifiable non-monetary asset without physical substance.

Interest cover A ratio that shows how much the profits of the company can fall before the interest payments are threatened.

Interest rate implicit in the lease The interest rate implicit in the lease is the discount rate that, at the inception of the lease, causes the aggregate present value of (a) the minimum lease payments and (b) the unguaranteed residual value to be equal to the fair value of the leased asset.

Inventories Inventories are assets: (a) held for sale in the ordinary course of business; (b) in the process of production for such sale; or (c) in the form of materials or supplies to be consumed in the production process or in the rendering of services.

Inventory holding period A measure of the average number of days which elapse between acquiring an item of inventory and then selling that item.

Inventory turnover A ratio that shows how quickly the company is turning over its stock during the year. This can give an indication of slow-moving stocks, or how efficient the stock control policy of the company is.

Investing activities Investing activities are the acquisition and disposal of long-term assets and other investments not included in cash equivalents.

Investment property Investment property is property (land or a building or part of a building, or both) held (by the owner or by the lessee under a finance lease) to earn rentals or for capital appreciation, or both.

J

Joint arrangement An arrangement of which two or more parties have joint control.

Joint operation A joint arrangement whereby the parties that have joint control of the arrangement have rights to the assets, and obligations for the liabilities, relating to the arrangement.

Joint venture This is where one company has a stake in another company and shares control jointly with others (venturers), through some contractual arrangement.

L

Lease A lease is an agreement whereby the lessor conveys to the lessee in return for a payment, or series of payments, the right to use an asset for an agreed period of time.

Lease term The lease term is the non-cancellable period for which the lessee has contracted to lease the asset, together with any further terms for which the lessee has the option to continue to lease the asset when at the inception of the lease it is reasonably certain that the lessee will exercise the option.

Liability A liability is a present obligation of the enterprise arising from past events, the settlement of which is expected to result in an outflow from the enterprise of resources embodying economic benefits.

Limited liability company A limited liability company is a company where the liability of the owners is limited to the amount of share capital subscribed for.

Liquidity risk The risk that an entity will encounter difficulty in meeting obligations associated with financial liabilities.

Local currency The currency in which the foreign company measures and records its transactions.

M

Market risk The risk that the fair value or future cash flows of a financial instrument will fluctuate due to changes in market prices.

Measurement The calculation of the value of an item to be recorded in the financial statements.

Minimum lease payments Minimum lease payments are the payments over the lease term that the lessee is required to make.

Monetary items These are usually items such as cash, accounts payable and receivable, bank overdrafts and loans.

N

Net investment in the lease Net investment in the lease is the gross investment in the lease discounted at the interest rate implicit in the lease.

Net profit margin A ratio that expresses profit before interest and tax (PBIT) as a percentage of sales. It shows how much profit is generated from sales.

Net realizable value Net realizable value is the estimated selling price in the ordinary course of business less the estimated costs of completion and the estimated costs necessary to make the sale.

Nominal value The nominal value is the amount stated on the face of a share certificate as the named value of the share when issued.

Non-controlling (minority) interest The proportion of a subsidiary not owned by the parent company. This non-controlling interest is accounted for and shown separately in the group statement of financial position.

Non-current (fixed) asset Any asset that does not meet the definition of a current asset. Also described as a fixed asset.

Non-current (long-term) liability A non-current or long-term liability is a liability that does not meet the definition of a current liability.

Non-distributable reserves Non-distributable reserves are reserves that cannot be distributed to shareholders (e.g. revaluation reserve, share premium account, capital redemption reserve).

Non-monetary items These usually comprise long- and short-term assets such as inventory, property, plant and equipment.

O

Off balance sheet finance An enterprise's obligations that are not recorded in its statement of financial position.

Operating activities Operating activities are the principal revenue-producing activities of the entity and other activities that are not investing or financing activities.

Operating gains Gains that arise as a result of trading operations.

Operating lease An operating lease is a lease other than a finance lease. The underlying substance of the transaction is a rental arrangement.

Operating leases (lease payments) Lease payments under an operating lease shall be recognized as an expense on a straight line basis over the lease term unless another systematic basis is more representative of the time pattern of the user's benefit.

Ordinary shares Ordinary shares are shares in a company that entitle the holder to a share of the dividend declared and a share in the net assets on a winding-up of the business.

P

Parent An entity that controls one or more subsidiaries.

Permanent capital Permanent capital comprises share capital plus non-distributable reserves.

Pre-acquisition profits and reserves These are profits and reserves that were in existence at the time the subsidiary was acquired. Such profits and reserves cannot be shown as part of the group reserves, and are capitalized as part of the cost of control.

Preference shares Preference shares entitle to the holders to preferential treatment in that they are entitled to a dividend before the ordinary shareholders. In general terms, the preference dividend is usually a fixed percentage.

Presentation currency The currency in which the financial statements of a company are presented.

Price/earnings ratio (PER) This ratio is a measure of how the stock market rates the company. It indicates how many times the earnings an investor is prepared to pay to buy a share.

Private company A private company ends its name with 'Limited' or 'Ltd'. Private companies will have a few shareholders and cannot offer their shares for sale on the stock exchange.

Profit vs cash flow The making of a profit does not necessarily result in an increased bank balance. Profit deals with revenues earned and expenses incurred, while cash flow is concerned with cash received and cash paid.

Property, plant and equipment Property, plant and equipment are tangible assets that are held for use rather than realization, and are intended to provide services or generate revenues over future accounting periods.

Provision A provision is a liability of uncertain timing or amount.

Public company A public company has 'plc' after its name. Such a company can offer shares for sale to the general public.

Q

Qualifying asset A qualifying asset is an asset that necessarily takes a substantial period of time to get ready for its intended use or sale.

Quick asset ratio The quick asset ratio, sometimes call the 'acid test' or 'liquidity ratio' is a refinement of the current ratio. It measures the extent to which an entity can meet its short-term obligations.

R

Ratio analysis Describes the relationship between two different accounting numbers taken from the financial statements.

Recognition of an asset Items of property, plant and equipment should be recognized as assets when it is probable that: (a) the future economic benefits associated with the asset will flow to the enterprise; and (b) the cost of the asset can be measured reliably.

Recognition of a liability A liability is recognized in the statement of financial position when: (a) it is probable that an outflow of resources embodying economic benefits will result from the settlement of a present obligation; and (b) the amount at which the settlement will take place can be measured reliably.

Recognized An item is recognized when it is included by means of words and amount within the main financial statements of an entity.

Recoverable amount Recoverable amount is the higher of an asset's net selling price and its value in use.

Regulatory framework The rules and regulations that govern financial reporting.

Replacement cost accounting A method of preparing financial statements in which all assets and related expenses e.g. depreciation, are valued at current replacement costs.

Research Research is original and planned investigation undertaken with the prospect of gaining new specific or technical knowledge and understanding.

Reserves Reserves represent the claims that the owners have on the assets of a company because the company has created new wealth for them over the period since it began.

Residual value The estimated amount that an entity would currently obtain from disposal of the asset, after deducting the estimated cost of disposal, if the asset were already of the age and in the condition expected at the end of its useful life.

Restructurings A restructuring is a programme that is planned and controlled by management and materially changes either: (a) the scope of a business undertaken by an entity; or (b) the manner in which that business is conducted.

Retained earnings These are the profits after tax (less any losses), which the company keeps within the business. These profits have not been paid out by way of dividend nor transferred to any other reserve. A company can choose to use some of these retained earnings to pay any future dividends.

Return on equity (ROE) A ratio that measures the return made by the organization from using its capital resources. This is sometimes referred to as the primary ratio and gives an indication of how efficient the organization is at generating profits from its capital.

Return on shareholders' capital (ROSC) A ratio that is similar in nature to *ROCE*, but considers the profit made by the company in relation to the capital contributed by shareholders.

Revaluation reserve Some non-current (fixed) assets may have been purchased several years ago and have risen in value over time. When this increase in value is recorded, it is put into the revaluation reserve.

Revenue The gross inflow of economic benefits during the period arising in the course of the ordinary activities of an entity when those inflows result in increases in equity, other than increases relating to contributions from equity participants.

S

Share-based payment transaction A transaction in which the entity receives or acquires goods or services either as consideration for its equity instruments or by incurring liabilities for amounts based on the price of the entity's shares or other equity instruments of the entity.

Share capital Share capital is the nominal value of shares either authorized by a company or actually issued to the members.

Share premium The share premium is the excess of issue price over nominal value.

Shareholders These are the owners of the shares and are entitled to receive a share of the profit of the company.

Statement of changes in equity IAS 1 requires a company to present a statement of changes in equity as a separate component of the financial statement. The statement reconciles the capital and reserves at the beginning of the period with those at the end.

Statement of comprehensive income IAS 1 sets out the minimum information to be presented on the face of the statement of comprehensive income. The statement will include all items of income and expense recognized in a period. The information may be presented in: (a) a single statement; (b) two statements – displaying the components of profit or loss.

Statement of financial position A snapshot of an entity's assets, liabilities and equity at a given point in time – usually period end.

Subsidiary company This is where one company has a substantial stake in another company, such that total control over the operating and financial policies can be exerted thus giving 'dominant influence' over the other company.

T

Tangible non-current asset Assets that have physical substance and are held for use in the production or supply of goods and serivces, for rental to others, or for administrative purposes on a continuing basis in the reporting entity's activities.

Tax base The tax base of an asset or liability is the amount attributed to that asset or liability for tax purposes.

Taxable profit Taxable profit (tax loss) is the profit (loss) for a period, determined in accordance with the rules established by the taxation authorities, upon which income taxes are payable (recoverable).

Taxable temporary differences Taxable temporary differences are temporary differences that will result in taxable amounts in determining taxable profit (tax loss) of future periods when the carrying amount of the asset or liability is recovered or settled.

Temporal method This is the method used to translate into the *functional currency*. It is used when the subsidiary company is seen as an extension of the parent company. All monetary items are translated at the rate of exchange ruling at the end of the reporting period. All non-monetary assets are translated at the rate ruling when the transaction was undertaken. All statement of comprehensive income items are translated at the average rate. Any exchange gain or loss is taken to profit or loss.

Temporary differences Temporary differences are differences between the carrying amount of an asset or liability in the statement of financial position and its tax base.

Trade payables payment period This ratio calculates how many days' credit the business is taking from suppliers.

Trade receivables collection period A ratio that measures how effective the business is in collecting its debts. The ratio is a measure of how many days' credit customers are taking to pay.

Transaction A transaction is an agreement to purchase or sell goods or services on credit or for cash. A transaction results in a decrease in the finances of the purchaser and an increase in the benefits of the sellers. In terms of foreign currency transactions, the buyer and the seller will usually be in different countries, using different currencies.

Translation The process of converting an amount from one currency to another. For example, US$15 translates (converts) to £10 when the exchange rate is £1 = US$1.5.

Translation reserve The specific reserve to which any exchange difference is put.

Treasury shares Treasury shares are an entity's own shares that have been purchased by the entity and held for sale at some future date.

U

Useful life Useful life is the period over which an asset is expected to be available for use by an entity, or the number of production or similar units expected to be obtained from the asset by an entity.

V

Value in use Value in use is the present value of the future cash flows expected to be derived from an asset or cash generating unit.

Vertical analysis This is done by equating the totals in a financial statement to 100 and then expressing the other figures as a percentage of the total and so produce a 'common size' statement.

Vesting period The period during which all the vesting conditions of a share-based payment arrangement are to be satisfied.

Z

Z-score A score developed by applying a specific weight to a number of accounting ratios. The resulting figure is called the Z-score and is used to predict the health of a company.

Index